Modern Real Estate Practice in North Carolina

SEVENTH EDITION

Fillmore W. Galaty

Wellington J. Allaway

Robert C. Kyle

Deborah B. Carpenter, DREI, Contributing Author

This publication is designed to provide accurate and authoritative information in regard to the subject matter covered. It is sold with the understanding that the publisher is not engaged in rendering legal, accounting, or other professional advice. If legal advice or other expert assistance is required, the services of a competent professional should be sought.

President: **Dr. Andrew Temte**

Chief Learning Officer: **Dr. Tim Smaby**

Vice President, Real Estate Education: **Asha Alsobrooks**

Development Editor: **Trude Irons**

Creative Director: **Kelly Utesch**

MODERN REAL ESTATE PRACTICE IN NORTH CAROLINA, SEVENTH EDITION

© 2009 by Dearborn Financial Publishing, Inc.®

Published by DF Institute, Inc., d/b/a Dearborn™ Real Estate Education
1905 Palace Street
La Crosse, WI 54603
www.dearbornRE.com

Printed in the United States of America

09   10   11   10   9   8   7   6   5   4   3   2   1

ISBN: 1-4277-8587-2

PPN: 1510-6607

Contents

Preface

Since its first printing in 1994, *Modern Real Estate Practice in North Carolina* has provided thousands of readers with valuable real estate information, presented in a logical and accessible manner. Specifically tailored to North Carolina law and practice, *Modern Real Estate Practice in North Carolina* sets the standard for real estate textbooks, whether it is used to prepare for the licensing examination, for a college or university program, or simply for personal knowledge.

■ FEATURES

Real estate students and instructors alike will appreciate the following features:

■ Each chapter opens with **learning objectives** that list what concepts and information you should be able to identify, describe, explain, and distinguish when you have finished.

■ **Key terms** are provided at the beginning of each chapter. This feature not only lets you know what terms you should watch for as you read but helps you study and review as well.

■ **Margin notes** serve as memory prompts for more efficient and effective studying.

■ **For example** scenarios help illustrate how issues of fair housing, agency, and brokerage affect real estate professionals and real estate transactions.

■ **Chapter review** and **sample exam questions** feature many fact-patterned problems that encourage you to understand and apply information rather than just memorize it.

■ **Chapter 20, "Real Estate Mathematics,"** helps you apply the basic math principles that real estate professionals use when working with clients or customers. In addition, **math rationales** are included for the chapter quizzes and sample exam to aid in reviewing and studying math concepts and applications.

■ **Chapter summaries** have been expanded to provide a convenient study tool of chapter concepts.

■ NEW TO THE SEVENTH EDITION

To make the Seventh Edition of *Modern Real Estate Practice in North Carolina* even more useful, we have added the following features:

■ **Legislative updates.** Content throughout the chapters and questions and answers reflects the latest changes to North Carolina Real Estate License Law and Commission Rules.

■ **More chapters.** Chapter 2, "Property Ownership and Interests," has been divided into two chapters, with the new Chapter 3 titled "Encumbrances on Real Property." The former Chapter 7, "Basic Contract Law and Agency Contracts," is now two chapters: Chapter 8, "Basic Contract Law," and Chapter 9, "Agency Contracts."

■ **Forms Appendix:** Important North Carolina forms subject to change are placed in a separate appendix in the order encountered in a basic residential sales transaction with other purpose forms following.

■ **Questions and answers** are extensively updated in the chapters and the practice exam to reflect the new seventh edition and the current economic climate.

■ **Web links** are grouped and placed at the end of each chapter for easy reference.

■ **New topics** have been added including: fee-for-service agencies, minimum level of services, do-not-call legislation, manufactured homes, and more.

■ **Content updates** are incorporated throughout the book and include: expanded coverage of the listing contract, North Carolina Residential Property Act and the Buyer Agency Agreement; HO-3 insurance policy; protected classes under Fair Housing laws; environmental protection laws; the Real Estate Financing Market—Federal Reserve, Primary Mortgage Market, and Secondary Mortgage Market; and computerized loan origination and automated underwriting.

■ **Study and exam tips** to help students prepare for, take, and pass the real estate exam are contained in **Appendix A,** preceding the practice exam.

One thing, however, has stayed the same. As in the first six editions, the goal of *Modern Real Estate Practice in North Carolina,* Seventh Edition, is to help you understand the dynamics of the real estate industry and prepare you for the licensing exam. In this edition, we have met that challenge, providing you with the critical information you need to pass the real estate examination, buy or sell property, or establish a real estate career.

Acknowledgments

■ CONTRIBUTING AUTHOR

The authors would like to thank Deborah B. Carpenter of Raleigh, North Carolina, who served as contributing author for the Seventh Edition of *Modern Real Estate Practice in North Carolina*. As lead instructor for the Raleigh Classroom of J.Y. Monk Real Estate Training Center, Deb's passion for teaching has helped countless students prepare for a career in real estate. Deb is the recipient of the North Carolina Educator of the Year Award and the NCREEA President's Award for Exceptional Service. She also holds the highly respected Distinguished Real Estate Educator (DREI) designation for excellence in classroom instruction. Deb has served with the Real Estate Educators Association (REEA) and the North Carolina Real Estate Educators Association (NCREEA) in many leadership positions, including past president of the NCREEA.

■ REVIEWERS

For their input in the development of the Seventh Edition, the authors wish to thank the following individuals:

Vicki Ferneyhough, DREI, Fonville Morisey Center for Real Estate Studies

Deborah H. Long, DREI, EdD, Long Talks and Fonville Morisey Center for Real Estate Studies

Dana S. Rhodes, DREI, Mingle School of Real Estate

Sandy Williams, DREI, J.Y. Monk Real Estate Training Center

CHAPTER

1

Basic Real Estate Concepts

- **describe** the physical and economic characteristics of real property; the concept of land use and development, including highest and best use; and the advantages and disadvantages of real estate investments.

- **identify** the various careers and areas of real estate specializations and the professional organizations that support them.

- **explain** the operation of supply and demand in the real estate market.

- **define** these *key terms:*

broker	highest and best use	provisional broker
business cycles	land	real estate
chattel	market	real property
demand	nonhomogeneity	situs
heterogeneity	personal property	supply
	personalty	

■ INTRODUCTION

It is important that real estate students understand the basic characteristics of real estate, how real estate is used, and the real estate market. This chapter presents those fundamental concepts and lays the foundation for the exciting and challenging study of real estate practice.

■ GENERAL CHARACTERISTICS OF REAL ESTATE

There are two major classifications of property: real property and personal property. The distinction between these two types of property is an important one. **Real property** is defined as the land, everything that is permanently attached to the land, and everything that is appurtenant to (or goes with) the land. **Personal property**, or **personalty**, is considered to be all property that does not fit the definition of real property. The primary characteristic of personal property is movability. Items of personal property, also referred to as **chattels**, include such tangibles as furniture, clothing, money, bonds, and bank accounts. In other words, a *chattel* is *an item of movable personal property*.

Land, Real Estate, and Real Property

The words *land, real estate*, and *real property* are often used interchangeably. However, for a full understanding of the nature of real estate and the laws that affect it, licensees need to be aware of subtle yet important differences in meaning.

Land. Land is defined as the earth's surface extending downward to the center of the earth and upward to infinity, including things permanently attached by nature, such as trees and water (see Figure 1.1).

Land includes the minerals and substances below the earth's surface together with the airspace above the land up to infinity. The surface, subsurface, and airspace can be owned separately as surface rights, subsurface rights, and air rights and can be severed by separate conveyance. A specific tract of land is commonly referred to as a *parcel*.

Real estate. Real estate, or realty, is defined as land at, above, and below the earth's surface, including all things permanently attached to it, whether natural or artificial (see Figure 1.1). The term *real estate* is therefore somewhat broader than the term *land* and includes not only the physical components of the land provided

FIGURE 1.1 **Land, Real Estate, and Real Property**

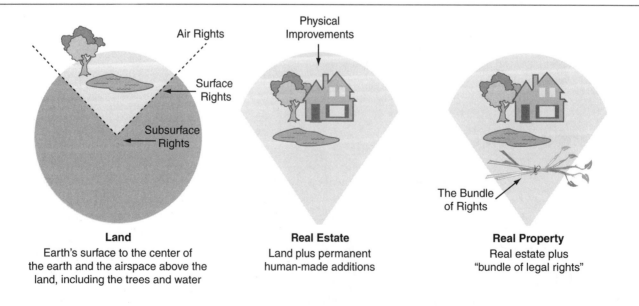

Land
Earth's surface to the center of the earth and the airspace above the land, including the trees and water

Real Estate
Land plus permanent human-made additions

Real Property
Real estate plus "bundle of legal rights"

by nature but also all human-made permanent improvements on and to the land. Land is referred to as *improved* when streets, utilities, sewers, and other improvements are brought to the land, therefore making the land suitable for building.

Real property.   **Real property** is defined as the land itself, the improvements thereon, and the interests, benefits, and rights inherent in the ownership of real estate (see Figure 1.1).

The broader term *real property* includes the physical surface of the land, what lies below it, what lies above it, and what is permanently attached to it, as well as all the rights of ownership that are usually referred to as the bundle of legal rights (including the right to possession and use, right to exclude others, the right to profit from the land, and the right to dispose of or encumber the land).

IN PRACTICE

When people talk about buying or selling houses, office buildings, land, and the like, they usually call all of these things real estate. For all practical purposes, the term is synonymous with real property, as defined here. Therefore, in everyday usage, real estate, or realty, includes the legal rights of ownership specified in the definition of real property.

Physical and Economic Characteristics of Real Property

Seven characteristics define the nature of real property and affect its use. These characteristics fall into two broad categories: physical characteristics and economic characteristics (see Figure 1.2).

FIGURE 1.2

Characteristics of Real Estate

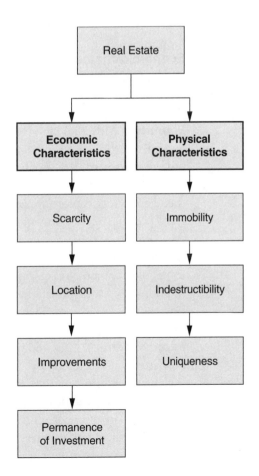

Physical characteristics.   Land has three physical characteristics that set it apart from other commodities: immobility, indestructibility, and uniqueness.

Immobility.   It is true that some of the substances of land are removable and that topography can be changed, but the geographic location of any given parcel of land can never be changed. Because land is immobile, the rights to use land are more easily regulated than are other forms of property use.

Indestructibility.   Land is durable and indestructible (or permanent). The permanence of land, coupled with the long-term nature of the improvements placed on it, has tended to stabilize investments in land. However, while land is indestructible, the improvements on it depreciate and can become obsolete, thereby reducing values—perhaps drastically. (Depreciation should not be confused with the fact that a given location can become undesirable economically, therefore creating a decrease in market value.)

> **Three Physical Characteristics of Real Estate**
> 1. Immobility
> 2. Indestructibility
> 3. Uniqueness

Uniqueness.   No two parcels of land are ever exactly the same. Although they may share substantial similarity, all parcels differ geographically. The uniqueness of land is also referred to as its **nonhomogeneity** or *heterogeneity*. In fact, it is the uniqueness of each parcel of land that gives rise to the remedy of specific performance for the breach of a real estate contract. Under the doctrine of *specific performance*, the party harmed by the breach of a real estate contract can ask a judge to force the breaching party to carry out the terms of the contract rather than ordering the breaching party to pay monetary damages. Because each parcel of land is unique, monetary damages cannot compensate the damaged party for the loss of that particular parcel.

Economic characteristics.   The basic economic characteristics of land are the factors that influence its value as an investment: scarcity, location, improvements, and permanence of investment. (*SLIP* is the mnemonic.)

Scarcity.   Although land is not thought of as a rare commodity, its total supply is fixed. Even though a considerable amount of land in the United States is still not used or inhabited, the supply of land in a given location (i.e., ocean front) or of a particular quality may be limited, therefore creating increased demand for that specific land. Because no more land can be produced, the increasing use of land has a positive impact on value.

Location (area preferences).   Area preference, sometimes called *location*, refers to people's choices and tastes regarding a given area. Location is one of the most important economic characteristics of land. **Situs** is a related term regarding location that takes into consideration social factors in addition to economic factors.

Improvements.   Any addition or change to land or a building that affects the property's value is referred to as an *improvement*. Improvements of a private nature, such as the house, fencing, and so on, are referred to as *improvements **on** the land*, whereas improvements of a public nature, such as sidewalks, sewer systems, curbing, and so on, are referred to as *improvements **to** the land*. Additions or alterations to the property that are merely repairs or replacements may not be considered to be improvements. Agents should be aware that the term *improved land* has two meanings. If buildings are constructed on the land, the buildings can be considered *improvements*. If the land has been prepared for development, such as with grading, installation of utilities, and so on, the land may be referred to as *improved land*.

Building an improvement on one parcel of land affects the value and utilization of neighboring tracts and can have a direct bearing on whole communities. For example, improving a parcel by constructing a shopping center or selecting it as the site for a nuclear power plant can directly influence a large area. Such land improvements can influence not only other parcels and other communities favorably or unfavorably, they may affect the use, value, and price of the land.

Permanence of investment.   Once land is improved, the total capital and labor used to build the improvement represents a large fixed investment. Although even a well-built structure can be torn down to make way for a newer building or another use of the land, improvements to the land such as drainage, electricity, and water and sewer systems remain because they generally cannot be dismantled or removed economically. The owner has no way to transfer the investment to another parcel of land. The return on such investments, therefore, tends to be long-term and relatively stable. This permanence generally makes improved real estate unsuitable for short-term, rapid-turnover investing.

Four Economic Characteristics of Real Estate
1. Scarcity
2. Location
3. Improvements
4. Permanence of investment

■ GENERAL CONCEPTS OF LAND USE AND INVESTMENT

The various characteristics of a parcel of real estate affect its desirability for a specific use. For example, contour and elevation of the parcel, and availability of transportation and natural resources, such as water, all affect the use that can be made of a property, and the way in which a property is used has a dramatic impact on the value of that property.

Highest and Best Use

The **highest and best use** is the use that will give the owners the greatest actual return on their investment. Extensive studies are often prepared to determine whether a property is being properly utilized. For example, a highest-and-best-use study may show that a parking lot in a busy downtown area or a farm surrounded by urbanized land is not the current highest and best use of the property.

If a property can be put to its highest and best use, its value will be maximized. For example, if the highest and best use of a piece of property is as a high-rise office building rather than as a parking lot, changing its use accordingly will increase its value and also will give the owners the highest return on their investment.

Although a property can have only one highest and best use at any given time, the highest and best use can change. Because of changes in socioeconomic conditions, a property's highest and best use may be a retail shopping center today but a large apartment complex five years from now.

Land-Use Controls

The potential uses of real property are limited by various land-use controls. Property owners cannot simply decide to tear down their single-family home and replace it with a convenience store. Chances are they would be violating a land-use law. The regulation of land use is accomplished through both public and private land-use controls, discussed in Chapter 6.

Real Estate as an Investment

Real estate, no matter what its use, is virtually always considered an investment. Customers often expect a real estate broker to act as an investment counselor. Though brokers should possess a basic knowledge of real estate investment, they should always refer a potential real estate investor to a competent accountant, lawyer, or investment specialist who can give expert advice regarding the investor's specific interest or objective.

So real estate practitioners can deal with customers on a basic level, real estate licensees should possess a rudimentary knowledge of real estate investment. Such knowledge begins with a brief examination of the traditional advantages and disadvantages of investing in real estate.

Advantages of real estate investment.   Historically, well-located and fairly-priced real estate investments have shown a good rate of return, often higher than the prevailing interest rate charged by mortgage lenders. Theoretically, this means that an investor can use the leverage of borrowed money to finance a real estate purchase and feel relatively sure that, if held long enough, the asset will yield more money than it costs to finance the purchase. It should be remembered that part of the return must make up for the value lost by a depreciating asset, such as a building.

Most real estate values tend to keep pace with the rate of inflation. Such an inflation hedge provides the prudent real estate investor with relative assurance that if the purchasing power of the dollar decreases, the value of the investor's assets will increase to offset the inflationary effects. In addition, real estate entrepreneurs may enjoy various tax advantages, which are discussed in more detail in Chapter 19.

Disadvantages of real estate investment.   Unlike stocks and bonds, real estate is not a liquid asset. This means that an investor may not be able to sell real estate quickly without taking a loss. Contrast this with the investor in stocks listed on the New York Stock Exchange, who needs only call a stockbroker to liquidate assets when funds are needed quickly. Even though a real estate investor may raise a limited amount of cash by refinancing the property, that property is usually listed with a real estate broker, and the investor may have to sell at a substantially lower price than full market value to facilitate a quick sale.

In addition, it is difficult to invest in real estate without some degree of expert advice. Investment decisions must be based on a careful study of all the facts in a given situation, reinforced by a broad and thorough knowledge of real estate and the manner in which it affects and is affected by the marketplace—the human element. Unsophisticated investors should seek legal and tax counsel before making any real estate investments.

Rarely can a real estate investor sit idly by and watch the invested money grow. Management decisions must be made. For example, should the investor manage the property personally or would it be preferable to hire a professional property manager? How much rent should be charged? How should repairs and tenant grievances be handled? Is sweat equity (physical improvements accomplished by the investor personally) required to make the asset profitable?

Finally, and most important, a high degree of risk often is involved in real estate investment. There is always the possibility that an investor's property will decrease in value during the period it is held or that it will fail to generate sufficient income to make it profitable. External influences beyond the investor's control may come into play in negative or positive ways, affecting the value of the investment.

■ THE SCOPE OF THE REAL ESTATE BUSINESS

Billions of dollars' worth of real estate is sold each year in the United States. Adding to this great volume of sales are rental collections by real estate management firms, appraisals of properties ranging from vacant land to modern office and apartment buildings, and the lending of money through mortgage loans on real estate.

Millions of people depend on some aspect of the real estate business for their livelihood. As the technical aspects of real estate activities become more complex, real estate offices require an increasing number of people properly trained to handle such transactions. Many professionals and business organizations, such as lawyers, architects, surveyors, accountants and tax specialists, banks, trust companies, and abstract and title insurance companies also depend on the real estate specialist.

Real Estate: A Business of Many Specializations

Despite the size and complexity of the real estate business, many people think of it as being comprised only of brokers. Actually, today's real estate industry employs millions of knowledgeable individuals who are well trained in specialty areas such as appraisal, property management, financing, development, counseling, and education. Each of these areas is a business unto itself, but every real estate professional must have a basic knowledge of all of these specializations to be successful.

Real estate brokerage.   The business of bringing together people interested in completing a real estate transaction is called *brokerage*. Usually, the **broker** acts as an agent who negotiates the sale, purchase, or rental of property on behalf of others for a fee or commission. In any transaction, there may be a **provisional broker** working on behalf of the broker. The commission, generally a percentage of the amount of the transaction, is usually paid by the seller in a sales transaction or by the owner in a rental transaction (although it can be paid by any party). Brokerage is further discussed in Chapter 7.

North Carolina's real estate license law (G.S. 93A-1 & 2) stipulates that a person must be licensed as a real estate broker if he or she lists or offers to list; sells or offers to sell; buys or offers to buy; auctions or offers to auction; negotiates the purchase, sale, or exchange of; leases or offers to lease; or rents or offers to rent any real estate for others for compensation or the promise of compensation. The license law also requires that a provisional broker that engages in any of these activities must be under the supervision of a real estate broker-in-charge.

Appraisal.   The process of estimating the value of a parcel of real estate is *appraisal*. Although brokers must have some understanding of valuation as part of their training, qualified appraisers are generally employed when property is financed or is sold by court order. The appraiser must have sound judgment, experience, a detailed knowledge of the methods of valuation, and be licensed as an appraiser. Appraisal is covered in Chapter 17.

Property management.   Someone who handles the operations of a property for its owner is involved in *property management*. The property manager may be responsible for soliciting tenants, collecting rents, altering or constructing new space for tenants, ordering repairs, and generally maintaining the property. The manager's basic responsibility is to protect the owner's investment and maximize the owner's return on the investment. Property management is discussed in Chapter 12.

Financing.   The business of providing the funds necessary to complete real estate transactions is called *financing*. Most transactions are financed by means of a loan secured by a mortgage or deed of trust by which the property is pledged as security for the eventual payment of the loan. This and other methods of real estate financing are examined in Chapter 13 and Chapter 14.

Property development.   This specialty includes the work of developers, or subdividers, who purchase raw land, divide it into lots, build roads, and install *sewer systems*. *Property development* also includes the skills of architects and builders, who improve the building lots with houses and other buildings and who sell the improved real estate, either themselves or through brokerage firms. Property development is discussed in Chapter 6. House construction is discussed in Chapter 16.

Counseling.   Providing competent independent advice and guidance on a variety of real estate problems is known as *counseling*. A counselor attempts to furnish the client with direction in choosing alternative courses of action. Increasing the client's knowledge is every counselor's function in rendering services.

Education.   *Education* is the provision of information to both the real estate practitioner and the consumer. Colleges, universities, private schools, and trade organizations conduct courses and seminars on all aspects of the business, from the principles of the prelicensing program to the technical aspects of tax and exchange law.

Other areas.   Many other specialties and professionals also are part of the real estate business. Practitioners associated with mortgage banking firms and those who negotiate mortgages for banks and savings associations are examples of professionals associated with these other areas of specialty. Members of corporate real estate departments as well as officials and employees of government agencies such as zoning boards and assessing offices are further examples.

Professional organizations.   The real estate business has many trade organizations, the largest being the National Association of REALTORS® (NAR). Organized in 1908, NAR sponsors various affiliated organizations that offer professional

T A B L E 1.1

National Association of REALTORS® Institutes and Sample Professional Designations

Institute	Designation(s)
National Association of REALTORS® (NAR)	Graduate REALTORS® Institute (GRI) Certified International Property Specialist (CIPS) Certified Property Manager® (CPM®) Accredited Buyer Representative® (ABR®)
American Society of Real Estate Counselors (ASREC)	Counselor of Real Estate (CRE)
Commercial Investment Real Estate Institute (CIREI)	Certified Commercial Investment Member (CCIM)
Institute of Real Estate Management (IREM)	Accredited Management Organization® (AMO®) Accredited Resident Manager® (ARM®)
REALTORS® Land Institute (RLI)	Accredited Land Consultant (ALC)
Society of Industrial and Office REALTORS® (SIOR)	Professional Real Estate Executive (PRE)
Women's Council of REALTORS® (WCR)	Leadership Training Graduate (LTG)

designations to brokers and others who complete required courses (see Table 1.1). NAR, along with the state and local boards, serves the interests of its members by keeping them informed of developments in their fields, publicizing the services of its members, improving standards and practices, and recommending or taking positions on public legislation or regulations affecting the operations of members and member firms.

The majority of local real estate associations throughout the United States and Canada are affiliated with NAR. Members of the North Carolina Association of REALTORS® (NCAR) and affiliated local boards subscribe to the association's strict Code of Ethics and are entitled to be known as REALTORS® or REALTOR-ASSOCI-ATES®. The term REALTORS® is a registered trademark. In North Carolina there are over 90,000 licensed brokers, of whom approximately 41,000 are REALTORS®. All REALTORS® are licensees, but not all licensees are REALTORS®. Please do not confuse NCAR with the North Carolina Real Estate Commission (NCREC), which is the regulatory licensing agency of the state.

Among the many other professional associations is the National Association of Real Estate Brokers (NAREB), whose members also subscribe to a code of ethics. Members of NAREB are known as *Realtists*.

Uses of Real Property

Five Categories of Real Property
1. Residential
2. Commercial
3. Industrial
4. Agricultural
5. Special-purpose

Just as there are many areas of specialization within the real estate industry, there are many different types of property in which to specialize. According to its use, real estate can generally be classified into one of five categories:

1. *Residential*—all property used for housing, from acreage to small city lots, both single-family and multifamily, in urban, suburban, and rural areas
2. *Commercial*—business property, including offices, shopping centers, stores, theaters, hotels, and parking facilities
3. *Industrial*—warehouses, factories, land in industrial districts, and power plants

4. *Agricultural*—farms, timberland, ranches, and orchards
5. *Special-purpose*—churches, schools, cemeteries, and government-held lands

The market for each of these types of properties can be further subdivided into the *sales market*, which involves the transfer of title, and the *rental market*, which involves the transfer of space on a rental basis.

IN PRACTICE   Although in theory a real estate broker or firm can perform all the services listed above and handle all five classes of property, this is rarely done except in small towns. Most real estate firms tend to specialize to some degree, especially in urban areas. In some cases, a real estate licensee may perform only one service for one type of property. Residential property brokers and industrial property managers are two examples of such specialization.

■ THE REAL ESTATE MARKET

In literal terms, a **market** is a place where goods are bought and sold, where value for those goods is established, and where it is advantageous for buyers and sellers to trade. The function of the market is to facilitate this exchange by providing a setting in which the supply and demand forces of the economy can establish market value. The real estate market is a free market and is local in nature.

Supply and Demand

> When supply increases and demand remains stable, prices go down. When demand increases and supply remains stable, prices go up.

The economic forces of supply and demand continually interact in the market to establish and maintain price levels. Essentially, when **supply** increases, prices drop as more producers compete for buyers; when **demand** increases, prices rise as more buyers compete for the product.

Production slows or stops during a period of oversupply. When the market cannot meet the demand, production increases to take advantage of demand. Supply and demand are balanced at what is called the *point of equilibrium*.

■ **FOR EXAMPLE** Here's how one broker describes market forces: "In my 17 years in real estate, I've seen supply and demand in action many times. When a car maker relocated its factory to my region a few years back, hundreds of people wanted to buy the few higher-bracket houses for sale at the time. Those sellers were able to ask ridiculously high prices for their properties, and two houses actually sold for more than the asking prices! On the other hand, when the naval base closed and 2,000 civilian jobs were transferred to other parts of the country, it seemed like every other house in town was for sale. We were practically giving houses away to the few people who were buying."

Supply and demand in the real estate market.   Characteristics of goods in the marketplace determine how quickly the forces of supply and demand will be able to achieve equilibrium. Such characteristics are the degree of standardization of the product, the mobility and financial stability of the product, and the mobility of the parties (buyer and seller).

Real estate is not a standardized product; no two parcels can ever be exactly alike. Each parcel of real estate is unique because it has its own geographic location.

Because real estate is fixed in nature (immobile), it cannot be moved from area to area to satisfy the pressures of supply and demand. Property buyers are also generally limited in their mobility—retirees are a major exception in regard to residences. For these reasons, the real estate business has tended toward local markets, where firms can maintain detailed familiarity with market conditions and available units. The increasing mobility of the population, the growing impact of new technologies in communication, and data handling have resulted in the geographic expansion of real estate firms.

Where standardization and mobility are relatively great, the forces of supply and demand balance relatively quickly. But because of real estate's characteristics of uniqueness and immobility, the real estate market is generally relatively slow to adjust. To a certain extent, the product can be removed from the market (as when a home offered for resale is withdrawn), yet an oversupply of product usually results in a lowering of price levels. Because development and construction of real estate take a considerable period of time from conception to completion, increases in demand also may not be met immediately. Building may occur in uneven spurts of activity owing to such factors.

Factors affecting supply.   Factors that tend to affect supply in the real estate market include the labor force, construction costs, government controls, and monetary or financial policies.

Labor force and construction costs.   A shortage of labor in the skilled building trades, an increase in the cost of building materials, or a scarcity of materials tends to decrease the amount of housing built or increase its cost. The impact of the labor force on price levels depends on the extent to which higher costs can be passed on to the buyer or renter in the form of higher purchase prices or rents. Technological advances that result in lower-priced materials and more efficient means of construction may tend to counteract some price increases.

Government controls and financial policies.   Government monetary policy can have a substantial impact on the real estate market. The Federal Reserve Board and government agencies such as the Federal Housing Administration (FHA) and Ginnie Mae (formerly the Government National Mortgage Association, GNMA), as well as Freddie Mac (formerly the Federal Home Loan Mortgage Corporation, FHLMC), can affect the amount of money available to lenders for mortgage loans (see Chapter 14). In addition, the government can influence the amount of money available for real estate investment through its fiscal and monetary policies. Such policies include the amount of money taken out of circulation, taxation, and the amount of money the government puts into circulation through spending programs ranging from welfare to farm subsidies.

At the local level, real estate taxation is one of the primary sources of revenue for government. Policies on taxation of real estate can have either positive or negative effects. Tax incentives have been one way for communities to attract new businesses and industries to their areas. And, of course, along with these enterprises come increased employment and expanded residential real estate markets.

Local governments also can affect market operations and the development and construction of real estate by applying land-use controls. Building codes and zoning ordinances are used by communities to control the use of land. Real estate values and markets are thereby stabilized. Community amenities—for example, churches, schools, and parks—and efficient government policies are influential factors affecting the real estate market. Local governments can negatively influence development by imposing excessive fees or overly restrictive zoning and building codes.

Factors affecting demand. Factors that tend to affect demand in the real estate market include population, demographics, and employment and wage levels.

Population. Because shelter (whether in the form of owned or rented property) is a basic human need, the general need for housing grows as the population grows. Even though the total population of the country may continue to increase, growth is not uniform. Some areas grow faster than others, and some do not grow at all. In some places, we almost have modern-day ghost towns, where the exhaustion of natural resources or the termination of an industrial operation has resulted in a mass exodus.

Demographics. Not only population but the makeup of that population—demographics—affects demand. Family size and the ratio of adults to children; the number of people moving into assisted care facilities and retirement communities; the effect of doubling up, where two or more families use one housing unit; and the changing number of single-parent households all contribute to the amount and type of housing needed. Also pertinent are the number of young people who would prefer to rent or own their own residences, but for economic reasons, have roommates or remain in their parents' homes.

Employment and wage levels. Home ownership and rental decisions are closely related to the ability to pay. Employment opportunities and wage levels in a small community can be affected drastically by decisions made by major employers in the area. Individuals involved in the real estate market in such communities must keep well informed about the business plans of local employers.

To estimate how changes in wage levels will affect people's decisions concerning real estate, it is also important to look for trends in how individual income is likely to be used. General trends in the economy (availability of mortgage money, interest rates, rate of inflation, and the like) will influence an individual's spending decisions.

Business cycles. The upward and downward fluctuations in business activity are called **business cycles**. Although business cycles often seem to recur within a certain number of years, they are actually caused primarily by forces such as population growth, taxes, interest rates, wars, and oil embargoes. A business cycle can generally be characterized by four stages: expansion, recession, depression, and revival. The movements of a cycle are usually gradual and indistinct.

The real estate cycle. As stated earlier, the real estate market is slow in adjusting to variations in supply and demand. Because one factor of a real estate cycle is building activity, the time lag between the demand for units and the completion of those units causes real estate cycles to peak after the rest of the economy does and to take longer to recover from depressed periods than do other economic sectors. The local character of the real estate market creates many local conditions that may not correspond to the general movement of a real estate cycle.

Governmental anticyclical efforts.   Ever since the Great Depression of the 1930s, the federal government has attempted to establish fiscal and monetary policies to prevent extreme fluctuations in the business cycle. By increasing government spending during times of recession and taking money out of circulation through taxation and control of lending institutions during times of inflation/expansion, the government attempts to promote steady, gradual economic growth.

■ RELATED WEB SITES

Building Owners and Managers Association International: *www.boma.org*
Commercial Investment Real Estate Institute: *www.ccim.com*
Counselors of Real Estate: *www.cre.org*
Institute of Real Estate Management: *www.irem.org*
National Association of Exclusive Buyers Agents: *www.naeba.org*
National Association of Independent Fee Appraisers: *www.naifa.com*
National Association of REALTORS®:   *www.realtor.org*
North Carolina Association of REALTORS®:   *www.ncrealtors.org*
North Carolina Real Estate Commission: *www.ncrec.state.nc.us*
Real Estate Buyer's Agent Council: *www.rebac.net*
Real Estate Educators Association: *www.reea.org*
REALTORS® Land Institute: *www.rliland.com*
Society of Industrial and Office REALTORS®:   *www.sior.com*
Women's Council of REALTORS®:   *www.wcr.org*

■ SUMMARY

The special nature of land as an investment is apparent in both its physical and economic characteristics. Physically, land is immobile, indestructible, and unique. Its economic characteristics are controlled by such factors as scarcity, location, improvements, and permanence of investment.

Although most people think of land as the surface of the earth, land is the earth's surface and everything under the earth and in the air above it. The term real estate further expands this definition to include all natural and human-made improvements attached to the land. Real property is the term used to include all the legal rights associated with ownership of real estate.

All property that does not fit the definition of real estate is classified as personal property, or personalty. Personal property can be moved. A chattel is an item of movable personal property.

The value of land is affected by its highest and best use and by the land-use controls that specify the possible uses of a parcel of land.

Although selling is the most widely recognized activity of the real estate business, the industry also involves many other services such as appraisal, property management, property development and subdivision, counseling, and property financing. Most real estate firms specialize in only one or two of these areas. However, the highly complex and competitive nature of our society requires that a real estate professional be an expert in a number of fields.

Real property can be classified according to its general use as residential, commercial, industrial, agricultural, or special-purpose. Although many brokers deal with more than one type of real property, they usually specialize to some degree.

A market is a place where goods and services can be bought and sold and price levels are established. The ideal market allows for a continual balancing of the forces of supply and demand. Because of its unique characteristics, real estate is relatively slow to adjust to the forces of supply and demand.

The supply of and demand for real estate are affected by many factors. Those that bear on supply include labor availability and construction costs as well as government monetary controls and fiscal policy. Elements that influence demand include population and demographics, employment and wage levels, interest rates and taxes. If demand is high and supply is low, there is a seller's market; if demand is low and supply is high, there is a buyer's market.

Fluctuations of business activity in this country are observed in cycles. Business cycles occur in four stages: expansion, recession, depression, and revival. The real estate cycle involves similar stages, but it tends to peak after the rest of the economy does and it takes longer to recover than other sectors of the business community.

QUESTIONS

1. Which of the following *BEST* defines real estate?
   a. Land and the air above it
   b. Land and the buildings permanently affixed to it
   c. Land and all things permanently affixed to it
   d. Land and the mineral rights in the land

2. Which of the following is *NOT* a physical characteristic of land?
   a. Indestructibility
   b. Scarcity
   c. Immobility
   d. Uniqueness

3. The term heterogeneity refers to which of the following?
   a. Scarcity
   b. Uniqueness
   c. Mobility
   d. Indestructibility

4. Situs refers to
   I. location preference.
   II. societal factors that are related to location.
      a. I only
      b. II only
      c. Both I and II
      d. Neither I nor II

5. Which of the following is *NOT* an economic characteristic of real estate?
   I. Indestructibility
   II. Scarcity
      a. I only
      b. II only
      c. Both I and II
      d. Neither I nor II

6. Which of the following physical and economic factors would a land developer take into consideration when determining the optimum use of a parcel of land?
   a. Transportation
   b. Available natural resources
   c. Contour and elevation
   d. All of the above

7. A theater or a hotel would be classified under the real estate category of
   a. residential.
   b. commercial.
   c. agricultural.
   d. industrial.

8. The demand for real estate is influenced by the
   a. number of real estate brokers in the area.
   b. ethnic makeup of neighborhoods.
   c. wage levels and employment opportunities in the area.
   d. price of new homes being built in the area versus the price of existing homes.

9. The designation REALTOR® refers to
   I. any licensed real estate broker.
   II. an active member of the National Association of REALTORS®.
      a. I only
      b. II only
      c. Both I and II
      d. Neither I nor II

10. Which of the following statements is/are *TRUE* of business cycles?
    I. Business cycles involve periods of expansion, recession, depression, and revival.
    II. The real estate business cycle is quicker to recover from depressed times than other business sectors.
       a. I only
       b. II only
       c. Both I and II
       d. Neither I nor II

11. All of the following factors tend to affect supply *EXCEPT*
    a. the labor force.
    b. construction costs.
    c. government controls.
    d. demographics.

12. Real estate can be a poor investment if
    a. the inflation rate is high.
    b. the investor plans to hold the investment for a long time.
    c. the investor needs ready cash.
    d. land values are appreciating in the area.

13. In general, when the supply of a certain commodity increases, prices
    a. tend to rise.
    b. tend to drop.
    c. tend to stabilize.
    d. can no longer be established.

14. In general terms, a market refers to which of the following?
    a. Place where goods are standardized for sell
    b. Amount of goods available at a given price
    c. Quality of goods available to the public
    d. Place where the value of goods is established

15. The demand for real estate in a particular community is LEAST affected by
    a. population.
    b. wage levels.
    c. employment.
    d. international trade.

16. The real estate market is considered local in character for all the following reasons EXCEPT
    a. land is fixed or immobile.
    b. consumers generally invest in real estate that is near their home or work.
    c. local controls can have a significant impact on the market.
    d. most people eagerly visit and invest in real estate in distant areas.

17. Highest and best use of real estate will
    a. maximize the property's value.
    b. stay constant throughout time.
    c. always be the property's current use.
    d. not be affected by local economic trends.

CHAPTER 2

Property Ownership and Interests

■ **LEARNING OBJECTIVES** *When you have finished reading this chapter, you should be able to*

■ **explain** the concept of the *bundle of legal rights*; the characteristics of real estate; the types of freehold estates.

■ **describe** all types of fixtures and be able to identify items that may or may not be fixtures by applying all parts of the Total Circumstances Test.

■ **describe** the different types of real property ownership.

■ **define** these *key terms:*

accretion	fructus industriales	remainder interest
agricultural fixtures	fructus naturales	remainderman
air rights	future interests	reversionary interest
appurtenance	joint tenancy	right of survivorship
avulsion	lateral support	riparian rights
bundle of legal rights	life estate	severalty
condominium ownership	life tenant	subjacent support
cooperative ownership	littoral rights	subsurface rights
emblements	manufactured home	surface rights
erosion	modular home	tenancy by the entirety
estovers	nonfreehold (leasehold)	tenancy in common
fee simple absolute	estates	time-share ownership
fee simple defeasible	North Carolina Condo-	Total Circumstances Test
fee simple determinable	minium Act of 1986	townhouse ownership
fee simple with condition	planned unit	trade fixture
subsequent	development (PUD)	Uniform Commercial
fixture	proprietary lease	Code (UCC)
foreshore	pur autre vie	waste
freehold estates	reliction	

■ THE CONCEPT OF PROPERTY

The unique nature of real estate has given rise to a distinctive set of laws and rights. Even the simplest of real estate transactions brings into play a complex body of laws, and licensees must understand not only the effect of these laws but also how the laws define real property.

The Bundle of Legal Rights

Real property is often described as a **bundle of legal rights.** This is a "legal relationship" between the owner and the property. In other words, a purchaser of real estate is actually buying the rights of ownership held by the seller. The rights of ownership (see Figure 2.1) include the

- right of *disposition* (to sell, will, transfer, or otherwise dispose of or encumber the property);
- right of *enjoyment* (to uninterrupted use of the property without interference of any third party claiming superior title);
- right of *exclusion* (to keep others from entering or using the property);
- right of *possession* (to use or occupy); and
- right of *control* (of the property and its profits within the framework of the law).

The concept of the bundle of rights comes from old English law and a population that, for the most part, could not read or write. Therefore, a seller transferred property by giving the purchaser a bundle of bound sticks from a tree on the property. This process was referred to as a *livery of seisin*. The purchaser who held the bundle also owned the tree from which the sticks came and the land to which the tree was attached. Because the rights of ownership can be separated and individually transferred, the sticks became symbolic of those rights.

Appurtenances

An **appurtenance** is defined as a right or privilege that goes with the ownership of land. These rights include subsurface rights (such as mineral rights), air rights, and water rights. A property owner is entitled to the right of lateral and/or subjacent support from adjacent landowners. The land may benefit from an appurtenant easement that will be discussed in Chapter 3. The protective benefit of restrictive covenants also "runs with the land" like other appurtenant rights and will be covered in Chapter 6. An appurtenance is generally transferred with the property to the new owner.

FIGURE 2.1

Bundle of Legal Rights

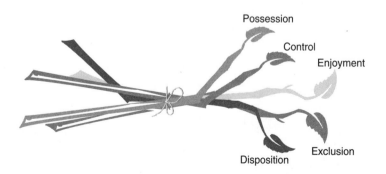

Possession

Control

Enjoyment

Exclusion

Disposition

Subsurface and Air Rights

Surface rights are simply the rights to use the surface of the earth. However, real property ownership also can include **subsurface rights**, which are the rights to use the space below ground level and to extract the natural resources lying below the earth's surface. Such natural resources might include minerals, coal, gas, oil, or water.

A transfer of surface rights may, however, be accomplished without the transfer of subsurface rights. For example, a landowner could sell the rights to any oil and gas found in the land to an oil company. The landowner then could sell his remaining interest, but reserve the rights to all coal found in the land. After the sale, three parties would have ownership interests in the real estate: the oil company would own all oil and gas, the seller would own all coal, and the new landowner would own the rest of the rights to the real property.

The rights to use the air above the land also may be sold or leased independently of the land. Such **air rights** are an increasingly important part of real estate, particularly in large cities, where air rights over railroads have been purchased to construct huge office buildings such as the Pan-Am Building in New York City and the Merchandise Mart in Chicago. To construct such a building, the developer must purchase not only the air rights but also numerous small portions of the land's surface for the building's foundation supports, called *caissons*.

Until the development of airplanes, a property's air rights were considered to be unlimited. Today, however, the courts permit reasonable interference with these rights, such as those necessary for aircraft, as long as the owner's right to use and occupy the land is not unduly lessened. Governments and airport authorities often purchase air rights adjacent to an airport to provide approach patterns for air traffic.

With the continuing development of solar power, air rights—more specifically, sun rights—have been redefined by the courts. They consider tall buildings that block sunlight from smaller solar-powered buildings to be interfering with the smaller buildings' sun rights.

In summary, one parcel of real property may be owned by many people, each holding a separate right to a different part of the real estate. These rights may be severed by separate conveyance. For example, there may exist at the same time

- an owner of the surface rights,
- an owner of the subsurface mineral rights,
- an owner of the subsurface gas and oil rights, and
- an owner of the air rights.

Water rights.   One of the interests that may attach to the ownership of real estate is the right to use adjacent bodies of water. In North Carolina, the ownership of water and the land adjacent to it is determined by the doctrine of riparian rights.

Riparian rights are granted to owners of land located along the course of a river, stream, or lake. Such an owner has the unrestricted right to use the water, provided such use does not harm owners upstream or downstream by interrupting

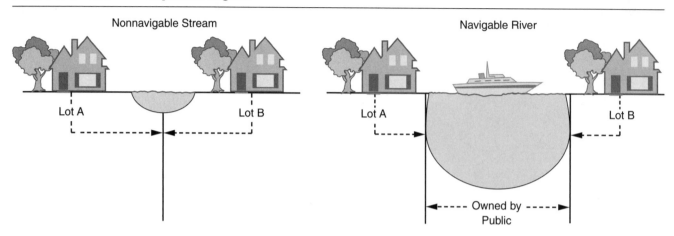

or altering the flow of the water or by contaminating it. In addition, an owner of land that borders a nonnavigable waterway owns the land under the water to the exact center of the waterway. In North Carolina, land adjoining navigable rivers is owned only to the banks of the river (see Figure 2.2). Navigable waters are considered public highways on which the public has an easement or a right to travel.

Closely related to riparian rights are the **littoral rights** of owners whose land borders oceans and large, navigable lakes that have a tide. Owners with littoral rights enjoy unrestricted use of navigable waters but own the land adjacent to the water only up to the mean high-water mark (see Figure 2.3). All land below this point is owned by the government. (The strip of land between high and low tide lines belongs to the state of North Carolina and is called the **foreshore**.)

Riparian and littoral rights are *appurtenant* (attached) to the land and cannot be retained when the property is sold. This means that the right to use the water belongs to whoever owns the bordering land and cannot be retained by a former owner after the land is sold.

The quantity of land can be affected by the natural action of the water. An owner is entitled to all land created by **accretion**, or an increase in land resulting from the deposit of soil by the water. If water recedes or disappears, new land is acquired by **reliction**. **Erosion**, the gradual wearing away of land caused by flowing water or other natural forces, may cause an owner to lose land. When a sudden act of nature such as a flood or avalanche removes soil, this is known as **avulsion**.

Support Rights

The owner of real property has the right to **lateral support,** or the right to have adjacent property support the natural boundaries of the land. Therefore, construction or excavation on a neighboring property should not cause the soil on the owner's property to subside.

As discussed above, occasionally the landowner severs the subsurface rights from the land and sells them. In such a situation, the property owner is entitled to **subjacent support** for the surface of the property from the owner of the

FIGURE   2.3   Littoral Rights

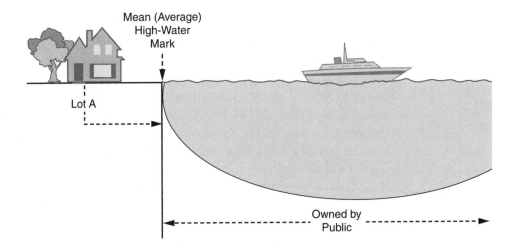

subsurface rights. Therefore, any subterranean mining projects must assure continued support of the land's surface.

Real Property Versus Personal Property

As discussed in Chapter 1, *real property* is defined as the land, everything attached to the land, and everything appurtenant to the land. *Personal property* is defined as everything that is not real property. While the distinction between real and personal property is important to all real estate transactions, it is not always obvious. For instance, is a pile of lumber in the backyard of a house personal property or part of the real property? What about the drapes or an antique mirror attached to the wall of a home? If these items are considered personal property, they can be taken by the seller when he or she moves out of the house. On the other hand, if these items are considered real property, the buyer becomes their new owner and the seller cannot remove them. Real estate agents must be careful to see that both parties to a real estate transaction understand clearly which items are real property and which items are personal property to prevent confusion and disappointment at closing.

Manufactured homes versus modular homes. A **manufactured home** is built according to the United States Department of Housing and Urban Development (HUD) construction standards and is defined by North Carolina General Statute §143-143.9(6) as:

> *A structure, transportable in one or more sections, which, in the traveling mode, is eight feet or more in width or is 40 feet or more in length, or when erected on site, is 320 or more square feet, and which is built on a permanent chassis and designed to be used as a dwelling with or without a permanent foundation when connected to the required utilities, and includes plumbing, heating, air conditioning, and electrical systems contained therein.*

A manufactured home, sometimes referred to as a mobile home or house trailer, can be either personal property or real property. While the manufactured home is still mobile with its own wheels and chassis, it has a Vehicle Identification Number registered with the NC Department of Motor Vehicles and is considered personal property. Manufactured housing is not considered real property just because the unit was placed on a residential lot. To convert the home into real property, the moving hitch, wheels and axles must be removed and the unit must be attached to a permanent foundation on land owned by the owner of the manufactured home. Once the owner files an affidavit confirming the aforementioned actions, the home is considered real property and an improvement to the lot.

Manufactured buildings, which include single-family **modular homes**, are governed by NC General Statute §143-139.1. These units are constructed in factories off-site according to state building codes and contain a label certifying compliance. Once the modular home is assembled on the home site, it is immediately considered to be real property.

Licensees should be able to differentiate between "manufactured homes" and "modular homes" when listing or selling such properties. The mandatory compliance labels from HUD for the manufactured housing and from the state for modular housing are usually found on the back exterior of the unit, under the kitchen sink, or near the electrical power box. Some older subdivisions have restrictive covenants that prohibit "house trailers," "mobile homes," or "manufactured homes" but do not strictly prohibit "modular homes."

The term used in law for plants that do not require annual cultivation (such as trees and shrubbery) is *fructus naturales* (fruits of nature); emblements are known in law as *fructus industriales* (fruits of industry or crops).

Plants. Plants generally fall into one of two classes. Trees, perennial bushes, and grasses that do not require annual cultivation (*fructus naturales*—fruits of nature) are considered real property. Annual crops, such as wheat, corn, vegetables, and fruit, are known as **emblements (*fructus industriales*—fruits of industry)** and are generally considered personal property. In a lease situation, a tenant may re-enter the land after lease termination, if necessary, to harvest crops that result from the tenant's labor. But in a sales transaction, if an annual crop is growing, it will be transferred as part of the real property if no special provision is made in the sales contract.

It is possible to change an item of real property to personal property by *severance*. For example, a growing tree is real estate until the owner cuts down the tree and thereby severs it from the earth. Similarly, an apple becomes personal property once it is picked from a tree, and a crop of wheat becomes personal property once it is harvested. Severance also may be the result of a contract. For example, if the owner of an apple orchard sells the apple crop while it is still ripening on the trees, the crop has been severed (and, therefore, turned into personal property) even though it is still physically attached to the trees.

It is also possible to change personal property into real property. If a landowner buys several azalea bushes, fertilizer, and mulch to landscape the front yard, the component parts, which were originally personal property, are converted into real property once planted and applied. They have become permanent improvements on the land. This process is called *annexation*.

Fixtures. In considering the differences between real property and personal property, it is important to be able to distinguish between a fixture and personal property.

An item that was once personal property but has been so affixed (or attached) to land or a building that the law construes it to be part of the real estate is a **fixture.** Examples of fixtures are heating plants, elevator equipment in highrise buildings, kitchen and bathroom cabinets, light fixtures, and plumbing fixtures. *If an item is a fixture, it automatically transfers with the property unless exempted by either party to the contract.* As a matter of fact, almost any item that has been added as a permanent part of a building is considered a fixture.

Legal tests of a fixture.   The **Total Circumstances Test** is a legal test applied by the courts to determine whether an item is a fixture (and, therefore, part of the real property) or personal property. All four parts of the test must be applied, but intention is the major part of the test. These four tests are easy to remember by using the mnemonic *IRMA*:

1. **Intention of the annexor:** Did the person who installed the item intend it to remain permanently or to be removable? (The courts look at objective evidence of the party's intent, not the party's subjective intent. In other words, the courts look at the facts surrounding the situation and determine what a reasonable person would have intended by them.)
2. **Relationship of the annexor:** Is the person making the attachment an owner or a tenant? It is presumed that an owner intends a permanent attachment (the item becomes a fixture), while a tenant intends a temporary attachment (the item remains personal property). The greater the legal relationship the annexor has to the real property, the greater the likelihood the item will be declared a fixture.
3. **Method of annexation:** How permanently was the item attached? Can it be removed without causing damage?
4. **Adaptation to real estate:** Has either the item or the property been tailored to facilitate working together? Has it been customized or built in to the property?

Four Legal Tests of a Fixture

1. Intention
2. Relationship
3. Method of annexation
4. Adaptation to real estate

Although these tests seem simple, court decisions have not been consistent regarding what constitutes a fixture. Articles that appear to be permanently affixed have sometimes been held by the courts to be personal property, whereas items that do not appear to be permanently attached have been held to be fixtures.

In the sale of property, the one certain way to avoid confusion over the nature of an article is for the parties to enter into a written agreement that establishes which items are considered part of the real property. A real estate broker should ensure that a sales contract includes a list of all articles that are being included in the sale, particularly if there is any doubt as to whether they are permanently attached fixtures. Articles that might cause confusion include freestanding appliances, invisible fencing and controls, light bulbs, above-ground pools, and swing sets.

IN PRACTICE

The NCAR Standard Form 2A-T, "The Offer to Purchase and Sales Contract," dated 2008, in paragraph 2, lists items that are normally fixtures and provides for items that may be exempted by the seller or buyer. "2. FIXTURES: The following items, if any, and if owned by the seller, are included in the purchase price free of liens: any built-in appliances, light fixtures, ceiling fans, attached floor coverings, blinds, shades, drapery rods and curtain rods, brackets and all related hardware, window and door screens, storm windows, combination doors, awnings, antennas, satellite dishes and receivers, burglar/fire/smoke alarms, pool and spa equipment, solar energy systems, attached fireplace screens, gas logs, fireplace inserts, electric garage door openers with controls, outdoor plants and trees (other than in movable containers), basketball goals, storage sheds, mailboxes, wall and/or door mirrors, attached propane gas tank, invisible fencing including all related equipment, lawn irrigation systems and all related equipment, water softener/conditioner and filter equipment, and any other items attached or affixed to the Property, *EXCEPT* any such items leased by the Seller and the following items: _____."

Trade fixtures.   An article owned by a tenant and attached to a rented space or building for use in conducting a business is a **trade fixture**, or a chattel fixture. Examples of trade fixtures are bowling alleys, store shelves, bars, and restaurant equipment. Do not confuse trade fixtures, items the tenant installs to further the tenant's business, with *up-fits*, such as walls or sinks installed by the landlord while preparing the property for the tenant's occupancy.

Trade fixtures differ from other types of fixtures in three ways:

1.   Fixtures are part of the real property and belong to the owner of that property. Trade fixtures are usually owned and installed by a tenant for personal use and remain the tenant's personal property.
2.   Fixtures are considered a permanent addition to a building, but trade fixtures are removable. Trade fixtures may be attached to a building in the same manner as other fixtures. However, due to the relationship of the parties (landlord and tenant), the law gives a tenant the right to remove trade fixtures, provided the removal is completed before the term of the lease expires and the rented space is restored to approximately its original condition.
3.   Because fixtures are legally construed to be real property, they are included in any sale or mortgage of the real property. Trade fixtures are not included in the sale or mortgage of real property except by special agreement.

Trade fixtures that are not removed at the end of the lease become the real property of the landlord. Acquiring the items in this way is known as *accession*.

■ **FOR EXAMPLE** Paul's Pizza leases space in a small shopping center. Paul bolts a large iron oven to the floor of the unit. When Paul's Pizza goes out of business or relocates, Paul will be able to take his pizza oven with him if he can repair the bolt holes in the floor; the oven is a trade fixture. On the other hand, if the pizza oven was brought into the restaurant in pieces, welded together, then set in concrete, Paul might not be able to remove it without causing structural damage. In that case, the oven might become a fixture.

Agricultural fixtures.   There is a special class of fixtures in North Carolina: **agricultural fixtures.** While fixtures used in a farming operation would seem to fall into the category of trade fixtures, agricultural fixtures are considered real property rather than personal property. Therefore, in North Carolina, if a tenant farmer installed feeding troughs during the tenancy, they would be considered real property and could not be removed by the tenant at the end of the lease without special written agreement.

Effect of the Uniform Commercial Code (UCC).   All brokers should be aware of the effect of the **Uniform Commercial Code (UCC)** on fixtures. According to the UCC, if a homeowner purchases an item on credit (a dishwasher, for example) and gives the creditor a security agreement, that item remains personal property and may be removed by the creditor in the event of default. When the item has been paid for in full, it becomes real property. Suppose the homeowner decides to sell her home before the dishwasher has been paid for. She could remove the dishwasher when she moves out of the house because it is still her personal property. On the other hand, she may leave the dishwasher behind and the buyer might assume that it is real property that was included in the purchase price. The buyer may be surprised to learn that he must pay the secured creditor the outstanding balance or risk having the appliance repossessed. All home buyers should make sure there are no security agreements filed on items within the home. This is normally included in the title search, which the buyer's lawyer will perform. The filing of the security agreement in effect makes the potential fixture an item of personal property until it is paid for in full.

■ ESTATES IN REAL PROPERTY

The amount and kind of interest that a person has in real property is called an *estate in land*. An *estate* may be defined as the degree, quantity, nature, and extent of interest one has in real property. Estates in land are divided into two major classifications: (1) nonfreehold estates or leasehold estates (those involving tenants) and (2) freehold estates (those involving ownership) (see Figure 2.4). (Nonfreehold estates are discussed in detail in Chapter 11.)

Freehold estates are estates of indeterminable length, such as those existing for a lifetime or forever. These include the

- fee simple estate (can pass by inheritance),
- defeasible fee estate (can pass by inheritance),
- *pur autre vie* estate (estate for the life of another) with remainder or reversion (can pass by inheritance), and
- ordinary conventional life estate with remainder or reversion (does not pass by inheritance).

The first three of these estates continue for an indefinite period and are inheritable by the heirs of the owner; they are called *estates of inheritance*. The fourth terminates on the death of the named person on whose life the estates are based, called the *measuring life*; they are called *estates not of inheritance*.

Nonfreehold, or **leasehold, estates,** which will be discussed thoroughly in Chapter 11, include any estate that is not a freehold estate. A leasehold estate exists on property in addition to a freehold estate when the property owner has rented the property to a tenant. The four types of leasehold estates are the

1. estate for years,
2. estate from year to year,
3. estate at will, and
4. estate at sufferance.

Fee Simple Estate

A holder of an estate in fee simple is entitled to all rights in the property. An estate in fee simple is the highest type of interest in real estate recognized by law. It is complete ownership. This estate is of potentially unlimited duration. When the owner dies, the estate passes to the owner's heirs or devisees (as provided in the owner's will). A fee simple estate is an estate of inheritance and is always legally transferable, but it is not always free of encumbrances. There are two major types of fee simple estates: *fee simple absolute* that basically has no ownership limitation and *fee simple defeasible* where the ownership can be terminated due to the actions of the current owner.

Fee simple absolute.   A fee simple ownership on which there are no limitations (other than governmental restrictions) is a **fee simple absolute** estate. In common usage, the terms *fee* and *fee simple* are used interchangeably with fee simple absolute. Owners of an estate in fee simple can do whatever they wish with the property as long as the use does not violate public land use regulations, deed restrictions, or the rights of others. This is the highest form of land ownership.

Fee simple subject to a condition subsequent: "on the condition that"

Fee simple determinable: "so long as" "while" "during"

Fee simple defeasible.   A **fee simple defeasible** (or *defeasible fee*) estate may be lost (or defeated) on the occurrence or nonoccurrence of a specified event. Also known as a *qualified fee estate*, the owner must stay *qualified* to own the estate by obeying deed restrictions imposed on the estate by a previous owner. Whether the restriction prohibits an activity or requires a specified land use will dictate which type of defeasible fee estate has been granted. Two types of defeasible estates are *fee simple subject to a condition subsequent* and *fee simple determinable*.

A **fee simple subject to a condition subsequent** estate dictates some action or activity that the new owner must not perform. The former owner retains a right of re-entry, called a *reversionary right*, so that if the condition is broken, the former owner can retake possession of the property through court proceedings. A fee simple estate with condition subsequent does not automatically revert to the original owner.

■ **FOR EXAMPLE** A grant of land on the condition that there be no sale of alcohol on the premises is a fee simple subject to a condition subsequent. If alcohol is sold on the property, the former owner has the right to reacquire full ownership. It will be necessary for the grantor (or the grantor's heirs or successors) to go to court to assert that right. There is no automatic right of reversion.

A **fee simple determinable** estate requires that a specified activity or land use continue. In a fee simple determinable estate, the ownership is held "so long as" or "during the period" the condition or limitation is maintained. The former owners, their heirs, or their successors retain the right of reversion that automatically reacquires full ownership if the special condition ceases to exist. No lawsuit is

FIGURE 2.4   **Freehold Estates and Interests in North Carolina**

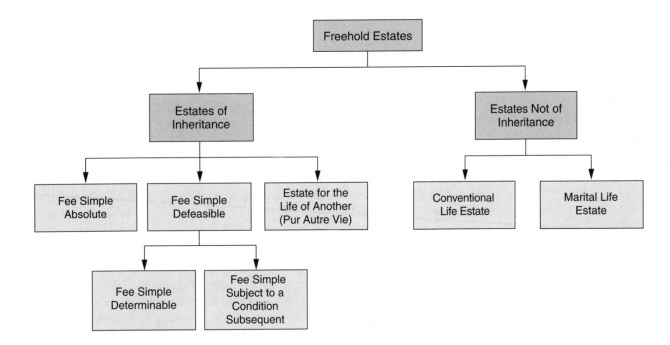

necessary for reversion. The use of the land has been pre-determined and the penalty for noncompliance has been predetermined.

■ **FOR EXAMPLE** A grant of land from Aunt Fran to her church so long as the land is used only for religious purposes is a fee simple determinable (with a special limitation). If the church uses the land for a nonreligious purpose, title automatically reverts back to Aunt Fran (or her heirs or successors).

Do not confuse the two estates. The difference between them is in the language used to create the estate and whether a court process is required for re-entry. A *fee simple estate subject to a condition subsequent* is conveyed *provided that*, or *on the condition that* some situation in the future does not happen. The language used for a *fee simple determinable estate* is based on time. It is conveyed *as long as*. Both of these defeasible estates are the same as far as possession and use are concerned. A real estate licensee is strongly encouraged to have competent legal advice when encountering any qualified estate scenario.

Because they will take effect only at some time in the future (if at all), the right of re-entry and the possibility of reversion are called **future interests.**

Life Estate

A **life estate** is a freehold estate in land that is limited in duration to the life of the owner or to the life or lives of some other designated person or persons. This form of ownership is occasionally called a partial estate because it does not last forever.

Conventional life estate. A conventional life estate is created by grant from the owner of the fee simple estate. The owner retains a reversionary interest in the property or names a *remainderman* that will ultimately receive fee simple absolute

FIGURE 2.5   Remainder Interest

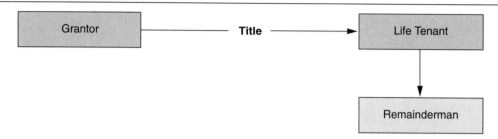

title (see Figure 2.5). A conventional life estate is limited to the lifetime of the owner of the life estate (the **life tenant**). An ordinary life estate ends with the death of the person to whom it was granted (see Figure 2.6). It is possible to have successive life estates.

■ **FOR EXAMPLE** Broderick wants his children ultimately to have ownership of a piece of property. But he wants his mother to be able to live on it for as long as she lives. So Broderick deeds the property to his mother for her life. Broderick's mother is the life tenant with her life being the measurement for how long she will own the estate; his children are the remaindermen. When she dies, the ownership of the property will automatically transfer to his children.

Life estate *pur autre vie.* There is also an estate known as an *estate for the life of another*; the legal term being *life estate **pur autre vie**. As with a conventional life estate, the life tenant owns the property. In this estate, it is owned for the lifetime of some named third party, called the *measuring life*. The measuring life has no present or future ownership in the property and only serves as the yardstick for the term of the life tenant's ownership. Upon the death of the measuring life, the estate would either revert to the original owner or become the property of the named remainderman. If the life tenant should die before the measuring life, the heirs of the deceased life tenant will inherit the life estate either by will or by descent.

■ **FOR EXAMPLE** Austin, a 67-year-old man, owns fee simple title to Blackacre Farms. He conveys a life estate in Blackacre Farms to his brother Carl for the life of Denise, Carl's daughter and Austin's niece. Carl has the right to enjoy the ownership of the property and is the life tenant, but Denise is the measuring life. Should Denise die, Carl's estate will terminate and revert to Austin, Austin's heirs, or to a named remainderman. Denise has no present or future ownership interest in the property.

While a conventional life estate is not considered an estate of inheritance, a life estate pur autre vie can be inherited by the life tenant's heirs, but only until the death of the measuring life. For example, if Carl died before Denise, Carl's heirs would inherit Carl's life estate. However, their life estate would terminate on the death of Denise.

F I G U R E   2.6   **Reversionary Interest**

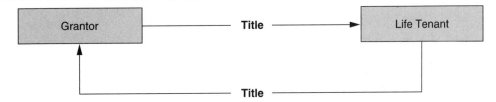

Remainder and reversion.   A fee simple owner who creates a life estate must consider the future ownership of the property after the termination of the life estate. The future interest may take one of two forms:

1. **Remainder interest:** The grantor names someone other than the grantor to receive title to the property when the life estate terminates. This occurred in our example with Broderick. He provided that his children would receive title when his mother's life estate terminated. The person(s) named (the children, in our example) is said to own a remainder interest and is called a **remainderman.** A **remainder interest** is a *nonpossessory estate*—a future interest. This interest can be sold. (See Figure 2.5)

2. **Reversionary interest:** If the grantor does not name a remainderman, then ownership returns to the grantor when the life estate terminates. This is called a **reversionary interest.** If the grantor is deceased when the life estate terminates, the property goes to the grantor's heirs or devisees. This interest or estate is called a *reversion* and is also a future interest. (See Figure 2.6)

When the life estate terminates, the holder of the future interest (the remainder or reversion) will be the owner of a fee simple estate.

Rights of life tenants.   A life tenant's interest in real property is a true ownership interest. In general, the life tenant is not answerable to the holder of the future interest as long as the property is maintained. A life tenant is entitled to all income and profits arising from the property during the life tenancy. A life tenant also may use some of the property's resources to maintain the property. For example, a life tenant may sell some of the timber growing on the property to pay for damages caused by a flood. This right to use property resources is referred to as estovers. A life tenant also can sell or mortgage a life tenancy, although there may be few parties willing to purchase or lend money that is secured by such a limited interest. Life tenants must pay real estate *ad valorem* taxes and special assessments that arise during the tenancy. They must also pay the interest, but not the principal, on any pre-existing debt secured by the property.

A life tenant's rights are not absolute, however. A life tenant can enjoy the rights of the land but cannot encroach on those of the reversioner or remainderman. In other words, the life tenant cannot perform any act that would permanently injure the land or property. For example, a life tenant would not be allowed to destroy an orchard on the property to avoid having to bother with it. This kind of injury to real estate is known in legal terms as **waste.** Those with a future interest in the property could bring legal action for damages or seek an injunction against the life tenant.

Marital life estate.   A marital life estate is one created by statute in some states. A marital life estate becomes effective automatically by operation of law on the occurrence of certain events. Dower and curtesy are the forms of marital life estate currently used in some states. *Dower* is a wife's right to a life estate in her husband's property after his death; *curtesy* is a husband's right to a life estate in his wife's property after her death.

In 1959, North Carolina abolished dower and curtesy, or marital life estates, and set up a system of intestate succession in their place. The North Carolina Intestate Succession Act provides for the distribution of the property of an intestate person, one who dies without a valid will. This statute allows for the equal division of property among eligible heirs, or, in the event of no heirs, having the property escheat to the North Carolina State Educational Assistance Authority. This statute does not override an active survivorship clause in a deed.

■ OWNERSHIP OF REAL PROPERTY

A fee simple estate in land may be held in (1) severalty, which means that title is held by one owner (sometimes referred to as *sole ownership*), or (2) co-ownership, co-tenancy, or concurrent ownership, where title is held by two or more persons at the same time.

The manner in which property is owned is important to the real estate broker for two reasons: (1) the form of ownership existing when a property is sold determines who must sign the various documents involved (listing contract, acceptance of offer to purchase or sales contract, and deed) and (2) the purchaser must determine in what form to take title. For example, a sole purchaser generally takes title in the purchaser's name alone, and a tenancy in severalty is created. However, if there are two or more purchasers, they may take title in a tenancy in common, in joint tenancy, or in tenancy by the entirety. When questions about these forms of ownership are raised by the parties to a transaction, the real estate broker should recommend that the parties seek legal and tax advice.

Ownership in Severalty   When title to real estate is vested in (presently owned by) one person or a single entity, such as a corporation, or limited liability company (LLC), that person or entity is said to own the property in **severalty.** This person or entity is also referred to as the *sole owner*.

Concurrent Ownership   When title to one parcel of real estate is vested in two or more persons or entities, those parties are said to be *concurrent owners*, or *co-owners*, of the property. There are several forms of co-ownership, each having unique legal characteristics. The three forms recognized in North Carolina are

1. tenancy in common,
2. joint tenancy, and
3. tenancy by the entirety.

Tenancy in common.   A parcel of real estate may be owned by two or more people in what is known as a **tenancy in common.** There are two important

FIGURE 2.7

Tenancy in Common

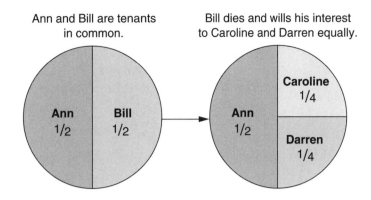

Ann and Bill are tenants in common.

Bill dies and wills his interest to Caroline and Darren equally.

characteristics of a tenancy in common. First, the ownership interest of a tenant in common is an undivided interest; there is a unity of possession among the co-owners. This means that although a tenant in common may hold, for example, a one-half or one-third interest in a property, it is impossible to distinguish physically which specific half or third of the property the tenant in common owns. The deed creating a tenancy in common may or may not state the fractional interest held by each co-owner; if no fractions are stated, the tenants are presumed to hold equal shares. For example, if five people hold title, each would own an undivided one-fifth interest. Although ownership interests are frequently equal shares, it is not a requirement of this type of ownership.

The second important characteristic of a tenancy in common is that each owner holds an undivided interest in severalty and can sell, convey, mortgage, or transfer that interest through the right of partition. On the death of a co-owner, that tenant's undivided interest passes to the heirs through a probate proceeding. The interest of a deceased tenant in common does not pass to another tenant in common unless the surviving co-owner is an heir or a purchaser (see Figure 2.7).

When two or more unmarried people acquire title to a parcel of real estate and the deed does not stipulate the type of tenancy created, by operation of law they acquire title as tenants in common.

Termination of co-ownership by partition suit.   Each co-owner of real estate has an absolute right to force a partition of the land by voluntary action and agreement, which will divide their real estate according to their interests. When a division among co-owners cannot be agreed on voluntarily, the division can be ordered by a court in a suit for partition. The court may actually divide the land into pro rata parcels or, if this cannot be done, may order the property sold and the proceeds divided proportionately among the owners.

Joint tenancy.   Most states recognize some form of **joint tenancy** in property owned by two or more people. With joint tenancy, the ownership shares are always equal with undivided possession. This type of ownership also requires that the joint tenants purchase the property together at the same time and that the names of all joint tenants appear on the deed. The main feature that distinguishes a joint

FIGURE 2.8

Joint Tenancy with Right of Survivorship

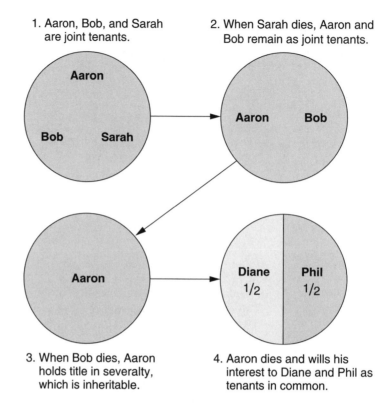

1. Aaron, Bob, and Sarah are joint tenants.

Aaron
Bob   Sarah

2. When Sarah dies, Aaron and Bob remain as joint tenants.

Aaron   Bob

3. When Bob dies, Aaron holds title in severalty, which is inheritable.

Aaron

4. Aaron dies and wills his interest to Diane and Phil as tenants in common.

Diane 1/2   Phil 1/2

tenancy from a tenancy in common is the possibility for the **right of survivorship**. With survivorship in place, the death of one of the joint tenants does not destroy the ownership unit; it only reduces by one the number of people who make up the unit. As each successive joint tenant dies, the surviving joint tenant(s) will acquire the interest of the deceased joint tenant. The joint tenancy continues until there is only one owner, who then holds title in severalty. The last surviving joint tenant has the same rights to dispose of the property as any sole owner (see Figure 2.8).

North Carolina does not favor the right of survivorship for a joint tenancy. The right of survivorship can be created if the deed is worded in exact compliance with North Carolina court decisions, making it clear that the right of survivorship is intended. Otherwise, North Carolina statutes provide that on the death of a joint tenant, the decedent's estate does not pass to the surviving joint tenant but instead goes to the heirs in the same manner as estates held by tenancy in common. In other words, unless the deed is worded exactly right, a joint tenancy can be created, but the right of survivorship does not apply. Note that where a right of survivorship is created, if one joint tenant owner conveys an interest to another person, that right of survivorship will be destroyed. The new owner becomes a tenant in common with the other owners because title is conveyed at a separate time (see Figure 2.9).

A lawyer should always be consulted if the parties to a transaction insist on the right of survivorship. There are many technical requirements that must be met before a North Carolina court will recognize a joint tenancy with a right to survivorship.

F I G U R E   2.9

Combination of Tenancies

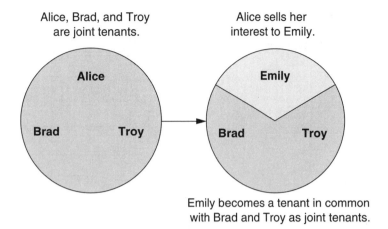

Alice, Brad, and Troy
are joint tenants.

Alice sells her
interest to Emily.

Emily becomes a tenant in common
with Brad and Troy as joint tenants.

Three Forms of Concurrent Ownership in North Carolina

1. Tenancy in common
2. Joint tenancy
3. Tenancy by the entirety

Tenancy by the entirety.   **Tenancy by the entirety** is a special form of tenancy in which the owners must be husband and wife. Each spouse has an equal, undivided interest in the property; each, in essence, owns the entire estate. On the death of one spouse, full title automatically passes to the surviving spouse through the right of survivorship without a probate hearing. The transfer of the interest of the deceased spouse may be recorded by filing a certificate of death, an affidavit, or a certificate of transfer, as provided by law.

The distinguishing characteristics of tenancy by the entirety are

■ the owners must be husband and wife when title is received;
■ the owners have rights of survivorship;
■ during the owners' lives, title can be conveyed only by a deed signed by both parties (one party cannot convey a one-half interest); and
■ there is generally no right to partition.

In North Carolina, any conveyance to a husband and wife by deed or by will creates a tenancy by the entirety by default unless specifically stated otherwise. A tenancy by the entirety may be terminated by the death of either spouse, by divorce (leaving the parties as tenants in common), or by the mutual agreement of both spouses. Note that a husband and wife can choose another form of ownership for property that is owned during marriage—tenancy by the entirety is not the only available option. Furthermore, property that is jointly owned before marriage (or owned in severalty by one of the spouses) does not automatically become a tenancy by the entirety simply by virtue of the fact of marriage. If a couple owned property before marriage as tenants in common, they will continue to own the property as tenants in common unless the husband and wife choose to legally change the form of ownership.

Common Interest Community Ownership

Some forms of ownership are called *common interest community ownership* because they contain elements of both ownership in severalty and concurrent ownership.

Condominium ownership.   The **condominium** form of ownership of apartment buildings was popular in Europe for many years before gaining wide acceptance in the United States. Condominium laws, often called *horizontal property acts*, have been enacted in every state, including North Carolina. Under these

Condominium Ownership

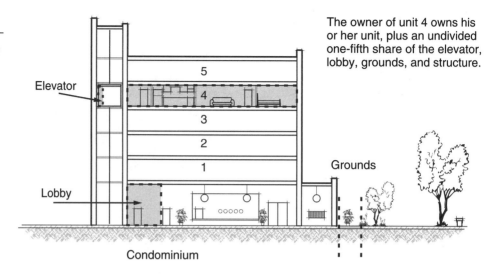

The owner of unit 4 owns his or her unit, plus an undivided one-fifth share of the elevator, lobby, grounds, and structure.

laws, the occupant/owner of each unit holds a fee simple title to the unit (which is often called *title to airspace*) and also a specified share of the indivisible parts of the building and land, known as the *common elements* or common areas (see Figure 2.10). The individual unit owners in a condominium own these common elements together as tenants in common. The individual unit owners pay their own separate property taxes and mortgage payments and typically belong to an owners' association that manages the common elements of the condominium complex.

The condominium form of ownership is usually used for apartment buildings. These may range from freestanding highrise buildings to townhouse-like arrangements. The common elements include such items as the land, exterior structure, hallways, elevators, stairways, and roof. In some instances, lawns and recreational facilities such as swimming pools, clubhouses, tennis courts, and golf courses also may be considered common areas. In addition, the condominium form of ownership is used for other types of properties such as commercial properties, office buildings, and multiuse buildings that contain offices and shops as well as residential units.

Creation of a condominium.   The **North Carolina Condominium Act of 1986** specifies that a condominium is created and established when the developer of the property executes and records a declaration of its creation in the county where the property is located. The declaration must include any covenants, conditions, or restrictions on the use of the property. The developer must file a plat map or plan of the condominium property, buildings, and any other improvements. The developer also must prepare a set of bylaws. The bylaws usually provide for

- the creation of a unit owners' association giving a vote to each unit owner,
- the election of a board of managers from among the unit owners,
- the duties of the board of managers,
- the compensation of its members,
- their method of election and removal,
- whether a managing agent is to be engaged, and
- the method of collecting the unit owners' association monthly dues from each member to cover the costs of management and maintenance of the common areas.

Consumer protection.   The North Carolina law also requires disclosure and other consumer protection measures in connection with new residential condominium unit sales in the form of public offering statements. The developer must disclose all ownership and other appropriate documents to the purchaser before the purchase contract is signed. The purchaser then has a seven-day rescission period, which begins after the purchase contract is signed. At any time during that seven-day period, the purchaser can cancel the sale and receive a full refund of any monies paid. On a resale unit (a sale of a condominium other than the original sale from the developer), a resale certificate detailing the monthly dues assessment and any other fees payable by a unit owner must be given to a purchaser prior to conveyance. There is no right to cancel in resale transactions.

Cooperative ownership.   Under the usual **cooperative** arrangement, title to land and building is held by a corporation (or partnership or land trust). The building management sets a price for stock shares for each unit in the building. Each tenant of a unit in the building purchases stock in the corporation when the tenant pays the agreed-on price for use of a specific apartment. The purchaser then becomes a shareholder of the corporation and, by virtue of that stock ownership, receives a **proprietary lease** to the unit for the life of the corporation.

The cooperative building's real estate taxes are assessed against the corporation as owner. Generally, the mortgage is signed by the corporation, creating one lien on the entire parcel of real estate. Taxes, mortgage interest, and principal, plus operating and maintenance expenses are shared by the tenants/shareholders in the form of monthly assessments.

While the cooperative tenants/owners do not actually own an interest in real estate (they own stock, which is personal property), for all practical purposes they control the property through their stock ownership and their voice in the management of the corporation. The bylaws of the corporation generally provide that each prospective purchaser of an apartment lease must be approved by an administrative board. This hybrid form of ownership has not enjoyed much popularity in North Carolina to date.

Townhouse ownership.   **Townhouse** projects are typically a group of two-story or three-story units that are horizontally attached to each other; that is, they share party walls. Each townhouse unit is individually owned; all unit owners have membership in the homeowner association that owns the common areas. The homeowners association will pay real property taxes on the common areas, while each individual unit owner will pay the real property taxes on the unit they own. Townhouse ownership is similar to condominium ownership with one fundamental difference: the owner of each townhouse unit also owns the land on which that unit is built. A developer may choose to build a townhouse project rather than a condominium project because of all the rules and regulations that govern condominiums.

Time-share ownership.   A **time-share** is any right to occupy a unit of real property during five or more separated time periods (usually consisting of one or two weeks) over a period of at least five years. Time-sharing permits multiple purchasers to buy interests in real estate—usually a unit of a resort hotel, an apartment, or a condominium—with each purchaser having a right to use the facility for a specific time period. For instance, a time-share owner may have the right to use an oceanfront apartment for the first three weeks of June every calendar year.

Due in large part to the historically high-pressure sales practices associated with the sale of time-shares, the North Carolina Time Share Act (G.S. 93A, Article 4) was passed to regulate the development and sale of time-shares. Despite the name given to a development project, if the format meets the definition in the Act, it will be classified a *time-share* and subject to its requirements. For example, all time-share projects must be registered with the state; developers must give prospective purchasers public offering statements prior to contract; and purchasers have a five-day cancellation or rescission period during which they can cancel the purchase without penalty. Time-share salespeople must be active real estate brokers operating under a project broker, who are subject to disciplinary action by the North Carolina Real Estate Commission. The Commission can also fine unlicensed time-share developers $500 for each violation of the Act or revoke the project's registration certificate. (See Appendix C.)

Planned unit development.   A **planned unit development (PUD)** is really a method of real estate development, not ownership. The major feature of a PUD is flexible zoning. It differs from a normal subdivision in that buildings may be clustered together (rather than complying with normal lot size and setback requirements), leaving more room for open spaces and recreational areas. Sometimes PUDs include a variety of land uses as well. For example, instead of being solely single-family residential, a PUD also may include some multifamily complexes as well as some retail or commercial uses. Typically, residential owners receive title to their individual units, while the homeowners' association typically has title to the common areas of the development.

■ RELATED WEB SITES

Manufactured Housing Institute: *www.manufacturedhousing.org*
Modular Today: *www.modulartoday.com*
Water Law in North Carolina:
  www.bae.ncsu.edu/programs/extension/publicat/arep/waterlaw.html
NC Department of the Secretary of the State/UCC laws:
  www.secretary.state.nc.us/ucc
NC Condominium Act:
  www.ncga.state.nc.us/gascripts/statutes/StatutesTOC.pl?Chapter=0047C

■ SUMMARY

Different rights to the same parcel of real estate may be owned and controlled by different parties, one owning surface rights, one owning air rights, and one or more owning subsurface rights. These rights can be severed by separate instruments.

When articles of personal property are permanently affixed to land, they may become fixtures. As such, they are considered a part of the real estate and become subject to any existing mortgage on the property. Personal property attached to real estate by a tenant for the purpose of his or her business is classified as a trade fixture and remains personal property of the tenant.

Although the sales contract is the best way to determine whether an item is a fixture, the Total Circumstances Test can be used if the contract is silent about the status of an item. Four legal tests determine if an item is a fixture or not: intent, relationship of the annexing party to the property, method of annexation, and adaptability. Intent is the most important test.

An estate is the degree, quantity, nature, and extent of interest a person holds in land. Ownership of freehold estates is of indeterminate length. Less-than-freehold estates are called nonfreehold, or leasehold, estates, and they involve tenants. A freehold and nonfreehold estate can exist on a single parcel of land at the same time if the landowner has leased the parcel to a tenant.

A freehold estate may be an estate of inheritance such as a fee simple estate or an estate not of inheritance such as a life estate. A fee simple estate can be absolute or defeasible on the happening of some event. A conventional life estate is created by the owner of a fee estate. The North Carolina Intestate Succession Laws have replaced marital life estates. Estates of inheritance include fee simple, fee simple determinable, fee simple subject to a condition subsequent, and life estate *pur autre vie*. Estates not of inheritance include conventional life estates.

Sole ownership, or ownership in severalty, indicates that title is held by one person or entity. Under concurrent ownership, there are several ways in which title to real estate can be held by more than one person. Co-ownership in North Carolina may be held by tenancy in common, joint tenancy, or tenancy by the entirety.

Common interest community ownership combines elements of ownership in severalty and concurrent ownership. Such forms of ownership include ownership of condominiums, cooperatives, time-shares, and townhouses and will include membership in an owners' association.

QUESTIONS

1. Real property is often referred to as a bundle of legal rights. Which of the following is *NOT* among these rights?
   a. Right of exclusion
   b. Right to override local zoning
   c. Right of enjoyment
   d. Right to sell or otherwise convey the property

2. A construction firm builds an office center over a railroad right-of-way. This means that
   a. trains can no longer operate during business hours because the noise would disturb occupants of the office center.
   b. the construction firm has built the office center using the subsurface rights to the property.
   c. the construction firm has built the office center using the air rights over the property.
   d. the construction firm is in violation of North Carolina law.

3. Aaron Heffner purchases a parcel of land and sells the mineral rights to an exploration company. Aaron sold which of the following rights?
   a. Air
   b. Surface
   c. Subsurface
   d. Air and subsurface

4. David owns property that is bordered by a small stream. His property ends
   a. at the stream edge.
   b. at the center of the stream.
   c. five feet before the stream edge.
   d. at the mean high-water mark of the stream.

5. Martha owns oceanfront property. Her property ends
   a. at the water's edge.
   b. at the edge of the dunes.
   c. at the low tide water mark.
   d. at the mean high-water mark.

6. Jordan Mims has placed a manufactured home on his lakefront lot. In order to make the home a legal part of the real estate, Jordan must do all of the following *EXCEPT*
   a. remove the trailer hitch, wheels, and axles.
   b. attach the home to a permanent foundation.
   c. remove the HUD label from the exterior of the home.
   d. cancel the motor vehicle title with an affidavit.

7. Which of the following is/are considered real property?
   I. A field of soybeans planted by a tenant farmer
   II. Ornamental trees planted in the yard by the owner
   a. I only
   b. II only
   c. Both I and II
   d. Neither I nor II

8. Which of the following would normally be considered a fixture?
   a. A portable basketball goal on the parking pad
   b. A custom-made mailbox attached to the house
   c. Curtains in the master bedroom that match the wallpaper
   d. A porch swing that is hanging from hooks on the front porch

9. A lumber dealer has just unloaded a truckload of lumber that will be used to build a porch on the property. At this point, the lumber is considered a(n)
   a. fixture.
   b. chattel.
   c. real property.
   d. improvement on real estate.

10. Which of the following would *NOT* be considered in determining if an item is a fixture?
    a. Intent
    b. Adaptability
    c. Value
    d. Method of attachment

11. Which of the following items would normally convey as a fixture with the property?
    a. Refrigerator and countertop microwave
    b. Free-standing butcher block table in the kitchen
    c. Decorative lights draped around the enclosed patio
    d. The large mirror bolted over the fireplace mantel

12. Anita Ferez is renting a single-family home under a one-year lease. With the landlord's approval, she installs awnings over the front windows to shade some delicate hanging plants. What is the status of the awnings at the end of the lease?
    a. Anita can remove the awnings when she vacates.
    b. The awnings are considered real property of the landlord and must stay.
    c. It is at the discretion of the landlord whether Anita can take the awnings.
    d. The awnings are considered trade fixtures and must stay.

13. A tenant firmly attaches appropriate appliances for his restaurant business on the leased premises. These appliances are
    I. trade fixtures.
    II. removable by the tenant within 30 days after the expiration of the lease agreement.
       a. I only
       b. II only
       c. Both I and II
       d. Neither I nor II

14. A purchaser of real estate learns that her ownership rights will continue forever and that no other person has any ownership control over the property. This person owns a
    a. fee simple interest.
    b. life estate pur autre vie.
    c. determinable fee estate.
    d. fee simple subject to a condition subsequent.

15. Qualified fee estate generally means that the estate will terminate on the death of
    I. the grantor.
    II. the grantee.
       a. I only
       b. II only
       c. Both I and II
       d. Neither I nor II

16. A fee simple estate has all the following characteristics EXCEPT that it is
    a. of indefinite duration.
    b. free of encumbrances.
    c. transferable by deed or by will.
    d. transferable with or without valuable consideration.

17. Which of the following statements is/are TRUE?
    I. A life estate is a freehold estate.
    II. A life estate pur autre vie can be an inheritable estate.
       a. I only
       b. II only
       c. Both I and II
       d. Neither I nor II

18. Which of the following describes a conventional life estate?
    a. Estate conveyed from Andrew to Betty until Betty dies
    b. Estate held by Andrew and Betty as co-owners with right of survivorship
    c. Estate conveyed to Betty for Jake's lifetime
    d. Fee simple estate

19. A freehold estate in land that will automatically extinguish upon the occurrence of a specified event is called a
    I. fee simple subject to a condition subsequent.
    II. fee simple determinable.
       a. I only
       b. II only
       c. Both I and II
       d. Neither I nor II

20. Geena wanted to donate a vacant lot she owned adjacent to a hospital to the hospital for expansion purposes. She wanted to make sure the land was used as she intended, so her attorney prepared the deed to convey ownership of the lot to the hospital "so long as it is used for hospital purposes." Upon receipt of the gift, the hospital owned a

    a. fee simple absolute estate.
    b. conventional life estate.
    c. fee simple determinable estate.
    d. leasehold estate.

21. Estevez has a freehold estate in a single-family home. He rents the home to a young couple.

    a. Estevez no longer has a freehold estate because a freehold estate and a leasehold estate cannot exist in the same property.
    b. Estevez must give up his freehold estate in order to rent the property to others.
    c. The tenants now hold the freehold estate in the property.
    d. Estevez has a freehold estate in the property, and the tenants have a leasehold estate in the property.

22. A life tenant can do all the following EXCEPT

    a. sell their lifetime rights.
    b. receive profits from the property.
    c. strip cut the timber on the property.
    d. use the resources of the property to maintain the property.

23. When title passes to a third party on the death of the life tenant, what is the third party's interest in the property?

    a. Remainder
    b. Reversionary
    c. Pur autre vie
    d. Redemption

24. When a fee simple estate in North Carolina is conveyed by a deed to two or more owners, other than husband and wife, without designating the nature of their co-ownership, they are assumed to be

    a. tenants by the entirety.
    b. joint tenants with survivorship.
    c. tenants in common.
    d. joint tenants without survivorship.

25. Ownership as a tenant in common must have

    a. undivided possessory interest.
    b. equal ownership interest.
    c. been bought by all owners at the same time.
    d. right of survivorship included.

26. If property is held by two or more owners as tenants in common, the interest of a deceased co-owner will pass to the

    a. remaining owner or owners.
    b. heirs of the deceased owner.
    c. trust under which the property was owned.
    d. state by the law of escheat, regardless of whether the deceased has any heirs.

27. What form of concurrent ownership can only be held by husband and wife?

    a. Tenants by the entirety
    b. Joint tenants with survivorship
    c. Tenants in common
    d. Joint tenants without survivorship

28. What form of concurrent ownership can be held by husband and wife?

    a. Tenants by the entirety
    b. Joint tenants with survivorship
    c. Tenants in common
    d. All the above

29. William, Frank, and Jane are joint tenants without the right of survivorship. Jane sells her interest to Lloyd, and then Frank dies. As a result,

    a. Frank's heirs, Lloyd and William, are joint tenants.
    b. Frank's heirs and William are joint tenants.
    c. William and Lloyd are tenants in common and are the only remaining owners of the property.
    d. William, Lloyd, and Frank's heirs are tenants in common.

30. Concerning concurrent ownership, which of the following statements is/are TRUE?

    I. Tenancy in common is not available to a married couple holding title on a property.
    II. Joint tenants must hold title to the property with equal, undivided interests.

       a. I only
       b. II only
       c. Both I and II
       d. Neither I nor II

31. A condominium is created when

   a. the construction of the improvements is completed.
   b. the owner/developer files a declaration of condominium in the public record.
   c. the condominium owners' association is established.
   d. all of the unit owners file documents in the public records asserting their decision.

32. Ownership that allows possession for only a specific time each period is a

   a. cooperative.
   b. time-share.
   c. condominium.
   d. syndicate.

33. A purchaser under the cooperative form of ownership receives

   I. a lease for the dwelling unit.
   II. stock in the cooperative corporation.
      a. I only
      b. II only
      c. Both I and II
      d. Neither I nor II

34. A buyer and a seller/developer executed a purchase contract for a new condominium on May 6, 2009, with the buyer giving $5,000 in earnest money. The buyer changed her mind and notified the seller on May 11, 2009, that she was rescinding the contract. Which of the following is true?

   a. The buyer can legally cancel the contract and have all the earnest money refunded.
   b. The buyer cannot cancel the contract because the three-day right of rescission has passed.
   c. The buyer can cancel only if she forfeits the earnest money.
   d. The buyer cannot cancel the contract because there is no right of rescission.

35. Which of the following statements is/are TRUE?

   I. A condominium owner individually owns only the "airspace" in the unit and no land.
   II. A townhouse owner individually owns the ground under the unit.
      a. I only
      b. II only
      c. Both I and II
      d. Neither I nor II

CHAPTER **3**

Encumbrances on Real Property

■ **identify** different types of encumbrances on real property.

■ **describe** different types of liens, easements, and encroachments.

■ **explain** property taxation laws and procedures; and how real property is assessed and taxed.

■ **define** these *key terms:*

ad valorem taxes	easement by prescription	mass appraisal
assessment	easement in gross	mechanics' lien
deed restrictions	encroachment	octennial reappraisal
dominant tenement	encumbrance	priority
easement	general lien	restrictive covenant
easement appurtenant	judgment	servient tenement
easement by condemnation	lien	special assessments
	lis pendens	specific lien
easement by necessity	Machinery Act	tax lien

■ ENCUMBRANCES ON REAL PROPERTY

A claim, charge, or liability that attaches to and is binding on real estate is called an **encumbrance.** An encumbrance is anything that affects title to real estate. It is a right or interest held by a party who is not the fee owner of the property. An encumbrance may affect the value or obstruct the use of the property, but it does not necessarily prevent a transfer of title.

Liens

A charge against property that provides security for a debt or an obligation of the property owner is a **lien.** If the obligation is not repaid, the lienholder, or creditor, has the right to have it paid out of the debtor's property, usually from the proceeds of a court sale. Real estate taxes, mortgages and trust deeds, judgments, and mechanics' liens all represent possible liens against an owner's real estate. A lien does not constitute ownership; it is a type of encumbrance. Note, however, that whereas all liens are encumbrances, not all encumbrances are liens.

Liens fall into several categories, based on how they are created. A voluntary lien is contractual or consensual and is created by the debtor's action, as when someone takes out a mortgage loan to buy real estate. An involuntary lien is created by law, such as a **tax lien** imposed by a municipality. Liens may be further classified as general or specific, as illustrated in Figure 3.1.

Specific liens.   A **specific lien** is secured by a specific parcel of property and affects only that particular property. Examples would be mortgage or deed of trust liens, real property taxes or special assessments liens, and mechanics' liens.

Mortgage and deed of trust liens.   In general, a *mortgage* or *deed of trust lien* is a voluntary specific lien on real estate given to a lender by a borrower as security for a real estate loan. It becomes a lien on real property when the lender records the mortgage or deed of trust in the office of the register of deeds in the county where the property is located. Mortgage and deed of trust liens are the most common form of lien or encumbrance. Mortgages and mortgage liens are discussed in detail in Chapter 14.

Real property tax and special assessment liens.   If a property owner fails to pay the taxes levied by a city or county on the property, the unpaid tax becomes a specific, involuntary lien on that property. The lien attaches to the property on the date the property is listed (January 1 of each year) and, as a superior lien, takes priority over all other liens. Real property is taxed on an *ad valorem* basis, which means *according to value.*

In addition to the ad valorem real estate taxes, special assessment (improvement) taxes may be levied against specific real property. The purpose of these taxes is to

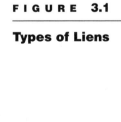

F I G U R E   3.1

Types of Liens

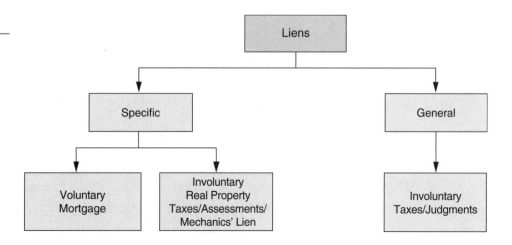

pay for an improvement that has benefited the taxed property, such as street paving or the installation of a sewer system.

Both ad valorem and special assessment tax liens are valid for ten years and have priority over other types of liens. (Property taxes are discussed in more detail later in this chapter.)

Mechanics' liens.   The purpose of the mechanic's lien is to give security to those who perform labor or furnish material in the improvement of real property. A **mechanic's lien** is a specific, involuntary lien and is available to contractors, subcontractors, architects, equipment lessors, surveyors, laborers, and others. This type of lien is filed when the property owner has not paid for the work or when the general contractor has been paid but has not paid the subcontractors or suppliers.

To be entitled to a mechanic's lien, the person who did the work must have had a contract (express or implied) with the owner or the owner's authorized representative. A person claiming a mechanic's lien must file the lien claim within 120 days after last furnishing the labor or materials; the lien takes effect from the date that person first furnished the labor or materials. The action to enforce a properly filed mechanic's lien must be brought within 180 days after a worker last furnished labor or materials.

General liens.   General liens affect all the property of a debtor, both real and personal, rather than a specific parcel of real property. Examples include judgments, personal property tax liens, and state and federal tax liens.

Judgments.   A **judgment** is a decree issued by a court. When the decree provides for the awarding of money and sets forth the amount of money owed by the debtor to the creditor, the judgment is referred to as a *money judgment.*

When a judgment is properly docketed in a county (entered and indexed in a judgment book), that judgment becomes an involuntary, general lien on all of the current and future real estate and personal property owned by the judgment debtor in that county. Real estate of the judgment debtor in other counties is not affected unless the judgment is docketed in those counties as well. A judgment lien is good for ten years from the date of the judgment.

Personal property tax liens.   A personal property tax is assessed on certain types of personal property. If unpaid, this tax becomes a general, involuntary lien against all the property owned by the taxpayer. Like real property tax liens, personal property tax liens have priority over other types of liens.

State tax liens.   Both unpaid state inheritance taxes and unpaid state income taxes give rise to general, involuntary liens against all property owned by the individual taxpayer. Both types of liens last for ten years.

Federal tax liens.   An Internal Revenue Service (IRS) tax lien results from a person's failure to pay any portion of federal IRS taxes, such as income and withholding taxes. A federal tax lien is a general, involuntary lien on all real and personal property held by the delinquent taxpayer. Its priority is based on the date of filing or recording; it does not supersede previously recorded liens.

Effects of liens on title.   Although the fee simple estate held by a typical real estate owner can be reduced in value by the lien rights of others, the owner is still free to convey title to a willing purchaser. The purchaser will, however, buy the property subject to any liens because liens run with the land; that is, they will bind successive owners if steps are not taken to clear the liens.

Remember, liens attach to the property, not to the property owner. Therefore, although a purchaser who buys real estate under a delinquent lien is not responsible for payment of the debt secured by the lien, the purchaser does face a possible loss of the property if the creditors take court action to enforce the payment of their liens.

Priority of liens.   Because property taxes and special assessments generally take **priority** over all other liens, they are called superior liens. Therefore, if the property is sold through a court-ordered sale to satisfy unpaid debts, outstanding real estate taxes, personal property taxes, and special assessments will be paid from the proceeds first. The remainder of the proceeds will be used to pay other outstanding liens in the order of the date and time they were filed. The first lien to be filed is the first lien to be paid. (This is called a *pure race system* of determining lien priority.) One exception to this rule is the mechanic's lien: the priority of a mechanic's lien dates back to the date the labor began or materials were first provided rather than to the date the lien was filed.

Deed Restrictions

Deed restrictions are another type of encumbrance on real property. Deed restrictions (also referred to as *covenants, conditions,* and *restrictions*) are private agreements placed in the public record that affect the use of land. They are usually imposed by an owner of real estate when property is sold and are included in the seller's deed to the buyer. Deed restrictions typically would be imposed by a developer or subdivider for the purpose of maintaining specific standards in a subdivision, and they would be listed in the original development plans for the subdivision filed in the public record. Deed restrictions are discussed further in Chapter 6.

Lis Pendens

A judgment or another decree affecting real estate is rendered at the conclusion of a lawsuit. Generally, there is a considerable time lag between the filing of a lawsuit and the rendering of a judgment. When any suit is filed that affects title to a specific parcel of real estate (such as a foreclosure suit), the person bringing the lawsuit may file a **lis pendens** (Latin for "litigation pending"). When a *lis pendens* is filed, anyone acquiring an interest in the property takes that interest subject to any judgment or decree the court may issue. *Lis pendens* is not a lien but rather a notice that there is an action or lawsuit pending that may adversely affect the title. The *lis pendens* acts more like an encumbrance against the title.

■ **FOR EXAMPLE** If a lender is filing a foreclosure suit against a property owner, it will file a *lis pendens* against the property. If the property owner should sell the property during the course of the legal action, the new purchaser would take title subject to the outcome of the foreclosure action.

Easements

A right to use the land of another for a particular purpose is called an **easement.** An easement is not a form of ownership; it merely grants the use of the property. There are two types of easements: *easement appurtenant* and *easement in gross*.

Easement appurtenant.   An easement that is annexed to the ownership of one parcel of land and used for the benefit of another parcel of land is an **easement appurtenant**. For an easement appurtenant to exist, two adjacent tracts of land must be owned by different parties. The tract over which the easement runs is known as the **servient tenement**; the tract that benefits from the easement is known as the **dominant tenement** (see Figure 3.2).

■ **FOR EXAMPLE** If Able and Baker own adjacent properties in a lake resort community and only Able's property borders the lake, Able may grant Baker an easement across Able's property so that Baker can have access to the lake. Able's property is the servient tenement; Baker's property is the dominant tenement. Baker's property benefits from the easement because it now has lake access, which did not exist before the easement was granted.

An easement appurtenant is considered part of both the dominant and the servient lands, and if either tract is conveyed to another party, the easement passes with the title. In legal terms, the easement *runs with the land*.

A *party wall* is an exterior wall of a building that straddles the boundary line between two owners' lots, with half of the wall on each lot. The lot owners own the half of the wall on their lot, and they have an easement appurtenant in the other half of the wall for support of their building. A written party-wall agreement should be used to create the easement rights. Expenses to build and maintain the wall are usually shared. A party driveway shared by adjoining owners and straddling the property boundary also should be created by written agreement, specifying responsibility for expenses.

Easement in gross.   A mere personal interest in or right to use the land of another is an **easement in gross**. The right of use belongs to an individual (whether a person or a corporation) and is not appurtenant to (attached to) any ownership estate in land. In other words, an easement in gross benefits a person or an entity, not a parcel of property. Examples of easements in gross are the easement rights a railroad has in its right-of-way or utilities easements (See Figure 3.2). Commercial easements in gross, such as the ones owned by the railroad company, may be assigned or conveyed and may be inherited. However, personal easements in gross usually are not assignable and terminate on the death of the easement owner.

Creating an easement.   To create an easement, there must be two separate parties, one of whom is the owner of the land over which the easement runs. It is impossible for the owner of a parcel of property to have an easement over that land. Thus, where a valid easement exists and the dominant tenement is subsequently acquired by the owner of the servient tenement, the easement is extinguished. The person who has the easement interest has a nonpossessory interest in the land. The owner of the land burdened by the easement has a possessory interest in the land (the owner can use and possess the land), but the owner cannot interfere with the easement holder's rights.

FIGURE   3.2   **Easement Appurtenant and Easement in Gross**

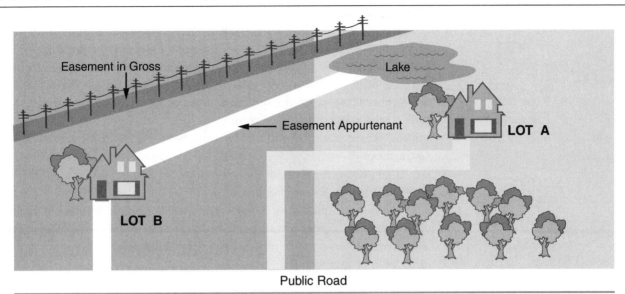

The owner of Lot B has an easement appurtenant across Lot A to gain access to the lake. Lot B is dominant and Lot A is servient. The utility company has an easement in gross across both parcels of land for its power lines.

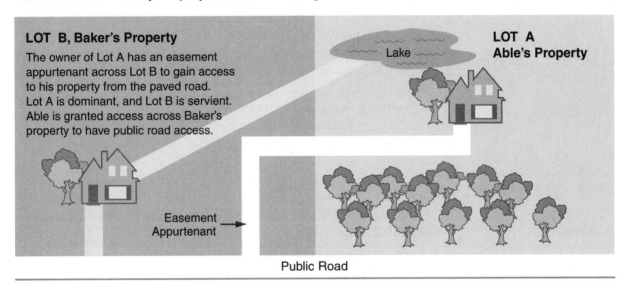

Easements may be created in the following ways:

- *Express grant.* An easement is commonly created by a written agreement between the parties establishing the easement right. Easements are often created in a deed from the owner of the property over which an easement will run. The North Carolina Statute of Frauds requires that easements be created in writing to be enforceable because they are an interest in real property.
- *Express reservation.* An easement can be created by the grantor in a deed of conveyance by reserving an easement over the sold land.
- *Necessity.* An **easement by necessity,** or easement by implication of law, arises because all owners must have rights of ingress to and egress from their land—they cannot be landlocked. If a grantor has conveyed property that

is completely surrounded by the grantor's property (thus landlocking the grantee), an easement by necessity will be created.

■ *Prescription*. When a claimant has made use of another's land for a certain period of time, as defined by state law, an **easement by prescription** is acquired. This prescriptive period is 20 years in North Carolina. The claimant's use must have been continuous, exclusive, and without the owner's approval. Additionally, the use must have been visible, open, and notorious, so that the owner could have readily learned of it. A property owner can prevent an easement by prescription from being created by giving permission to the user.

■ *Condemnation*. An **easement by condemnation** is acquired for a public purpose through the power of eminent domain. *Eminent domain* is the power of a government or quasi-government entity to take property for a public use, after paying the owner just compensation. Examples are taking land to put in a school or widen a road. In both cases, the owner must be compensated for any loss in property value.

Terminating an easement.   An easement may be terminated

■ when the purpose for which the easement was created no longer exists;
■ if the easement holder becomes the owner of the land where the easement is located (a situation called a *merger*);
■ by release of the right of easement to the owner of the servient tenement;
■ by abandonment of the easement (the intention of the parties is the determining factor);
■ by non-use of a prescriptive easement;
■ by adverse possession by the owner of the servient tenement;
■ by destruction of the servient tenement, as in the demolition of a party wall;
■ by nonrecordation;
■ by lawsuit (an action to quiet title) against someone claiming the easement; or
■ by excessive use, as when a residential easement is converted to commercial purposes.

Encroachments

An **encroachment** arises when an improvement or any portion of an improvement, such as a building, a fence, or a driveway illegally extends beyond the land of its owner and covers some land of an adjoining owner, a street, or an alley. For instance, two landowners are neighbors. The garage of one landowner actually extends one foot onto the neighbor's property. This is an encroachment.

Encroachments are usually disclosed by either a physical inspection of the property or a location survey. A location survey shows the location of all improvements on a property and determines whether any improvements extend over the lot lines. If the building on a lot encroaches on neighboring land, the neighbor may be able either to recover damages or to secure removal of the portion of the building that encroaches. Encroachments of long standing (for the prescriptive period of 20 years in North Carolina) may give rise to easements by prescription. The primary reason for a property survey is to ensure no encroachments have occurred. The legal effect of an encroachment is to potentially make both titles unmarketable.

IN PRACTICE
Because an undisclosed encroachment could render a title unmarketable, the existence of an encroachment should be noted in a listing agreement, and the sales contract governing the transaction should be made subject to the existence of the particular encroachment. Encroachments are not disclosed by the usual title evidence provided in a real estate sale unless a survey is submitted while the examination is being made. Mortgage lenders may resist loans on properties with encroachments.

■ PROPERTY TAXATION IN NORTH CAROLINA

The ownership of real estate is subject to certain government powers. One of these powers is the right of state and local governments to impose tax liens for the support of their governmental functions. This power to tax comes from the state constitution and is considered to be a constitutional power rather than a police power. Because the location of real estate is permanently fixed, the government can levy taxes with a high degree of certainty that the taxes will be collected. Furthermore, because the lien for taxes levied on real estate has priority over other previously recorded liens, the tax lien will be the first lien to be paid from the proceeds of a court-ordered sale of the real estate.

Real estate taxes fall into two categories: (1) general real estate, or ad valorem, taxes and (2) special assessment, or improvement, taxes. Both of these taxes are levied against specific parcels of property and automatically become liens on those properties.

General Tax (Ad Valorem Tax)

General real estate taxes are levied for the general support of the government agency authorized to impose the levy. These taxes are known as **ad valorem taxes** because the amount of the tax varies in accordance with the value of the property being taxed. In North Carolina, the Machinery Act governs ad valorem taxes.

Property subject to taxation. All real property in North Carolina is subject to taxation. Although counties and municipalities determine real estate property tax rates within their jurisdictions, the **Machinery Act** regulates standards for real property taxation, standards for tax assessment, standards for tax appraisal, and requirements for tax-exempt status. Property generally considered tax-exempt or eligible for special tax treatment includes that owned by nonprofit religious, educational, and charitable organizations; property owned by the elderly and handicapped; agricultural, horticultural, and forest lands; and some properties with energy-efficient heating and cooling systems.

Taxation timetable. In January of each tax year, all taxable real property must be listed in the county in which it is located. All listed property is assessed at its fair market value. Real property is appraised based on a statutory schedule and then is reappraised every eight years, a process referred to as **octennial reappraisal**. Real property may be reassessed more frequently than every eight years. In addition, the county or city may choose to make horizontal adjustments in the fourth year after reappraisal. This means the values of certain types of property or of properties within certain areas may be uniformly adjusted to current value by applying an *across the board* percentage increase or decrease.

Each county or municipality determines the appropriate tax rate every year as part of its budgeting process. The rate is calculated by dividing the total amount of revenue needed by the total assessed value of all the property in the county or city. A new property tax rate must be established by July 1 of each year or the tax rate from the previous year will stand. Tax rates are usually expressed as a certain dollar amount per $100 of assessed value. Per the Machinery Act (NCGS §105-271), assessed value is supposed to be equal to market value, at least at the time the assessment is established.

■ **FOR EXAMPLE** If a city has an annual budget of $705,600 and has property within its jurisdiction with assessed value of $78,400,000, this year's tax rate would be

$$\$705,600 \div \$78,400,000 = \$0.90 \text{ per } \$100 \text{ of valuation}$$

If the tax rate were $0.90 per $100 of value, a $90,000 home would get a tax bill for $810.

$$\$90,000 \div \$100 \times 0.90 = \$810$$

If the tax rate were only $0.80 per $100 of value, the same $90,000 home would get a tax bill for $720.

$$\$90,000 \div \$100 \times 0.80 = \$720$$

Each year's property taxes are legally due and payable on September 1. However, because interest does not begin accruing until early in January of the following year, most people pay their real property taxes in late December. The last day that current real property taxes can be paid without penalty is January 5 of the following year. It is worth noting that even though cities and counties operate under a fiscal year (beginning on July 1 and ending on June 30), taxes are prorated based on the calendar year (see Figure 3.4).

Property tax liens. As noted earlier, property taxes are liens that attach to real property as of the listing date. In other words, even though property taxes are not due until September 1 of any given year, the tax lien takes effect the previous January 1. Remember, this tax lien takes priority over all other liens.

Appraisal and Assessment

The *appraisal* of real property may be defined as a process or an opinion as to value of property and how that value is communicated (see Chapter 17). The **assessment** is an official valuation of property for the purpose of establishing assessed value for tax purposes. Even though similar in concept, the techniques used in appraisal and assessment are quite different. Tax assessors do not have the time to assess individual properties like appraisers for reasons such as loan applications. In

FIGURE 3.3

Taxation Timetable

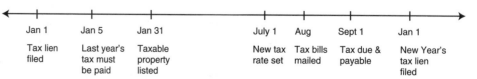

Jan 1	Jan 5	Jan 31	July 1	Aug	Sept 1	Jan 1
Tax lien filed	Last year's tax must be paid	Taxable property listed	New tax rate set	Tax bills mailed	Tax due & payable	New Year's tax lien filed

the assessment process one method routinely used is the **mass appraisal** technique that determines assessed value for all lands in a given area by applying an overall percentage increase or decrease. This method is often used in conjunction with a *horizontal adjustment*. Real property may be subject to reassessment if substantial improvements are added to the property.

Special Assessments

Special assessments, the second category of real estate taxes, are special taxes levied on real estate for public improvements made to that real estate.

Property owners of properties that benefit directly from the improvements are required to pay for them. Special assessments are authorized for the installation of paved streets, curbs, gutters, sidewalks, storm sewers, street lighting, beach erosion drainage projects, and water control, to mention just a few. Because these improvements increase the value of the affected properties, the owners are, in effect, merely reimbursing the taxing entity for that increase. Either a county or a city may levy the special assessment, and statutes regulate how the assessment is to be prorated and levied. The assessment could be based on the cost per front foot or on the total area of the land that benefits. Large assessment bills may be prorated over several years.

Like ad valorem taxes, special assessment liens enjoy priority over other types of liens. (However, they do not take precedence over ad valorem taxes.)

■ SUMMARY

Encumbrances against real estate may be in the form of specific and general liens, deed restrictions, easements, and encroachments. A fee simple estate is always transferable but may not always be free of encumbrances.

Liens are claims, or charges, of creditors or tax officials against the real and personal property of a debtor. Liens are either general, covering all current and future real and personal property of a debtor/owner, or specific, covering only the specific property described in the mortgage, tax bill, or other document. The life of a general lien is usually ten years from the rendering of the judgment.

With the exception of real and personal property tax liens, special assessment liens, and mechanics' liens, the priority of liens is determined by the order in which they are placed in the public record of the county in which the debtor's property is located. Property tax liens are superior liens that are given priority over other liens. Special assessment liens also are given priority over all but property tax liens. The priority of a mechanics' lien is established from the first day of labor or delivery of material instead of date of recordation. Mechanics' liens are also unique in that the creditor has 120 days to record the lien after the last day of labor or delivery of materials.

Deed restrictions are private use conditions placed on real property by the owner of the real estate. Developers use **restrictive covenants** or protective covenants to maintain uniform standards in a subdivision in order to protect property values.

An easement is the right acquired to use another's real estate. There are two types of easements: easement appurtenant and easement in gross. An appurtenant easement involves two separately owned tracts. The tract benefited is known as the dominant tenement; the tract subject to the easement is called the servient tenement. An appurtenant easement is an encumbrance to the servient estate and a benefit to the dominant estate. An easement in gross is a personal right, such as that granted to individuals or to utility companies to maintain poles, wires, and pipelines. A personal easement in gross is not transferable and ends with the death of the grantee; a commercial easement in gross is transferable. There are multiple ways to create and terminate easements. An encroachment is an unauthorized use of another's real estate. Encroachments are frequently created accidentally due to inattention to property lines when placing improvements near the property boundary. The net effect of an encroachment is to possibly make titles to both properties unmarketable. A survey is the best way to discover encroachments.

In North Carolina, the Machinery Act governs *ad valorem* taxes by regulating standards and requirements used by counties and municipalities throughout the state. Real estate taxes are levied annually by local taxing authorities based on real property's assessed value. The octennial reappraisal requirement assures that assessed value is reappraised every eight years. Payments are required before stated dates, after which penalties accrue. Tax rates are usually expressed as a dollar amount per $100 of assessed value.

Special assessments are levied by county or local municipalities to allocate the cost of public improvements such as new sewers, sidewalks, curbs, or paving to the real property that benefits from them.

QUESTIONS

1. Which of the following is an example of a specific lien?
   a. Judgment lien
   b. Special assessment lien
   c. Personal property tax lien
   d. IRS income tax lien

2. Which of the following is an example of a general lien?
   a. Mortgage lien
   b. Real estate tax lien
   c. Mechanics' lien
   d. State income tax lien

3. A mechanics' lien
   a. must be filed within 180 days after last day of labor.
   b. is a general lien that is good for ten years.
   c. is used to collect payment from the general contractor.
   d. gives security to persons that work on real property owned by others.

4. According to typical lien priority, which of the following would be paid first from proceeds from a court-ordered sale?
   a. Mortgage lien
   b. Judgment lien
   c. Real property tax lien
   d. Special assessment lien

5. Which of the following liens typically would be given higher priority?
   a. Mortgage dated last year
   b. Current real estate taxes
   c. Mechanics' liens for work started before the mortgage was made
   d. Judgments rendered yesterday

6. Under city contract, ABC Paving Company paved a dirt road that runs adjacent to your property. As property owner, you would pay for this in the form of
   a. ad valorem real property taxes.
   b. personal property taxes.
   c. an invoice from the contractor.
   d. a special assessment.

7. *Lis pendens* is a
   I. recorded document that prohibits the transfer of title.
   II. legal notice of pending litigation that might affect the property title.
   a. I only
   b. II only
   c. Both I and II
   d. Neither I nor II

8. Ed Roberts has the legal right to pass over the land owned by his neighbor. Ed holds an
   a. easement.
   b. emblement.
   c. estate in land.
   d. encroachment.

9. After moving into his new home, Marco discovers that his neighbor gets to his workshop by regular use of Marco's driveway. Marco's lawyer explains that the neighbor's lot owns an easement over Marco's driveway. Marco's property is called
   a. the servient estate.
   b. a leasehold estate.
   c. a pur autre vie estate.
   d. the dominant estate.

10. All of the following terms are related to easements *EXCEPT*
    a. appurtenant.
    b. assessment.
    c. by necessity.
    d. by prescription.

11. In North Carolina, all real property *MUST* be reassessed every
    a. four years.
    b. six years.
    c. eight years.
    d. ten years.

12. The ad valorem property tax rates may be adjusted every

    a. year.
    b. two years.
    c. four years.
    d. five years.

13. What is the assessed value of a house located in the city limits if the city tax rate is $0.80 per $100, the county tax rate is $0.50 per $100, and the owner's annual taxes are $1,600?

    a. $123,077
    b. $200,000
    c. $208,000
    d. $320,000

14. What is the monthly tax liability on a property assessed at $133,000 if the published tax rate is $1.678 per $100 of assessed value?

    a. $66.05
    b. $185.98
    c. $792.61
    d. $2,231.74

15. If you recently paid $2,000 in annual property taxes and the assessed value of your house is $183,500, what is the tax rate?

    a. $.9175 per $100
    b. $1.09 per $100
    c. $9.12 per $100
    d. $10.90 per $100

16. Property is appraised at $129,000. If property is assessed at 75 percent of the appraised value, what is the assessed value of the property?

    a. $69,750
    b. $96,750
    c. $129,000
    d. $172,000

17. Betty's house was appraised at $389,000 for tax purposes. It was assessed at 85 percent of the appraised value. The taxes were $1.10 per $100 of value. How much were the annual taxes?

    a. $281.35
    b. $356.58
    c. $3,637.15
    d. $4,279.00

18. Market value for a property outside the city limits of Greensboro is $295,000. Assessed value is calculated at 80% of market value. The city tax rate is $.84 per $100 and the county tax rate is $.63 per $100. What is the monthly tax liability for this property?

    a. $123.90
    b. $154.88
    c. $289.10
    d. $361.38

19. The city of Pleasant Valley has an annual budget of $7,248,000. If the city has taxable property that has an assessed value of $1,123,500,000, what tax rate per $100 of assessed value must be levied to raise the necessary money to meet the budget?

    a. $0.65
    b. $1.56
    c. $6.40
    d. $15.63

CHAPTER 4

Property Description

■ **LEARNING OBJECTIVES** *When you have finished reading this chapter, you should be able to*

- ■ **explain** the importance of an accurate legal description and list those documents requiring legal descriptions.

- ■ **discuss** the legally acceptable methods of property description used in North Carolina, give examples, and know the characteristics of each.

- ■ **learn** the various land measurements used in real estate practices and the importance of a survey.

- ■ **define** these *key terms*:

call	plat map	survey
legal description	point of beginning (POB)	topographic survey
metes-and-bounds description	reference to a recorded plat (lot-and-block or recorded plat system)	
monuments		

■ DESCRIBING LAND

One of the essential elements of a valid deed is an accurate legal description of the land being conveyed. The real estate involved must be identifiable from the wording of the deed and with reference to only the documents named in the deed. The courts have usually held that a description of land is legally sufficient if a competent surveyor can locate the real estate in question.

A **legal description** is an exact way of describing real estate in a contract, a deed, a mortgage, or another document that will be accepted by a court of law. While street addresses are not sufficient legal descriptions, the legal description in a deed or mortgage may be followed by the words *commonly known as* and the street address. The street address standing alone is referred to as an *informal description or reference*.

A typical parcel of land has been conveyed and transferred many times in the past. The description of the land in a deed, a mortgage, or another instrument should be the same as that used in the previous instrument of conveyance. Discrepancies, errors, and legal problems can be avoided or reduced if this practice is followed in drawing up subsequent conveyances.

IN PRACTICE   One of the most frequent causes of lawsuits against licensees is inaccurate monuments and lot lines. Buyers need to be confident that the property they are purchasing is in fact what they believe they are buying. Relying on old surveys is not a good idea; the property should be resurveyed by a competent land surveyor, whether or not the lender requires it. Brokers should be very careful when stating the location of boundary lines. Licensees should encourage prospective buyers to hire a registered land surveyor if they plan to install fences or add to the buildings on their property. Recent flooding in North Carolina points out the need to be sure that buyers are informed about whether their property is in a flood plain that can also be determined by an appropriate survey.

METHODS OF DESCRIBING REAL ESTATE

There are four basic methods of legally describing real estate: (1) metes and bounds, (2) reference to recorded plat (lot and block), (3) reference to a publicly recorded document that contains a legal description, and (4) the rectangular (government) survey, *which is not used in North Carolina*. A combination of methods also may be used.

Metes and Bounds

A **metes-and-bounds description** is the earliest form of legal description used in the United States and is still the primary method of describing property in the original 13 colonies. It makes use of the boundaries and measurements of the land in question. This description shows the boundaries of the parcel and where they meet. Such a description starts at a definitely designated place called the **point of beginning (POB)** and proceeds around the boundaries of the tract (clockwise or counterclockwise) by reference to linear measurements and compass directions, referred to as **calls.** Each call gives the distance (metes) and direction (bounds). Each call begins with either North or South (the cardinal directions), then the number of degrees East or West, using a surveyor's compass. A metes-and-bounds description always ends at the POB so that the tract being described has closure.

In a metes-and-bounds description, the actual distance between monuments takes precedence over any linear measurement set forth in the description if the two measurements differ. **Monuments** are fixed objects used to establish real estate boundaries. Natural objects such as stones, large trees, lakes, and streams, as well as streets, highways, and markers placed by surveyors, are commonly used as

Metes-and-Bounds Tract

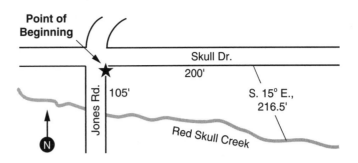

monuments. Measurements often include the words *more or less*; the location of the monuments is more important than the distance stated in the wording. Problems are created in some instances when a monument has shifted or disappeared over the years.

An example of a metes-and-bounds description of a parcel of land (pictured in Figure 4.1) follows:

> *A tract of land located in _____, _____, described as follows: Beginning at the intersection of the east line of Jones Road and the south line of Skull Drive; thence north 90° east along the south line of Skull Drive 200 feet; thence south 15° east 216.5 feet, more or less, to the center thread of Red Skull Creek; thence north 4° west along the center line of said creek to its intersection with the east line of Jones Road; thence north 105 feet, more or less, along the east line of Jones Road to the place of beginning.*

When used to describe property within a town or city, a metes-and-bounds description may begin as follows:

> *Beginning at a point on the southerly side of Kent Street, 100 feet easterly from the corner formed by the intersection of the southerly side of Kent Street and the easterly side of Broadway; thence . . .*

In this description, the POB is given by reference to the intersection. The description must close by returning to the POB.

Metes-and-bounds descriptions may be very complex and should be handled with extreme care. When they include compass directions of the various lines and concave or convex curved lines, they can be difficult to understand. In such cases, the advice and counsel of a professional surveyor should be sought.

Reference to a Recorded Plat (Lot and Block)

The second method of land description used in North Carolina is by **reference to a recorded plat (lot-and-block** or **recorded plat system).** It is a system that uses lot and block numbers—referred to as a *plat* or *subdivision*—placed in the Registry of Deeds of the county where the land is located. This is the most common and worry-free method of describing property in urban areas.

The first step in subdividing land is the preparation of a **plat map**—by a licensed surveyor or engineer—as illustrated in Figure 4.2.

FIGURE 4.2   **Subdivision Plat Map**

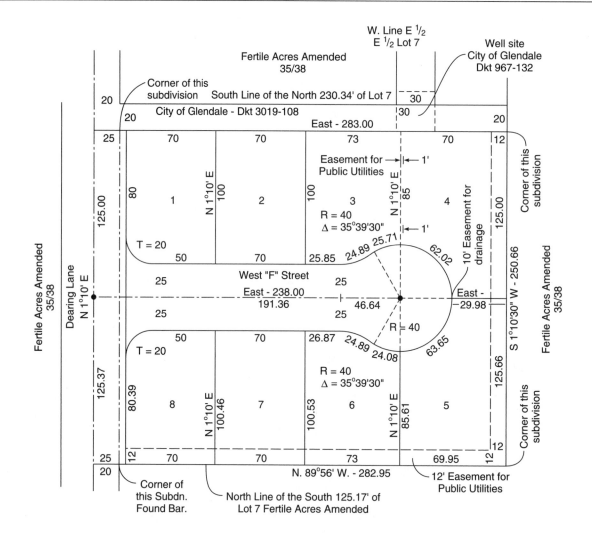

On this plat map, the land is divided into numbered or lettered blocks and lots, and streets or access roads for public use are indicated. Lot sizes and street details must be indicated completely and must comply with all local ordinances and requirements. When properly signed and approved, the subdivision plat must be recorded in the public records in the county where the land is located to be a legally acceptable property description. In describing a lot from a recorded subdivision plat, the lot and block number, name or number of the subdivision plat, and name of the county and state are used. For example:

> *Being all of Lot Number Forty-one (41) as shown and designated on a certain map prepared by John Doe, C.E., dated May 16, 1980, entitled "Plan of Bradford Extension," which said map is duly recorded in Map Book 7 at Page 32, in the Office of the Register of Deeds of Craven County, to which map reference is hereby made for a further and better description. Less and except any existing road right of ways of record.*

Reference to a Recorded Deed

The third method of land description used in North Carolina is by reference to a publicly recorded document, usually an earlier deed to the identical property. This deed typically contains a legal description of the property that is to be conveyed. For example, if a deed dated September 17, 1993, included the previous description by reference to a recorded plat, a deed prepared four years later that conveyed the same property could incorporate that same description by referring to the previous deed. Deeds do not make reference to buildings on the property.

IN PRACTICE   When filling in the blanks of a sales contract, an agent should exercise great care to ensure that a proper and accurate legal description is used. Never list the legal description as *N/A* for "not applicable."

Because legal descriptions of newly subdivided land, once recorded, affect title to real estate, they should only be prepared by a professional land surveyor or a lawyer. Real estate licensees who attempt to draft legal descriptions create potential risks for themselves and their clients and customers. (See G.S. 93A-6 (a)(11), and Rule A.0111.) Furthermore, when entered on a document of conveyance, legal descriptions should be copied with care. For example, an incorrectly worded legal description in a sales contract may obligate the seller to convey or the buyer to purchase more or less land than either one intended. Title problems can also arise for the buyer who seeks to convey the property at a future date.

Informal References

The use of informal references in describing property can often lead to legal problems, but informal references may be sufficient if they enable a surveyor to precisely locate the parcel of real estate. A street address is a good example of an informal reference and is often used in a listing contract and short-term rental agreements. Any contract to convey a real property interest and any type of deed should always contain a legally acceptable description.

Preparation and Use of a Survey

Legal descriptions should not be changed, altered, or combined without adequate information from a competent authority such as a surveyor or title lawyer. Legal descriptions should always include the name of the county and state in which the land is located.

A professional land surveyor is trained and licensed to locate a given parcel of land and to determine its legal description. The surveyor does this by preparing a **survey,** which sets forth the legal description of the property, and a *survey sketch*, which shows the location and dimensions of the parcel. When a survey also shows the location, size, and shape of buildings located on the lot, it is referred to as a *physical survey*, a *mortgage location survey*, or an *identification survey*. When a survey shows the *lay of the land*, such as where there are hills and valleys, it is called a **topographic survey** or *topo survey*. Surveys are required in many real estate transactions, such as when conveying a portion of a given tract of land, conveying real estate as security for a mortgage loan, showing the location of new construction, locating roads and highways, and determining the legal description of the land on which a particular building is located. When underwriting a real estate loan, the lender might require an up-to-date survey of the collateral property to make sure that there are no encroachments on the property because an encroachment could render the title to the property unmarketable. Encroachments could cross boundary lines, easements, or setbacks. Title insurance routinely excludes coverage of title defects that would have been discovered by a survey, if a survey was not conducted.

MATH CONCEPTS

LAND ACQUISITION COSTS

To calculate the cost of purchasing land, use the same unit in which the cost is given. Costs quoted per square foot must be multiplied by the proper number of square feet; costs quoted per acre must be multiplied by the proper number of acres; and so on.

To calculate the cost of a parcel of land of three acres at $1.10 per square foot, convert the acreage to square feet before multiplying:

43,560 square feet per acre × 3 acres = 130,680 square feet

130,680 square feet × $1.10 per square foot = $143,748

To calculate the cost of a parcel of land of 17,500 square feet at $60,000 per acre, convert the cost per acre into the cost per square foot before multiplying by the number of square feet in the parcel:

$60,000 per acre ÷ 43,560 square feet per acre =

$1.38 (rounded) per square foot

17,500 square feet × $1.38 per square foot = $24,150

■ RELATED WEB SITE

North Carolina Society of Surveyors: *www.ncsurveyors.com*

■ SUMMARY

Documents affecting or conveying interests in real estate must contain accurate legal descriptions of the property involved. Four methods of legal description of land are used in the United States: (1) metes and bounds, (2) reference to recorded plat (lot and block), (3) reference to publicly recorded document (deed), and (4) rectangular (government) survey. The last method is not used in North Carolina. An informal reference, such as the street address, is only adequate on listing agreements or short-term leases; any transfer of title or interest in real estate should use an adequate legal description obtained through one of the four methods mentioned above. A property's description should always be the same as the one used in previous documents.

The primary method of property descriptions in the original 13 colonies is the metes-and-bounds method. In a metes-and-bounds description, the actual location of monuments takes precedence over the written linear measurement in a document. When property is described by metes and bounds, the description must always enclose a tract of land; that is, the boundary line must end at the point at which it started (POB).

Land in every state can be subdivided into lots and blocks by means of a recorded plat of subdivision. An approved plat of survey that shows the division into blocks, giving the size, location, and designation of lots and specifying the location and size of streets to be dedicated for public use, is filed for recordation in the Register of Deeds' office of the county in which the land is located. It is possible to re-subdivide portions of a previously recorded subdivision.

The services of professional land surveyors are necessary in the conduc
estate business. A plat prepared by a surveyor is the usual method of cei
legal description of a certain parcel of land. Mortgage location (or iden
surveys are strongly encouraged to discover encroachments. Title insurance policies usually exclude coverage of title defects that would have been discovered in a
survey, if no survey was made.

QUESTIONS

1. In a sales contract, which of the following is an acceptable legal description of property?
   a. MLS number of the listed property
   b. "Johnson property on Maple Street"
   c. Metes and bounds description
   d. Lot number

2. A monument is used in which of the following types of legal descriptions?
   a. Lot and block
   b. Metes and bounds
   c. Rectangular survey
   d. Government survey

3. In describing real estate, the system that uses feet, degrees, and natural markers is the
   a. rectangular survey.
   b. metes-and-bounds description.
   c. government survey.
   d. lot and block system.

4. If the property being transferred is residential property within an established subdivision, the most commonly used legal description would be
   a. street address.
   b. metes-and-bounds.
   c. reference to a recorded plat.
   d. reference to a recorded deed.

5. A street address would be adequate property description for a
   a. short-term lease.
   b. sales contract.
   c. special warranty deed.
   d. deed of trust.

Answer questions 6 through 9 according to the information given on the plat of Mountainside Manor in Figure 4.3.

6. Which of the following statements is true?
   a. Lot 9, Block A is larger than Lot 12 in the same block.
   b. The plat for the lots on the southerly side of Wolf Road between Goodrich Boulevard and Carney Street is found on Sheet 3.
   c. Lot 8, Block A has the longest road frontage.
   d. Lot 11, Block B has more frontage than Lot 2, Block A.

7. Which of the following lots has the most road frontage on Jasmine Lane?
   a. Lot 10, Block B
   b. Lot 11, Block B
   c. Lot 7, Block A
   d. Lot 2, Block A

8. "Beginning at the intersection of the east line of Goodrich Boulevard and the south line of Jasmine Lane and running south along the east line of Goodrich Boulevard a distance of 230 feet; thence east parallel to the north line of Wolf Road a distance of 195 feet; thence northeasterly on a course N 22° E a distance of 135 feet; and thence northwesterly along the south line of Jasmine Lane to the point of beginning." Which lots are described here?
   a. Lots 13, 14, and 15, Block A
   b. Lots 9, 10, and 11, Block B
   c. Lots 1, 2, 3, and 15, Block A
   d. Lots 7, 8, and 9, Block A

9. On the plat, how many lots have easements?
   a. One
   b. Two
   c. Three
   d. Four

10. If the local market value of undeveloped land is $25,000 per acre, what is the value of a lot that has 21,780 square feet?
    a. $12,500
    b. $15,755
    c. $215,422
    d. $544,500

FIGURE 4.3   Plat of Mountainside Manor Subdivision

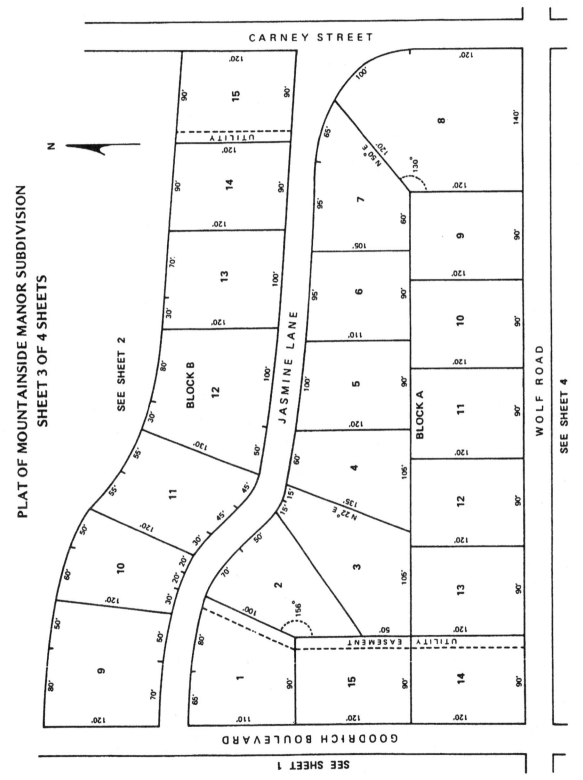

PLAT OF MOUNTAINSIDE MANOR SUBDIVISION
SHEET 3 OF 4 SHEETS

Recorded January 14, 1969 in plan book volume 351, page 15, in Beaver County, Pennsylvania.

CHAPTER 5

Transfer of Title to Real Property

■ **LEARNING OBJECTIVES** *When you have finished reading this chapter, you should be able to*

- ■ **identify** and understand the methods of transferring title, and the essential and nonessential elements of a deed.

- ■ **calculate** excise tax due when property is transferred.

- ■ **describe** the three major types of deeds used in North Carolina.

- ■ **explain** the processes of title examination and recordation.

- ■ **define** these *key terms*:

abstract of title	deed	marketable title
adverse possession	delivery and acceptance	Marketable Title Act
alienation	eminent domain	North Carolina Intestate
ALTA policy	escheat	Succession Act
chain of title	excise tax	quitclaim deed
cloud on the title	general warranty deed	recording
condemnation	grantee	special warranty deed
Conner Act	granting clause	title
constructive notice	grantor	title insurance
covenant	intestate	title search
		will

■ METHODS OF TRANSFERRING TITLE

Title to real estate means the right to or ownership of the land. The word *title* also is used to refer to the documentary evidence of the right of ownership, such as a deed. The word *title* refers to a summation of all the things property owners possess to prove and protect their ownership interest in property. The term *title* has two functions: (1) it represents the bundle of legal rights the owner possesses in the real estate, and (2) it denotes the facts that, if proven, enable a person to recover or retain ownership or possession of a parcel of real estate.

A parcel of real estate may be transferred voluntarily by sale or gift, or it may be taken involuntarily by operation of law. In addition, it may be transferred by will or descent after a person has died. Transfer of title is referred to as **alienation**, which means the act of transferring property to another.

Voluntary Alienation

Most transactions utilizing real estate agents involve voluntary alienation. Voluntary alienation (transfer) of title may be made by either gift or sale with the wishes and consent of the property owner. To transfer title by voluntary alienation during an owner's lifetime, that owner must use some form of deed.

A **deed** is a written instrument by which an owner of real estate intentionally conveys right, title, or interest in the parcel of real estate to another. A deed is evidence of title. The owner is referred to as the **grantor,** and the person who receives title is called the **grantee** (see Figure 5.1). A deed is executed (signed) only by the grantor(s). The grantee(s) does not usually sign the deed.

Requirements for a valid conveyance.   A valid deed in North Carolina must contain certain essential elements, including the following:

- The deed must be in writing.
- The grantor must have the legal capacity to execute a deed.
- Both the grantor and the grantee must be identified.
- There must be adequate words of conveyance.
- There must be an accurate legal description of the property conveyed.
- The deed must be signed by the grantors.
- The deed must be delivered to and voluntarily accepted by the grantee.

In writing.   All deeds must be in writing, in accordance with the requirements of the North Carolina Statute of Frauds, which states "an oral deed cannot be enforced."

FIGURE 5.1

Legal Terms for Parties in Real Estate Transactions

In reference to parties to a real estate instrument, such as a deed, the parties are referred to in legal terms such as *grantor* and *grantee.* The "OR" is the giver of the paper, and the "EE" is the receiver of the paper.

Type of Document	Giver	Receiver
Deed	Grantor (Seller)	Grantee (Buyer)
Offer	Offeror (Buyer)	Offeree (Seller)
Counteroffer	Offeror (Seller)	Offeree (Buyer)
Lease	Lessor (Landlord)	Lessee (Tenant)
Mortgage	Mortgagor (Buyer)	Mortgagee (Lender)
Option	Optionor (Seller)	Optionee (Buyer)
Installment Contract	Vendor (Seller)	Vendee (Buyer)
Will	Devisor (Deceased)	Devisee (Heir)

Grantor. A grantor must have a legal existence, be of lawful age, and be legally competent in order to convey title to real estate. A minor (a person who has not reached the age of majority) does not have legal capacity to transfer title, so any attempted conveyance by a minor is voidable by that minor upon reaching 18 years of age in North Carolina.

A grantor generally is held to have sufficient mental capacity to execute a deed if that grantor is capable of understanding the action. A deed executed by a person while mentally impaired (for example, by intoxication) is only voidable—it is not void. A deed executed by a person who has been judged legally incompetent is considered to be void.

> A **grantor** conveys property to a grantee.
>
> A **grantee** receives property from a grantor.
>
> A **deed** is the instrument that conveys property from a grantor to a grantee.

Identification of grantor and grantee. To be valid, a deed must name both the grantor and the grantee in such a way that they are readily identifiable. Furthermore, the grantee must be a real person, either a natural person or an artificial person, such as a corporation. A deed naming as the grantee a fictitious person, a company that does not exist, or a society or club that is not properly incorporated is considered void. The grantee cannot be a dead person.

Words of conveyance. A deed of conveyance transfers a present interest in real estate, and it must contain words that state the grantor's intention to convey the property at this time. An expression of intent to convey at some future time is inadequate. Such words of conveyance are often called the **granting clause**. Depending on the type of deed and the obligations agreed to by the grantor, the wording is generally *convey and warrant; grant; grant, bargain, and sell;* or *remise, release, and quitclaim.*

Legal description. To be valid, a deed must contain an acceptable, accurate, legal description of the real estate conveyed. Land has been described adequately if a competent surveyor could locate the property from the description used. The rules relative to describing real estate were discussed in Chapter 4.

Signature of grantor. To be valid, a deed must be signed by all the grantors (or their authorized agents) named in the deed. If the grantor is married, both the grantor and the grantor's spouse must sign the deed even if only one spouse is named in the deed. The grantee does not usually sign the deed.

Delivery. Before a transfer of title by conveyance can take effect, there must be **delivery and acceptance;** that is, actual *delivery* of the deed by the grantor and either actual or implied *acceptance* by the grantee. Delivery may be made by the grantor to the grantee personally or to a third party who is authorized by the grantee to accept the deed (such as a lawyer). Title is said to *pass* when a deed is delivered and voluntarily accepted. In North Carolina, recordation of the deed by the buyers or their agent is recognized as acceptance. The effective date of the transfer of title from the grantor to the grantee is the date of delivery of the deed itself.

Elements that are not required. Nonessential elements often appear in deeds, but are not required for validity. Nonessential elements include the following:

■ Deeds do not have to be *witnessed.*

- Deeds do not have to be *dated* (although, for practical matters, it may be wise to do so).
- Deeds do not have to include a statement as to the amount of *consideration* (the amount of money that was paid for the property).
- Deeds do not have to be *acknowledged* (i.e., *notarized*).
- Deeds do not have to be *recorded* to be valid but, under the Conner Act, the grantees must record the valid deed to protect their interest as to third parties under the law.
- Effective in 1999, deeds do not have to be *sealed* in North Carolina to be valid. Standard deed forms may continue to have the word *seal* after the signature; however, it is no longer required to create a valid deed. Signing *under seal* does have certain legal advantages such as extending the statute of limitations protecting the parties' rights from three years to ten years.

Note that acknowledgment (or notarization) is necessary before a deed can be recorded, and recording a deed is necessary to protect the grantee's interests in the property. Recording is discussed later in this chapter.

Types of Deeds

Three common forms of deeds—the general warranty deed, the special warranty deed, and the quitclaim deed—and several types of special-purpose deeds are used in North Carolina.

General warranty deed.   For a purchaser of real estate, a **general warranty deed** provides greater protection than any other deed. It is the best deed for the grantee, but it gives the grantor the greatest degree of liability. It is referred to as a *general warranty deed* or simply a *warranty deed* because the grantor is legally bound by certain basic **covenants** or warranties:

> **General Warranty Deed**
>
> *Four covenants:*
> 1. Covenant of seisin
> 2. Covenant against encumbrances
> 3. Covenant of quiet enjoyment
> 4. Covenant of warranty forever

- *Covenant of seisin and the right to convey:* The grantor warrants that he or she is the legal owner of the property and has the right to convey title to it. Delivery of seisin is the actual transfer of title.
- *Covenant against encumbrances:* The grantor warrants that the property is free from any liens or encumbrances except those of record. Encumbrances would generally include such items as mortgages, mechanics' liens, real estate tax liens, protective covenants, and easements.
- *Covenant of quiet enjoyment:* The grantor guarantees that the grantee's title will be good against third parties who might bring court actions to establish superior title to the property. If the grantee's title is found to be inferior, the grantor is liable for damages.
- *Covenant of warranty forever:* The grantor guarantees that if at any time in the future the title fails, he or she will compensate the grantee for the loss sustained. However, it is in the best interest of the grantee to obtain title insurance because at the time of a later claim, the grantor may be dead or financially insolvent.

These covenants in a general warranty deed are not limited to matters that occurred during the time the grantor owned the property; they extend back to its origin. An example of a general warranty deed appears in Figure 5.2. Note that the first three covenants are most important.

FIGURE 5.2 **General Warranty Deed**

NORTH CAROLINA GENERAL WARRANTY DEED

Excise Tax: _____

Parcel Identifier No._____ Verified by _____ County on the ____ day of_____, 20__
By:_____

Mail/Box to: _____

This instrument was prepared by:_____

Brief description for the Index: _____

THIS DEED made this _____ day of _____, 20___, by and between

GRANTOR	GRANTEE

Enter in appropriate block for each party: name, address, and, if appropriate, character of entity, e.g. corporation or partnership.

The designation Grantor and Grantee as used herein shall include said parties, their heirs, successors, and assigns, and shall include singular, plural, masculine, feminine or neuter as required by context.

WITNESSETH, that the Grantor, for a valuable consideration paid by the Grantee, the receipt of which is hereby acknowledged, has and by these presents does grant, bargain, sell and convey unto the Grantee in fee simple, all that certain lot or parcel of land situated in the City of _____, _____ Township, _____ County, North Carolina and more particularly described as follows:

The property hereinabove described was acquired by Grantor by instrument recorded in Book _____ page _____.

A map showing the above described property is recorded in Plat Book_____ page _____.

NC Bar Association Form No. 3 © 1976, Revised © 1977, 2002   + James Williams & Co., Inc.
Printed by Agreement with the NC Bar Association - 1981   www.JamesWilliams.com

F I G U R E   5.2   **General Warranty Deed (continued)**

TO HAVE AND TO HOLD the aforesaid lot or parcel of land and all privileges and appurtenances thereto belonging to the Grantee in fee simple.

And the Grantor covenants with the Grantee, that Grantor is seized of the premises in fee simple, has the right to convey the same in fee simple, that title is marketable and free and clear of all encumbrances, and that Grantor will warrant and defend the title against the lawful claims of all persons whomsoever, other than the following exceptions:

IN WITNESS WHEREOF, the Grantor has duly executed the foregoing as of the day and year first above written.

_____   _____(SEAL)
                (Entity Name)

By:_____   _____(SEAL)
        Title:_____

                                                                                        _____(SEAL)

By:_____   _____(SEAL)
        Title:_____

By:_____
        Title:_____

USE BLACK INK ONLY

SEAL-STAMP   State of North Carolina - County of _____

I, the undersigned Notary Public of the County and State aforesaid, certify that _____
_____ personally appeared before me this day and acknowledged the due execution of the foregoing instrument for the purposes therein expressed. Witness my hand and Notarial stamp or seal this _____ day of _____, 20__.

My Commission Expires:_____   _____
                                                                            Notary Public

SEAL-STAMP   State of North Carolina - County of _____

I, the undersigned Notary Public of the County and State aforesaid, certify that _____
_____ personally came before me this day and acknowledged that _he is the _____ of _____,
a North Carolina or _____ corporation/limited liability company/general partnership/limited partnership (strike through the inapplicable), and that by authority duly given and as the act of each entity, _he signed the forgoing instrument in its name on its behalf as its act and deed. Witness my hand and Notarial stamp or seal this _____ day of _____, 20__.

My Commission Expires:_____   _____
                                                                            Notary Public

SEAL-STAMP   State of North Carolina - County of _____

I, the undersigned Notary Public of the County and State aforesaid, certify that _____
_____

Witness my hand and Notarial stamp or seal this _____ day of _____, 20__.

My Commission Expires:_____   _____
                                                                            Notary Public

The foregoing Certificate(s) of _____ is/are certified to be correct.
This instrument and this certificate are duly registered at the date and time and in the Book and Page shown on the first page hereof.

_____   Register of Deeds for _____ County

By:_____   Deputy/Assistant - Register of Deeds

NC Bar Association Form No. 3 © 1976, Revised © 1977, 2002   * James Williams & Co., Inc.
Printed by Agreement with the NC Bar Association - 1981   www.JamesWilliams.com

Special warranty deed (limited warranty deed). A conveyance that carries only two covenants is called a **special warranty deed** (also known as a *limited warranty deed*). The grantor warrants that he or she received title to the land and that the property was not encumbered during the time he or she held title except as noted in the deed. Special warranty deeds generally contain the words *remise, release, alienate,* and *convey* in the granting clause. Any additional warranties to be included must be specifically stated in the deed. An example of a special warranty deed appears in Figure 5.3.

Quitclaim deed (non-warranty deed). A **quitclaim deed** (non-warranty deed) provides the grantee with the least protection of any deed. It carries no covenant or warranties and conveys only such interest, if any, that the grantor may have when the deed is delivered. By a quitclaim deed, the grantor only *remises, releases, and quitclaims* an interest in the property to the grantee. The deed might convey an easement; it might re-convey equitable title back to a seller; it might convey nothing at all. An example of a quitclaim deed appears in Figure 5.4.

If the grantor under a quitclaim deed has no interest in the property described, the grantee acquires nothing by virtue of the quitclaim deed; nor does the grantee acquire any right of warranty against the grantor. A quitclaim deed can convey title as effectively as a warranty deed if the grantor has good title when the deed is delivered, but it provides none of the guarantees of a warranty deed.

A quitclaim deed is frequently used to cure a defect, called a **cloud on the title**, in the recorded history of a real estate title. For example, if the name of the grantee is misspelled on a warranty deed placed in the public record, a quitclaim deed with the correct spelling may be executed to the grantee to perfect the title. A quitclaim deed is sometimes used to convey ownership rights from one spouse to the other in a divorce agreement. A quitclaim deed also is used when a grantor allegedly has inherited property but is not certain of the validity of the title of the decedent from whom the property was inherited. The use of a warranty deed in such an instance could carry with it obligations of warranty, while a quitclaim deed would convey only the grantor's interest.

IN PRACTICE A licensed real estate agent in North Carolina is prohibited from drafting a deed for others and is also prohibited from filling in the blanks of a deed form for others. While a licensed real estate agent may prepare a deed to convey the agent's own property, an attorney should be consulted for all deed preparations.

Special-Purpose Deeds

There are many specialized forms of deeds used in North Carolina for various specific purposes. A few significant examples of these are discussed below.

Correction deed. A correction deed is used when there has been an error in a previous deed. For example, if the description of the property in the original deed was incorrect, a correction deed will be used to make the correction. Errors in names or dates would also be corrected by this deed.

Deed of gift. When a grantor conveys property as a gift (that is, no consideration or only token consideration has been accepted for the property), a deed of gift is used. A deed of gift must be recorded within two years or it becomes void. Because no consideration is exchanged, there is no need to pay excise tax.

FIGURE 5.3   Special Warranty Deed

NORTH CAROLINA SPECIAL WARRANTY DEED

Excise Tax: _____

Parcel Identifier No. _____ Verified by _____ County on the ____ day of _____, 20__
By: _____

Mail/Box to: _____

This instrument was prepared by: _____

Brief description for the Index: _____

THIS DEED made this _____ day of _____, 20___, by and between

GRANTOR	GRANTEE

Enter in appropriate block for each party: name, address, and, if appropriate, character of entity, e.g. corporation or partnership.

The designation Grantor and Grantee as used herein shall include said parties, their heirs, successors, and assigns, and shall include singular, plural, masculine, feminine or neuter as required by context.

WITNESSETH, that the Grantor, for a valuable consideration paid by the Grantee, the receipt of which is hereby acknowledged, has and by these presents does grant, bargain, sell and convey unto the Grantee in fee simple, all that certain lot or parcel of land situated in the City of _____, _____ Township, _____ County, North Carolina and more particularly described as follows:

The property hereinabove described was acquired by Grantor by instrument recorded in Book _____ page _____.

A map showing the above described property is recorded in Plat Book_____ page _____.

NC Bar Association Form No. 6 © 1977, 2002   + James Williams & Co., Inc.
Printed by Agreement with the NC Bar Association - 1981   www.JamesWilliams.com

F I G U R E   5.3   **Special Warranty Deed (continued)**

TO HAVE AND TO HOLD the aforesaid lot or parcel of land and all privileges and appurtenances thereto belonging to the Grantee in fee simple.

And the Grantor covenants with the Grantee, that Grantor has nothing to impair such title as Grantor received, and Grantor will warrant and defend the title against the lawful claims of all persons claiming by, under or through Grantor, other than the following exceptions:

IN WITNESS WHEREOF, the Grantor has duly executed the foregoing as of the day and year first above written.

_____   _____(SEAL)
(Entity Name)

By:_____   _____(SEAL)
        Title:_____

By:_____   _____(SEAL)
        Title:_____

By:_____   _____(SEAL)
        Title:_____

USE BLACK INK ONLY

SEAL-STAMP | USE BLACK INK ONLY

State of North Carolina - County of _____

I, the undersigned Notary Public of the County and State aforesaid, certify that _____
_____ personally appeared before me this day and acknowledged the due execution of the foregoing instrument for the purposes therein expressed. Witness my hand and Notarial stamp or seal this _____ day of _____, 20__.

My Commission Expires:_____   _____
                                                                                      Notary Public

SEAL-STAMP

State of North Carolina - County of _____

I, the undersigned Notary Public of the County and State aforesaid, certify that _____
_____ personally came before me this day and acknowledged that _he is the _____ of _____,
a North Carolina or _____ corporation/limited liability company/general partnership/limited partnership (strike through the inapplicable), and that by authority duly given and as the act of each entity, _he signed the forgoing instrument in its name on its behalf as its act and deed. Witness my hand and Notarial stamp or seal this _____ day of _____, 20__.

My Commission Expires:_____   _____
                                                                                      Notary Public

SEAL-STAMP

State of North Carolina - County of _____

I, the undersigned Notary Public of the County and State aforesaid, certify that _____
_____ personally appeared before me this day and acknowledged the due execution of the foregoing instrument for the purposes therein expressed. Witness my hand and Notarial stamp or seal this _____ day of _____, 20__.

My Commission Expires:_____   _____
                                                                                      Notary Public

The foregoing Certificate(s) of _____ is/are certified to be correct.
This instrument and this certificate are duly registered at the date and time and in the Book and Page shown on the first page hereof.
_____ Register of Deeds for _____ County
By:_____ Deputy/Assistant - Register of Deeds

NC Bar Association Form No. 6 © 1977, 2002   + James Williams & Co., Inc.
Printed by Agreement with the NC Bar Association - 1981   www.JamesWilliams.com

F I G U R E   5.4   **Quitclaim Deed (Non-Warranty Deed)**

NORTH CAROLINA NON-WARRANTY DEED

Excise Tax:

Parcel Identifier No._____ Verified by _____ County on the _____ day of_____, 20__
By:_____

Mail/Box to: _____

This instrument was prepared by:_____

Brief description for the Index: _____

THIS DEED made this _____ day of _____, 20___, by and between

GRANTOR	GRANTEE

Enter in appropriate block for each party: name, address, and, if appropriate, character of entity, e.g. corporation or partnership.

The designation Grantor and Grantee as used herein shall include said parties, their heirs, successors, and assigns, and shall include singular, plural, masculine, feminine or neuter as required by context.

WITNESSETH, that the Grantor, for a valuable consideration paid by the Grantee, the receipt of which is hereby acknowledged, has and by these presents does grant, bargain, sell and convey unto the Grantee in fee simple, all that certain lot or parcel of land situated in the City of _____, _____ Township, _____ County, North Carolina and more particularly described as follows:

The property hereinabove described was acquired by Grantor by instrument recorded in Book _____ page _____.

A map showing the above described property is recorded in Plat Book_____ page _____.

NC Bar Association Form No. 7 © 1977, 2002   + James Williams & Co., Inc.
Printed by Agreement with the NC Bar Association - 1981   www.JamesWilliams.com

F I G U R E   5.4   **Quitclaim Deed (Non-Warranty Deed) (continued)**

TO HAVE AND TO HOLD the aforesaid lot or parcel of land and all privileges and appurtenances thereto belonging to the Grantee in fee simple.

The Grantor makes no warranty, express or implied, as to title to the property hereinabove described.

IN WITNESS WHEREOF, the Grantor has caused this instrument to be duly executed and delivered.

_____   _____(SEAL)
(Entity Name)

By:_____   _____(SEAL)
Title:_____

By:_____   _____(SEAL)
Title:_____

By:_____   _____(SEAL)
Title:_____

USE BLACK INK ONLY

SEAL-STAMP

State of North Carolina - County of _____
I, the undersigned Notary Public of the County and State aforesaid, certify that _____
_____ personally appeared before me this day and acknowledged the due execution of the foregoing instrument for the purposes therein expressed. Witness my hand and Notarial stamp or seal this _____ day of _____, 20__.
My Commission Expires:_____   _____
Notary Public

SEAL-STAMP

State of North Carolina - County of _____
I, the undersigned Notary Public of the County and State aforesaid, certify that _____
_____ personally came before me this day and acknowledged that _he is the _____ of _____, a North Carolina or _____ corporation/limited liability company/general partnership/limited partnership (strike through the inapplicable), and that by authority duly given and as the act of each entity, _he signed the forgoing instrument in its name on its behalf as its act and deed. Witness my hand and Notarial stamp or seal this _____ day of _____, 20__.
My Commission Expires:_____   _____
Notary Public

SEAL-STAMP

State of North Carolina - County of _____
I, the undersigned Notary Public of the County and State aforesaid, certify that _____
_____ personally appeared before me this day and acknowledged the due execution of the foregoing instrument for the purposes therein expressed. Witness my hand and Notarial stamp or seal this _____ day of _____, 20__.
My Commission Expires:_____   _____
Notary Public

The foregoing Certificate(s) of _____ is/are certified to be correct.
This instrument and this certificate are duly registered at the date and time and in the Book and Page shown on the first page hereof.
_____ Register of Deeds for _____ County
By:_____ Deputy/Assistant - Register of Deeds

NC Bar Association Form No. 7 © 1977, 2002
Printed by Agreement with the NC Bar Association - 1981

+ James Williams & Co., Inc.
www.JamesWilliams.com

Deed of release.   A deed of release is used to release a parcel of property from a mortgage or deed of trust lien when the real estate loan has been paid in full.

Deed in lieu of foreclosure.   A deed in lieu of foreclosure is used when a borrower has defaulted on the mortgage loan and wants to avoid a foreclosure action. With the lender's agreement, the debtor simply gives the lender a deed in lieu of (instead of) foreclosure and, therefore, is spared both the foreclosure procedure and the possibility of a deficiency judgment (see Chapter 13). Significant tax issues can arise when a deed in lieu of foreclosure is used; competent legal or tax advice always should be obtained.

Trustee's deed.   A deed of conveyance executed by a trustee is a trustee's deed and is used when a trustee named in a will, trust agreement, or trust deed conveys the real estate to anyone other than the trustor. The trustee's deed sets forth the fact that the trustee executes the instrument in accordance with the powers and authority granted to him or her by the trust instrument. A trustee's deed is generally used to transfer title after a foreclosure auction.

Timber or mineral deed.   As discussed in Chapter 2, some ownership rights can be severed from the land and transferred by deed, such as the harvesting of timber or minerals located on the property.

Deeds executed pursuant to court order.   This classification covers deeds such as a sheriff's deed, a tax deed, a guardian's deed, and an executor's deed. These deeds are used to convey title to property that is transferred by court order or by will.

One characteristic of these special-purpose deeds is that the full consideration is usually stated in the deed. This is done because the deed is executed pursuant to a court order; because the court has authorized the sale of the property for a given amount of consideration, this amount should be exactly stated in the document.

Excise Tax

All sellers of real property in North Carolina must pay an **excise tax** that is based on the sales price of the property. The statute states, "There is levied an excise tax on each deed, instrument, or writing by which any interest in real property is conveyed to another person." Prior to year 2000, actual *revenue stamps* were affixed to each deed as proof that this excise tax had been paid. Now, because the Registrar of Deeds must mark the document to show the tax amount paid prior to recording the document, the term *revenue stamps* has been discontinued. The amount of the tax is $1 for every $500 of consideration or fraction thereof and always is expressed as a whole dollar amount. The type of financing used, if any, has no effect on the calculation of excise tax.

The statute establishing the payment of excise tax exempts certain types of conveyances, such as transfer by a government entity, transfer by will or intestate succession because of death, transfer by deed of gift when no consideration is paid, transfer by merger or consolidation, transfer by lease for a term of years, and transfer by instruments securing a debt, such as a mortgage and/or deed of trust.

MATH CONCEPTS   **CALCULATE EXCISE TAX**

To calculate the amount of the excise tax, if the sales price is not an even $500 amount, round the sales price up to the nearest $500, divide by 500, and multiply by $1. For example, suppose the purchase price is $89,250. Round up the price to $89,500, and divide by 500 which equals 179. Multiply 179 by $1 and you have determined that the seller will need to pay $179 in excise tax.

As another example, suppose the purchase price is $94,750. Round up the price to $95,000, and divide by 500 which equals 190. Multiply 190 by $1. The seller will need to pay $190 in excise tax.

Involuntary Alienation

Title to property also can be transferred by involuntary alienation—that is, without the owner's wishes or consent (see Figure 5.5). Such transfers are usually carried out by operation of law and range from government condemnation of land for public use to the sale of property to satisfy delinquent tax or mortgage liens.

Escheat. When a person dies **intestate** (without a will) and leaves no heirs, the title to that person's real estate passes to the state by the state's power of **escheat**.

Eminent domain. Federal, state, and local governments; school boards; some government agencies; and certain public and quasi-public corporations and utilities have the power of **eminent domain**. Under this power, private property may be taken for public use through a suit for condemnation. **Condemnation** is the

F I G U R E 5.5   **Involuntary Alienation**

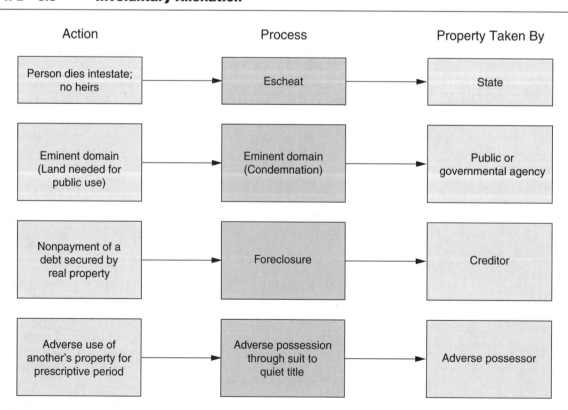

process by which the power of eminent domain is exercised. The exercise of eminent domain is subject to a court's determination of three necessary conditions: (1) that the use is for the benefit of the public; (2) that an equitable amount of compensation, as set by the court, will be paid to the owner; and (3) that the rights of the property owner will be protected by due process of law. North Carolina also recognizes a *quick take* method of condemnation. When authorized by law, title and possession of private property can immediately be transferred to the public authority.

Lien foreclosure.   Land also may be transferred without an owner's consent to satisfy debts contracted by the owner that have become liens against the real property. In such cases, the liens are foreclosed, the property is sold, and the proceeds of the sale are applied to pay off the debts. Debts that could be foreclosed include mortgage loans, real estate taxes, mechanics' liens, and general judgments against the property owner.

Adverse possession.   **Adverse possession** is another means of involuntary transfer. For persons to make a claim of ownership under adverse possession they must have some reason to believe the land is theirs. Owners who do not use or inspect their land for a number of years may lose title to another person who makes a claim to the land, takes possession, and, most importantly, uses the land. The mnemonic *OCEAN* reminds us that the possession of the claimant must be

> **Requirements for**
> **Adverse Possession**
> Open
> Continuous
> Exclusive
> Adverse
> Notorious

- Open (well known to others),
- Continuous (uninterrupted for the required period),
- Exclusive (not shared with another),
- Adverse to the true owner's possession (the adverse possessor must intend to claim that the land occupied is his or her own), and
- Notorious/hostile (without the permission of the owner).

In North Carolina, the required period of continuous possession varies widely, depending on the circumstances. If the adverse possessor is trying to acquire privately owned property and has color of title (a faulty document that purports to give the adverse possessor title), the period of possession is 7 years. If there is no color of title, the period of possession is 20 years. Property owned by the government is not subject to acquisition by adverse possession.

Even if the adverse possessor fulfills all the legal requirements for adverse possession, he or she must go to court to get clear title to the property. This is done with a quiet title action. It is difficult to prove title by adverse possession, and until a court decides that title has been acquired, the claimant's title is considered to be unmarketable.

Transfer of a Deceased Person's Property

By descent (intestate succession).   Every state, including North Carolina, has a law known as a *statute of descent and distribution.* When a person dies intestate (without having left a will), the decedent's real estate and personal property pass to the decedent's heirs according to this statute. In effect, the state makes a will for anyone who did not do so. A court appoints a person to distribute the deceased's property according to the provisions of the **North Carolina Intestate Succession Act.** This person is called an *administrator* if a man or an *administratrix* if a woman. As noted previously, if the property owner dies intestate and leaves no heirs, the property will escheat to the state of North Carolina. North Carolina's provisions for intestate succession are quite complicated, and a lawyer should be consulted when intestate succession questions arise.

Transfer of title by will. A **will** is an instrument made by a mentally competent owner to convey title to real and personal property on the owner's death. A will takes effect only after death; until that time, any property covered by the will can be conveyed by the owner and thus removed from the owner's estate. An ownership interest that contains survivorship rights cannot be affected by a will. In North Carolina, if a husband and wife own property as tenants by the entirety, that property cannot pass by will. Neither spouse can disinherit the other spouse by will.

The gift of real property by will is known as a *devise*, and a person who receives real property by will is known as a *devisee*. Technically, an heir is one who takes property by the law of descent, but the term is commonly used to include devisees as well. A legacy or *bequest* is a gift of personal property; the person receiving personal property is known as a *beneficiary*.

■ TITLE ASSURANCE

Under the terms of a typical real estate sales contract, the seller is required to deliver **marketable title** to the buyer at the closing. To be marketable, a title must meet five criteria: (1) be free from any significant liens and encumbrances; (2) disclose no serious defects; (3) be free of doubtful questions of law or fact to prove its validity; (4) protect a purchaser from the hazard of litigation or any threat to quiet enjoyment of the property; and (5) convince a reasonably well-informed and prudent person, acting on business principles and willful knowledge of the facts and their legal significance, that the property could in turn be sold or mortgaged at a fair market value.

Most people spend more money on the purchase of real estate than on any other single item. Therefore, it is understandable that buyers want to be sure they get what they pay for—marketable title to the property. So while a deed might contain several warranties of title, the buyer should insist on a title search and a property survey to make sure he or she is getting marketable title.

Title Search

A **title search** is the examination of all public records that might affect a title. The title examiner tries to establish a **chain of title,** which shows the record of ownership of the property over a period of time, depending on the length of the title search. In the United States, chains of title in colonial states frequently date back to a grant from the king of England. In those states admitted to the Union after the formation of the United States, the deeds of conveyance in the chain of title generally stem from the patent issued by the U.S. government. A lawyer or a trained paralegal can perform a title search, or title examination, but only attorneys may give an opinion of title. In North Carolina, real estate agents are prohibited from giving an opinion on the condition of a title.

Through the chain of title, the ownership of the property can be traced backward from its present owner to its source; this thorough, condensed history of the title is called an **abstract of title**. Frequently, the title examination is conducted for a shorter period of time based on local custom or practical considerations. Most title defects are revealed in a search that traces back 30 to 60 years, especially if title insurance has been in place. Ownership is traced by means of searching the *grantee and grantor indexes* that are kept in the Register of Deeds' offices. Under this system, all documents relating to a parcel of property are indexed under the names of the grantors and the grantees, not under the property itself.

If there is a period for which ownership is unaccounted, there is a gap in the chain. In such cases, it is usually necessary to establish ownership by a court action called a *suit to quiet title*. The court's judgment, following a proceeding in which all possible claimants are allowed to present evidence, can be filed. A suit to quiet title may be required when, for instance, a grantor has acquired title under one name and conveyed title under a different name. Title acquired by adverse possession also can be established of record by a quiet title action.

When a title examination is conducted, the title examiner lists each instrument in chronological order along with information relative to taxes, judgments, special assessments, surveys, easements, and the like. The title examiner concludes with an opinion of title indicating which records were examined and when, and stating the examiner's opinion of the quality of the title. The grantor and grantee index system is used in North Carolina to examine the title. Any defect of title will appear in the grantor index.

Marketable Title Act.   North Carolina's **Marketable Title Act** provides that if a chain of title can be traced back for 30 years and no other claim has been recorded during that time, the title becomes a marketable title. Any conflicting claims predating the 30-year chain of title may be extinguished. The practical effect of this act is to eliminate obsolete defects in the chain of title.

Title Insurance

A **title insurance** policy is a contract by which a title insurance company agrees, subject to the terms of its policy, to indemnify (to compensate or reimburse) the insured (the owner, the mortgagee, or another interest holder) against any losses sustained as a result of defects in a title that existed at the time the policy was issued, other than those exceptions listed in the policy.

Title companies issue various forms of title insurance policies; the most common are the owner's title insurance policy and the mortgagee's title insurance policy. As the names indicate, each type of policy is issued to insure specific interests. An owner's policy insures an owner's interest in property; a mortgagee's policy insures a lender's interest in property. The owner's coverage is usually the face amount of the purchase price and the owner is permanently protected. The lender's coverage is limited to the loan amount and is of a *diminishing liability*. Lender's coverage ends with the payoff of the mortgage loan.

A standard coverage policy usually insures against defects that may be found in the public records plus many defects not found there. The extended coverage provided by an **ALTA** (American Land Title Association) **policy** includes all the protection of a standard policy plus additional protection to cover risks that may be discovered only through inspection of the property (including rights of persons in actual possession of the land, even if unrecorded) or revealed by examination of an accurate survey. The company does not insure against any defects in or liens against the title that are found by the title examination and listed in the standard policy.

The ALTA owner's title insurance policy protects the owner against title defects not found in the public records, such as

- falsification of the records;
- misrepresentation of the true owner(s) of the land;
- old unsettled estates;
- forged deeds, releases, or wills;
- instruments executed under a fabricated or expired power of attorney;
- errors in copying and indexing;
- deeds delivered after the death of a grantor or grantee or without consent of the grantor;
- mistakes in recording legal documents;
- undisclosed or missing heirs;
- birth or adoption of children after the date of the will;
- deeds by persons of unsound mind;
- deeds by persons supposedly single but secretly married; and
- deeds by minors.

The consideration for the policy (the premium) is paid once at closing for the life of the policy. The maximum loss for which the company may be liable cannot exceed the face amount of the policy (unless the amount of coverage has been extended by use of an inflation rider). When a title company settles a claim covered by a policy, it can then step into the shoes of the insured party and seek compensation from anyone responsible for the settled claim.

With the owner's title insurance policy, if the insured owner were to lose title because of a covered claim, the title company would pay the owner the value of the property up to the face amount of the policy (plus the amount covered in the policy's available inflation clause). The title company also assumes any costs incurred in the defense of the title. ALTA coverage is summarized in Table 5.1.

North Carolina is considered an approved attorney state. That means that title searches are usually performed by an attorney rather than by a title insurance company. When the title search is completed, the attorney submits a preliminary opinion on title to the title insurance company, which, in essence, serves as an application for title insurance. Based on the preliminary opinion on title, the title insurance company issues a title commitment. The title commitment includes a description of the title insurance policy; the name of the insured party; the legal description of the real estate; the estate or interest covered; a schedule of all exceptions, consisting of encumbrances and defects found in the public records; and conditions and stipulations under which the commitment is issued. The title commitment is used at closing as assurance of a clear title to the property in question.

TABLE 5.1	Standard Coverage	Extended Coverage	Not Covered by Either Policy
Owner's Title Insurance Policy	1. Defects found in public records 2. Forged documents 3. Incompetent grantors 4. Incorrect marital statements 5. Improperly delivered deeds	Standard coverage plus defects discoverable through: 1. Property inspection, including unrecorded rights of persons in possession 2. Examination of survey 3. Unrecorded liens not known by policyholder	1. Defects and liens listed in policy 2. Defects known to buyer 3. Changes in land use brought about by zoning ordinances 4. Defects that would have been shown by an accurate survey, if a survey was not done

After closing, the attorney issues a final opinion on title, which includes recording information for the deed and deed of trust and so forth. The final opinion on title goes to the title insurance company, which issues the title insurance policy based on this information. Under the title insurance policy, the title insurance company promises to defend the title as insured, as well as to pay any claims against the property if the title proves to be defective. The opinion issued by the attorney is just that, an *opinion* based on the search of public records. It is not a guarantee of good title.

IN PRACTICE   Before a lender will forward money on a loan secured by real estate, it normally orders a title search at the expense of the borrower to assure itself that there are no recorded liens superior in priority to its mortgage on the property. The lender also typically requires the borrower to purchase a title insurance policy to protect the lender's interest. The owner-borrower may also purchase an "owner's policy." An owner's policy is highly recommended, but the owner-borrower must request this policy since it is not automatic.

Title Recordation

Both title insurance and title examinations depend on the fact that all conveyances of real property, as well as most other interests in real property, must be recorded to be enforceable. All owners or parties interested in real estate need to record, or file, all documents affecting their interests in the real estate to give public notice to the world of those interests. This public notice is called **constructive notice.** Physically taking possession of the property is *actual notice.*

Necessity for recording.   Through the process of **recording,** documents that affect property ownership are readily available as matters of public record. Therefore, a person can inspect the documents that affect a property before making a decision about purchasing it. A potential purchaser can verify that the seller can probably convey good title to the property as well as what liens and encumbrances affect that title.

■ **FOR EXAMPLE**   A purchaser offering cash for a property might want to be sure, before the settlement takes place, that the seller has paid in full all of the debts outstanding against the property. By inspecting the recorded documents, the purchaser could determine what debts encumber the property.

To serve as public notice, all instruments in writing affecting any estate, right, title, or interest in land must be recorded with the Register of Deeds in the county where the land is located. Everyone interested in the title to a parcel of property can, therefore, receive notice of the various interests of all other parties. Because North Carolina is a pure race state (see below), recording gives legal priority to those interests that are recorded first.

Conner Act.   The **Conner Act** is a state law that provides that many types of real estate documents are not valid as to third parties unless they are recorded. The documents covered include deeds, mortgages, installment land contracts, assignments, options, leases of more than three years, easements, and restrictive covenants. Under the Conner Act, if a purchaser fails to record a deed but a subsequent purchaser does, the subsequent purchaser's title takes precedence over the first purchaser's title. This kind of recording statute is called a *pure race statute*: whoever records first prevails, even if that purchaser had personal knowledge of a previous interest that was unrecorded.

■ **FOR EXAMPLE** Suppose Zackermann sells her property to Sands. Sands fails to record his deed. Two weeks later, Zackermann sells the same property (even though it is no longer hers) to Hanson. Hanson suspects that Zackermann no longer owns the property but accepts the deed and quickly records it. Because Hanson recorded his deed, he now has marketable title to the property, and Sands is out of luck.

■ RELATED WEB SITE

American Land Title Association: *www.alta.org*

■ SUMMARY

Title to real estate is the right to and evidence of ownership of the land. It may be transferred by voluntary alienation, involuntary alienation, will, or descent.

The voluntary transfer of an owner's title is made by a deed. Requirements of a valid deed include parties with the legal capacity to contract, a readily identifiable grantee, a granting clause, an adequate legal description of the property, delivery and acceptance, and the signature of the grantor. Deeds are subject to a state excise tax when they are recorded. Title to the property passes when the grantor delivers a deed to the grantee and it is accepted.

The obligations of a grantor are determined by the form of the deed—general warranty deed, special warranty deed, or quitclaim deed. A general warranty deed binds the grantor to certain covenants or warranties. The general warranty deed gives the grantor the greatest degree of liability, while it gives the grantee the greatest degree of protection. The standard sales contract states that the grantor will provide a general warranty deed to the grantee at closing. A special warranty deed warrants only that since the grantor received title to the property, the real estate was not encumbered by the grantor, except as stated in the deed.

A quitclaim deed carries with it no warranties whatsoever and conveys only the interest, if any, that the grantor possesses in the property.

An owner's title may be transferred without the owner's permission by a court action such as a foreclosure or judgment sale, a tax sale, condemnation under the right of eminent domain, adverse possession, or escheat. These are forms of involuntary alienation. Eminent domain is the right of the government to take private property for the public good with fair compensation paid to the private property owner; condemnation is the process by which it is done. Adverse possession occurs when a party claims ownership to land owned by another party. If the claimant meets all the legal requirements of adverse possession (open, continuous, exclusive, adverse, and notorious), the court may grant quiet title action. Escheat is the right of the state to receive a descendant's property if the property owner died intestate with no heirs.

The real estate of an owner who makes a valid will (who dies testate) passes to the devisees through the probating of the will. The title of an owner who dies without a will (intestate) passes according to the provisions of the North Carolina Intestate Succession Act. The purpose of recording deeds is to give legal, public, and constructive notice to the world of the parties' interests in real estate. The recording provisions have been standardized to give order in the transfer of real estate. Without them, it would be virtually impossible to transfer real estate from one party to another. Although recordation is not essential to make a document valid, the Conner Act requires recordation to protect the owner against claims from third parties.

Title evidence shows whether a seller is conveying marketable title. Marketable title is generally one that is so free from significant defects that the purchaser can be insured against having to defend the title. The Marketable Title Act extinguishes old title defects if the chain of title can be traced for 30 years without problem. Title insurance protects the policy owner from defects in the title, except those specifically excluded from the insurance policy. The title insurance premium is a one-time cost, usually paid at closing by the buyer, and owner's coverage remains in effect permanently, while the lender's coverage diminishes until it is extinguished upon the payoff of the loan balance.

QUESTIONS

1. In North Carolina, the statutory period for adverse possession (without color of title) is an uninterrupted period of how many years when trying to acquire privately owned property?
   a. 3
   b. 7
   c. 20
   d. 30

2. When property is sold for $75,000, the excise tax would be
   a. $75.
   b. $125.
   c. $135.
   d. $150.

3. Mario sold his property for $185,900 and let the buyer assume his loan balance of $125,000. How much excise tax will Mario pay at closing?
   a. $121.80
   b. $122.00
   c. $371.80
   d. $372.00

4. Title to real estate may be transferred during a person's lifetime by which of the following means?
   a. Escheat
   b. Descent
   c. Alienation
   d. Devise

5. What type of deed might an owner of real estate use to voluntarily transfer a right, a title, or an interest in real estate?
   a. Sheriff's deed
   b. Warranty deed
   c. Foreclosure deed
   d. Trustee's deed

6. Hank owned property as a tenant in common with his two best friends. Years later, Hank was adjudged legally incompetent and moved into a nursing home. During his stay at a nursing home, Hank wrote a will leaving his entire estate to the nursing assistant assigned to his care. Hank was survived by three children when he died. After his death, his real estate interests passed to
   a. his two best friends due to ownership rights.
   b. the nursing assistant named in his will.
   c. his children by the law of intestate succession.
   d. the state by escheat.

7. Excise taxes on real estate conveyances in North Carolina are usually paid
   I. by the grantee.
   II. based on the sales price minus any loan assumptions.
      a. I only
      b. II only
      c. Both I and II
      d. Neither I nor II

8. Which of the following is NOT a means of title transfer by involuntary alienation?
   a. Eminent domain
   b. Escheat
   c. Foreclosure
   d. Will

9. Deeds conveying North Carolina real estate require the signature of the
   I. grantor.
   II. grantee.
      a. I only
      b. II only
      c. Both I and II
      d. Neither I nor II

10. Which of the following *BEST* describes the covenant of quiet enjoyment?
    a. The grantor promises to obtain and deliver any instrument needed to make the title good.
    b. The grantor guarantees that if the title fails in the future, the grantor will compensate the grantee.
    c. The grantor warrants that the grantor is the owner of the property and has the right to convey title to it.
    d. The grantor ensures that the title will be good against the title claims of third parties.

11. A purchaser went to the Registry of Deeds to check the public records. She found that the seller was the grantee in the last recorded deed and that no mortgage was ever on record against the property. Therefore, the purchaser may assume which of the following?
    a. All taxes are paid, and no judgments are outstanding.
    b. The seller has good title.
    c. The seller probably did not mortgage the property.
    d. Probably no one else is occupying the property.

12. The person who examines the chain of title and prepares an opinion of title for a parcel of real estate
    a. writes a brief history of the record of ownership of the property.
    b. ensures the condition of the title.
    c. inspects the physical condition of the property.
    d. issues a guarantee as to the quality of the title.

13. Instruments affecting real estate are recorded in the public records of the county where the property is located because
    I. recording gives constructive notice to the world of the rights and interests in a particular parcel of real estate.
    II. the instruments must be recorded to comply with the terms of the Statute of Frauds.
       a. I only
       b. II only
       c. Both I and II
       d. Neither I nor II

14. Chain of title refers to a
    a. summary of all instruments and legal proceedings affecting a specific parcel of land.
    b. series of links measuring 7.92 inches each.
    c. document that protects the insured parties against defects and hidden risks such as forgeries, undisclosed heirs, errors in the public records, and so forth.
    d. succession of conveyances from some starting point whereby the present owner derives title.

15. A title insurance policy with standard coverage generally covers all of the following *EXCEPT*
    a. forged documents.
    b. incorrect marital statements.
    c. rights of parties in possession.
    d. incompetent grantors.

16. Condemnation is
    a. the right of the government to take private property.
    b. rezoning of private property.
    c. the process by which eminent domain is exercised.
    d. adverse possession with just compensation.

17. Which of the following is *NOT* a necessary condition of eminent domain?
    a. Use benefits the public.
    b. Property is to be given to the owner of a quasi-public corporation.
    c. Property owner is protected by due process of law.
    d. Just compensation is paid to the property owner.

18. Which of the following real estate documents is *LEAST* likely to be recorded?
    a. Deed
    b. Month-to-month lease
    c. Option contract
    d. Land contract

19. Which of the following should be discoverable in a search of the public records?
    a. Encroachments
    b. Rights of any party in possession
    c. Inaccurate surveys
    d. Easements

20. In North Carolina, the statutory period of possession required to acquire title of privately owned property by adverse possession with color of title is how many years?

a. 7
b. 12
c. 20
d. 30

6

CHAPTER

Land-Use Controls

■ **LEARNING OBJECTIVES** *When you have finished reading this chapter, you should be able to*

■ **identify** different types of public and private land-use controls and their effect on property use.

■ **understand** the development of the master (comprehensive) plan and how it affects the development, control, and use of property.

■ **explain** the basic stages in developing a subdivision, including compliance with zoning, regulations, building codes, and the approval process.

■ **understand** land-use controls and real estate agents' disclosure responsibilities.

■ **define** these *key terms:*

aesthetic zoning	extra-territorial jurisdictions (ETJs)	nonconforming use
Americans with Disabilities Act (ADA)	Federal Emergency Management Agency (FEMA)	overlay district
buffer zones		plat map
building codes	flood hazard area	police power
building permit	historic preservation zoning	property report
certificate of occupancy		protective covenant
conditional-use permit	Interstate Land Sales Full Disclosure Act	restrictive covenant
declaration of restrictive covenants	laches	spot zoning
enabling act	master plan	subdivision
		variance
		zoning ordinances

The regulation of land use is accomplished through public land-use controls, private land-use controls (deed restrictions), and public ownership of land—including parks, schools, and expressways—by federal, state, and local governments.

■ PUBLIC LAND-USE CONTROLS

The **police power** of the states is their inherent authority to create and adopt regulations necessary to protect the public health, safety, and general welfare of the citizenry. The states, in turn, allow counties, cities, and towns to make regulations in keeping with general laws. The largely urban population and the increasing demands placed on our limited natural resources have made it necessary for cities, towns, and villages to increase limitations on the private use of real estate. There are now controls over noise, air, and water pollution, as well as population density.

Public land-use controls include

■ planning,
■ zoning,
■ subdivision regulations,
■ building codes, and
■ environmental protection legislation.

The Master Plan

The primary method by which local governments recognize development goals is through the formulation of a comprehensive **master plan,** also commonly referred to as a *general plan.* Cities and counties develop master plans to ensure that social and economic needs are balanced against environmental and aesthetic concerns.

The master plan is both a statement of policies and a presentation of how those policies can be realized. As created by the city, county, or regional *planning commission,* a typical master plan provides for

■ *land use,* including standards of population density and economic development;
■ *public facilities,* including schools, civic centers, and utilities;
■ *circulation,* including public transportation and highways;
■ *conservation* of natural resources; and
■ *noise abatement.*

Both economic and physical surveys are essential in preparing a master plan. Countywide plans also must include the coordination of numerous civic plans and developments to ensure orderly city growth with stabilized property values. City plans are put into effect by the enactment and enforcement of zoning ordinances.

Zoning

The provisions of the master plan are implemented by zoning ordinances. **Zoning ordinances** are laws imposed by local government authorities (such as cities and counties) that regulate and control the use of land and structures within designated districts or zones. Zoning regulates and affects such things as use of the land, lot sizes, types of structures permitted, building heights, *setbacks* (the minimum distance away from streets or sidewalks that structures may be built), and density (the ratio of land area to structure area or population).

Zoning powers are conferred on municipal governments by North Carolina's **enabling act** through the General Assembly. There are no nationwide or state-wide zoning ordinances; zoning is local in nature. (State and federal governments may, however, regulate land use through special legislation, such as scenic easement or coastal management laws.) Because there is no conformity of zoning codes or definitions, it is critical for licensees to check with local municipalities before answering any questions about zoning.

Zoning ordinances generally divide land use into general use classification such as: residential, commercial, industrial, and agricultural. There are usually many specific sub-classifications under each general use category. Many communities now include *cluster zoning* and *multiple-use zoning;* the latter permits planned unit developments (PUDs).

To ensure adequate control, land-use areas are further divided into subclasses. Residential areas may be subdivided to provide for detached single-family dwellings, semi detached structures containing not more than four dwelling units, walkup apartments, or highrise apartments. Some communities require the use of **buffer zones**—such as landscaped parks and playgrounds—to separate and screen residential areas from nonresidential areas.

Adoption of zoning ordinances.   Today, almost all cities have enacted comprehensive zoning ordinances governing the use of land located within corporate limits. North Carolina General Assembly has enacted legislation that allows a municipality to regulate development in areas adjacent to, but not within, the corporate limits. These areas outside the incorporated limits, but subject to the zoning restrictions of a municipality, are called **extra-territorial jurisdictions (ETJs)**. Population of the municipality will determine if the regulatory power extends one mile or up to three miles from the corporate limits.

Zoning ordinances must not violate the rights of property owners (as provided under the due-process provisions of the Fourteenth Amendment to the U.S. Constitution) or the various provisions of the North Carolina State Constitution. If the means used to regulate the use of property are destructive, unreasonable, arbitrary, or confiscatory, the legislation is usually considered void. Tests commonly applied in determining the validity of ordinances require that

- the power be exercised in a reasonable manner;
- the provisions be clear and specific;
- the ordinance be free from discrimination;
- the ordinance promote public health, safety, and general welfare under the police power concept; and
- the ordinance apply to all property in a similar manner.

When land is taken for public use by the government's power of eminent domain, the owner must receive fair compensation. When *downzoning* occurs in an area—for instance, when land zoned for residential construction is rezoned for conservation or recreational purposes only—the state is ordinarily not responsible for compensating property owners for any resulting loss of value. However, if the courts find that a *taking* has occurred, the downzoning will be held to be an unconstitutional attempt to use the power of eminent domain without providing fair compensation to the property owner. (See Chapter 5 for a discussion of eminent domain.)

Zoning laws are generally enforced by requiring that building permits be obtained before property owners can build on their land. A permit will not be issued unless a proposed structure conforms to the permitted zoning, among other requirements.

Legal nonconforming use.   It is not unusual to find real property uses that were legally established before the adoption of the current zoning plan. This *grandfathered* use is referred to as a legal **nonconforming use** (or simply "nonconforming use") of the property. Nonconforming use can apply to the way the land is used, the type of structure that is on the property, the way the structure is used, or even the lot size itself. For instance, a small factory building may be the last one left in a neighborhood that was once industrial but has since been zoned for residential use. The factory owner has a *matter of right* to continue this nonconforming pre-existing use.

Nonconforming uses are generally not permitted to continue indefinitely. Zoning statutes may prohibit the reconstruction of a building that is destroyed by fire or otherwise dismantled if it does not conform to current zoning requirements. Generally, nonconforming use property can only be maintained, not improved nor enlarged, since the zoning authority usually desires eventual conformity by all property. Compliance with current zoning requirements may also be required upon transfer of title. A real estate licensee should never guarantee the continuance of a nonconforming use after a purchase; refer the buyer to the zoning power for verification.

Illegal nonconforming use.   An illegal nonconforming use (or simply "illegal use") is one that violates the zoning laws at the time it is put into place. For example, opening a gas station in a single-family residential zone would be an illegal use. The zoning body (city or county) can go to court to stop an illegal use at any time, even if the unpermitted use has been in place for an extensive period of time. To create an illegal nonconforming use is a misdemeanor.

Zoning variations.   Each time a master plan is created or a zoning ordinance enacted, some owners are inconvenienced and want to change the use of their property. Zoning boards of adjustment have been established in most communities to hear complaints about the effects of zoning ordinances on specific parcels of property. Petitions may be presented to the board for variances or exceptions to the zoning law. Generally, such owners may appeal for either a conditional-use permit or a variance to allow a use that does not meet current zoning requirements.

Conditional-use permits allow nonconforming, but related land uses.

Variances permit prohibited land uses to avoid undue hardship.

A **conditional-use permit,** or *special-use permit,* is provided for in the zoning laws. It is granted to a property owner who wishes to use property in a special way that is in the public interest—such as a church or hospital in a residential district. A **variance** may also be sought to allow a deviation from an ordinance due to unique circumstances. As discussed in Chapter 1, under highest and best use, it is in the public interest to put land to use rather than have it lie fallow. To get a variance, the property owner must prove that there is no other reasonable use for the property and the property owner will suffer a substantial hardship if the variance is not granted. The hardship also must not have been created by the property owner.

■ **FOR EXAMPLE** If an owner's lot is level next to a road but slopes steeply 30 feet away from the road, the zoning board may allow a variance so the owner can build closer to the road than the setback requirement allows. Otherwise, the lot could not be used.

A property owner can change the zoning classification of a parcel of real estate by obtaining an amendment to the official zoning map, which is part of the original zoning ordinance for the area. The proposed amendment must be brought before a public hearing on the matter and approved by the governing body of the community. When local officials fail to grant the desired relief from zoning regulations, the unhappy property owner can appeal to the courts, which may override the local officials and even the voters.

Overlay districts.   An **overlay district** is a type of zoning that is superimposed over another type of zoning. The overlay zone can modify the use of the original zone. A common example is when an area that is zoned single-family residential is also designated as a flood zone. This means that additional restrictions and regulations are imposed on developments and improvements in that area. Two other examples of overlay districts are historic preservation and aesthetic zoning.

Historic preservation zoning.   The purpose of **historic preservation zoning** is to preserve historic buildings and sites that are irreplaceable. An owner whose property falls within a historic preservation zone may have difficulty changing or upgrading the exterior of a structure on the property.

Before making material changes to a property located in a designated historic district or to individual property designated as a historic property, the owner must obtain a *certificate of appropriateness* from the appropriate regulatory entity. This certificate confirms that the local historic preservation commission, or other appropriate entity, has approved of the changes to be made to the property.

Aesthetic zoning.   In North Carolina, an area can be zoned strictly for aesthetic or appearance considerations. Therefore, a property's value can be increased or decreased for the public good of an aesthetically-pleasing neighborhood. Exterior surfaces of structures being restricted to a particular color palette or construction material would be an example of **aesthetic zoning**.

Spot zoning.   When a particular property or group of properties is rezoned to permit a use different from the neighboring properties' use, it is referred to as **spot zoning**. Whether spot zoning is legal or illegal in any particular case depends on whether the spot zoning is truly in the public interest rather than being for the benefit of a single property owner (or a few property owners) at the expense of neighboring property owners or the community at large. Some of the factors considered by North Carolina courts when determining the legality of spot zoning include: (1) the size of the rezoned area—rezoning a single lot is more questionable than rezoning multiple tracts; (2) the degree of compatibility of the different zoning with the government's adopted plans for the area; (3) the impact of the rezoning on the landowner(s), neighboring landowners and the surrounding community; and (4) the degree of difference between the zoning of the surrounding area and the new zoning for the tract(s) in question.

Agent's Duty to Disclose Zoning

Agents' responsibilities concerning knowledge of land-use controls vary. Agents working with urban properties—both commercial and residential—usually have more responsibilities and require more knowledge than agents working in more rural areas. Residential agents may require more knowledge of subdivision regulations, street disclosure laws, and protective covenants than commercial agents, who may require more knowledge about rezoning, variances, and special-use permits.

Agents should be able to recognize situations such as mixed use and property alterations where a closer check of zoning may be necessary. An agent should never make assumptions about the current or future zoning of a property on behalf of a client or customer. Purchasers are strongly encouraged to verify with the regulatory power any property use that is material to their desire for the property in question. Proper disclosure of zoning and protective covenants should be routinely made before the buyer signs an offer to purchase. A listing agent should acquire copies of any deed restrictions and protective covenants at the time of taking the listing.

Subdivision Regulations

Subdivision Regulations

1. Land is divided into two or more lots.
2. Cities and counties implement subdivision regulations.
3. Planning boards have administrative responsibilities.
4. Subdividing must have preliminary plat approval before selling lots.
5. Final plat must be recorded prior to closing.
6. Subdivision must comply with street disclosure laws.
7. Protective covenants are enforceable.

There is *no uniform planning and land development legislation that affects the entire country.* Laws governing subdividing and land planning are controlled by the state and by local governing bodies of the county, city, town, or village where the land is located. Local regulations are by no means uniform but reflect customs and local climate, health, and hazardous conditions. Despite the local nature of land-use laws, rules and regulations developed by government agencies such as the Federal Housing Administration (FHA) have provided certain *minimum standards* that have served as usable guides. A large number of local governments have established higher standards for subdividers of land under their jurisdiction.

In North Carolina, state law defines the term **subdivision** as "all divisions of a tract or parcel of land into two or more lots, building sites, or other divisions for the purpose of sale or building development (whether immediate or future) and includes all division of land involving the dedication of a new street or a change in existing streets." There are a few exceptions to this definition of subdivision. The following two types of parcels are not considered subdivisions: (1) a division of land if each parcel has more than ten acres with no street right-of-way dedication and (2) a division of land no larger than two acres into no more than three lots with no street right-of-way dedication involved, when the parcel is owned by a single entity.

Although an approved preliminary plat of subdivision of land prior to public sale for residential or commercial use is required, land planning precedes the actual subdividing process. The land development plan must comply with the overall master plan adopted by the county, city, town, or village. The basic city plan and zoning requirements are not inflexible, but long, expensive (and frequently complicated) hearings are usually required before alterations can be authorized. Approval of the subdivision **plat map** by local authorities is, however, a necessary step before recording. Actual transfer of title cannot occur until the final plat has been recorded.

Most cities, villages, and other areas that are incorporated under state laws have *planning commissions*. Depending on how the particular group is organized, such a committee or commission may have only an advisory status to the council or trustees of the community. In other instances, the commission may have authority to approve or disapprove plans.

Communities establish strict criteria before approving new subdivisions. Frequent requirements are *dedication* of land for streets, schools, and parks; assurance by *bonding* that sewer and street costs will be paid or that such improvements will be completed before construction begins; and *compliance with zoning ordinances* governing use and lot size, along with fire and safety ordinances.

Because of the fear that they may pollute streams, rivers, lakes, and underground water sources, septic tank systems are no longer authorized in many areas, and an environmentally approved sewage-disposal arrangement must be included in a land development plan. The shortage of water has caused great concern, and local authorities usually require that land planners submit information on how they intend to satisfy sewage-disposal and water-supply requirements. Development and septic tank installation may first require a *soil evaluation test* of the soil's absorption and drainage capacities. Frequently, a planner will also have to submit an *environmental impact report*.

Subdivision process.   The process of subdivision normally involves three distinct stages of development: (1) the initial planning stage, (2) the final planning stage, and (3) the disposition, or start-up.

During the *initial planning stage*, the subdivider seeks out raw land in a suitable area. Once the land is located, the property is analyzed for its highest and best use, and preliminary subdivision plans are drawn up accordingly. Close contact is initiated between the subdivider and local planning and zoning officials. If the project requires zoning variances, negotiations for these begin. The subdivider also locates financial backers and initiates marketing strategies.

The *final planning* stage is basically a follow-up of the initial stage. Final plans are prepared, approval is sought from local officials, permanent financing is obtained, the land is purchased, final budgets are prepared, and marketing programs are designed.

The *disposition*, or *start-up*, carries the subdividing process to a conclusion. Subdivision plans are recorded with local officials, and streets, sewers, and utilities are installed. Buildings, open parks, and recreational areas are constructed and landscaped if they are part of the subdivision plan. Marketing programs are then initiated, and title to the individual parcels of subdivided land is transferred as the lots are sold.

A developer of a subdivision must have streets approved, based on construction standards set by the North Carolina Department of Transportation, and must declare the streets to be for public or private use. Developers and their agents must disclose to buyers whether new subdivision streets will be public or private prior to selling or conveying the lot, pursuant to North Carolina disclosure laws (G.S. 136-102.6). Regardless of the age of the subdivision, real estate licensees should determine if the streets are public or private before making any statements to that effect. Also, just because streets have been dedicated for public use and approved by the North Carolina Department of Transportation, does not mean that the state will immediately take possession of the roads. There is usually a minimum population requirement prior to state adoption.

Real estate licensees should be well aware of the needed verification of approved subdivisions, especially in regards to selling recently subdivided lots. Before selling or listing lots in newly subdivided land, an agent should check with the Register of Deeds Office in the county where the lot is located to ensure the plat has been properly recorded. Approval must be granted by the proper county agency (usually a planning board) before recordation can take place. North Carolina now allows the acceptance of monies and contracts on subdivision parcels once the preliminary plat has been approved. However, if there are any material changes from the preliminary to the final plat map, a buyer is allowed to cancel any existing contract and receive a refund of all monies. An agent who closes a sale on a lot before final approval of the subdivision is granted and recorded may be subject to a civil lawsuit or may be criminally prosecuted as well as face disciplinary action by the North Carolina Real Estate Commission.

Plat of subdivision. The subdivider's completed plat of subdivision, a map of the development indicating the location and boundaries of individual properties, must contain all necessary approvals of public officials and must be recorded in the county where the land is located.

The plat will be the basis for future conveyance, so the subdivided land should be measured carefully, with all lot sizes and streets noted by the surveyor and entered accurately on the document. Survey monuments should be established, and measurements should be made from these monuments, with the location of all lots carefully marked. As noted above, brokers engaged to sell subdivided land should be certain that the subdivision has been approved by the appropriate government body.

Covenants and restrictions. Deed restrictions, discussed in more detail later in this chapter, are usually originated and recorded by a subdivider as a means of controlling and maintaining the desirable quality and character of the subdivision. These restrictions can be included in the subdivision plat or they may be set forth in a separate recorded instrument, commonly referred to as a declaration of restrictions.

Deed restrictions may include the size of structures that can be built; the cost—often the minimum cost—of structures that can be built; the number of structures that can be built; or even architectural styles, fence heights, setbacks, or outbuildings that can be built on the land. Almost anything that is not illegal can be set forth in the restrictive covenants.

FHA standards.   FHA minimum standards have been established for residential-area subdivisions that are to be submitted for approval for FHA loan insurance. The primary minimum standards established by the FHA deal with the actual development and infrastructure of the subdivision.

FHA standards also apply to building construction. Since 1986, in recognition of the more stringent local codes in effect, the FHA has allowed local building codes (where pre-approved by HUD—the Department of Housing and Urban Development) to serve as the standards. Exceptions generally include site condition standards, thermal (insulation) standards, and certain other material standards.

Interstate Land Sales Full Disclosure Act

To protect consumers from fraudulent and "overenthusiastic" sales promotions in interstate land sales, Congress passed the **Interstate Land Sales Full Disclosure Act** in 1968. The law requires those engaged in the interstate sale or leasing of subdivision lots to file a *statement of record* and register the details of the land with HUD. The Act exempts the sale of lots in a subdivision containing fewer than 25 lots. Interstate sales or leasing activities include out-of-state mailers, newspaper ads, television advertising directed to out-of-state buyers, and out-of-state telephone solicitation. Licensees involved in interstate selling of lots across state lines that come under this Act should seek legal advice to ensure full compliance.

If a development contains 25 or more lots, the developer must furnish prospective buyers with a **property report** containing all essential information about the property, such as

- distance over paved roads to nearby communities,
- number of homes currently occupied,
- soil conditions affecting foundations and septic systems,
- type of title a buyer receives, and
- existence of liens.

The property report must be given to a prospective purchaser prior to signing a lease or sales contract.

A purchaser of a lot covered by the Act has seven days to reconsider the sale. The purchaser can revoke, or rescind, the sales contract—at the purchaser's option— until midnight of the seventh day following the signing of the contract. If a buyer signs a contract to purchase a lot covered by the Act and fails to receive a property report, the purchaser has two years in which to revoke the contract.

If the seller misrepresents the property in any sales promotion, anyone induced to purchase a lot by the promotion can sue the seller for civil damages. Failure to comply with the law also may subject a seller to criminal penalties of fines and imprisonment.

Building Codes

North Carolina has enacted a series of statewide **building codes** containing requirements as to construction standards, and the primary purpose is safety. Most cities, towns, and counties have enacted ordinances that enforce these *minimum construction standards* that must be met when repairing or erecting buildings. This enforcement is through the local building inspectors certified by the North Carolina Department of Insurance (NCDI). These building codes set the requirements for kinds of materials, sanitary equipment, electrical wiring, fire prevention standards, and the like.

Most communities require the issuance of a **building permit** by the city clerk or another official before a person can build a new structure or alter or repair an existing building on property within the municipality. The permit requirement allows officials to verify compliance with building codes and zoning ordinances as they examine the plans and inspect the work. Once the completed structure has been inspected and found satisfactory, the city inspector issues a **certificate of occupancy (CO).** Not securing a building permit can make the property uninsurable for hazard insurance purposes until the oversight has been rectified. Some municipalities will allow retroactive approval of permits; some will require total removal of the improvement or repair. Unpermitted space should not be included in heated, living square footage quoted by real estate licensees, but the lack of a necessary permit should be disclosed as a material fact to all parties.

If the construction violates a private deed restriction (discussed later in this chapter), the issuance of a building permit will not cure this violation. A building permit is merely evidence of the applicant's compliance with municipal regulations.

Flood Hazard Regulations and Insurance

The Federal Emergency Management Agency (FEMA) has designated many areas bordering on rivers and streams as **flood hazard areas**, which are subject to federal regulations concerning improvements and construction in those areas. FEMA produces maps that designate these flood hazard areas, and flood insurance is required under the National Flood Insurance Program (NFIP) if a federally related mortgage loan is to be used for properties within those areas. The lender will insist on appropriate flood insurance, which the buyer can purchase through most regular insurance companies that sell homeowners' policies. The standard homeowners' policies do not cover flood damage. Flood insurance is a separate policy from the federally operated NFIP but is brokered through local insurance companies. Land located in these flood hazard areas is subject to restrictions in terms of location, types of improvements, and elevations of the improvements. Real estate licensees should inform any potential buyers of possible flood areas and have them review the latest version of the flood maps compiled by the Army Corps of Engineers.

Highway Access Restrictions

Access to a public road or street is important to any buyer, and the agent should make sure that public road access is available. If any government entity takes away road access, the owner must be compensated under eminent domain. If there is any planned construction of new highways, freeways, loop roads, etc., real estate licensees are expected to be aware of this and make full disclosure to any potential customer or client. Changes in road access have a great impact on value and usability of the property. Failure of a real estate licensee to properly disclose material facts about road access could lead to disciplinary action by the North Carolina Real Estate Commission [see G.S. 93A-6(a)(1)].

IN PRACTICE   The subject of city planning, zoning, and restriction of the use of real estate is extremely technical, and interpretation of the law is not altogether clear. Real estate agents should never offer advice on whether a particular use will be allowed or whether a variance or special-use permit will be granted. Questions concerning any of these subjects in relation to real estate transactions should always be referred to the appropriate authority or legal counsel.

Environmental Protection Legislation

Federal and state legislators have passed a number of environmental protection laws in an attempt to respond to the growing public concern over the improvement and preservation of America's natural resources. (See Chapter 21 for further discussion on environmental issues.) The various states also have responded to the environmental issue by passing a variety of local environmental protection laws regarding all forms of pollution—air, water, noise, and solid-waste disposal. Many states have enacted laws that prevent builders or private individuals from considering septic tanks or other waste disposal systems in certain areas, particularly where streams, lakes, and rivers are affected. In addition to the state and federal governments, cities and counties frequently pass environmental legislation. A licensee should stay informed of local environmental concerns so they may inform consumers.

Americans with Disabilities Act (ADA)

The federal government has recently mandated that new commercial buildings and older public buildings that undergo remodeling must meet the standards of the **Americans with Disabilities Act (ADA).** The purpose of this legislation is to facilitate accessibility and mobility by ramp construction, safety rails, wider doors, and other accommodations. (See Chapter 20 for further discussion on ADA.) ADA does not apply to residential housing.

■ PRIVATELY IMPOSED LAND-USE CONTROLS

Private land-use controls are put in place by individual property owners, usually when they transfer property. When property is conveyed, a property owner can include restrictions in the deed that limit the new owner's use of the property. For example, the property may be conveyed on the condition that it is used only as a bird sanctuary. The most common examples of private land-use controls are the restrictions imposed by subdivision developers. All those who purchase lots in a subdivision promise to abide by the developer's restrictions, which usually include provisions requiring regular property maintenance and restrictions on parking, fences, architectural details, and so on.

There is a distinction between restrictions on the grantee's right to *sell* and restrictions on the grantee's right to *use*. In general, provisions in a deed conveying a fee simple estate with restrictions on the grantee's right to sell, mortgage, or convey it are void. Such restrictions attempt to limit the basic principle of the *free alienation (transfer) of property*; the courts consider them against public policy and, therefore, unenforceable.

A developer may establish limitations on the right to use land through a covenant in a deed or by reference to a separate recorded declaration, called a **declaration of restrictive covenants**. When a lot in that subdivision is conveyed by an owner's deed, the deed refers to the plat and declaration of restrictions and incorporates these restrictions as limitations on the title conveyed by the deed. In this manner, the restrictive covenants are included in the deed by reference and become binding on all grantees. Such covenants or restrictions usually relate to type of building; use to which the land may be put; type of construction, height, setbacks, and square footage; and possibly cost. Private use restrictions are used primarily to protect property values and need not pass the test of promoting the public welfare, the test that public use restrictions must pass.

IN PRACTICE

The term **restrictive covenant** is being replaced by the term **protective covenant.** Both have essentially the same meaning, which is defined by the North Carolina Real Estate Commission as follows: "Protective covenants are enforceable conditions that restrict the manner in which an owner may use his/her property" (1997-1998 Update Course). The term *protective covenant* is a more modern term and better implies the intended use, which is to protect owners from uses that may have an adverse effect on value or enjoyment.

Use restrictions usually are considered valid if they are reasonable and are for the benefit of all property owners in the subdivision. However, if such restrictions are so broad in their terms that they prevent the free transfer of property, they may not be enforceable. If any restrictive covenant or condition is considered ineffective by a court, the property is freed from the invalid covenant or condition. Note that deed restrictions can be more restrictive on an owner's use than zoning ordinances. When zoning and covenants are in conflict, the more restrictive of the two takes precedence.

Generally, a subdivision developer will transfer the covenant enforcement rights to an established owners association at some predetermined time. Subdivision restrictions give the owners association and each lot owner the right to apply to the court for an injunction or legal action to prevent a neighboring lot owner from violating the recorded restrictions. If granted, the court injunction directs the violator to stop or remove the violation on penalty of being in contempt of court. The court retains the power to punish the violator for failure to obey the court order. If adjoining lot owners stand idle while a violation is being committed, they can *lose the right* to petition for injunctive relief by their inaction; the court might claim their right was lost through **laches**—that is, loss of a right through undue delay or failure to assert it.

Responsibilities of Real Estate Agents

When a licensee knows, or should have known, that the property in question is subject to protective covenants, there are certain obligations that the broker has to the prospective buyer. The agent should inform the buyer that since the property might be subject to private use restrictions, the buyer should obtain and carefully read a copy of the most recent version of the covenants before making an offer on the property. In a note under Provision 1 in the NCAR/NCBA Standard Form 2-T Offer to Purchase and Contract (see Appendix D, Form 11), the purchaser is cautioned to review Restrictive Covenants, if any, plus any governing documents for the subdivision or any established owners' association. The additional documents should clarify under what conditions the current covenants might be amended. Although a prudent broker should always volunteer general knowledge of the possible existence of land use restrictions, there are some situations that would require a licensee to actively disclose and notify the buyer of possible problems. If the broker is aware of an intended use of the property by the buyer that is typically restricted in many residential communities, the broker should recognize this as a "red flag" situation, point out the potential for conflict with most residential subdivision covenants, assist the buyer in obtaining a copy of the covenants, and suggest that the buyer consult a competent attorney for clarification if necessary. A broker is strongly cautioned to refrain from stating whether or not a particular use of the property will be allowed or if a certain act will be in violation of the covenants. Also, making assumptions about allowed activities or uses based on what other property owners have done is a recipe for liability disaster! Some aberrant uses may have been legally grandfathered and some may be illegal violations of the current covenants. Always have the consumer consult an attorney if there is any uncertainty about a proposed land use.

■ GOVERNMENT OWNERSHIP

Over the years, the government's general policy has been to encourage private ownership of land. A certain amount of land is owned by the government for such uses as municipal buildings, state legislative houses, schools, and military stations. Such direct public ownership is a means of land control.

Publicly owned streets and highways serve a necessary function for the entire population. Public land is often used for recreational purposes as well. National and state parks and forest preserves create areas for public use and recreation and at the same time help to conserve our natural resources. At present, the federal government owns approximately 775 million acres of land, nearly one-third of the total area of the United States. At times, the federal government has held title to as much as 80 percent of the nation's total land area.

■ RELATED WEB SITES

Federal Emergency Management Authority: *www.fema.gov*
North Carolina Department of Insurance: *www.ncdoi.com*
North Carolina Department of Transportation projects: *www.ncdot.org/projects*
North Carolina Flood Mapping Program: *www.ncfloodmaps.com*

■ SUMMARY

The control of land use is exercised in three ways: through public controls, private (or nongovernment) controls, and government ownership of land.

Public controls are ordinances based on the states' police powers to protect the public health, safety, and welfare. Through power conferred by state enabling acts, local governments enact comprehensive master plans, and any zoning must be in accordance with the master plan.

Zoning ordinances carrying out the provisions of the master plan segregate residential areas from business and industrial zones and control not only land use but also density of populations and height and bulk of buildings. Zoning enforcement issues involve boards of adjustment, conditional-use permits, variances, and non-conforming uses. Zoning ordinances are local in nature. There are no statewide zoning ordinances and there is no conformity in zoning regulations or codes.

A subdivider buys undeveloped acreage, divides it into smaller parcels, and develops or sells it. A builder builds homes on the lots and sells them through the builder's own sales organization or through local real estate brokerage firms. A developer may be a subdivider or a builder who also subdivides. Land development must comply with the master plans adopted by counties, cities, towns, or villages. Development may entail approval of land-use plans by local planning committees or commissioners.

The process of subdivision includes dividing the tract of land into lots and blocks and providing for utility easements, as well as laying out street patterns and widths. A subdivider must record a completed plat of subdivision, with all necessary approvals of public officials, in the county where the land is located. Subdividers usually place restrictions on the use of all lots in a subdivision as a general plan for the benefit of all lot owners. Closing the sale of a lot in an unapproved subdivision or nondisclosure of subdivision street status by a real estate licensee will subject the licensee to disciplinary action by the North Carolina Real Estate Commission and possible civil or criminal lawsuit.

Subdivided land sales are regulated on the federal level by the Interstate Land Sales Full Disclosure Act. This law requires that developers engaged in interstate land sales or leasing for a subdivision containing 25 or more lots register the details of the land with HUD. Before any sales contract is signed, such developers also must provide prospective purchasers with a property report containing all essential information about the property. Subdivided land sales are also regulated by individual state and local statutes.

State building codes specify minimum standards for construction, plumbing, sewers, electrical wiring, and equipment to ensure safety. Local municipalities may require building codes that are more restrictive than the state codes.

In addition to land-use control on the local level, state governments and the federal government have passed laws regarding flood hazard insurance and highway access restrictions. They also have occasionally intervened when necessary to preserve natural resources through environmental legislation.

Private controls are exercised by owners, generally developers, who control use of subdivision lots by deed restrictions designed to apply to all lots. Property owners' associations or adjoining-lot owners may enforce recorded restrictions by obtaining a court injunction to stop a violator. Private restrictions need not promote the public welfare and safety like public restrictions. If there is a conflict between private restrictions and zoning restrictions, whichever regulations are stricter will take precedence.

Public ownership is a land use control that provides land for such public purposes as parks, highways, schools, and municipal buildings.

QUESTIONS

1. A provision in a subdivision declaration used as a means of forcing the grantee to live up to the terms under which the grantee holds title to the land is a
   a. protective covenant.
   b. reversion clause.
   c. loss through laches.
   d. conditional-use permit.

2. Tests commonly applied in determining the validity of zoning ordinances require all of the following *EXCEPT* that the
   a. power be exercised in a reasonable manner.
   b. ordinance be free from discrimination.
   c. ordinance apply to all property in a similar manner.
   d. ordinance causes a loss of property value for the public good.

3. Public land-use controls include all of the following *EXCEPT*
   a. subdivision regulations.
   b. restrictive covenants.
   c. environmental protection laws.
   d. master plan specifications.

4. Zoning powers are conferred on municipal governments by
   I. state enabling acts.
   II. eminent domain.
      a. I only
      b. II only
      c. Both I and II
      d. Neither I nor II

5. Zoning laws are generally enforced by
   a. homeowner associations.
   b. nonissuance of building permits to properties that do not conform to zoning.
   c. restrictive covenants.
   d. the North Carolina Secretary of State.

6. Zoning boards of adjustment are established to hear complaints about
   a. protective covenants.
   b. the effects of a zoning ordinance.
   c. state building codes.
   d. the effects of public ownership.

7. The zoning allows regulation of all of the following *EXCEPT*
   a. number of buildings.
   b. size of buildings.
   c. building ownership.
   d. building occupancy.

8. The purpose of a building permit is to
   I. maintain municipal control over the volume of building.
   II. provide evidence of compliance with municipal building codes.
      a. I only
      b. II only
      c. Both I and II
      d. Neither I nor II

9. Dinwiddie owns a vacant lot in a residential neighborhood. His friends in the city government manage to change the zoning on his lot to commercial, so he can increase his profits on the property. This type of zoning is called
   a. spot zoning.
   b. a nonconforming use.
   c. an illegal use.
   d. a variance.

10. The grantor of a deed may place effective restrictions on the
    I. right to sell the land.
    II. use of the land.
       a. I only
       b. II only
       c. Both I and II
       d. Neither I nor II

11. A new zoning code is enacted. A building that is permitted to continue in its current use even though that use does not conform to the new zoning is an example of a(n)
    a. legal nonconforming use.
    b. hardship variance.
    c. conditional use.
    d. inverse condemnation.

12. To determine whether a location can be put to future use as a retail store, one would examine the
    a. building code.
    b. current use.
    c. housing code.
    d. zoning code.

13. A list of deed restrictions probably would NOT include
    a. types of buildings that may be constructed.
    b. allowable ethnic origins of purchasers.
    c. activities that are not to be conducted at the site.
    d. minimum size of buildings to be constructed.

14. A seller's deed restriction may be enforced by
    a. court injunction.
    b. zoning board of adjustment.
    c. city building commission.
    d. state legislature.

15. J & J Enterprises just purchased a vacant lot next to their retail shop. They plan to expand their shop onto the newly acquired lot. The architectural plans extend the addition two feet into the setback requirements for that location. To construct the building legally, the owners must obtain a
    a. license.
    b. variance.
    c. nonconforming-use permit.
    d. permit issued by the state.

16. To control and maintain the quality and character of a subdivision, a developer will establish which of the following?
    I. Deed restrictions
    II. Building codes
       a. I only
       b. II only
       c. Both I and II
       d. Neither I nor II

17. A residential neighborhood in Central City consists of homes built in the late 1800s. The neighborhood is subject to special zoning that prohibits property owners from tearing down a current home and replacing it with a modern one. This type of zoning is called
    a. historic preservation zoning.
    b. spot zoning.
    c. zoning amendments.
    d. eminent domain.

18. A drawing showing the sizes and locations of streets, utility easements, and lots in a subdivision is called a
    a. gridiron pattern.
    b. topographic survey.
    c. plat map.
    d. property report.

19. The property report required by the Interstate Land Sales Full Disclosure Act, would NOT need to include
    a. soil conditions affecting foundations.
    b. original purchase price paid by developer.
    c. number of homes currently occupied.
    d. existence of liens.

20. When other property owners in an established subdivision wish to remedy a violation of a restrictive covenant by a neighbor, they should
    a. appeal to the zoning commission.
    b. write the city council.
    c. complain to the developer.
    d. hire an attorney and sue the offender.

21. Due to the strange shape of Dewey's lot, present zoning restrictions about parking space requirements will cause an undue hardship for Dewey's planned use of the property as an office building. If there are no other reasonable uses for the property, Dewey may be allowed to proceed with his plans under

    a. nonconforming use.
    b. a variance.
    c. spot zoning.
    d. a special-use permit.

22. Mr. Jones has owned and operated a gas station at the edge of town for 20 years. Pursuant to a new comprehensive plan, the city rezones the land as residential. Which of the following statements is *TRUE*?

    a. The gas station can probably continue to operate under a variance.
    b. If Mr. Jones sells the station, the new owner can continue to operate under the grandfather clause.
    c. The city can force Mr. Jones to close the gas station immediately.
    d. Mr. Jones can continue to operate the station as long as he does not enlarge the building.

23. Which of the following statements is/are *TRUE* about subdivision regulations?

    I. A subdivision consists of at least five parcels of land for the purpose of sale or development now or in the future.
    II. A licensee can create a sales contract on lots in a new subdivision only after the final subdivision plat has been recorded.
    a. I only
    b. II only
    c. Both I and II
    d. Neither I nor II

24. Flood insurance is

    a. part of most homeowner hazard insurance policies.
    b. required on all FHA loans if the property is located in a flood hazard area.
    c. sold only by agents of the Federal Emergency Management Agency.
    d. coverage for all property damage caused by any water source.

Real Estate Brokerage and the Law of Agency

LEARNING OBJECTIVES *When you have finished reading this chapter, you should be able to*

- **identify** all types of agency relationships and characteristics of each (single, subagency, dual agency, and designated dual agency) and explain how fiduciary relationships are established and terminated.

- **differentiate** between client-level and customer-level responsibilities of the agent.

- **explain** agency disclosure requirements in North Carolina; how, when, and to whom proper agency disclosures must be made.

- **explain** the duties and liabilities of principals to their agents and third parties.

- **define** these *key terms*:

agency	fee-for-service	negligent omission
agent	fiduciary	oral buyer agency
antitrust laws	first substantial contact	price-fixing
broker	fraud	principal
brokerage	general agent	provisional broker
broker-in-charge	implied agreement	puffing
caveat emptor	independent contractor	ratification
client	in-house sale	special agent
commingling	LOADS	stigmatized properties
commission	material facts	subagent
cooperating broker	multiple listing service (MLS)	tort
customer		universal agent
designated dual agency	National Do Not Call Registry	willful misrepresentation
dual agency		willful omission
employee	negligent misrepresentation	*Working with Real Estate Agents*
express agreement		

■ INTRODUCTION TO BROKERAGE AND AGENCY

The nature of real estate brokerage services, particularly those provided in residential sales transactions, has changed significantly over the years. Through the 1950s, real estate brokerage firms were primarily one-office, minimally staffed, family-run operations. The broker listed the owner's property for sale and found a buyer without assistance from other companies. Then the sale was negotiated and closed. It was relatively clear that the broker represented the seller's interests.

In the 1960s, however, the ways buyers and sellers were brought together in a transaction began to change. Brokers started to share information about properties they had listed, which resulted in two brokers/firms cooperating with one another to sell a property. Brokers formalized this exchange of information by creating **multiple-listing services (MLSs)**. By increasing exposure to potential buyers, the MLS expedited sales and, therefore, became a widely used industry service.

Unfortunately, confusion quickly arose over whom the broker represented in these cooperative co-brokered transactions. With two different brokers/firms involved in a sale, the natural assumption was that there was a clear division of responsibility. The broker who had the property listed for sale represented the seller; the broker who found the buyer represented the buyer. However, this was not the case. In these shared transactions, both brokers represented the seller. Generally, the MLSs provided for a *unilateral subagency*, which was created when a seller listed property with a listing broker or firm. The listing broker then submitted the listing to the MLS so the listing could be shared with other MLS members. These MLS members immediately became subagents of the seller; the seller became their client or principal. This common *traditional view* of agency began to erode when buyers became concerned about having their own representation.

Such misunderstandings ultimately led buyers to question exactly how their interests were being protected. This helped spur a growing trend in which buyer consumers began to demand that their rights be protected so that they could make informed decisions. In many states, lawmakers have departed from the common-law doctrine of **caveat emptor**—let the buyer beware—toward greater consumer protection. Buyers seek not only accurate, factual information but also advice, particularly as real estate transactions have become much more complex. Buyers view the real estate licensee as the expert on whom they can rely to guide them. Today, most buyers seek and obtain representation. However, North Carolina is still considered to be a *caveat emptor* state.

■ THE LAW OF AGENCY

The basic framework of the law that governs the legal responsibilities of the broker to the people the broker represents—known as the *law of agency*—has not changed. However, its *application* has. Brokers are re-evaluating their services. They are determining whether they will represent the seller, the buyer, or both (if permitted by state law) in the sale or rental of property. They also must decide how they will cooperate with other brokers in a transaction. In short, the brokerage business is undergoing many changes as brokers focus on ways to enhance their services to buyers and sellers.

The North Carolina Real Estate Commission (NCREC) strongly encourages the **broker-in-charge (BIC)** of a real estate firm to have a written office policy as to the type(s) of agency the firm will practice. The firm is technically the agent in a transaction. The company policy should cover whether the firm will practice seller single agency only, buyer single agency only, or dual and designated agency. Which party the firm will represent is a decision that is largely based on economics. For instance, a single-agency practice could result in a loss of income in certain areas of the state. Whichever form of representation the firm adopts, the written policy should clearly state how that type of agency representation will be exercised. The written policy also should explain how the firm will enter into cooperative relationships among other firms, how it will arrange commission splits, and how it will implement disclosure requirements.

■ GENERAL AGENCY DEFINITIONS

Real estate brokers are commonly referred to as agents. Legally, however, the term refers to a strictly defined legal relationship. In the real estate industry, it is the relationship a party has with buyers and sellers. In the *law of agency*, the body of law that governs these relationships, the following terms have specific definitions:

> An *agent* is a person authorized to act on behalf of another.

- **Agent**—the individual who is authorized and consents to represent the interests of another person. In the real estate industry, principals are hiring an entire company to represent them. Even though *the firm* is the agent, the broker-in-charge would be personally accountable for agency law compliance.
- **Subagent**—one who is employed by a person already acting as an agent (such as a provisional broker licensed under a broker-in-charge who is employed under the terms of a listing agreement). Simply stated, a *subagent* is *an agent of an agent.*
- **Principal**—the person who hires and delegates to the agent through a brokerage contract the responsibility of representing that person's best interests. In the real estate business, the principal can be the buyer, seller, landlord, or tenant.
- **Agency**—the fiduciary relationship between the principal and the agent.
- **Subagency**—the fiduciary relationship between the subagent and the principal.
- **Fiduciary**—a relationship in which the agent is placed in the position of trust and confidence to the principal.
- **Client**—the principal.
- **Customer**—the third party for whom some level of service is provided by an agent of another party, but who is not represented by the agent.

The principal-agent relationship evolved from the master-servant relationship under English common law. The servant owed absolute loyalty to the master. This loyalty superseded the servant's personal interest as well as any loyalty the servant might owe to others. The agent owes the principal similar loyalty. As masters used the services of servants to accomplish what they could not or did not want to do for themselves, the principal uses the services of the agent. The agent is regarded as an expert on whom the principal can rely for specialized professional advice.

An agent works for the *client* and with the *customer*.

There is a distinction between the level of services that agents provide to clients and the level they provide to customers. The client is the principal to whom the agent gives advice and counsel. The agent is entrusted with certain *confidential information* and has *fiduciary responsibilities* (discussed in greater detail later in this chapter) to the principal. In contrast, the customer is entitled to factual information and fair and honest dealings as a consumer but does not receive advice and counsel or confidential information about the principal. The agent works *for* the principal and *with* the customer. Essentially, the agent is an advocate for the principal.

The relationship between the principal and agent must be consensual: the principal *delegates* authority; the agent *consents* to act. The parties must mutually agree to form the relationship. An agent may be authorized by the principal to use the assistance of others, called subagents of the principal.

■ BROKERAGE DEFINED

Before discussing the intricacies of agency, it is important to look more closely at the parties who provide the client and customer services in a real estate agency relationship.

Brokerage is the business of bringing buyers and sellers together in the marketplace. Buyers and sellers in many fields of business employ the services of brokers to facilitate complex business transactions. In the real estate business, a **broker** is defined as a person who is licensed to list, lease, buy, exchange, auction, negotiate, or sell interest in real property for others and to charge a fee for services. The **provisional broker** works on behalf of, and is licensed to represent, the broker (see G.S. 93A-1, G.S. 93A-2).

The principal who employs the firm may be a seller, a prospective buyer, an owner (landlord) who wishes to lease out property, or a person (tenant) seeking property to rent. The real estate firm or broker-in-charge acts as the agent of the principal, and the licensees employed by the firm act as the subagents of the principal. The principal usually compensates the firm with a **commission,** contingent on the firm successfully performing the service for which it was employed. That service generally involves negotiating a transaction with a prospective purchaser, seller, landlord, or tenant who is ready, willing, and able to complete the contract. However, the source of compensation does not necessarily dictate the agency relationship.

In a typical real estate listing contract, the seller will authorize the firm to use licensees employed by the firm as well as other **cooperating brokers/**firms (members of the MLS). Cooperating brokers may act as subagents of the principal and may in turn employ their own licensees. The relationship of a licensee to an employing broker/firm is also an agency relationship. The licensee is, therefore, the agent of the firm in addition to being the subagent of the principal.

REALTOR® Board/Association MLSs may not require that members make blanket offers of subagency to other members. Instead, MLS members must offer cooperation with compensation to other members. Thus, other members of the MLS may find a buyer for listed property while working as a subagent of the listing agent or as an agent of the buyer. The cooperating agent then will receive a portion of the commission when the sale closes. While all offers of cooperation must be accompanied by an offer of compensation, the listing broker may offer differing amounts to subagents and to buyer agents.

Classification of Agency Relationships

An agent may be classified as a universal agent, a general agent, or a special agent, based on the nature of the agent's authority.

A **universal agent** is a person who is empowered to do anything the principal could do personally. There are virtually no limits to the universal agent's authority to act on behalf of the principal. An unlimited power of attorney would be an example of universal agency. This type of agency is seldom practiced in a typical real estate transaction.

A **general agent** may represent the principal in a broad range of matters *related to a particular business or activity*. The general agent may, for example, bind the principal to any contracts within the scope of the agent's authority. This type of agency can be created by a *general power of attorney*, which makes the agent an *attorney-in-fact*. A real estate broker typically does not have this scope of authority as an agent in a real estate sales transaction. A property manager may be hired to be a general agent for the landlord in the management of certain properties.

A **special agent** is authorized to represent the principal in only one specific act or business transaction, and under limited, detailed instructions. A real estate broker is usually a special agent. If hired by a seller, the broker's duty is limited to finding a "ready, willing, and able buyer" for the property. A special agent for a buyer has the limited responsibility of finding a property that fits the buyer's criteria. As a special agent, the broker cannot bind the principal to any contract. A *special power of attorney* is another means of authorizing an agent to carry out only a specified act or acts. It is important to remember that a special agency gives *limited authority*.

■ **FOR EXAMPLE** Andrew, a real estate investor, hires Cami, a real estate broker, to locate and purchase an investment property for him at the coast. Andrew gives Cami authority to choose any property that meets his general parameters of location, price, and property type. Cami also is given a limited power of attorney for the purpose of completing this purchase. Cami is authorized to make binding decisions on Andrew's behalf and is acting as a general agent of Andrew. Later, Andrew hires Karl, a real estate broker in the mountains, to help facilitate Andrew's purchase of an office building in Boone. Karl acts as a courier and general right-hand man for Andrew, but Andrew is making all the decisions and will personally sign all documents in the transaction for himself. Karl is acting as Andrew's special agent.

Creation of Agency

Agents are employed for their expertise. However, provision of services does not in itself create an agency relationship. No agency exists without mutual consent between the principal and the agent. The agent consents to undertake certain duties on behalf of the principal, subject to the principal's control. The principal authorizes the agent to perform these acts when dealing with others.

Common-law agency relationships can be created in the following ways:

- With a written listing contract whereby a seller employs an agent to produce a buyer for the property; the seller is the principal, the firm/broker is the seller's agent
- With a buyer agency contract whereby a prospective buyer hires a firm/broker to locate properties for the buyer with buyer representation; the buyer is the principal, the firm/broker is the buyer's agent
- With a dual-agency contract whereby the agent legally represents both parties; both seller and buyer are principals, firm/broker is agent to both, but written informed consent from both parties is required
- With a property management contract whereby the owner of rental properties engages the services of an agent to rent and manage the property; the owner is the principal and the firm/broker is the property manager/agent
- With an in-house brokerage employment contract whereby a licensee signs an employment agreement with a firm/broker that defines the legal and agency relationship between them; the firm/broker is the principal and the licensee is the agent
- By the conduct of the parties (implied agency)

(Examples of these agency agreements are fully discussed in Chapter 9.)

Scope of Authority

Under general agency law principles, an agency relationship can be created by either an oral or a written agency agreement between the principal and the agent. It also can be implied from words or conduct. To ensure that all parties have a clear understanding of the agency relationship, it is in everyone's best interest to create an agency relationship through an expression of agreement rather than through implication. Principal and agent should make an **express agreement** (written or oral).

Agency also can be created by **implied agreement** when principal and agent, without formally agreeing to the agency, act as if one exists. However, an implied contract will not be established simply on trade custom and practice. There must be sufficient evidence to show that the principal authorized the agent to perform acts under circumstances in which a reasonable principal would be expected to compensate the agent for the services. The fact that a seller simply allows a broker to show the property is not sufficient to create an implied agency agreement, nor are implied agency agreements permitted under North Carolina real estate license law.

When someone claims to be an agent but there is no agreement, the *principal* can establish an agency relationship by **ratification** (apparent authority)—in other words, by performing any act that accepts (ratifies) the conduct of the agent as that of an agent.

If someone has stated incorrectly that another person is as the person's agent and a third person has relied on that representation, an agency relationship may have been created by estoppel. In such an event, in dealing with the *agent*, the *principal* cannot later deny the existence of an agency.

Compensation.   Because the source of an agent's compensation does not necessarily determine whether an agency relationship exists between two parties, an agent does not necessarily represent the party who pays the commission. In theory, an agency relationship can exist even if there is no fee involved (a gratuitous agency); however, such situations are rare, especially in real estate transactions. Buyers and sellers can make any agreement with a firm/broker they choose about compensating the firm/broker, regardless of which one is the agent's principal. For example, the seller could agree with the listing firm/broker to pay a commission to the broker who is the buyer's agent. The agency agreement should state how the agent is being compensated.

Termination of Agency

When an agent completes an assignment, the agency relationship ends, as does all responsibility to that former principal. An agency agreement may be terminated at any time for any of the following reasons:

- Completion or fulfillment of the purpose for which the agency was created
- Expiration of the terms of the agency
- Mutual agreement to terminate the agency
- Breach by one of the parties, such as abandonment by the agent or revocation by the principal (The breaching party might be liable for damages.)
- By operation of law, as in a bankruptcy of the principal (because title to the property would be transferred to a court-appointed receiver)
- Destruction or condemnation of the property
- Death or incapacity of either party (Notice of death is not necessary. Note that if a property is listed with a brokerage firm, the firm must dissolve to "die." If the individual listing licensee dies, the listing would not be terminated because the listing belongs to the firm rather than to the deceased listing agent.)

■ AGENCY RELATIONSHIPS

A variety of agency relationships may be created. The distinctions between them are not always clear. When consumers feel their individual interests have not been adequately protected, licensees may face legal and ethical problems. The broker-in-charge must decide the agency policies and procedures for the firm, determine who will be represented, disclose the agency alternatives to each party, and then act according to the agency relationship defined.

In North Carolina every agreement for brokerage services in real estate transactions must be in writing [see Rule A.0104(a)]. Real estate agency relationships typically are created with a listing agreement, a property management agreement, a buyer-agency agreement, or a tenant-agency agreement. Listing agreements and buyer-agency agreements will be discussed in detail in Chapter 9.

Single Agency

In a single-agency situation, the firm/broker exclusively represents either the buyer or the seller in a transaction. The agent represents one client; any third party is a customer. In the past, particularly in residential sales, firms almost always represented the seller. The firm served the seller as the client, and agents in the firm were subagents of the seller. In this case, prospective buyers do not have a client-based relationship with anyone. Rather, they are the customers (the third parties) who are not represented by the seller's agent (i.e., the listing firm/broker). Consequently, in this situation, buyers must take responsibility for protecting their own interests in a transaction—in essence, buyers are represented by no one other than themselves. Firms/brokers may choose to exclusively represent buyers as their clients. In this case, the sellers are the third parties. Because of the growing awareness that buyers also deserve the degree of representation available in a client-based relationship, more buyers are seeking brokers to represent them.

A *single agent* represents either the buyer or the seller in a transaction.

A single-agency firm/broker may represent either the seller or the buyer in any particular transaction. However, in single agency, the broker never represents both parties in the same transaction. This limitation avoids conflicting fiduciary duties and results in client-level service and loyalty to only one client. Single agency precludes selling one's own listings if the firm is acting as a buyer's agent. For this reason, few brokerage firms elect to practice seller agency only or buyer agency only; those that do usually practice buyer agency only. There are some single agency firms that represent both sellers and buyers, just not in the same transaction, as their company policy states that they will not practice dual agency.

Buyer Agency

When a buyer contracts with a firm/broker to locate property and represent the buyer's interests in the transaction, the buyer is the principal—the broker's client. The broker as agent is strictly accountable to the buyer. The seller is the third party.

In the past, it was simple: brokers always represented sellers, and buyers were expected to look out for themselves. With the widespread use of MLSs and subagency, a buyer often had the mistaken impression that the subagent was the buyer's agent, although the reality was that both agent and subagent represented the seller's interest. Today, however, many residential brokers recognize the opportunities afforded by buyer representation. Some brokers have become specialists in the field of buyer brokerage, representing buyers exclusively. Real estate regulatory agencies (including the North Carolina Real Estate Commission) across the country have developed rules and procedures to regulate such buyers' brokers, and local real estate associations have developed agency representation forms and other materials for them to use. The agency agreement forms are discussed in Chapter 9. Professional organizations offer assistance, certification, training, and networking opportunities for buyers' agents.

A buyer-agency or tenant-agency relationship is established in the same way as any other agency agreement: by *express* contract or agreement, *which may be oral initially, but which must be reduced to writing no later than the time an offer is extended by any party to the transaction. If the agent seeks to restrict the buyer's right to work with other agents or independently or to bind the client to the agent for any specified period, then the buyer-agency agreement must be in writing from the formation of the restricted relationship.* The buyer's agent may receive a flat fee or a share of the listing commission or both, depending on the terms of the agency agreement.

Subagency

A subagency is created when one broker/firm, usually the seller's agent, appoints other brokers/firms (with the authority of the seller) to assist in performing client-based functions on the principal's behalf. These cooperating brokers/firms have

FIGURE 7.1

Subagency

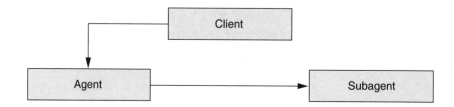

A *subagent* is the agent of an agent. The person designated by an agent to assist in performing client-based functions on behalf of the principal.

the same fiduciary obligations to the seller-principal as the listing broker, assisting in producing a ready, willing, and able buyer for the property. The listing broker and the seller now become potentially liable for the conduct of all of the cooperating brokers/firms and their licensees in protecting the fiduciary responsibility to the seller (see Figure 7.1). It is also important to note that when a real estate broker/firm becomes an agent under an agency agreement with a principal, all individual real estate licensees affiliated with the broker/firm automatically become subagents of the principal, unless there is a specific agreement to the contrary.

■ **FOR EXAMPLE** In our previous example, Andrew authorized Cami to act as his general agent in the purchase of coastal investment property. While working on this purchase for Andrew, Cami was hospitalized with food poisoning for several days. Cami hired one of her colleagues, Duncan, to supervise inspections and repairs on the property during her illness. Duncan acted as a subagent, the agent of an agent. Duncan owed Andrew the same loyalty and obedience as Cami did since they both ultimately work for Andrew.

Dual and Designated Dual Agency

The appropriate paragraphs of NC Real Estate Commission Rule A.0104 are quoted below.

> (d) *A real estate broker representing one party in a transaction shall not undertake to represent another party in the transaction without the written authority of each party. Such written authority must be obtained upon the formation of the relationship except when a buyer or tenant is represented by a broker without a written agreement in conformity with the requirements of paragraph (a) of this rule. Under such circumstances, the written authority for dual agency must be reduced to writing not later than the time that one of the parties represented by the broker makes an offer to purchase, sell, rent, lease, or exchange real estate to another party.*

> (i) *A firm which represents more than one party in the same real estate transaction is a dual agent and, through the brokers associated with the firm, shall disclose its dual agency to the parties.*

> (j) *When a firm represents both the buyer and seller in the same real estate transaction, the firm may, with the prior express approval of its buyer and seller clients, designate one or more individual agents associated with the firm to represent only the interest of the seller and one or more other individual brokers associated with the firm to represent only the interests of the buyer in the transaction. The authority for designated agency must be reduced to writing not later than the time that the parties are required to reduce their dual agency agreement to writing in accordance with subsection (d) of this rule. An individual broker shall not be so designated and shall not undertake to represent only the interest of one party if the broker has actually received confidential*

information concerning the other party in connection with the transaction. A broker-in-charge shall not act as a designated agent for a party in a real estate sales transaction when a provisional broker under his supervision will act as a designated agent for another party with a competing interest.

(k)   *When a firm acting as a dual agent designates an individual broker to represent the seller, the broker so designated shall represent only the interest of the seller and shall not, without the seller's permission, disclose to the buyer or a broker designated to represent the buyer:*

(1)   *that the seller may agree to a price, terms, or any conditions of sale other than those established by the seller;*

(2)   *the seller's motivation for engaging in the transaction unless disclosure is otherwise required by statute or rule; and*

(3)   *any information about the seller which the seller has identified as confidential unless disclosure of the information is otherwise required by statute or rule.*

(l)   *When a firm acting as a dual agent designates an individual broker to represent the buyer, the broker so designated shall represent only the interest of the buyer and shall not, without the buyer's permission, disclose to the seller or a broker designated to represent the seller:*

(1)   *that the buyer may agree to a price, terms, or any conditions of sale other than those offered by the buyer;*

(2)   *the buyer's motivation for engaging in the transaction unless disclosure is otherwise required by statute or rule; and*

(3)   *any information about the buyer which the buyer has identified as confidential unless disclosure of the information is otherwise required by statute or rule.*

(m)   *A broker designated to represent a buyer or seller in accordance with Section (j) of this Rule shall disclose the identity of all of the brokers so designated to both the buyer and the seller. The disclosure shall take place no later than the presentation of the first offer to purchase or sell.*

(n)   *When an individual broker represents both the buyer and seller in the same real estate sales transaction pursuant to a written agreement authorizing dual agency, the parties may provide in the written agreement that the broker shall not disclose the following information about one party to the other without written permission from the party about whom the information pertains:*

(1)   *that a party may agree to a price, terms, or any conditions of sale other than those offered;*

(2)   *the motivation of a party for engaging in the transaction, unless disclosure is otherwise required by statute or rule; and*

(3)   *any information about a party which that party has identified as confidential, unless disclosure is otherwise required by statute or rule.*

Dual Agency

A *dual agent* represents two principals with opposing interests in the same transaction.

In a **dual agency** situation, the broker/firm represents the buyer and the seller in the same transaction. Dual agency requires that the agent be equally loyal to two separate principals at the same time. The challenge is to fulfill the fiduciary obligations to one principal without compromising fiduciary obligations to the other. Under the strict terms of the law of agency, dual agency seems to be a logical impossibility. How can one person serve two masters, especially when their interests are not only separate but may also be opposite? Because agency originates with the broker/firm, dual agency arises when the broker/firm is the agent of both parties in the same transaction. The firm licensees, as agents of the broker, have fiduciary responsibilities to the same principals as well. A real estate firm/broker representing one party in a transaction shall not undertake to represent another party in the same transaction without the express approval of both parties.

■ **FOR EXAMPLE** Mark, a real estate broker, is the agent for the owner of Roomy Manor, a large mansion. Jennifer, a prospective buyer, comes into Mark's office and asks him to represent her in her search for a modest home. After several weeks of activity, including two offers unsuccessfully negotiated by Mark, Jennifer spots the For Sale sign in front of Roomy Manor. She tells Mark that she wants to make an offer and asks for his advice on a likely price range. Mark is now in the difficult position of being a dual agent; Mark represents the seller (who naturally is interested in receiving the highest possible price) and the buyer (who is interested in making a successful low offer).

Undisclosed dual agency.   A broker/firm may not intend to create a dual agency situation. However, by a broker associate's words and actions, it can occur *unintentionally* or *inadvertently*. Sometimes the cause is carelessness. Other times the subagent does not fully understand the fiduciary responsibilities. Some licensees lose sight of other responsibilities when they focus intensely on bringing buyers and sellers together. For example, a licensee representing a seller might tell a buyer that the seller will accept less than the listing price, which is a breach of the duty of loyalty (discussed later in this chapter). Giving a buyer any specific advice on how much to offer can lead the buyer to believe that the licensee is an advocate for the buyer. This would create an *implied agency* with the buyer and violate the duties of loyalty and confidentiality to the principal/seller. Because neither party has been informed of the situation or given the opportunity to seek separate representation, the interests of both are jeopardized. This undisclosed dual agency violates licensing laws [see G.S. 93A-6(a)(4)]. It can result in rescission of the sales contract, forfeiture of the commission, or the filing of a suit for damages.

■ **FOR EXAMPLE** Using the previous Roomy Manor example, if Mark does not tell Jennifer that he represents the seller of the property, he will be an undisclosed dual agent. Mark has two options. First, knowing Jennifer's comfortable financial situation and intense desire for the property, Mark might choose not to tell Jennifer about the dual-agency situation. Instead, he could tell her that Roomy Manor's owner will accept nothing less than the full asking price. While this will ensure that Mark receives the maximum possible commission, it will also subject him to severe penalties for violating the state's licensing laws. Alternatively, Mark should disclose his relationship with the seller and work out a dual-agency agreement with both parties in which he legally represents both parties' interests.

A more common example of dual agency would be if Mark employed two licensees, Rob and Susan. Rob is the listing agent for Roomy Manor, and Susan meets and begins representing the buyer, Jennifer. Because both Rob and Susan are associated with Mark's real estate brokerage, Mark and his licensees will still be construed as dual agents and have to enter into a legal disclosed dual-agency agreement with the parties.

Disclosed dual agency. Dual agency should be purposely created. In North Carolina, the key to *lawful* dual agency is that *all parties (seller/buyer, lessor/lessee)* must be *informed* and must *consent* to the broker representing both of them in the same transaction. In North Carolina, a firm that represents more than one party in the same real estate transaction is a dual agent and must disclose its dual agency status to the parties. The written authority for dual agency must be *obtained upon the formation of the relationship, except when an agent is working with a buyer or tenant under an oral agency agreement pursuant to A.0104(a), in which event the express oral authority for dual agency must be reduced to writing not later than the time that one of the parties represented by the agent makes an offer to purchase, sell, rent, lease, or exchange real estate to another party.* Though the possibility of conflict of interest still exists, the disclosure is intended to minimize the risk for the broker and ensure that both principals are aware of its effect on their respective interests.

Designated dual agency. **Designated dual agency,** sometimes called *designated agency,* might be used when a transaction is an **in-house sale.** It involves appointing one or more licensees of a firm to exclusively represent the seller and appointing another licensee of the same firm to exclusively represent the buyer in the same real estate transaction. However, it must be done with prior express approval of both parties. The firm continues to act as a dual agent; the individually designated licensees do not. The major advantage of designated dual agency is that both of the firm's clients (the seller and the buyer) receive a fuller and direct representation from their respective designated agent.

> *Designated dual agency occurs in an in-house transaction when the broker-in-charge (BIC) appoints one agent to exclusively represent the buyer and appoints another agent to exclusively represent the seller. The firm stays in dual agency providing impartial representation to both principals.*

If a firm wants to practice the designated dual agency option, the broker-in-charge (BIC) must establish a comprehensive written company policy on designated agency, and this policy must comply with North Carolina Real Estate Commission (NCREC) Rules. Firms electing to practice designated dual agency must specify who within the firm is authorized to appoint designated agents. This person is normally the BIC.

If a firm practices dual agency and designated dual agency, full written disclosure of this practice should be given to clients and customers at the earliest opportunity. When a firm enters into an agency contract with the seller/client or buyer/client, the client must be given an opportunity to indicate in writing which agency relationship he or she is authorizing. *The authority for designated agency must be reduced to writing not later than the time that the parties are required by NCREC rule to reduce their dual agency agreement to writing.*

The BIC must follow current legal restrictions when appointing the designated dual agents. *If the BIC represents one of the parties as a designated dual agent, the BIC can appoint only a licensed nonprovisional broker as the designated dual agent for the other party.* The BIC cannot appoint a provisional broker as a designated dual agent if the BIC represents the other party [see Rule A.0104(j)]. The BIC may, however, appoint a licensed nonprovisional broker to represent one party and appoint a licensed provisional broker to represent the other party.

NCREC rules impose another major restriction on the appointment of a designated dual agent. Namely, if a licensee has received *confidential information* about one party to the transaction, that agent has an obligation to refuse an appointment as the designated dual agent of the other party to the transaction. After a licensee has been appointed as a designated agent for one of the firm's clients, the designated agent exclusively represents that principal in the transaction. Therefore, if the agent learns any confidential information about the other principal in the transaction after being designated, the designated agent must disclose that information to the client that they exclusively represent. This is a major reason that firms should protect the transfer of information within the firm. An agent who illegally becomes a designated dual agent when already in possession of confidential information about the opposite principal in the transaction creates potential legal liability for the firm as well as becoming subject to possible disciplinary action by the NCREC. Note that while a client's confidential information must be kept confidential, agents must always disclose any information required by law to be disclosed, such as material facts about the property. Further, the company may have legal exposure if the post-designation receipt of confidential information occurs in-house.

Some important points about dual and designated dual agency include the following:

- To become a dual agent, there must be a client relationship with both the seller and the buyer within the same firm.
- There cannot be designated dual agency unless dual agency exists first.
- The firm owes the same fiduciary duties to both parties which has the effect of neutralizing the firm and its agents when acting as dual agents, but designated dual agents owe their fiduciary duties primarily to the party they are designated to represent, even though the firm has an equal obligation to both parties.
- Designated dual agency is a form of dual agency that is optional, but it has the potential to result in both of the firm's clients receiving better representation.
- To practice designated dual agency, the firm's policy must authorize it and both parties must give their written consent.

Throughout any discussion of agency duties, it is important to remember that an agent's duties to the principal are greater than the agent's duties to the customer (third person). However, a dual agent represents both parties. Therefore, the agent is generally restricted by the dual agency agreement from disclosing to either client information that does not relate directly to the property, such as the personal situation of either party, the financial status of either party, the prices willing to be offered or accepted by either party, any unusual pressure on either party to buy or sell, and so on. As mentioned earlier, a dual agent *is required by law* to disclose all material facts about the property to both principals, but is absolved from disclosing confidential information about either principal by the terms of the dual agency agreement.

Agency relationships in real estate rentals.   Another type of brokerage contract that creates an agency relationship is the Property Management Agreement, which is entered into by a management firm/broker and a property owner who wishes to hire someone to manage rental properties. *As with all agency agreements involving a property owner, the property management agreement must be in writing from the formation of the relationship.* The property manager/broker becomes the agent and the property owner becomes the principal. The fiduciary—agency—relationship between the property manager/broker and the property owner is the same as that between the broker and the property seller or buyer. Any licensed employees of the property manager/broker become subagents of the property owner. Prospective tenants *are* customers (or third parties) of the property manager, who owes certain duties *to the tenants* imposed by North Carolina Real Estate Law (N.C.G.S. Chapter 93A), fair housing laws (discussed in Chapter 20), and landlord/tenant laws (discussed in Chapter 11). *A property manager of residential property usually will represent only the property owner and will not seek to represent the tenant as well, which would cause the agent to become a dual agent. However, whenever an agent seeks to establish an agency relationship with a tenant thereby making the tenant a client,* the agreement for brokerage services between the broker and the tenant shall be express and shall be reduced to writing not later than the time any party makes an offer to rent or lease property.

■ AGENCY DISCLOSURE

To resolve some of the potential confusion surrounding agency relationships, North Carolina requires that real estate agents must disclose their agency status to both buyers and sellers in every real estate sales transaction. At the first substantial contact with a buyer or seller, an agent must provide the buyer or seller with a copy of the mandatory NCREC-published brochure entitled **Working with Real Estate Agents**. The text of this brochure is shown in Figure 7.2.

In every real estate *sales* transaction (residential and commercial) the agent shall provide the brochure to a prospective buyer or seller no later than **first substantial contact**. First substantial contact occurs when conversation between a licensee and a consumer shifts from facts about the property to possible confidential information about the consumer's needs, wishes, and abilities or when the consumer or licensee begins to act as if there is a fiduciary relationship. The agent must review the brochure with the buyer or seller and make a determination if the agent will act as the agent of the seller or the agent of the buyer. An agency relationship cannot be formed without this review. The nature and obligations of an agency relationship must be clearly explained to the consumer so that the consumer understands that the agent owes all client-level fiduciary duties only to the client/principal. The purpose of the agency disclosure brochure is informed consent by the consumer as to the best agency relationship for them. Always make agency disclosure prior to showing property to a buyer consumer; first substantial contact with a prospective buyer occurs no later than the time information is gathered to use in the selection of properties for viewing.

Each prospective seller and buyer must be given a copy of the mandatory brochure no later than first substantial contact. The brochure contains information on the various agency relationships available such as (1) seller's agent, (2) dual agent, (3) buyer's agent, and (4) seller's agent working with a buyer. If the first substantial contact does not occur *face-to-face*, then the brochure must be mailed, faxed, or e-mailed to the prospective buyer or seller as soon as possible, but in no event later than three calendar days from the date of first substantial contact. Then, the agent must review the contents of the brochure with the prospective seller

FIGURE 7.2   **Text from the *Working with Real Estate Agents* Brochure**

WORKING WITH REAL ESTATE AGENTS

When buying or selling real estate, you may find it helpful to have a real estate agent assist you. Real estate agents can provide many useful services and work with you in different ways. In some real estate transactions, the agents work for the seller. In others, the seller and buyer may each have agents. And sometimes the same agents work for both the buyer and the seller. It is important for you to know whether an agent is working for you as **your** agent or simply working **with** you while acting as an agent of the other party.

This brochure addresses the various types of working relationships that may be available to you. It should help you decide which relationship you want to have with a real estate agent. It will also give you useful information about the various services real estate agents can provide buyers and sellers, and it will help explain how real estate agents are paid.

Be sure to read and understand the listing agreement before you sign it.

SELLERS

Seller's Agent

If you are selling real estate, you may want to "list" your property for sale with a real estate firm. If so, you will sign a "listing agreement" authorizing the firm and its agents to represent you in your dealings with buyers as your *seller's agent*. You may also be asked to allow agents from other firms to help find a buyer for your property.

Duties to Seller: The listing firm and its agents must • promote your best interests • be loyal to you • follow your lawful instructions • provide you with all material facts that could influence your decisions • use reasonable skill, care and diligence, and • account for all monies they handle for you. Once you have signed the listing agreement, the firm and its agents may not give any confidential information about you to prospective buyers or their agents without your permission so long as they represent you. **But until you sign the listing agreement, you should avoid telling the listing agent anything you would *not* want a buyer to know.**

Services and Compensation: To help you sell your property, the listing firm and its agents will offer to perform a number of services for you. These may include • helping you price your property • advertising and marketing your property • giving you all required property disclosure forms for you to complete • negotiating for you the best possible price and terms • reviewing all written offers with you and • otherwise promoting your interests.

For representing you and helping you sell your property, you will pay the listing firm a sales commission or fee. The listing agreement must state the amount or method for determining the commission or fee and whether you will allow the firm to share its commission with agents representing the buyer.

them to represent both you and the seller at the same time (as a **dual agent**). Or you may agree to let them represent only the seller (**seller's agent** or **subagent**). Some agents will offer you a choice of these services. Others may not.

Dual Agent

You may even permit the listing firm and its agents to represent you **and** a buyer at the same time. This "dual agency relationship" is most likely to happen if an agent with your listing firm is working as a *buyer's agent* with someone who wants to purchase your property. If this occurs and you have not already agreed to a dual agency relationship in your listing agreement, your listing agent will ask you to sign a separate agreement or document permitting the agent to act as agent for both you and the buyer.

It may be difficult for a *dual agent* to advance the interests of both the buyer and seller. Nevertheless, a *dual agent* must treat buyers and sellers fairly and equally. Although the *dual agent* owes them the same duties, buyers and sellers can prohibit *dual agents* from divulging **certain** confidential information about them to the other party.

Some firms also offer a form of dual agency called "designated agency" where one agent in the firm represents the seller and another agent represents the buyer. This option (when available) may allow each "designated agent" to more fully represent each party.

If you choose the "dual agency" option, remember that since a dual agent's loyalty is divided between parties with competing interests, it is especially important that you have a clear understanding of • what your relationship is with the *dual agent* and • what the agent will be doing for you in the transaction.

BUYERS

When buying real estate, you may have several choices as to how you want a real estate firm and its agents to work with you. For example, you may want them to represent only you (as a **buyer's agent**). You may be willing for

Buyer's Agent

Duties to Buyer: If the real estate firm and its agents represent you, they must • promote your best interests • be loyal to you • follow your lawful instructions • provide you with all material facts that could influence your decisions • use reasonable skill, care and diligence, and • account for all monies they handle for you. Once you have agreed (either orally or in writing) for the firm and its agents to be your *buyer's agent*, they may not give any confidential information about you to sellers or their agents without your permission so long as they represent you. **But until you make this agreement with your buyer's agent, you should avoid telling the agent anything you would *not* want a seller to know.**

Unwritten Agreements: To make sure that you and the real estate firm have a clear understanding of what your relationship will be and what the firm will do for you, you may want to have a written agreement. However, some firms may be willing to represent and assist you for a time as a *buyer's agent* without a written agreement. But if you

Continued on the back

Source: Reproduced with permission of the North Carolina Real Estate Commission.

F I G U R E   7.2   **Text from the** *Working with Real Estate Agents* **Brochure (continued)**

Seller's Agent Working With a Buyer

If the real estate agent or firm that you contact does not offer *buyer agency* or you do not want them to act as your *buyer agent*, you can still work with the firm and its agents. However, they will be acting as the *seller's agent* (or "subagent"). The agent can still help you find and purchase property and provide many of the same services as a *buyer's agent*. The agent must be fair with you and provide you with any "material facts" (such as a leaky roof) about properties.

But remember, the agent represents the seller—not you— and therefore must try to obtain for the seller the best possible price and terms for the seller's property. Furthermore, a *seller's agent* is required to give the seller any information about you (even personal, financial or confidential information) that would help the seller in the sale of his or her property. Agents must tell you *in writing* if they are *sellers' agents* before you say anything that can help the seller. But until you are sure that an agent is not a *seller's agent*, you should avoid saying anything you do *not* want a seller to know.

Sellers' agents are compensated by the sellers.

The North Carolina Real Estate Commission
P.O. Box 17100 • Raleigh, North Carolina 27619-7100
919/875-3700 • Web Site: www.ncrec.state.nc.us
REC 3.45 3/1/02

00,000 copies of this public document were printed at a cost of $.00 per copy.

oral) buyer agency agreement, your *buyer's agent* will ask you to sign a separate agreement or document permitting him or her to act as agent for both you and the seller. It may be difficult for a *dual agent* to advance the interests of both the buyer and seller. Nevertheless, a *dual agent* must treat buyers and sellers fairly and equally. Although the *dual agent* owes them the same duties, buyers and sellers can prohibit *dual agents* from divulging **certain** confidential information about them to the other party.

Some firms also offer a form of dual agency called "designated agency" where one agent in the firm represents the seller and another agent represents the buyer. This option (when available) may allow each "designated agent" to more fully represent each party.

If you choose the "dual agency" option, remember that since a *dual agent's* loyalty is divided between parties with competing interests, it is especially important that you have a clear understanding of • what your relationship is with the *dual agent* and • what the agent will be doing for you in the transaction. This can best be accomplished by putting the agreement in writing at the earliest possible time.

decide to make an offer to purchase a particular property, the agent must obtain a written agency agreement. If you do not sign it, the agent can no longer represent and assist you and is no longer required to keep information about you confidential. Furthermore, if you later purchase the property through an agent with another firm, the agent who first showed you the property may seek compensation from the other firm.

Be sure to read and understand any agency agreement before you sign it.

Services and Compensation: Whether you have a written or unwritten agreement, a *buyer's agent* will perform a number of services for you. These may include helping you • find a suitable property • arrange financing • learn more about the property and • otherwise promote your best interests. If you have a **written** agency agreement, the agent can also help you prepare and submit a written offer to the seller.

A *buyer's agent* can be compensated in different ways. For example, you can pay the agent out of your own pocket. Or the agent may seek compensation from the seller or listing agent first, but require you to pay if the listing agent refuses. Whatever the case, be sure your compensation arrangement with your *buyer's agent* is spelled out in a buyer agency agreement before you make an offer to purchase property and that you carefully read and understand the compensation provision.

Dual Agent

You may permit an agent or firm to represent you **and** the seller at the same time. This "dual agency relationship" is most likely to happen if you become interested in a property listed with your *buyer's agent* or the agent's firm. If this occurs and you have not already agreed to a dual agency relationship in your (written or or buyer at the earliest opportunity thereafter. The brochure can be reformatted to allow for various means of communication, but the text cannot be changed. It must be exactly as printed by the NCREC. The brochure is not designed to replace the review and explanation of agency by the agent, but rather to facilitate this explanation. The brochure contains a *tear-off* panel for the buyer or seller to sign, acknowledging receipt and review of the contents by the agent. Because the consumer cannot be forced to sign the panel, the licensee shall note on the panel if the consumer refuses to sign the acknowledgment panel. The agent must keep this panel on file as proof of compliance with Rule A.0104 for three years. (See Rule A.0108.)

Rule A.0104(e) also requires a seller's agent or subagent working with a prospective buyer to disclose, *in writing* at first substantial contact, the agency status of representing the seller. If first substantial contact occurs other than a face-to-face meeting where it is not practical to provide written disclosure, the broker shall immediately disclose by similar means whom he or she represents and shall immediately, but in no event later than three calendar days from the first substantial contact, mail or otherwise transmit a copy of the written disclosure to the buyer. Note that this written disclosure of seller agency or subagency to the prospective buyer now may be accomplished merely by the buyer initialing the box at the bottom of the tear-off panel of the *Working with Real Estate Agents* brochure (see Figure 7.2).

■ **FOR EXAMPLE** Broker Sergio is holding an open house for a seller-client of his firm. Many prospective buyers tour the listed property during the afternoon. Does Sergio have to provide and review the **Working with Real Estate Agents** publication with the prospective buyers? If so, at what point must the agency disclosure occur? Most prospective buyers will tour the open house without requesting or disclosing any confidential information; if all conversation between the consumer and Sergio is strictly facts about the property, first substantial contact has not been reached and agency disclosure is not mandated. However, if the consumer begins asking more specific or personal questions, the brochure must be reviewed and Sergio and prospective buyer must determine and agree in what capacity Sergio will work with the buyer—whether as a seller's subagent or as a dual agent (since his firm already has an agency relationship with the seller). If the buyer consumer is not ready or willing to enter into an agency relationship with Sergio and his firm, the prospective buyer must initial the "Disclosure of Seller Subagency" at the bottom of the brochure panel before Sergio continues to provide assistance. If the buyer-consumer is ready and willing to enter some form of buyer agency with Sergio and his firm, they must determine whether the buyer and dual agency agreement will be written or oral, and whether designated agency is authorized. Full disclosure of agency options to consumers as soon as possible should always be the preferred action.

Oral buyer agency is an agency option a firm may use when the consumer is unwilling to commit to an exclusive written buyer agency relationship. A real estate broker may enter into an oral buyer agency agreement at first substantial contact with a prospective buyer [Rule A.0104(a)]. An agent who works with and represents a buyer initially under an oral agreement must do so in a *nonexclusive capacity*. *All* oral buyer agency agreements are nonexclusive. Any buyer agency agreement that seeks to bind the buyer to the agent or firm for a particular time period or that prohibits the buyer from working with other agents or firms must be in writing from the start. Under the oral buyer agency agreement, a buyer is free to enter into similar agreements with other firms and agents. An oral agreement is considered to be of indefinite duration and can be terminated at the will of either party at any time.

■ **FOR EXAMPLE** Bull Broker is contacted by a prospective buyer to look at properties for sale. During the initial interview, Bull merely hands the brochure to the buyer without any explanation or review and tells the buyer he will represent the buyer as her agent during this transaction. Has a buyer agency been formed? The answer is no. The brochure must be reviewed and the agent and prospective buyer must determine and agree in what capacity the agent will work with the buyer—whether as a seller's subagent or as a buyer's agent, and if the latter, whether under an oral or written buyer agency agreement.

Rule A.0104(a) also states, "A broker shall not continue to represent a buyer or tenant without a written agreement when such agreement is required by this rule." An agent must enter into a written buyer agency agreement no later than the time the first offer to purchase is presented. A buyer's agent working under oral agency *cannot* actually present the offer to the seller's agent unless the buyer/client first has signed a *written* buyer agency agreement. Although an agent may enter into an oral buyer agency agreement at first substantial contact, the rule does not prohibit the agent from getting an agency agreement in writing at first substantial contact. The written agency agreement does not have to be exclusive, but the agent should attempt to get the agency agreement in writing as soon as possible.

■ **FOR EXAMPLE** Bubba Broker has given the prospective buyer the brochure at first substantial contact, has reviewed it with the buyer, and has entered into an oral buyer agency agreement with the buyer. The buyer finds a home and wants to make an offer. After the offer has been prepared and before presentation to the seller or seller's agent, Bubba attempts to get the buyer agency agreement in writing and signed by the buyer as required by Rule A.0104(a). The buyer refuses to sign the buyer agency agreement. At this time, Bubba can no longer represent the buyer, but can present the offer acting as the seller's subagent with the buyer's permission. Of course, as the seller's subagent, Bubba must share information about the buyer/customer with the seller/client and is no longer required to keep information about the buyer confidential.

In the above example the broker must follow very specific conditions in order to present the offer as a seller's agent or subagent:

- The broker must clearly explain to the buyer that the broker will now represent the seller and will have a duty to the now *seller/client* to convey any information, confidential or not, about the now *buyer/customer* that the broker learned during their relationship as buyer agent under the previous oral agreement.
- The broker must officially terminate the oral buyer agency agreement in writing, which should include the former buyer/client's consent to do so, and an understanding that confidential information must be revealed.
- The broker must have the consent from the listing firm to act as a seller's subagent and must provide written disclosure of his seller subagency status to the buyer.

Note: Prior to switching to seller subagency, the oral buyer agent should consider entering into a written buyer agency agreement limited solely to that property, which few reasonable buyers should refuse.

Because an agent may work with a buyer under an oral buyer agency agreement, the rule of necessity also allows an agent to enter into an oral dual agency agreement that must also be put in writing no later than the time an offer is presented. In order to work under oral dual agency, the dual agency arrangement must have been discussed and the prospective buyer must orally agree for the agent to be a dual agent at the time the oral buyer agency is established. The same applies to oral designated dual agency.

The following may be used as a five-point checklist to properly follow disclosure rules:

1. The agency disclosure brochure must be given to prospective sellers and buyers upon first substantial contact in all real estate sales transactions.
2. The agent must review the brochure and a determination of agency status must take place. The buyer/seller can acknowledge receipt by signing the tear-off panel to be retained by the agent.
3. Listing agreements are *required to* be in writing from the start.
4. The rule *allows* for an agent to act as a buyer's agent, a dual agent, or a designated dual agent under an oral agreement, until such time as the agreements must be put in writing, which is not later than the time an offer is going to be presented.
5. Any buyer agency agreement that sets forth agency exclusivity or a definite period of time must be in writing from the start.

■ DUTIES AND LIABILITIES OF AGENTS

Agent's Responsibilities to Principal

As mentioned earlier, an agency relationship is a **fiduciary** relationship, one of trust and confidence between the broker and the principal. In a fiduciary relationship, the broker, by law, owes the principal specific duties—the duties of loyalty, obedience, accounting, disclosure of information, and skill, care, and diligence, easily remembered by the acronym **LOADS** (see Figure 7.3). These duties are described below. Note that such duties are not simply moral or ethical obligations; they are the law of agency.

Loyalty. The broker/firm owes the principal the utmost loyalty. That means placing the principal's interests above those of all others, including the broker's own. The agent must be particularly sensitive to any possible conflicts of interest. *Confidentiality* about the principal's personal affairs is a key element of loyalty. An agent may not, for example, disclose the principal's financial condition. When the principal is the seller, the agent may not reveal such things as the principal's willingness to accept less than the listing price or any anxiousness to sell unless the principal has authorized the disclosure. If the principal is the buyer, the agent may not disclose, for instance, that the buyer will pay more than the offered price if necessary, or that the buyer is under a tight moving schedule or any other fact that might harm the principal's bargaining position. (These are several reasons why

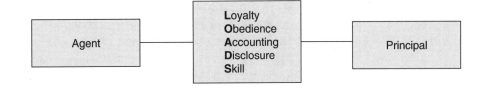

FIGURE 7.3

Agent's Responsibilities to Principal

undisclosed dual agency could result in rescission, monetary damages, forfeiture of commission, and disciplinary action by the NCREC.)

Because the agent may not act out of self-interest, the negotiation of a sales contract must be conducted without regard to how much the agent will earn in commission. All states forbid agents to buy property listed with them for their own use or in which they have a personal interest without first disclosing that interest and receiving the principal's consent. An agent must disclose to a client any personal or business relationship the agent may have with another party to the transaction, even if it is a former relationship. North Carolina Real Estate License Law and agency law require a buyer's agent to disclose to the buyer/client any personal interest that agent may have in the property. If the licensee is a seller's agent, there is no duty to disclose to the buyer the licensee's personal interest.

■ **FOR EXAMPLE** Broker Larry's sister owns a piece of property that she bought several years ago with Larry acting as her agent. She now wants to sell it as a For Sale by Owner. She asks Larry to help her sell at the highest possible price, even though the property is not listed with Larry. Larry has a buyer/client who is interested in the property and wants to make an offer to purchase. Larry does not reveal his relationship with the seller and tries to get the buyer to make a higher-than-market-value offer. Larry has clearly violated his loyalty to his principal, the buyer.

Obedience

The fiduciary relationship obligates the broker to act in good faith at all times, obeying the principal's instructions in accordance with the contract. That obedience is not absolute, however. The broker may not obey any instructions that are unlawful or unethical. For example, the broker may not follow instructions to make the property unavailable to members of a minority group or to conceal a defect in the property. Because illegal acts do not serve the principal's best interest, obeying such instructions violates the broker's duty of loyalty, not to mention other laws making the conduct illegal. On the other hand, a broker who exceeds the authority assigned in the contract is liable for any losses that the principal suffers as a result.

Accounting

The broker must be able to account for all funds received from, or on behalf of, the principal. Real estate license laws require that brokers give accurate copies of all documents to all parties affected by them and keep copies of such documents on file for three years (see Rule A.0108). In addition, the license laws generally require that the broker deposit immediately all trust funds entrusted to the broker in a special trust account (see Rule A.0107). It is illegal for the broker to commingle such monies with personal funds. **Commingling** is a term used to describe when trust funds and the firm/broker's personal/business funds are placed in the same account.

■ **FOR EXAMPLE** A broker has accepted an earnest money deposit in connection with an offer to purchase and deposits that money into his business account. The broker receives an earned commission check from another firm and deposits that check into the trust account. Both are examples of commingling, a mixing of trust funds with non-trust funds. Licensing law in North Carolina prohibits commingling.

Disclosure of information. Another very important duty of an agent to his/her principal is the duty of disclosure of information. It is the firm/broker's duty to keep the principal fully informed at all times of all facts or information the broker obtains that could affect the principal's decision in the transaction. A broker who fails to disclose such information may be held liable for any damages that result. A licensee must also disclose any personal benefit from the transaction because making a secret profit out of a transaction is prohibited.

The real estate agent also may be liable for facts he or she *should have known* and revealed to the principal but did not. This duty of *discovery* includes facts favorable or unfavorable to the principal's position, even if the disclosure of those facts would end the transaction.

Examples of facts an agent for the seller has a duty to disclose to the seller include:

■ all offers (See Rule A.0106);
■ the identity of the prospective purchasers, including the agent's relationship, if any, to them (such as a relative of the broker being a participating purchaser);
■ the ability of the purchaser to complete the sale or offer a higher price;
■ any relationship the broker has with the buyer (such as an agreement for the broker to manage the buyer's property after it is purchased); and
■ the buyer's intention to resell the property for a profit.

An agent for the buyer must disclose deficiencies of a property as well as factors that may adversely affect a property's value or desirability. The agent should disclose information that could affect the buyer's ability to negotiate the lowest purchase price, such as how long a property has been listed or why the seller is selling, if known by the agent.

North Carolina requires that sellers of most residential properties give the buyer a mandatory residential property disclosure statement. While the real estate agent cannot fill out the form, the agent is required to inform the seller of the agent's responsibilities in regard to the property disclosure. Property disclosure is discussed in more detail in Chapter 9.

Skill, care, and diligence. The broker must exercise a reasonable degree of skill, care, and diligence while transacting the business entrusted by the principal. The principal is entitled to expect the agent's skill and expertise in real estate matters to be superior to that of the average person.

The most fundamental way in which the broker meets this standard is to use the broker's skill and knowledge on the principal's behalf. Whether acting as a buyer's agent or as a seller's agent, the broker has an affirmative duty to try to discover and disclose to the principal all facts that are pertinent to the principal's decision-making process in the transaction. If the broker represents the seller, the broker's duties include helping the seller arrive at an appropriate and realistic listing price, discovering and disclosing facts that affect the seller, and properly presenting the contracts that the seller signs. Skill, care, and diligence also means making reasonable efforts to market the property, such as advertising and holding open houses, as well as helping the seller evaluate the terms and conditions of all offers to purchase.

A broker who represents the buyer will be expected to help the buyer locate suitable property and evaluate property values, neighborhood and property conditions, and financing alternatives, as well as to prepare offers and counteroffers with the buyer's best interest in mind.

A broker who does not make a reasonable effort to properly represent the interests of the principal could be found negligent. The firm/broker is liable to the principal for any loss resulting from negligence or carelessness.

Agent's Responsibilities to Third Parties

Even though an agent's primary responsibility is to the principal, the agent also has duties to third parties. The duties of an agent to a third party come from three sources: (1) North Carolina license law, (2) the North Carolina Unfair or Deceptive Trade Practices Act, and (3) court cases. These duties include

- being honest and fair, and
- complying with North Carolina Real Estate License Law and NCREC rules, including disclosure of material facts relating to a property or transaction about which the agent has knowledge or should reasonably have acquired knowledge.

When working with a buyer, a broker (as an agent of the seller) must exercise extreme caution and have knowledge of the laws and ethical considerations that affect this relationship. For example, brokers must be careful about the statements they or their agents make about a parcel of real estate. General statements of opinion are permissible as long as they are offered as opinions and without any intent to deceive.

Statements of fact, however, must be accurate. Opinion statements that exaggerate a property's benefits are called **puffing.** Although puffing is legal and a common practice, it must not constitute a misrepresentation of the property. Brokers must ensure that none of their statements can be interpreted as involving **fraud.** Fraud is the *intentional* misrepresentation of a material fact in such a way as to harm or take advantage of another person. In addition to false statements about a property, the concept of fraud covers intentional concealment or nondisclosure of important facts. If a contract to purchase real estate is obtained as a result of fraudulent misstatements made by a seller's agent, the contract may be disaffirmed or renounced by the purchaser. In such a case, the client loses a contract and the broker will lose a commission. If either party suffers loss because of a broker's misrepresentations, the broker can be held liable for damages. If the broker's misstatements are based on the owner's own inaccurate statements to the broker, however, and the broker had no independent duty to investigate their accuracy, the broker may be entitled to a commission even if the buyer rescinds the sales contract.

Agents must also be careful not to make any misrepresentations or omissions where **material facts** are concerned. As noted previously, the common law of agency requires an agent to disclose to the principal *any facts that might affect the principal's decision in a transaction.* To determine an agent's duty to disclose material facts to a third party, one must look to the North Carolina Real Estate Licensing Law, which requires disclosure of material facts to all parties to the transaction regardless of whom the licensee represents in the transaction. Per the *North Carolina Real Estate Manual,* the NCREC has historically interpreted *material facts to be disclosed to any party* under the Real Estate License Law to include at least

- *facts about the property itself* (i.e., significant physical characteristics such as square footage or acreage, a structural defect, or defective mechanical systems);
- *facts relating directly to the property* (usually factors outside the property that may directly affect value, use, or desirability of the property, such as a pending zoning change or planned highway construction in the immediate vicinity)
- *facts relating directly to the ability of the agent's principal to complete the transaction* (such as a pending foreclosure sale or buyer's inability to qualify for financing); and
- *facts known to be of specific importance to a party* (most likely to be items of special interest to a purchaser's intended use of the property, such as zoning allowing home businesses or covenants allowing multiple pets).

Some issues have been declared to be material facts by the North Carolina Real Estate Commission. For example if a residence has ever been clad in an exterior insulating and finishing system commonly called "EIFS" or "synthetic stucco," that will remain a material fact for that property forever. Also, if a residence has ever had leaking polybutylene pipes, this must be disclosed. Finally, if a property was the site of a meth lab, this also must be disclosed.

Prohibited Conduct

North Carolina real estate licensing law specifically prohibits the following types of acts in the agent's relationship with any party to the transaction [G.S. 93A-6(a) (1)]:

- *Willful misrepresentation:* intentionally misinforming any party involved in a transaction about a material fact
- *Negligent misrepresentation:* unintentionally misinforming any party involved in a transaction about a material fact
- *Willful omission:* intentionally failing to disclose a material fact to any party involved in a transaction
- *Negligent omission:* unintentionally failing to disclose a material fact to any party involved in a transaction

Willful Misrepresentation

Willful misrepresentation takes place when agents who have *actual knowledge* of a material fact deliberately misinform a buyer, seller, tenant, or landlord concerning such fact. Willful misrepresentation also takes place when an agent who does *not* have actual knowledge of a matter material to the transaction intentionally provides information concerning such matter to a buyer, seller, tenant, or landlord without regard for the truthfulness of the information. (See the examples that follow.) This is an act that is intentional on the part of the agent. An agent could also be involved in *indirect misrepresentation*, which occurs when an agent misrepresents a material fact to a subagent who in turn passes it on to a third party. If a material fact is misrepresented, courts could provide relief to the injured party in the form of damages or rescission of the contract. An agent guilty of misrepresentation could also face disciplinary action by the NCREC.

■ **FOR EXAMPLE**

- ■ An agent tells a buyer the cost of utilities is very reasonable without verification from the owner. If the costs are very high, the agent could be guilty of willful misrepresentation.
- ■ An agent tells a buyer the foundation of a house is sound and has been properly built, when the agent knows the foundation is substandard and improperly constructed.
- ■ A builder explains to an agent that the poor exterior wall insulation resulted from the developer's overall goal of containing cost. When this agent's buyer/client asks about the insulation, the agent replies that the builder was highly reputable and he was certain the insulation met the necessary standards.
- ■ A buyer signs a buyer agency agreement with an agent. The buyer wants to purchase property with low taxes. The agent informs the buyer that a particular property has annual taxes of $600 when in fact the agent knows the new assessed value will increase taxes to $1,200.

Negligent Misrepresentation

Negligent misrepresentation takes place when agents *unintentionally* misinform a buyer, seller, tenant, or landlord concerning a material fact because they do not have actual knowledge of the fact, because they have incorrect information, or because of a mistake by the agent. If the agent *should reasonably have known* the truth of the matter that was misrepresented, then the agent may be guilty of *negligent misrepresentation* even though acting in good faith. The fact that the agent was ignorant about the issue is no excuse. If a buyer relies on the agent's statement, the agent is liable for any damages that may result. If a buyer's agent relies on incorrect information provided by a listing (seller's) agent through the MLS property data, even with disclaimers, the buyer's agent may be held liable if the agent should reasonably have known the information was incorrect.

■ **FOR EXAMPLE**

- ■ A listing agent relies on a recent appraiser's report that a house has 2,500 square feet of heated living floor space and enters that information into the MLS property data. However, the house actually has 2,000 square feet. Although the *Residential Square Footage Guidelines* written by the NCREC (see Appendix B) allows a broker to "reasonably rely" on a recent report from a qualified appraiser, a prudent and knowledgeable agent in this case should have recognized a 500-square-foot error (i.e. 25% error). If the agent unreasonably relied on the appraiser's report and informed a buyer the house has 2,500 square feet, she has made a negligent misrepresentation. A buyer's agent also should recommend that a buyer measure a property if square footage is important to the buyer.

■ An agent tells a buyer/client that the home being shown has Levelor blinds throughout, without actually checking the brand name. The blinds are actually cheap, imported imitations of Levelor blinds.

Willful Omission

Willful omission takes place when agents have *actual knowledge* of a material fact and a duty to disclose such fact to a buyer, seller, tenant, or landlord, but deliberately fail to disclose such fact.

■ **FOR EXAMPLE**

■ An agent knows that a highway relocation is pending that would adversely affect value and use of a property a buyer wants to purchase but does not reveal this to the buyer.

■ An agent lists a property in midwinter knowing that the air-conditioning system does not operate properly but does not reveal that fact to a prospective buyer.

Negligent Omission

Negligent omission takes place when agents do *not* have actual knowledge of a material fact but *should reasonably have known* of such fact. If they fail to disclose this fact to a buyer, seller, tenant, or landlord, they may be guilty of *negligent omission*, even though they acted in good faith in the transaction.

Agents have an obligation to *discover and disclose* material facts about the property that any prudent agent would reasonably have discovered during the transaction. A listing agent would be held more accountable than would a selling agent in discovery and disclosure of defects in the property because of the listing agent's direct fiduciary relationship with the seller and the fact that the listing agent inspected the property and should be more familiar with the property than the selling agent.

■ **FOR EXAMPLE** An agent has listed a property in a neighborhood where a vacant lot is being considered by the city for installation of a garbage recycling system. The plan has been well publicized in the news media, which also has given much publicity to the fact that the neighbors have filed legal action against the city. The agent does not reveal this information to a buyer and, when questioned, states that he was not aware of these plans.

Frequently, the buyer or the buyer's mortgage lender will request inspections or tests to determine the presence or level of environmental risks. If environmental risk questions arise in a transaction, licensees should recommend that their client/customer obtain advice from state and local authorities responsible for environmental regulation or other appropriate experts, whenever toxic waste dumping, contaminated soil or water, nearby chemical or nuclear facilities, or health hazards such as radon, asbestos, and lead paint may be present.

IN PRACTICE NCREC has published other examples of these prohibited acts in the License Law and Rule Comments section of *North Carolina Real Estate Licensing Law and Commission Rules* (Appendix C), to which the student is referred. Students should be thoroughly familiar with these topics.

Stigmatized Properties

Over the years, brokers have encountered what are called **stigmatized properties**, those properties branded by society as undesirable because of events that occurred there. Some properties are typically marked by a criminal event: a homicide, suicide, or other violence; illegal drug or gang-related activity; or other events that render the property socially unmarketable in the community's view. Another psychologically impacted property would be a purported haunted house, which is not a material fact.

Under current North Carolina law (G.S. 39–50 and G.S. 42–14.2), the death—even the violent death—or serious illness of a previous owner or resident of a residential property is not a material fact. Therefore, it need not be voluntarily disclosed to a prospective buyer or tenant. If the prospective buyer specifically asks the agent about the death or illness, the agent can refuse to answer. Any answer the agent chooses to give, however, must be truthful. The one exception to this rule is if the death or illness is AIDS-related. Because persons with AIDS (or HIV infection) are considered legally handicapped under fair housing laws, an agent cannot disclose this condition, even if asked. Instead, the agent should tell the person who asked the question that the agent is prohibited by law from answering the question.

Sex Offender Disclosure

The above-mentioned General Statutes, also provide that the fact that a registered sex offender (or any other person convicted of a crime requiring registration by the Sex Offender and Public Protection Registration Programs) resides in or near a property for sale or lease is not a material fact requiring disclosure by licensees. The real estate licensee's agency status in the transaction will have no effect on the requirement to disclose either the presence of the sex offender in the area or the existence of the state sex offender registry. It does not matter if the licensee is a seller's agent, a landlord's agent, a buyer's agent, a tenant's agent, or a dual agent. If a licensee chooses to *voluntarily* disclose the presence of the registered sex offender, or to advise a prospective buyer or tenant to visit the sex offender registry, it will not be a violation of the Real Estate Licensing Law. Providing false or misleading information when asked about the presence of sex offenders in a given area will be construed by NCREC as a violation of the Real Estate Licensing Law.

IN PRACTICE

Because real estate licensees have, under the law, enormous exposure to liability, some brokers purchase errors and omissions insurance policies for their firms. Similar to malpractice insurance in the medical field, such policies generally cover liability for errors, mistakes, and negligence in the usual listing and selling activities of a real estate office. Individual agents, likewise, should be insured. Note that no insurance will protect a licensee from litigation arising from criminal acts such as fraud. Also, insurance companies normally exclude coverage for violation of civil rights laws. Nor will errors and omission insurance relieve a licensed agent from disciplinary action by the NCREC.

Liabilities and Consequences of Breach of Duty

Any agent who breaches an agent's duties to either the principal or a third party must bear the consequences of that breach. These consequences may include any (or all) of the following:

■ Disciplinary action by NCREC. Any violation of a duty owed to the principal or third parties is grounds for disciplinary action by NCREC. If the Commission finds that the agent did in fact violate the license law, that agent's license may be revoked or suspended.

- A civil action in court brought by the injured party. If the breach of duty harms either the principal or a third party, the agent may be sued and found liable for the damages caused by the breach. Note that if the agent's improper behavior is deemed to be within the scope of the agent's duties, the agent's principal also may be held liable for the damages caused by the agent. The principal can in turn sue the agent for reimbursement for those damages.
- Criminal prosecution brought by the district attorney. A violation of a provision of the real estate license law is also a misdemeanor (see G.S. 93A-8). If the agent's breach of duty also is a criminal act, such as fraud or embezzlement, the district attorney may bring a criminal action against the agent.

■ DUTIES AND LIABILITIES OF PRINCIPALS

Duties to Agent

The principal has two basic duties to the agent:

1. To act in good faith (to cooperate with the agent and refrain from hindering the agent's efforts). For example, if the seller-client refuses to let the agent show the property, this is a breach of good faith.
2. To pay the agent the agreed-on compensation when the agent finds a ready, willing, and able buyer. Once the agent brings the seller a buyer who is ready, willing, and able to purchase the property on the seller's terms, the agent has earned a commission, whether or not the seller decides to sell the home.

Duties to Third Parties

Historically, real estate transactions were governed by the doctrine of caveat emptor, or let the buyer beware. The principal was liable to a buyer only if the principal willfully misrepresented the property. It was up to the buyer to thoroughly examine and research the property, and the buyer was, for all intents and purposes, expected to purchase the property *as is*. Property owners had no affirmative duty to reveal defects about the property. This is still true in North Carolina. However, this principle has been gradually eroded by both court decisions and consumer protection laws. Sellers are always liable for fraudulent misrepresentations.

Liabilities and Consequences of Breach of Duty

The principal who violates the principal's duties either to the agent or to a third party is liable for the damage caused. The principal may be subject to both a civil lawsuit and criminal prosecution (if so warranted). The principal also may be held liable and accountable for the agent's misconduct, referred to as a **tort,** which is a wrongful act by an agent while representing the principal and *acting within the scope of the employment agreement that created the agency.*

■ NATURE OF THE BROKERAGE BUSINESS

Even if affiliated with a national franchise or marketing organization, a real estate broker is an independent businessperson who sets the policies of the broker's office. A broker may engage employees and licensees, determine their compensation, and direct their activities. A broker is free to accept or reject agency relationships with principals. This is an important characteristic of the brokerage business: *a broker has the right to reject agency contracts that, in the broker's judgment, violate the ethics or high standards of the office.* However, once a brokerage relationship has been established, the broker represents the principal and owes that person the duty to exercise care, skill, and integrity in carrying out instructions.

Broker-in-Charge–Licensed Associate Relationship

Although brokerage firms vary widely in size, few brokers today perform their agency duties without the assistance of other licensees. Consequently, much of the business's success hinges on the *broker-in-charge–licensed associate relationship.*

A provisional broker is any person licensed to perform real estate activities on behalf of a licensed real estate broker. The broker-in-charge is fully responsible for the actions performed in the course of the real estate business by all persons affiliated with the broker. In turn, *all of a provisional broker's activities must be performed in the name of the supervising broker* (see NCREC Rule A.0506). A nonprovisional broker associate has more autonomy in brokerage activities.

The provisional broker can carry out only those responsibilities assigned by the broker with whom the provisional broker is licensed and can receive compensation only from that broker (see G.S. 93A-6(a)(5)). As an agent of the broker, the provisional broker has no authority to make contracts with or receive compensation directly from any other party, whether the principal, another broker, a buyer, or a seller.

Independent contractor versus employee. The employment agreement between a broker-in-charge and a licensed associate preferably should be in writing and should define the obligations and responsibilities each has in the relationship. The broker-in-charge is responsible for supervising all provisional brokers in any brokerage activity and may be answerable to the Real Estate Commission for the conduct of those provisional brokers. A broker-in-charge has fewer supervisory responsibilities for the associated nonprovisional brokers, who are held more accountable for their own acts, thereby reducing the broker-in-charge's exposure to disciplinary action by the Real Estate Commission for the conduct of the associated nonprovisional brokers. The real estate *company* remains civilly liable for the acts of all of its associated brokers, whether provisional or nonprovisional.

Associated brokers with an active license may be paid for tax purposes either as a Form W-2 **employee** or as a Form 1099 **independent contractor**. This distinction is relevant primarily for tax purposes and is determined by tests set forth by the Internal Revenue Service (IRS) as to the degree of control exercised by the employer/principal over its employees/agents. The primary distinction for the employer/principal is that the employer is liable for withholding and paying Social Security and income taxes to the IRS for persons who are paid as Form W-2 employees, whereas Form 1099 independent contractors are responsible for reporting their income and paying estimated taxes with no contribution from the employer/principal. An employer may pay certain benefits on behalf of its employees, but not its independent contractors, and generally will be required to pay unemployment compensation tax on the wages of its employees, but not its independent contractors.

Regardless of whether associated brokers are paid as employees or independent contractors, the real estate company has the right to determine company policy and to dictate certain procedures or rules governing how its associated agents will conduct their brokerage business, as they are engaging in brokerage as agents of the company which remains liable for its agents' conduct.

IN PRACTICE   The Internal Revenue Service (IRS) often investigates the independent-contractor-versus-employee situation in real estate offices. Under the *qualified real estate agent* category in the Internal Revenue Code, three requirements can establish independent contractor status: (1) The individual must have a current real estate license. (2) The individual must have a written contract with the broker containing the following clause: "The salesperson will not be treated as an employee with respect to the services performed by such salesperson as a real estate agent for federal tax purposes." (3) Ninety percent or more of the individual's income as a licensee must be based on sales production and not on the number of hours worked. The broker should have a standardized agreement drawn up or reviewed by a lawyer to ensure its compliance with these federal dictates. The broker should also be aware that written agreements mean little to an IRS auditor if the actions of the parties are contrary to the document's provisions.

Antitrust Laws

The real estate industry is subject to federal and state **antitrust laws.** Generally, these laws prohibit monopolies and contracts, combinations, and conspiracies that unreasonably restrain trade. The most common antitrust violations are price-fixing, group boycotting, and allocation of customers or markets.

Price-fixing is the practice of setting prices for products or services rather than letting competition in the open market establish those prices. In real estate it occurs when brokers agree to set sales commissions, fees, or management rates, and it is illegal. Brokers must independently determine commission rates or fees only for their own firms. These decisions must be based on the broker's business judgment and revenue requirements without input from other brokers.

Multiple-listing organizations, Boards of REALTORS®, and other professional organizations may not set fees or commission splits. Nor are they allowed to deny membership to brokers based on the fees the brokers charge. Either practice could lead the public to believe that the industry sanctions not only the unethical practice of withholding cooperation from certain brokers but also the illegal practice of restricting open-market competition.

The broker's challenge is to avoid any impression of attempts at price-fixing as well as the actual practice. Hinting in any way to prospective clients that there is a *going rate* of compensation implies that rates are, in fact, standardized. A broker must clarify to clients that the rate stated is only what the firm charges. Likewise, discussions of rates among licensees from different firms could be construed as a price-fixing activity and should be avoided scrupulously.

NCREC is specifically prohibited by law (G.S. 93A-3) from making rules and regulations that regulate or dictate commissions, salaries, or fees to be charged by licensees. Commission Rule A.0109(f) states: "The Commission shall not act as a board of arbitration and shall not compel parties to settle disputes concerning such matters as the rate of commission, the division of commissions, pay of salesmen, and similar matters." All commission arrangements between an agent and a principal must be made in a way that shows they have been negotiated between the principal and agent.

Group boycotting occurs when two or more businesses conspire against other businesses or agree to withhold their patronage to reduce competition. Group boycotting is illegal under the antitrust laws.

Allocating markets or customers involves an agreement between brokers to divide their markets and refrain from competing with each other for business. Allocations have been made on a geographic basis, with brokers agreeing to specific territories within which they will operate exclusively. The division might occur by markets, such as by price range. These agreements conspire to eliminate competition and are illegal.

The penalties for such acts are severe. For example, under the Sherman Antitrust Act people who are found guilty of fixing prices or allocating markets may be punishable by a maximum $100,000 fine and three years in prison. For corporations, the penalty may be as high as $1 million. In a civil suit, a person who has suffered a loss because of the antitrust activities of a guilty party may recover triple the value of the actual damages plus attorney's fees and costs.

Fee-for-Services

The Internet has revolutionized the real estate profession in many ways. One of the more notable impacts of the Internet is that it has allowed buyers and sellers to have tremendous access to information about real estate, housing, financing, and law. The Internet has caused a radical shift in that the average consumer is now much more knowledgeable about real estate matters. With knowledge and information, a consumer is more innovative and independent. The advent of the Internet also has meant that the consumer is privy to information immediately. Consumers now want instant access to real estate information.

Successful licensees will understand and encourage consumers' innovation. In the process, it is critical for licensees to identify what services can be provided and to underscore the value of those services. While emphasizing the services that licensees provide, it may be important for licensees to think of themselves as consultants. While consumers are more independent, real estate expertise is almost always needed.

It may be more important for licensees to be more flexible and open to seeing their occupation as a *bundle of services* that can be unbundled. Note that unbundling fee-for-services is different from discounted real estate services. **Fee-for-services** is the arrangement where the consumer decides which services are needed and then works with and pays the licensee solely for those services. Discounted real estate services is the arrangement where a consumer receives all of the real estate services, but for a discounted price.

Unbundling services means offering services in a piecemeal fashion. For example, a consultant may want to offer a seller the following services:

- Helping the seller prepare the property for sale
- Performing a comparative market analysis (CMA) and pricing the property

- Assisting with marketing the property using the MLS and any other Web sites
- Locating and screening a buyer
- Completing an offer to purchase agreement and helping with negotiations
- Assisting with closing a transaction

Other services include those for a buyer. For example, a consultant may offer a buyer the following services:

- Consulting on renting versus owning
- Helping a buyer with a mortgage preapproval
- Consulting on a buyer's desired location
- Visiting properties with a buyer and checking property information
- Completing an offer to purchase agreement and helping with negotiations
- Assisting with closing a transaction

Note the discussion below regarding minimum level of services and the problems that can occur when providing a limited service.

While licensees want to encourage consumers to use all of their services (full-service) for a commission rate, when it becomes apparent that a consumer wants help with one or several services only, then it would be helpful for the licensee to have in mind the best compensation model. Many licensees use either an hourly rate or a flat fee for particular services. In determining a flat fee, licensees consider the amount of hours it would take to do a particular task and multiply that by an hourly rate. In order to avoid a price-fixing claim, it is important that brokers independently establish their fees and do not develop their fees based on a "norm" in the industry.

Licensees may also want to develop their own lists of services for sellers and buyers, as well as a list of specific services to help those consumers selling their home on their own (FSBOs).

Communicating with consumers and identifying their real estate needs are important factors. Licensees provide an array of valuable services from which consumers can pick and choose. Knowledgeable and independent consumers can seem threatening to a licensee; however, the licensee has the opportunity to emphasize the value and variety of real estate services offered, for varying fees. Remember that it is ultimately the broker who decides whether an unbundling of services is good for the company.

■ **FOR EXAMPLE** Chris wants to buy a house without contracting with a licensee for a full range of brokerage services but needs help writing an offer. Chris asks Sally, a broker friend of hers, to write an offer to purchase. Sally enters into a written buyer agency agreement with Chris for this limited service, writes the offer to purchase, and charges Chris a set fee for her service.

Minimum Level of Service

Problems have emerged with the growing number of brokerages offering limited-service listing agreements. These agreements stipulate that a listing broker offers no services other than that of placing a listing in the MLS. When sellers enter into this kind of agreement, the sellers are essentially representing themselves.

The seller may well be aware of this; however, when questions emerge involving the transaction, the seller sometimes turns to the buyer's agent for answers. Seller questions and licensee answers of this type should be handled carefully or they could lead to a claim of undisclosed dual agency. In response to this problem, some states have enacted legislation defining an exclusive brokerage agreement. Other states have proposed regulations that define the minimum level of services a consumer should expect from a licensee. North Carolina has no laws or rules on this issue; however, the NCREC has shared some insight in the 2008-2009 Edition of the *North Carolina Real Estate Manual*. While there is currently no standard limited services listing contract form, a carefully worded limited services listing agreement drafted by an attorney is perfectly legal in North Carolina. Although a broker may limit by contract the services that will be provided to a client, the broker may not limit or waive duties under NC License Law. The major duties of a listing agent that may not be waived or limited include: disclosure of any material fact to any party; avoidance of false promises; avoidance of undisclosed conflict of interest; proper accounting for trust funds; competence in performance of duties; prompt delivery of all offers and contracts; and compliance with the Residential Property Disclosure Act.

National Do Not Call Registry

In 2003, federal do-not-call legislation was signed into law, and real estate professionals must comply with the provisions of the **National Do Not Call Registry**. The registry is managed by the Federal Trade Commission; it is a list of telephone numbers from consumers who have indicated their preference to limit the telemarketing calls they receive. The registry applies to any plan, program, or campaign to sell goods or services through interstate phone calls. The registry does not limit calls by political organizations, charities, or telephone surveyors.

A real estate licensee may call a consumer with whom they have an established business relationship for up to 18 months after the consumer's last purchase, delivery, or payment, even if the consumer is listed on the National Do Not Call Registry. A licensee also may call a consumer for up to three months after the consumer makes an inquiry or submits an application. Note that if a consumer asks a company not to call, even if there is an established business relationship, the company must abide by the consumer's wishes. Federal authorities have ruled that calling owners of "for sale by owner" properties or owners of expired listings with another firm are subject to the Act.

On the National Do Not Call Registry, the only information accessible (for a fee) from the registry is a registrant's telephone number. Telemarketers and sellers are now required to search the registry at least once every 31 days and drop registered consumer phone numbers from their call lists. North Carolina's Do Not Call statute mirrors the federal rules and piggybacks on the federal registry. Penalties on the federal level are up to $11,000 per call and North Carolina fines range from $500 to $5,000 depending on the violation.

■ RELATED WEB SITES

Association of Real Estate Licensing Law Officials: *www.arello.org*
National Do Not Call Registry: *www.donotcall.gov*
North Carolina Department of Justice: No Calls NC: *www.nocallsnc.com*
North Carolina Real Estate Commission: *www.ncrec.state.nc.us*
North Carolina Sexual Offender Registry: *http://ncfindoffender.com*
US Department of Internal Revenue: *www.irs.gov*
US Department of Justice, Antitrust Division: *www.usdoj.gov.atr*

■ SUMMARY

Real estate brokerage is the business of bringing together, for a fee or commission, people who wish to buy, sell, exchange, or lease real estate. An important part of real estate brokerage is the law of agency. A real estate broker/firm may be hired by a seller or a buyer to sell or find a particular parcel of real estate. The broker represents the person who hired him. The person who hires the broker/firm is the principal or client. The principal and the agent have a fiduciary relationship under which the agent owes the principal the duties of loyalty, obedience, accounting, confidentiality, disclosure, and skill, care, and diligence.

The common law of agency is the primary body of law governing the principal-agent relationship. Agency relationships may be either express, by oral or written agreement of the parties, or implied by their actions. In single-agency relationships, the broker/agent represents one party, either the property owner or the buyer/lessee, in the transaction. If the agent solicits the assistance of other brokers/firms who cooperate in the transaction, the other brokers are subagents of the principal. Representing two opposing parties in the same transaction is dual agency. Licensees must be careful not to create a dual agency when none was intended. Illegal, unintentional, or inadvertent dual agency may result in the sales contract being rescinded and the commission forfeited, or it may result in a lawsuit. Disclosed dual agency requires that both principals be informed and that both consent in writing to the broker's multiple representation. In any case, the prospective parties in the transaction should be informed about the agency alternatives and how client-level versus customer-level services differ.

Real estate agents must discuss their agency options with both buyers and sellers in all real estate sales transactions. This disclosure must be done by giving the buyer or seller the mandatory *Working with Real Estate Agents* brochure no later than first substantial contact. The agent must review and determine with the buyer or seller what their agency relationship will be. An agent with the consent of the buyer may act as a buyer agent, dual agent, and/or designated dual agent under an oral buyer and/or dual agency agreement up until such time as the buyer wishes to make an offer. The oral agreement must be nonexclusive in nature and have no time limit. The buyer agency or dual agency relationship must be confirmed in writing prior to presentation of first offer. An agency agreement with a property owner must be in writing from the formation of the relationship, namely, at the time the listing is taken or the property management arrangement is made.

In dual agency situations, the clients occasionally are not willing to forfeit the advocacy of exclusive representation and advice. One way some firms have been able to continue to provide such full client-level services during an in-house transaction is the use of designated dual agency. In designated agency, the firm appoints one or more agents to exclusively represent each of the clients while the rest of the firm remains in dual agency. The only combination of designated agents that is not allowed is the broker-in-charge opposite a provisional broker under their supervision. A licensee also is not eligible to be designated if they already possess confidential information about the opposite side of the transaction. Confidentiality of information is critical.

Licensees also have certain duties and obligations to third parties or customers. Customers are entitled to fair and honest dealings and information that is necessary for them to make informed decisions. This includes voluntarily disclosing material facts about property.

A broker/firm may hire sales agents, whether provisional brokers or nonprovisional brokers, to assist in this work. These licensees work on the broker's behalf as salaried employees or as independent contractors.

Many of the general operations of a real estate brokerage are regulated by the real estate license laws. In addition, state and federal antitrust laws prohibit brokers from conspiring to fix prices, boycott other firms, or allocate customers or markets. Licensees should never imply that commission rates are standardized. Some firms are offering a "menu" of specific brokerage services with various fees in addition to the traditional full service approach. Compliance with state and federal Do Not Call laws is stressed.

Any violation of agency law is also considered to be a violation of North Carolina Real Estate License Law.

QUESTIONS

1. A real estate broker acting as the agent of the seller

    a. is obligated to render faithful service to the seller.
    b. has a fiduciary duty to the buyer.
    c. can agree to a change in price without the seller's approval.
    d. can accept a bonus from the buyer without the seller's approval.

2. A broker is entitled to collect a commission from both the seller and the buyer when the broker

    I. is a member of MLS.
    II. acts as a disclosed dual agent.
        a. I only
        b. II only
        c. Both I and II
        d. Neither I nor II

3. Fiduciary refers to

    a. the independent contractor status of an agent.
    b. the relationship of trust between the agent and the principal.
    c. the seller's subagent that is working with the buyer.
    d. the principal in an exclusive agency relationship.

4. While in the employ of a real estate broker, a provisional broker has the authority to

    a. act as an agent for the seller.
    b. assume responsibilities assigned by the broker.
    c. accept a commission from another broker.
    d. advertise a property on his or her own behalf.

5. A person who has the authority to enter into contracts concerning all business affairs of another is called a(n)

    a. universal agent.
    b. secret agent.
    c. special agent.
    d. attorney.

6. The legal relationship between broker and seller is usually a

    a. universal agent.
    b. special agent.
    c. dual agent.
    d. general agent.

7. A real estate broker hired by an owner to sell a parcel of real estate must comply with

    I. all lawful instructions of the buyer.
    II. the law of agency.
        a. I only
        b. II only
        c. Both I and II
        d. Neither I nor II

8. McCarthy, a real estate broker, learns that her neighbor Smith wishes to sell his house. McCarthy knows the property well and is able to persuade Jones to make an offer for the property. No listing agreement has been made. McCarthy then asks Smith if she can present an offer to him, and Smith agrees. At this point,

    a. Smith is not obligated to pay McCarthy a commission.
    b. Jones is obligated to pay McCarthy for locating the property.
    c. Smith must pay McCarthy a commission.
    d. McCarthy has become a subagent of Jones.

9. A real estate firm who engages licensees as independent contractors must

    a. withhold income tax from all commissions they earn.
    b. provide insurance plans offered to firm employees.
    c. withhold Social Security from all commissions they earn.
    d. still supervise the licensees and remain civilly liable for the brokerage activities of the licensees.

10. Single agency occurs when a real estate agent
    a. represents only one party in a transaction.
    b. represents both the buyer and the seller in a transaction.
    c. chooses to be a designated dual agent.
    d. has both the listing and the sales sides of a transaction.

11. An agent who breaches the fiduciary duties may be subject to all of the following *EXCEPT*
    a. a civil lawsuit.
    b. disciplinary action by the Real Estate Commission.
    c. suspension of licensure by the Board of REALTORS®.
    d. criminal prosecution.

12. The principal owes the agent
    I. the duty of acting in good faith.
    II. payment of compensation.
        a. I only
        b. II only
        c. Both I and II
        d. Neither I nor II

13. In North Carolina, the doctrine of caveat emptor
    a. has been completely replaced by case law and consumer protection laws.
    b. is still intact for property owners in real estate transactions.
    c. is applicable only if the agent acts as a dual agent.
    d. is overridden by agents' disclosure laws.

14. Under the common law of agency, a real estate broker owes all of the following duties to the principal *EXCEPT*
    a. care.
    b. obedience.
    c. disclosure.
    d. novation.

15. An agency relationship may be legally terminated by all of the following means *EXCEPT*
    a. the owner decides not to sell the house.
    b. the broker discovers that list price will not yield an adequate commission.
    c. the owner dies.
    d. the broker secures a ready, willing, and able buyer for the seller's property.

16. Maude represents the seller at an open house. When should she disclose her agency relationship to a potential buyer at the open house?
    a. After answering questions for the buyer about the house
    b. As soon as the buyer enters the open house
    c. When preparing an offer for the buyer
    d. At first substantial contact

17. A disclosure of agency status should be made by a buyer's agent to the seller
    I. with a written confirmation in the offer to purchase and contract.
    II. at the initial contact with the seller or seller's agent, orally or in writing.
        a. I only
        b. II only
        c. Both I and II
        d. Neither I nor II

18. Barbara is representing the property seller. She is showing the property to Luis, a prospective buyer customer. Luis likes the house but does not want to pay as much as the seller wants. He asks Barbara if the seller would take less than the listing price. Barbara knows that the seller is very anxious to sell and would probably agree to $7,000 less than his asking price. Barbara suggests that Luis make an offer at $5,000 less than the listing price. In this situation, Barbara
    a. has done a good job securing an acceptable offer for the seller.
    b. has violated her fiduciary duties to the seller.
    c. will now be considered a designated dual agent.
    d. is making a secret profit from the transaction.

19. Michael is representing the seller, Bart. He shows Bart's house to his cousin, Samantha, who is very interested in buying it. Michael presents Samantha's full-price offer to Bart, who eagerly accepts it. Both Bart and Samantha are very happy with the transaction. Which statement is true?

a. Because both parties are happy with the transaction, it doesn't matter whether Michael disclosed his relationship with Samantha to Bart.

b. Bart cannot complain about Michael's actions because Samantha's offer was for the full listing price.

c. Michael has violated his fiduciary duties to Bart by failing to disclose his relationship with Samantha and could be subject to disciplinary action.

d. Michael has done nothing wrong; he was not required to disclose his relationship with Samantha.

20. The seller tells the listing agent about a latent defect in the property. The listing agent tells the buyer's agent about the defect, but the buyer's agent does not inform the buyer. Who would most likely be held responsible for the omission?

a. The seller because he made no representation on the Residential Property Disclosure form regarding the defect

b. The listing agent because he has the duty to inform the buyer personally of any latent defects

c. The listing firm because the listing firm is liable for all disclosures in a sale transaction

d. The buyer's agent because he should not withhold information from his client

21. If a broker's misrepresentation causes loss or financial injury to a buyer customer, which of the following could be found liable?

I. Principal
II. Broker

a. I only
b. II only
c. Both I and II
d. Neither I nor II

22. Which of the following statements about dual agency is/are correct?

I. Dual agency can occur within one firm if a licensee shows his buyer-client his or her own listing.

II. Dual agency can occur within one firm if a licensee has become a buyer's agent and is showing a property listed by the broker-in-charge.

a. I only
b. II only
c. Both I and II
d. Neither I nor II

23. Under License Law and Commission Rules, which of the following is/are *TRUE* concerning designated agency?

I. The broker-in-charge cannot be a designated agent.

II. An agent cannot be appointed as a designated agent if she has prior confidential knowledge about the other party to the transaction.

a. I only
b. II only
c. Both I and II
d. Neither I nor II

24. It is discovered after a sale that the land parcel is 10 percent smaller than the owner represented it to be. The broker who passed the erroneous information on to the buyer is

a. not liable as long as she only repeated the seller's data.

b. not liable if the misrepresentation was unintentional.

c. not liable if the buyer actually inspected what she was getting.

d. liable if the broker knew or should have known of the discrepancy.

25. Kris is representing the property seller. Maurice, an agent at the same firm, is representing a buyer. Kris and Maurice confer during a sales meeting and discover the compatible needs of the clients. All of the following are true *EXCEPT*

    a. Kris is being diligent in trying to find a buyer for the seller.

    b. Maurice has performed his fiduciary duties to the buyer.

    c. the broker-in-charge must designate two other licensees who did not attend the meeting to represent the clients.

    d. if the parties have consented to dual agency, the broker-in-charge can allow Kris and Maurice to continue their representation in brokering this transaction.

26. Which of the following situations would be considered a material fact that would require disclosure by a listing agent?

    a. Owner's son committed suicide in the basement of the property

    b. An upstairs bedroom is believed to be haunted

    c. A group home for unwed mothers is located down the street

    d. The house was totally replumbed after a polybutylene pipe broke in the master bathroom.

27. Provisional broker Mischa of Paradise Realty is Sue Lin's exclusive buyer agent. In accordance with NCREC Rules, Mischa has a written agency agreement with Sue Lin. When co-brokering a transaction with a listing agent at Roy Realty, Mischa is *NOT* allowed to

    a. be compensated from the commission paid by the seller to Roy Realty.

    b. require Sue Lin to compensate Mischa's firm.

    c. be compensated directly by Sue Lin.

    d. negotiate compensation with Sue Lin because the seller has already negotiated commission with the listing agent.

28. Agent Parul is Lindsay's listing agent. Parul has Lindsay's permission to practice dual agency. Ross, another agent in Parul's firm, is holding an open house at Lindsay's property on Sunday. Kermit attends the open house, but never shows an interest in Lindsay's property. Kermit begins to discuss his specific needs for property with Ross. Ross must

    a. disclose that the firm is a dual agent since Kermit is sharing his needs.

    b. refuse to represent Kermit since Ross already works for Lindsay.

    c. stop Kermit's information sharing until they have reviewed the *Working with Real Estate Agents* brochure and decided their agency relationship.

    d. require Kermit to initial the acknowledgement panel on the *Working with Real Estate Agents* brochure.

8

CHAPTER

Basic Contract Law

■ **LEARNING OBJECTIVES** *When you have finished reading this chapter, you should be able to*

■ **define** all types of contracts and give the requirements for a valid contract.

■ **identify** the essential elements of contracts and their legal effect if absent.

■ **define** statutes that apply to contract law and the legal remedies on breach of a contract.

■ **define** these *key terms:*

assignment	express contract	rescission
auction	implied contract	specific performance
bilateral contract	legality of object	statute of frauds
breach of contract	legally competent parties	statute of limitations
compensatory damages	liquidated damages	time is of the essence
consequential damages	"meeting of the minds"	unenforceable contract
consideration	mutual assent	unilateral contract
contract	novation	valid contract
counteroffer	offer	voidable contract
earnest money deposit	offer and acceptance	void contract
executed contract	parol evidence rule	
executory contract	reality of consent	

■ CONTRACTS

In the course of their business, brokers use many types of contracts and agreements to carry out their responsibilities to sellers, buyers, landlords, tenants, and the general public. Among these are listing contracts, buyer agency contracts, sales contracts, option contracts, land installment contracts, and leases. The general body of law that governs the operation of such contracts is known as *contract law*. This chapter discusses basic contract law that applies to all types of contracts.

A **contract** is a *legally enforceable promise or set of promises between legally competent parties, supported by legal consideration, to do (or refrain from doing) a legal act that must be performed and for which the law provides a remedy if a breach of promise occurs.* A contract must be

- *voluntary*—no one may be forced into a contract,
- *an agreement or a promise*—a contract is essentially a legally enforceable promise,
- *made by legally competent parties*—the parties must be viewed by the law as capable of making a legally binding promise,
- *supported by legal consideration*—a contract must be supported by some valuable thing that induces a party to enter into a contract and that must be legally sufficient to support a contract, and
- *about a legal act*—no one may make a legal contract to do something illegal.

Depending on the situation and the nature or language of the agreement, a contract may be express or implied, unilateral or bilateral, executory or executed, valid, unenforceable, voidable, or void.

Express and Implied Contracts

Depending on how a contract is created, it may be *express* or *implied*. In an **express contract,** the parties state the terms and show their intentions in words to that effect. An express contract may be either oral or written. In an **implied contract,** the agreement of the parties is demonstrated by their actions or conduct. In a seller-agency relationship, a listing agreement is a written, express contract between the seller and the broker/firm, naming the broker/firm as the fiduciary representative of the seller.

■ FOR EXAMPLE
- Hugh approaches his neighbor, Bob, and says, "I will paint your house today for $500." Bob replies, "If you paint my house today, I will pay you $500." Hugh and Bob have entered into an express contract.
- Ken goes into a restaurant and orders a meal. Ken has entered into an *implied contract* with the restaurant to pay for the meal, even though payment was not mentioned before the meal was ordered.

Bilateral and Unilateral Contracts

Contracts may also be classified as either *bilateral* or *unilateral*. In a **bilateral contract,** both parties promise to do or refrain from doing something; one promise is exchanged for another. ("I will do this, and you will do that.") A real estate sales contract is a bilateral contract because the seller promises to sell a parcel of real estate and deliver title to the property to the buyer, who promises to pay a certain sum of money for the property. Most real estate-related contracts are bilateral in nature.

TABLE 8.1	Classification of Contract	Legal Effect	Example
Legal Effects of Contracts	Valid	Binding and enforceable on both parties	Agreement complies with essentials of a valid contract
	Void	No legal effect	Contract for an illegal purpose
	Voidable	Valid but may be disaffirmed by one party	Contract with a minor
	Unenforceable	Valid between the parties, but neither party may force performance	Certain oral agreements

In a **unilateral contract,** one party makes a promise to induce a second party to do something. The second party is not legally obligated to act; however, if the second party does comply, the first party is obligated to keep the promise. ("I will do this if you do that.") For example, if a person runs a newspaper ad offering a reward for the return of a lost pet, that person is promising to pay if the act of returning the pet is fulfilled.

Executed and Executory Contracts

A contract may be classified as either *executed* or *executory,* depending on whether the agreement has been performed completely. An **executed contract** is one in which all parties have fulfilled their promises and, therefore, fully performed the contract. (Do not be confused by the fact that the word *execute* is also used to refer to the signing of a contract.) An **executory contract** exists when something remains to be done by one or both parties. A sales contract, signed and accepted, pending closing, is an example of an executory contract.

Validity of Contracts

A contract can be described as *valid, void, voidable,* or *unenforceable* (see Table 8.1), depending on the circumstances.

A **valid contract** complies with all the essential elements of a contract, which will be discussed later in this chapter, and is binding and enforceable on both parties.

A **void contract** is one that has no legal force or effect. It is unenforceable in a court of law because it does not meet the essential elements of a contract. However, a void contract may be fully executed unless one of the parties disaffirms it.

■ **FOR EXAMPLE** Two persons enter into a "contract" where one party agrees to murder someone if the other party pays him. This calls for an illegal act to take place; therefore, the contract is void at law and could not be enforced in a court of law.

A **voidable contract** is one that seems, on the surface, to be valid but may be rescinded, or disaffirmed, by one or both parties, based on some legal principle.

If someone makes a contract while drugged or intoxicated, the contract is voidable by that person. A voidable contract will be considered by the courts to be valid if the party who has the option to disaffirm the agreement does not do so within a prescribed period of time. A contract with a minor, for instance, is usually voidable by the minor upon reaching the age of majority. A contract entered into with a person who is known to be mentally ill is usually voidable during the mental illness. On the other hand a contract entered into with a person who is insane (as determined by the courts) is void.

An **unenforceable contract** has all the elements of a valid contract; however, neither party can sue the other to force performance. Unenforceable contracts are said to be *valid as between the parties* because once the agreement is fully executed and both parties are satisfied, neither has reason to initiate a lawsuit to force performance. For example, an oral agreement for the sale of a parcel of real estate would be unenforceable, because the Statute of Frauds (discussed later) requires that real estate sales contracts be in writing to be enforceable. However, if both the seller and the buyer perform their obligations under the oral agreement, a valid transfer can occur, but if one of the parties refuses to perform, there is nothing the other party can do to compel performance.

Essential elements of a valid contract.   In general, the four essentials of a valid contract are as follows:

1. **Legally competent parties**: Both parties to the contract must be of legal age and have sufficient mental capacity. In North Carolina, 18 is the age of contractual capacity. Persons younger than 18 years of age are deemed *infants* or minors. Generally, minors' contracts are voidable by the minor or may be canceled before or within a reasonable time after the minor reaches age 18. (In other words, an adult cannot hold a minor to a contract, but a minor can hold an adult to a contract.) A broker should inquire carefully into the ages of both the purchaser and the seller of real estate. Advanced age, in contrast, may be an indication of a person's incapacity to contract as a result of senility. In questions of legal competency, it may be desirable to consult with the client's lawyer. A party who understands the nature and effect of the contract has sufficient mental capacity. Mental capacity is not the same as medical sanity.
2. **Mutual assent or deliberate agreement**: An offer by one party that is accepted by the other party. **Offer and acceptance** means that there must be a **meeting of the minds**. Courts look to the objective intent of the parties to determine whether they intended to enter into a binding agreement. The terms of the agreement must be fairly definite and understood by both parties. Furthermore, the acceptance must be actually communicated to the offeror. (The methods of making and receiving offers, the counteroffer, the acceptance, and communication will be discussed in detail in Chapter 10.)
3. **Legality of object**: To be valid, a contract must not contemplate a purpose that is illegal or against public policy. If a contract calls for immoral performance, discrimination, or a criminal act to take place, the contract is void.
4. **Consideration**: Courts will not enforce gratuitous (free) promises. Consideration is something of legal value, bargained for and given in exchange for a promise or an act. Any return promise to perform that has been bargained for and exchanged is legally sufficient to satisfy the consideration element;

A contract may be
- **valid**—has all legal elements; is fully enforceable;
- **void**—lacks one or all elements; has no legal force or effect;
- **voidable**—has all legal elements; may be rescinded or disaffirmed; or
- **unenforceable**—has all legal elements; is enforceable only between the parties.

Four Elements of a Valid Contract

1. Legally competent parties
2. Mutual assent or deliberate agreement
3. Legality of object
4. Consideration

for example, the purchase price is the consideration in exchange for the transfer of the property in a real estate contract. A binder or an earnest money deposit is merely an expression of good faith and is not an essential element of a contract.

Absence of undue influence, duress, misrepresentation, and mistake. Contracts signed by a person under duress or undue influence are voidable by that person or by a court. Extreme care should be taken when one or more of the parties to a contract are elderly, sick, in great distress, or under the influence of alcohol or drugs, both legal and illegal. To be valid, every contract must be signed as the free and voluntary act of each party. Misrepresentation, fraud, or mistake of fact could render a contract voidable by the injured party. In the absence of these factors, **reality of consent** has been reached.

Revocation of an offer. An offer may be *revoked* or withdrawn by the offeror (the party making the offer, usually the buyer) at any time prior to acceptance if the revocation is communicated directly to the offeree (the party in receipt of the offer, usually the seller) by the offeror. It also can be revoked if the parties are notified through their agents.

Any attempt by the offeree to change any of the terms proposed by the offeror creates a **counteroffer**. The offeror is relieved of the original offer because the offeree has, in effect, rejected it by making changes. The offeror can accept the offeree's counteroffer, reject it, or, if the offeror wishes, make another counteroffer. Any change in the most recent offer results in another counteroffer, until one party agrees to the other party's counteroffer and both parties sign the final contract. Counteroffers may be made by *pen and ink* changes as long as each individual change within the offer is initialed and dated by all parties in addition to the signatures and dates necessary at the bottom of the contract. To avoid confusion and mistakes, signing a new offer to purchase and contract form that incorporates all the changes is the preferred practice.

An offer or a counteroffer *may be revoked at any time before it has been accepted* (even if the person making the offer or counteroffer agreed to keep the offer open for a set period of time. The offeree, or the offeree's agent, must receive notification of the revocation. The contract should stipulate the manner of acceptance; generally, an offer is not considered accepted until the person making the offer has been *notified of the other party's acceptance* (signature).

When the parties communicate through an agent or at a distance, questions may arise regarding whether an acceptance, a rejection, or a counteroffer has effectively taken place. The real estate broker should transmit all offers, acceptances, or other responses as soon as possible to avoid such problems. In North Carolina, these notifications should be delivered as soon as possible, but in no event later than five days after execution [see G.S. 93A-6(a)(13) and Rule A.0106]. Remember that as an agent, a real estate licensee stands in the shoes of the principal. Communication of acceptance or revocation to an agent is the same as communication directly to the principal.

■ **FOR EXAMPLE** A buyer who is represented by an agent has presented an offer to the seller on Monday. On Tuesday, the seller decides to accept the offer. The seller signs the offer to purchase, and on Tuesday night, the seller's agent tells the buyer's agent that the seller has accepted the buyer's offer. Because it is so late, the buyer's agent decides to wait until Wednesday to tell the buyer that the seller has accepted the offer. Early Wednesday morning, the buyer changes his mind and decides to revoke the offer. It is too late. The communication of the seller's acceptance to the buyer's agent is deemed to be communication to the buyer. Because the offer has been accepted (signed) and communicated, the buyer can no longer revoke his offer. They are under contract.

Agreement in writing and signed.   Not all contracts must be in writing to be enforceable; however, every state has adopted the common-law doctrine known as the **statute of frauds**, which requires that certain types of contracts be in writing to be enforceable in a court of law.

The North Carolina Statute of Frauds requires that to be enforceable in a court of law, conveyances of interests in real property—such as deeds, contracts for sale, mortgages, options, easements, and certain leases (those that are for longer than three years from their making)—must be in writing and signed by the party to be bound or by the party's legally authorized agent. A listing agreement or a buyer representation agreement is an employment contract and is not covered by the North Carolina Statute of Frauds; however, North Carolina Real Estate Commission rules require that agency agreements be in writing (Rule A.0104). The purpose of the North Carolina Statute of Frauds is to prevent fraudulent proof of an oral contract.

The **parol evidence rule**, another heritage of the common law, is a rule of evidence that dictates that no oral agreements that contradict the terms of a written contract may be considered in a lawsuit based on the written agreement. The written contract is assumed to be the complete manifestation of the agreement of the parties. The many exceptions to the rule include evidence that a contract was entered into illegally or evidence intended to clarify ambiguous contract terms. The party who drafted the ambiguous terms would most likely be ruled against in a court hearing.

IN PRACTICE   If there is any ambiguity in a contract, the courts generally will interpret the agreement against the party who prepared it. For example, if the seller prepares the offer to purchase and contract, and one of the terms is ambiguous, the court will interpret that term in favor of the buyer.

■ CONTRACT LAW AND AUCTION SALES

The familiar procedure of a buyer making an offer to purchase, which the real estate agent then presents to the seller for acceptance or rejection, is avoided with an **auction.** Instead of merely presenting the offer to the seller, an auctioneer actually accepts the offer on behalf of the seller. (The typical real estate agent virtually never has the authority to accept an offer on behalf of the seller.) After the auctioneer accepts the offer, or bid, the buyer and seller formalize their oral agreement with a written document (to satisfy the Statute of Frauds) [see Rule A.0104(h)].

A real estate auctioneer must have two licenses: (1) a real estate license and (2) an auctioneer's license. The mere crier of sales is exempt from real estate licensure [see G.S. 93A-2(a)].

There are two types of auctions:

1. *Auctions with reserve*: The seller reserves the right to stop the bidding if it becomes apparent that the high bid will be unacceptable to the seller. The seller must reject all bids before the auction is concluded and the auctioneer accepts a bid.
2. *Auctions without reserve*: the seller agrees to accept the high bid, no matter what the terms of that bid. This is also called an *absolute auction* in North Carolina.

Note that when the seller accepts any bid at any auction, no matter what type, the property is sold. A seller should fully understand that once the auctioneer declares a bid accepted, the property is sold on those terms because the auctioneer can bind the seller.

■ PERFORMANCE OF CONTRACT

Under any contract, each party has certain rights and duties to fulfill. The question of when a contract must be performed is an important factor. Many contracts call for a specific time at or by which the agreed-on acts must be completely performed. In addition, many contracts state that **time is of the essence**. This means that the contract must be performed within the time limit specified, and any party who has not performed on time is liable for breach of contract. If an offeror includes *time is of the essence* in the offer, the offeror can still revoke the offer at any time prior to acceptance.

When a date is noted in a contract but is not followed by the phrase, "time is of the essence," the date is a general target date that all parties should attempt to meet. If the promised action is not completed by the *target date*, the contract is not automatically terminated or made voidable. As long as the action is completed within a reasonable time, the contract will probably still be binding on all parties. The definition of *a reasonable time* would necessitate a court ruling. When a contract does not specify a date for performance, the acts it requires should be performed within a reasonable time (as determined by the court, if a conflict arises). The interpretation of what constitutes a reasonable time will depend on the situation. Generally, if the act can be done immediately—such as a payment of money—it should be performed immediately unless the parties agree otherwise.

IN PRACTICE Despite the best efforts of buyer and seller, it may be impossible to close a transaction on the date stipulated. The seller may not be able to complete necessary repairs before that date. The buyer's lender may be swamped with loan applications and unable to provide funding on the date requested. Buyer and seller can adjust the closing date (or any other contract term) by a modification of the contract—a written addendum signed by all parties. The broker may negotiate the new term(s) but may not sign the modification on behalf of any of the parties. Contingencies must be anticipated to allow sufficient time for completion when contracts are executed.

Assignment and Novation

Assignment = substitution of *parties*

Novation = substitution of *contracts*

Occasionally, after a contract has been entered into, one party wants to withdraw without actually terminating the agreement. This may be accomplished through either assignment or novation.

Assignment refers to a transfer of rights or duties under a contract to a third party. In North Carolina, rights in a contract may be assigned to a third party unless the agreement forbids such an assignment. Duties may also be assigned (delegated), but the original obligor remains secondarily liable for them (after the new obligor) unless specifically released from this responsibility. The exception to this rule is a contract for personal services, which may not be assigned. Most contracts include a clause that either permits or forbids assignment. The North Carolina Association of REALTORS®/North Carolina Bar Association Standard Offer to Purchase and Contract is not assignable without mutual written consent. An assignment does not terminate the contract or change the terms of the contract.

Novation is another way to avoid the terms of an existing contract without breaching that contract. *Nova* means new, and *novation* is the substitution of a new contract for an existing agreement with the intent of extinguishing the old contract. The new agreement may be between the same parties, or a new party may be substituted for either (*novation of the parties*). The parties' intent must be to discharge (cancel) the old obligation; therefore, it does terminate the original contract. The new agreement must be supported by consideration and must conform to all the essential elements of a valid contract. For example, a business owner who recently signed a long-term lease for office space finds another office location that he prefers. If the business owner can find another tenant for the currently leased office space, the landlord might accept a new lease with the new tenant in place of the business owner's existing lease agreement. This would effectively cancel the business owner's obligation to continue to lease the space.

Discharge of Contract

A contract may be performed completely, with all terms carried out, or it may be breached (broken) if one of the parties defaults. A contract also may be discharged (canceled) by various other methods. These include the following:

- *Partial performance* of the terms of the contract. This is sometimes referred to as *accord and satisfaction*. When one party accepts something less than agreed on as complete performance, the contract is considered discharged.
- *Substantial performance*, in which one party has substantially performed the contract but does not complete all the details exactly as the contract requires. Such performance—for example, under construction contracts—may be sufficient to force payment, with certain adjustments for any damages suffered by the other party.
- *Impossibility of performance*, in which an act required by the contract cannot be accomplished.
- *Mutual agreement* of the parties to cancel.
- *Operation of law*, as in the voiding of a contract by a minor, as a result of fraud or the expiration of the statute of limitations (discussed later in this chapter), or as a result of the alteration of a contract without the written consent of all parties involved. Bankruptcy can also discharge a contractual obligation.

Default—Breach of Contract

A **breach of contract** is a violation, without legal excuse, of any of the terms or conditions of a contract, as when a seller breaches a sales contract by not delivering title to the buyer under the conditions stated in the agreement. The nondefaulting party has certain rights.

If a party to a contract defaults, the nondefaulting party has the following alternatives:

- The injured party may *sue the breaching party for money damages* or **compensatory damages**. Money damages are awarded to the injured party to compensate him or her for the breach of the contract, not to punish the party who breached the contract. The amount of the money damages should be only what is necessary to *make the party whole*—that is, put the party in the position he or she would have been in if the contract had been performed as agreed. For example, the buyer can be sued for compensatory damages if his earnest money is not adequate to cover the seller's losses.
- The injured party may be entitled to collect **liquidated damages**. *Liquidated damages* are defined as *the amount of money that will compensate the injured party for breach, which the parties agree to at the time they enter into the contract.* For example, the **earnest money deposit** is considered liquidated damages in the event the buyer breaches the contract. The seller is entitled to keep the amount of the deposit as compensation for any injuries caused by the buyer's breach of contract.
- **Consequential damages** are special damages that might be obtained if the damages upon breach were reasonably foreseeable to the breaching party at the time of making the contract. It also allows the injured party to sue for lost profits.
- The injured party may file a court action, known as a suit for **specific performance,** to force the other party to perform the contract as agreed. Specific performance is ordered only when the subject matter of the contract is not readily available from another source and when each party has the ability to perform the contractual obligations. Because every parcel of real estate is considered unique, a suit for specific performance brought by the buyer or seller under a purchase and sales contract may be successful.
- The injured party may *rescind the contract,* which means the contract is declared invalid and both parties return to the position they were in before they entered into the contract. **Rescission** may be appropriate when facts were misrepresented or one party entered the contract under duress. A right of rescission may be written into the contract or may be stipulated by law, such as the five-day right of rescission for a time-share purchase or the seven-day right of rescission for a new condominium purchase.

Statute of Limitations

North Carolina law allows a specific time limit during which parties to a contract may bring legal suit to enforce their rights. The **statute of limitations** varies for different legal actions, and any rights not enforced within the applicable time period are lost.

■ BROKER'S AUTHORITY TO PREPARE DOCUMENTS

A licensed real estate broker is not authorized to practice law and may be disciplined under G.S. 93A-6(a)(11) for attempting to perform any legal service. Because drafting (preparing) legal documents for others is considered to be a legal service, Rule A.0111 of the North Carolina Real Estate Commission states that an agent "in a real estate transaction shall not draft offers, sales contracts, options, leases, promissory notes, deeds, deeds of trust or other legal instruments by which rights of others are secured." A broker is, however, permitted to fill in the blanks on certain approved preprinted documents (such as sales contracts and leases) when authorized to do so by the parties, provided the licensee does not charge a separate fee for completing such forms.

IN PRACTICE Licensees are permitted to use electronic, computer, or word processing equipment to store preprinted approved forms; however, the form may not be altered in any way before the form is presented to the parties to the contract. Licensees may, however, make written notes, memoranda, or correspondence recording negotiations of the parties to the transaction as long as they do not constitute binding agreements. The parties to the instruments may delete or change provisions, but the change or deletion must be marked to so indicate.

Contract forms. *Preprinted forms* are used for many kinds of contracts because most transactions are consistently similar in nature. The use of preprinted forms raises three issues: (1) how to *fill in the blanks*, (2) what printed matter is not applicable to a particular sale and is to be *ruled out* by drawing a line through the unwanted words, and (3) what additional clauses or agreements (called *riders* or *addenda*) are to be included. All changes and additions should be dated and must be initialed in the margin or on the rider by both parties when the contract is executed.

■ SUMMARY

A contract is defined as a legally enforceable promise or set of promises that must be performed and for which the law provides a remedy if a breach occurs.

In general, contracts may be classified as express or implied; bilateral or unilateral; executed or executory; or, according to their legal enforceability, as valid, void, voidable, or unenforceable. The essential elements of a valid contract are legally competent parties, mutual assent, legality of object, and consideration. A valid real estate contract must include an adequate legal description of the property. North Carolina Statute of Frauds requires that contracts which convey interests in real property must be in writing and signed by all parties. Therefore, to be valid, contracts that convey real property will not only be express, but written as well.

Offers may be revoked by the offeror any time before contract formation by delivering notification of the revocation to the offeree. Communication to the party's agent is considered equivalent to communication to the principal. A counteroffer is considered a rejection of the original offer and the creation of a new offer.

In a number of circumstances where contingencies are used, a contract may be canceled before it is performed fully. Furthermore, in many types of contracts, either party may transfer rights and obligations under the agreement by assignment of the contract or novation (i.e., substitution of a new contract). The best way to terminate a contract is by full performance.

Contracts frequently used in the real estate business include agency agreements, offers to purchase and contract, installment land contracts, leases, and options. In most contracts, missing a target date does not automatically terminate the contract. If the term *time is of the essence* follows a date, the date becomes absolute. If such a date is missed, the contract may allow the nonbreaching party to terminate the contract.

Breach of contract can lead to a suit for compensatory damages, consequential damages, specific performance, or rescission of the contract. Most real estate contracts request liquidated damages in the form of earnest money deposits.

A real estate auctioneer has the power to bind the seller by accepting a bid during the auction sale. The real estate auctioneer needs a real estate license as well as an auctioneer's license, if acting as the owner's agent for any service other than crying the sale. There are two types of auctions in North Carolina: auctions with reserve and auctions without reserve (absolute auctions).

A real estate broker does not have the authority to draft documents for others in a transaction. It is acceptable for a licensee to fill in the blanks on a pre-printed form without crossing into the unauthorized practice of law. Significant changes or additions to the standard forms should be prepared by an attorney.

QUESTIONS

1. To be enforceable, contracts for the purchase and sale of real estate would need all of the following *EXCEPT*
   a. mentally capable parties that understand the terms of the contract.
   b. earnest money deposit must accompany the contract.
   c. mutually acceptable terms of the agreement.
   d. in writing and signed by all parties to be charged.

2. A real estate license gives the licensee the right to
   a. draft offers to purchase for a client.
   b. fill in the blanks on pre-printed standard forms.
   c. act as a principal to the contract.
   d. perform as a notary public.

3. The injured party in a real estate transaction with the right to a suit for specific performance is the
   a. broker.
   b. buyer.
   c. title company.
   d. lender.

4. To be enforceable, a contract must be entered into by a person who is at least
   a. 16 years old.
   b. 18 years old.
   c. 21 years old.
   d. 25 years old.

5. A contract is said to be bilateral if
   a. one of the parties is a real estate licensee.
   b. the contract has yet to be fully performed.
   c. only one party to the agreement is bound to act.
   d. all parties to the contract are bound to act.

6. During the period of time after a valid real estate sales contract is created, but before title actually passes, the status of the contract is
   a. void.
   b. executory.
   c. executed.
   d. unilateral.

7. Anita is under contract to buy property but would rather let her friend Laura buy it. Unless the contract prohibits it, Laura can take over Anita's obligation by the process known as
   a. assignment.
   b. substantial performance.
   c. subordination.
   d. mutual consent.

8. All of the following persons would have the potential of creating a voidable contract *EXCEPT*
   a. a seller that was taking strong pain medication after surgery.
   b. a seller that drank a bottle of champagne prior to signing the contract.
   c. a buyer that does not read well.
   d. a buyer that will turn 18 after closing the transaction.

9. Kay drives into a gas station and fills her gas tank. She is obligated to pay for the fuel through what kind of contract?
   a. Express
   b. Implied
   c. Voluntary
   d. Executed

10. Nick and Kelly sign a valid contract under which Nick will convey Raptor Manor to Kelly. Nick changes his mind, and Kelly sues for specific performance. What is Kelly seeking in the lawsuit?
    a. Money damages
    b. New contract
    c. Deficiency judgment
    d. Conveyance of the property

11. In which of the following situations has reality of consent been reached?
    a. Seller signed sales contract at gunpoint.
    b. Buyer's spouse threatened divorce if buyer did not buy property.
    c. Listing agent lied about completion dates of recreational amenities.
    d. Seller lied about her motivation for selling.

12. A buyer submits an offer to purchase property through the use of his exclusive buyer's agent, Gerri. After Gerri has delivered the offer to the listing agent at the other firm, the buyer calls and asks Gerri to cancel the offer since he has located a different property that he likes better. Gerri cannot revoke the offer if the
    a. listing agent has already presented the offer to the seller.
    b. seller has already signed the offer but has not told anyone.
    c. listing agent has sent an e-mail to Gerri saying that the seller signed the offer.
    d. seller signed the offer after making one change about removing a ceiling fan.

13. A contract states that closing will take place on or before June 22 of this year, *time is of the essence.* If the buyer cannot close until June 26,
    I. the buyer has breached the contract.
    II. the seller has the potential of terminating the contract.
        a. I only
        b. II only
        c. Both I and II
        d. Neither I nor II

14. A builder/seller advertising a selling bonus to any selling agent is an example of a(n)
    a. voidable contract.
    b. unilateral contract.
    c. bilateral contract.
    d. open listing contract.

CHAPTER 9

Agency Contracts

■ **LEARNING OBJECTIVES** *When you have finished reading this chapter, you should be able to*

■ **describe** the different types of agency contracts and the procedures for using agency contracts.

■ **identify** different types of compensation and disclosure requirements.

■ **understand** how to be entitled to and calculate compensation.

■ **describe** the typical listing process including calculations for seller net and minimum sales price.

■ **understand** the requirements of the North Carolina Residential Property Disclosure Act.

■ **define** these *key terms:*

buyer-agency agreement	extender clause	procuring cause
comparative market analysis (CMA)	listing agreement	protection agreement
employment contract	multiple listing service (MLS)	puffing
exclusive-agency listing	net listing	ready, willing, and able buyer
exclusive-right-to-sell listing	open listing	retainer fee
	override clause	success fee

■ AGENCY CONTRACTS AND PRACTICES FOR WORKING WITH SELLERS

As mentioned in Chapter 7, an agency agreement for brokerage services creates a special agency relationship between the principal (seller, buyer, landlord, or tenant) and the agent (broker/firm), wherein the agent is authorized to represent the principal and the principal's property to third parties, including submitting or receiving offers for the property. Per NCREC Rule A.0104(a & b), all written agency agreements must (1) be signed by all parties; (2) include the licensee's license number; (3) have a definite termination date; and (4) contain the prescribed nondiscrimination provision. This chapter will review in depth the different standardized agency agreements used in sales transactions and closely examine a typical listing process. Entering into an agency agreement follows the agency disclosure discussed in Chapter 7. *Note:* Forms referenced in this and other chapters are located in Appendix D, North Carolina Real Estate Forms.

Why Use a Listing Agreement?

Just as a supermarket without inventory will have no customers, the real estate industry without inventory will have no business. To acquire inventory, most brokers obtain listings of properties for sale (although some work with properties for lease, rent, exchange, or option). Under the provisions of North Carolina's real estate license laws, only a broker/firm having an active license can act as an agent to list, sell, or rent another person's real estate.

The first type of contract an agent is likely to encounter is the **listing agreement.** As with most agency agreements, the listing agreement is an **employment contract** rather than a real estate contract. With a listing agreement, the broker/firm is hired to represent the seller-principal, but real property is not transferred. An agreement for brokerage services between a broker and an owner of real property must be in writing from the outset of the relationship [see Rule A.0104(a)]. Under NCREC rules, *an oral agency agreement with a property owner—whether a listing contract with a seller or property management agreement with an owner— is not permitted.* The agreement must be in writing before any brokerage services are provided. There is only one exception to this rule: if a seller did not originally give permission for dual or designated dual agency in the listing agreement, the seller can orally amend their written listing agreement to authorize either type of dual agency at a later date. This oral consent to dual agency must be reduced to writing prior to submission of the first offer on the property.

Note: Throughout this chapter, unless otherwise stated, the terms *broker, agent,* and *firm* are intended to include both a nonprovisional broker and a provisional broker working under the broker. However, only the broker/firm has the direct authority to provide services to a principal; the individual licensees will usually provide services as a subagent (i.e., as an affiliated agent of the company serving as agent).

Broker's Entitlement to a Commission

The listing broker's/firm's compensation is specified in the listing agreement. The most widely-used type of compensation is a commission, or brokerage fee, computed as a *percentage of the final accepted gross sales price*. A flat-fee commission is another way to receive compensation. The commission payment, usually considered earned when the broker has accomplished the work for which the broker was hired, is due at the closing of the transaction. Most sales commissions are paid when all terms of the purchase contract have been fulfilled.

To be entitled to collect a commission, an agent must be actively licensed, must be employed by the principal under a valid written agency agreement, or be the procuring cause of the sale, and must produce a **ready, willing, and able buyer**. Licensed provisional brokers can only be paid directly by their employing brokers, not directly by a principal. Commission Rule A.0109 further stipulates that a licensee in a sales transaction cannot receive any compensation, incentive, bonus, or other consideration from any party or person without full and timely disclosure of the compensation to the broker's principal. Timely disclosure must be confirmed in writing prior to making or accepting any offer. (See Appendix D, Form 10.)

Once a broker obtains an offer from a ready, willing, and able buyer that meets the seller's terms, the seller is technically liable for the broker's commission. A ready, willing, and able buyer is one who is *financially qualified, prepared to buy on the seller's terms, and ready to take positive steps toward consummation of the transaction by showing willingness to enter into an enforceable contract.* But even if the transaction is not consummated, the broker still may be entitled to a commission when the seller

- has a change of mind and refuses to sell,
- has a spouse who refuses to sign the deed,
- has a title with uncorrected defects,
- commits fraud with respect to the transaction,
- is unable to deliver possession within a reasonable time,
- insists on terms not in the listing (for example, the right to restrict the use of the property), or
- has a mutual agreement with the buyer to cancel the transaction.

In other words, *a broker generally is due a commission if a sale is not consummated because of the principal's unjustified default.* Even if the buyer backs out without legal cause after the seller has accepted the offer, the broker may be entitled to a commission, but collecting it may be difficult. To be considered the **procuring cause** of sale, the broker must have taken action to start (or cause) a chain of events that resulted in the sale. A broker who causes or completes such action without a written agency contract that promises compensation is deemed a *volunteer* and has no legal claim to compensation.

The rate of a broker's commission is negotiable in every case. For members of the profession to attempt, however subtly, to impose uniform commission rates is a clear violation of federal antitrust laws. The important point is for broker and client to agree on a rate before the agency relationship is established. If no amount or percentage rate of commission is stated in the listing contract and a legal action results, the court may determine a reasonable commission by evidence of the custom in a particular community. NCREC is prohibited by law from regulating the amount of commission charged by licensees [see G.S. 93A-3(c)].

Historically, under terms of the traditional real estate agency relationship, the brokerage fee was paid by the seller to the listing broker/firm, who then shared a portion of that fee with the licensee who managed the listing. If another company

MATH CONCEPTS

SHARING COMMISSIONS

Many people might share a commission: the listing broker/firm, the listing licensee, the selling broker/firm, and the selling licensee. Drawing a diagram can help you determine which person is entitled to receive what amount of the total commission.

Agent Eve, while working for ABC Realty, took a listing on a $189,000 house at a 6% commission rate. Agent Ted, while working for Homes Realty, found the buyer for the property. The property sold for the listed price, and the listing firm and the selling firm shared the commission equally. If the selling firm kept 45% of what it received, how much did agent Ted receive? (If the firm retained 45% of the commission split that it received, its licensee would receive the balance of the split: 100% − 45% = 55%.)

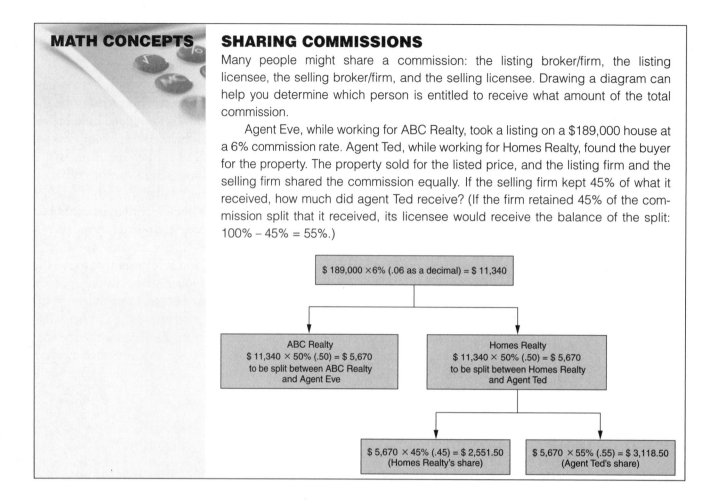

found the buyer of the property, the broker also would split the fee with that cooperating broker/firm. However, as the practice of buyer agency has become more widespread, earning compensation has become a little more confusing.

Naturally, to earn any compensation, the buyer's broker must have an active real estate license and have a valid written buyer-agency contract. The terms of that buyer-agency agreement will control how much compensation is to be paid to the buyer's agent and which party will pay that compensation. (There are currently no points of law or court cases in North Carolina to provide legal guidance on the question of how to pay a buyer agent.)

Buyers' agents may be compensated by *retainer fees* and *success fees*. The **retainer fee** is typically a small amount of compensation, usually paid up front by the buyer/client when the buyer-agency agreement is established. This fee is advanced partial compensation for services. The **success fee** is due and payable by the buyer/principal on the signing and acceptance of an offer to purchase property found by the buyer's agent. Typically, however, it is actually paid at closing. The buyer-agency agreement normally states that the buyer's agent will first try to recover the success fee from the listing firm (see Appendix D, Form 8, Provision 4).

Types of Listing Agreements

The forms of listing agreements generally used are (1) open listing, (2) exclusive-agency listing, and (3) exclusive-right-to-sell listing.

Open listing.   In an **open listing**, the seller retains the right to employ any number of brokers as agents; it is a nonexclusive-type of listing. The brokers can act simultaneously, and the seller is obligated to pay a commission only to that broker who successfully produces a ready, willing, and able buyer. If the seller personally sells the property *without the aid of any of the brokers*, the seller is not obligated to pay any broker a commission; the seller can compete with the agents for the commission. If the owner or any of the brokers sells the property, all other open listing agreements on that property will terminate the authority given to those brokers. A broker who was in any way a procuring cause of the transaction, however, may be entitled to a commission if the procuring cause of sale can be proved.

Open Listing

- There are multiple agents.
- Only selling agent is entitled to a commission.
- Seller retains the right to sell independently without obligation.

Exclusive-agency listing.   In an **exclusive-agency listing**, one broker is specifically authorized to act as the exclusive agent of the principal. The seller under this form of agreement *retains the right to sell the property*, without obligation to the broker; the seller can compete with the agent to save the commission. If the seller sells through his or her own efforts, the exclusive agency of the broker is automatically terminated. The seller is obligated to pay a commission to the broker if the broker has been the procuring cause of a sale or if any broker sells the property with or without the assistance of the exclusive listing broker.

Exclusive-Agency Listing

- There is one authorized agent.
- Broker receives a commission if any broker is procuring cause.
- Seller retains the right to sell without obligation to listing broker.

Exclusive-right-to-sell listing.   In an **exclusive-right-to-sell listing**, one broker is appointed as sole agent of the seller and is given the exclusive right, or *authorization*, to represent the property in question. Under this form of listing contract, the seller must pay the broker a *commission regardless of who sells the property* if it is sold while the listing agreement is in effect. In other words, if the seller gives a broker an exclusive-right-to-sell listing but finds a buyer without the broker's assistance, the seller still must pay the broker a commission. In North Carolina, this is the most common form of listing agreement. Please note that the listing agreement contains specific language stating that the broker is entitled to the commission regardless of who actually sells the property. Claiming a commission as the procuring cause of the sale has no legal effect. The term *exclusive right to sell* does not imply that the broker has the authority to enter into a *sales contract* on behalf of the property owner. The listing agreement is not an offer to sell the property; it is an *employment* agreement. The seller cannot be forced to sell the property even if the offer matches the terms of the listing agreement exactly; the seller is only required to pay the earned commission to the broker.

Exclusive-Right-to-Sell Listing

- There is one authorized agent.
- Broker receives a commission regardless of who sells the property.

Protection agreement.   When a particular property is not currently listed with any real estate brokerage firm, a **protection agreement** is used to guarantee a broker a commission if that particular property is sold to a specific buyer. The agreement does not create a general listing. When the broker is an exclusive buyer agent, the broker may use the protection agreement to guarantee the seller's payment of the sales commission without creating any agency relationship with the seller. The North Carolina Association of REALTORS® created the Unrepresented Seller Disclosure and Fee Agreement (Std. Form 150) to address required agency disclosure to a property owner selling their own property, and compensation by that property owner to a buyer's agent. (See Appendix D, Form 9.)

■ **FOR EXAMPLE** A broker may use a protection agreement when she has a client who is interested in a specific type of property. The broker knows this buyer would be interested in a particular house that is "For Sale by Owner." However, the broker does not want to suggest that the buyer view the house because the broker could lose the opportunity to earn a commission. Instead, the broker might first approach the homeowner/seller and ask whether he would agree to pay her a commission if her client decided to purchase the home.

Multiple Listing Services

A *multiple-listing clause* is usually included in an exclusive listing. Brokers who are members of a **multiple listing service (MLS)** agree to pool their listings. The multiple-listing provision gives additional authority to the listing broker to *distribute the listing to other brokers who belong to the MLS*. The contractual obligations among the member brokers of a multiple listing organization vary widely. Most listing agreements include what is called *an offer of compensation and cooperation*. Under this provision, the commission is divided between the listing broker and the selling broker, regardless of which party the selling broker represents.

Under most MLS contracts, the broker who secures a listing is not only authorized but *obligated* to submit the listing to the MLS within a definite period of time so that it can be distributed to the other member brokers. The length of time during which the listing broker can offer the property exclusively without notifying the other member brokers varies by REALTOR® board.

A multiple listing provision offers advantages to both the broker and the seller. Brokers develop a sizable inventory of properties to be sold and are ensured a portion of the commission if they list a property or participate in its sale. Sellers also gain under this form of listing agreement because all members of the multiple listing organization are eligible to sell their property and are made aware of its availability. Many MLS agreements now allow all members to upload all the MLS entries onto their firm Web sites for even more exposure to the properties.

Information needed when listing properties in MLS.   It is important to obtain as much information as possible concerning a parcel of real estate when taking a listing. It is wise to complete a physical inspection of the property in the presence of the seller and collect all the physical data necessary to submit to the MLS for inclusion in its property data block. Of course, it is important to make sure all data is accurate. (*Puffing,* which is the use of exaggerated comments or opinions, is not permitted.) The agent should point out any defects to the seller that may need correcting before the property can be shown. Also, during this phase of the listing procedure, the agent should identify all items of personal property the seller may wish to leave behind and identify any fixtures the seller may wish to remove. This process ensures that all possible contingencies are anticipated and provided for, particularly when the listing will be shared with other brokers in a multiple-listing agreement.

As part of the MLS agreement, listing brokers in North Carolina are required to use a separate information form, known as a profile or data sheet, for recording many of the property's features. This information generally includes the following (where appropriate):

- Names, addresses, and relationship, if any, of the owners
- Legal description of the property
- Size of the improvements (square footage)
- Age of the improvements and their type of construction
- Number and general dimensions of rooms
- Lot size (frontage and depth) as well as information concerning the facilities, services, and institutions (e.g., schools, parks and recreational areas, churches, public transportation) available in the neighborhood where the property is located
- Information on any existing loans, including name and address of each lender; type of loan; loan number; loan balance; interest rate; monthly payment and what it includes (principal, interest, real estate tax impounds, hazard insurance impounds, mortgage insurance premiums); whether the loan may be assumed by the buyer and, if so, under what circumstances; whether the loan may be prepaid without penalty; and so forth
- Possibility of seller financing
- Amount of any outstanding special assessments and whether they will be paid by the seller or assumed by the buyer
- Zoning classification of the property
- Current (or most recent year's) property taxes
- Any real property to be removed from the premises by the seller and any personal property to be included in the sale for the buyer (both the listing contract and the subsequent purchase contract should be explicit on these points)
- Any additional information that would make the property appealing and marketable
- Any required disclosures concerning agency representation, property condition, known defects in the property, and the like

Termination of Listings A listing agreement may be terminated for any of the following reasons:

- Completion or fulfillment of the purpose for which the agency was created (the best way to terminate a listing)
- Expiration of the terms of the agency
- Mutual agreement to terminate the agency
- Breach by one of the parties, such as abandonment by the agent or revocation by the principal (The breaching party might be liable for damages.)
- By operation of law, as in bankruptcy of the principal (because title to the property would be transferred to a court-appointed receiver)
- Destruction or condemnation of the property
- Death or incapacity of either party (Notice of death is not necessary. Note that if a property is listed with a brokerage firm and the listing licensee dies, the listing would not be terminated because the listing belongs to the firm.)

A listing agreement is a *personal service contract* with the broker/firm (not the individual licensee), and its success depends on the personal efforts of the broker who is party to the agreement. The broker cannot turn over the listing to another broker. If the broker abandons the listing by failing to work toward its fulfillment or if he or she revokes the agreement, the property owner cannot force the broker to comply with it. The property owner can, however, sue the broker for damages.

The property owner could fail to fulfill the terms of the agreement by refusing to cooperate with reasonable requests of the broker (such as allowing tours of the property by prospective buyers) or by refusing to proceed with a sales contract. A property owner who cancels the listing agreement could be liable for damages to the broker.

The Listing Contract Form

A wide variety of listing contract forms is available today. Some brokers have attorneys draft contracts for their firm's use; some use forms prepared by their MLS; some use forms produced by the North Carolina Association of REALTORS®. No matter which form is used, most listing contracts require similar information because the same considerations arise in almost all real estate sales transactions. A copy of the North Carolina Association of REALTORS® Exclusive Right to Sell Listing Agreement, Form 101, (provisions of which will be referenced in this section) is contained in Appendix D, Form 1.

All listing agents should make sure the listing contract form is filled in properly and approved by the firm and/or the broker-in-charge. Note that a broker/firm can draft the listing form because broker/firm is a party to that agreement; a listing form is an employment agreement between the broker and the seller, not a contract between the buyer and the seller. However, the broker-in-charge should have an attorney approve the form. The listing agreement also must comply with NCREC rules.

Agency disclosure.   As previously discussed in Chapter 7, the real estate agent at first substantial contact with a buyer or seller in all real estate sales transactions must give and review the agency disclosure brochure, *Working with Real Estate Agents*, and determine agency status. The tear-out panel on the brochure must be completed appropriately, hopefully signed by the buyer/seller, and a copy retained by the agent for three years. Review of this mandatory brochure will facilitate understanding of the need for agency-related decisions within the listing agreement, such as cooperation with and compensation to other firms or possible authorization of dual agency. Agency disclosure must happen before a broker begins to gather information to complete a listing agreement.

Description of the property.   All listing agreements should include a clear and precise description of the real estate to be sold. While the legal description does not have to be included for the listing agreement to be valid, it is always wise to do so to avoid confusion and ambiguity (Provision 1).

Note that in addition to the real property, all items of personal property that are to be included in the sale should be adequately described. Most listing agreements include a section (Provision 3) that lists the items of personal property that will be left with the real estate when it is sold and the items of real property (fixtures) the seller expects to remove at the time of sale (Provision 2). Each item should be explicitly identified (brand name, serial number, color), even though some items may become points of negotiation should a ready, willing, and able buyer be found. Examples of items to address in these provisions are major appliances, pool and spa equipment, fireplace accessories, storage sheds, stacked firewood, stored heating fuel, leased equipment, window hardware and treatments, and so on.

Listing price.   A listing agreement always should state the price the seller wants for the listed property (Provision 6). The other terms of the sale also should be included. For example, whether the price is to be paid in cash or financed is an important term. If the seller's mortgage cannot be assumed or if the seller refuses to offer any type of seller financing, then the seller must be paid in cash. Most buyers must get a mortgage loan in order to pay the seller cash, so the type of loan might be important to the seller because of loan requirements for the financed property. Remember, if the broker procures a buyer who is ready, willing, and able to purchase on the terms stated in the listing agreement, the broker will be deemed to have earned the commission whether or not the seller accepts the offer. For this reason, it is critical to clarify all terms of the listing, including acceptable sales price and how it will be paid.

Note that the listing price is the proposed gross sales price. The seller should understand that any outstanding obligations, such as unpaid real estate taxes, special assessments, and mortgage and trust deed debts, remain the seller's responsibility and must be paid from the proceeds of the sale unless otherwise contractually agreed to by the buyer.

Term of listing agreement.   In North Carolina, *all written agency agreements must specify a definite termination date* of the agency relationship [NCREC Rule A.0104(a)]. The listing form must provide for a definite period of time with an automatic termination date (Provision 7). If the property has not been sold by midnight of the termination date, the listing agreement is automatically terminated without notification being required of either party. If mutually acceptable, the listing can be either extended or renewed in writing. Automatic extension or renewal clauses are prohibited in all agency agreements except for property management agreements that allow the landlord to terminate with notice at the end of any contract period.

Brokerage fee.   The listing agreement must specify the compensation to be paid to the broker (Provision 8). The brokerage fee must be freely negotiable between the parties (therefore, it cannot be preprinted on a standard form). To comply with federal antitrust laws, real estate agents cannot state or imply that the brokerage fee is set by law, by an MLS, or a Board of REALTORS®, nor can they state that it is the standard or customary fee. The agreement should also address the possibility of and the permission for additional compensation to the firm. As noted earlier, NCREC Rule A.0109 requires written notification to the client prior to making or receiving any offer if such a fortuitous situation arises. The NCAR Confirmation of Additional Compensation form (see Appendix D, Form 10) has been created to satisfy this Rule requirement and is referenced in the listing agreement.

Brokerage fees can be calculated as a commission (a percentage of the gross sales price), a flat fee (a specific sum of money to be paid at some specified time), or a net amount. If the listing calls for a net fee, the agreement is referred to as a **net listing**. A net listing provision refers to the amount of money the seller will receive if the property is sold. The seller's property is listed for this net amount, and the broker is free to offer the property for sale at any price higher than the listing price. If the property is sold, the broker receives from the seller any proceeds exceeding the stipulated net amount to be retained by the seller. Although not illegal in North Carolina, *this type of listing is not recommended* because of an obvious conflict of interest. *The question of fraud frequently is raised because of uncertainty over the sales price set or compensation received by the broker.* The term *net amount* is often misunderstood and disputed. This type of listing is strongly discouraged.

The listing agreement should also establish the listing firm's authority from the seller to cooperate with other real estate firms in the procurement of a buyer for the seller's property. The seller-client must also grant permission for the listing firm to compensate other firms through the sharing or splitting of the brokerage fee. Whether or not the listing firm and/or the seller-client will agree to cooperate with and compensate only other firms that represent the buyer or whether they will extend seller sub-agency to other firms is a very important issue. Since a principal may be held liable for the actions of their agent under the law of tort (mentioned in Chapter 7), there is potential for vicarious liability for the listing firm and seller-client due to the actions of the cooperating firm's licensees when they are acting as a subagent of the seller.

Override or extender clause.   Some listing contracts contain an **override** or **extender clause** (Provision 8c), which provides that the property owner will pay the listing broker a commission if, within a specified number of days after the listing expires, the owner sells, rents, leases, or options the property to or exchanges the property with someone the owner originally met or made contact with through the broker. This clause protects the broker who introduces two parties and is the procuring cause of a sale, only to have the parties intentionally delay entering into a contract and complete the transaction after the listing expires. The override clause usually parallels the terms of the listing agreement; for example, a six-month listing might carry a broker protection clause of six months after the listing's expiration. To enforce this clause, the listing broker must provide the seller, within a specified time, the names of potential buyers who looked at the property during the listing period. However, to protect the owner and prevent owner liability for two separate commissions, most of these clauses stipulate that they cannot be enforced if the property is listed under a new listing agreement, either with the original listing broker or with another broker.

Authority to cooperate with other firms.   Since the major advantages of belonging to a multiple listing service are the sharing of listed property information and the offer of shared agent compensation, it is critical that the seller-client understands and authorizes how other firms will be paid if they sell the listed property (Provision 9). Seller is cautioned about sharing confidential information with other brokers that might have to disclose that information to the buyer.

Firm's duties.   The agreement should state the obligations the broker promises to fulfill (Provision 10). These include but are not limited to advertising, showing the property, submitting the listing information to an MLS, presenting all offers, and accounting for funds received on behalf of the seller. The broker should comply with the principles of the agency's fiduciary duties discussed in Chapter 7.

Broker also needs permission from the seller for certain marketing activities (Provision 11). For example, according to the terms of the agreement, will the broker be able to place a sign on the property? Advertise and market the property using the broker's best efforts? Submit the listing to an MLS? Show the property at reasonable times and on reasonable notice to the seller? Place a lockbox on the property and accept earnest money deposits on behalf of the seller? Advertise the property on the Internet? Conduct an open house? Without written consent of the seller, the broker cannot undertake any such activities. If the seller does not wish to have the property advertised via the Internet, which has become a prime advertising tool, they must opt-out of this service by signing an *Internet Advertising Addendum* (Appendix D, Form 4) and attaching it to the listing agreement.

All brokerage services must be delivered without discriminatory practices or intentions. Licensees should always be conscious of performing brokerage activities in compliance with federal, state, and local fair housing laws, which will be covered in detail in Chapter 20. Inclusion of the following prescribed nondiscriminatory language is required in all agency agreements in North Carolina: *"The agent shall conduct all brokerage activities in regard to this agreement without respect to the race, color, religion, sex, national origin, handicap or familial status of any party or prospective party."* (Provision 10)

Seller's duties.   Since the listing agreement is a bilateral contract, it should also state the obligations the seller promises to fulfill (Provision 12). These include completing the Residential Property Disclosure Report, unless the property is exempt from the Act (Appendix D, Form 5); complying with the Lead-Based Paint Hazard Reduction Act if the property was built prior to 1978 (Appendix D, Form 6); making the property available for showing; and cooperating with the firm in good faith. The seller is asked to disclose information concerning flood hazard potential (Provision 13), previous use of synthetic stucco (Provision 14), existence of a termite bond (Provision 16), and if the property is subject to an owner's association (Provision 15). The seller also is responsible for providing good, marketable title to convey the property and promises there are no circumstances to prevent that transfer. The seller should disclose any situation that might prevent conveyance of a clear title; and, if the property is subject to participation in a **short sale**, seller should complete the Short Sale Addendum (Appendix D, Form 12) as part of the listing agreement. Seller acknowledges receipt of sample copies of the Offer to Purchase and Contract and the Professional Services Disclosure and Election form (Appendix D, Form 7) for review purposes.

Handling of earnest money.   The firm's policies for holding and crediting of any earnest money needs to be disclosed as well as the disbursement of any forfeited earnest money (Provision 17). Traditionally, the listing firm deposits any earnest money offered with a sales contract into its trust account in accordance with NCREC rules. Any forfeited earnest money may be given in its entirety to the seller or split between the seller and the listing firm.

Acknowledgement of agency disclosure and relationship.   Seller should acknowledge receipt and review of the *Working with Real Estate Agents* brochure and address whether or not to authorize the practice of dual agency in any form

(Provision 21). A concise review of the treatment of information and availability of advice from the listing agent during dual agency is noted. Election of the designated agent option requires the seller's initials.

Miscellaneous provisions. Other provisions of the listing agreement address whether the seller authorizes a home inspection; and agreement for mediation in the event of a dispute between the firm and the seller. There also is a provision for customized terms or conditions to be included in the agreement. The seller can acknowledge receipt of several standardized informational brochures on various topics. At the end of the agreement, both the seller(s) and the agent of the firm must sign and share contact information. The broker also must include the broker's individual license number for NCREC Rule compliance.

Due diligence by agent. Since the real estate broker is responsible for the disclosure of any material information regarding the property, it is important to get as much initial information from the seller as possible. It is sometimes necessary to ask penetrating and possibly embarrassing questions to save both principal and agent from potential legal difficulties. If applicable, the seller must be informed of the seller's duty to give the buyer a property disclosure statement under the North Carolina Residential Property Disclosure Act, which is discussed later in this chapter. If the property is a residential structure built prior to 1978, the agent must also explain the requirement for lead-based paint disclosure. The agent should also gather such pertinent information as legal descriptions.

The agent's duty to *discover and disclose* material facts, including defects in the property, begins with a thorough personal inspection of the property. It is also good business practice to use other sources to verify information provided by the seller. In the listing of industrial, commercial, and agricultural properties, pertinent information may be extensive and detailed. An agent experienced in these areas would be best qualified to gather the information in a complete and accurate manner.

The agent should also collect copies of all of the seller's legal documents concerning the property, such as the deed and survey, and verify the following: (1) the seller's interest in the property, (2) any land-use restrictions that may apply, (3) the size (acreage or square feet) of the land, and (4) the square footage of all the buildings.

Determining Square Footage

In North Carolina, square footage is not considered a material fact that must be disclosed. However, the listing agent is traditionally expected to report the square footage of all buildings located on the listed property. Of primary importance is the residential dwelling. The square footage is normally reported as the *heated living area*, that is, the living area heated by the primary heating system. Measurements for heated living area are derived from exterior measurement to the extent possible. If interior measurements must be utilized, a licensee should add six inches to include the exterior wall width. When measuring attached housing such as townhouses, duplexes, and condominiums, additional measuring challenges may be encountered. Per the NCREC "Residential Square Footage Guidelines," a licensee should add six inches for the common walls in townhouses or duplexes, but add nothing for exterior walls in condos, since the unit does not include the exterior walls. Any deviations, alterations, or changes should be given special mention.

North Carolina Real Estate License Law does not require that agents advertise or report the square footage, but if agents do communicate square footage, the NCREC expects the information to be verifiable and accurate. There are several guidelines for measuring properties available that agents may use. See Appendix B of this text for the North Carolina Real Estate Commission's "Residential Square Footage Guidelines." These guidelines or comparable guidelines should be used when calculating square footage. Such guidelines will assist a licensee if a party to the transaction challenges their reported square footage. These guidelines contain specific procedures for measuring and reporting square footage, for which an agent would be held accountable by the NCREC.

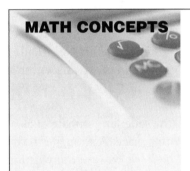

MATH CONCEPTS

CALCULATING SALES PRICES, COMMISSIONS, AND NETS TO SELLER

When a property sells, the sales price equals 100% of the money being transferred. Therefore, if a broker is to receive a 6% commission, 94% will remain for the seller's other expenses and equity. To calculate a commission using a sales price of $80,000 and a commission rate of 6%, multiply the sales price by the commission rate:

$$\$80,000 \times 6\% = \$80,000 \times 0.06 = \$4,800 \text{ commission}$$

To calculate a sales price using a commission of $4,550 and a commission rate of 7% (0.07 as a decimal), divide the commission by the commission rate:

$$\$4,550 \div 7\% = \$4,550 \div 0.07 = \$65,000 \text{ sales price}$$

To calculate a commission rate using a commission of $3,200 and a sales price of $64,000, divide the commission by the sales price:

$$\$3,200 \div \$64,000 = 0.05 \text{ as a decimal} = 5\% \text{ commission rate}$$

To calculate the net to the seller using a sales price of $85,000 and a commission rate of 8% (0.08 as a decimal), multiply the sales price by 100% minus the commission rate:

$$\$85,000 \times (100\% - 8\%) = \$85,000 \times 92\% = \$78,200 \text{ net to seller}$$

The same result could be achieved by calculating the commission ($85,000 × 0.08 = $6,800) and deducting it from the sales price ($85,000 − $6,800 = $78,200). However, this involves unnecessary extra calculations.

Sales price × commission rate = commission
Commission ÷ commission rate = sales price
Commission ÷ sales price = commission rate
Sales price × (100% − commission rate) = net to seller

Pricing the Property

Once a listing decision is secured and all necessary information obtained, the pricing of the real estate is of primary importance. It is the responsibility of the broker to advise and assist, but ultimately it is the *seller* who must determine the listing price for the property. Because the average seller does not usually have the background to make an informed decision about a fair market value, real estate agents must be prepared to offer their knowledge, information, and expertise in this area.

A broker can help the seller determine a listing price for the property by means of a **comparative market analysis (CMA)**. Essentially, a CMA compares the prices of recently sold and/or listed properties that are similar in location, style, and amenities to the subject property. If no such comparisons can be made, or if the seller feels the property is unique in some way, a full-scale real estate appraisal—a detailed estimate of a property's value by a professional certified appraiser—may be warranted.

> A real estate agent performs a CMA to estimate property value, whereas an appraiser would prepare a detailed full appraisal report.

Whether a CMA or formal appraisal is used, the figure sought is the subject property's market value. *Market value*, as will become clear in Chapter 17, is the most probable price the property will bring in an arm's-length transaction under normal conditions on the open market. A broker performing a CMA (sometimes called a *broker price opinion* or *BPO*) will estimate market value as likely to fall within a range (for example, $135,000 to $140,000).

At this point, the agent should also prepare and give the seller an estimate of closing costs, which might help the seller establish the listing price. Although it is the property owner's privilege to set the asking price, a broker may reject any listing in which the price is substantially exaggerated. Once the listing price has been established, only this price can be quoted to a prospective buyer unless seller gives permission to share another price.

■ THE NORTH CAROLINA RESIDENTIAL PROPERTY DISCLOSURE ACT

Property Disclosure Statement

North Carolina law requires that the sellers of most residential properties containing one to four units give the buyer a Residential Property Disclosure Statement, if required. There are properties that are excluded from compliance with this Act. The most common exclusions that real estate agents will encounter are new construction, foreclosure sales, and any rent-to-own scenarios. The statement must be given to the buyer *no later than the time the buyer makes an offer on the property*. The property disclosure statement may be included in the sales contract, in an addendum to the contract, or in a separate document (see Appendix D, Form 5). The form is a state-mandated form and must be used when required. No other form can be substituted. Additional forms may be used, however, such as a copy of a home inspection.

The statement includes disclosures about items relative to the condition of the property about which the owner has actual knowledge. The Residential Property Disclosure Act also allows the owner to make no representations as to the condition of the property except as otherwise provided in the purchase and sale agreement. As befits a *caveat emptor* state, an owner who decides to make *no representation* as to the condition of the property has no duty to disclose those defects, whether or not the owner knows about them.

If the property owner does not deliver the disclosure statement to the buyer prior to or at the time the purchaser makes an offer, the purchaser may cancel, or rescind, any resulting real estate contract. North Carolina G.S. 47E-5(b) addresses the buyer's right of rescission as follows:

> *The purchaser's right to cancel shall expire if not exercised prior to the following, whichever occurs first:*
> *(1) The end of the third calendar day following the purchaser's receipt of the disclosure statement*
> *(2) The end of the third calendar day following the date the contract was made*
> *(3) Settlement or occupancy by the purchaser in the case of a sale or exchange*
> *(4) Settlement in the case of a purchase pursuant to a lease with option to purchase*

If the buyer decides to rescind the sales contract, the buyer must give the seller written notice of the withdrawal within the three-day period. The buyer who exercises this rescission right is entitled to a full refund of any earnest money deposit given to the seller.

The disclosure statement should be kept accurate throughout the listing period. If, after the seller delivers the disclosure statement to the buyer, the disclosure statement is rendered inaccurate (or discovered to be inaccurate) in a material way, the seller must promptly deliver a corrected disclosure statement to the buyer. If the seller fails to deliver the corrected disclosure statement or fails to make any repairs necessary to make the original disclosure statement correct, the buyer may have a legal action for damages.

Review of agent's responsibilities.   Nondisclosure by the seller in no way relieves licensees from their *statutory duty to discover and disclose all material facts to all parties in the transaction.* As noted previously, the listing agent is responsible for informing the seller that it is the seller's responsibility to complete and provide the mandatory disclosure form to all prospective buyers. Although licensees are prohibited from actually completing the form, they can provide insight and advice to the seller. The broker should also assist the seller in providing a complete and up-to-date form to the buyer or their agent. It is common practice around the state for this disclosure form to be available in the listed property and/or as an additional page of information on the MLS listing. All licensees in the transaction, regardless of whom they represent, have an obligation to ensure the delivery of the mandated form to the buyer in a timely manner.

■ WORKING WITH BUYERS

Working as a Seller's Subagent

If the buyer-consumer chooses not to be represented by any type of buyer agency, after proper review by the broker of all agency choices in the *Working with Real Estate Agents* brochure, the buyer must initial the "Disclosure of Seller Subagency" statement at the bottom of the brochure panel authorizing the broker to work as a seller's subagent. In this situation, the broker is in a fiduciary relationship with the seller, *not the buyer*; therefore, the buyer should be very careful what information is shared with the broker that must communicate everything to the seller-client.

Working as a Buyer's Agent

Nonexclusive buyer-agency agreement. Under this type of buyer-agency contract, the buyer does not have exclusive representation from one particular agent. The potential buyer is free to enter into other buyer-agency contracts with other brokers/firms. This also frees the buyer to view and purchase property through a seller's subagent or to purchase property directly from a property owner. Buyer agent compensation under this type of contract may involve a retainer fee or success fee, as previously discussed.

Oral buyer agency. NCREC Rule A.0104(a) permits licensees to work initially as a buyer or tenant agent under an express *oral* buyer or tenant agency agreement. After proper review of agency options in the *Working with Real Estate Agents* brochure, a buyer consumer may wish representation but elect to postpone the execution of a written buyer-agency agreement. Minimally, the oral agreement should address issues of compensation and whether the client authorizes dual agency, if the situation arises. All oral buyer/tenant agency agreements are *nonexclusive*, which means the client may work with other agents or independently and the relationship may be terminated by the agent or the client with notice at any time. Any oral buyer-agency agreement must, by NCREC Rule, be open-ended with no definite termination date. If the agent seeks to restrict the buyer/tenant's ability to work with other agents or to bind the client for a specified period, then the agreement must be in writing from the outset of the restricted relationship. *At the latest,* an oral buyer/tenant agency agreement must be reduced to writing not later than the time any party to the transaction makes an offer to buy, sell, rent, lease, or exchange property to another. Virtually any written buyer-agency agreement will satisfy the Rule's requirement for written agency, whether the agreement is nonexclusive or limited to one particular property. An agent shall *not* continue to act as a buyer or tenant agent if the client refuses to enter into a written buyer-agency agreement when required by the rule. If the buyer refuses to reduce the oral buyer agency to writing, the only way the agent can go forward in the transaction is if the buyer will allow the agent to switch to acting as a seller's subagent. This change must be agreeable to the seller as well as the buyer.

Exclusive buyer-agency agreement. Under this type of buyer-agency contract, one broker/firm is selected by a potential buyer to represent him or her in the purchase of a property on an exclusive basis. The buyer agrees not to work with any other broker/firm in the purchase of a property. The employed broker is the *only real estate firm* with whom the buyer can work to locate and purchase property. When the buyer has signed an exclusive buyer-agency contract, all agents working for that firm become subagents of that buyer. The buyer, however, may not be restricted from buying directly from a property owner, but language in the contract can still require the buyer to pay the broker a success fee. Some buyers who are resistant to an exclusive agency agreement may be more willing to sign if the agreement is short in time duration or limited to a particular property. An exclusive buyer-agency agreement must be in writing from the formation of the exclusive agency. A buyer-agency agreement terminates no later than the date stated in the agreement, unless renewed by that expiration date. It also terminates upon the closing of a purchase obtained by the buyer's agent. The Exclusive Right to Represent Buyer Agreement (Appendix D, Form 8) is an example of an exclusive buyer-agency agreement.

Buyer agent's responsibilities.   A buyer's agent must

- give and review the *Working with Real Estate Agents* brochure with the buyer;
- explain agency duties and responsibilities;
- ensure that a proper agency contract is executed;
- properly qualify the prospective buyer/client;
- obtain and verify information about the property;
- disclose agency status to all parties to the transaction;
- discover and disclose material facts about the property;
- assist in the preparation, presentation, and negotiation of offers submitted by and on behalf of the buyer/client; and
- assist the buyer/client with preparation for closing the transaction.

The Buyer Agency Agreement

Since all agency agreements must comply with NCREC Rules, there are many similarities between a seller's listing agreement and a **buyer agency agreement**. There are provisions dealing with similar issues such as duration of the agreement, broker's compensation, descriptions of the duties of the firm and the client, non-discrimination clause, acknowledgement of receipt of agency disclosure brochure, and the possible practice of dual agency. There are, of course, several unique issues with buyer agency that need to be addressed in the agency agreement. The provisions that are substantially different from the listing agreement will be reviewed using the North Carolina Association of REALTORS® Exclusive Right to Represent Buyer form (Appendix D, Form 8).

Type of property.   Since the primary purpose of the buyer's agent is to help the buyer locate and purchase an acceptable property, it seems obvious that general property requirement parameters need to be established (Provision 1). These parameters may be very general, such as residential property within a specific county, or very specific, such as residential property that allows multiple horses within five miles of a major interstate road. The agreement may even be restricted to a particular property.

Other professional advice.   Buyer is advised to seek professional advice as needed about different matters involved in a real estate purchase from subject matter experts, such as attorneys, surveyors, engineers, etc (Provision 10). Although the broker may provide suggestions of available subject matter experts, the buyer agrees not to hold the broker/firm responsible for the buyer's selection of advisors or the actions of the advisors. Buyer acknowledges receipt of multiple standard publications for review and educational purposes.

Confidentiality issues.   Unless otherwise noted in the agency agreement, the buyer authorizes the broker to disclose the buyer's name(s) as necessary (Provision 5). The buyer also is advised that although licensees are prohibited from disclosing terms of any offer without the express permission of the offering party, the seller is under no such restriction (Provision 15).

■ DUAL AGENCY AGREEMENTS

Dual Agency

A real estate brokerage firm whose policy allows dual agency, electing to represent both the buyer(s) and the seller(s) in the same transaction, must use a written dual agency agreement—no later than the making of the first offer—to modify existing relationships that were created when entering into either a listing contract or a buyer-agency contract. The most recent versions of the listing and buyer-agency agreements have the dual agency agreement incorporated into the form.

IN PRACTICE

Firms practicing dual agency will normally require that their agents, when entering into either a listing agreement or a buyer's agreement, have the client (buyer or seller) authorize dual agency in the agency agreement. This meets the requirement for written informed consent and ideally should be obtained when the agency relationship is established. The dual agency provision basically gives a blanket authorization for dual agency, if needed later in the transaction.

The dual agency authorization in the standard agency agreements contains:

■ Provisions for agreeing to dual agency;
■ The Broker's role as a dual agent;
■ The Seller's and the Buyer's roles; and
■ Provisions for the option of designated dual agency.

A dual agency agreement can be drafted by an attorney to create dual agency and provide written informed consent if written agency has not been previously entered into by the respective parties to be represented by the broker. Such an agreement is required when a broker brings together a potential buyer and a potential seller in hopes of negotiating a successful transaction, but neither party has signed any agency agreement with the broker.

■ SUMMARY

A listing agreement or property management agreement is an employment contract between a broker/firm and a property owner. In the typical real estate transaction, the broker is hired to find either a ready, willing, and able buyer or tenant for the property. All agency agreements with property owners must be in writing from the formation of the relationship to be valid under NCREC rules [see Rule A.0104(a)].

In order to earn a commission, an agent must be actively licensed in North Carolina, working under a valid agency agreement to provide the duties required in the agency agreement. A listing agent must provide a ready, willing and able buyer on terms acceptable to the seller. A buyer's agent must locate an acceptable property type detailed in the buyer-agency agreement. In some cases, a broker may claim that a commission is earned even if a sales contract is not created nor closing reached.

The listing agreement types include open listings, exclusive-agency listings, and exclusive-right-to-sell listings. An open listing is one in which, to obtain a commission, the broker must find a buyer before the property is sold by the seller or another broker. Under an exclusive-agency listing, the broker is given the exclusive right to represent the seller, but the seller retains the right to sell the property without the broker's help and to owe the broker no commission. With an exclusive-right-to-sell listing, the seller employs only one broker and must pay that broker a commission regardless of whether the broker or the seller finds a buyer—provided the buyer is found within the listing period. There are numerous ways to terminate a listing agreement with the best being full performance of the defined duties.

The listing contract should include a description of the property (both real and personal), an acceptable listing price, a description of the agent's and the principal's duties, a nondiscriminatory clause, compensation agreement, authorization for type of agency to be practiced including any form of dual agency, and a definite term with an automatic expiration. While gathering property information for listing and marketing the property, the licensee should use great care to discover and disclose material facts. Although square footage is not a material fact in North Carolina, accuracy is imperative if an agent advertises the heated living area of a house.

The North Carolina Residential Property Disclosure Act is a state law requiring most residential property sellers to give a completed mandatory property report form to potential buyers before presentation of the first offer. If the form is not delivered in a timely manner, the buyer may have the ability to cancel any resulting contract and receive a refund of all deposits paid. Since North Carolina is still a *caveat emptor* state, the owner is allowed to mark a *No Representation* option on the form even if they are aware of defects. Nondisclosure by the seller does not relieve any licensee in the transaction from their affirmative duty to discover and disclose material facts. An agent is prohibited from completing the form on behalf of the property owner. An agent's duty, whether working for the buyer or the seller, is to make the client aware of the statute, assure proper delivery of the form, and assist the client with interpretation of the data on the form. The most common exceptions from this Act are new home construction, foreclosures, and lease with option to purchase.

The employment contract with the buyer is called a Buyer-Agency Agreement that can be either exclusive or nonexclusive. While all agency agreements with property owners must be written from the outset, oral buyer agency is possible if the relationship is nonexclusive for an unknown time period. Oral buyer agency must be reduced to writing prior to the presentation of the first offer. Dual and designated agency is also possible as a verbal agreement until time for presenting an offer. Authorization of the practice of any type of dual agency has been incorporated into the agency agreements.

QUESTIONS

1. A listing agreement
   a. can allow automatic renewal until either party gives notice.
   b. with an override clause protects the listing firm's commission in all situations for the prescribed time period.
   c. is allowed to be oral prior to presentation of an offer.
   d. is required by North Carolina License Law to be written from formation.

2. How are an exclusive-agency listing and an exclusive-right-to-sell listing alike?
   a. The seller retains the right to sell the real estate without the broker's help and without paying the broker a commission.
   b. The seller authorizes only one particular agent to show the property.
   c. The responsibility of representing the seller is given to one broker only.
   d. There is no similarity between the two listing types.

3. All of the following would terminate a listing EXCEPT
   a. expiration of the contract period.
   b. death or incapacity of the seller.
   c. nonpayment of the commission by the seller.
   d. destruction of the improvements on the property.

4. The parties to the listing contract are the
   a. seller and the buyer.
   b. seller and the broker.
   c. buyer and the broker.
   d. broker and the MLS.

5. A listing taken by a real estate licensee belongs to the
   a. firm.
   b. seller.
   c. agent.
   d. agent and firm equally.

6. A seller's residence is listed with a broker, and the seller stipulates that she wants to receive $85,000 from the sale, but the broker can sell the property for as much as possible and keep the difference as the commission. The broker agrees. This is what type of listing?
   a. Exclusive right to sell
   b. Exclusive agency
   c. Open listing
   d. Net listing

7. Seller has listed his property under a standard exclusive-agency listing with broker Baker. If the seller sells his property himself during the term of the listing without Baker's services, he will owe the listing firm
   a. no commission.
   b. full commission.
   c. partial commission.
   d. only reimbursement for expenses.

8. A real estate commission rate is set by the
   a. local real estate board.
   b. North Carolina Real Estate Commission.
   c. principal and the agent.
   d. local multiple listing service.

9. In a sales transaction, which of the following statements is/are TRUE of a listing agreement?
   I. It must be in writing to be legal and enforceable.
   II. It requires the seller to sell the property if terms of an offer match the terms in the listing.
      a. I only
      b. II only
      c. Both I and II
      d. Neither I nor II

10. A listing contract contains a clause that gives the broker the right to collect a commission after the listing contract terminates if the owner sells the property to someone the broker introduced to the property. This is what type of clause?
    a. Extender
    b. Subordination
    c. Exclusivity
    d. Procurement

11. A broker listed a property at an 8% commission rate. After the sale closed, the seller discovered that the broker had been listing similar properties at a 7% commission rate. Based on this information, which of the following statements is/are *TRUE*?

    I. The broker has violated antitrust laws.
    II. The seller can cancel the listing agreement without penalty.
    a. I only
    b. II only
    c. Both I and II
    d. Neither I nor II

12. A broker gets a commission if her listed property is sold, no matter who sells it, if she used what type of listing agreement?

    a. Net
    b. Open
    c. Exclusive agency
    d. Exclusive right to sell

13. Under the North Carolina Residential Property Disclosure Act, the seller must

    I. provide a completed property disclosure form to the buyer before the buyer makes an offer.
    II. disclose all known property defects on the mandatory form.
    a. I only
    b. II only
    c. Both I and II
    d. Neither I nor II

14. Which of the following statements is *NOT* true about the North Carolina Residential Property Disclosure Act?

    a. If the form is not provided per the statute, the buyer may be able to cancel any resulting contract.
    b. If the seller marks *No Representation* on the form, the licensee is relieved of their duty to discover and disclose material facts.
    c. If the buyer rescinds the contract within the allowed time period, all deposit monies will be refunded to the buyer.
    d. Act compliance is required of the seller even if there is no real estate licensee involved in the transaction.

15. The seller has signed a listing agreement with ABC Realty that authorizes the listing firm to collect a 6% commission. According to company policy, ABC Realty offers 40% of the total commission to any cooperating broker that sells the listing. If another firm sells the listing for $125,000, what commission amount will ABC Realty retain?

    a. $3,000
    b. $4,500
    c. $5,000
    d. $7,500

16. Lisa Listing Agent received $4,287.50 as her portion of the commission earned on the sale of her listing. She received 70% of the commission retained by the listing firm. The firm split the 5% listing commission equally with the selling firm. What was the sales price of the property?

    a. $245,000
    b. $171,500
    c. $122,500
    d. $120,000

17. A seller needs $120,000 to pay off their mortgage loan and $1,000 for other closing expenses, plus he would like to net $50,000 to use to purchase his next home. If the listing firm charges a 5% listing fee, what is the minimum sales price that will meet these requirements?

    a. $162,450
    b. $171,000
    c. $179,550
    d. $180,000

18. The seller wants to net $85,000 cash from the sales transaction. The sales commission is 7%, the seller's closing costs are $1,000, and the seller's loan payoff figure is $65,000. What must the sales price be to accomplish the seller's goal?

    a. $151,000
    b. $155,000
    c. $161,750
    d. $162,366

Sales Contracts and Practices

When you have finished reading this chapter, you should be able to

- ■ **determine** when a contract has been formed and explain how to handle modifications and counteroffers.

- ■ **identify** the purpose of the Uniform Electronic Transactions Act.

- ■ **describe** all required provisions of a sales contract and be able to determine when certain addenda are required.

- ■ **explain** the features and uses of the installment land contract.

- ■ **define** the following *key terms:*

acceptance	offer	optionor
backup offer	offeree	right of first refusal
contingency	offeror	Uniform Electronic
installment land contract	option	Transaction Act (UETA)
mailbox rule	optionee	

■ THE SALES CONTRACT

A *real estate sales contract* sets forth *all* details of the agreement between a buyer and a seller for the purchase and sale of a parcel of real estate. Depending on the state or locality, this agreement may be known as *an offer to purchase, a contract of purchase and sale, a purchase agreement, an earnest money agreement, a deposit receipt,* or another variation of these titles. In North Carolina the most common title is Offer to Purchase and Contract.

Whatever the form is called, when it has been prepared and signed by the purchaser, it is an offer to purchase the subject real estate. Later, if the document is accepted and signed by the seller, it becomes, or *ripens into*, a contract of sale. The most commonly used sales contract in North Carolina is the Standard Form 2-T Offer to Purchase and Contract approved jointly by the North Carolina Association of Realtors® (NCAR) and the North Carolina Bar Association (NCBA).

Any offer-to-purchase form offered for use by a real estate licensee in North Carolina must meet the provisions and standards of Rule A.0112 of the North Carolina Real Estate Commission (NCREC) (see Figure 10.1). Another type of sales contract discussed in this chapter is the installment land contract that incorporates seller-financing provisions.

IN PRACTICE   NCREC Rule A.0112 outlines the provisions that must appear in any offer to purchase and contract form suggested for use in North Carolina by real estate licensees. License law strictly prohibits real estate agents from drafting *sales* contracts that bind other people. The NCREC does not *create or approve* contract forms. The contract forms used in this textbook are NCAR standard forms that have been jointly approved by NCBA and NCAR and are utilized in most residential sales transactions in North Carolina.

> The contract of sale is the most important document in the sale of real estate because it sets the terms of the agreement between buyer and seller and establishes each party's legal rights and obligations.

Every sales contract requires at least two parties—a seller (the vendor) and a buyer (the vendee). The same person cannot be both buyer and seller because a person cannot legally contract with himself or herself. *The contract of sale is the most important document in the sale of real estate* because it sets the parameters of the agreement between the buyer and the seller and establishes their legal rights and obligations. It is more important than the deed itself because *the contract*, in effect, *dictates the contents of the deed*.

Issues to be addressed in a real estate sales contract are price, terms, legal description of the property, kind and condition of the title, form of deed the seller will deliver, kind of title evidence required, who will provide title evidence, and how defects in the title, if any, are to be eliminated. The contract must state all the terms of the agreement and spell out all **contingencies** and/or conditions.

In situations where a contract is vague or ambiguous in its terms and one party sues the other based on one of these terms, the courts may refuse to enforce a contract for the parties. The real estate broker must be aware that the responsibilities and legal rights of the parties to a sale are governed by the terms of the contract that must be adequately prepared.

Contracts in Writing

The statute of frauds provides that no action may be brought on any contract for the sale of real estate unless the contract is in writing and signed by the parties to be bound by the agreement. The offer to purchase and contract, therefore, must be in writing to be enforceable. The written requirement has encountered some new interpretations in recent years. In the year 2000, the General Assembly enacted North Carolina's version of the federal *E-sign* legislation, **Uniform Electronic Transactions Act (UETA),** that addresses electronic commerce which clearly includes real estate transactions. Under the scope of this Act, contracts can be created by electronic means such as e-mail and faxes. Also of major importance

F I G U R E   10.1   Rule A.0112

A.0112 Offers and Sales Contracts

(a) A broker acting as an agent in a real estate transaction shall not use a preprinted offer or sales contract form unless the form describes or specifically requires the entry of the following information:

  (1) the names of the buyer and seller;

  (2) a legal description of the real property sufficient to identify and distinguish it from all other property;

  (3) an itemization of any personal property to be included in the transaction;

  (4) the purchase price and manner of payment;

  (5) any portion of the purchase price that is to be paid by a promissory note, including the amount, interest rate, payment terms, whether or not the note is to be secured, and other material terms;

  (6) any portion of the purchase price that is to be paid by the assumption of an existing loan, including the amount of such loan, costs to be paid by the buyer or seller, the interest rate and number of discount points and a condition that the buyer must be able to qualify for the assumption of the loan and must make every reasonable effort to qualify for the assumption of the loan;

  (7) the amount of earnest money, if any, the method of payment, the name of the broker or firm that will serve as escrow agent, an acknowledgment of earnest money receipt by the escrow agent, and the criteria for determining disposition of the earnest money, including disputed earnest money, consistent with Commission Rule .0107 of this Subchapter;

  (8) any loan that must be obtained by the buyer as a condition of the contract, including the amount and type of loan, interest rate and number of discount points, loan term, and who shall pay loan closing costs; and a condition that the buyer shall make every reasonable effort to obtain the loan;

  (9) a general statement of the buyer's intended use of the property and a condition that such use must not be prohibited by private restriction or governmental regulation;

  (10) the amount and purpose of any special assessment to which the property is subject and the responsibility of the parties for any unpaid charges;

  (11) the date for closing and transfer of possession;

  (12) the signatures of the buyer and seller;

  (13) the date of offer and acceptance;

  (14) a provision that title to the property must be delivered at closing by general warranty deed and must be fee simple marketable title, free of all encumbrances except ad valorem taxes for the current year, utility easements, and any other encumbrances specifically approved by the buyer, or a provision otherwise describing the estate to be conveyed, and encumbrances, and the form of conveyance;

  (15) the items to be prorated or adjusted at closing;

  (16) who shall pay closing expenses;

  (17) the buyer's right to inspect the property prior to closing and who shall pay for repairs and improvements, if any;

  (18) a provision that the property shall at closing be in substantially the same condition as on the date of the offer (reasonable wear and tear excepted), or a description of the required property condition at closing, and

  (19) a provision setting forth the identity of each real estate agent and firm involved in the transaction and disclosing the party each agent and firm represents.

The provisions of this Rule shall apply only to preprinted offer and sales contract forms which a broker acting as an agent in a real estate transaction proposes for use by the buyer and seller. Nothing contained in this Rule shall be construed to prohibit the buyer and seller in a real estate transaction from altering, amending or deleting any provision in a form offer to purchase or contract; nor shall this Rule be construed to limit the rights of the buyer and seller to draft their own offers or contracts or to have the same drafted by an attorney at law.

(b) A broker acting as an agent in a real estate transaction shall not use a preprinted offer or sales contract form containing the provisions or terms listed in Subparagraphs (b)(1) and (2) of this Rule. A broker or anyone acting for or at the direction of the broker shall not insert or cause such provisions or terms to be inserted into any such preprinted form, even at the direction of the parties or their attorneys:

  (1) any provision concerning the payment of a commission or compensation, including the forfeiture of earnest money, to any broker or firm, or

  (2) any provision that attempts to disclaim the liability of a broker for his representations in connection with the transaction.

for the real estate industry is that under the legislation, an electronic signature is binding. The statute defines an electronic signature as "an electronic sound, symbol, or process attached to, or logically associated with, a record and executed or adopted by a person with the intent to sign the record." Therefore, a faxed signature on an offer or contract will probably be just as effective as ink on paper. Despite this Act, the North Carolina Real Estate Commission does not recommend that real estate transactions be consummated in this way since there have been no defining court cases to test the enforceability of the Act.

The Offer and Acceptance

One of the essential elements of a contract being formed (discussed in Chapter 8) was that of *mutual assent* or *deliberate agreement*. To form a valid real estate sales contract there must be an *offer* made, an *acceptance* of that offer, and communication of the acceptance to the other party (the offeror).

The offer.   Anyone who makes an **offer** to purchase property is known as the **offeror**—the person making the offer. Anyone who receives an offer is known as the **offeree.**

■ **FOR EXAMPLE** Betty Buyer makes an offer to purchase Sam Seller's house by having her agent, Cooper, prepare a Standard Form 2-T. Once the form is properly filled out with the terms of Betty's offer, she signs it as the buyer and asks Cooper to present the offer to Sam, through Sam's agent, Cindy. At this point Betty is the offeror and Sam is the offeree.

In the previous example, a contract is not yet formed; there is merely an offer to buy that has been made by an offeror to an offeree. Those preparing an offer must make certain there are no ambiguities with respect to the language or construction of the offer because the intent of the offer is to bind the parties when it is accepted. An offer must be definite and precise in its terms; it cannot be of an illusory, or deceptive nature. Mere advertisements of a property for sale do not constitute an offer, nor does the typical listing contract constitute an offer. Preliminary negotiations also do not constitute an offer.

Many times an offer may contain conditions and/or contingencies. In other words, the offeror is saying to the offeree, "This is my offer, if the following conditions or contingencies can be met."

■ **FOR EXAMPLE** Betty Buyer, in the above example, is making an offer of $100,000 contingent on her ability to obtain financing based on an $80,000 loan and other specific loan requirements. If Betty does not qualify for the loan based on contract terms, even after an offer acceptance, she is relieved from the terms of the contract.

The acceptance.   For an offer to become a binding contract, it must be communicated to and accepted by the offeree according to the exact terms and conditions of the offer. An **acceptance** occurs when the offeree signs the offer without making any changes to it, thereby evidencing his acceptance and willingness to be bound by and perform all terms of the offer. If an acceptance of exact terms and conditions takes place (mirror-image) and that acceptance is properly communicated back to the offeror, a binding contract is formed. If the offeree changes *any* terms or conditions of the offer, no matter how slight or small, an acceptance does not take place; instead a counteroffer has been made. Any earnest money that was presented with the offer to purchase must be handled in accordance with NCREC Rule A.0107. If no contract is ever formed, the full earnest money is returned to the offeror.

The counteroffer.   As discussed in Chapter 8, when the offeree receives the offer and makes any change to that offer, it constitutes a counteroffer, which is a rejection of the first offer. When the counteroffer takes place, the original offer cannot be revived. The offeree also cannot later reconsider and *accept* the original offer. *It has been rejected; it no longer exists*.

> A counteroffer rejects the original offer and constitutes a new offer, not a revision of the original offer.

■ **FOR EXAMPLE** When Betty made her offer, she entered $100,000 as the offered purchase price. Sam changed the purchase price to $105,000 with a pen and ink change, dated and initialed the change and signed the form as the seller. At this time, Sam becomes the offeror, making a new offer back to Betty, who is now the offeree. Once this new offer is communicated to Betty, if she accepts it by initialing and dating the form, she has accepted the offer from Sam. When her acceptance is properly communicated to Sam, a contract has been formed.

If Betty changes the $105,000 to $103,000 and initials and dates the change, a counter-counteroffer has taken place. Betty is once again the offeror and Sam is once again the offeree. This process of countering the previous offer can continue for an indefinite period until total agreement between parties has been reached.

Methods of Communicating Offers and Acceptance

There are various ways that offers and acceptance may be communicated. Probably the most common and the most acceptable way is to communicate in writing; the offeror signs the written offer and communicates it to the offeree, and the offeree signs the written offer, denoting acceptance. When the acceptance is properly communicated back to the offeror, a contract is formed.

Communication of the acceptance to the offeror may be either oral—by telephone, voice mail, or in person—or by personal delivery of the written acceptance by the offeree or by another person on behalf of the offeree. Communication to either party's agent is deemed communication to that party.

Traditional, special, or electronic mail are acceptable ways to communicate an offer or an acceptance. If an acceptance is placed into the mail service to the other party or that party's agent, it is considered as having been delivered when mailed, not necessarily when actually received; this is known as the **mailbox rule.** The parties cannot revoke the offer once the acceptance is mailed because it is now a contract. The telegraph and telegram are other means of communicating an acceptance, although they are seldom used today in the real estate business. Facsimiles (fax machine, e-mail, telecopier, etc.) are acceptable means of communicating offer and acceptance. Acceptance of an offer becomes complete, and a contract is formed, when communication of acceptance is received by the offeror's communication device. This form of communicating the offer and acceptance is commonplace in the real estate business.

Termination of Offers

There are several ways to terminate an offer (remember that an offer is not a contract, which is terminated in other ways). Termination of offers can take place

- if the offeree rejects the offer and/or creates a counteroffer;
- if the offeree fails to accept within the prescribed time stipulated in the offer;
- within a reasonable time, if a time of acceptance is not prescribed;
- prior to acceptance, if the offeror communicates a revocation of the offer; or
- by the death of the offeror or offeree.

Major Contract Provisions

All real estate sales contracts can be divided into a number of general parts. Although each form of contract will contain these divisions, their location within a particular contract may vary. Generally speaking, sales contract forms, including the predominate standard offer to purchase and contract form used in North Carolina (Form 2-T, see Appendix D, Form 11) will include at least the following items:

- Names and marital status of the buyer and seller and the obligations of both parties—the buyer's obligation to purchase the property and the seller's obligation to convey the property. There also should be a statement indicating how the buyer intends to take title.
- Legal description of the property and, if appropriate, the street address.
- Purchase price and how the purchaser intends to pay for the property, including earnest money deposits, additional cash from the purchaser, and the conditions of any mortgage financing the purchaser intends to obtain or assume.
- Provision for any contingencies (delays in obtaining financing, inability to obtain financing, purchaser's inability to sell a property to finance the current transaction, seller's inability to acquire another desired property, inability of the seller to clear the title). If a contingency is not met, neither party is bound to carry out the agreement. For example, if the buyer cannot obtain the type of financing described in the agreement, the buyer does not have to proceed with the transaction. If the purchaser makes the sale contingent on selling another home first, the seller may insist on an escape clause. Such a provision allows the seller to look at a more favorable offer, with the original purchaser retaining the right (if challenged) either to firm up the first sales contract by eliminating the contingency or to void the contract.
- Contingency clause providing for completion of the contract should the property be damaged or destroyed between the time the contract is signed and the date of closing. In some instances, destruction of improvements makes performance of a sales contract by the seller impossible.
- Provisions for closing the transaction and transferring possession of the property to the purchaser. A realistic closing date should be included in the offer to purchase.
- Proration of (adjustment for) real estate taxes, rents, fuel, owner association dues, and other closing costs.
- Provision regarding the quality of title the seller must provide.
- Provision for remedies should either party default on the contract (including liquidated damages and the right to sue for specific performance or damages).
- Signatures of all parties and execution date on which the contract is signed. The signature of a witness is not essential to a valid contract.

Miscellaneous Provisions in a Contract

While a sales contract may address a wide variety of matters related to the sale, the following additional miscellaneous items are included in the NCBA/NCAR Standard Form 2-T Offer to Purchase and Contract (Appendix D, Form 11), which is widely used in North Carolina:

- Identification of any personal property to be left on the premises for the purchaser (such as major appliances, lawn ornaments, and garden equipment). Often, personal property items are sold along with the real estate. These items should be specifically described in the purchase agreement, possibly include brand name, model number, and serial number, if appropriate. Custom dictates that when there are many such items, they should be enumerated in a bill of sale, which is evidence of ownership. By describing the personal property in the contract, a broker minimizes any potential conflict between the purchaser and seller as to what constitutes personal property and what constitutes fixtures. NCREC cautions that merely referencing a property's MLS list of personal property is not adequate or advised because the entry is not a legal part of the sales contract and can be changed. It is good practice for a licensee to bring to the attention of the parties any property that potentially may fall into this difficult classification.
- Identification of any real property to be removed by the seller prior to closing (such as storage sheds). As noted in the previous bullet about inclusion of personal property, just referencing the MLS entry is inadequate.
- Purchase by the buyer of fuel in any tanks on the property.
- Transfer or payment of any outstanding special assessments.
- Provision for seller to provide a homeowner warranty program.
- Provision that the contract can be terminated by the purchaser if the property appraises for less than the contracted sales price.
- Purchaser's right to certain inspections and reports such as a structural engineering report, pest control infestation report, or habitability report within a specified number of days.
- Purchaser's right to a purchased option period to investigate and evaluate the property and determine willingness to proceed with the transaction.
- Purchaser's right to inspect the property shortly before the closing or settlement—often called the *walk-through*.
- Agreement as to what documents will be provided by each party and when they will be delivered.

Addenda

Several standard addenda have been approved for use with the standard sales contract when appropriate (see Figure 10.2). These addenda address specific issues that may be too complicated to include in the space allowed for *other provisions*. The agent should use these approved addenda when dealing with these issues because they increase the chances of proper preparation and negate any suspicion that the agent may be illegally practicing law by drafting a contract. For example, an FHA/VA Financing Addendum must be used when the buyer is going to apply for an FHA or a VA loan; a Seller Financing Addendum must be used when the seller is providing part or all of the financing; a Buyer Possession Before Closing Agreement Addendum must be used when the buyer wishes to move onto the property before the closing date; and a Lead-Based Paint Disclosure Addendum must be used when the property is a residence built prior to 1978.

FIGURE   10.2

**Addenda Forms
Approved by NCAR
and NCBA**

2A1-T	Backup Contract Addendum
2A2-T	Contingent Sale Addendum
2A3-T	New Construction Addendum
2A4-T	FHA/VA Financing Addendum
2A5-T	Seller Financing Addendum
2A6-T	Loan Assumption Addendum
2A7-T	Buyer Possession Before Closing Agreement Addendum
2A8-T	Seller Possession After Closing Agreement Addendum
2A9-T	Lead-Based Paint or Lead-Based Paint Hazard Addendum
2A11-T	Additional Provisions Addendum
2A12-T	Owner's Association Addendum
2A13-T	Vacation Rental Addendum
2A14-T	Short Sale Addendum

**Submitting Offers
to Seller**

Real estate agents are obligated by licensing law [93A-6(a)(13)] and Commission Rule A.0106 to disclose all offers to sellers immediately, but no later than five days from the date of the offer. Simply telephoning the offeree with the terms of an offer is not sufficient delivery, according to the NCREC 2008-9 Update material. Furthermore, listing agents must disclose any additional information they have that may affect a seller's decision to accept an offer. This includes information about the offeror's financial ability to close the transaction, as well as the possibility of other offers that may be presented shortly.

An agent can neither reject nor accept an offer on behalf of a seller, nor can an agent screen offers presenting only those offers that the agent feels have merit. All offers, written or verbal, must be communicated to the seller. It is up to the seller to accept or reject any offer that is made, however unreasonable that offer is. Agents also must present those offers that may be at a disadvantage to them.

■ **FOR EXAMPLE** One buyer may offer the seller $90,000 in cash for the seller's home, while another buyer offers the seller $95,000, contingent on obtaining financing. The agent must present both offers as soon as possible, even though if the seller accepts the first offer (because it is in cash), it will mean a smaller commission for the agent.

Backup offers.   An agent may receive a **backup offer** on a listed property that is under contract—an offer that is made after the owner has already signed a contract to sell the property but before the sale has closed. In that case, the agent should inform the offeror that there is an existing contract and inquire whether he or she wishes to withdraw the offer. If the offeror still wants to make an offer on the property, the agent must submit the offer to the seller. The agent should advise the seller to seek legal counsel if the seller is interested in accepting the offer. Backup offers that are contingent on the first sale falling through always should be drafted by an experienced attorney. There is an approved Backup Contract Addendum (NCAR Standard Form 2A1-T) to address this issue. Note again that the agent is required to submit all offers, including backup offers, to the seller immediately.

**Handling Offer
to Purchase
Modifications
and Counteroffers**

Frequently, a seller wants certain changes to be made to an offer before accepting it. For example, instead of a $1,000 earnest money deposit, the seller may demand a $5,000 earnest money deposit. As discussed earlier, once the offeree makes any material change in the offer, the offeree has *rejected* that offer and created a *counteroffer*. No contract has been formed at this stage. It is up to the original offeror to accept or reject the counteroffer. If the original offeror accepts the counteroffer *with a few changes,* another counteroffer has been created and the process begins again.

Negotiations between a buyer and seller may consist of a series of counteroffers before final terms are agreed on. Any changes to the original offer must be made in writing and initialed by both parties. Unfortunately, if all the changes are written into the initial offer form, the contract can become virtually unreadable. It is a good idea for the agent to fill in a new standard form with the final terms and have both parties sign and date it. This avoids later confusion over which terms were changed and how.

An alternative to making *pen and ink* changes to the original offer is for the seller to utilize the NCAR Response to Buyer's Offer (Std. Form 340-T, Appendix D, Form 13). The form allows the seller to list terms that would be more acceptable and suggest the buyer (offeror) consider them when revising the original offer. The response form rejects the original offer but does not create a counteroffer; this allows the seller to be free to accept any new offers while the original offeror is deciding how to proceed with negotiations. This form is also an excellent way to respond to multiple offers simultaneously without binding the seller to any one offer.

The fact that there are multiple offers on a property is not considered a material fact that must be disclosed. However, if one of the offering parties is notified of the existence of a competing offer, then all offering parties must receive the same notification. This maintains a "level playing field" for all offerors. Also, as of July 1, 2008, NCREC Rule A.0115 prohibits any broker from disclosing the price or any other material term in any offer to purchase, sell, lease, rent, or option real property to a competing party without the express authority of the offeror. "Shopping the offer" by agents has long been considered unethical and is now also illegal in North Carolina. Of course, unlicensed principals in the transaction are not bound by this rule.

Furnishing Copies of Offers and Contracts to Buyer and Seller

According to Commission Rule A.0106, real estate agents must provide all parties with a copy of any instrument they sign at the time of execution, or no later than five days after execution. It is important to remember that a contract may have been created long before the offeror receives a written copy of the signed contract.

■ **FOR EXAMPLE** When a buyer signs an offer to purchase, the agent must immediately provide the buyer with a copy of that offer. Then if the seller signs the offer, the agent must immediately provide the seller with a copy of that signed offer. And of course, the agent also must give a copy of the offer to purchase and contract—with both signatures—to the buyer. Per the Rule, *immediately* has its common meaning, with the outside limit being no later than five days from execution.

It is standard practice to create six copies of the forms, sometimes called *counterparts.* (Note that a *signed copy becomes an original.*) One copy goes to each of the following: the buyer, the seller, the listing real estate office, the selling real estate office, the closing attorney, and the lender. Despite the practice of multiple "originals," only one signed original is necessary to create a contract.

■ INSTALLMENT LAND CONTRACT

A real estate sale can be made under an **installment land contract,** sometimes called a *land contract* or *contract for deed.* An installment land contract is not only a sales contract but also a financing instrument. The seller agrees to owner financing with some type of installment payment method for the buyer. Under an installment land contract, the seller, also known as the *vendor,* retains legal ownership, while the buyer, known as the *vendee,* secures possession of and an equitable interest in the property. The buyer holds equitable title, and the contract is a cloud on the seller's title.

The buyer usually agrees to give the seller a down payment and pay regular monthly installments of principal and interest over a number of years. The buyer also agrees to pay real estate taxes, insurance premiums, repairs, and upkeep on the property. While the buyer obtains possession when the contract is signed by both parties, *the seller is not obligated to execute and deliver a deed to the buyer until a future date, which may not be until all the terms of the contract have been satisfied.*

There is no standard approved form for an installment land contract; therefore, all interested parties should consult an attorney for advice and drafting expertise. All installment land contracts must be in writing to be valid and enforceable, as required by the statute of frauds, and must be recorded, as required by the Conner Act (see page 82).

Typical Provisions

Most installment land contracts contain the following provisions:

■ Full names of the parties;
■ Date when the contract is signed;
■ Legal description of the property to be conveyed;
■ Contract price of the property conveyed;
■ Amount of the purchaser's down payment;
■ Amount and due date of each installment payment;
■ Interest rate on the unpaid balance and the method of computing the interest;
■ Seller's promise to deliver a general warranty deed on completion of the contract;
■ Fact that the purchaser is responsible for the payment of taxes, assessments, and other charges against the property from the date of the contract unless agreed to the contrary;
■ Whether the contract is assignable; and
■ What happens in the event of default.

Advantages and Disadvantages

For the seller. The typical land contract is advantageous to the seller for a number of reasons. There is an income tax benefit that comes from receiving the sales price in installments over several years instead of in a lump sum. The seller gets to retain legal title, which makes the seller feel more secure. If the buyer defaults, many land contracts provide forfeiture as a remedy. Forfeiture means that all the monthly payments the buyer has made are forfeited as well as all rights in the property. Finally, the land contract may be the only way to make property desirable and/or attainable to buyers when interest rates are high or institutional loans are hard to obtain.

On the other hand, sellers often receive small down payments under a land contract, and a seller may prefer to be *cashed out*—that is, to get immediate cash for the equity. For example, the seller may need cash to make a down payment on a new home.

For the buyer. If the buyer has a poor credit rating, a history of foreclosures or bankruptcies, or marginal income, a land contract may be the only way to finance a transaction. The down payment and the closing costs are usually lower than in institutional financing arrangements. The purchaser also has the tax advantages that come with ownership of real estate. All these are obvious advantages for the buyer.

However, if the buyer defaults under the contract for deed, the forfeiture remedy available to the seller is extremely harsh for the buyer. The buyer can lose all the payments made under the contract in addition to the property itself. Also, because the buyer does not get legal title to the property until the end of the contract term, the buyer will find it virtually impossible to use the property as collateral for interim financing needs.

■ OPTION TO PURCHASE REAL ESTATE

A conventional **option** is a *contract by which an* **optionor** *(generally an owner) gives an* **optionee** *(a prospective purchaser or lessee) the irrevocable right to buy or lease the owner's property at a fixed price within a stated period of time*. An option to purchase has two considerations: (1) the option fee when the option is given and (2) the agreed-on sales price when the option is exercised. The option fee is normally nonrefundable if the option is not exercised. The optionee must decide, within the specified time, either to exercise the option right (to buy or lease the property) or to allow the option right to expire. At the time the option is signed by the parties, the optionor does not sell, nor does the optionee buy. They merely agree that the optionee will have the right to buy and the owner will be obligated to sell *if* the optionee decides to exercise the option. An option is enforceable by only one party—the optionee. Because the seller is prohibited from selling the property to anyone else during the option period, it would probably be in the optionor's best interest to clearly terminate the optionee's rights by using the term *time is of the essence* regarding the option date. A common application of an option is a lease that includes an option for the tenant to purchase the property. Options on commercial real estate frequently depend on the fulfillment of specific conditions, such as obtaining a zoning change or a building permit. The optionee is usually obligated to exercise the option if the conditions are met.

Requirements of Options

All options for real property are required to be in writing under the statute of frauds. Under the Conner Act, an option must be recorded to be enforceable against the claims of third parties.

There is currently no standard approved Option to Purchase Contract. If a licensee has parties that desire a conventional option to purchase agreement, an attorney should be contacted to draft the appropriate contract. A licensee should never attempt to create an option contract.

The option should describe the manner in which the optionee will notify the optionor of the decision to exercise the option. Not only should the option spell out the terms under which the optionee can buy the property, it also should describe the major terms of the sale itself, such as the purchase price, financing terms, and type of deed that will be used to convey title. The consideration for the option (the option fee) also must be stated clearly. Furthermore, the option should explain whether the price the optionee paid for the option right will be applied toward the purchase price.

Right of First Refusal

An option should not be confused with a right of first refusal. A **right of first refusal** is created when a property owner promises to give the contracting party the first chance to buy the property or to match the bona fide offer of a third party, should the owner decide to sell. Rights of first refusal are commonly found in leases. In a lease situation, a right of first refusal might give the tenant the right either to purchase the property, if offered for sale, or to renew the lease or lease adjoining space. In some condominiums, the association of unit owners retains the right of first refusal on any sale of a unit.

Note that with a right of first refusal, the property owner does not promise to sell the property at all—merely promises that *should* the decision is made to sell, the other party will get the first opportunity to buy. This is different from the option, where the owner promises to sell should the optionee choose to buy.

■ OPTION TO TERMINATE

In the NCAR/NCBA Standard Form 2-T Offer to Purchase and Contract (Appendix D, Form 11), the parties to the contract are given alternatives for handling property inspections and repairs in Provision 16.

Alternative 1 provides the historic practice of allowing the buyer to inspect the property and request eligible repairs. The seller then has the choice of making those repairs and binding the buyer, or refusing to make the repairs, thereby allowing the buyer to terminate the contract. Alternative 2 allows the purchaser to pay a nonrefundable fee directly to the seller for the option of terminating the contract for any or no reason prior to a specified date and time. If the buyer elects to continue in the contract, the option fee will be credited to the buyer's closing expenses. The option fee should not be confused with the earnest money deposit that serves as the liquidated damages.

The Alternative 2 option is significantly different from the conventional option to purchase contract discussed in the preceding section. Whereas a conventional option is the right to purchase by a certain date, the Alternative 2 option is a right to *NOT* purchase by a certain date. Instead of exercising a right to *opt in* and create a purchase contract, the buyer under Alternative 2 is *opting out* of a contract to purchase. Prior to the Option Termination Date, the buyer is encouraged to make a thorough investigation of the property and negotiate any repairs or changes in contract terms the buyer deems necessary. If the buyer and seller cannot reach an agreement regarding repairs or terms, the buyer can give written notice to the seller that buyer is exercising the right to terminate the contract prior to the Option Termination Date (Form 350-T, Appendix D, Form 15). If the buyer does not exercise the option to terminate by the Option Termination Date, the buyer must proceed with the purchase of the property in its current condition unless a repair agreement has been signed, such as the Repair Request and Agreement (Form 310-T, Appendix D, Form 14). Please note that *time is of the essence* regarding the Option Termination Date and notice of termination must be delivered to the seller or listing company by the stated date and time or the buyer has lost the right to unilaterally terminate.

■ RELATED WEB SITES

Electronic Signatures in Global and National Commerce Act (E-SIGN):
 www.ftc.gov/os/2001/06/esign7.htm
Uniform Electronic Transactions Act: *www.nccusl.org*

■ SUMMARY

An offer to purchase, once accepted, binds a buyer and a seller to a definite sales transaction, as described in detail in the resulting contract. The buyer is bound to purchase the property for the amount stated in the agreement. The seller is bound to deliver a good and marketable title, free from liens and encumbrances (except those allowed by the contract).

Real estate sales contracts must be in writing to be enforceable per the Statute of Frauds. The most used sales contract, the NCAR/NCBA Standard 2-T, complies with requirements of Rule A.0112 that any pre-printed offer to purchase form used by a real estate licensee include the 19 pieces of noted information. The form begins use as an offer, which may *mature* into a contract. The offeror is the person making the offer (could be buyer or seller), and the offeree is the person who is receiving the offer (could be buyer or seller). If either party to the offer makes a change, it constitutes a counteroffer that rejects the original offer and creates a new offer. Modifications to an offer can be done by pen-and-ink changes or by the drafting of a completely new offer. Pen-and-ink changes must be initialed by all parties and should be dated. If contract terms are vague or ambiguous, the resulting contract may be unenforceable. Signatures and contracts that are faxed, scanned, or e-mailed will probably be considered valid due to the Uniform Electronic Transactions Act.

Offers can be terminated in the following ways: withdrawal by offeror, rejection by offeree, expiration of time period, or creation of a counteroffer. Use of the *Response to Buyer's Offer* form is suggested in a multiple offer scenario. A contract is created once all parties to the contract have signed it and the last party to sign has communicated this acceptance to the opposite party. Communication of acceptance can be accomplished orally or in writing.

The installment land contract serves two legal purposes: (1) it is a contract to convey, and (2) it is a financing device for seller financing. Under an installment land contract, the buyer takes immediate possession of the property and pays off the purchase price over a period of years, while the seller retains legal title until the purchase price is paid in full.

Under a conventional option contract, the optionee purchases from the optionor, for a limited time period, the exclusive right to purchase or lease the optionor's property. While the seller may not sell the property to anyone other than the optionee during the option period, the optionee/buyer is not obligated to purchase or lease the property; the optionee who elects to exercise the option to purchase or lease the property must notify the seller in writing of the decision to purchase/ lease *before* the option period expires. In a right of first refusal, all that is promised is a guarantee to be given the first opportunity to buy with no terms negotiated.

Under Paragraph 16, Alternative 2 of the NCAR/NCBA 2-T Offer to Purchase and Contract, the buyer pays the seller directly a nonrefundable option fee for the right to terminate the contract for any or no reason prior to the Option Termination Date. If the buyer does not opt out of the contract, the option fee will be credited to the purchase price.

QUESTIONS

1. To sell his property the seller has entered into a contract. While the sale is pending, the listing agent receives another offer to purchase the property from a different firm. Which of the following statements is *TRUE*?
   a. The agent does not have to present this offer to the seller.
   b. The agent must present this offer to the seller.
   c. The agent has to present this offer only if its terms are better than the terms of the pending sale.
   d. The agent must tell the offeror that offers are prohibited while a sale is pending.

2. Which of the following statements is *TRUE* of a conventional option to purchase contract?
   a. It need not recite a set amount of consideration for purchase of the property.
   b. It must be exercised within a specified time period by the optionee.
   c. It does not allow negotiation on changes to contract terms during the option period.
   d. It is enforceable by both the optionor and the optionee.

3. At 1:30 pm, an agent from Alana Realty faxed an offer to purchase to her seller client. At 2:00 PM, after considering the offer, the seller called and informed his agent that he wanted to increase the earnest money deposit by $1000. To make the seller's requested change for additional earnest money, the seller's agent need only
   I. change the term in the original offer, initial, and date the one change on behalf of the seller.
   II. prepare a new offer and, with the seller's permission, sign on behalf of the seller.
      a. I only
      b. II only
      c. Both I and II
      d. Neither I nor II

4. The buyer's offer is made on the condition that the buyer's present home sells in the next 30 days. This condition is called a(n)
   a. first right of refusal.
   b. contingency.
   c. unilateral offer.
   d. option.

5. The buyer's offer is made on the condition that the buyer is able to obtain an 80% institutional loan at a specified interest rate by a specified date. If the buyer notifies the seller in writing of the inability to obtain such a loan, the buyer will
   a. have to go ahead with the purchase anyway.
   b. not have to purchase the home, but will forfeit the whole earnest money deposit.
   c. not have to purchase the home, but will forfeit half of the earnest money deposit.
   d. not have to purchase the home and will be entitled to a full refund of the earnest money deposit.

6. An offer to purchase is submitted on a listing while the property owner is out of town on business. The offer is faxed to the owner and the owner signs the faxed copy of the offer with no changes in terms. If the signed offer is then faxed to the listing agent who calls the buyer's agent with this information, which of the following statements is *TRUE*?
   a. The seller is under contract to sell his property since faxed signatures are binding.
   b. The original signatures of both buyer and seller must appear on the same copy of the offer; therefore, a contract does not exist.
   c. No contract exists yet since the buyer has not been personally told of the contract acceptance.
   d. No contract exists since no one on the buyer's side of the transaction has seen the seller's signature.

7. Which of the following statements is/are *TRUE* when an offer to purchase has been signed by the buyer and then given to the seller's broker with an earnest money deposit check for the seller to consider?

   I. The earnest money check must be deposited immediately into the listing firm's trust account.

   II. If the buyer withdraws the offer before it is accepted by the seller, the earnest money will be forfeited.

     a. I only
     b. II only
     c. Both I and II
     d. Neither I nor II

8. An offer to purchase real estate can be terminated by all of the following reasons *EXCEPT*

     a. failure to accept the offer within a prescribed period.
     b. revocation by the offeror communicated to the offeree after acceptance.
     c. acceptance of the offer by the offeree after making one change in terms.
     d. death of the offeror or offeree.

9. Which of the following statements is *TRUE* of Alternative 2 of the NCAR/NCBA 2-T offer to purchase and contract?

     a. The option fee is applied to the purchase price at closing.
     b. It requires all the systems of the property to be functioning adequately.
     c. The earnest money check is paid directly to the seller.
     d. Within three business days after option period expires, the buyer must notify the seller of the buyer's decision to proceed with the contract.

10. When a buyer and seller have entered into an installment land contract,

   I. the seller retains an interest called legal title.

   II. the buyer acquires an immediate interest in the property known as equitable title.

     a. I only
     b. II only
     c. Both I and II
     d. Neither I nor II

11. Carl and Hannah enter into a real estate sales contract. Under the contract terms, Carl will pay Hannah $500 a month for ten years. Hannah will continue to hold legal title to the property. Carl will live on the property and pay all real estate taxes, insurance premiums, and regular upkeep costs. What kind of contract do Carl and Hannah have?

     a. Option to purchase contract
     b. Contract for mortgage
     c. Unilateral contract
     d. Installment land contract

12. The Taylors offer in writing to purchase a house owned by the Shorts for $120,000, including the draperies, with the offer to expire on Saturday at noon. The Shorts reply in writing on Thursday, accepting the $120,000 offer, but excluding the draperies. On Friday, while the Taylors consider this response, the Shorts reconsider the original offer, and decide to accept the original offer in writing, including the draperies. Since it is before Saturday noon, the Taylors

     a. are legally bound to buy the house including the draperies.
     b. are not bound to buy because they are not under contract.
     c. must buy the house and are not entitled to the draperies.
     d. must buy the house, but may deduct the value of the draperies from the $120,000.

13. Robert signs a contract under which he may purchase a house for $80,000 any time within the next three months. Robert pays the current owner $500 at the time the contract is signed. Which of the following best describes this contract?

     a. Contingency
     b. Option to purchase
     c. Installment land contract
     d. Contract for deed

14. A for-sale-by-owner signs a written offer to purchase without making any changes to the offer. The seller then mails the signed offer to the buyer by express mail without any further contact with the buyer. Before receipt of the envelope from the seller, the buyer changes her mind about purchasing the property and calls the seller to withdraw the offer. Which of the following statements is *TRUE*?

    a. Buyer cannot withdraw offer, because she is already under contract.
    b. Buyer can withdraw offer since she has not received the signed contract yet.
    c. Buyer was under contract as soon as the seller signed the offer to purchase.
    d. Contract has been formed but is unenforceable since real estate licensees were not involved.

15. A seller receives two offers to purchase on her property at the same time. One offer is for full listing price but wants a delayed closing that is not in the seller's best interest. The second offer has terms that are very agreeable to the seller but offers less than full price for the property. Without any knowledge or consent of the first offeror, the listing agent contacts only the second offeror and tells them that there is a full price offer on the table and asks if they would like to increase the purchase price in their offer. Listing agent is

    a. honoring his fiduciary duty to the seller by soliciting a higher offer.
    b. in violation of Commission Rules because he must also respond to the first offeror.
    c. in violation of Commission Rules because he illegally revealed offer terms.
    d. working within Commission Rules as long as his actions were at the direction of his seller client.

CHAPTER

11

Landlord and Tenant

■ **LEARNING OBJECTIVES** *When you have finished reading this chapter, you should be able to*

- ■ **identify** and explain the characteristics of the four types of nonfreehold estates.

- ■ **explain** the concepts of the Residential Rental Agreements Act, the Tenant Security Deposit Act, the Doctrine of Retaliatory Eviction, and the NC Vacation Rental Act.

- ■ **describe** the various types of leases and their purposes; the requirements and general conditions of a valid lease; and how a lease may be terminated.

- ■ **explain** the general provisions of leases as they relate to possession, recording, improvements, maintenance, assignment and subleasing, and breach.

- ■ **understand** the major provisions of NCAR's Standard Residential Rental Contract form.

- ■ **define** these *key terms:*

constructive eviction	implied warranty of	privity of contract
covenant of quiet	habitability	privity of estate
enjoyment	index lease	Residential Rental
estate at sufferance	law of negligence	Agreements Act
estate at will	lease	retaliatory eviction
estate for years	leasehold estate	sandwich lease
estate from period to	lessee	security deposit
period	lessor	self-help eviction
fixed rental lease	net lease	subleases
full-service lease	North Carolina Vacation	summary ejectment
graduated lease	Rental Act	Tenant Security Deposit
gross lease	novation	Act
ground lease	percentage lease	
holdover tenant	periodic tenancy	

■ LEASING REAL ESTATE

A **lease** is a conveyance from a landlord, an owner of real estate (known as the **lessor**), to a tenant (the **lessee**) that transfers the right of possession and use of the owner's property to the tenant for a specified period of time. A *lease* is also a contract that generally sets forth the length of time the contract is to run, the amount to be paid by the lessee for the right to use the property, and other rights and obligations of the parties.

> A lease covers the conditions upon which a tenant may possess, occupy, and use the property.

A lease is said to have a *dual legal personality*—it is a contract and it also conveys an interest in real property. Because of this dual purpose, both the owner and the tenant have certain rights and duties from two sources: (1) **privity of estate** (which comes from traditional property law) and (2) **privity of contract** (which comes from the terms of the contract itself). Privity means the *mutual or successive relationship to the same rights of property*. For example, the lessee has the exclusive right of possession under privity of estate, but the lessor may be granted the right to reenter the premises under the terms of the contract.

Since a lease is a bilateral agreement, both parties have rights and obligations under the lease. The landlord grants the tenant the right to occupy the premises and use them for purposes stated in the lease. In return, the landlord retains the right to receive payment for the use of the premises as well as a reversionary right to retake possession after the lease term has expired. The lessor's interest in leased property is called a *leased fee estate plus reversionary right*.

■ RESIDENTIAL RENTAL AGREEMENTS ACT

In North Carolina, residential leases and the landlord-tenant relationship are governed by the **Residential Rental Agreements Act** (NCGS §42-38 et. seq.). The primary purpose of this Act is to ensure that only habitable residential units are rented. A failure to comply with the terms of this Act has potentially serious consequences. The Act does not apply to transient quarters such as hotels or motels, nor does it apply to commercial or rent-free properties.

Obligations of Landlord and Tenant Are Mutually Dependent

The Residential Rental Agreements Act makes *the obligations of the landlord and the tenant mutually dependent*. That is, if either the landlord or the tenant fails to fulfill a duty, the other party is no longer responsible for fulfilling an equivalent duty. For example, if the landlord fails to provide the tenant with habitable premises, the tenant does not have to remain in the premises for the full lease term. Furthermore, the statutory duties of the landlord according to this Act cannot be waived or altered by lease provision or other agreement between landlord and tenant. For example, the landlord is not allowed to lease the property for reduced rent in exchange for the tenant accepting the property in an "as is" condition. If a real estate licensee is acting as an agent for a landlord, the court sees the licensee as a *landlord* under the Act.

Landlord's Statutory Duties

The Act provides that the landlord's primary duty is **implied warranty of habitability**—to supply *fit* and *habitable* premises to the tenant. This means the premises must be fit for human occupancy. The landlord must comply with current building and housing codes; make all necessary repairs to keep the premises in a habitable condition; keep all common areas safe; and maintain all electrical, plumbing, sanitary, heating, ventilating, and other facilities. The landlord must also provide operable smoke detectors, installing and maintaining in accordance with established standards. The landlord must repair smoke detectors within 15 days of receiving notice of necessary repairs.

If the landlord fails to keep the premises fit, the tenant can invoke the protection of the common-law doctrine of **constructive eviction**. This doctrine gives the tenant the right, in effect, to cancel the remainder of the lease and vacate the premises without penalties. The tenant gives the landlord notice that the premises are uninhabitable. If the situation is not corrected within a reasonable time, the tenant can leave the premises and is no longer responsible for paying future rent. In effect, the tenant evicts himself or herself by building a case to prove the landlord's breach of the bilateral lease agreement. Of course, the tenant is responsible for paying rent up to and including the last day of occupancy. Tenant is unilaterally forbidden to withhold rent while in possession of the unit. The tenant security deposit, if any, is to be returned to the tenant.

Law of Negligence

Tenants, or their guests, are sometimes injured on leased property, and the question arises as to whether the landlord can be held accountable for those injuries. The common **law of negligence** holds that the landlord is liable for injuries that occur in common areas—hallways, stairways, elevators, sidewalks, and parking lots—when the landlord has negligently failed to maintain safe conditions in those areas. Therefore, if a tenant or guest has the right to be on the premises and is injured because of the landlord's failure to maintain the common areas, the injured party may be able to recover damages from the landlord.

However, if the injury occurs in the area exclusively occupied by the tenant—such as an apartment or office space—the results are different. Generally, the landlord is not liable for injuries that occur within the leased premises. The only exception to this rule is if the landlord failed to keep the premises in a habitable condition. Under the Residential Rental Agreements Act, the fact that the landlord failed to maintain the leased premises in a fit and habitable condition can be presented in court as evidence of the landlord's negligence. The negligence could mean that the landlord would be held liable for the injury.

With the increase in crime, the landlord's liability for criminal acts that occur on leased premises or the common areas of rental property has become an issue. In North Carolina, a landlord is not generally liable for criminal acts committed against tenants unless the landlord knew or should have known of a dangerous situation and did nothing to protect the tenants. For instance, if a rental property is in a high crime area and the landlord knows that the security system is grossly inadequate, the landlord may be liable if a tenant is injured in a mugging in a building hallway.

Tenant's Statutory Duties

The Act states that the tenant's primary duty is to *maintain the dwelling unit*. This means the tenant must keep the occupied premises clean and safe, dispose of all garbage and other waste, keep the plumbing fixtures clean, comply with the obligations imposed on tenants by current housing and building codes, replace batteries in smoke detectors as needed during the tenancy, refrain from deliberately or negligently damaging the premises, and take responsibility for any damage that does occur.

Tenant Prohibited from Unilaterally Withholding Rent

Under the Residential Rental Agreements Act, tenants do not have the right to withhold rent before they obtain a court order giving them that right. Thus, even when the tenant has a legitimate complaint against the landlord, the tenant cannot decide to withhold all or a portion of the rent as a remedy. Note that this provision does not alter the tenant's right to vacate the premises and stop paying future rent on the basis of constructive eviction. A tenant who withholds the rent but retains possession of the property has violated the rental agreement, giving the landlord the right to evict.

IN PRACTICE

Despite several written requests from the tenant, the landlord has not had the heating system in the tenant's unit repaired. Tired of waiting on the landlord, the tenant hires a HVAC repairperson to fix the unit and pays for the service call himself. The tenant then deducts the cost of the repair from the rent check for that month. This might be considered *withholding rent* because the entire rent payment was not submitted. Furthermore, a tenant does not have the right to make changes or repairs to the landlord's property without the landlord's permission (preferably in writing).

Residential Eviction Remedies

The only possible legal eviction remedy is that provided for by statute through the court system; in other words, a landlord cannot use self-help eviction remedies, no matter how peaceful. For example, the landlord cannot change the locks on the doors to prevent the tenant from entering the premises, cut off the tenant's utilities, or seize the tenant's possessions. Instead, the landlord must bring an eviction action in court before a magistrate. A state statute (NCGS §42-21.1) sets forth public policy against the **self-help eviction** procedure and replaces it with a procedure called **summary ejectment**. This hearing before a magistrate in small claims court is the only legal way a landlord can evict a tenant. The law (NCGS §42-25.7) also provides direction on the appropriate disposal of an evicted tenant's abandoned personal property. Expedited eviction is possible when the tenant, their family member, or guest has engaged in criminal activity in the leased unit; landlord should seek legal assistance before filing for expedited eviction.

Retaliatory Eviction Prohibited

An important provision of this Act is known as the *doctrine of retaliatory eviction*. Under the **retaliatory eviction** provision (NCGS §42-37), a tenant cannot be evicted because the tenant has asserted a legal right against the landlord. Therefore, a landlord cannot evict a tenant who, in good faith, requests that the landlord make required repairs, exercises legal rights against the landlord, becomes involved in a tenants' rights association, or complains to a government entity about a landlord's violation of landlord-tenant law. If the landlord tries to evict a tenant within 12 months after the tenant tried to assert a protected legal right, the tenant can use this doctrine as a defense in the eviction action. The doctrine does not require the landlord to renew the lease.

■ TENANT SECURITY DEPOSIT ACT

In North Carolina, the **Tenant Security Deposit Act** (NCGS §42-50 et. seq.) regulates the amount of money that can be required as a **security deposit** and what the landlord can do with that deposit. The amount of the security deposit depends on the term of the tenancy. The maximum amount of security deposit is the equivalent of

- two weeks' rent if the tenancy is from week to week,
- one and one-half months' rent if the tenancy is from month to month, and
- two months' rent if the tenancy is longer than month to month.

The landlord may do one of two things with the security deposit: (1) the security deposit can be placed in a trust account with an insured North Carolina bank or savings institution or (2) the landlord can obtain a bond as a guarantee for the deposit. The landlord must tell the tenant either the name of the bank or savings institution or the name of the bonding company. (*If a real estate agent is handling the deposit, the agent has only one option: the security deposit must be deposited into a trust account* [see NCREC Rule A.0107].)

The Tenant Security Deposit Act provides that a security deposit on a residential unit may be used only to reimburse the landlord for nonpayment of rent, damage to the premises (other than "ordinary wear and tear"), nonfulfillment of the rental period, unpaid bills that may create a lien on the property due to the tenant's occupancy, cost of removing and storing tenant's property, costs of re-renting after a breach, or court costs in connection with an eviction action. If a tenant breaches the lease and abandons the property, the landlord is obligated to diligently attempt to find a new tenant as soon as possible. If the property is re-rented, the landlord can withhold only the part of the security deposit that covers the *lost* rent plus costs of re-renting. The remainder of the deposit must be returned to the breaching tenant. If the security deposit does not entirely cover the rent lost due to breach, the landlord may retain the entire deposit and employ other legal methods to recoup the loss of rent.

Upon the termination of the lease, the landlord or his agent must account for the tenant security deposit to the tenant in writing within 30 days. An itemized account of any permitted deductions from the deposit with the return of any unused money must be sent to the last known address of the tenant.

If pets are allowed on the premises, the landlord is allowed to charge a separate, reasonable pet fee that can be nonrefundable. If the animal is a service animal, such as a Seeing Eye dog, it would not be regarded as a *pet* and a pet fee would *not* be allowed because a service animal is considered to be an extension of the handicapped person.

Damages to the Premises

Even though the tenant security deposit may be retained in whole or in part to pay for damages to the premises, the landlord cannot use the deposit to pay for damages that may be classified under the broad term *ordinary wear and tear*. Real estate law in North Carolina does not define what may constitute ordinary wear and tear versus what may constitute actual damages to the premises. NCREC has published consumer information on tenant security deposits that provides excellent guidance to landlords, property managers, and tenants. Common examples of *ordinary wear and tear* are

- dirty carpet or carpet worn from long use;
- peeling, faded, and cracked paint;
- dirty walls and windows;
- leaking plumbing and worn plumbing fixtures; and
- frayed curtains and broken blind strings.

Examples of other damages for which use of the deposit is permitted are

- large holes in the walls;
- crayon marks;
- broken plumbing fixtures, windows, and counter tops;
- burned places and stains on carpeting;
- bizarre or unauthorized paint colors;
- appliances requiring extraordinary cleaning due to excessive filth; and
- extraordinary cleaning of the unit due to excessive filth.

■ CONSTITUTIONAL RIGHTS OF TENANTS IN PUBLIC HOUSING

The tenants of government-subsidized low-income housing (sometimes called "Section 8 Housing") have some additional rights. These tenants have an entitlement to continued occupancy and cannot be evicted unless there is *good cause*. There must be a finding of fault on the tenant's part, not merely circumstances that are beyond the tenant's control (such as loss of a job). Tenants are entitled to due process. The landlord must maintain property in habitable condition or risk being suspended from future program participation.

■ NORTH CAROLINA VACATION RENTAL ACT

The **North Carolina Vacation Rental Act** (NCGS §42A) went into effect January 1, 2000, and is modeled after the Residential Rental Agreement Act. The statute establishes uniform rules for landlords, tenants, and their agents involved in the handling of short-term rentals under 90 days in length where the tenant has a primary residence elsewhere. The Act applies to all landlords (using an agent or not) who rent residential property for the purposes of vacation, recreation, or leisure. It is important to note that a vacation rental property manager, like other types of property managers for others, must be a licensed real estate broker. A licensee may pay a *referral fee* to an unlicensed travel agent (*defined in the statute*) for procuring a tenant *only for vacation rentals, according to certain guidelines found in NCREC Rule A.0109(e), and* provided that no other acts of real estate brokerage requiring a license are performed by the travel agent (motels, hotels, etc., are exempt). The Vacation Rental Act authorizes

- all rental agreements to be in writing;
- the landlord to collect payments in advance of the tenancy, but monies must be placed in an escrow account (no later than three banking days after receipt of these payments;

- the landlord to refund tenant's payments if fit and habitable premises cannot be provided;
- regulations for the use of monies collected as security deposits;
- the new owner to take title subject to rentals for the next 180 days, if the property is sold;
- an expedited eviction procedure;
- the landlord to provide tenants with fit premises and keep property repaired and safe;
- the tenants to maintain the property and not damage the premises; and
- upon compliance, the tenants to be given a refund of their rent if tenants are ordered by authorities to evacuate, unless the tenants had been offered evacuation insurance to cover the potential risk.

■ OTHER LANDLORD/TENANT RULES

Landlords must comply with federal and state fair housing laws and must not discriminate unlawfully. (Fair housing rights are discussed in Chapter 20.) Violation of the Residential Rental Agreements Act may also constitute a violation of the Unfair and Deceptive Business or Trade Practices Act that can result in the payment of treble damages if found guilty. NCREC also can discipline a licensee for violation of these laws. Landlords must comply with *sexual harassment statutes*, which prohibit unsolicited overt demands for sexual favors when negotiating a lease or determining rights under a lease. Landlords also must comply with the Americans with Disabilities Act (see Chapter 20).

■ LEASEHOLD (NONFREEHOLD) ESTATES

When a landowner leases real estate to a tenant, the tenant's right to occupy the land for the duration of the lease is called a **leasehold estate**. A leasehold estate is an estate in land that is generally considered personal property, because no ownership of the real property has changed hands.

In the discussion of interests and estates in Chapter 2, freehold estates were differentiated from leasehold estates. Just as there are several types of freehold (ownership) estates, there are also various leasehold estates. The four most important are *estate for years, estate from period to period, estate at will,* and *estate at sufferance* (see Table 11.1). The major difference between the various leasehold estates is the way each is terminated. One parcel of property can be held in both a nonfreehold and freehold estate at the same time.

Estate for Years (Tenancy for Years)

Estate for years = Any definite period.

A leasehold estate that continues for a *definite period of time*, whether for years, months, weeks, or even days, is an **estate for years.** An estate for years always has a specific starting and ending time, and it may be for a term of less than one year. It automatically terminates at the end of the lease period. No notice is required to terminate the lease at the end of the lease period. When the lease period expires, the lessee is required to vacate the premises and surrender possession to the lessor. A lease for years may be terminated prior to the expiration date by the mutual consent of both parties, but otherwise neither party may terminate

TABLE 11.1	Type of Estate	Distinguishing Characteristics
Leasehold Estates	Estate for years	Automatic termination after a definite period of time
	Estate from period to period	Automatic renewal after a definite initial period, until terminated by either party with required notice
	Estate at will	Terminated by either party at any time with no required notice
	Estate at sufferance	Landlord must evict illegal holdover tenant

without showing that the lease agreement has been breached. As is characteristic of all leases, an estate for years gives the lessee the right to occupy and use the leased property—subject, of course, to the terms and covenants contained in the lease agreement itself.

Estate from Period to Period (Periodic Tenancy)

An **estate from period to period,** or a **periodic tenancy**, is created when the landlord and tenant enter into an agreement that continues for a specific period, *being automatically renewed for an indefinite time without a specific ending date.* Rent is payable at definite intervals. Such a tenancy is generally created by agreement or operation of law to run for a certain amount of time, such as week-to-week, month-to-month, or year-to-year. A typical residential lease sets up a periodic tenancy. The agreement is automatically renewed for similar succeeding periods until one of the parties gives notice to terminate. In effect, the payment and acceptance of rent extend the lease for another period. In North Carolina, the minimum notice-of-termination periods are as follows:

- For a week-to-week tenancy, the notice period is two days.
- For a month-to-month tenancy, the notice period is seven days.
- For a year-to-year tenancy, the notice period is one month.

Estate from period to period = Indefinite term; automatically renews.

A month-to-month tenancy generally is created when a tenant takes possession with no definite termination date and pays rent monthly. This is usually a valid agreement.

IN PRACTICE

A common residential apartment lease is originally for the period of one year and then converts to a month-to-month lease. As long as the tenant makes the rent payment on time and the landlord accepts the payment, the lease is extended for another monthly period. With a thirty-day notice, either the landlord or the tenant can terminate this lease.

A tenancy from period to period also may be created when a tenant with an estate for years remains in possession, or holds over, after the expiration of the lease term. If no new lease agreement has been made, the landlord may evict the tenant or treat the **holdover tenant** as being under a periodic tenancy. Acceptance of rent is usually considered conclusive proof of the landlord's acquiescence in a periodic tenancy.

Estate at Will

An estate that gives the tenant *the right to possess property with the consent of the landlord for a term of unspecified or uncertain duration* is an **estate at will,** or a tenancy at will. It may be created by express agreement or by operation of law, and during its existence the tenant has all the rights and obligations of a lessor/lessee relationship.

Estate at will = Indefinite term; possession with landlord's consent.	■ **FOR EXAMPLE** At the end of a lease period, a landlord informs a tenant that in a few months the city is going to demolish the apartment building to make way for an expressway. The landlord gives the tenant the option to occupy the premises until demolition begins. If the tenant agrees to stay, a tenancy at will is created.

An estate at will can be terminated at any time, *at the will* of either party. All that is required is for one party to declare that the tenancy is over. No prior notice is required. However, if the tenancy at will is for agricultural land and the tenant has planted crops, the tenant is entitled to return to the premises to harvest those crops under the *doctrine of emblements*.

Estate at Sufferance

An **estate at sufferance,** or a *tenancy at sufferance*, arises when a tenant who lawfully came into possession of real property continues, after the tenant's rights have expired, to hold possession of the premises *without the consent of the landlord.* An example of an estate at sufferance is when a tenant for years *fails to surrender* possession at the expiration of the lease. The *holdover tenant* has no rights in the property, and the landowner can have him or her evicted at any time, without advance notice. This is not a trespass situation because the tenant originally took possession with the consent of the lessor. This is the lowest estate in real estate.

Estate at sufferance = Tenant's previously lawful possession continued without landlord's consent.

If a tenant has an estate at will or an estate at sufferance and pays the landlord rent monies that the landlord accepts, a periodic tenancy is re-created. If the landlord wishes to end the tenant's estate, consideration cannot be accepted under either the estate at will or the estate at sufferance.

■ TYPES OF LEASES

The manner in which rent is determined indicates the type of lease that is in force (see Table 11.2).

Fixed Rental Lease

In a **fixed rental lease,** the tenant's obligation is to pay a *fixed rental amount*, and the landlord pays all taxes, insurance premiums, mortgage payments, repair costs, and the like connected with the property (usually called *property charges*). This type of lease is most often used for residential rentals and is sometimes called a flat or **gross lease.**

Percentage Lease (Retail Lease)

A **percentage lease** provides for rental based on a *percentage of the gross or net income* received by a tenant doing business on the leased property. This type of lease is usually used in the rental of retail business locations. The percentage lease usually provides for a smaller than normal fixed rental fee (base rent) plus a percentage of that portion of the tenant's gross or net business income that exceeds a stated minimum.

TABLE 11.2   **Characteristics of Lease Types**

Lease Type	Generally Used for	Lease Characteristics
Fixed rental lease	Residential leases	Tenant pays a fixed amount of rent but none of the property charges
Percentage lease	Commercial leases	Tenant pays a percentage of the gross or net income as rent
Net lease	Commercial leases	Tenant pays rent plus all or some of the property charges
Graduated lease	Commercial leases	Tenant pays rent, which increases at predetermined dates
Ground lease	Commercial leases	Tenant typically pays rent on land and builds on it

■ **FOR EXAMPLE** A lease might provide for a fixed base monthly rental of $1,500, with a further agreement that the tenant pays an additional amount each month equivalent to 4 percent of all gross sales in excess of $30,000. The percentage charged in such leases varies widely with the nature of the business and is negotiable between landlord and tenant. A tenant's bargaining power is determined by the volume of business. Percentages also vary with the location of the property and general economic conditions.

MATH CONCEPTS

CALCULATING PERCENTAGE LEASE RENTS

Percentage leases usually call for a fixed base monthly rent plus a percentage of gross sales income exceeding a stated monthly or annual amount. For example, a lease might require minimum rent of $1,300 per month plus 5% of the annual sales of the business that exceed $160,000. On an annual sales volume of $250,000, the annual rent would be calculated as follows:

$1,300 base rent per month × 12 months = $15,600

$250,000 − $160,000 = $90,000 subject to percentage rent

$90,000 × .05 (5%) = $4,500

$15,600 base rent + $4,500 percentage rent = $20,100 total annual rent

Net Lease

A **net lease** provides that, in addition to the rent, *the tenant pays all or some of the property charges such as maintenance, property taxes, and insurance.* This type of lease is sometimes called a *triple net lease* if the tenant pays *all* of the property charges. Commercial agents frequently referred to these charges as TICAM (**t**axes, **i**nsurance, and **c**ommon **a**rea **m**aintenance). The monthly rental paid to the landlord is in addition to these charges and is net income for the landlord after operating costs have been paid. Leases for entire commercial or industrial buildings and the land on which they are located, ground leases, and long-term leases are frequently net leases.

Graduated Lease

A **graduated lease** provides for *increases in rent to occur at set future dates.* Graduated leases are often used in the rental of office space for multiple-year terms. Sometimes called a step-up lease.

■ **FOR EXAMPLE** A three-year office lease may provide for the rent to be $1,000 a month for the first year, $1,200 a month for the second year, and $1,400 a month for the third year.

Index Lease

An **index lease** allows *rent to be increased or decreased periodically,* based on changes in a stipulated index, such as the government cost-of-living index or some other named index.

Ground Lease

When a landowner leases land to a tenant who agrees to *erect a building* on the land, the lease is usually referred to as a **ground lease.** Ground leases usually involve separate ownership of land and building. Such a lease must be for a long enough term to make the transaction desirable to the tenant investing in the building. These leases are generally net leases that require the lessee to pay rent as well as real estate taxes, insurance, upkeep, and repairs. Ground leases often run for terms of 99 years or longer. Such leases should be very clear about ownership of the improvements on the land at the end of the lease.

Oil and Mineral Lease

When oil companies lease land to explore for oil, gas, and other minerals, a special lease agreement must be negotiated. Usually, the landowner receives a cash payment for executing the lease. If minerals are found, the property owner usually receives a portion of the value of the minerals as a royalty. The North Carolina Statute of Frauds states that any mineral lease, regardless of duration, must be in writing to be enforceable.

Full-Service Lease

Full-service leases are commercial leases that are often used in large office or multi-tenant buildings such as shopping centers where the tenants share in overall operating expenses for the common areas and the building(s). Under a full-service lease, the landlord will provide most or all services related to the lease, such as utilities, cleaning services, grounds maintenance, etc. Usually rent is paid as a base amount plus a prorated share of the complex's operating expenses.

■ LEASE PROVISIONS

Most leases are complex documents that should be carefully prepared, and both landlords and tenants should not hesitate to seek legal advice if they have questions about the application of certain provisions. Real estate agents are allowed only to fill in the blanks in preprinted forms and it is critically important that a real estate agent use a form appropriate to the specific rental situation. Only a form drafted specifically by an attorney and/or approved forms promulgated by reputable trade organizations should be utilized plus a lawyer should prepare any additional clauses inserted into a standard lease.

Essential Provisions for a Valid Lease

The requirements for a valid lease are basically the same as those for any other contract. Generally, the four essentials of a valid lease are as follows:

> **Four Essentials of a Valid Lease**
> 1. Mutual agreement
> 2. Consideration
> 3. Capacity to contract
> 4. Legal objectives

1. *Mutual agreement.* The parties must reach a mutual agreement on all material terms of the contract (i.e., time of possession, amount of rent, due date for rent, etc.), usually accomplished by means of offer and acceptance.
2. *Consideration.* All leases, being contracts, must be supported by valid consideration. In the leasing of real estate, rent is the normal consideration granted for the right to occupy the leased premises.
3. *Capacity to contract.* The parties must have the legal capacity to contract. That is, they must be of sound mind, sober, and of legal age.
4. *Legal objectives.* The objectives of the lease must be legal.

When the statute of frauds applies (lease over three years from the making thereof), an oral lease is considered to be unenforceable. A description of the leased premises should be stated clearly. If the lease covers land, the legal description of the real estate should be used. If the lease is for part of a building, such as office space or an apartment, that part of the property should be described clearly and carefully. If supplemental space is to be included, the lease should clearly identify it.

Common Major Provisions

Many other provisions are commonly found in lease agreements. Although the attorneys of the landlord and/or the tenant usually draft commercial leases to satisfy the unique requirements of the individual leasing situation, many of the following provisions will still be included. A copy of North Carolina's Association of REALTORS® Residential Rental Contract (Form 410-T) is shown in Appendix D, Form 17.

Tenant's use of premises.   A lessor may restrict a lessee's use of the premises through provisions included in the lease. This is especially important in leases for stores or commercial space. For example, a lease may provide that the leased premises are to be used *only* for the purpose of a real estate office *and for no other purpose*. Tenant uses that could result in environmental concerns are addressed below. In the absence of such limitations, a lessee may use the premises for any lawful purpose. The tenant may also impose use restrictions in the lease, such as the lease being subject to rezoning approval for specific tenant use. The tenant may request use exclusivity, such as being the only restaurant in a small shopping center.

Environmental concerns.   Industrial leases will frequently restrict or forbid the production, use, discharge, and/or storage of hazardous materials on the property due to environmental concerns. Since some state and federal regulations will hold the landowner liable for environmental contamination even if they did not create the problem, it is vital to contractually agree to the handling or disposal of any allowed contaminants. Lease provisions for periodic inspection of compliance with governmental regulations for the handling of hazardous materials would be appropriate. Lessee should conduct a thorough environmental evaluation of the site before signing any lease that would make them liable for all environmental clean-up expenses upon termination of the lease since contamination from a previous use might already exist.

Fixtures.   Neither the landlord nor the tenant is required to make any improvements to the leased property. In the absence of an agreement to the contrary, the tenant may make improvements with the landlord's express permission. Any such alterations generally become the property of the landlord; that is, they become fixtures. However, as discussed in Chapter 2, a tenant may be given the right by the terms of the lease to install trade fixtures. It is customary to stipulate that such trade fixtures may be removed by the tenant before the lease expires, provided the tenant restores the premises to pre-lease condition, normal wear and tear excluded.

Repairs (nonresidential property).   Unlike the landlord obligations under the Residential Rental Agreement Act, if the leased property is nonresidential and no lease provision exists to the contrary, landlords are generally not obligated to make any repairs to leased premises. Nonresidential tenants are generally deemed to have accepted the property with no implied promise that the premises are safe or suitable for the use intended. Landlords may be responsible for repairing *hidden*, or *latent, defects*, since a diligent inspection by the prospective tenant would not have revealed the defect. Tenants typically are required to make ordinary repairs or be held liable for *waste* of the property. Generally the tenant is required to return the premises in the same condition in which they were received, with allowance for ordinary use.

Upfitting improvements (commercial leases).   A commercial landlord will usually provide for the initial customization of leased space for a new tenant. The tenant is frequently allowed, within cost parameters, to specify customizing preferences, such as wall and floor covering selection, location of interior walls, and placement of doors. If the tenant wants improvements that exceed the *upfit allowance*, the tenant usually negotiates their inclusion in the rent or pays for the excess expense. Occasionally, in an effort to retain a desirable tenant, the landlord may offer upfitting improvements to renovate the tenant's current space.

Assignment and subleases.   The lessee may assign or sublease the lease if the lease terms do not prohibit it. Most leases prohibit the lessee from assigning or subletting without the lessor's written consent. The lessor, therefore, retains control over the occupancy of the leased premises but must not unreasonably withhold consent. With an *assignment*, a tenant transfers all leasehold interests, which include both the entire term of the lease and all premiums. One who transfers less than all of the leasehold interests by leasing them to a new tenant **subleases** and retains a reversionary interest to re-enter the property prior to the end of the original lease period. In effect, a sublease is the making of a new lease, wherein the original lessee (tenant) becomes a sublessor and the new tenant becomes a sublessee.

In most cases, the sublease or assignment, of a lease does not relieve the original lessee of the obligation to make rental payments unless the landlord agrees to waive such liability. When a lease is assigned, the original tenant retains *secondary liability* for paying the rent unless the original tenant is granted a **novation** by the landlord releasing the lessee from further liability. When a lease is sublet, the original tenant retains *primary liability* for paying the rent. The sublessor's (original lessee's) interest in the real estate is known as a **sandwich lease**.

Term of the lease and lease renewal.   The term of a lease is the period for which the lease will be in effect, and it should be set out precisely. The date of the beginning of the term and the date of its ending should be noted, together with a statement of the total period of the lease; for example, "for a term of three years beginning December 1, 2009, and ending November 30, 2012."

Unless specifically provided for in the lease, a lessee typically has no right to renew a lease. A renewal clause should stipulate when the lessee must notify the lessor that the lease will be renewed, how the lessor must be notified, and the length of the new lease period. A provision permitting automatic renewals should address timely termination notification requirements by either party.

Default. As with all well-written contracts, a provision should address legal remedies in the case of default by either party. The most common examples of default are by the lessee through nonpayment of rent, damage to the property, or abandonment of the property. Although the landlord can be in default, it is less likely. The remedies for default are limited to the conditions of the lease or applicable statutes.

Options to purchase or first right of refusal. Many leases contain an option that grants the lessee the right to purchase the leased premises at the end of the lease; this provision is particularly likely in a ground lease where the tenant has significantly improved the landlord's property. Usually, the price of the property is agreed to in advance, but sometimes the parties agree to abide by an estimate of value compiled by a selected group of appraisers done at the time of the purchase. Every option should state the purchase price or the exact method used to determine the purchase price. Instead of an option to purchase, a lease may contain a *right of first refusal* (see Chapter 10).

Landlord's right to enter and the covenant of quiet enjoyment. Once a valid lease has been executed, the lessor, as the owner of the real estate, is usually bound by the **covenant of quiet enjoyment** that is implied by law. Under this covenant, the lessor guarantees that the lessee may take possession of the leased premises and that no one, including the landlord, will interfere with the tenant's possession or use of the property. This covenant also means that the tenant will not be affected by any defects in the landlord's title. (This right comes from the *privity of estate*.)

The landlord has no right to enter the leased premises during the lease term unless the lease specifically gives the landlord or their agent this right (through *privity of contract*). Usually, the landlord retains the right to enter to inspect the property, to make necessary repairs, to show the property to potential tenants, and in case of an emergency. Most leases provide that the landlord or their agent must give the tenant a certain amount of notice before entering the premises.

Termination of Leases

As with any contract, a lease is discharged when the contract terminates. Termination can occur when all parties have fully performed their obligations under the agreement. The landlord and tenant may mutually agree to cancel the lease, but if the tenant simply abandons the property, the tenant remains liable for the terms of the lease—including the payment of rent. Leases may be terminated in the following ways:

- The parties to a lease may mutually agree to cancel the lease.
- When the lease term expires, the lease is terminated automatically.
- A tenancy may be terminated by operation of law, as in a bankruptcy or condemnation proceeding.
- If one of the parties fails to perform a material obligation, such as the tenant fails to pay rent or the landlord fails to maintain habitable condition, the other party can terminate the lease.

If the tenant fails to pay rent, the landlord can evict the tenant. If the tenant refuses to leave the premises voluntarily, the landlord must bring an eviction action in court (summary ejectment) to have the tenant removed. If the landlord fails to maintain the premises in habitable condition, the tenant is considered *constructively evicted* and may move out and stop paying future rent.

Note that when the owner of leased property dies or the property is sold, *the lease does not terminate*. The heirs of a deceased landlord are bound by the terms of existing valid leases. In addition, if a landlord conveys leased real estate, the new landlord takes the property subject to the rights of the tenants.

Statute of Frauds and Recordation

Any lease that lasts for *more than three years from the date of execution* must be in writing and signed by the landlord and the tenant to comply with the North Carolina Statute of Frauds. For instance, a lease signed on January 1, 2009, and terminating on December 31, 2009, does not have to be in writing. Generally, oral leases for three years or less are enforceable. But a lease signed on January 1, 2009, and terminating on January 31, 2012, does have to be in writing to be enforceable.

Under the Conner Act, leases required to be in writing under the North Carolina Statute of Frauds must be recorded to be enforceable against third parties. If the lease is not recorded and a third party buys the property, that person is not required to honor the terms of the lease. Failure to observe the statutory requirements in recording a lease does not in any way affect its validity between the parties, just third parties.

IN PRACTICE   Even though an oral lease may be enforceable, such as a lease for one year commencing the day of agreement, it is always better practice to put lease agreements in writing and to have the writing signed by all parties to the agreement. The lease document should be as inclusive as possible, for reasons that will become apparent from reading this chapter.

■ RELATED WEB SITES

National Association of Independent Landlords: *http://nail-usa.com*
National Landlord Tenant Guide: *www.rentlaw.com*
North Carolina General Assembly (search by name of Act):
    www.ncga.state.nc.us/gascripts/statutes/Statutes

■ SUMMARY

A lease is an agreement that grants one person the right to use the property of another for a certain period in return for consideration called rent. The lease agreement is a combination of a conveyance creating a leasehold interest in the property and a contract outlining the rights and obligations of the landlord and the tenant.

The primary intent of the Residential Rental Agreement Act is to provide habitable residential units. The obligations of the landlord and the tenant under this Act are mutually dependent and cannot be waived. The Act allows for the right of constructive eviction by the tenant if the landlord violates his duties and prohibits retaliatory eviction on the part of the landlord. Tenant is prohibited from withholding rent while in possession of the landlord's property. Any residential lease that violates the Residential Rental Agreements Act is void. If the tenant violates their duties under the Act, the landlord can evict them through summary ejectment. The landlord can be held liable for injuries suffered in the common areas of the rental property under the law of negligence if the landlord did not maintain the property in good, safe condition.

Tenant Security Deposit Act regulates the amount and use of money that can be required as a security deposit for rental property and how the landlord holds that deposit. The maximum amount of the deposit depends on the term of the tenancy; the equivalent of two months' rent is the most that can ever be charged. The landlord, or the property manager, must return the deposit or provide to the tenant a detailed accounting of the deposit within 30 days of termination of a lease.

The North Carolina Vacation Rental Act applies to residential properties leased for less than 90 days for recreation or leisure purposes and the tenant has a primary residence elsewhere. The Act requires maintained habitability of the rental units and allows for expedited evictions, if necessary. Purchaser of a vacation rental property must honor any reservations for the next 180 days that are in place at the time of the purchase.

A leasehold estate that runs for a definite period of time creates an estate for years that terminates automatically; one that runs for an indefinite number of terms creates a periodic estate (year-to-year, month-to-month) that needs notice to terminate. An estate at will runs for a period of time established by the tenant and landlord, and it needs no notice for termination. An estate at sufferance is possession by a holdover tenant without the consent of the landlord, and it will probably necessitate eviction proceedings. The requirements of a valid lease include mutual assent, consideration, legal capacity to contract, and legal objectives. The Statute of Frauds generally requires that any lease of more than three years from the date of its making must be in writing, while the Conner Act requires those same leases to be recorded for protection from third parties. Most leases also include clauses relating to rights and obligations of the landlord and tenant such as the use of the premises, provision for subletting and assignment, improvements and repairs, and the landlord's right to enter the premises.

Leases may be terminated by the expiration of the lease period, the mutual agreement of the parties, or a breach of the lease by either landlord or tenant. It is important to note that, in most cases, neither the death of the landlord nor the landlord's sale of the rental property terminates a lease.

The several basic types of leases include net leases, gross leases, graduated leases, index leases, and percentage leases. These leases are classified according to the method used in determining the rental rate of the property. The most common residential lease is a gross fixed rent lease. Percentage leases are commonly used in retail lease situations.

QUESTIONS

1. If a lease is for longer than three years in duration, the lease must be recorded to be
   I. valid between the parties.
   II. enforceable against third parties.
      a. I only
      b. II only
      c. Both I and II
      d. Neither I nor II

2. A landlord may enter leased premises to make repairs if the landlord
   a. knocks first to give notice of intent to enter.
   b. is given this right in the lease.
   c. gives 48 hours notice of intent to enter.
   d. gives written notice of intent to enter 24 hours in advance.

3. For the tenant to terminate a tenancy from month to month, according to standard protocol, the tenant
   a. must give notice to the landlord prior to termination.
   b. need not give notice to the landlord about vacating the leased premises.
   c. must give 45 days' notice to the landlord prior to termination.
   d. must ask for the security deposit before vacating the leased premises.

4. A lease calls for a base rent of $1,200 per month plus 4 percent of the annual gross business exceeding $150,000. This is what type of lease?
   a. Gross
   b. Graduated
   c. Percentage
   d. Net

5. The requirements of a valid lease include
   a. mutual assent.
   b. consideration.
   c. capacity to contract.
   d. all of the above.

6. An agreement in which the tenant pays a fixed rent and the landlord pays all taxes, insurance, and maintenance on the property is a
   a. net lease.
   b. gross lease.
   c. index lease.
   d. ground lease.

7. A percentage lease provides for a
   a. long-term rental of a certain percentage of the space in a building.
   b. definite monthly rent not to exceed a stated percentage of the building's value.
   c. definite monthly rent plus a percentage of the tenant's gross receipts in excess of a certain amount.
   d. monthly graduated rent amount not to exceed a stated percentage of the original rent.

8. A tenant who transfers the remaining term of a lease to a third party is
   a. a sublessee in a sandwich lease.
   b. assigning the lease.
   c. relieved of any further obligation under the lease.
   d. giving the third party a gross lease.

9. If a tenant complains to the authorities about a housing code violation in the apartment building that affects her health, the landlord may
   I. reduce the rent as the remedy.
   II. evict the tenant for filing a compliant.
      a. I only
      b. II only
      c. Both I and II
      d. Neither I nor II

10. A property owner sells his mountain chalet that he has been renting to vacationing ski fanatics for years. At the time of the sale, there are already 20 different week-long reservations in place for the upcoming ski season that starts in a couple of months. The purchaser of the chalet

    a. must honor any of the reservations that occur within the next six months.
    b. does not have to honor any of the reservations since they are with the old owner.
    c. must honor all reservations in place at the time of closing regardless of when they occur.
    d. does not have to honor any reservations as long as a 30-day advance written notice is given to the tenant.

11. If a landlord fails to repair the broken heating system in a timely manner, the tenant may

    a. stay in the premises and withhold rent until the repair is complete.
    b. personally pay for the repair and deduct the expense from the monthly rent.
    c. withhold rent and deposit it in an escrow account at a bank until the repair is complete.
    d. leave the premises and stop paying rent.

12. The Residential Rental Agreement Act requires the landlord to keep the

    I. apartment building in habitable condition.
    II. common areas in the rental property in safe condition.
        a. I only
        b. II only
        c. Both I and II
        d. Neither I nor II

13. A ground lease is usually

    a. short term.
    b. for 5 to 10 years.
    c. for 99 years.
    d. automatically renewable.

14. The rental amount in an index lease

    I. will adjust based on the appraiser's estimate of current rent value.
    II. is allowed to increase or decrease periodically.
        a. I only
        b. II only
        c. Both I and II
        d. Neither I nor II

15. If a lessor sells the leased premises, the new owner

    a. can negotiate new rental payments with the tenants if the leases were recorded.
    b. takes the property subject to the terms of the tenants' leases.
    c. must wait to take title until all the leases expire.
    d. can change any of the lease terms after a two-month waiting period.

16. With a month-to-month tenancy, the landlord can require a maximum security deposit equal to

    a. seven days' rent.
    b. two weeks' rent.
    c. one and one-half months' rent.
    d. two months' rent.

17. If a residential tenant breaches the lease by not paying rent, the landlord may

    a. change the locks and prevent the tenant from entering the premises.
    b. turn off the tenant's utilities until rent is paid.
    c. file a summary ejectment with the courts.
    d. seize and sell the tenant's possessions to raise the rent money.

18. Constructive eviction occurs when the

    a. landlord forcibly removes the tenant from the premises after obtaining a court order.
    b. tenant moves out because the landlord fails to keep the premises in habitable condition.
    c. tenant fails to pay rent on time and the landlord changes the locks.
    d. landlord retaliates against the tenant for complaining to a state authority.

19. An estate for years
    a. renews itself automatically unless notice to terminate is given.
    b. terminates automatically at the expiration of the lease term.
    c. requires no notice to terminate.
    d. cannot be renewed.

20. An estate at sufferance usually terminates
    a. only with prior notice.
    b. on its second automatic renewal.
    c. through a summary ejectment.
    d. automatically on its expiration date.

21. Dan's landlord has sold his building to the state so that a freeway can be built. Dan's lease has expired, but the landlord is letting him remain until the time the building will be torn down. Dan is part of a
    a. holdover tenancy.
    b. first right of refusal.
    c. tenancy at sufferance.
    d. tenancy at will.

22. If the landlord of an apartment building breaches her lease with one of the tenants and the tenant's unit becomes uninhabitable, which of the following would probably result?
    a. Suit for possession
    b. Constructive eviction
    c. Tenancy at sufferance
    d. Covenant of quiet enjoyment

23. Which of the following statements about the Tenant Security Deposit Act is NOT true?
    a. A property manager may be bonded for security deposits if the bonding company is located in North Carolina.
    b. The landlord has 30 days after the end of the lease to account for the use of the deposit money and/or return the funds to the tenant.
    c. The deposit money may be used to repair holes in the walls and stains in the carpet.
    d. A landlord can charge a deposit that is the equivalent of two months' rent for a one-year lease.

24. Jody has a one-year leasehold interest in Harbor House. The interest automatically renews itself at the end of each year. Jody's interest is referred to as a tenancy
    a. for years.
    b. from period to period.
    c. at will.
    d. at sufferance.

25. Mary has assigned her apartment lease to Ben, and the landlord has agreed to the assignment. If Ben fails to pay the rent, who is liable?
    a. Ben is primarily liable; Mary is secondarily liable.
    b. Mary is primarily liable; Ben is secondarily liable.
    c. Mary is solely liable.
    d. Ben is solely liable.

26. Which event would automatically terminate a residential lease?
    a. Destruction of the property
    b. Sale of the property
    c. Failure of the tenant to pay rent
    d. Death of the lessor

27. Which transaction would best be described as involving a ground lease?
    a. A landowner agrees to let a tenant search and drill for oil on a property for 99 years.
    b. With the landowner's permission, a tenant builds a shopping center on a rented property at the tenant's own expense.
    c. A landlord charges a commercial tenant separate rent amounts for the land and buildings under a lease.
    d. A tenant pays a base amount for the property, plus a percentage of business generated income.

28. The landlord is charging a monthly base rent of $900 plus 4 percent of the tenant's annual gross sales that exceed $150,000. If the tenant's business has annual gross sales of $275,000, the total annual rent would be
    a. $ 5,000.
    b. $ 11,000.
    c. $ 15,800.
    d. $ 21,800.

12 CHAPTER

Property Management

■ **explain** the need for property management as an industry specialization, and the functions and responsibilities of property managers.

■ **identify** the basic elements of a property management agreement.

■ **calculate** earned property management fees.

■ **explain** how to budget for operating expenses.

■ **define** these *key terms*:

property management   property manager
  agreement

■ PROPERTY MANAGEMENT

The need for specialized property managers became apparent during the 1930s as lending institutions took possession of numerous foreclosed income properties. Lacking the expertise to administer these properties, they looked to the real estate industry for expert management assistance. In recent years the increased size of buildings; the technical complexities of construction, maintenance, and repair; and the trend toward absentee ownership by individual investors and investment groups have led to the expanded use of professional property managers for both residential and commercial properties. Property management has become so important that many brokerage firms maintain separate management departments staffed by carefully selected, well-trained people. A number of corporate and institutional owners of real estate have also established property management departments. Despite this trend, some real estate investors still manage their own property and therefore must acquire the knowledge and skills of a property manager. Although property owners have always had the privilege of managing their own property without the need of licensure, they cannot compensate any unlicensed friend, relative, or neighbor for assistance in the management. This includes showing the units and collecting rents. Only title-holding owners can manage their property without an active North Carolina real estate license.

In North Carolina, a property manager who is the owner's *agent* must have an active nonprovisional real estate broker's license. A property manager who is the employee of the owner is still required to have a real estate license unless the *owner* of the property is a Chapter C or Subchapter S corporation. If there is a corporate owner and the property is titled in the corporation's name, then a salaried employee without a real estate license will be allowed to manage the property.

The property manager broker can utilize the services of other licensees and/or unlicensed salaried employees with limited authority. Onsite leasing agents that show available units and collect rent payments are frequently unlicensed employees of the property manager. G.S. 93A-2(c)(6), quoted below, grants licensing exemptions if the employee does not negotiate any lease terms.

> *Any salaried person employed by a licensed real estate broker, for and on behalf of the owner of any real estate or the improvements thereon, which the licensed broker has contracted to manage for the owner, if the salaried employee is limited in his employment to: exhibiting units on the real estate to prospective tenants; providing the prospective tenants with information about the lease of the units; accepting applications for lease of the units; completing and executing preprinted form leases; and accepting security deposits and rental payments for the units only when the deposits and rental payments are made payable to the owner or the broker employed by the owner. The salaried employee shall not negotiate the amount of security deposits or rental payments and shall not negotiate leases or any rental agreements on behalf of the owner or broker.*

With the huge increase in the number of homeowner and property owner associations in recent years, there has been a commensurate increase in the demand for association management services. Although licensed property management firms manage some communities, there is currently no real estate license requirement to provide association management. Of course, if a licensee is involved in association management, they will be held to the higher level of conduct than an unlicensed manager and subject to license law.

■ FUNCTIONS OF THE PROPERTY MANAGER

In the simplest terms, a **property manager** is someone who *preserves the value of an investment property while generating income as an agent for the owner.* The agency relationship is created by the *property management contract.* The fiduciary relationship that exists between the property manager and the property owner based on the same relationship of trust that exists between a real estate broker and a seller or buyer, which was discussed in Chapter 7. A property manager usually serves the property owner as a general agent.

> A property manager's primary function is to preserve the value of an owner's investment property while generating income for the owner.

The property manager is expected to merchandise the property and control operating expenses in order to maximize income. With this expectation in mind, the property manager chooses the best possible means to carry out an agent's responsibilities and has more authority and discretion than an employee. The manager should maintain and modernize the property to preserve and enhance the owner's capital investment. The manager carries out these objectives by securing suitable tenants, collecting the rents, caring for the premises, budgeting and controlling expenses, hiring and supervising employees, keeping proper accounts, and making periodic reports to the owner. Property managers do not perform functions such as making capital improvements, reinvesting profits, paying the owner's income tax, or establishing a depreciation schedule.

Securing Management Business

In today's market, property managers may look to corporate owners, apartment and condominium associations, homeowners' associations, investment syndicates, trusts, and absentee owners as possible sources of management business. In securing business from any of these sources, word of mouth is often the best advertising. A manager who consistently demonstrates the ability to increase property income over previous levels should have no difficulty finding new business.

The Property Management Agreement

The first step in taking over the management of any property is to enter into a **property management agreement** with the owner. This agreement creates an agency relationship between the owner and the property manager. A property manager is usually considered to be a *general agent*, whereas a residential real estate broker is usually considered to be a *special agent*. As an agent, the property manager is charged with the same agency responsibilities as the listing broker—*loyalty, obedience, accounting, disclosure,* and *skill, care, and diligence* (LOADS). (Agency responsibilities are discussed at length in Chapter 7.)

Per Commission Rule A.0104, all property management agreements must be in writing from its inception. Unlike other agency agreements, the Commission rule allows property management agreements to contain an automatic renewal clause if the property owner can terminate with notice at the end of any contract period. The NCAR "Exclusive Property Management Agreement" (Form 401, Appendix D, Form 16) will be referenced to show provisions that a good agreement should include.

- *Description* of the property (Provision 1).
- *Contract period* (Provision 2) should have definite beginning and ending dates but can allow for automatic term renewal if parties have the opportunity to terminate the agreement at the end of any term period.
- *Management fee* (Provision 3). The fee can be based on a percentage of gross income or net operating income, a commission on new rentals, a fixed fee, or a combination of these. For example, the manager may get 3% of all monthly rentals collected. Both the owner and manager must ensure that the agreement is very specific as to how the management fee will be determined. If the manager will collect additional fees, such as application fees

or late payment fees, the ownership of those monies must be clarified in the agreement (Provision 4).

■ *Definition of management's responsibilities* (Provision 5). All of the manager's duties should be stated in the contract; exceptions should be noted. Important inclusions are to whom the rent and security deposit are paid; the method used in returning security deposits; and the method of paying mortgages, utility costs, and other bills. Adherence to all fair housing laws required.

■ *Extent of the manager's authority as an agent* (Provision 5). This provision should state what authority the manager is to have in such matters as hiring, firing, and supervising employees; establishing rental rates; making expenditures; and authorizing repairs within the limits set previously with the owner. (Repairs that exceed a certain expense limit may require the owner's written approval.) Authorization for marketing and/or cooperating with or compensating other agents also would be necessary (Provisions 6 & 7). Making capital improvements would be the owner's responsibility.

■ *Reporting* (Provision 5(e, f)). Agreement should be reached on the frequency and detail of the manager's periodic reports on operations and financial position. These reports enable the owner to monitor the manager's work and serve as a basis for both the owner and the manager to assess trends that can be used in shaping future management policy.

■ *Responsibilities of owner* (Provision 8). This provision should clarify the duties that the property owner retains including proper insurance coverage, adherence to fair housing laws, adequate provision of funds for management and maintenance of the property. Allocation of the property management expenses, such as fees for custodial help, advertising, supplies, and repairs, should state which are to be charged to the property's expenses versus which are to be paid by the owner.

■ *Duties upon termination* (Provision 13). Both parties agree to act promptly to settle financial and record-keeping accounts, some of which might include the transfer of funds and notifications of tenants.

■ *Miscellaneous provisions.* Additional provisions should address tenant security deposits and trust-account management (Provision 9 &10); entry of the leased unit by owner or agent during the lease period (Provision 11); and Lead-Based Paint Hazard Reduction Act disclosure compliance (Provision 12). Agent should receive notification of sale of property (Provision 14) and owner should receive notification if the agent assigns or sells ownership right in the property management firm (Provision 24). Owner needs to acknowledge that the manager is only a real estate professional and other service experts might be indicated (Provision 26).

After entering into an agreement with a property owner, a manager handles the property as the owner would. In all activities, the manager's first responsibility is *to realize the highest return on the property that is consistent with the owner's instructions.* Before contracting to manage any property, the professional property manager should be certain that the owner has realistic income expectations and is willing to spend money on necessary maintenance. Attempting to meet impossible owner demands by dubious methods can endanger the manager's reputation and make it difficult to obtain future business.

■ PROPERTY MANAGEMENT FEE

As mentioned earlier, the property management fee can be based on a percentage of gross or net income, a commission on new rentals, a fixed fee, or a combination of these.

■ **FOR EXAMPLE** Assume a property management agreement provides that the property manager gets 9 percent of all rents collected from a ten-unit apartment building. Two of the units are studio apartments that each rent for $250 a month. Six of the units are one-bedroom apartments that each rent for $325 a month. The remaining two units are two-bedroom apartments that each rent for $400 a month. Because of vacancies and collection losses, the property manager collects the rent for both studio apartments but for only five of the one-bedroom apartments and only one of the two-bedroom units. The property manager's fee is calculated as follows (Note: the fee is based only on money actually collected):

$$
\begin{array}{ll}
\$250 \times 2 \text{ units} = & \$\ \ 500 \\
\$325 \times 5 \text{ units} = & \$1,625 \\
\$400 \times 1 \text{ unit} = & \underline{\$\ \ 400} \\
& \$2,525 \text{ total rents collected} \times 0.09 \\
& \text{percentage of rents collected} \\
& = \$227.25 \text{ manager's fee for} \\
& \text{this month}
\end{array}
$$

As with real estate sales commission rates, all management fees must be negotiable between the parties. It is a violation of federal antitrust laws for property managers to conspire to set standard rates for their local areas. It is recommended that brokers should have a clear understanding with the owner of all the services to be rendered and who will pay for particular advertising and operating expenses prior to negotiating a property management fee.

■ MANAGEMENT CONSIDERATIONS

A property manager must live up to both the letter and the spirit of the property management agreement. The owner must be kept well informed on all matters of policy, as well as on the financial condition of the property and its operation. A manager must stay in contact with others in the field, therefore becoming increasingly knowledgeable and keeping informed on current policies pertaining to the profession.

Budgeting Expenses

Before attempting to rent any property, a property manager should develop a yearly operating budget based on anticipated revenues and expenses and reflecting the long-term goals of the owner. The wise property manager makes projections based on figures from a number of years. In preparing a budget, the manager should begin by allocating money for continuous, fixed expenses—employees' salaries, real estate taxes, and insurance premiums. Although budgets should be as accurate an estimate of costs as possible, adjustments may be necessary, especially in the case of new properties.

Next, the manager should establish a cash reserve fund for variable expenses such as repairs, decorating, and supplies. The amount allocated for the reserve fund can be estimated from previous yearly totals of variable expenses.

Capital expenditures.   If an owner and a property manager decide that modernization or renovation would enhance the property's value, the manager should budget money to cover the costs of remodeling. The property manager should be thoroughly familiar with the *principle of contribution* (discussed in Chapter 17) or should seek expert advice when estimating any increase in value expected by an improvement. In the case of large-scale construction, the expenses charged against the property's income should be spread over several years. The property owner decides to make capital improvements based on projections and advice from the property manager.

Renting the Property

The role of the property manager should not be confused with that of a broker acting as a leasing agent. The property manager may use the services of a leasing agent, but that agent does not undertake the full responsibility of maintaining and managing the property. The manager must be concerned with the long-term financial health of the property; the leasing broker is concerned solely with renting space. Note that in renting residential properties and dealing with residential tenants, property managers must be sure to follow the requirements of the Residential Rental Agreements Act and Tenant Security Deposit Act (discussed in Chapter 11).

Setting rental rates.   In establishing rental rates for a property, a manager must be concerned that, in the long term, the income from the rentable space will cover the property's fixed charges and operating expenses, plus provide a fair return on the investment. Consideration must be given to the prevailing rates in comparable buildings and the current level of vacancy in the property to be rented—supply and demand. Once the manager makes a detailed survey of the competitive space available in the neighborhood, rental prices should be adjusted for differences between these neighboring properties and the subject property. Annual rent adjustments are usually warranted. Note that although residential apartment rental rates are stated in monthly amounts per unit, office and commercial space rentals may be stated according to the annual or the monthly rate per square foot of space.

In establishing rental rates, the property manager has four long-term considerations:

1. The rental income must be sufficient to cover the property's fixed charges, such as taxes and insurance, and operating expenses, such as maintenance. (Note that debt service [principal and interest payment] on a mortgage loan is not an operating expense.)
2. The rental income must provide a fair return on the owner's investment.
3. The rental rate should be in line with prevailing rates in comparable properties. It may be slightly higher or slightly lower, depending on the strength of the property.

4. The current vacancy rate in the property is a good indicator of how large a rent increase is advisable. A building with a low vacancy rate (that is, few vacant units) is a better candidate for an increase than one with a high vacancy rate.

If a high level of vacancy exists, an immediate effort should be made to determine why. *A high level of vacancy does not necessarily indicate that rents are too high.* The trouble may be inept management or defects in the property. The manager first should attempt to identify the problem (if any) and correct it, rather than automatically lowering rents. Conversely, *even though a high percentage of occupancy may appear to indicate an effective rental program, it could also mean that rental rates are too low.* With an apartment or office building, any time the occupancy level exceeds 95 percent, an analysis should be made to be certain that the building rates are not below market.

MATH CONCEPTS

RENTAL COMMISSIONS

Rental commissions are usually based on the annual rent from a property. For example, if an office unit rents for $475 per month and the commission rate is 8%, the commission is calculated as follows

$475 per month x 12 months = $5,700

$5,700 x 0.08 (8%) = $456 annual commission

Marketing the property.   One of the property manager's duties is to market the property to potential suitable tenants. The property management agreement generally authorizes the placement of signs on the property in compliance with any zoning or restrictive covenants. Advertising on the Internet as well as print media also will expose the property to the general public. It should be noted that any advertising and/or marketing activities must comply with all federal, state, and local fair housing laws.

Selecting tenants.   Generally, the highest rents can be secured from satisfied tenants. A residential broker dealing only with sales may sell a property and then have no further dealings with the purchaser, but much of a property manager broker's success depends on retaining sound, long-term relationships. The first and most important step is selection. In selecting a prospective commercial or industrial tenant, a manager should be certain that (1) *the size of the space* meets the tenant's requirements (each business *fits the space*), (2) the tenant has the *ability to pay* for the space, (3) the *tenant's business is compatible* with the building and the other tenants' businesses, and (4) if the tenant is likely to expand in the future, *expansion space will be available.* Once a prospect becomes a tenant, the manager must be certain that the tenant remains satisfied in all respects commensurate with fair business dealings.

Note that in selecting *residential* tenants, the property manager must comply with all federal, state, and local fair housing laws (discussed in Chapter 20). Lease application requirements and rental policies that are uniformly applied to all lease applicants are not discriminatory in nature and constitute good business practices. Requiring all applicants to pay an application fee that will purchase a criminal records background check and a credit report can reduce the likelihood of renting to an "unqualified" tenant. A property manager's desire for a high level of occupancy should not override good judgment in accepting only those tenants who can be expected to meet their financial obligations to the property owner. The property manager should uniformly investigate financial references given by the prospect, by local credit bureaus, and, when possible, by the prospective tenant's former landlords.

Collecting rents.   The best way to minimize problems with rent collection is to make certain that the property manager has "qualified" all prospective tenants in the first place. The terms of rental payment should be spelled out in detail in the lease agreement. The property manager should establish a consistent, enforced collection plan with a sufficient system of notices and records. In cases of delinquency, every attempt must be made to make collections without resorting to legal action. For those cases in which legal recourse is required (i.e., summary ejectment), the property manager must be prepared to promptly initiate and follow through in conjunction with legal counsel.

It is important that property managers scrupulously follow all state laws, rules, and regulations when it comes to collecting and accounting for rents. The North Carolina Real Estate License Law and NCREC's Rules require that property managers deposit funds into trust accounts by mandated deadlines and maintain detailed and accurate trust account records (see NCREC Rule A.0107). The Tenant Security Deposit Act limits the amount of security deposits for residential property that can be required and mandates how they must be handled (discussed in Chapter 11). The property manager can collect tenant security deposits only if authorized in the property management agreement.

Performing landlord's duties under the lease.   The property manager broker is considered by many leases to "be" the landlord as pertains to conducting actions or providing services to the tenants. The establishment and implementation of rules and regulations dealing with a multitude of issues within multi-tenant properties will help ensure satisfied tenants and landlords. The manager would be expected to coordinate and provide negotiated tenant services on behalf of the landlord, such as janitorial services, required repairs and grounds maintenance. Instituting legal actions, such as eviction proceedings, would also fall to the capable hands of the property manager.

Accountability and record keeping.   It is crucial that property managers maintain accurate records of all monies received and handled on behalf of the landlord. Records of leases and compliance with various laws, such as the Lead-Based Paint Hazard Reduction Act, must also be maintained for a minimum of three years from the date of last activity. Unless otherwise negotiated in the property management agreement, the manager should render monthly accounting to the landlord. The property manager broker will be held responsible for compliance with all trust account maintenance laws even if daily trust fund activities were delegated to another person, such as a bookkeeper.

Maintaining the Property

One of the most important functions of a property manager is the supervision of property maintenance. The manager must learn to balance the services provided with the costs they entail in order to satisfy the tenants' needs while minimizing operating expenses. Assuring that tenants are being charged for repairs needed to correct damage occurring during tenancy helps minimize out-of-pocket expense for the property owner. Completion of a "property condition checklist" prior to possession by a new tenant can be compared to a newly-completed checklist immediately before tenant is due to vacate the premises. This will aid in the proper and accurate damage assessment in the leased property.

Efficient property maintenance demands accurate assessment of the needs of the building and the number and kinds of personnel that will meet these needs. Because staffing and scheduling requirements will vary with the type, size, and regional location of the property, the owner and the manager usually agree in advance on maintenance objectives for the property. For one property, the most viable plan may be to operate with a low occupancy level and minimal expenditures for services and maintenance. Another property may be more lucrative if kept in top condition and operated with all possible tenant services because it can then command premium rental rates.

The manager first must protect the physical integrity of the property to ensure that the condition of the building and its grounds is kept at present levels over the long term. For example, preserving the property by repainting the exterior or replacing the heating system will help keep the building functional and decrease routine maintenance costs.

Property maintenance encompasses four areas: (1) preventive maintenance, (2) repair or corrective maintenance, (3) routine maintenance and cleaning, and (4) construction.

Preventive maintenance includes regularly scheduled activities—such as regular painting and periodic lubrication of gears and motors—that will maintain the structure so that the long-range value and physical integrity of the building are preserved. Most authorities agree that preventive upkeep is the most critical, but most neglected maintenance responsibility.

Preventive maintenance helps prevent problems and expenses.

Repair or corrective maintenance involves the actual repairs that keep the building's equipment, utilities, and amenities functioning as contracted for by the tenants. Repairing a boiler, fixing a leaky faucet, and mending a broken air-conditioning unit are acts of repair maintenance.

Corrective maintenance corrects problems after they've occurred.

The property manager must also *supervise routine maintenance and cleaning* throughout the building, including such day-to-day duties as cleaning common areas; performing minor carpentry and plumbing tasks; and providing regularly scheduled upkeep of heating, air-conditioning, and landscaping.

Finally, property maintenance requires new or renovative *construction*. Especially when handling commercial or industrial space, the property manager often is called on to make tenant improvements—alterations to the interior of the building to meet the functional demands of the tenants. These alterations may range from repainting to completely gutting the interior and redefining the space. Tenant improvements are especially important when renting new buildings because the interior is usually left as an unfinished shell so that it can be customized for individual tenants.

Supervision of modernization or renovation of buildings that have become functionally obsolete (discussed in Chapter 17) and unsuited to today's building needs also is important. The renovation of a building often increases the building's marketability and therefore its income potential.

Hiring employees versus contracting for services.   One of the major decisions a property manager faces is whether to contract for maintenance services from an outside firm (outsourcing) or to hire on-site employees to perform such tasks. This decision should be based on a number of factors, including size of the building and land area, complexity of tenants' requirements, and availability of suitable, affordable labor.

Handling Environmental Concerns

With the proliferation of federal and state laws and the increase in local regulation, environmental concerns have become a major responsibility of the property manager and will require increased management time and attention in the future. Although property managers are not expected to be experts in all of the disciplines necessary to operate a modern building, they are expected to be knowledgeable in many diverse subjects, most of which are technical in nature. Environmental concerns awareness is one such subject that will be discussed further in Chapter 21.

The property manager must be able to respond to a variety of environmental problems. She may manage structures containing asbestos, mold, or radon, or be asked to arrange an environmental audit of a property. Note that lead-based paint disclosures (discussed in Chapter 21) are required for residential tenant-occupied property built prior to 1978. The manager must see that hazardous wastes produced by her employer or a building's tenants receive proper disposal. Even the normally nonhazardous waste of an office building must be controlled to avoid violation of laws requiring segregation of types of wastes. In areas where recycling is practiced, the property manager must provide the facilities and see that tenants sort their trash properly.

The Americans with Disabilities Act

The Americans with Disabilities Act (ADA) has had a significant impact on the responsibilities of the property manager, both in building amenities and in employment issues.

Title I of the ADA provides for the employment of qualified job applicants regardless of their disability. Any employer with 15 or more employees must adopt nondiscriminatory employment procedures. In addition, employers must make reasonable accommodations to enable individuals with disabilities to perform essential job functions.

Property managers must also be familiar with Title III of the ADA, which prohibits discrimination in commercial properties and public accommodations. The ADA requires that managers ensure that people with disabilities have full and equal access to facilities and services. The property manager typically is responsible for determining whether a building meets the ADA's accessibility requirements. The property manager must also prepare a plan for retrofitting a building that is not in compliance when removal of existing barriers is *readily achievable*—that is, can be performed without much difficulty or expense. There are some tax advantages available to help offset the expense of complying with ADA requirements. ADA experts may be consulted, as may architectural designers who specialize in accessibility issues.

To protect owners of existing structures from the massive expense of extensive remodeling, the ADA recommends *reasonably achievable accommodations* to provide access to the facilities and services. New construction and remodeling, however, must meet higher standards of accessibility and usability because it costs less to incorporate accessible features in the design than to retrofit. Though the law intends to provide for people with disabilities, many of the accessible design features and accommodations benefit everyone.

IN PRACTICE   The U.S. Department of Justice has ADA specialists available to answer general information questions about compliance issues. The ADA Information Line is at 800-514-0301 (TTY 800-514-0383). The ADA Web site is noted at the end of the chapter.

Existing barriers must be removed when this can be accomplished in a *readily achievable* manner—that is, with little difficulty and at low cost. The following are typical examples of readily achievable modifications:

- Ramping or removing an obstacle from an otherwise accessible entrance
- Lowering wall-mounted public telephones
- Adding raised letters and Braille markings on elevator buttons
- Installing auditory signals in elevators
- Reversing the direction in which doors open

Alternative methods can be used to provide reasonable accommodations if extensive restructuring is impractical or if retrofitting is unduly expensive. For instance, installing a cup dispenser at a water fountain that is too high for an individual in a wheelchair may be more practical than installing a lower unit.

IN PRACTICE   Federal, state, and local laws may provide additional requirements for accommodating people with disabilities. Licensees should be aware of the full range of laws to ensure that their practices are in compliance.

■ RELATED WEB SITES

American With Disabilities Act: *www.ada.gov*
Building Owners and Managers Association: *www.boma.org*
Institute of Real Estate Management: *www.irem.org*
National Association of Residential Property Managers: *www.narpm.org*

■ SUMMARY

Property management is a specialized service to owners of income-producing properties in which the managerial function may be delegated to an individual or a firm with particular expertise in the field. The manager, as agent of the owner, becomes the administrator of the project and assumes the executive functions required for the care and operation of the property.

Property management for others necessitates an active North Carolina real estate nonprovisional broker's license. The property manager broker can hire other licensees and/or unlicensed salaried employees to perform daily activities. Leasing agents are frequently unlicensed employees that are not allowed to negotiate any lease terms. There is no licensing requirement to manage property associations.

A written property management agreement establishing the agency relationship between owner and manager must be carefully prepared to define and authorize the manager's duties and responsibilities from the inception of the agency relationship. A property management agreement is the only agency contract that is allowed by the NCREC to have an automatic renewal clause. The manager's duties include establishing a rental schedule, preparing an operating budget, marketing and renting the property, collecting rents and security deposits, initiating any necessary legal actions, maintaining the property, performing the landlord's duties under the lease, maintaining insurance, maintaining records, and reporting regularly to the owner.

Property managers' duties do not normally include reinvesting profits, making capital improvements, establishing a depreciation schedule, or paying the owner's income tax.

Projected expenses, combined with the manager's analysis of the condition of the building and the rent patterns in the neighborhood, form the basis on which rental rates for the property are determined. Once a rent schedule is established, the property manager is responsible for soliciting tenants whose needs are suited to the available space and who are financially capable of meeting the proposed rents. Generally, the manager is obligated to collect rents, maintain the building, hire necessary employees, pay taxes for the building, and handle tenant problems.

Maintenance includes safeguarding the physical integrity of the property, performing routine cleaning and repairs, and making tenant improvements—adapting the interior space and overall design of the property to suit tenants' needs and the demands of the market.

The property manager must comply with ADA requirements to ensure that facilities provide for reasonably achievable accommodations for persons with disabilities.

QUESTIONS

1. Apartment rental rates are usually expressed
   a. in monthly amounts.
   b. on a per-room basis.
   c. in square feet per month.
   d. in square feet per year.

2. In preparing for variable expenses in a budget, the property manager should set up a(n)
   a. control account.
   b. floating allocation.
   c. cash reserve fund.
   d. asset account.

3. An important concern in setting rents is
   I. prevailing rates in the area.
   II. current vacancy rates.
      a. I only
      b. II only
      c. Both I and II
      d. Neither I nor II

4. Which of the following might suggest that rents are too low?
   a. Poorly maintained building
   b. Many For Lease signs in the area
   c. High occupancy rate
   d. High vacancy level

5. Repairing a boiler is classified as which type of maintenance?
   a. Preventative
   b. Corrective
   c. Routine
   d. Construction

6. In renting units in an apartment building, a property manager must comply with all of the following EXCEPT
   a. the terms of the management agreement.
   b. the lawful instructions of the owner.
   c. fair housing laws.
   d. the AMA Code of Ethics.

7. If the leasing agent gets an 8 percent commission on rents collected, what would his annual commission be if he leases 20 offices at $750 a month?
   a. $ 1,200
   b. $ 9,000
   c. $14,400
   d. $15,000

8. Generally, the provisions of the management agreement should include all of the following EXCEPT
   a. a definition of the manager's responsibilities.
   b. a listing of previous owners of the property.
   c. the extent of the manager's authority as an agent.
   d. the calculation of management fees.

9. When selecting a tenant, consideration should be given to all of the following EXCEPT
   a. size of the space versus the tenant's requirements.
   b. tenant's ability to pay.
   c. racial and ethnic background of the tenant.
   d. compatibility of the tenant's business with other tenants' businesses.

10. A property manager is usually responsible for
   I. developing a budget and controlling expenses.
   II. communicating with the owner about physical problems with a building.
      a. I only
      b. II only
      c. Both I and II
      d. Neither I nor II

11. Last year your firm managed a 48-unit apartment building. Two units were four-bedroom,
penthouse units renting for $1,000 per month
with no vacancies. Twenty-five units with three
bedrooms rented for $850 per month and carried
a 5 percent vacancy factor. Ten two-bedroom
units rented for $750 per month and carried a
5 percent vacancy factor. Eleven one-bedroom
apartments with balconies rented for $650 per
month and carried a 10 percent vacancy factor.
The management fee is 12 percent. How much
commission did your firm gross last year managing this building?

   a. $ 45,480
   b. $ 50,036
   c. $ 51,476
   d. $ 53,136

12. When a property manager is establishing a budget for the building, all of the following should be
included as an operating expense EXCEPT

   a.   cleaning supplies.
   b.   management fees.
   c.   debt service payments.
   d.   routine repairs.

13. An active real estate license will be needed if the
property manager is

   a.   an employee of a partnership that owns the
property to be managed.
   b.   part owner of the property.
   c.   an employee of a corporation that owns the
property to be managed.
   d.   a general partner of the partnership that
owns the property to be managed.

14. A property manager who enters into a management agreement with an owner is usually a

   a.   special agent.
   b.   general agent.
   c.   universal agent.
   d.   designated agent.

CHAPTER 13

Real Estate Financing: Principles

■ **LEARNING OBJECTIVES** *When you have finished reading this chapter, you should be able to*

■ **distinguish** between title theory and lien theory states.

■ **identify** the basic provisions of security and debt instruments and rights and duties of lenders and borrowers.

■ **explain** the characteristics of various types of loan repayment plans.

■ **define** the effect of discount points on yield and calculate mathematically how to determine the number of points and the dollar amount of points to be paid by the borrower.

■ **define** these *key terms:*

acceleration clause	equitable title	negotiable instrument
adjustable-rate mortgages (ARMs)	equity	power of sale foreclosure
	equity of redemption	prepayment penalty
alienation clause	foreclosure	principal
amortized loans	graduated payment mortgage (GPM)	promissory note
balloon payment		satisfaction of mortgage
beneficiary	grantor/trustor	shared-appreciation mortgage (SAM)
debt service	hypothecation	
deed in lieu of foreclosure	interest	statutory redemption period
deed of trust	judicial foreclosure	
default	lien theory	statutory right of redemption
deficiency judgment	loan origination fee	
direct reduction loans	mortgage	term loan
discount points	mortgagee/mortgagor	title theory
due-on-sale clause	negative amortization	usury
		yield

■ BASIS MORTGAGE TERMS AND CONCEPTS

There are two different legal theories about the effect of mortgaging property—the title theory and the lien theory. Under the **lien theory**, which is the older, more traditional approach, a two-party mortgage instrument is used as security for the debt. The borrower (**mortgagor**) retains both legal and equitable title to the property. The lender (**mortgagee**) is given the right to have the property sold through the **judicial foreclosure** process and the proceeds applied to the debt, should the borrower **default** under the terms of the mortgage loan.

Title theory uses the three-party deed of trust instrument (a form of mortgage) as security for the debt. The borrower (**grantor** or **trustor**) actually conveys legal title to the **trustee** (third party) to hold for the lender (**beneficiary**) until the debt is satisfied. The borrower retains **equitable title** to the property. This means that the borrower has the right to use and possess the property as if he or she owned it and to demand the return of the legal title when the debt is repaid. Upon request of the lender, the trustee can initiate the **power of sale foreclosure** to sell the property if the debt is not paid per the terms of the promissory note. The lender's legal ownership is subject to termination on full payment of the debt or performance of the obligation. North Carolina follows the title theory.

> In a lien theory state, the borrower retains both legal and equitable title.
>
> In a title theory state, the borrower retains equitable title and conveys legal title to a trustee until the debt has been satisfied.

The legal differences between title theory and lien theory are of little significance today. Under both theories, if a borrower defaults, the lender may foreclose the lien, offer the property for sale, and apply the funds received from the sale to reduce or extinguish the obligation. As protection to the borrower, most states allow a statutory redemption period during which the borrower in default can redeem the property.

■ SECURITY AND DEBT

Generally, any interest in real estate that may be sold may also be pledged as security or collateral for a debt. A basic principle of property law—that a person cannot convey greater rights in property than the person actually has—applies equally to the right to mortgage. So, the owner of a fee simple estate can mortgage the fee, and the owner of a leasehold or subleasehold can mortgage that leasehold interest. For example, a large retail corporation renting space in a shopping center may mortgage its leasehold interest to finance remodeling work.

Mortgage Loan Instruments

Two parts to a mortgage loan exist—the debt itself and the security for the debt. When a property is to be mortgaged, the owner must execute, or sign, two separate instruments:

1. The **promissory note**, or financing instrument, is the written promise or agreement to repay a debt in definite installments with interest. The mortgagor executes one or more promissory notes to reflect the amount of the debt.
2. The **mortgage** or **deed of trust**, that is, the security instrument, is the document that pledges the property to the lender as security or collateral for a debt.

FIGURE 13.1

Mortgages

Mortgage —Two Parties

When the Money Is Borrowed

Mortgagor
(Borrower)

Note and
Mortgage   Loan $

Mortgagee
(Lender)

When the Money Is Repaid

Mortgagor
(Borrower)

Pays the   Satisfaction
Loan $ of Mortgage

Mortgagee
(Lender)

A mortgagor is a borrower who gives a mortgage to a lender, the mortgagee, in return for the money. The relationship between mortgagor and mortgagee is shown in Figure 13.1.

Hypothecation is the act of pledging real property as security for payment of a loan without giving up possession of the property. A pledge of security—a mortgage—cannot be effective legally unless there is a debt to secure. Both the note and the mortgage must be executed (signed) to create an enforceable mortgage loan.

Deeds of trust.   In some areas of the country, including North Carolina, lenders prefer to use a three-party security instrument known as a deed of trust, or trust deed (see Figure 13.2), rather than a mortgage document. In a deed of trust, the borrower conveys naked title or bare legal title (title without the right of possession) to the real estate as security for the loan from the borrower to a third party, called the trustee. The trustee then holds title on behalf of the lender, known as the beneficiary, who is the legal owner and holder of the promissory note. The wording of the conveyance sets forth actions that the trustee may take if the borrower, known as the grantor or trustor, defaults under any of the deed of trust terms. The procedure for foreclosing a deed of trust is simpler and faster than the procedure used to foreclose a mortgage, because the deed of trust contains an

FIGURE 13.2

Deed of Trust

Deed of Trust—Three Parties

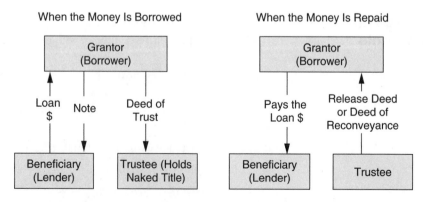

automatic power-of-sale clause that, in case of the borrower's default, gives the trustee the power to sell the property in a nonjudicial foreclosure. Note that the term mortgage loan is commonly used to refer to a loan secured by either a mortgage or deed of trust.

■ THE PROMISSORY NOTE

When a real estate purchase is financed with a mortgage loan, the borrower must sign a promissory note. The promissory, or mortgage, note is legal evidence of the debt between the borrower and lender.

Essential Elements of a Valid Note

The essential elements of a note are (1) term, (2) promise to pay, and (3) signature of the borrower(s). A promissory note is a simple document that states the amount of the debt, the time and method of payment, and the rate of interest. The note may also refer to or repeat several of the clauses that appear in the mortgage document. The borrower is called the maker, or payor, or obligor, and the lender is called the payee. The note, like the mortgage, should be signed by all parties who have an interest in the property (for example, both spouses should sign the note). Remember that (1) only the borrowers (makers) of the note sign it, (2) it is not recorded (only the security instrument is recorded), and (3) there is only one original that is signed at the closing (although there may be copies given to the various parties).

A promissory note is usually a **negotiable instrument**—that is, a written promise or order to pay a specific sum of money. An instrument is said to be negotiable when its holder, the payee, may transfer the right to receive payment to a third party. This may be accomplished by signing the instrument over to the third party or, in some cases, merely by delivering the instrument to that person. Other examples of negotiable instruments include checks and bank drafts. It is important for the promissory note to be negotiable because lenders often sell their mortgage loans in the secondary mortgage market.

To be negotiable, or freely transferable, an instrument must meet certain requirements of the law. The instrument must be in writing, made by one person to another, and signed by the maker. It must contain an unconditional promise to pay a sum of money on demand or at a set date in the future. In addition, the instrument must be payable to the order of a specifically named person or to the bearer (whoever has possession of the note). Instruments that are payable to order must be transferred by endorsement; those payable to bearer may be transferred by delivery. A nonnegotiable note does not contain to order or to bearer but is payable to a named person. It is neither transferable nor assignable. The vast majority of real estate notes are negotiable, and therefore transferable.

It is important to understand the difference between the negotiability of a note—that is, whether a note is transferable from one lender to another—and the negotiability of the terms (such as the interest rate) of a note. The original parties to the note may negotiate the terms of the loan, but once those terms are determined, they are binding on the parties to the note, whether or not the note itself is transferred to another party.

Special Note Provisions

Virtually all promissory notes used by institutional lenders contain three additional provisions:

1. **Acceleration clause.** The **acceleration clause** provides that if a borrower defaults, the lender has the right to accelerate the maturity of the debt—to declare the entire debt (plus accrued interest and costs) due and payable immediately—even though the terms of the mortgage originally allow the borrower to amortize the debt in regular payments over a period of years. Without the acceleration clause, the lender would have to sue the borrower every time a payment became due and in default (late).

2. **Prepayment penalty clause.** When a loan is paid in installments over a long term, the total interest paid by the borrower can exceed the principal of the loan. If such a loan is paid off before its full term, the lender collects less interest from the borrower. For this reason, some lenders include a prepayment penalty clause in the promissory note, requiring that the borrower pay a **prepayment penalty** against the unearned portion of the interest for any payments made ahead of schedule. A loan that does not have a prepayment penalty clause will include a prepayment privilege clause, which allows the borrower to prepay a portion or all of the outstanding balance without penalty. Lenders in North Carolina are not permitted to charge a prepayment penalty on any residential loan with an original balance of $150,000 or less that is the first lien on the borrower's primary residence. Also, federal law prohibits lenders from charging a prepayment penalty on any FHA-insured VA-guaranteed loan.

3. **Due-on-sale clause.** Frequently, when a conventional real estate loan is made, the lender wishes to prevent some future purchaser of the property from being able to assume that loan without the lender's permission, particularly at its original rate of interest. For this reason, some lenders include a **due-on-sale clause**, also known as an **alienation clause**, in the note. A due-on-sale clause provides that on sale of the property by the borrower to a buyer who wants to assume the loan, the lender has the choice of either declaring the entire debt to be due and payable immediately or permitting the buyer to assume the loan at current market interest rates. Use of this clause triggers the acceleration clause. The absence of a due-on-sale clause would permit a loan assumption without the lender's prior consent.

Principal and Interest (Debt Service)

A charge for the use of money borrowed (the **principal**) is called **interest**. Loan payments are usually described as principal and interest payments (P&I) or **debt service** payments. Interest may be due either at the end of each payment period (known as *payment in arrears*) or at the beginning of each payment period (*payment in advance*). Whether interest is charged in arrears or in advance is specified in the note, but the interest on the vast majority of mortgage loans is payable in arrears. In practice, the distinction becomes important if the property is sold before the debt is repaid in full, as will become evident in Chapter 15. Note that the interest charged on real estate loans is simple interest, and it is charged only on the outstanding loan balance.

Most mortgage loans are **amortized loans**. That is, as regular level payments are made, each payment is broken down and applied first to the interest owed, with the rest of the payment applied to the principal amount—over a term of perhaps 15 years or 30 years. At the end of the term, the full amount of the principal and all interest due is reduced to zero. Some mortgage loans require a fixed amount of principal to be paid in each payment with the amount applied to interest varying as the balance is reduced. Such loans are called **direct reduction loans**.

Each month, in addition to paying P&I, the borrower is normally required by the lender to pay one-twelfth of the annual real property taxes and one-twelfth of various annual insurance premiums, such as for homeowner's, flood, or mortgage insurance policies. **Principal, interest, taxes, and insurance** is referred to as PITI. The taxes and insurance portion (TI) of the monthly payment is placed into the lender's escrow account and held until those bills are due. The lender receives the tax and insurance bills and pays those items from its escrow account on behalf of the borrower.

Most amortized mortgage loans are paid in monthly installments; some, however, are payable biweekly, quarterly, or semiannually. These payments may be computed based on a number of payment plans, which tend alternately to gain and lose favor with lenders and borrowers as the cost and availability of mortgage money fluctuates. Some of these basic payment plans are described in the following subsections.

Fully amortized fixed-rate mortgage.   The fully amortized fixed-rate mortgage requires that the mortgagor pay a constant amount, usually monthly, that will completely pay off the loan amount with the last equal payment. The mortgagee first credits each payment to the interest due and then applies the balance to reduce the principal of the loan. Therefore, while each debt service payment remains the same, the portion applied toward repayment of the principal grows and the interest due declines as the unpaid balance of the loan is reduced (Figure 13.3).

Partially amortized fixed-rate mortgage.   With a partially amortized loan, the monthly principal and interest payments are a constant amount, but that payment amount is not sufficient to completely pay off the loan within the loan term. At maturity, a balloon payment will be due to pay the remaining principal. A **balloon payment** is a payment of an amount that is larger than the previous regular payments.

FIGURE 13.3

Level-Payment Amortized Loan

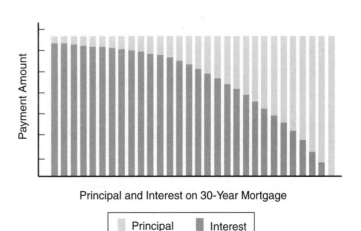

Principal and Interest on 30-Year Mortgage

Principal   Interest

Straight-line amortized mortgage. With straight-line amortization as in a direct reduction mortgage loan, the mortgagor may pay a different amount for each installment, with each payment consisting of a fixed amount credited toward the principal plus an additional amount for the interest due on the principal outstanding since the last payment was made.

MATH CONCEPTS

CALCULATING SIMPLE INTEREST

To compute simple interest, use the formula $I = P \times R \times T$, where

$$I = \text{interest}$$
$$P = \text{principal}$$
$$R = \text{rate}$$
$$T = \text{time}$$

Apply this formula to a $30,000 loan (P) at 7% interest (R) to be repaid over 15 years (T). To calculate the interest owing for the first month, perform the following calculations:

$$I = \$30,000 \times 0.07 \times 15$$
$$I = \$31,500$$

$31,500 total interest ÷ 15 years = $2,100 yearly interest payment

(Note: After the borrower makes the first principal payment, the loan total will be reduced and therefore the interest payment also will be reduced.)

$2,100 ÷ 12 months = $175 first monthly interest payment

Interest and principal credited from amortized payment. Lenders charge borrowers a certain percentage of the principal as interest for each year a debt is outstanding. The amount of interest due in a particular payment is calculated by computing the total yearly interest based on the unpaid balance and dividing that figure by the number of payments made each year. There are numerous software programs that will generate an amortization schedule showing the payment split between the principal and interest portions.

■ **FOR EXAMPLE** Assume the current outstanding balance of a loan is $70,000. The interest rate is 6¾ percent per year, and the monthly P&I payment is $454.30. Based on these facts, the interest and principal due on the next payment would be computed as shown:

$70,000 loan balance × 0.0675 annual interest rate = $4,725 annual interest
$4,725 annual interest ÷ 12 months = $393.75 monthly interest
$454.30 monthly P&I payment – $393.75 monthly interest =
$60.55 monthly principal
$70,000 beginning loan balance – $60.55 monthly principal =
$69,939.45 remaining loan balance after payment

This process is followed with each payment over the term of the loan. The same calculations are made each month, starting with the declining new loan balance figure from the previous month.

Usury.   The maximum rate of interest legally charged on loans may be set by state usury laws. Charging interest in excess of this rate is called **usury** and is illegal. Lenders are penalized for making usurious loans. Usury laws were enacted primarily to protect consumers from unscrupulous lenders that charge unreasonably high interest rates. In some states, a lender that makes a usurious loan is permitted to collect the borrowed money, but only at the legal rate of interest. In other states, a usurious lender may lose the right to collect any interest or may lose the entire amount of the loan in addition to the interest. Loans made to corporations are generally exempt from usury laws.

Usury laws are state laws, but federal law preempted state law in this situation when the Depository Institutions Deregulation and Monetary Control Act of 1980 specifically exempted from state interest limitations all federally-related residential first mortgage loans made after March 31, 1980. This Act was passed to continue the availability of mortgage loans in the early 1980s when interest rates hit 18 percent while most state usury limits were below that rate. Federally related loans are those made by federally chartered institutions or those insured or guaranteed by a federal agency. The exemption includes loans used to finance manufactured housing (the federal term for mobile homes) and the acquisition of stock in a cooperative housing corporation. North Carolina exempts all residential first deeds of trust from state usury laws.

Usury laws are complicated, and any licensee who has questions about state or federal usury laws should consult a lawyer.

Discount points.   The return or profit on a loan is sometimes called the **yield**. A large part of the yield comes from the interest rate the lender charges on the loan. However, the rate of interest that a lender charges for a mortgage loan might be less than the rate of return required by the lender or by an investor who might purchase that loan from the lender. For this reason, the lender can charge **discount points** to make up the difference between the mortgage interest rate and the required investor yield.

One discount point equals 1 percent of the original loan amount and increases the yield of a loan by approximately one-eighth percent.

The number of points charged varies, depending on the difference between the interest rate and the required yield and on the average time the lender expects the loan to be outstanding. While most loans have an average term of 30 years, the average life of all loans is actually 11 years to 12 years because loans are usually paid off much sooner, when the borrower sells the property or refinances the loan. Lenders calculate that it takes an average of six to eight discount points to increase the yield 1 percent, with eight points being the rule of thumb; therefore, it is said that one point will increase the yield about one-eighth percent. Points can be charged on FHA-insured, VA-guaranteed, and conventional loans.

■ **FOR EXAMPLE** Suppose a lender wants to increase its yield on a $100,000 loan by one-half percentage point. If eight points equals a yield increase of one percentage point, to increase the yield by one-half percentage point, the lender would have to charge four points.

The cost to the borrower of a point equals 1 percent of the loan amount and is charged as prepaid interest at the closing. Thus, points charged on the $100,000 loan would be $4,000 ($100,000 × 4%). In this situation, the lender would actually fund $96,000 (the $100,000 principal amount of the loan minus the $4,000 for points), but $100,000 would have to be repaid by the borrower, thereby increasing the investor's yield (a $96,000 loan receiving interest calculated on $100,000).

MATH CONCEPTS

DISCOUNT POINTS

From the borrower's standpoint, one discount point equals 1% of the loan amount. To calculate the net amount of a $75,000 loan after a three-point discount is taken, multiply the loan amount by 100% minus the discount:

$$\$75,000 \times (100\% - 3\%)$$
$$\$75,000 \times 97\%$$
$$\$75,000 \times 0.97 = \$72,750$$

Or deduct the dollar amount of the discount from the loan:

$$\$75,000 - (\$75,000 \times 3\%)$$
$$\$75,000 - (\$75,000 \times .03)$$
$$\$75,000 - 2,250 = \$72,750$$

Investor Yield

From the standpoint of the investor, one discount point received increases the yield on the loan by one-eighth percent. Two points would increase the yield by one-fourth percent, four points by one-half percent, six points by three-quarter percent, and eight points by 1%. For example, if a loan carried an interest rate of 9½% and a discount of 6 points, the yield to the investor would be calculated as follows:

6 discount points = ¾% increase in yield
9½% interest per the contract + ¾% increase from the discount =
10¼% yield to the investor

If an investor requires a 10½% yield on a loan with a 10¼% interest rate, the number of discount points needed would be calculated as follows:

10½% = 10⅘%; 10⅘% required yield − 10²⁄₈% interest rate = ²⁄₈% difference;
²⁄₈% = 2 discount points

Discount points should not be confused with the **loan origination fee** charged by most lenders, which is an administrative expense for generating the loan. Unlike points, loan origination fees are not prepaid interest; they are an expense that must be paid to the lender, typically 1 percent of the loan amount regardless of any discount points that might also be charged.

IN PRACTICE

Interest payments made under a mortgage loan secured by a first or second home are deductible for federal income tax purposes if the combined loan amounts do not exceed $1 million. This deduction, in effect, reduces the borrower's total cost of housing for the year. Interest deductions are limited, however, to the interest paid on an initial loan amount or refinancing no greater than the purchase price of the home plus capital improvements, unless the loan proceeds are used for qualified medical or educational purposes. Points (prepaid interest) paid at the time of financing a home purchase are fully deductible for the year paid by the buyer. Points on a loan to finance property improvements also are fully deductible for the year paid. Points paid on a loan refinancing may be deductible. If advance payments of loan principal are made, there is no increase in the deduction. If the entire loan is prepaid, however, any undeducted points may be deducted for that year. A tax expert should be consulted to accurately determine all tax liability and advantage.

■ MORTGAGE LOAN REPAYMENT PLANS

Fixed rate-level payment mortgage.   The most popular repayment plan, the fixed rate-level payment mortgage, was discussed earlier under fully amortized fixed-rate mortgage. This may also be referred to as a level-payment, simple interest loan. Mortgagors tend to prefer this repayment plan since there are no payment surprises during the course of the loan. Both the interest rate and the debt service amount are set for the duration of the loan.

Interest-only mortgage (term loan).   A mortgagor may choose an interest-only payment plan that calls for periodic payments of interest only, with the *principal to be paid in full at the end of the loan term*. This is known as a **term loan**, or a *straight loan*. Historically, such plans were used for construction loans and second mortgages, but consumers occasionally used them for residential first mortgage loans. Prior to the 1930s, the only form of mortgage loan available was the straight-payment loan, payable in full after a relatively short term, such as three years to five years. The high rate of foreclosure on such loans in the depression years prompted the introduction and use of the more manageable long-term amortized loans that are now the norm. The popularity of term loans in recent years as first mortgages for primary residences in combination with very low or no down payment requirements is thought to have contributed to the huge number of foreclosures currently being experienced.

Adjustable-rate mortgage (ARM).   Adjustable-rate mortgages (ARMs) generally originate at one rate of interest, with the rate fluctuating up or down during the loan term based on the movement of a *published index*. Because the interest may change, so may the mortgagor's loan payments. Details of how and when the rate of interest on the loan might change are included in the provisions of the mortgage note.

Generally, interest rate adjustments are limited to one per period, and a maximum amount of increase or decrease may be made over the life of the loan. Certain regulations may enable a lender to adjust the interest rate on a monthly basis. The borrower is usually given the right to repay the loan in full without penalty whenever the interest rate changes. (See the discussion of prepayment penalties earlier in this chapter.)

Common components of an ARM include the following:

■ **Note rate (contract rate).** The original rate charged, which is stated in the closing documents, is called the note rate.
■ **Index.** The interest rate on the outstanding balance of the loan is increased or decreased according to the movements of a named publicly published

index. A very popular index used by lending institutions is the short-term U.S. Treasury bill rate, but many other indices are available and used.

■ **Margin.** The amount of interest a lender charges over and above the index rate is called the margin. For example, if the most recent one-year Treasury bill rate was 3.25 percent, the lender could add a 2 percent margin and charge the borrower a 5.25 percent interest rate on the outstanding loan balance. The amount of the margin remains fixed for the entire life of the loan; it is the movement of the index rate that causes the ARM interest rate to fluctuate.

■ **Interest rate caps.** Rate caps limit the amount the interest rate may increase or decrease in any one adjustment period, called the *anniversary* or *periodic interest rate cap*. They also limit the amount the interest rate can increase over the entire life of the loan, which is called the *lifetime* or *life of loan cap*.

■ **Payment cap.** The payment cap, which sets a maximum amount for payment changes, protects the mortgagor against the possibility of individual payments that the mortgagor cannot afford. With a payment cap, a rate increase can result in **negative amortization**—an increase in the loan balance. For instance, suppose a borrower's rate increases a full 1 percent. For this borrower a 1 percent rate increase translates into a payment increase of $65 a month. However, the payment cap limits the increase to $45 a month. During that adjustment period, the borrower will be paying $20 a month less than the amount required to pay the full principal and interest payment. So, each month, $20 is added to the principal balance. This is negative amortization.

■ **Adjustment period.** This establishes how often the loan rate may change. Common adjustment periods are every year (a 1-year ARM), every three years (a 3-year ARM), and every five years (a 5-year ARM), or some combination.

■ **Conversion option.** Lenders may offer a conversion option, which permits the mortgage to be converted from an adjustable-rate to a fixed-rate loan at certain intervals during the life of the mortgage. The option is subject to certain terms and conditions for the conversion.

Figure 13.4 illustrates the effect interest rate fluctuations and periodic caps have on an adjustable-rate mortgage. Obviously, without rate caps and payment caps, a mortgage's interest rate could fluctuate wildly over several adjustment periods, depending on the behavior of the index to which it is tied. In Figure 13.4, the borrower's rate ranges from a low of 5.9 percent to a high of 9.5 percent. Such unpredictability makes personal financial planning difficult. On the other hand, if the loan had a lifetime rate cap of 7.5 percent, the borrower's rate would never go above that level, regardless of the index's behavior. Similarly, a lender would want a floor to keep the rate from falling below a certain rate (here, 6.5 percent). The shaded area in the figure shows how caps and floors protect against dramatic changes in interest rates.

Graduated payment mortgage (GPM). A flexible payment plan, such as a **graduated payment mortgage** (GPM), allows a mortgagor to make lower monthly payments for the first few years of the loan (typically the first five years) and larger payments for the remainder of the term, when the mortgagor's income is expected to have increased. The interest on a GPM is fixed throughout the life of the loan.

FIGURE 13.4

Adjustable-Rate Mortgage

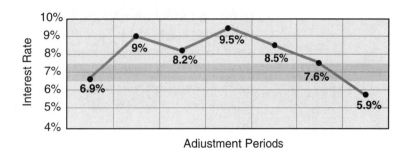

However, in the early years of the loan, the monthly payments are lower than the payments required to fully amortize the loan. This results in *negative amortization.* As each payment is made, the unpaid interest is added to the principal balance, resulting in an increasing loan balance for the first few years. The monthly payments then increase at stated intervals throughout the loan term, eventually making up for the negative amortization and paying off the loan in full by the end of the loan term. Generally, this type of loan is used to enable first-time buyers and buyers in times of high interest rates to purchase real estate.

Balloon payment loan.   When a mortgage loan requires periodic payments that will not fully amortize the amount of the loan by the end of the loan term, the final payment is an amount that is larger than the previous payments—a balloon payment. Examples would be a partially amortized loan and a term loan.

■ **FOR EXAMPLE** A loan for $80,000 at 10 percent interest may be computed on a 30-year amortization schedule but paid over a 20-year term, with a final balloon payment due at the end of the 20th year. In this case, each monthly payment would be $792.24 (the amount taken from a 30-year amortization schedule), with a final balloon payment of $56,340 (the amount of principal still owing after 20 years).

MATH CONCEPTS

INTEREST-ONLY BALLOON PAYMENT LOAN

Consider a loan with the following terms: $80,000 at 8% interest, with only interest payable monthly and the loan fully repayable in 15 years. To calculate the amount of the final balloon payment:

$80,000 × 0.08 = $6,400 annual interest
$6,400 annual interest ÷ 12 months = $533.33 monthly interest payment
$80,000 principal payment + $533.33 monthly interest =
$80,533.33 final balloon payment

It is frequently assumed that if payments are made promptly, the lender will extend the balloon payment for another limited term. The lender, however, is in no way legally obligated to grant this extension and can require payment in full when the note is due. The borrower may have to refinance the loan with another lender.

A loan that requires a balloon payment is called a *partially amortized* loan and is quite common in seller-financing situations. When sellers finance part or all of the purchase price, they often want to be *cashed out*—that is, have the seller financing paid off—within three to five years of the sale.

Growing-equity mortgage (GEM). The *growing-equity mortgage*, or rapid-payoff mortgage, makes use of a fixed interest rate, but payments of principal are increased according to an index or a schedule. The total payment, therefore, increases, but the borrower's income is expected to keep pace, and the loan is paid off more quickly. (*Note:* **equity** is the borrower's financial interest in the property; that is, the value of the property minus all outstanding mortgages and other liens.)

Biweekly loans. Biweekly loans require that the borrower make a loan payment every two weeks instead of once a month. The amount of the payment is half of what the monthly payment required for 30-year amortization would have been. This payment plan results in the borrower's paying the equivalent of one extra monthly payment a year. (The borrower makes 26 biweekly payments—the equivalent of 13 monthly payments.) Because of this, most biweekly loans are paid off in about 20 or 21 years instead of 30 years. Because the loan is paid off earlier, the borrower pays less interest over the life of the loan, and lenders often offer biweekly loans at slightly lower interest rates than standard 30-year loans.

Shared-appreciation mortgage (SAM). Under a shared-appreciation mortgage, the lender originates the mortgage at a favorable interest rate (several points below the going rate) in return for a guaranteed share of any gain the borrower realizes when he or she eventually sells the property. This type of loan was originally made to developers of large real estate projects, but in times of expensive mortgage money, it has appeared in the residential finance market. The specific details of the shared-appreciation agreement are set forth in the mortgage or trust deed and note documents.

■ THE MORTGAGE (OR DEED OF TRUST) INSTRUMENT

A mortgage or deed-of-trust document is typically a little more complicated than a promissory note. The mortgage or deed of trust must refer to the terms of the promissory note and clearly establish through the use of a mortgaging clause that the property is intended to be security for a valid debt. It must identify the lender and the borrower (who must have the capacity to contract) and must include an accurate, adequate legal description of the property. It must be in writing and signed by all parties who have an interest in the real estate. (The lender does not sign the mortgage or deed of trust.) Finally, the mortgage or deed of trust must be recorded and delivered to and accepted by the lender or trustee (see Figure 13.5).

Rights and Duties of the Borrower

The borrower (mortgagor or grantor) is required to fulfill many obligations. These usually include

■ payment of the debt in accordance with the terms of the note;
■ payment of all real estate taxes on the property given as security;
■ maintenance of adequate insurance to protect the lender if the property is destroyed or damaged by fire, windstorm, or another hazard;
■ maintenance of the property in good repair at all times; and
■ lender authorization before making any major alterations or demolishing any building on the mortgaged property.

Failure to meet any of these obligations can result in a borrower's default on the note. When this happens, the loan documents may provide for a grace period (e.g., 30 days) for the borrower to correct the default, after which the lender has the right to foreclose the mortgage or deed of trust and collect on the note. The most frequent cause of default is the borrower's failure to meet monthly payment installments.

The borrower has the right to possess and enjoy the property during the loan term, with no interference from the lender. The borrower also has the right (*right of defeasance*) to have legal title to the property transferred back to him or her when the loan is paid in full. Under the provisions of the mortgage or deed of trust, when the note has been fully paid, the trustee is required to execute a **satisfaction of mortgage**, also known as a deed of release, reconveyance deed, release of mortgage, or mortgage discharge. This document reconveys to the borrower all interest in the real estate that was conveyed to the lender by the original recorded mortgage or deed of trust document. By having this release entered in the public record, the owner shows that the mortgage lien has been removed from the property.

Rights of the Lender

A lender has the right to assign the mortgage debt as well as the right to foreclose the mortgage or deed of trust if the borrower defaults.

As mentioned earlier, because a note is a negotiable instrument, it may be sold to a third party without the consent of the borrower. The lender endorses the note to the third party and also executes an assignment of mortgage. The assignee becomes the new owner of the debt and security instrument with all the rights and obligations of the original lender. This assignment must be recorded. On payment in full, or satisfaction of the debt, the assignee is required to execute the satisfaction, or release, of the security instrument (discussed earlier). In the event of a foreclosure, the assignee is required to file the suit. The note and mortgage cannot be assigned if the loan is in default.

When a borrower defaults in making payments or fulfilling any of the obligations set forth in the mortgage or deed of trust, the lender can enforce its rights through a **foreclosure**. Such a default may include failure to make payments, destruction of all or part of the property, or failure to pay current insurance premiums or real property taxes. Foreclosure is the process of selling the mortgaged real estate to repay the debt from the proceeds of the sale. The foreclosure procedure brings the rights of the parties and all junior lienholders to a conclusion and passes title in the subject property to the highest acceptable bidder at a foreclosure sale. Property thus sold is free of the mortgage and all junior liens, but it still may have other encumbrances. Note that the purpose of foreclosure is to cut off the borrower's equity of redemption rights (discussed below).

Methods of foreclosure. Three general types of foreclosure proceedings exist—judicial, nonjudicial, and strict. The specific provisions of each method vary from state to state.

1. **Judicial foreclosure.** Mortgages are foreclosed through a court process called **judicial foreclosure**. A judicial foreclosure proceeding provides that the property pledged as security may be sold by court order after the mortgagee

NORTH CAROLINA DEED OF TRUST

SATISFACTION: The debt secured by the within Deed of Trust together with the note(s) secured thereby has been satisfied in full.

This the _____ day of _____, 20____

Signed:_____   _____

_____   _____

Parcel Identifier No._____ Verified by _____ County on the ____ day of_____, 20__

By:_____

Mail/Box to: _____

This instrument was prepared by:_____

Brief description for the Index: _____

THIS DEED of TRUST made this _____ day of _____, 20___, by and between:

GRANTOR	TRUSTEE	BENEFICIARY

Enter in appropriate block for each party: name, address, and, if appropriate, character of entity, e.g. corporation or partnership.

The designation Grantor, Trustee, and Beneficiary as used herein shall include said parties, their heirs, successors, and assigns, and shall include singular, plural, masculine, feminine or neuter as required by context.

WITNESSETH, That whereas the Grantor is indebted to the Beneficiary in the principal sum of _____
_____ Dollars ($_____),
as evidenced by a Promissory Note of even date herewith, the terms of which are incorporated herein by reference. The final due date for payments of said Promissory Note, if not sooner paid, is_____, 20___.

FIGURE   13.5   North Carolina Deed of Trust (continued)

NOW, THEREFORE, as security for said indebtedness, advancements and other sums expended by Beneficiary pursuant to this Deed of Trust and costs of collection (including attorneys fees as provided in the Promissory Note) and other valuable consideration, the receipt of which is hereby acknowledged, the Grantor has bargained, sold, given and conveyed and does by these presents bargain, sell, give, grant and convey to said Trustee, his heirs, or successors, and assigns, the parcel(s) of land situated in the City of _____, _____ Township, _____ County, North Carolina, (the "Premises") and more particularly described as follows:

TO HAVE AND TO HOLD said Premises with all privileges and appurtenances thereunto belonging, to said Trustee, his heirs, successors, and assigns forever, upon the trusts, terms and conditions, and for the uses hereinafter set forth.

If the Grantor shall pay the Note secured hereby in accordance with its terms, together with interest thereon, and any renewals or extensions thereof in whole or in part, all other sums secured hereby and shall comply with all of the covenants, terms and conditions of this Deed of Trust, then this conveyance shall be null and void and may be canceled of record at the request and the expense of the Grantor.

If, however, there shall be any default (a) in the payment of any sums due under the Note, this Deed of Trust or any other instrument securing the Note and such default is not cured within ten (10) days from the due date, or (b) if there shall be default in any of the other covenants, terms or conditions of the Note secured hereby, or any failure or neglect to comply with the covenants, terms or conditions contained in this Deed of Trust or any other instrument securing the Note and such default is not cured within fifteen (15) days after written notice, then and in any of such events, without further notice, it shall be lawful for and the duty of the Trustee, upon request of the Beneficiary, to sell the land herein conveyed at public auction for cash, after having first giving such notice of hearing as to commencement of foreclosure proceedings and obtained such findings or leave of court as may then be required by law and giving such notice and advertising the time and place of such sale in such manner as may then be provided by law, and upon such and any resales and upon compliance with the law then relating to foreclosure proceedings under power of sale to convey title to the purchaser in as full and ample manner as the Trustee is empowered. The Trustee shall be authorized to retain an attorney to represent him in such proceedings.

The proceeds of the Sale shall after the Trustee retains his commission, together with reasonable attorneys fees incurred by the Trustee in such proceedings, be applied to the costs of sale, including, but not limited to, costs of collection, taxes, assessments, costs of recording, service fees and incidental expenditures, the amount due on the Note hereby secured and advancements and other sums expended by the Beneficiary according to the provisions hereof and otherwise as required by the then existing law relating to foreclosures. The Trustee's commission shall be five percent (5%) of the gross proceeds of the sale or the minimum sum of $_____ whichever is greater, for a completed foreclosure. In the event foreclosure is commenced, but not completed, the Grantor shall pay all expenses incurred by Trustee, including reasonable attorneys fees, and a partial commission computed on five per cent (5%) of the outstanding indebtedness or the above stated minimum sum, whichever is greater, in accordance with the following schedule, to-wit: one-fourth (¼) thereof before the Trustee issues a notice of hearing on the right to foreclosure; one-half (½) thereof after issuance of said notice, three-fourths (¾) thereof after such hearing; and the greater of the full commission or minimum sum after the initial sale.

And the said Grantor does hereby covenant and agree with the Trustee as follows:

1. INSURANCE. Grantor shall keep all improvements on said land, now or hereafter erected, constantly insured for the benefit of the Beneficiary against loss by fire, windstorm and such other casualties and contingencies, in such manner and in such companies and for such amounts, not less than that amount necessary to pay the sum secured by this Deed of Trust, and as may be satisfactory to the Beneficiary. Grantor shall purchase such insurance, pay all premiums therefor, and shall deliver to Beneficiary such policies along with evidence of premium payments as long as the Note secured hereby remains unpaid. If Grantor fails to purchase such insurance, pay premiums therefor or deliver said policies along with evidence of payment of premiums thereon, then Beneficiary, at his option, may purchase such insurance. Such amounts paid by Beneficiary shall be added to the principal of the Note secured by this Deed of Trust, and shall be due and payable upon demand of Beneficiary. All proceeds from any insurance so maintained shall at the option of Beneficiary be applied to the debt secured hereby and if payable in installments, applied in the inverse order of maturity of such installments or to the repair or reconstruction of any improvements located upon the Property.

2. TAXES, ASSESSMENTS, CHARGES. Grantor shall pay all taxes, assessments and charges as may be lawfully levied against said Premises within thirty (30) days after the same shall become due. In the event that Grantor fails to so pay all taxes, assessments and charges as herein required, then Beneficiary, at his option, may pay the same and the amounts so paid shall be added to the principal of the Note secured by this Deed of Trust, and shall be due and payable upon demand of Beneficiary.

3. ASSIGNMENTS OF RENTS AND PROFITS. Grantor assigns to Beneficiary, in the event of default, all rents and profits from the land and any improvements thereon, and authorizes Beneficiary to enter upon and take possession of such land and improvements, to rent same, at any reasonable rate of rent determined by Beneficiary, and after deducting from any such rents the cost of reletting and collection, to apply the remainder to the debt secured hereby.

4. PARTIAL RELEASE. Grantor shall not be entitled to the partial release of any of the above described property unless a specific provision providing therefor is included in this Deed of Trust. In the event a partial release provision is included in this Deed of Trust, Grantor must strictly comply with the terms thereof. Notwithstanding anything herein contained, Grantor shall not be

NC Bar Association Form No. 5 © 1976, Revised © September 1985, 2002   + James Williams & Co., Inc.
Printed by Agreement with the NC Bar Association - 1981   www.JamesWilliams.com

entitled to any release of property unless Grantor is not in default and is in full compliance with all of the terms and provisions of the Note, this Deed of Trust, and any other instrument that may be securing said Note.

5. WASTE. The Grantor covenants that he will keep the Premises herein conveyed in as good order, repair and condition as they are now, reasonable wear and tear excepted, and will comply with all governmental requirements respecting the Premises or their use, and that he will not commit or permit any waste.

6. CONDEMNATION. In the event that any or all of the Premises shall be condemned and taken under the power of eminent domain, Grantor shall give immediate written notice to Beneficiary and Beneficiary shall have the right to receive and collect all damages awarded by reason of such taking, and the right to such damages hereby is assigned to Beneficiary who shall have the discretion to apply the amount so received, or any part thereof, to the indebtedness due hereunder and if payable in installments, applied in the inverse order of maturity of such installments, or to any alteration, repair or restoration of the Premises by Grantor.

7. WARRANTIES. Grantor covenants with Trustee and Beneficiary that he is seized of the Premises in fee simple, has the right to convey the same in fee simple, that title is marketable and free and clear of all encumbrances, and that he will warrant and defend the title against the lawful claims of all persons whomsoever, except for the exceptions hereinafter stated. Title to the property hereinabove described is subject to the following exceptions:

8. SUBSTITUTION OF TRUSTEE. Grantor and Trustee covenant and agree to and with Beneficiary that in case the said Trustee, or any successor trustee, shall die, become incapable of acting, renounce his trust, or for any reason the holder of the Note desires to replace said Trustee, then the holder may appoint, in writing, a trustee to take the place of the Trustee; and upon the probate and registration of the same, the trustee thus appointed shall succeed to all rights, powers and duties of the Trustee.

☐   **THE FOLLOWING PARAGRAPH, 9. SALE OF PREMISES, SHALL NOT APPLY UNLESS THE BLOCK TO THE LEFT MARGIN OF THIS SENTENCE IS MARKED AND/OR INITIALED.**

9. SALE OF PREMISES. Grantor agrees that if the Premises or any part thereof or interest therein is sold, assigned, transferred, conveyed or otherwise alienated by Grantor, whether voluntarily or involuntarily or by operation of law [other than: (i) the creation of a lien or other encumbrance subordinate to this Deed of Trust which does not relate to a transfer of rights of occupancy in the Premises; (ii) the creation of a purchase money security interest for household appliances; (iii) a transfer by devise, descent, or operation of law on the death of a joint tenant or tenant by the entirety; (iv) the grant of a leasehold interest of three (3) years or less not containing an option to purchase; (v) a transfer to a relative resulting from the death of a Grantor; (vi) a transfer where the spouse or children of the Grantor become the owner of the Premises; (vii) a transfer resulting from a decree of a dissolution of marriage, legal separation agreement, or from an incidental property settlement agreement, by which the spouse of the Grantor becomes an owner of the Premises; (viii) a transfer into an inter vivos trust in which the Grantor is and remains a beneficiary and which does not relate to a transfer of rights of occupancy in the Premises], without the prior written consent of Beneficiary, Beneficiary, at its own option, may declare the Note secured hereby and all other obligations hereunder to be forthwith due and payable. Any change in the legal or equitable title of the Premises or in the beneficial ownership of the Premises, including the sale, conveyance or disposition of a majority interest in the Grantor if a corporation or partnership, whether or not of record and whether or not for consideration, shall be deemed to be the transfer of an interest in the Premises.

10. ADVANCEMENTS. If Grantor shall fail to perform any of the covenants or obligations contained herein or in any other instrument given as additional security for the Note secured hereby, the Beneficiary may, but without obligation, make advances to perform such covenants or obligations, and all such sums so advanced shall be added to the principal sum, shall bear interest at the rate provided in the Note secured hereby for sums due after default and shall be due from Grantor on demand of the Beneficiary. No advancement or anything contained in this paragraph shall constitute a waiver by Beneficiary or prevent such failure to perform from constituting an event of default.

11. INDEMNITY. If any suit or proceeding be brought against the Trustee or Beneficiary or if any suit or proceeding be brought which may affect the value or title of the Premises, Grantor shall defend, indemnify and hold harmless and on demand reimburse Trustee or Beneficiary from any loss, cost, damage or expense and any sums expended by Trustee or Beneficiary shall bear interest as provided in the Note secured hereby for sums due after default and shall be due and payable on demand.

12. WAIVERS. Grantor waives all rights to require marshaling of assets by the Trustee or Beneficiary. No delay or omission of the Trustee or Beneficiary in the exercise of any right, power or remedy arising under the Note or this Deed of Trust shall be deemed a waiver of any default or acquiescence therein or shall impair or waive the exercise of such right, power or remedy by Trustee or Beneficiary at any other time.

13. CIVIL ACTION. In the event that the Trustee is named as a party to any civil action as Trustee in this Deed of Trust, the Trustee shall be entitled to employ an attorney at law, including himself if he is a licensed attorney, to represent him in said action and the reasonable attorney's fee of the Trustee in such action shall be paid by the Beneficiary and added to the principal of the Note secured by this Deed of Trust and bear interest at the rate provided in the Note for sums due after default.

14. PRIOR LIENS. Default under the terms of any instrument secured by a lien to which this Deed of Trust is subordinate shall constitute default hereunder.

15. OTHER TERMS.

NC Bar Association Form No. 5 © 1976, Revised © September 1985, 2002
Printed by Agreement with the NC Bar Association - 1981

+ James Williams & Co., Inc.
www.JamesWilliams.com

F I G U R E   13.5   North Carolina Deed of Trust (continued)

IN WITNESS WHEREOF, the Grantor has duly executed the foregoing as of the day and year first above written.

_____   _____(SEAL)

_____(Entity Name)_____

By:_____   _____(SEAL)

     Title:_____

By:_____   _____(SEAL)

     Title:_____

By:_____   _____(SEAL)

     Title:_____

_____(SEAL)

_____(SEAL)

_____(SEAL)

USE BLACK INK ONLY

SEAL-STAMP

State of North Carolina - County of _____

I, the undersigned Notary Public of the County and State aforesaid, certify that _____
_____ personally appeared before me this day and acknowledged the due execution of the foregoing instrument for the purposes therein expressed. Witness my hand and Notarial stamp or seal this _____ day of _____, 20___.

My Commission Expires:_____   _____
                                            Notary Public

SEAL-STAMP

State of North Carolina - County of _____

I, the undersigned Notary Public of the County and State aforesaid, certify that _____
_____ personally came before me this day and acknowledged that _he is the _____ of _____,
a North Carolina or _____ corporation/limited liability company/general partnership/limited partnership (strike through the inapplicable), and that by authority duly given and as the act of each entity, _he signed the forgoing instrument in its name on its behalf as its act and deed. Witness my hand and Notarial stamp or seal this _____ day of _____, 20___.

My Commission Expires:_____   _____
                                            Notary Public

SEAL-STAMP

State of North Carolina - County of _____

I, the undersigned Notary Public of the County and State aforesaid, certify that _____
_____

Witness my hand and Notarial stamp or seal this _____ day of _____, 20___.

My Commission Expires:_____   _____
                                            Notary Public

The foregoing Certificate(s) of _____ is/are certified to be correct. This instrument and this certificate are duly registered at the date and time and in the Book and Page shown on the first page hereof.
_____ Register of Deeds for _____ County

By:_____ Deputy/Assistant - Register of Deeds

NC Bar Association Form No. 5 © 1976, Revised © September 1985, 2002   * James Williams & Co., Inc.
Printed by Agreement with the NC Bar Association - 1981   www.JamesWilliams.com

has given sufficient public notice. On a borrower's default, the lender may accelerate the due date of all remaining monthly payments. The lender's lawyer can then file a suit to foreclose the lien. On presentation of the facts in court, the property is ordered sold. A public sale is advertised and held, and the real estate is sold to the highest acceptable bidder. The new owner receives title to the property by means of a *sheriff's deed*.

2. **Nonjudicial foreclosure.** A deed of trust does not have to be foreclosed through a court action, so this type of foreclosure is called a *nonjudicial foreclosure* or foreclosure under power of sale. Nonjudicial foreclosure is made possible by the power-of-sale clause in the deed of trust. The power-of-sale clause gives the trustee the power to sell the property and use the proceeds to repay the debt. (Note that a mini-hearing is required before the clerk of the court; otherwise, the property cannot be sold.)

   To institute a nonjudicial foreclosure, the trustee or lender must record a notice of default at the county courthouse in the Clerk of Court's office within a designated time period to give notice to the public of the intended auction. Generally, this official notice is accompanied by advertisements published in local newspapers that state the total amount due and the date of the public sale. The trustee then conducts the sale and transfers title to the high bidder by means of a *trustee's deed*. North Carolina exercises power of sale foreclosure.

3. **Strict foreclosure.** Although the judicial and nonjudicial foreclosure procedures are the prevalent practices today, in a few states it is still possible for a lender to acquire the mortgaged property by a strict foreclosure process. After appropriate notice has been given to the delinquent borrower and the proper papers have been prepared and filed, the court establishes a specific time period during which the balance of the defaulted debt must be paid in full. If this is not done, the court usually awards full legal title to the lender. Strict foreclosure is not used in North Carolina.

Deed in lieu of foreclosure.   An alternative to foreclosure is for the lender to accept a **deed in lieu of foreclosure** from the borrower. This is sometimes known as a *friendly foreclosure* because it is accomplished by agreement rather than by civil action. The major disadvantage to this manner of default settlement is that the mortgagee takes the real estate subject to all junior liens; foreclosure eliminates all such liens.

Distribution of proceeds.   After the property is sold at the foreclosure sale, the proceeds are distributed in the following five-step order:

1. To pay all costs of the sale, including court costs or trustee fees, legal fees, advertising fees, and so on
2. To pay any outstanding real and personal property taxes or assessments
3. To pay the mortgage(s) or deed(s) of trust debt (assuming this debt has first priority over any other liens) in order of recordation
4. To pay off any other liens in order of priority
5. To pay any surplus (equity) to the borrower

Redemption.   Defaulting borrowers usually have a chance to redeem their property. In most cases, redemption takes one of two forms—equity right of redemption or **statutory right of redemption.**

Historically, the **equity of redemption** (also called the *equity right of redemption*) is inherited from the old common-law proceedings in which the foreclosure process extinguished the borrower's right to regain the property. Adopted by statutory law, this concept provides that if, during the course of a foreclosure proceeding but before the confirmation of the foreclosure sale, the borrower pays the lender the total amount due, plus costs, then the borrower retains the property. The borrower who redeems will be required to repay the accelerated loan in full (see Figure 13.6).

During a ten-day **statutory redemption period** after the auction (the *upset bid period*), a mortgagor (borrower) can try to raise the necessary funds to redeem the property. During the upset bid period, any qualified bidder can submit an upset bid, a bid to purchase the property for an amount that exceeds the foreclosure sale price by a specific margin. Each upset bid triggers a new ten-day period. If the defaulted borrower can pay all that is owed to the lender (including accrued interest and penalties plus cost of foreclosure sale) anytime prior to confirmation of sale, the borrower redeems the property, receives legal title, and eliminates the previous winning bid. The foreclosure sale becomes final at the end of any ten-day period when no new bid is filed and the borrower's right to redeem the property is terminated.

Deficiency judgment.   If the foreclosure sale of the real estate secured by a mortgage or trust deed does not produce sufficient proceeds to pay the loan balance and accrued unpaid interest plus costs of sale, the lender may be entitled to a personal judgment against the maker of the note for the unpaid balance. Such a judgment is called a **deficiency judgment**. It also may be obtained against any endorsers or guarantors of the note and any owners of the mortgaged property who may have assumed the debt by written agreement. Deficiency judgments are prohibited in certain cases, such as when a purchase-money deed of trust (seller financing) is used. If the seller is holding a purchase-money mortgage/deed of trust, the seller has a special priority in lien payoffs in the foreclosure.

If any surplus proceeds exist from the foreclosure sale after real estate taxes, the mortgage debt, and all junior liens (second mortgage, mechanics' liens, and so on) are paid off and expenses and interest are deducted, these proceeds (equity) are paid to the borrower.

Buying Subject to or Assuming a Seller's Mortgage

When a person purchases real estate that is subject to an outstanding mortgage or deed of trust, the buyer may take the property in one of two ways. The property may be purchased subject to the mortgage, or the buyer may assume the mortgage and agree to pay the debt. This technical distinction becomes important if the buyer defaults and the mortgage or deed of trust is foreclosed.

When the property is sold *subject to the mortgage*, the buyer will not be personally obligated to pay the debt in full. The buyer takes title to the real estate knowing that he or she must make payments on the existing loan. On default, the lender forecloses and the property is sold by court order to pay the debt. If the sale does not pay off the entire debt, the purchaser is not liable for the difference. In some circumstances, however, the original seller might continue to be liable, if sale proceeds do not cover the entire debt.

FIGURE 13.6

Redemption

In contrast, a buyer who purchases the property and assumes the seller's debt becomes personally obligated for the payment of the entire debt. If the mortgage is foreclosed and the court sale does not bring enough money to pay the debt in full, a deficiency judgment against the assumptor and the original borrower may be obtained for the unpaid balance of the note. If the original borrower received a release from liability by the lender, only the assumptor is liable.

■ **FOR EXAMPLE**

■ When Jennifer bought her house a short time ago, interest rates were very low. Now Jennifer has been unexpectedly transferred out of the country and needs to sell the house quickly. Because interest rates have risen dramatically since the time of Jennifer's loan, buyers may be attracted by the prospect of assuming her low-interest mortgage. Clearly, if a buyer were to take out a new mortgage now, the rate would be higher and the cost of home ownership would be increased. By assuming an existing loan with a more favorable interest rate, a buyer can save money.

■ Dylan purchased his house when interest rates were high. In the short time since then, rates have fallen precipitously. If Dylan must sell quickly, he may find that buyers are not interested in assuming a high-interest mortgage. A buyer might purchase Dylan's property subject to the existing mortgage. That is, the buyer would purchase Dylan's equity; Dylan still would be liable for the mortgage; and the bank could foreclose on the property to recover a default. If the foreclosure sale failed to satisfy the debt, Dylan would be liable for the shortfall.

In most cases, a mortgage loan may not be assumed without lender approval. The lending institution requires the assumptor to qualify financially, and many lending institutions charge a transfer fee to cover the costs of changing the records. The purchaser usually pays any loan assumption charge.

■ RELATED WEB SITES

Mortgage Bankers Association: *www.mbaa.org*
Mortgage Bankers Association of the Carolinas: *www.mbac.org*
North Carolina Association of Mortgage Professionals: *www.ncmortgage.org*
North Carolina Banking Commission: *www.nccob.org*

■ SUMMARY

Real estate loans provide the principal source of financing for real estate transactions. After a lending institution has received, investigated, and approved a loan application, it issues a commitment to make the loan. The borrower is required to execute a promissory note, agreeing to repay the debt, and a mortgage or deed of trust, which secures the note by pledging the property as collateral for the loan. The security instrument—mortgage or deed of trust— is recorded to give constructive notice to the world of the lender's interest in the property. The promissory note usually contains certain special provisions: the acceleration clause, the due-on-sale clause, and the prepayment penalty clause. Two types of security instruments exist: (1) a mortgage, which involves a borrower (the mortgagor) and a lender (the mortgagee), and (2) a deed of trust, which involves a borrower (the grantor or the trustor), a lender (the beneficiary), and an independent third party (the trustee). The mortgage allows the borrower to retain both legal and equitable title and is used in a lien theory state. The deed of trust conveys legal title to the property to the trustee, who has the power to sell the property on behalf of the lender if the borrower defaults on the loan; borrower retains equitable title. Deeds of trust are used in a title theory state such as North Carolina.

There are many repayment plans for mortgage loans. Examples would include adjustable-rate mortgage, graduated payment mortgage, term loan, and balloon payment mortgage. The most common residential home mortgage is the fully amortized fixed-rate level-payment mortgage.

The note's payment in full entitles the borrower to a satisfaction, or release, of mortgage, which is recorded to clear the lien from the public records. Default by the borrower may result in acceleration of payments, a foreclosure sale, and loss of title. Three types of foreclosure sales exist: judicial foreclosure, power of sale (nonjudicial) foreclosure, and strict foreclosure. Proceeds from the foreclosure sale first pay cost of sale expenses, then ad valorem taxes and assessments, then mortgages and liens in order of recordation. Any equity is returned to the defaulted borrower; any shortfall will prompt a deficiency judgment from the professional creditor wanting satisfaction. Holder of a purchase money deed of trust is not allowed to file for a deficiency judgment.

QUESTIONS

1. North Carolina is characterized as a(n)
   a. lien theory state.
   b. title theory state.
   c. mortgage theory state.
   d. escrow theory state.

2. Which of the following statements is *TRUE* of a prepayment penalty in a mortgage instrument?
   a. It usually penalizes early payment of the mortgage loan.
   b. It is prohibited in all residential and commercial mortgage loans in North Carolina.
   c. It can never be waived, even if the buyer's mortgage is with the same lender as the seller's.
   d. It penalizes the lender when the mortgagor pays off the loan early.

3. A deed of trust
   a. is evidence of a debt.
   b. uses real estate as security for the repayment of a debt.
   c. is sometimes called a promissory note.
   d. is evidence of both legal and equitable title.

4. A charge to a borrower of three discount points on a $120,000 loan is
   a. $450
   b. $3,600
   c. $4,500
   d. $116,400

5. The person who obtains a real estate loan by signing a deed of trust is called the
   a. grantee.
   b. grantor.
   c. trustee.
   d. beneficiary.

6. All of the following components are common in an adjustable rate mortgage *EXCEPT*
   a. a payment cap.
   b. a life of the loan cap.
   c. an escrow cap.
   d. an anniversary cap.

7. Laws that limit the amount of interest that can be charged to the borrower are called
   a. truth-in-lending laws.
   b. usury laws.
   c. equal credit opportunity laws.
   d. RESPA legislation.

8. If a borrower pays $2,700 for points on a $90,000 loan, how many points is the lender charging for this loan?
   a. Two
   b. Three
   c. Five
   d. Six

9. Before the foreclosure sale, the borrower who has defaulted on the loan seeks to pay off the debt plus any accrued interest and costs under the right of
   a. redemption.
   b. defeasance.
   c. reentry.
   d. survivorship.

10. The clause in a promissory note that gives the lender the right to demand that all future installment payments become due on default is the
    a. escalation clause.
    b. defeasance clause.
    c. alienation clause.
    d. acceleration clause.

11. Which of the following statements is/are *TRUE* about a deed of trust?
    I. Foreclosure is conducted through the power of sale clause.
    II. It pledges the property as collateral for securing the loan.
    a. I only
    b. II only
    c. Both I and II
    d. Neither I nor II

12. Pledging property for a loan without giving up possession is best described as
    a. hypothecation.
    b. defeasance.
    c. alienation.
    d. novation.

13. Discount points on a mortgage are computed as a percentage of the
    a. selling price.
    b. amount borrowed.
    c. closing costs.
    d. down payment.

14. The clause in a deed of trust that allows the lender to call in the loan when the property is transferred is called the
    a. acceleration clause.
    b. prepayment penalty clause.
    c. alienation clause.
    d. defeasance clause.

15. Proceeds from a foreclosure sale first pay
    a. mortgages in the order of recordation.
    b. outstanding property taxes.
    c. junior liens in the order of recordation.
    d. the cost of the foreclosure sale.

16. In a deed in lieu of foreclosure situation,
    a. the lender is obligated to accept the deed.
    b. the lender takes the real estate subject to all junior liens.
    c. a civil action is required.
    d. all encumbrances on the property are extinguished.

17. A deficiency judgment on a promissory note may be granted to a
    a. holder of a purchase-money mortgage.
    b. creditor whose loan was satisfied by the foreclosure sale.
    c. lender whose note was not fully satisfied by the foreclosure sale.
    d. mortgagor of the note.

18. Which of the following statements is/are *TRUE* if a buyer purchases property subject to the seller's loan and then defaults on the loan?
    I. The buyer is personally liable for the underlying debt.
    II. The seller remains personally liable for the underlying debt.
    a. I only
    b. II only
    c. Both I and II
    d. Neither I nor II

19. A term loan requires that the borrower pay
    a. only the interest during the loan term.
    b. both principal and interest during the loan term.
    c. an interest rate that adjusts during the loan term.
    d. increasing amounts of principal during the loan term.

20. A mortgage loan that calls for a substantially larger than normal payment at the end of the loan term is a(n)
    a. index loan.
    b. graduated payment loan.
    c. balloon payment loan.
    d. adjustable rate loan.

21. Interest charges by the lender on a fixed-rate conventional level payment loan are
    a. subject to periodic changes.
    b. almost always simple interest.
    c. usually paid in advance.
    d. all of the above.

22. A deficiency judgment is
    a. a court decision declaring that a debt is excused if a foreclosure sale does not satisfy the debt.
    b. a court decision for the balance owed on a debt after the security has been sold to apply toward the debt.
    c. a specific lien.
    d. a general lien with a life of five years.

23. Which of the following mortgages features increasing payments with the increases applied directly to the principal?

a. Shared appreciation
b. Growing equity
c. Adjustable rate
d. Graduated payment

24. A promissory note must be signed by the

I. borrower.
II. lender.

a. I only
b. II only
c. Both I and II
d. Neither I nor II

25. A deed of trust is a

a. two-party instrument.
b. three-party instrument.
c. promissory note.
d. security instrument that requires a judicial foreclosure.

26. A buyer has purchased a home under an agreement that made the buyer personally obligated to continue making payments under the seller's existing mortgage. If the buyer defaults and the court sale does not satisfy the debt, the buyer will be liable for making up the deficiency. The buyer has

a. purchased the home subject to the seller's mortgage.
b. assumed the seller's mortgage.
c. adjusted the alienation clause in the seller's mortgage.
d. benefited from the defeasance clause in the seller's mortgage.

CHAPTER 14

Real Estate Financing: Practices

■ **LEARNING OBJECTIVES** *When you have finished reading this chapter, you should be able to*

■ **understand** some of the components of the recent financial crisis.

■ **define** the prevailing criteria for (1) conventional, (2) FHA-insured, and (3) VA-guaranteed mortgage loans.

■ **identify** other types of financing techniques and special purpose loans.

■ **describe** how the secondary mortgage market operates, including the three major agencies, and federal legislation that affects mortgage lending practices.

■ **explain** residential lending practices and procedures.

■ **define** these *key terms*:

annual percentage rate (APR)	Federal Reserve System	Real Estate Settlement Procedures Act (RESPA)
blanket mortgage	FHA-insured loan	
buydown	Freddie Mac	Regulation Z
certificate of reasonable value (CRV)	Ginnie Mae	reverse-annuity mortgage (RAM)
	home equity loans	
	jumbo loan	sale and leaseback
conforming loan	loan-to-value ratio (LTV)	secondary mortgage market
construction loan	open-end mortgages	
conventional loan	package loan	short sale
Department of Housing and Urban Development (HUD)	Predatory Lending Act	subordination agreement
	primary mortgage market	subprime mortgage
	private mortgage insurance (PMI)	trigger terms
Equal Credit Opportunity Act (ECOA)	purchase-money mortgage	Truth-in-Lending Act
Fair Credit Reporting Act		VA-guaranteed loan
Fannie Mae		wraparound loan

■ INTRODUCTION TO THE REAL ESTATE FINANCING MARKET

The real estate financing market has the following three basic components:

1. Government influences, primarily the Federal Reserve System, but also the Home Loan Bank System and the Office of Thrift Supervision,
2. The primary mortgage market, and
3. The secondary mortgage market.

Under the umbrella of the financial policies set by the Federal Reserve System, the primary mortgage market originates loans that are bought, sold, and traded in the secondary mortgage market. It is important to have a clear understanding of the market in which mortgage loans exist.

The Federal Reserve System

The role of the **Federal Reserve System** (the Fed) is to maintain sound credit conditions, help counteract inflationary and deflationary trends, and create a favorable economic climate. The Federal Reserve System divides the country into 12 Federal Reserve Districts, each served by a Federal Reserve Bank. All nationally chartered banks must join the Fed and purchase stock in its district reserve banks.

The Fed regulates the flow of money and interest rates in the marketplace through its member banks by controlling their reserve requirements and discount rates. The Fed also can regulate the money supply through the Federal Open Market Committee, which buys and sells U.S. government securities on the open market. The sale of securities removes the money paid by buyers from circulation. When it buys them, it infuses its own reserves back into the general supply.

Reserve requirements.   The Federal Reserve System requires that each member bank keep a certain amount of assets on hand as reserve funds. These reserves are unavailable for loans or any other use. This requirement not only protects customer deposits, but it also provides a means of manipulation for the flow of cash in the money market.

By increasing its reserve requirements, the Fed in effect limits the amount of money that member banks can use to make loans. When the amount of money available for lending decreases, interest rates rise. By causing interest rates to rise, the government can slow down an overactive economy by limiting the number of loans that would have been directed toward major purchases of goods and services. The opposite is also true—by decreasing the reserve requirements, the Fed can encourage more lending. Increased lending causes the amount of money circulated in the marketplace to rise, while simultaneously causing interest rates to drop.

Discount rates.   Federal Reserve member banks are permitted to borrow money from the district reserve banks to expand their lending operations. The discount rate is the rate charged by the Fed when it lends to its member banks. The federal funds rate is the rate recommended by the Fed for the member banks to charge each other on short-term loans. These rates form the basis on which the banks determine the percentage rate of interest they will charge their loan customers. The prime rate, the short-term interest charged to a bank's largest, most creditworthy customers, is strongly influenced by the Fed's discount rate. In turn, the prime rate is often the basis for determining a bank's interest rate on other loans, including mortgages. These rates are usually higher than the prime rate. In theory, when the Fed's discount rate is high, bank interest rates are high. When bank interest rates are high, fewer loans are made and less money circulates in the marketplace. On the other hand, a lower discount rate results in lower overall interest rats, more bank loans, and more money in circulation.

The Primary Mortgage Market

The **primary mortgage market** is made up of the lenders that originate mortgage loans. These lenders make money available directly to borrowers. From a borrower's point of view, a loan is a means of financing an expenditure; from a lender's point of view, a loan is an investment. All investors look for profitable returns on their investments. For a lender, a loan must generate enough income to be attractive as an investment. Income on the loan is realized from the following two sources:

1. Finance charges collected at closing, such as loan origination fees and discount points
2. Recurring income, that is, the interest collected during the term of the loan

An increasing number of lenders look at the income generated from the fees charged in originating loans as their primary investment objective. Once the loans are made, they are sold to investors. By selling loans to investors in the secondary mortgage market, lenders generate funds with which to originate additional loans. In addition to the income directly related to loans, some lenders derive income from servicing loans for other mortgage lenders or investors who have purchased the loans. Servicing involves such activities as

- collecting payments (including insurance and taxes),
- accounting,
- bookkeeping,
- preparing insurance and tax records,
- processing payments of taxes and insurance, and
- following up on loan payment and delinquency.

The terms of the servicing agreement stipulate the responsibilities and fees for the service.

Some of the major lenders in the primary market include the following:

- *Savings associations, or thrifts, and commercial banks.* These institutions are known as fiduciary lenders because of their fiduciary obligations to protect and preserve their depositors' funds. Mortgage loans are perceived as secure investments for generating income and enable these institutions to pay interest to their depositors. Fiduciary lenders are subject to standards and regulations established by government agencies such as the Federal Deposit Insurance Corporation (FDIC) and the Office of Thrift Supervision (OTS). These agencies govern the practice of fiduciary lenders. The various government regulations are intended to protect depositors against the reckless lending that characterized the savings and loan industry in the 1980s.
- *Insurance companies.* Insurance companies amass large sums of money from the premiums paid by their policyholders. While a certain portion of this

money is held in reserve to satisfy claims and cover operating expenses, much of it is invested in profit-earning enterprises, such as long-term real estate loans. Although insurance companies are not considered primary lenders, they tend to invest their money in large, long-term loans that finance commercial, industrial, and larger multifamily properties rather than single-family home mortgages.

■ *Credit unions.* Credit unions are cooperative organizations in which members place money in savings accounts, usually at higher interest rates than other savings institutions offer. In the past, most credit unions made only short-term consumer and home improvement loans, but in recent years they have been branching out to longer-term first and second mortgages and trust deed loans.

■ *Pension funds.* Pension funds usually have large amounts of money available for investment. Because of the comparatively high yields and low risks offered by mortgages, pension funds have begun to participate actively in financing real estate projects. Most real estate activity for pension funds is handled through mortgage bankers and mortgage brokers.

■ *Endowment funds.* Many commercial banks and mortgage bankers handle investments from endowment funds. The endowments of hospitals, universities, colleges, charitable foundations, and other institutions provide a good source of financing for low-risk commercial and industrial properties.

■ *Investment group financing.* Large real estate projects, including highrise apartment buildings, office complexes, and shopping centers, are often financed as joint ventures through group financing arrangements such as syndicates, limited partnerships, and real estate investment trusts (REITs).

■ *Mortgage banking companies.* Mortgage banking companies originate mortgage loans with money belonging to insurance companies, pension funds, and individuals, and with funds of their own. They make real estate loans with the intention of selling them to investors and receiving a fee for servicing the loans. Mortgage banking companies are generally organized as stock companies. As a source of real estate financing, they are subject to fewer lending restrictions than are commercial banks or savings associations. Mortgage banking companies often are involved in all types of real estate loan activities and often serve as intermediaries between investors and borrowers. They are NOT mortgage brokers.

■ *Mortgage brokers.* Mortgage brokers are NOT lenders. They are intermediaries who bring borrowers and lenders together. Mortgage brokers locate potential borrowers, process preliminary loan applications, and submit the applications to lenders for final approval. Frequently, they work with or for mortgage banking companies. They do not service loans once the loans are made. Mortgage brokers also may be real estate brokers who offer these financing services in addition to their regular real estate brokerage activities. Many state governments are establishing separate licensure requirements for mortgage brokers to regulate their activities.

IN PRACTICE

A growing number of consumers apply for mortgage loans via the Internet. Many major lenders have Web sites that offer information to potential borrowers regarding their current loan programs and requirements. In addition, online brokerage or match-making organizations link lenders with potential borrowers. Some borrowers prefer the Internet for its convenience in shopping for the best rates and terms, accessing a wide variety of loan programs, and speeding up the loan approval process.

The Secondary Mortgage Market

The **secondary mortgage market** purchases, services, and sometimes re-sells existing mortgages and mortgage-backed securities created by the primary market lenders. This process replenishes funds to the primary mortgage market so they can originate more mortgage loans for the house-buying public, thereby helping homeownership become more affordable for all Americans. There are three major institutions in the secondary market: Fannie Mae, Ginnie Mae, and Freddie Mac. **Fannie Mae**, originally named the Federal National Mortgage Association (FNMA), is a privately-owned corporation that issues its own common stock and provides a secondary market for mortgage loans—conventional loans as well as FHA and VA loans. (Fannie Mae was once a government agency, and even though it is now a privately-owned corporation, it is still considered quasi-governmental or a government-sponsored enterprise (GSE) because it can borrow money from the U.S. Treasury.) Fannie Mae buys a *block* or *pool* of mortgages from a lender in exchange for *mortgage-backed securities* that the lender may keep or sell. Fannie Mae was instrumental in developing the uniform underwriting guidelines that helped assure investors of the quality of the mortgage-backed securities. These underwriting guidelines are now an accepted part of mortgage loan underwriting procedures and are regularly used to determine a loan applicant's creditworthiness. As the oldest and largest of the secondary mortgage market institutions, Fannie Mae has taken a leadership role in this arena. A visit to the Fannie Mae Web site will yield a wealth of information.

Ginnie Mae, originally called the Government National Mortgage Association (GNMA), exists as a corporation without capital stock and is a division of HUD. Ginnie Mae is designed to administer special-assistance programs and work with Fannie Mae in secondary market activities. Fannie Mae and Ginnie Mae can join forces in times of tight money and high interest rates through their tandem plan. Basically, the *tandem plan* provides that Fannie Mae can purchase high-risk, low-yield (usually FHA) loans at full market rates, with Ginnie Mae guaranteeing payment and absorbing the difference between the low yield and current market prices.

Ginnie Mae also guarantees investment securities issued by private offerors (such as banks, mortgage companies, and savings associations) and is backed by pools of FHA and VA mortgage loans. The Ginnie Mae pass-through certificate lets small investors buy shares in a pool of mortgages that provides for a monthly *pass through* of principal and interest payments directly to certificate holders. Ginnie Mae guarantees such certificates.

Freddie Mac, originally the Federal Home Loan Mortgage Corporation (FHLMC), functioning similar to Fannie Mae, provides a secondary market for mortgage loans, primarily conventional loans originated by savings associations. Freddie Mac has the authority to purchase mortgages, pool them, and sell bonds in the open market with the mortgages as security. Note, however, that Freddie Mac does not guarantee payment of these mortgages.

Many lenders use the standardized forms and follow the guidelines issued by Freddie Mac because use of these forms is mandatory for lenders that wish to sell mortgages in the agency's secondary mortgage market. The standardized documents include loan applications, credit reports, and appraisal forms.

The recent financial crisis.   On September 6, 2008, due to the recent financial crisis in the mortgage lending industry and overwhelming concern for the continued stability of the secondary market, the federal government placed both Fannie Mae and Freddie Mac into a governmental conservatorship under the newly formed Federal Housing Finance Agency. At that time, the two mortgage giants together owned or guaranteed over $5.3 trillion-worth of mortgages—nearly half of the American mortgage market. In addition to placing Fannie and Freddie back into governmental control, the U.S. Department of the Treasury has agreed to provide up to $100 billion of capital to ensure continued liquidity to the housing and mortgage markets. The ultimate stated goal of the conservatorship is to begin reducing the size of the mortgage portfolios of both Fannie and Freddie by 10 percent per year beginning in 2010 when the housing market is projected to be recovering. Federal officials have stated that such a step is necessary to strengthen the housing market and stabilize the financial market. The governmental programs to help stabilize and strengthen the housing and lending industries will be found on a newly posted Web site: *www.financialstability.gov*.

Much speculation has abounded and many fingers have been pointed to locate the exact cause of the lending industry crisis. Was it the lack of oversight on the part of the federal government; predatory lending practices and low qualifying requirements by the lenders; borrowers overextending themselves financially; appraisers overvaluing collateral properties; Wall Street strongly backing subprime mortgage securities; or real estate agents pushing up the high costs of housing? Perhaps the best explanation is a mixture of all the possible answers.

One major component of what has been termed a "financial meltdown" must be the huge surge and rapid decline in the popularity of the **subprime mortgage** market. As Fannie Mae and Freddie Mac were pressured to serve more of the consumer market, the qualifying standards became more and more liberal for borrowers and financing products became more flexible and creative. The secondary market created, endorsed, and purchased products such as 100 percent LTV loans, interest-only loans, hybrid (or exploding) ARMs, pay-option ARMs, and 40-year term loans. Lenders targeting subprime borrowers with relatively low credit scores flourished due to *stated income loans* (a loan where borrowers are asked to state their income and the lender believes them without verification) and/or *no documentation loans* (a loan with few to no documentation requirements, though easier to qualify for, generally carried a significantly higher interest rate); the number of subprime loans increased by over 300 percent from early 2000 to 2005. During the early years of the new century, escalating property values in many housing markets around the country offset the high risk of the subprime loans. If the rapidly increasing payments became burdensome, the borrower refinanced to access the newly acquired equity in the property or sold at a profit and financed a more expensive property.

Early 2005 saw the beginning of the housing market slowdown in some parts of the country. From the spring of 2005 to the fall of 2006, subprime mortgaged properties experienced a huge downward spiral in value with an increase in payment amounts that could not be corrected by refinancing. In early 2007, Freddie and Fannie stopped purchasing hybrid ARM loans and greatly reduced the number of no-doc or stated income loans (nicknamed "liar loans") that they would purchase.

By the summer of 2007, the subprime crisis exploded when several of the largest subprime lenders went bankrupt, leaving remaining subprime lenders suffering with huge drops in stock value. Banks absorbed millions of dollars in bad loans and began seriously restricting the money flow. According to RealtyTrac, which conducts and reports foreclosure statistics nationally, August 2007 saw an all-time record high number of foreclosures with one in every 557 households filing for foreclosure. Perhaps the final blow was at the end of 2008 when billions of dollars in subprime loans reset at greatly increased repayment terms causing even more widespread foreclosures. According to RealtyTrac, almost 3.2 million foreclosure filings were reported nationally in 2008 which is an 81 percent increase over 2007 and a 225 percent increase over 2006. The five states posting the highest foreclosure rates in 2008 were Nevada, Florida, Arizona, California and Colorado; North Carolina ranked 27th in foreclosure rates with a total of 41,750 filings in 2008. The beginning of 2009 has shown a hopeful turn in the right direction for North Carolina homeowners with a 7 percent drop in foreclosure rates from December to January; this represents a 29 percent decrease from January of 2008.

■ TYPES OF MORTGAGE LOANS

The various types of mortgage loans that are available today can be divided roughly into private conventional loans and government-sponsored loans.

Conventional Loans

A **conventional loan** is a loan that is not *backed*—that is, made, insured, or guaranteed—by any government agency. In other words, the lender bears all the risk of borrower default when making a conventional loan. A conventional loan is viewed as the most secure loan because its *loan-to-value ratio* is lowest. A mortgage loan is generally classified based on its **loan-to-value ratio (LTV)**, which is the ratio of debt to value of the property. *Value* is the sales price or the appraised value, whichever is less. The *lower* the ratio of debt to value, the *higher* the down payment by the borrower will be. For the lender, the higher down payment means a more secure loan, which minimizes the lender's risk. For instance, if a property is worth $100,000, an 80 percent loan would equal $80,000, and the borrower would make a $20,000 down payment.

MATH CONCEPTS

DETERMINING LTV

If a property has an appraised value of $100,000, secured by a $90,000 loan, the LTV is 90% (*Note:* if appraised value and sales price differ, the lender will use the lesser of the two to determine LTV.):

$90,000 loan ÷ $100,000 value = 0.90, or 90% LTV

Lenders that originate conventional loans usually intend to sell those loans to the secondary mortgage market once the transaction closes. Fannie Mae and other secondary market institutions will only purchase mortgage loans that conform to their lending guidelines to ensure that loans that are packaged together for purchase have similar characteristics.

Conforming loan guidelines for first mortgages secured by one to four family unit residences include a maximum loan amount; a minimum down payment; limits on seller contributions; and borrower qualifying ratios. The maximum loan amounts are set annually based on a formula utilizing average house prices. Loan limits have historically been uniform for the contiguous states with higher limits for Alaska, Guam, Hawaii, and the U.S. Virgin Islands. The Housing and Economic Recovery Act of 2008 has expanded the definition of "conforming loan" to allow higher loan limits in *high cost areas* as determined by the Federal Housing Finance Agency. Due to this change, maximum loan limits should be verified for specific areas. Most guidelines require a 5 percent minimum down payment (although some have required less) that necessitates the purchase of private mortgage insurance (PMI). Generally, the borrower must personally provide at least 5 percent of the purchase price even if family members contribute additional down payment. Maximum contributions by the seller (or any third party) vary with different loan conditions, but are capped at 6 percent of the sales price. Borrower qualification requirements will be discussed later in the chapter.

Mortgage loans that do not meet all these guidelines are called *nonconforming loans*. Subprime loans made to borrowers who cannot meet the qualification requirements for a "conforming loan" are a good example of nonconforming loans. In addition, nonconforming loans include loans that exceed the maximum loan limits for conforming loans and are called **jumbo loans**.

Private mortgage insurance.   One way a borrower can obtain a conventional mortgage loan with a smaller down payment is under a **private mortgage insurance (PMI)** program. When the LTV ratio is higher than a specified percentage, the lender requires additional security to minimize its risk. The borrower purchases insurance from a PMI company as additional security to insure the lender against borrower default. LTVs of up to 95 percent of the appraised value of the property are possible with PMI. PMI protects a certain percentage of a loan, usually 20 percent to 30 percent, against borrower default. Normally, the borrower is charged a fee for the first year's premium at closing and a monthly renewal fee while the insurance is in force. The premium may be financed or the fee at closing may be waived in exchange for slightly higher monthly payments. When a borrower has limited funds for investment, these alternative methods of reducing closing costs are very important. Because only a portion of the loan is insured, once the loan is repaid to a certain level (usually 75 percent or 70 percent of the value of the property), the lender may agree to allow the borrower to terminate the coverage. Practices for termination vary from lender to lender. In order to avoid purchasing private mortgage insurance during recent years, some borrowers would utilize *piggyback loans*. By taking out a first and second mortgage simultaneously, the PMI requirement could be avoided. The most common arrangements were either 80/10/10 or 80/15/5; both used a first mortgage LTV of 80 percent, a second mortgage LTV of either 10 percent or 15 percent, and then down payment in the amount of 10 percent or 5 percent.

IN PRACTICE

Effective in July 1999, a federal law required that PMI automatically terminate if a borrower

■   has accumulated at least 22% equity in the home; and
■   is current on mortgage payments.

Under the Homeowners Protection Act, a borrower with a good payment history will have PMI canceled when he or she has built up equity equal to 20 percent of the purchase price or the appraised value. Lenders are required by the law to inform borrowers of their right to cancel PMI. Before this law was enacted, lenders could (and often did) continue to require monthly PMI payments long after borrowers had built up substantial equity in their homes and the lender no longer risked a loss from the borrower's default.

FHA-Insured Loans

The Federal Housing Administration (FHA) was created in 1934 under the National Housing Act to encourage improvement in housing standards and conditions, provide an adequate home-financing system through insurance of housing credit, and exert a stabilizing influence on the mortgage market. The FHA was the government's response to the lack of housing, the excessive foreclosures, and the collapsed building industry that occurred during the Great Depression.

The FHA, which operates under the **Department of Housing and Urban Development (HUD)**, neither builds homes nor lends money to purchase single-family housing. Rather, *it insures loans on real property made by approved lending institutions*. The FHA does not insure property; it insures lenders against loss in case of borrower default. An **FHA-insured loan**, then, refers not to a loan that is made by the agency but to a loan that is insured by it. FHA-insured loans are made by FHA-approved lenders, which are free to set the interest rates on the loans.

The most popular FHA program is Title II, Section 203(b), fixed-interest-rate loans for 10 years to 30 years on one-family to four-family residences. The FHA does not fix interest rates on these loans. These rates can be lower than those on conventional loans because the protection of FHA mortgage insurance makes them of less risk to lenders. Technical requirements established under congressional authority must be met before the FHA will issue the insurance. Three of these requirements are as follows:

1.   In addition to paying interest, the borrower pays a *one-time mortgage insurance premium for the FHA insurance*. This amount (currently 1.5 to 3.0 percent of the loan amount depending on loan requirements, but subject to change) may be paid at closing by the borrower or someone else, or it may be added to the loan amount. (For example, on a $100,000 loan, the one-time premium would equal $1,500, to be either paid in cash at closing or added to the loan amount.) Also, the borrower is charged an annual renewal premium of one-half of 1 percent of the loan amount.

2.   The mortgaged real estate must be appraised by an *approved FHA appraiser*. The loan amount generally cannot exceed either of the following: (1) 98.75 percent for loans over $50,000 (for loans less than $50,000, the buyer must contribute 3 percent of the sales price to the down payment and closing costs) or (2) 97.75 percent of the sales price or appraised value, whichever is less. Note that if the purchase price exceeds the FHA-appraised value,

the buyer may pay the difference in cash as part of the down payment. In addition, the FHA has set maximum loan amounts for various regions of the country. (Contact your regional HUD office for such amounts in your area.) FHA regulations require that both buyer and seller sign a statement indicating that they have examined the FHA appraisal.

3. The FHA regulations set standards for type and construction of buildings, quality of neighborhood, and credit requirements for borrowers.

For a more thorough review of the FHA-insured loan requirements, limits, and options, visit the HUD Web site.

Prepayment privileges.   When a mortgage loan is insured by the FHA and the real estate given as security is a single-family dwelling or an apartment building with no more than four units, the borrower has the privilege of prepaying the debt without penalty. On the first day of any month before the loan matures, the borrower may pay the entire debt or an amount equal to one or more monthly payments on the principal. The borrower must give the lender written notice of intention to exercise this privilege at least 30 days beforehand; otherwise, the lender has the option of charging up to 30 days' interest in lieu of such notification.

Assumption rules.   The assumption rules for FHA-insured loans vary, depending on the date that the loan was originated, as seen in the following examples:

■ Loans originated prior to December 15, 1989, generally have no restriction on their assumption. Anyone can assume these loans with no qualifications.

■ For loans originated December 15, 1989, and thereafter, no assumptions are allowed without complete buyer qualification, and investor loans are no longer allowed. All FHA loans made under the 203(b) program are for owner-occupied properties only.

Other FHA loan programs.   In addition to loans made under Title II, Section 203(b), FHA-insured loans are granted under the following programs:

■ *Title I:* Home improvement loans are covered under this title. Such loans are for relatively low amounts and have repayment terms of no longer than 7 years and 32 days.

■ *Title II, Section 234:* Loans made to purchase condominiums are covered under this program, which in most respects is similar to the basic 203(b) program.

■ *Title II, Section 245:* Graduated payment mortgages, as discussed in Chapter 13, are allowed under this program. Depending on interest rates, the LTV ratio of such loans might range from 87 percent to 93 percent.

■ *Title II, Section 251:* Adjustable-rate mortgages (ARMs) are allowed under this program. The interest rate cannot change more than 1 percent per year or more than 5 percent over the life of the loan.

Points.   The lender of an FHA-insured loan can charge discount points in addition to a 1 percent loan origination fee. The payment of points is a matter of negotiation between the seller and the buyer. However, if the seller pays more than 6 percent of the costs normally paid by the buyer—such as discount points, the loan origination fee, the mortgage insurance premium, buydown fees, prepaid items, impound or escrow amounts, and the like—the lender is to treat such payments as sales concessions, and the price of the property for purposes of the loan must be reduced.

Interest rates.   Neither HUD nor the FHA regulates the interest rates paid on FHA-insured loans. The rates fluctuate from lender to lender, and the buyer is responsible for obtaining the lowest interest rate possible.

Lead paint notification.   HUD now requires that a lead paint notification form be given to residential buyers to sign on or before the date the purchaser executes (signs) the sales contract. The FHA requires that the lender be provided with a copy of the notification form at the time of the loan application (Appendix D, Form 6). In the event the purchaser does not receive and sign the form on or before the date the sales contract is executed, the contract must be re-executed. This HUD guideline is required for FHA-insured loans on homes built prior to 1978.

VA-Guaranteed (GI) Loans

Under the Servicemen's Readjustment Act of 1944 and subsequent federal legislation, the Department of Veterans Affairs (VA) is authorized to guarantee loans to purchase or construct homes for eligible veterans. Eligibility status varies and is determined by length of service during peace or war times. Nonactive veterans wishing to use their entitlement cannot have received a dishonorable discharge from the military. The VA also guarantees loans to purchase mobile homes and plots on which to place them. GI loans assist veterans in financing the purchase of homes with little or no down payment at comparatively low interest rates. From time to time, the VA issues rules and regulations setting forth the qualifications, limitations, and conditions under which a loan may be guaranteed. (Table 14.1 compares VA and FHA loan programs.)

Like the term *FHA loan, VA loan* is something of a misnomer. Normally, the VA does not lend money itself; it guarantees loans made by lending institutions approved by the agency. The term **VA-guaranteed loan**, then, refers not to a loan that is made by the agency, but to one that is guaranteed by it. The guarantee works to protect the lender in case of default much like private mortgage insurance or FHA's MIP. The regional VA office for North Carolina is located in Winston-Salem and can be reached at 800-827-1000. Extensive information about VA loan benefits and requirements is available at the VA Web site.

To determine what portion of a mortgage loan the VA will guarantee, the veteran must apply for a *certificate of eligibility*. This certificate does not mean that the veteran will automatically receive a mortgage. It merely sets forth the maximum guarantee the veteran is entitled to, which is frequently called the *entitlement* or *eligibility*. Note that the maximum amount of the guarantee refers to the amount the lender would receive from the VA in case of default and foreclosure if the sale did not bring enough to cover the outstanding balance.

Ordinarily, a veteran obtains a loan from a VA-approved lending institution; only in locations where financing is not reasonably available, such as in isolated rural areas, does the VA actually lend money. Although there is no maximum VA loan amount, lenders will generally loan up to four times a veteran's available entitlement without a down payment. Although an eligible veteran's basic entitlement is currently $36,000, the guaranty in loans over $144,000 can be increased to a maximum of $89,912 thereby allowing a 100 percent loan of up to $359,650 ($89,912 max. guaranty × 4 = $359,648). The loan amount can be larger if the veteran is willing and able to make a down payment.

Maximum loan terms are 30 years for one-family to four-family dwellings and 40 years for farms. Residential property (up to a four-family unit) purchased with a VA loan must be owner-occupied. Interest rates are freely negotiable between the lender and the borrower. The VA also will issue a **certificate of reasonable value (CRV)** for the property being purchased, stating its current market value based on a VA-approved appraisal. The CRV places a ceiling on the amount of a VA loan allowed for the property; if the purchase price is greater than the amount cited in the CRV, the veteran may either pay the difference in cash or terminate the purchase agreement without penalty. Also, the seller may agree to lower the

	FHA	VA
TABLE 14.1 **Comparison of FHA and VA Loan Programs**	1. Financing is available to veterans and nonveterans. 2. Financing programs are for owner-occupied (1-family to 4-family), residential dwellings. 3. Requires a larger down payment than VA. 4. Different valuation methods; like VA, there are prescribed valuation procedures for the approved appraisers to follow. 5. FHA valuation sets the maximum loan FHA will insure but does not limit the sales price. 6. No prepayment penalty. 7. On default foreclosure and claim, the FHA lender usually gets U.S. debentures. 8. Insures the loan by way of mutual mortgage insurance; premiums paid by buyer or seller. If by buyer, may be paid in cash or added to note. 9. No secondary financing is permitted until after closing. 10. Buyer pays a 1 percent loan origination fee. 11. Loans made prior to 12/1/86 are fully assumable; seller remains liable until the loan is paid off. Loans made between 12/1/86 and 12/15/89 are fully assumable after 12 months on owner-occupied loans; seller remains liable for 5 years. Loans made since 12/15/89 require prior approval of assumptor; seller is released from liability.	1. Financing available only to veterans and certain unremarried widows and widowers. 2. Financing is limited to owner-occupied residential (1-family to 4-family) dwellings; must sign occupancy certificate on two separate occasions. 3. Normally does not require down payment. 4. Methods of valuation differ. VA issues a certificate of reasonable value (CRV). 5. With regard to home loans, the law requires that the VA loan not exceed the appraised value of the home. 6. No prepayment penalty. 7. Following default, foreclosure, and claim, the lender usually receives cash (if VA elects to take the house). 8. Guarantees loans according to a sliding scale. 9. Secondary financing is permitted in exceptional cases. 10. Buyer may pay discount points but cannot finance them in the loan; he or she can pay a 1 percent loan origination fee. 11. A funding fee from 0.05 to 3.33 percent must be paid to VA in addition to other fees. It may be paid by the seller or buyer. If paid by the buyer, it may be paid in cash or added to the note. 12. VA loan can be assumed by nonveteran without VA approval for loans made prior to 3/1/88; otherwise, approval is required. 13. For loans originated after 3/1/88, release of liability is automatic if VA approves the assumption.

purchase price to the amount named in the CRV, or both the buyer and the seller may renegotiate the sale and each make a concession on the price.

Assumption rules.   VA loans made prior to March 1, 1988, remain freely assumable by veterans and nonveterans, but a nominal assumption processing fee is charged. All loans made on or after that date require lender approval of the buyer and an assumption agreement. Even when a VA loan is assumed, the original veteran borrower remains personally liable for the repayment of the loan unless the lender approves a release of liability.

To obtain a release of liability, the veteran must meet three requirements. First, the loan must be up-to-date (there are no past-due payments). Second, the assumptor must have sufficient income and a good enough credit history to qualify for the loan. Third, the assumptor must agree to assume the veteran's obligation for the loan. Note that any release of economic liability issued by the lender does not release or restore the veteran's entitlement that is tied to the loan. This must be obtained separately from the VA.

Restoration of entitlement.   Even though a veteran has used a veteran's entitlement to purchase a home once, the veteran still may be eligible for another VA loan. If the veteran is selling a current VA-financed home, entitlement can be restored. For instance, if the first house is sold and the original VA loan is paid off, the veteran's entitlement will be restored and the veteran will be eligible for another VA home loan that can be used to purchase a replacement home. A veteran's entitlement also can be restored if the veteran sells the home to another veteran who is willing to assume the existing loan and if the buyer's entitlement is substituted for the entitlement of the selling veteran. The basic rule, with little exception, is that veterans can only have one property in their name at a time that is or was financed by a VA-guaranteed loan.

Prepayment.   As with an FHA-insured loan, the borrower under a VA-guaranteed loan can prepay the debt at any time without penalty.

Points.   Points are payable by either the veteran borrower or the seller. There also is a funding fee, which the veteran pays the VA at closing. The funding fee is a sliding fee, ranging from 0.5 percent to 3.33 percent. The funding fee can be added to the note.

IN PRACTICE   Regulations and requirements regarding FHA and VA loans change frequently. Before making an offer based on FHA and/or VA financing, agents working with buyers as clients or customers should always first check with local FHA-approved and VA-approved lenders as well as with local FHA and VA offices from time to time for current information regarding these government-backed loan programs. Sellers' agents should further check on *hidden fees* that sellers may be required to pay if they accept an offer based on FHA and/or VA financing.

Rural Economic and Community Development Services

The Rural Economic and Community Development Services is a federal agency of the Department of Agriculture. This agency offers programs to help purchase or operate family farms. It also provides loans to help purchase or improve single-family homes in rural areas—generally areas with a population of fewer than

10,000 that are not suburbs of urban areas. Loans are made to low-income and moderate-income families, and the interest rate charged can be as low as 1 percent, depending on the borrower's income. The loan programs fall into two categories—*guaranteed loans*, made and serviced by a private lender and guaranteed by the agency, and *direct loans* from the agency.

The Farm Service Agency (FSA) has farm loan programs designed to help family farmers who are unable to obtain commercial private credit. These farmers may be beginning farmers, those who suffered financial setbacks such as natural disasters, or those with limited resources to maintain a profitable operation. Some farmers can satisfy their credit needs through the use of loan guarantees. The money is borrowed from a local agricultural lender that makes and services the loan, and FSA guarantees the lender against default loss up to a maximum of 90 percent. If a farmer cannot qualify for a guaranteed loan, FSA also makes direct loans, which are serviced by FSA. Eligible applicants may obtain a direct loan up to a $200,000 maximum, whereas a guaranteed loan may be as high as $300,000. Both have a maximum repayment period of 40 years.

The Rural Housing Service Agency, a branch of FSA, administers housing programs for low- to moderate-income rural residents. These types of loans include Direct Single Family Housing Loans, Guaranteed Single Family Housing Loans, and Repair Loans and Grants.

The Direct Single Family Housing Loan is designed for families with low to very low income—80 percent or less of county median income. These loans can be used to buy, build, improve, or repair rural homes. Eligibility requirements include (1) a rural area with a population of less than 10,000, (2) families who are without safe and decent housing, and (3) families to whom financing is not otherwise available. Availability of funds is based on annual appropriations. Loans may be made up to 100 percent of the appraised value. Interest rates are normally set at market rate, and the term of the loan is typically 33 years, but may be as long as 38 years. Applicants pay some costs, such as the credit report fee, appraisal fee, and closing costs, and the applicant must have good credit.

The Guaranteed Single Family Housing Loan is designed for moderate-income families who have limited down payment capability. Loans are processed by approved lenders and guaranteed by the U.S. government. Eligibility requirements are similar to the direct loan as discussed above. Maximum loan amounts range from $78,660 to $116,850, depending on the county in which the property is located. Interest rates are negotiable and fixed, with a 30-year loan term.

Repair Loans and Grants are designed for very-low-income individuals—those who earn 50 percent or less of the county median income. Funds can be used for repairs, installation of essential features, or to remove health and safety hazards. To qualify, the applicant must (1) live in a rural area of less than 10,000 population, (2) meet the income standards, and (3) be unable to get financing elsewhere. Grants are available only if the applicant is at least 62 years old. The interest rate is 1 percent annual percentage rate (APR), terms are up to 20 years, and there are no fees. The applicant must have a reasonable credit history.

Other Types of Loans

By altering the terms of the basic mortgage and note, a borrower and a lender can tailor financing instruments to best suit the type of transaction and the financial needs of both parties.

Purchase-money mortgages.   A **purchase-money mortgage** is owner-financing given at the time of purchase to facilitate the sale and refers to the instrument *given by the purchaser to a seller who takes back a note and mortgage for part or all of the purchase price.* *Takes back* refers to the fact that the seller has taken back some interest in the property in exchange for financing. It may be a first or second deed of trust, and it becomes a lien on the property when the title passes. The borrower holds title under a purchase-money mortgage. In the event of foreclosure on a purchase-money mortgage, this lien takes priority over judgment liens against the borrower and over mechanics' liens. In North Carolina, a seller-lender is not entitled to a deficiency judgment.

Package loans.   A **package loan** includes not only the real estate, but also all fixtures and appliances installed on the premises. In recent years, this type of loan has been used extensively in financing furnished condominium units. Such loans usually include the kitchen range, refrigerator, dishwasher, garbage disposal, washer and dryer, freezer, and other appliances, as well as furniture, drapes, and carpets. In other words, the lender has *packaged* both real and personal property in the same loan.

Blanket mortgages.   A **blanket mortgage** covers *more than one parcel of land* and usually is used to finance subdivision developments, though it can be used to finance the purchase of improved properties as well. These loans usually include a provision, known as a *partial release clause*, so that the borrower may obtain the release of any one lot or parcel from the lien by repaying a definite amount of the loan at closing without triggering a due-on-sale clause for the rest of the financed property.

Wraparound loans.   A **wraparound loan**, also known as an *overriding* or *all-inclusive mortgage*, enables a borrower who is paying off an existing mortgage to obtain additional financing from a second lender or the seller. *The new lender, which could be the seller, assumes payment of the existing loan and gives the borrower a new, increased loan at a higher interest rate.* The total amount of the new loan includes the existing loan as well as the additional funds needed by the borrower. The borrower makes payments to the new lender or seller on the larger loan, and the new lender or seller makes payments on the original loan. The original loan cannot contain a due-on-sale clause.

■ **FOR EXAMPLE** Suppose Brown is selling his house for $75,000. He has an outstanding mortgage on the property in the amount of $30,000 at 6 percent interest. The buyer, Morgan, does not want to get an institutional loan, so Brown agrees to extend $65,000 in financing to Morgan at 7 percent interest. Morgan makes a $10,000 down payment, and then makes monthly payments to Brown. Brown takes a portion of each payment he receives from Morgan, uses it to make the mortgage payment on his $30,000 loan, and pockets the rest of the monthly payment.

A wraparound mortgage frequently is used as a method of refinancing real property or financing the purchase of real property when an existing mortgage cannot be prepaid. It also is used to finance the sale of real estate when the buyer wishes to put up a minimum of initial cash for the sale. The buyer takes title subject to the existing mortgage. The buyer also executes a wraparound document to the seller, who collects payments on the new loan and continues to make payments on the old loan. The buyer should require a protective clause in the document granting the right to make payments directly to the original lender in the event of a default on the old loan by the seller.

IN PRACTICE   A wraparound loan is possible only if the original loan permits such a refinancing. An acceleration, an alienation, or a due-on-sale clause in the original loan documents may prevent a sale under such terms. A real estate licensee should neither encourage nor assist in any financing that violates loan provisions. To do so could result in suspension or revocation of the agent's license.

Open-end mortgages. Open-end mortgages act as a *line of credit* or *equity line*, allowing the mortgagee to make additional future advances of funds to the mortgagor, and are generally set up as home equity loans (discussed below). The mortgagee may have a prior lien for the amount of additional future advances if the mortgagee is obligated to make advances, as in construction loans. For unobligated future advances, the lien may be subordinate to other liens that may be created before the additional advancements are made.

Construction loans. A construction loan is made to *finance the construction of improvements* on real estate—homes, apartments, office buildings, and so forth. Under a construction loan, the lender commits the full amount of the loan but makes *partial installment payments* or *draws* as the building is being constructed.

Installment payments are made to the *general contractor* for that part of the construction work that has been completed since the previous payment. Prior to each payment, the lender inspects the construction site. The general contractor must provide the lender with adequate waivers of lien releasing all mechanic's lien rights (see Chapter 2) for the work covered by the payment. This kind of loan generally bears a higher interest rate because of the risks assumed by the lender. These risks include the inadequate releasing of mechanics' liens just referred to, possible delays in completing the building, and the financial failure of the contractor or subcontractors. The lender always runs the risk that the loan funds will run out before the construction has been completed. Construction financing is generally *short-term*, or *interim, financing*. The borrower is expected to arrange for a *permanent loan*—also known as an *end loan* or a *take-out loan*—that will repay, or *take out*, the construction financing lender when the work is completed. Construction loans normally pose a greater degree of risk to lenders than any other types of loans.

Sale and leaseback. Sale-and-leaseback arrangements are used rather extensively as a means of financing large commercial or industrial plants. The land and building, usually used by the seller for business purposes, are sold to an investor such as an insurance company. The real estate is then leased back by the investor to the seller, who continues to conduct business on the property as a tenant. The buyer becomes the lessor, and the original owner becomes the lessee. This enables a business firm that has money invested in real property to free that money so it can be used as working capital.

Sale-and-leaseback arrangements are very complex. They involve complicated legal procedures, and their success is usually related to the effects the transaction has on a firm's tax situation. A real estate broker should advise the parties to a sale-and-leaseback arrangement to consult with legal and tax experts when involved in this type of transaction.

Buydowns.   A **buydown** is a way to lower the initial interest rate on a mortgage or deed of trust loan. Perhaps a homebuilder wishes to stimulate sales by offering a lower-than-market interest rate. Or, a first-time residential buyer may have trouble qualifying for a loan at the prevailing rates; relatives or the sellers might want to help the buyer qualify. In any case, a lump sum is paid in cash to the lender at closing. The payment offsets (and so reduces) the interest rate and monthly payments during the mortgage's first few years. Typical buydown arrangements reduce the interest rate by 1 percent to 3 percent over the first year to third year of the loan term. After that, the rate rises. The assumption is that the borrower's income also will increase and that the borrower will be more able to absorb the increased monthly payments. A common type of buydown is called the *3-2-1 buydown*. The interest rate is bought down by 3 percent in the first year, 2 percent in the second year, and 1 percent in the third year. For the fourth and succeeding years, the interest rate is the fixed note rate.

Home equity loans.   **Home equity loans** are a source of funds for homeowners who wish to finance the purchase of expensive items; consolidate existing installment loans on credit card debt; or pay for medical, educational, home improvement, or other expenses. This type of financing has been used increasingly, partly because tax laws no longer allow deductibility of interest on debts not secured by real estate (*consumer interest*). Home equity loans are secured by the borrower's residence, and some or all of the interest charged may be deductible.

A home equity loan can be taken out as a fixed loan amount or as an equity line of credit. With the home equity line of credit (HELOC), the lender extends a line of credit that the borrowers can use whenever they want. The borrowers receive their money through checks sent to them, deposits made in a checking or savings account, or a book of drafts the borrowers can use, up to their credit limit.

Reverse-annuity mortgages.   A **reverse-annuity mortgage (RAM)** is one in which regular monthly payments are made *to the borrower*, based on the equity the homeowner has invested in the property given as security for the loan. A reverse-annuity mortgage allows senior citizens on fixed incomes to utilize the equity buildup in their homes without having to sell the property. The borrower is charged a fixed rate of interest, and the loan is eventually repaid from the sale of the property or from the borrower's estate on the borrower's death.

Mortgage Priorities

Mortgages and other liens normally have priority in the order in which they have been recorded. A mortgage on land that has no prior mortgage lien on it is a *first mortgage*. When the owner of this land executes another loan for additional funds, the new loan becomes a *second mortgage*, or a *junior mortgage*, when recorded. The second lien is subject to the first lien; the first has prior claim to the value of the land pledged as security. Because second loans represent greater risk to lenders, they are usually issued at higher interest rates and for shorter terms.

The normal recordation priority of mortgage liens may be changed by the execution of a **subordination agreement**, in which the first lender subordinates its lien to that of the second lender. To be valid, such an agreement must be signed by both lenders. Subordination agreements may be contained in the mortgage itself or they may be separate agreements filed for recordation.

■ RESIDENTIAL LENDING PRACTICES AND PROCEDURES

All mortgage lenders require that prospective borrowers file an application for credit that provides the lender with the basic information needed to evaluate the acceptability of the proposed loan. The application includes information regarding the purpose, the amount, the rate of interest, and the proposed terms of repayment of the loan. This is considered a preliminary offer of a loan agreement; final terms may require lengthy negotiations.

Application for Credit

A prospective borrower must submit personal information to the lender, including employment, earnings, assets, and financial obligations. Details of the real estate that will be the security for the loan must generally be provided, including legal description, improvements, title, survey, and taxes. For loans on income property or those made to corporations, additional information is required, such as financial and operating statements, schedules of leases and tenants, and balance sheets.

The lender carefully investigates the application information—studying credit reports and scores and an appraisal of the property—before deciding whether to grant the loan. The lender's acceptance of the application is written in the form of a loan commitment, which creates a contract to make a loan and sets forth the details.

IN PRACTICE

Because interest rates and loan terms change frequently, check with local sources of real estate financing on a regular basis to learn of specific loan rates and terms. As a licensee, you can better serve your customers and clients if you can knowledgeably refer buyers to local lenders offering the most favorable terms.

Prequalifying Buyers

Every real estate agent should have a basic understanding of the loan standards lenders use as they decide whether or not to approve a loan. These loan standards, called *underwriting guidelines* or *qualifying standards*, can then be used by the agent to prequalify the agent's buyers. By prequalifying a buyer, the agent is more likely to avoid the disappointment of a rejected loan application. Note that agent prequalification is not the same as a lender's loan approval.

Qualifying standards are fairly complex; however, the basics are easy to understand and remember. The major element of any prequalification procedure is measuring the adequacy of a buyer's income. A lender will never approve a loan if the applicant does not have enough income to meet the monthly loan payments. Until an agent knows how large a loan payment the buyer can afford, the agent will not be able to effectively assist the buyer in selecting an affordable home.

MATH CONCEPTS

DETERMINING MAXIMUM AFFORDABILITY

You can use loan qualifying ratios to determine the price range of housing a prospective buyer can afford. Let's look at the Harrisons, whose gross monthly income is $3,900. To determine what kind of house they can afford, multiply their monthly income by a given standard debt ratio, 36%, for example.

$$\$3,900 \times 0.36 = \$1,404$$

Now subtract their recurring expenses, which total $475.

$$\$1,404 - \$475 = \$929$$

The maximum housing payment they can afford under this ratio is $929, including principal, interest, taxes, and insurance (PITI). Tax and insurance costs will vary according to location, but for purposes of this example, we will assume that 10% of the maximum payment is devoted to taxes and insurance. Deduct this 10% from the maximum payment.

$$\$929 \times 0.10 = \$92.90$$
$$\$929 - \$93 \text{ (rounded up)} = \$836$$

The Harrisons can afford to pay $836 a month in principal and interest. If current interest rates are 7%, they would qualify for a loan amount of $125,714. (You can use a financial calculator to determine this loan amount, or use a loan factor of 6.65. To use a loan factor, divide the principal and interest payment by the rate factor and multiply by 1,000.) Assuming that the Harrisons have $12,650 for a down payment, they could afford to purchase a home for $138,364.

$$\$125,714 \text{ maximum loan amount} + \$12,650 \text{ down payment} = \$138,364$$

Computerized Loan Origination and Automated Underwriting

A computerized loan origination (CLO) system is an electronic network for handling loan applications through remote computer terminals linked to several lenders' computers. With a CLO system, a buyer can select a lender and apply for a loan right from the brokerage office.

On the lender's side, new automated underwriting procedures can shorten loan approvals from weeks to minutes. Automated underwriting also tends to lower the cost of loan application and approval by reducing lender's time spent on the process by as much as 60 percent. Complex or difficult mortgages can be processed in less than 72 hours. Such speed in the loan approval process can allow a buyer to submit proof of loan approval with offers to purchase; therefore, strengthening their negotiating position.

Scoring and automated underwriting.   Lenders have been using credit scoring systems to predict prospective borrowers' likelihood of default for many years. When used in automated underwriting systems, the application of credit scores can become somewhat controversial. Critics of scoring are concerned that without human discretion the scores may result in more difficulty for low-income borrowers to qualify. Human judgment should be consulted especially when the loan application in a higher risk.

Each of the three major types of loan programs has a different way of measuring the adequacy of a buyer's income.

Conventional conforming loans.   Conventional lenders usually apply two ratios (income ratio and debt ratio) to the buyer's income to measure adequacy. First, the proposed monthly housing expense can usually be no more than 28 percent of the borrower's monthly gross income. Note that the proposed monthly housing expense includes principal and interest payments, plus monthly property taxes, insurance payments, and homeowner association dues, if applicable. Second, the proposed monthly housing expense plus the buyer's other long-term recurring monthly debts can usually total no more than 36 percent of the buyer's monthly gross income. Recurring monthly debts include items such as charge card payments, child support payments, personal loan payments, and car payments. These qualifying ratios can change, depending on the LTV ratio of the loan. The borrower must qualify on both ratios or they do not qualify for the loan. The larger the down payment the borrower makes, the easier it will be to qualify.

■ **FOR EXAMPLE** The Harrisons are seeking an 80% loan. They make $3,900 a month. Their recurring monthly payments include a $300 car payment, a $75 charge card payment, and a $100 college loan payment. They want to qualify for an $850 monthly loan payment, including principal, interest, taxes, and insurance (PITI).

First, add the three recurring monthly expenses, which total $475, to the $850 proposed housing expense to determine the total monthly expenses of $1,325.

If you divide $1,325 (total monthly expenses) by $3,900 (monthly income), you discover that the Harrisons' total monthly expenses equal about 34% of their monthly income. Therefore, they would qualify for the proposed loan under the second ratio because 34% is less than the debt ratio maximum of 36%. If you divide $850 (monthly PITI) by $3,900 (monthly income), you discover that the Harrisons' proposed housing expense is about 22% of their monthly income. This is well within the 28% income ratio maximum. Because both income standards are met, the Harrisons have a good chance of qualifying for the loan.

Let's assume the Harrisons want a more expensive home that would require a loan of $250,000. How much annual income would the Harrisons need to qualify using the 28:36 ratios if the estimated monthly PITI will be $1,665 and they have other monthly recurring obligations of $2,000? The first step would be to add up all monthly debts, then divide by the 36% debt ratio to get monthly income required; then multiply by 12 months.

$1,665 + $2,000 = $3,665 ÷ 0.36 = $10,180.56 monthly income × 12 months = $122,166.72 annual income

Let's take an example of determining maximum housing expenses that another couple could have with an annual income of $36,000 and recurring obligations (not including housing expenses) of $400 per month, using the 28:36 percent ratios to qualify.

$36,000 annual income ÷ 12 months = $3,000 monthly income × 0.36 = $1,080 maximum recurring obligation, not including housing. Their actual other monthly recurring obligations are $400. Their maximum monthly housing expenses would be $680 ($1,080 − $400 = $680).

FHA loans. The FHA also uses the same two ratios (income and debt) as in conventional loans to qualify its borrowers; however, the maximum proposed-housing-expense-to-income ratio is 29 percent, and the maximum proposed-total-monthly-debt-to-income ratio is 41 percent. These ratios are calculated in the same manner as the conventional ratios discussed above. The FHA ratios are not dependent on the loan's LTV ratio, unlike conventional ratios. FHA ratios remain constant, regardless of the amount of the down payment. Note that FHA standards are somewhat easier to meet than conventional standards.

VA loans. The VA uses a slightly different method to qualify its borrowers. The VA uses only the total-monthly-debt-to-income ratio, which the VA has set at 41 percent of the borrower's monthly income. Instead of a second ratio, the VA uses the *residual-income method*. With this qualifying method, buyers must have a certain amount of cash left over after paying their monthly housing expenses and other recurring debts. The VA publishes a table of how much residual income is required for buyers. The amount varies, depending on the number of dependents the buyer has and the geographic region in which the buyer lives. As with the two ratios used by conventional and FHA lenders, VA borrowers must qualify under both the total-monthly-debt-to-income ratio and the residual-income method before the loan will be approved.

■ **FOR EXAMPLE** A married couple with two children living in Raleigh with a combined annual gross income of $43,200 wants to apply for a $100,000 loan. The VA Cost of Living Table shows their required residual income is $964 for loan amounts above $70,000 for a family of four. Monthly withholding taxes and Social Security taxes are estimated to be $900 per month. Shelter expenses, which include principal, interest, taxes, and insurance (PITI), along with maintenance and utilities, are estimated to be $920. Other monthly obligations with six or more monthly payments left total $600.

$3,600	Monthly gross income
− 900	Taxes and Social Security
− 920	Shelter costs
− 600	Other debt obligations
$1,180	Residual income

The actual residual income exceeds the table amount, so the couple qualifies under this method.

Now let's take a look at whether the applicant couple from the previous example meets the 41% income ratio test. First add the total monthly obligations together.

$920	Shelter expense
+600	Other debt obligations
$1,520	Total monthly obligations

Then divide the total monthly obligations by the gross monthly income.

$$\$1,520 \div \$3,600 = 0.42 = 42\%$$

Because this ratio is more than the 41% maximum, the applicant does not qualify under this ratio.

If the applicant's residual income exceeds the required amount by more than 20%, the applicant may qualify for the loan, even if the applicant's total-monthly-debt-to-income ratio exceeds the 41% maximum.

■ **FOR EXAMPLE** The applicant couple's residual income in the previous example was $1,180. They were required to have only $964 in residual income.

$1,180 residual income – $964 required residual income =
$216 excess residual income

To find the percentage of excess residual income, divide the excess residual income by the required amount.

$216 excess residual income ÷ $964 required residual income =
0.224 or 22% of excess residual income

So even if the applicant couple's income ratio had been higher than 41%, they still might have qualified because they had a substantial amount of residual income.

■ FINANCING LEGISLATION

The federal government regulates the lending practices of mortgage lenders through the Truth-in-Lending Act, the Equal Credit Opportunity Act, and the Real Estate Settlement Procedures Act.

Truth-in-Lending Act and Regulation Z

Regulation Z, which was promulgated pursuant to the **Truth-in-Lending Act**, requires that credit institutions inform borrowers of the true cost of obtaining credit so that the borrowers can compare the costs of various lenders and avoid the uninformed use of credit. Regulation Z applies when credit is extended to individuals for personal, family, or household uses and when the amount of credit is $25,000 or less. Regardless of the amount, Regulation Z always applies when a credit transaction is secured by a residence.

Regulation Z requires that the consumer be fully informed of all finance charges as well as the true annual interest rate before a transaction is consummated. The finance charges must include any loan fees, finder's fees, service charges, and points, as well as interest. In the case of a mortgage loan made to finance the purchase of a dwelling, the lender also must compute and disclose the **annual percentage rate (APR)** but does not have to indicate the total interest payable during the term of the loan. APR is frequently thought to be the interest rate because both are expressed as percentages. APR is the relationship of all finance charges to the loan amount and will always be higher than the interest rate. Also, the lender does not have to include as part of the finance charge such actual costs as title fees, legal fees, appraisal fees, credit report fees, survey fees, and closing expenses.

In total, the lender must disclose to the borrower (1) the loan's APR, (2) all finance charges associated with the loan, (3) the total number and amount of all payments, and (4) the total amount financed. These are called the *four chief disclosures* that must appear in a heavily outlined section, called the *Federal Box*, of the financing disclosure paperwork.

Advertising.   Regulation Z provides strict regulation of real estate advertisements that include mortgage financing terms. General phrases like *liberal terms available* may be used, but if specifics, called **trigger terms**, are given, the advertiser must comply with this regulation. Generally, if any numbers related to the loan are disclosed, a trigger term has been hit and total financing term disclosure is mandatory. Under the provisions of Regulation Z, the APR—which includes all finance charges—rather than the interest rate alone must be stated. The total finance charge must be specified as well.

Specific credit terms, such as *down payment, monthly payment, dollar amount of the finance charge,* or *term of the loan,* may not be advertised unless the following information is set forth as well: cash price; required down payment; number, amounts, and due dates of all payments; and APR. The total of all payments to be made over the term of the mortgage must also be specified unless the advertised credit refers to a first mortgage or deed of trust to finance the acquisition of a dwelling.

Penalties.   Regulation Z sets the penalties for noncompliance. The penalty for violation of an administrative order enforcing Regulation Z is $10,000 for each day the violation continues. A fine of up to $10,000 may be imposed for engaging in an unfair or a deceptive trade practice. In addition, a creditor may be liable to a consumer for twice the amount of the finance charge, for a minimum of $100 and a maximum of $1,000, plus court costs, lawyer's fees, and any actual damages. Willful violation is a misdemeanor punishable by a fine of up to $5,000 or one year's imprisonment or both.

Federal Equal Credit Opportunity Act

The federal **Equal Credit Opportunity Act (ECOA)**, in effect since 1975, prohibits lenders and others who grant or arrange credit to consumers from discriminating against credit applicants on the basis of race, color, religion, national origin, sex, marital status, age (provided the applicant is of legal age), dependence on public assistance, or exercise of the consumer's rights under this Act. In addition, lenders and other creditors must inform all rejected credit applicants, in writing, within 30 days, of the principal reasons why credit was denied or terminated.

Fair Credit Reporting Act

The federal **Fair Credit Reporting Act**, effective since 1970, gives individuals the right to check their own credit reports and demand that mistakes be corrected. Credit bureaus are required to limit the credit information they provide to the previous seven years (except for bankruptcies, which can stay on credit records for ten years). Individuals who have been denied credit based on information found in a credit report can examine their credit report at no charge. Under the Fair and Accurate Credit Transaction Act (FACT Act), individuals who have not been denied credit but want to examine their credit report may now receive one free credit report per year from each of the national credit bureaus. At this time, here are the three major credit bureaus where consumers can access their credit report and learn about protecting their credit identity: Equifax, Experian, and TransUnion. There is also a joint Web site for ordering the free annual report.

Predatory Lending Act

The **Predatory Lending Act** is a recent North Carolina law that applies to lenders and addresses permissible fees that may be charged in connection with home loans secured by the first mortgage or first deed of trust. The Act's main provisions include the following:

- To impose restrictions and limitations on high-cost loans
- To revise the permissible fees and charges on certain loans
- To prohibit unfair or deceptive practices by mortgage brokers and lenders
- To provide for public education and counseling about predatory lenders

Loan Fraud Legislation

Loan fraud involves making any false representations in order to obtain a loan for a larger amount of money than the borrower is entitled to under the lender's guidelines. Misrepresentations may involve value of the collateral land, amount of down payment, personal information about the borrower, amount of closing expenses, undisclosed rebates or credits to a party, or occupancy. In almost every loan fraud, some false documentation was submitted to lenders, closing attorneys, real estate licensees, or other involved parties. Federal loan fraud statutes apply to all residential and commercial real estate transactions. *Any false statement to a lender is a federal felony crime punishable by fines up to $1,000,000 and/or imprisonment for up to 30 years.*

Real Estate Settlement Procedures Act

The federal **Real Estate Settlement Procedures Act (RESPA)** was created to ensure that the buyer and seller in a residential real estate transaction involving a new first mortgage loan have knowledge of all settlement costs. This important federal law will be discussed in detail in Chapter 15.

RESPA requires that all transaction charges to the parties be clearly itemized on the HUD-1 closing statement that makes loan fraud harder to conceal.

■ RELATED WEB SITES

AARP; reverse mortgage info: *www.aarp.org/money/revmort/*
Source for free annual credit report: *www.annualcreditreport.com*
Equifax Credit Bureau: *www.equifax.com*
Experian Credit Bureau: *www.experian.com*
Fair Isaac: *www.myfico.com*
Fannie Mae: *www.fanniemae.com* and *www.efanniemae.com*
Federal Reserve Board: *www.federalreserve.gov*
Freddie Mac: *www.freddiemac.com*
Ginnie Mae: *www.ginniemae.gov*
National Reverse Mortgage Lenders Association: *www.reversemortgage.org*
Realty Trac: *www.realtytrac.com*
Transunion Credit Bureau: *www.tuc.com*
U.S. Department of Agriculture; RECD loans: *www.rurdev.usda.gov*
U.S. Department of Housing and Urban Development (HUD): *www.hud.gov*
U.S. Department of Veterans Affairs: *www.homeloans.va.gov*
US Treasury Department: *www.financialstability.gov*

■ SUMMARY

Many types of mortgage loans exist, including conventional loans and those insured by the FHA or guaranteed by the VA. FHA-insured and VA-guaranteed loans must meet certain requirements for the borrower to obtain the benefits of the government backing, which induces the lender to lend its funds. The interest rates for these loans may be lower than those charged for conventional loans. Lenders competitively set the interest rates on all three loan types. Other types of real estate financing include seller-financed purchase-money mortgages or deeds of trust, blanket mortgages, wraparound mortgages, open-end mortgages, construction loans, sale-and-leaseback agreements, buydowns, and home equity loans.

Loan underwriters for each type of loan must evaluate the borrower's creditworthiness and the specific loan's degree of risk in order to make a lending decision. Generally, the credit history, qualifying ratios, and income of the borrower as well as the property appraisal and goodness of title will influence the willingness to grant the loan and the terms of the loan.

The federal government affects real estate financing money and interest rates through the Federal Reserve Board's discount rate and reserve requirements; it also participates in the secondary mortgage market. Generally, the secondary market is composed of those investors that ultimately purchase and hold the loans as investments. These include insurance companies, investment funds, and pension plans. Fannie Mae, Ginnie Mae, and Freddie Mac take an active role in creating a secondary market by regularly purchasing mortgage and deed of trust loans from primary market loan originators and retaining, or warehousing, them until investment purchasers are available.

Regulation Z, implementing the federal Truth-in-Lending Act, requires that lenders inform prospective borrowers who use their homes as security for credit of all finance charges involved in such a loan. Severe penalties are provided for noncompliance. The federal Equal Credit Opportunity Act prohibits creditors from discriminating against credit applicants on the basis of race, color, religion, national origin, sex, marital status, age, or dependence on public assistance. The Fair Credit Reporting Act allows a consumer to review personal credit history held by the credit bureaus and correct any errors. Predatory Lending Act is a North Carolina law that strives to protect the desperate borrowing public from unscrupulous lenders. Loan fraud legislation is growing as this crime gains more visibility; penalties are harsh. Any intentional misrepresentation of information to a lender for the purpose of borrowing more than the borrower is entitled to per underwriting guidelines is loan fraud. The Real Estate Settlement Procedures Act requires that lenders inform both buyers and sellers in advance of all fees and charges required for the settlement or closing of a residential real estate transaction. Compliance with these statutes will make loan fraud harder to perpetrate.

QUESTIONS

1. Which of the following defines the secondary mortgage market?
   a. Markets in which loans are bought and sold after they have been originated
   b. Lenders that deal exclusively in second mortgages
   c. Markets in which loans are originated
   d. Lenders that offer VA and FHA financing

2. The Carters purchased a residence for $95,000. They made a down payment of $15,000. The Carters financed the remaining $80,000 of the purchase price by executing a mortgage and note to the seller. This type of loan is called a
   a. purchase-money mortgage.
   b. package mortgage.
   c. balloon mortgage.
   d. term mortgage.

3. Which of the following statement(s) is/are true about private mortgage insurance?
   I. Conventional lenders will usually require it on any loan over 80% LTV.
   II. It can be discontinued when the borrower's equity in the home exceeds 22% if he or she is current on the loan payments.
      a. I only
      b. II only
      c. Both I and II
      d. Neither I nor II

4. A borrower obtains a mortgage loan to make repairs on her home. The loan is not insured or guaranteed by a government agency, and the mortgage document secures the maximum amount of funds to be used for the current home repairs as well as any future funds to be advanced to the borrower by the lender. This borrower has obtained a(n)
   a. wraparound mortgage.
   b. conventional open-end loan.
   c. installment contract.
   d. shared equity mortgage.

5. Regulation Z requires that lenders
   a. properly inform buyers and sellers of commercial property of all settlement costs in a real estate transaction.
   b. inform prospective borrowers of all charges, fees, and interest involved in making a home mortgage loan.
   c. not discriminate in the lending of credit based on protected class.
   d. study the economic market before they decide what interest rate to charge on residential mortgages.

6. A veteran's VA entitlement can be restored
   a. by letting a non-veteran assume the current VA home loan.
   b. once the equity in the property exceeds 25 percent of the market value.
   c. selling the property to a qualified veteran.
   d. by paying off the original VA loan that was secured by the entitlement.

7. Aunt Fran continues to live in the home she purchased 40 years ago, but she now receives monthly loan installment checks from her mortgage lender thanks to her
   a. shared-appreciation mortgage.
   b. adjustable-rate mortgage.
   c. reverse-annuity mortgage.
   d. sale-leaseback agreement.

8. The McManns are purchasing an ocean-front summer home in a new resort development. The house is completely furnished, and the McManns have obtained a mortgage loan that covers the purchase price of the residence, including furnishings and appliances. This kind of financing is called a
   a. wraparound loan.
   b. package loan.
   c. blanket loan.
   d. home equity loan.

9. All of the following are true about the Rural Economic and Community Development loans *EXCEPT*

a. Loans are insured by the federal government through Ginnie Mae.

b. Loans are for low- to moderate-income homebuyers.

c. The financed properties must be located in sparsely populated areas.

d. Loans may be made for up to 100% of appraised value.

10. A developer received a loan that covers five parcels of real estate and provides for the release of the mortgage lien on each parcel when certain payments are made on the loan. This type of loan arrangement is called a

a. construction loan.

b. blanket loan.

c. package loan.

d. wraparound loan.

11. Funds for Federal Housing Administration (FHA) loans are usually provided by

a. the FHA.

b. the FDIC.

c. qualified lenders.

d. FNMA.

12. Under the provisions of the Truth-in-Lending Act (Regulation Z), the annual percentage rate (APR) of a finance charge does *NOT* include

a. discount points.

b. title preparation fees.

c. loan origination fee.

d. loan interest rate.

13. With proper notification of the lender, a prepayment penalty cannot be imposed on a(n)

I. VA-guaranteed mortgage loan.

II. FHA-insured mortgage loan.

    a. I only

    b. II only

    c. Both I and II

    d. Neither I nor II

14. Which of the following is *NOT* a participant in the secondary market?

a. FHLMC

b. GNMA

c. FNMA

d. RESPA

15. As a general policy, conventional lenders require that a borrower qualify on which of the following ratios before they can be approved?

I. Monthly housing expense-to-income ratio

II. Monthly long-term recurring expenses-to-debt ratio

    a. I only

    b. II only

    c. Both I and II

    d. Neither I nor II

16. All the following statements about junior mortgages are true *EXCEPT*

a. "Their interest rates are usually higher than rates charged on first mortgages."

b. "They are always purchase money mortgages."

c. "They are more subject to default than first mortgages."

d. "They are usually for a shorter term than first mortgages."

17. The Sosas are applying for a home loan that will have a monthly loan payment of $750 (including taxes and insurance). Their recurring monthly expenses equal $500. How much monthly income do they need to qualify for a conventional loan using ratios of 28/36?

a. $2,083

b. $2,679

c. $3,472

d. $4,464

18. All of the following financing information statements are trigger terms under Regulation Z of the Truth-in-Lending Act *EXCEPT*

a. "Great assumable low interest rate loan"

b. "Only $500 down and $750 a month"

c. "FHA loan at 5% annual interest"

d. "Easy qualifying on this 30-year loan"

19. The interest rate on FHA loans is set by the
    a. FHA.
    b. FNMA.
    c. lender.
    d. Federal Reserve.

20. All the following statements about Fannie Mae are true EXCEPT
    a. "She was originally a HUD agency."
    b. "She helped to standardize loan underwriting guidelines."
    c. "She was the first secondary market institution."
    d. "She makes mortgage loans directly to the consumer."

21. Mortgage bankers (companies) play an important role as a source of real estate financing. Their primary functions include all of the following EXCEPT
    a. servicing mortgage loans they sell to investors.
    b. originating all types of loans.
    c. charging service fees to investors and origination fees to loan applicants.
    d. using just their own funds from deposit assets to originate mortgage loans.

22. Which of the following loans exposes the lender to the greatest degree of risk?
    a. FHA
    b. Conventional, with 95 percent LTV ratios
    c. Construction
    d. VA, with no down payment

23. The main purpose of the Truth-in-Lending Act is to
    a. give a full disclosure of credit charges.
    b. regulate the practice of redlining.
    c. ensure that lenders give good-faith estimates of closing costs.
    d. establish legal usury limits.

24. For which type of loan would the buyer have to produce a CRV?
    a. FHA
    b. Conventional
    c. VA
    d. Reverse annuity

25. The major difference between a purchase-money mortgage and an installment land contract is
    a. only one can be used for seller financing.
    b. the time at which the buyer gets possession and use of the property.
    c. the time at which delivery of the deed is made.
    d. There is no difference.

26. A buyer purchased a new home for $175,000. The buyer made a down payment of $15,000 and obtained a $160,000 mortgage loan. The builder-seller of the house paid the lender 2% of the loan balance for the first year and 1% of the loan balance for the second year. This represented total savings for the buyer of $4,800. What type of arrangement does this represent?
    a. Wraparound mortgage
    b. Purchase-money mortgage
    c. Blanket mortgage
    d. Buydown mortgage

27. The federal Equal Credit Opportunity Act prohibits lenders from discriminating against potential borrowers on the basis of all of the following EXCEPT
    a. marital status.
    b. gender.
    c. dependence on public assistance.
    d. amount of income.

28. If a lender agrees to make a loan based on an 80 percent LTV, what is the amount of the loan if the property appraises for $114,500 and the sales price is $116,900?
    a. $80,000
    b. $91,600
    c. $92,560
    d. $93,520

29. In determining LTV, value is
    a. 80 percent of the sales price or less.
    b. 95 percent of the appraised value.
    c. appraisal value or price, whichever is less.
    d. price or appraisal value, whichever is more.

30. Using the 28:36 qualifying ratios, what is the minimum annual income needed to qualify for a $120,000 loan at 6 percent annual interest rate for 30 years if the proposed PITI will be $847 and the borrower has other monthly recurring debts of $745?

    a. $28,233
    b. $36,300
    c. $53,067
    d. $68,229

31. What is the maximum loan a borrower can qualify for using the 28:36 ratios if her annual income is $60,000, the mortgage loan factor is 6.67, the estimated monthly taxes and insurance (TI) is $160, and her monthly nonhousing recurring debts total $700?

    a. $140,929.53
    b. $144,072.00
    c. $164,917.54
    d. $185,907.04

32. If a borrower has an annual gross income of $42,000 and will have monthly recurring debts of $500, not including housing expenses, what will be the maximum monthly housing expenses using the 28:36 ratios?

    a. $760
    b. $920
    c. $980
    d. $1,260

CHAPTER

15

Closing the Real Estate Transaction

■ **LEARNING OBJECTIVES** *When you have finished reading this chapter, you should be able to*

■ **describe** closing, the preliminaries that must take place before actual closing, and the settlement meeting.

■ **describe** the steps involved in preparing a closing statement and the steps involved in the transfer of title and funds.

■ **list** RESPA requirements.

■ **calculate** all types of prorations and prepare a detailed closing statement worksheet.

■ **define** these *key terms:*

accrued items	prepaid items	soil suitability test
closing	prorations	survey
closing agent	Real Estate Settlement	Uniform Settlement
closing statement	Procedures Act	Statement (HUD-1)
credit	(RESPA)	walk-through
debit	settlement	

■ PRECLOSING PROCEDURES

Everything a licensee does in the course of a real estate transaction, from securing clients to presenting offers and coordinating inspections, leads to one final event: closing. **Closing**, or **settlement**, is the consummation of the real estate transaction. Closing actually involves three events: (1) the promises made in the sales contract are fulfilled, (2) the mortgage loan funds (if any) are distributed to the buyer for use, and (3) other settlement costs or funds are disbursed. It is the time when the title to the real estate is transferred in exchange for payment of the purchase price. Closing marks the end of any successful real estate sales transaction. Before the property changes hands, however, there are important issues that must be resolved.

Buyer's Issues

Closing is the point at which ownership of a property is transferred in exchange for the selling price.

The buyer needs to be assured that the title that will be delivered by the seller at closing is without defect, or *cloud*. To establish the marketability of the title, the buyer's attorney will usually conduct a title search to verify clear chain of title and to discover encumbrances such as liens, deed restrictions, protective covenants, or easements. A property survey should also be obtained to verify the physical size and shape of the property, the location of improvements upon the parcel, and the absence of encroachments involving surrounding parcels.

The buyer should also utilize various professional inspections to determine the condition of the property. If the buyer and the seller agreed to Alternative 1 in Provision 16 of the North Carolina Association of REALTORS® (NCAR) Standard Form 2-T Offer to Purchase and Contract (Appendix D, Form 11), a property inspection should uncover any mandatory repairs of covered systems of the house. Other inspections may be required to determine the presence of pest infestation, radon, friable asbestos, or unusual drainage affecting the structure. Please note that the buyer bears the responsibility for hiring the various inspectors for the specific individual inspections the buyer may desire. Unless otherwise stated in the contract, if there are required repairs or corrective measures dictated by Alternative 1, the seller has three options: (1) complete them, (2) provide for their completion, or (3) refuse to complete them. If the seller refuses to complete the repairs, the buyer has two options: (1) accept the property in its present condition or (2) terminate the contract.

If the buyer and the seller have agreed to Alternative 2 in Provision 16 of the NCAR Standard Form 2-T Offer to Purchase and Contract, the buyer may have anything inspected at the buyer's expense during the option period and negotiate acceptable corrective measures or repairs on anything that is discovered. The seller is not bound to any mandatory repairs or corrective measures under Alternative 2. Remember that repair negotiations under Alternative 2 must be resolved prior to the termination of the option period because if the buyer does not exercise the right to terminate the contract prior to the Option Termination Period, the buyer must accept the property in its then current condition.

Soil suitability test.   If property is unimproved and does not have access to a central sewage disposal system, the buyer should order a **soil suitability test**. This test measures the soil's ability to absorb and drain water. Soil must percolate (i.e., perk) properly before approval will be given to install a septic system for on-site sewage disposal. In North Carolina, the buyer customarily pays for this soil evaluation test, formerly called the percolation test.

Property survey.   A property **survey** gives the purchaser information about the exact location and size of the property. The buyer normally pays for the survey, although the sales contract can specify otherwise. It is usual for the survey to denote the location of all buildings, driveways, fences, and other improvements located on the premises being purchased. Any improvements located on adjoining property that may encroach on the premises being bought also are noted. The survey should describe in detail any existing easements and encroachments. Whether or not the sales contract calls for a survey, lenders occasionally require one. The buyer is strongly encouraged to secure an updated survey even if the lender does not require one or if the parcel was recently surveyed because encroachments can occur at any time and make the title unmarketable until resolved.

Final property inspection.   Shortly before the closing takes place, the buyer's agent and the buyer usually make a final inspection of the property often called the **walk-through**. Through this physical inspection, the buyer can ensure that necessary repairs have been made, that the property has been adequately maintained since contract, and that all fixtures are in place with no unauthorized removal or alteration of any part of the improvements.

Note: The request for a preclosing walk-through should be in the contract to purchase. This clause usually provides that the buyer has an option to a final walk-through inspection within approximately 24 hours prior to actual closing or at a date and time agreed on with the seller. The NCAR Standard Form 2-T Offer to Purchase and Contract contains this clause.

IN PRACTICE   Licensees should avoid recommending one individual or one specific source for any inspections or testing services. If the buyer suffers any injury as a result of a provider's negligence, the licensee also may be liable. At least three sources of each type of professional service provider should be recommended to give the parties free choice. Agents should recommend a full set of inspections even if the purchase is made with no financing contingency involved.

Seller's Issues

Obviously, the seller's main interest is receiving payment for the property. The seller needs to be sure that the buyer has obtained the necessary financing and has sufficient funds to complete the sale. The seller also needs to be certain that all the requirements of the sales contract are met so the transaction can be completed.

Both parties will want to inspect the closing statement to ensure that all monies involved in the transaction have been accounted for properly. Both parties may be accompanied to closing by their attorneys although it is uncommon in North Carolina for the seller to have an attorney present at closing.

IN PRACTICE   Depending on local custom, the broker's role at closing can vary from simply being present to conducting the proceedings. A broker's service generally continues after the sales contract is signed—the broker advises the parties in practical matters and makes sure all details are taken care of so that the closing can proceed smoothly. (Remember, a real estate broker is not authorized to give legal advice or otherwise engage in the practice of law.) The broker might make arrangements for such items as title evidence, surveys, appraisals, termite inspections, and repairs, or the broker might recommend sources of these services to the parties. The broker also is held responsible by the North Carolina Real Estate Commission (NCREC) for the accuracy and delivery of the closing statement either at closing or within five days after closing [see G.S. 93A-6(a)(14)].

Title Procedures

Both the buyer and the buyer's lender want assurance that the seller's title complies with the requirements of the sales contract. After a thorough title search, the closing attorney usually submits a preliminary opinion on title to the title insurance company. Based on this opinion, the title insurance will issue a title commitment. This is a commitment to issue a title insurance policy if the final title search confirms that the seller's title is marketable.

On the date of the closing meeting (the date of delivery of the deed), the buyer has a title commitment that was probably issued several days or weeks before the closing. For this reason, the final opinion on title and the title insurance policy are issued after closing (see Chapter 5).

Unless the buyer is assuming the seller's mortgage loan, the seller's existing loan is paid in full and a mortgage release should be recorded. The exact amount required to pay off the existing loan is provided in a current *payoff statement* from the lender, effective on the date of closing. This payoff statement states the unpaid amount of principal, interest due through the date of payment, the fee for issuing the certificate of satisfaction or release, credits (if any) for tax and insurance reserves, and the amount of any prepayment penalties. The same procedure is followed for any other liens that must be released before the buyer takes title. If there is an escrow account for the mortgage loan, it could be applied to the balance owed or it may be refunded after closing.

For transactions in which the buyer assumes the seller's existing mortgage loan, the closing attorney needs to know the exact balance of the loan as of the closing date. It is customary for the closing attorney to obtain information from the lender that includes the terms of the mortgage loan being assumed. The closing attorney will have the buyer sign the assumption documents accepting the terms of the loan and the responsibility to repay the loan. The seller may also be required to execute an *affidavit of lien waiver* (*affidavit of title*). This is a sworn statement in which the seller assures the title insurance company and the buyer that there have been no judgments, bankruptcies, or divorces involving the seller since the date of the title examination. The affidavit promises that no unrecorded deeds or contracts were made, no repairs or improvements were made that have not been paid for, and the seller knows of no defects in the title. If the seller is the builder, the affidavit should address the payment of any subcontractors used in the construction process. The seller also affirms that he or she is in possession of the premises. This form is normally required before the title insurance company will issue an owner's policy to the buyer. The affidavit gives the title insurance company the right to sue the seller if the seller's statements in the affidavit are incorrect.

■ CONDUCTING THE CLOSING

In North Carolina, closings are conducted by gathering the parties together and exchanging copies of the documents. This kind of closing is called the *closing meeting* (or a *face-to-face closing*). Current practice in North Carolina is that a lawyer frequently represents the buyer although the settlement agent does not have to be an attorney. The seller also may be represented by a different lawyer but usually is not. The attorney/closing agent, normally selected and paid by the buyer, also represents the lender's interest.

A closing involves the resolution of two issues. First, the promises made in the sales contract are fulfilled. Second, the buyer's loan is finalized and the mortgage lender or closing attorney/agent disburses the loan funds. Closings are most often held in the attorney's office; however, they may be held at any number of locations, including the office of the lending institution or the broker. Those persons attending a typical residential closing may include

- the buyer;
- the seller;
- the real estate brokers (both the buyer's and the seller's agents);
- the seller's and the buyer's attorneys;
- representatives of the lending institutions involved with the buyer's new mortgage loan, the buyer's assumption of the seller's existing loan, or the seller's payoff of an existing loan; and
- the representative of the title insurance company (although this seldom happens in North Carolina).

Escrow Type Closing

The closing agent may use the escrow-type closing if the parties cannot attend the closing meeting. The parties can agree in advance who will act as escrow/closing agent, and all funds and paperwork are delivered *into escrow*. The designated escrow agent is an impartial third party who conducts the closing. When the deed has been prepared and delivered to the escrow agent, it is considered to have been legally delivered to the buyer under what is called the *relation back doctrine*. This type of closing is seldom used in North Carolina. In other states that practice this type of closing, title insurance companies and lending institutions often act as escrow agents.

Closing Agent or Closing Officer

One person called the **closing agent** or officer usually conducts the proceedings at a closing and calculates the division of income and expenses between the parties (called settlement). In North Carolina, the closing agent has historically been the buyer's attorney because so many of the functions performed at closing are of a legal nature. In 2003, the North Carolina State Bar ruled in an ethics opinion that an attorney does not have to physically preside over the closing meeting. A nonlawyer assistant under the direct supervision of an active member of the Bar may conduct the closing meeting (identify documents to be signed, indicate the correct place to sign, and disburse proceeds) as long as that person does not engage in the unauthorized practice of law. The supervising attorney must be available to answer any legal concerns that may arise such as the need for legal advice on how to take title or the legal status of the title. NCREC strongly cautions that any real estate licensee who conducts a closing meeting under the above situation will be held fully responsible for all aspects of the closing.

The Exchange

When the parties are satisfied that everything is in order, the exchange is made. All pertinent documents then are recorded *in the correct order* to ensure continuity of title. For instance, if the seller is paying off an existing loan and the buyer is obtaining a new loan, the seller's satisfaction of mortgage should be recorded before the seller's deed to the buyer is recorded. The buyer's new mortgage or deed of trust must be recorded *after* the deed because the buyers cannot pledge the property as security for the loan until they own it. The transaction is *closed* when all documents have been recorded.

IRS Reporting Requirements

Every real estate transaction must be reported to the IRS by the closing agent on Form 1099-S. Information includes the sales price, the amount of property tax reimbursement credited to the seller, and the seller's Social Security number. If the closing agent does not notify the IRS, the responsibility for filing the form falls on the mortgage lender, although the brokers or the parties to the transaction ultimately could be held liable.

Lender's Interest in Closing

Whether a buyer is obtaining new financing or assuming the seller's existing loan, the lender wants to protect its security interest in the property. The lender has an interest in making sure that the buyer receives good, marketable title and that tax and insurance payments are maintained. Lenders want their mortgage liens to have priority over other liens. They also want to ensure that the insurance will be current if the property is damaged or destroyed. For this reason, a lender generally requires proof that the buyer has purchased both a title insurance policy for the benefit of the lender and a hazard insurance policy. In addition, a lender may require that the borrower provide additional information: a survey, a termite or other inspection report, or a certificate of occupancy (for newly constructed buildings). The lender also may request that a reserve or escrow account be established for tax and insurance payments. Lenders sometimes even require representation by their own attorney(s) at closings.

■ RESPA REQUIREMENTS

The federal **Real Estate Settlement Procedures Act (RESPA)** was enacted to protect consumers from abusive lending practices. RESPA also aids consumers during the mortgage loan settlement process. It ensures that consumers are provided with important, accurate, and timely information about the actual costs of settling or closing the transaction. It also eliminates *kickbacks* and other referral fees that tend to inflate the costs of settlement unnecessarily. RESPA prohibits lenders from requiring excessive escrow account deposits.

RESPA's Consumer Protections
- CLO regulation
- CBA disclosure
- Settlement cost booklet
- Good-faith estimate of settlement costs
- Uniform Settlement Statement
- Prohibition of kickbacks and unearned fees

RESPA requirements apply when the purchase is financed by a federally related mortgage loan. *Federally related loans* are loans made by banks, savings associations, or other lenders whose deposits are insured by federal agencies. The term also covers loans insured by the FHA or guaranteed by the VA; loans administered by HUD; or loans intended to be sold by the lender to Fannie Mae, Ginnie Mae, or Freddie Mac. RESPA is administered by HUD.

RESPA regulations apply to first-lien residential mortgage loans made to finance the purchase of one-family to four-family homes, cooperatives, and condominiums. RESPA also governs second or subordinate liens for home equity loans. RESPA does not normally cover a transaction financed solely by a purchase-money mortgage taken back by the seller, an installment contract (contract for deed), or the buyer's assumption of the seller's existing loan. However, if the terms of the assumed loan are modified or if the lender charges more than $50 for the assumption, the transaction will be subject to RESPA.

IN PRACTICE

While RESPA's requirements are aimed primarily at lenders, some of its provisions affect real estate brokers as well. Real estate licensees fall under RESPA when they refer buyers to particular lenders, title companies, attorneys, or other providers of settlement services. Licensees who offer computerized loan origination (CLO) services also are subject to regulation. Remember: buyers have the right to select their own providers of settlement services; therefore, the required use of a specific service provider is prohibited.

Controlled Business Arrangements

For the real estate consumer, a service that continues to increase in popularity is one-stop shopping. A real estate firm, title insurance company, mortgage broker, home inspection company, and even a moving company may agree to offer a package of services to consumers. RESPA permits such a controlled business arrangement (CBA) *as long as the consumer is clearly informed of the relationship among the service providers and that other providers are available*. Required use of a particular service provider is prohibited by RESPA. Fees may not be exchanged among the affiliated companies simply for referring business to one another. This may be a particularly important issue for licensees who offer *computerized loan origination (CLO)* services to their clients and customers. While a borrower's ability to comparison shop for a loan may be enhanced by a CLO system, the range of choices must not be limited. Consumers must be informed of the availability of other lenders.

Disclosure Requirements

RESPA mandates that lenders and settlement agents have the following disclosure obligations at the time of loan application and loan closing:

■ *Special information booklet:* Lenders must provide a copy of a special informational HUD booklet to every person from whom they receive or for whom they prepare a loan application (except for refinancing). The HUD booklet must be given at the time the application is received or within three days afterward. The booklet provides the borrower with general information about settlement (closing) costs. It also explains the various provisions of RESPA, including a line-by-line explanation of the Uniform Settlement Statement.

■ *Good-faith estimate of settlement costs:* No later than three business days after the receipt of the loan application, the lender must provide to all borrowers a good-faith estimate of the settlement costs the borrower is likely to incur. This estimate may be either a specific figure or a range of costs based on comparable past transactions in the area. In addition, if the lender requires that a particular attorney or title company be used to conduct the closing, the lender must state whether it has any business relationship with that firm and must estimate the charges for this service.

■ *Uniform Settlement Statement (HUD Form 1):* RESPA requires that a special HUD form (shown in Figure 15.1 on pages 299–300) be completed to itemize all charges to be paid by the borrower and seller in connection with settlement. The **Uniform Settlement Statement (HUD-1)** includes all charges paid in connection with the transaction, whether required by the lender or by a third party. Items not required by the lender that are paid by the borrower and seller outside closing, such as repairs, must be included on HUD-1. Charges required by the lender that are paid for before closing are indicated as *paid outside closing (POC)* but are not reflected in the *bottom line* totals of HUD-1. RESPA prohibits a lender from requiring that a borrower deposit amounts in escrow accounts for taxes and insurance that exceed certain limits, to prevent the lender from taking advantage of the borrower. The *seller* is also prohibited from requiring, as a condition of the sale, that the buyer purchase title insurance from a particular company.

The settlement statement must be made available for inspection by the borrower *at or before settlement*. Borrowers have the right to inspect the completed HUD-1, to the extent that the figures are available, *one business day before the closing*. (Sellers are not entitled to this privilege.)

Lenders must retain these statements for two years after the date of closing. In addition, state law requires that real estate licensees retain all records of a transaction for a three-year period (see Rule A.0108). The Uniform Settlement Statement may be altered to allow for local custom, and certain lines may be deleted if they do not apply in the area.

Kickbacks and Referral Fees

RESPA *prohibits the payment of kickbacks*, or *unearned fees*, incident to or as part of a real estate settlement service. It prohibits referral fees *when no services are actually rendered*. The payment or receipt of a fee, kickback, or anything of value for referrals for settlement services is prohibited for activities such as making mortgage loans, title searches, title insurance, or services rendered by attorneys, surveyors, home inspectors, or appraisers. Violators of RESPA requirements are currently subject to a fine up to $10,000, one-year imprisonment, or both.

Preliminaries to Closing

Preparation for closing involves ordering and reviewing an array of documents. The closing attorney has the responsibility for ensuring that all legal documents are prepared and properly delivered. Legal documents required to close a residential transaction include items listed below.

Documents sellers are responsible for providing (either directly or through their attorney) include the following:

- The deed (usually prepared by the closing attorney)
- Affidavit as to mechanics' liens
- Bill of sale of personal property (If any of the seller's personal property is being transferred to the buyer, ownership can be shown by a bill of sale.)
- Leases and related documents (if the property being transferred is currently leased)
- Statement from the seller's lender (A current loan balance payoff figure must be available as of the day of closing.)
- Proof of repairs or services (If any repairs were necessary, the seller must bring proof to the closing that the repairs have been done.)

Documents buyer is responsible for providing (either directly or through the closing attorney) include the following:

- Financing documents (The closing attorney receives a closing package from the lender with instructions on how to prepare the financing documents, including the deed of trust and the promissory note.)
- Title insurance policy (issued after the attorney's opinion of good title)

- Property insurance policy (The buyer is required to bring a current policy to the closing.)
- Wood-destroying insect inspection report (The buyer normally pays for this unless the transaction is financed with a VA loan, in which case the seller normally pays.)
- Property survey

■ PREPARATION OF CLOSING STATEMENT

A typical real estate transaction involves expenses for both parties in addition to the purchase price. These include items prepaid by the seller for which he or she must be reimbursed (such as taxes) and items of expense the seller has incurred but for which the buyer will be billed (such as assumed mortgage interest paid in arrears). The financial responsibility for these items must be *prorated*, or divided equitably, between the buyer and the seller. All expense items and prorated items are accounted for on the settlement statement. This is how the exact amount of cash required from the buyer and the net proceeds to the seller are determined (see Table 15.1). The closing statement worksheet and/or the HUD-1 form are not considered to be legal documents and may be prepared by a licensed real estate broker.

Regardless of who prepares the closing statement, NCREC will hold the real estate licensees responsible for accuracy and delivery. NCREC can take appropriate disciplinary action against a broker who fails to provide complete and accurate closing statements and to ensure proper delivery [see G.S. 93A-6(a)(14)].

How the Closing Statement Works

The completion of a **closing statement** involves an accounting of all the parties' debits and credits as of the time of closing. A **debit** is a charge; an amount that a party owes and must pay at the closing. A **credit** is an amount entered in a person's favor—an amount that has already been paid, an amount being reimbursed, or an amount the buyer promises to pay in the form of a loan.

The closing statement only reflects the accounting of the two parties to the transaction (the buyer and the seller). If both parties are involved with a bill or expense, it will be posted as a double entry. If an expense is between one of the principals and a third party (such as the surveyor), it will appear as a single entry.

> A *debit* is an amount to be paid by the buyer or seller; a *credit* is an amount payable to the buyer or seller.

To determine the amount the buyer needs at the closing, the buyer's debits are totaled. Any expenses and prorated amounts for items prepaid by the seller are added to the purchase price. Then the buyer's credits are totaled. These include the earnest money (already paid), the balance of the loan the buyer is obtaining or assuming, and the seller's share of any prorated items that the buyer will pay in the future (see Table 15.2). Finally, the total of the buyer's credits is subtracted from the total debits to arrive at the actual amount of certified funds the buyer must bring to the closing. Usually the buyer brings a certified or official bank check or has the funds wired to the closing attorney's escrow account. Although cash is definitely *certified funds*, the buyer who brings a bag of money to pay the bills at closing may encounter resistance from the closing agent because large amounts

T A B L E 15.1   **Allocation of Expenses**

Item	Paid by Seller	Paid by Buyer
Broker's Commission	✗ by agreement	✗ by agreement
Attorney's fees	✗ by agreement	✗ by agreement
Recording expenses	✗ to clear title	✗ transfer charges
Excise tax	✗ deed transfer tax	
Title expenses	✗ quitclaim deed if necessary to clear title defect	✗ attorney title examination and title insurance
Loan fees	✗ prepayment penalty (seller's loan)	✗ origination fee/assumption fee
Tax and insurance reserves (escrow or impound accounts)		✗ if required by lender
Appraisal fees		✗ if requested
Survey fees		✗ if requested

of cash (typically over $10,000) will trigger paperwork requirements by either banking regulations and/or the Patriot Act.

A similar procedure is followed to determine how much money the seller actually will receive. The seller's debits and credits are totaled separately. The credits include the purchase price plus the buyer's share of any prorated items that the seller has prepaid. The seller's debits include expenses, the seller's share of prorated items to be paid later by the buyer, and the balance of any mortgage loan or other lien that the seller is paying off. Finally the total of the seller's debits is subtracted from the total credits to arrive at the amount the seller will receive.

Broker's commission. The responsibility for paying the broker's commission is determined by signed agency agreement. If the broker is the agent for the seller, the seller is usually responsible for paying the commission. If the listing firm entered the property into a multiple listing service (MLS), the compensation of the selling agent (whether a buyer's agent or a seller's subagent) is generally disclosed in the MLS entry. Most of the time, the listing firm will split the commission earned from the seller with a cooperating firm that brings the buyer to the transaction. If the listing firm or seller refuses to pay the buyer's agent, most buyer agency agreements state that the buyer is then responsible for the agent's compensation at a preset rate or figure.

Attorney's fees. If either of the parties' attorneys is to be paid from the closing proceeds, that party is charged with the expenses on the closing statement. The attorney's fee may include preparation or review of documents, title search and opinion, or representation of the parties at settlement.

Recording expenses. The *seller* usually pays for recording charges (filing fees) necessary to clear all defects in order to furnish the purchaser with a marketable title. Items customarily charged to the seller include the recording of release deeds or satisfaction of mortgages, quitclaim deeds, affidavits, and satisfaction of mechanic's lien claims. The *purchaser* pays for recording charges that arise from the actual transfer of title.

TABLE 15.2 **Credits and Debits**

Item	Credit to Buyer	Debit to Buyer	Credit to Seller	Debit to Seller	Prorated
Principal amount of new mortgage	✗				
Payoff of existing mortgage				✗	
Unpaid principal balance if assumed mortgage	✗			✗	
Accrued interest on existing assumed mortgage	✗			✗	✗
Tenants' security deposits	✗			✗	
Purchase-money mortgage	✗			✗	
Unpaid real estate tax or utility bills	✗			✗	✗
Buyer's earnest money	✗				
Selling price of property		✗	✗		
Fuel oil on hand (valued at current market price)		✗	✗		
Prepaid insurance and tax escrow for mortgage assumed by buyer		✗	✗		
Refund to seller of prepaid water charges and similar utility expenses		✗	✗		✗
Prepaid real estate taxes		✗	✗		✗
Excise tax (revenue stamps)				✗	

Usually such items include recording the deed that conveys title to the purchaser and the mortgage or deed of trust executed by the purchaser. If the NCAR Standard Form 2-T Offer to Purchase and Contract is used, recordation of the deed is required by contract to complete the closing process.

Excise tax. North Carolina requires an excise tax (formerly known as revenue stamps) on the gross revenue generated by the sale of real estate. This tax, sometimes called a *deed transfer tax*, is levied at a rate of $1 per $500 of value, or portion thereof. The excise tax will always round up to the next whole dollar amount if the calculation includes cents. This expense is borne by the seller.

Title expenses.   Custom usually requires that the buyer obtain and pay the title examination. Most of the time, this charge will be included in the attorney's fee.

Evidence of title relied on in the purchase of a parcel of real estate includes a title guaranty or a fee policy of title insurance. The title guaranty and fee policy of title insurance are one-time premium charges for insurance that insures the purchaser's title during the period of ownership of real estate. Some lenders request an American Land Title Association (ALTA) policy that insures the mortgagee for the amount of the mortgage loan, called a *lender's policy*. A buyer may also purchase an owner's policy to protect the entire purchase price; this higher level of coverage is always a good investment.

Loan fees.   When the buyer secures a new loan to finance the purchase, the lender ordinarily charges an administrative fee called a loan origination fee of about 1 percent of the loan value. The borrower usually pays the fee at the time the transaction closes. The lender also may charge discount points to permanently buydown the interest rate. In order to prove creditworthiness, the buyer will pay for a credit report at the time of loan application that will show up as *paid outside of closing (POC)* on the HUD-1. If the buyer assumes the seller's existing financing, there will usually be an assumption fee. Also, under the terms of some mortgage loans, the seller may be required to pay a prepayment charge or penalty for paying off the mortgage loan in advance of its due date. Overnight mailing expenses to the lenders of both parties is very common because it saves additional days of interest for both parties.

Tax reserves and insurance reserves (escrow or impound accounts). Most mortgage lenders require that borrowers provide a reserve fund or escrow account to pay future real estate taxes and insurance premiums, especially when the loan-to-value ratio exceeds specified percentages. These payments are often referred to as *prepaids*. The borrower usually starts the account at closing by depositing funds to cover at least two months of taxes and hazard insurance. The borrower's monthly loan payment includes the loan principal and interest plus one-twelfth of the estimated taxes and insurance (PITI) for the escrow account. The taxes and insurance are held by the lender in the escrow or impound account until the bills are due. Some lenders also use the escrow account for collecting private mortgage insurance premium and maintenance fees that are payable on a recurring basis to an owner's association. Although sellers occasionally agree to pay all or some of the buyer's closing expenses, the lender will almost always require the borrower to pay for prepaids.

Appraisal fees.   Generally, the purchaser pays the appraisal fees because it is customary for the lender to require an appraisal as a condition of the loan. If the fee is paid at the time of the loan application, it is reflected on the HUD-1 settlement statement as having been *paid outside closing (POC)*.

Survey fees.   The purchaser who benefits from the information shown on a survey will customarily pay the survey fees. Clearing up any title defects that arise from the survey, such as eliminating an encroachment, would be the seller's responsibility. As discussed previously, some lenders will require a new survey as a condition of financing.

Option fee.   If the parties to the contract agreed to Alternative 2 in Provision 16 of the NCAR Standard Form 2-T Offer to Purchase and Contract, the buyer must pay a nonrefundable option fee directly to the seller for the right to terminate the contract for any or no reason. There is no contract if the option fee has not been paid. Per the contract, the option fee will be credited to the buyer at closing and will be debited from the seller's side because the seller already received it outside of closing. This fee is not to be confused with earnest money that serves as liquidated damages.

Additional fees.   Because each real estate transaction is unique, it is not uncommon to have additional fees or expenses charged to either party dependent on the sales contract. An FHA borrower owes a lump sum for payment of the mortgage insurance premium (MIP) if it is not being financed as part of the loan. A VA borrower pays a funding fee directly to the VA at closing. If a conventional loan carries private mortgage insurance, the buyer prepays one year's insurance premium at closing. Charges for specialized inspections such as home inspections, radon tests, structural inspections, or environmental evaluations are becoming more commonplace. Because some service providers require payment at the time of service, those charges often appear on the closing statement as POC (paid outside of closing). Any charge that seems unusual should be questioned by the licensee or principal to verify its purpose.

Accounting for Expenses

Expenses paid out of the closing proceeds are debited, or charged, only to the party making the payment. Occasionally the buyer and the seller may share an unpaid expense item such as current real estate taxes. In that case, the parties are debited for their share of the expense.

■ PRORATIONS

Most closings involve a division of financial responsibility between the buyer and seller for such items as loan interest, taxes, rents, and fuel or utility bills. These allowances are called **prorations.** Closing computations typically mean that each party pays for what they used or for the time they occupied the property during the appropriate period (month or year). Prorations are necessary to ensure that expenses are divided fairly between the seller and the buyer. For example, the seller may owe current taxes that have not yet been billed; the buyer will want this settled at the closing. If real property taxes have been paid in advance, the seller is entitled to a rebate at the closing. If the buyer assumes the seller's existing mortgage or deed of trust, the seller usually owes the buyer an allowance for accrued interest through the date of closing. The seller is normally responsible for prorated expenses owed on the day of closing, except for the buyer's daily interim interest on a new loan that would be a single entry debit to the buyer.

Accrued items are unpaid items to be prorated (such as unpaid current real estate taxes or interest on an assumed mortgage) that are owed by the seller but will be paid later by the buyer. The seller therefore pays for the seller's portion of the bill by giving the buyer credit for it at closing. The seller receives a debit for that prorated share, and the buyer is given an equal amount as a credit.

Prepaid items are expenses that have already been paid by the seller prior to closing and the buyer needs to rebate that portion to the seller. Examples would be real estate taxes already paid by the seller for the current year prior to closing or prepaid homeowner association dues. The item is prorated and the buyer's allocated portion is reflected as a credit to the seller and as a debit to the buyer.

The Arithmetic of Prorating

Accurate prorating involves four considerations:

1. The nature of the item being prorated (i.e., annual versus monthly expense, calendar versus fiscal year)
2. Whether it is an accrued item (unpaid) that requires the determination of an earned amount (i.e., an advance payment to the buyer)
3. Whether it is a prepaid item (overpaid) that requires that the unearned amount (i.e., a refund to the seller) be determined
4. What arithmetic processes must be used (see different methods below)

There are several different ways to prorate items that require a division of funds among the parties (the buyer and the seller). Those listed below are the most common ways to prorate, but the buyer and seller may agree to any other method.

360-day year/30-day month method.   This method is referred to as the *banker's year/banker's month method* (sometimes as the *statutory method*) and is, perhaps, the easiest to use, but probably not the most accurate. (This is the method used for all prorations in the textbook and on the North Carolina Real Estate State Licensing Examinations.) The year is treated as having 360 days with each month having 30 days.

365-day year method/Actual-days-in-the-month method.   This method is the most accurate and normally will be used in actual real estate closings. If the closing takes place in a leap year, then a 366-day year is used. Using this method, the actual days in the month are used. For instance, January would have 31 days and November would have 30 days.

The final proration figure will vary slightly, depending on which computation method is used. (Note that whichever method is used, the seller is responsible for the day of closing on all prorations involving the seller unless otherwise agreed.) The final figure also will vary according to the number of decimal places to which the division is carried. *All of the computations in this textbook and on the North Carolina Real Estate Licensing Examinations are computed by carrying the division to three decimal places.* The third decimal place is rounded off to cents only after the final proration figure is determined.

Accrued Items

When the real estate tax is levied for the calendar year (from January to December) and is payable either during that year or in the following year, the accrued portion is for the period from January 1 through and including the day of closing. If the current tax bill has not yet been issued, the parties must agree on an estimated amount based on the previous year's bill and any known changes in assessment or tax levy for the current year, referred to as the *best estimate* method.

Sample proration calculation (30-day month/360-day year method).   For example, assume a sale is to be closed on April 17 and current real estate taxes of

$1,200 are to be prorated accordingly. The accrued period, then, is 107 days (from January 1 through April 17).

January	30
February	30
March	30
April	17
Total	107 days

First determine the prorated cost of the real estate tax per day:

$$\$1,200 \div 360 = \$3.333 \text{ per day}$$

Next, multiply this figure by the accrued period to determine the prorated real estate tax:

$$\$3.333 \quad \text{per day}$$
$$\times 107 \quad \text{days}$$
$$\$356.63 \quad \text{real estate tax}$$

Therefore, the accrued real estate tax for 107 days is $356.63. This amount represents the seller's accrued earned tax. It is a *credit to the buyer* and a *debit to the seller* on the closing statement because the seller must give his portion of the tax bill to the buyer who will eventually pay the entire bill when it becomes due and payable.

IN PRACTICE

Many title insurance companies provide proration charts that detail tax factors for each day in the year. To determine a tax proration using one of these charts, multiply the factor given for the closing date by the annual real estate tax.

Prepaid Items

A tax proration could be a *prepaid item*. Because the real estate tax is due and payable on September 1, it may be paid before a closing takes place. Tax prorations calculated for closings taking place later in the year may reflect the fact that the seller has already paid the tax. The buyer then has to reimburse the seller for the buyer's portion of the taxes; the proration would be *credited to the seller* and *debited to the buyer*.

Sample prepaid item calculation (30-day month/360-day year method).   Assume that closing is to take place on November 13 and the seller received the annual real estate tax bill of $1,850 in August and has paid the entire bill. Because the seller's liability for taxes is only for the period of January 1 through and including the day of closing, the seller should get back the taxes for the remainder of the year (buyer's portion).

$1,850 annual tax bill ÷ 360	=	$5.139 per day
January 1 – November 13 = 313 days × $5.139	=	$1,608.507
$1,850.00 total bill – $1,608.51 seller's portion	=	$241.49 credit seller/debit buyer

Sample prepaid homeowner's insurance calculation (30-day month/360-day year method). The closing takes place on June 18, and the sellers had purchased and paid for an annual homeowner's insurance policy on February 1 in the amount of $720. The loan is to be assumed and the insurance policy is to be assigned to the buyers. (Note that insurance premiums are normally paid on a fiscal year basis.) As a practical matter, insurance companies rarely permit the assignment of a seller's homeowner's insurance policy to a buyer. A residential buyer almost always must obtain a new insurance policy.

$720 annual premium ÷ 360	=	$2 daily premium
February 1 – June 18 = 138 days × $2	=	$276 seller's portion
$720 – $276	=	$444 credit seller/ debit buyer

General Rules for Prorating

The following are some general prorating guidelines for preparing the closing statement:

■ In North Carolina, the seller owns the property on the day of closing (regardless of what time of day the closing meeting is scheduled), and prorations or apportionments are usually made *through and including the day of closing*.

■ Always prorate for the seller first. If prorating an accrued item, once the seller's portion is computed, the buyer's amount will be the same, but an opposite entry: if a debit to the seller, it is a credit to buyer, and it is the same amount of money. (Think of the entries as if they represented a personal check from one party payable to the other party . . . the check amount is the same when it is written and when it is received.)

■ If prorating a prepaid item, subtract the seller's portion from the total bill to determine the buyer's portion. The buyer's portion will be the same amount on the seller's entry: a credit to the seller and a debit to the buyer.

■ Accrued or prepaid *real estate taxes* are usually prorated at the closing. When the amount of the current real estate tax cannot be determined definitely, the proration is usually based on the last obtainable tax bill.

■ *Special assessments* for municipal improvements such as sewers, water mains, or streets are usually paid in annual installments over several years, with annual interest charged on the outstanding balance of future installments. The seller normally pays the entire balance due, unless the buyer and seller have agreed otherwise in the sales contract. *The special assessment generally is not prorated at the closing*. The contract of sale must address the manner in which special assessments are to be handled at settlement.

■ *Rents* are usually adjusted on the basis of the *actual* number of days in the month of closing in real life situations. It is customary for the seller to receive the rents for the day of closing and to pay all expenses for that day. If any rents for the current month are uncollected when the sale is closed, the buyer often will agree by a separate letter to collect the rents if possible and remit the pro rata share to the seller. If the seller is holding a tenant security deposit, it can be transferred to the buyer by a double-entry (debit seller/ credit buyer). The tenant security deposit is not prorated because it is the tenant's money . . . not the seller's.

Sample rent prorations (30-day month/360-day year method).   Assume the monthly rent is $600, the closing takes place on June 21, and the seller has received the rent for the month of June (paid in advance).

$600 monthly rent ÷ 30 days = $20 per day

21 days (when property owned by seller) × $20 = $420 seller's share

$600 – $420 = $180 buyer's share (debit seller/credit buyer)

Now assume that the monthly rent is $675, the closing takes place on June 5, and the seller has not collected the rent prior to closing (paid in arrears). The buyer will collect the entire month's rent of $675.

$675 monthly rent ÷ 30 days = 22.50 per day

5 days (when property owned by seller) × $22.50 = $112.50 seller's share (debit buyer/credit seller)

Mortgage loan interest.   Interest paid on almost all mortgage loans is simple interest. On almost every mortgage loan, because the interest is paid *in arrears*, buyers and sellers must understand that the mortgage payment due on June 1, for example, includes interest due for the month of May. Thus, if the buyer is getting a new loan, the lender will start charging interest on the day of closing and will normally collect interim interest for the day of closing through the last day of the closing month from the buyer (single entry debit to buyer) at closing. The buyer will usually have at least one day of interim interest but never more than one month's worth. The buyer will not make a monthly payment until the first of the second month. Furthermore, the buyer who assumes a mortgage on May 18 and makes the June payment will be paying for the time the seller occupied the property and should be credited with the seller's part of the month's interest.

Sample interest on a new loan (interim interest) (30-day month/360-day year method).   Pretend that closing is April 12, and the buyer's first mortgage payment will be due on June 1. The buyer will owe for the day of closing through the remainder of the month: 19 days. The loan amount is $95,600 and the interest rate is 6 percent. This is a simple interest example.

$95,600 × 0.06 interest rate = $5,736 annual interest

$5,736 ÷ 360 days = $15.933 daily interest

19 days × $15.933 = $302.73 interest owed by buyer (debit buyer)

Note that this is not a prorated item. It is a cost to be paid only by the buyer to the buyer's lender; therefore, the day of closing belongs to the buyer. *Interim interest adjustment is the only time the buyer will pay for the closing day.*

Sample assumed loan interest proration (30-day month/360-day year method).   The loan amount to be assumed is $105,555 at 7 percent interest. The day of closing is May 18. The first step is to calculate the daily amount of interest, then multiply that by the number of days the seller owned the property during that month. This is a simple interest example.

$105,555 × 0.07 interest rate   = $7,388.85 annual interest

$7,388.85 ÷ 360 days   = $20.525 daily interest

18 days × $20.525   = $369.45 seller's share of interest
(debit seller/credit buyer)

Security deposits.   Security deposits made by tenants to cover the last month's rent of the lease or to cover the cost of repairing damage caused by the tenant are generally transferred in their entirety by the seller to the buyer (debit seller/credit buyer), not prorated.

Summary of Items to Be Prorated

Real estate taxes, unpaid	Debit seller/credit buyer
Real estate taxes, prepaid	Credit seller/debit buyer
Rents collected by seller	Debit seller/credit buyer
Rents to be collected by buyer	Credit seller/debit buyer
Interest on assumed loan	Debit seller/credit buyer
Owner's association dues, unpaid	Debit seller/credit buyer
Owner's association dues, prepaid	Credit seller/debit buyer

Note: A homeowner's insurance policy premium may be prorated if the policy is to be assigned to the buyer, which is extremely rare. Entries would be credit seller/debit buyer for the buyer's prorated share of the premium because insurance premiums are usually paid in advance.

Summary of Other Double-Entry Items

Sales price	Credit seller/debit buyer
Assumption of seller's loan	Debit seller/credit buyer
Purchase-money mortgage	Debit seller/credit buyer
Transfer of seller's escrow account	Credit seller/debit buyer
Alternative 2 option fee	Debit seller/credit buyer
Tenant security deposit, assigned	Debit seller/credit buyer
Fuel oil or gas	Credit seller/debit buyer
Cost of separately sold personal property	Credit seller/debit buyer

Normal Single-Entry Items to Seller

Seller's personal property taxes to be paid at closing	Debit seller
Pay off seller's existing loan	Debit seller
Deed preparation fee	Debit seller
Excise tax (revenue stamps)	Debit seller
Recordation fee, satisfaction of seller's mortgage	Debit seller
Broker's commission	Debit seller
Delinquent real/personal property taxes	Debit seller
IRS tax liens	Debit seller

Normal Single-Entry Items to Buyer

Homeowner's policy, if new	Debit buyer
Loan origination fee	Debit buyer
Financing documents preparation fee	Debit buyer
Deed/mortgage recording fees	Debit buyer
Title insurance premium	Debit buyer
Property survey fee	Debit buyer
Title examination/attorney fee	Debit buyer
Advanced escrow deposits	Debit buyer
Interim interest on buyer's new loan	Debit buyer
Loan discount points	Debit buyer
Earnest money deposit	Credit buyer
New first mortgage loan	Credit buyer
New second/third mortgage loan	Credit buyer

Note: If taxable personal property (such as a farm tractor) is to be conveyed to the buyer along with real property, the personal property taxes on the item would be prorated per the terms of the NCAR Standard Form 2-T Offer to Purchase and Contract form.

Note: Real property taxes may be handled as a *double-debit* under certain circumstances: (1) agreement of the buyer and seller, (2) seller has received the tax bill, (3) the taxes have not been paid, and (4) the taxes are to be paid at closing to satisfy the tax lien.

Example: The closing date is December 15, annual taxes are $1,260, and the double-debit method will be used.

$1,260 annual tax ÷ 360 days	= $3.50 daily taxes
January 1 – December 15	= 345 days
345 days × $3.50	= $1,207.50 debit seller
$1,260 – $1,207.50	= $52.50 debit buyer

■ SAMPLE CLOSING STATEMENT

There are many possible formats for settlement computations. The remaining portion of this chapter illustrates a sample transaction using the HUD Uniform Settlement Statement in Figure 15.1.

Basic Information of Offer and Sale

John and Joanne Iuro listed their home at 3045 North Racine Avenue in Riverdale, North Carolina, with the Open Door Real Estate Company. The listing price was $118,500, and possession could be given within two weeks after all parties had signed the contract. Under the terms of the listing agreement, the sellers agreed to pay the broker a commission of 6 percent of the gross sales price.

On April 18 the Open Door Real Estate Company submitted an offer to the Iuros from Brook Redeman, a bachelor, presently residing at 22 King Court, Riverdale.

F I G U R E   15.1   RESPA Uniform Settlement Statement

A. **Settlement Statement**   U.S. Department of Housing and Urban Development   OMB Approval No. 2502-0265 (expires 9/30/2006)

B. Type of Loan

					6. File Number:	7. Loan Number:	8. Mortgage Insurance Case Number:
1.	FHA	2.	FmHA	3.	Conv. Unins.		
4.	VA	5.	Conv. Ins.				

C. Note: This form is furnished to give you a statement of actual settlement costs. Amounts paid to and by the settlement agent are shown. Items marked "(p.o.c.)" were paid outside the closing; they are shown here for informational purposes and are not included in the totals.

D. Name & Address of Borrower:	E. Name & Address of Seller:	F. Name & Address of Lender:
Brook Redeman 22 King Court Riverdale, NC	John & Joanne Iuro 3045 Racine Ave. Riverdale, NC	Thrift Federal Savings 1100 Fountain Plaza Riverdale, NC

G. Property Location:	H. Settlement Agent:	
3045 Racine Ave. Riverdale, NC	Place of Settlement: Open Door Real Estate Company 720 Main Street, Riverdale, NC	I. Settlement Date: June 15

J. Summary of Borrower's Transaction		K. Summary of Seller's Transaction	
100. Gross Amount Due From Borrower		**400. Gross Amount Due To Seller**	
101. Contract sales price	115,000.00	401. Contract sales price	115,000.00
102. Personal property		402. Personal property	
103. Settlement charges to borrower (line 1400)	5,289.45	403.	
104.		404.	
105.		405.	
Adjustments for items paid by seller in advance		**Adjustments for items paid by seller in advance**	
106. City/town taxes to		406. City/town taxes to	
107. County taxes to		407. County taxes to	
108. Assessments to		408. Assessments to	
109.		409.	
110.		410.	
111.		411.	
112.		412.	
120. Gross Amount Due From Borrower	120,289.45	**420. Gross Amount Due To Seller**	115,000.00
200. Amounts Paid By Or In Behalf Of Borrower		**500. Reductions In Amount Due To Seller**	
201. Deposit or earnest money	23,000.00	501. Excess deposit (see instructions)	
202. Principal amount of new loan(s)	92,000.00	502. Settlement charges to seller (line 1400)	7,245.00
203. Existing loan(s) taken subject to		503. Existing loan(s) taken subject to	
204.		504. Payoff of first mortgage loan	78,395.56
205.		505. Payoff of second mortgage loan	
206.		506.	
207.		507.	
208.		508.	
209.		509.	
Adjustments for items unpaid by seller		**Adjustments for items unpaid by seller**	
210. City/town taxes to		510. City/town taxes to	
211. County taxes 1/1 to 6/15	695.18	511. County taxes 1/1 to 6/15	695.18
212. Assessments to		512. Assessments to	
213.		513.	
214.		514.	
215.		515.	
216.		516.	
217.		517.	
218.		518.	
219.		519.	
220. Total Paid By/For Borrower	115,695.18	**520. Total Reduction Amount Due Seller**	86,336.31
300. Cash At Settlement From/To Borrower		**600. Cash At Settlement To/From Seller**	
301. Gross Amount due from borrower (line 120)	120,289.45	601. Gross amount due to seller (line 420)	115,000.00
302. Less amounts paid by/for borrower (line 220)	(115,695.18)	602. Less reductions in amt. due seller (line 520)	(86,336.31)
303. Cash [X] From [ ] To Borrower	4,594.27	**603. Cash** [X] To [ ] From Seller	28,663.69

Section 5 of the Real Estate Settlement Procedures Act (RESPA) requires the following: • HUD must develop a Special Information Booklet to help persons borrowing money to finance the purchase of residential real estate to better understand the nature and costs of real estate settlement services; • Each lender must provide the booklet to all applicants from whom it receives or for whom it prepares a written application to borrow money to finance the purchase of residential real estate; • Lenders must prepare and distribute with the Booklet a Good Faith Estimate of the settlement costs that the borrower is likely to incur in connection with the settlement. These disclosures are manadatory.

Section 4(a) of RESPA mandates that HUD develop and prescribe this standard form to be used at the time of loan settlement to provide full disclosure of all charges imposed upon the borrower and seller. These are third party disclosures that are designed to provide the borrower with pertinent information during the settlement process in order to be a better shopper.

The Public Reporting Burden for this collection of information is estimated to average one hour per response, including the time for reviewing instructions, searching existing data sources, gathering and maintaining the data needed, and completing and reviewing the collection of information.

This agency may not collect this information, and you are not required to complete this form, unless it displays a currently valid OMB control number.

The information requested does not lend itself to confidentiality.

Previous editions are obsolete   Page 1 of 2   form **HUD-1** (3/86)
ref Handbook 4305.2

F I G U R E   15.1   RESPA Uniform Settlement Statement (continued)

L. Settlement Charges

			Paid From Borrowers Funds at Settlement	Paid From Seller's Funds at Settlement
700. Total Sales/Broker's Commission based on price $ 115,000 @ 6.0 % =				
Division of Commission (line 700) as follows:				
701. $	to			
702. $	to			
703. Commission paid at Settlement				6,900.00
704.				
800. Items Payable In Connection With Loan				
801. Loan Origination Fee	1 %		920.00	
802. Loan Discount	2 %		1,840.00	
803. Appraisal Fee	$300.00 to Swift Appraisal		POC	
804. Credit Report	$ 60.00 to Acme Credit		POC	
805. Lender's Inspection Fee				
806. Mortgage Insurance Application Fee to				
807. Assumption Fee				
808.				
809.				
810.				
811.				
900. Items Required By Lender To Be Paid In Advance				
901. Interest from 6/15 to 6/30 @$ 18.528	/day 16 days 7.25%		296.45	
902. Mortgage Insurance Premium for	months to			
903. Hazard Insurance Premium for	1 years to Hite Insurance		345.00	
904.	years to			
905.				
1000. Reserves Deposited With Lender				
1001. Hazard insurance	2 months@$ 28.75	per month	57.50	
1002. Mortgage insurance	months@$	per month		
1003. City property taxes	months@$	per month		
1004. County property taxes	7 months@$ 126.50	per month	885.50	
1005. Annual assessments	months@$	per month		
1006.	months@$	per month		
1007.	months@$	per month		
1008.	months@$	per month		
1100. Title Charges				
1101. Settlement or closing fee	to			
1102. Abstract or title search	to			
1103. Title examination	to			
1104. Title insurance binder	to			
1105. Document preparation	to Attorney			75.00
1106. Notary fees	to			
1107. Attorney's fees	to Attorney		350.00	
(includes above items numbers:	)			
1108. Title insurance	to		290.00	
(includes above items numbers:	)			
1109. Lender's coverage	$ 210.00			
1110. Owner's coverage	$ 80.00			
1111.				
1112.				
1113.				
1200. Government Recording and Transfer Charges				
1201. Recording fees: Deed $ 20.00	; Mortgage $ 25.00	; Releases $ 20.00	45.00	20.00
1202. City/county tax/stamps: Deed $	; Mortgage $			
1203. State tax/stamps: Deed $ 230.00	; Mortgage $			230.00
1204. Recording fees to clear title				20.00
1205.				
1300. Additional Settlement Charges				
1301. Survey to			175.00	
1302. Pest inspection to			85.00	
1303.				
1304.				
1305.				
1400. Total Settlement Charges (enter on lines 103, Section J and 502, Section K)			5,289.45	7,245.00

Redeman offered $115,000, with earnest money/down payment of $23,000 and the remaining $92,000 of the purchase price to be obtained through a new conventional loan. No private mortgage insurance will be necessary because the loan-to-value ratio will not exceed 80 percent. The Iuros signed the contract on April 29. Closing was set for June 15 at the office of the Open Door Real Estate Company, 720 Main Street, Riverdale.

The unpaid balance of the Iuros' mortgage as of June 1 will be $78,200. Debt service payments are $540 per month with interest at 6 percent per annum on the unpaid balance.

The title insurance policy paid for by the buyer at the time of closing cost $290, including $210 for lender's coverage and $80 for homeowner's coverage. Recording charges of $20 were paid for the recording of two instruments to clear defects in the sellers' title. State excise tax in the amount of $230 ($1 per $500 of sales price or fraction thereof) was paid by the sellers. In addition, the sellers must pay an attorney's fee of $75 for preparation of the deed. This amount will be paid from the closing proceeds.

The buyer must pay an attorney's fee of $350 for examination of the title evidence and legal representation. There is also a $20 fee to record the deed. These amounts also will be paid from the closing proceeds.

Real estate taxes in Riverdale are paid in arrears. Taxes for this year, estimated at last year's figure of $1,518, have not been paid. According to the contract, prorations are to be made on the basis of the 360-day year/30-day month method.

Computing the Prorations and Charges

The following list illustrates the various steps in computing the prorations and other amounts to be included in the settlement to this point.

1. *Closing date:* June 15
2. *Commission:* 6% × $115,000 (sales price) = $6,900
3. *Sellers' mortgage interest:*
   6% × $78,200 (principal after June 1 payment) = $4,692 interest per year
   $4,692 ÷ 360 days = $13.033 interest per day
   15 days of accrued interest to be paid by the sellers
   15 × $13.033 = $195.495, or $195.50 interest owed by the sellers
   $78,200 + $195.50 = $78,395.50 payoff of sellers' mortgage
4. *Real estate taxes* (estimated at $1,518):
   $1,518 ÷ 360 days = $4.217 per day
   January 1 through June 15 equals 165 days
   165 days × $4.217 = $695.81 debit seller/credit buyer
5. *Excise tax* ($1 per $500 of consideration or fraction thereof):
   $115,000 ÷ $500 = $230
   $230 × $1 = $230 excise tax, debit seller

The sellers must pay an additional $20 to record the mortgage release. The buyer's new loan is from Thrift Federal Savings, 1100 Fountain Plaza, Riverdale, in the amount of $92,000 at 7¼ percent interest. In connection with this loan, Redeman will be charged $300 to have the property appraised by Swift Appraisal. The Acme Credit Bureau will charge $60 for a credit report. (Because appraisal and credit reports are performed prior to loan approval, they are paid at the time of loan application, whether or not the transaction eventually closes. These items will be noted as *POC* on the settlement statement.) In addition, Redeman will pay for interim interest on his loan for the remainder of the month of closing: 16 days at $18.528 per day, or $296.45. His first full payment (including July's interest) will be due August 1. He must deposit $885.50 into a tax escrow account with the lender. That is seven-twelfths of the anticipated county real estate tax of $1,518. A one-year hazard insurance premium at $3 per $1,000 of appraised value ($115,000 ÷ $1,000 × 3 = $345) paid at closing to Hite Insurance Company. An insurance reserve to cover the premium for two months is also deposited in an escrow account with the lender. Redeman will have to pay an additional $25 to record the deed of trust and $175 for a survey. He will also pay a loan origination fee of $920 and two discount points, plus $85 for a pest inspection.

The Uniform Settlement Statement

The Uniform Settlement Statement is divided into 12 sections. Sections J, K, and L contain particularly important information. The borrower's and seller's summaries (J and K) are very similar. In Section J, the buyer/borrower's debits are listed in lines 100 through 112. They are totaled on line 120 (Gross Amount Due From Borrower). The total of the settlement costs itemized in Section L on line 1400 of the statement is entered on line 103 as one of the buyer's charges. The buyer's credits are listed on lines 201 through 219 and totaled on line 220 (Total Paid By/For Borrower). The buyer's credits then are subtracted from the charges to arrive at the cash due from the borrower to close (line 303).

In Section K, the seller's credits are entered on lines 400 through 412 and totaled on line 420 (Gross Amount Due To Seller). The seller's debits are entered on lines 501 through 519 and totaled on line 520 (Total Reduction Amount Due Seller). The total of the seller's settlement charges from line 1400 is on line 502. The debits then are subtracted from the credits to arrive at the cash due the seller to close (line 603).

Section L is a summary of all the settlement charges for the transaction; the buyer's expenses are listed in one column and the seller's expenses in the other. If an attorney's fee is listed as a lump sum in line 1107, the settlement should list by line number the services that were included in that total fee. Copies of the Uniform Settlement Statement (HUD-1) are available in PDF format online in HUD's forms library.

■ RELATED WEB SITES

HUD site for forms: *www.hud.gov/hudclips*
Dept. of Housing and Urban Development: RESPA:
   www.hud.gov/offices/hsg/sfh/res/respa_hm.cfm

■ SUMMARY

Closing a real estate sale involves both title procedures and financial matters. Although North Carolina has relaxed its requirement that all closings be overseen by attorneys, an attorney still generally acts as the closing agent at the closing meeting. Due to the fiduciary duties that an agent owes their client, the North Carolina Real Estate Commission maintains that the real estate broker should be present at the closing to oversee the transfer of title and the accounting of all monies in the transaction. North Carolina licensing law holds the broker responsible for the accuracy and delivery of the HUD-1 settlement statement regardless of who prepared it.

The closing agent has the primary responsibility for reporting the seller's closing proceeds to the IRS on Form 1099-S.

The federal Real Estate Settlement Procedures Act (RESPA) requires disclosure of all settlement costs when a residential real estate purchase is financed by a federally related mortgage loan. RESPA requires that lenders (1) provide an informational booklet to the consumer within three days of loan application, (2) provide a good-faith estimate of closing costs, and (3) use a Uniform Settlement Statement (HUD-1) to detail the financial particulars of a transaction. RESPA also prohibits kickbacks or referral fees from settlement service providers.

The closing statement is a detailed report of all monies in a real estate transaction. It lists the sales price, expenses, credits, and prorations between buyer and seller. The purpose of this statement is to determine the net amount due the seller at closing and the amount of certified funds the buyer must bring to the closing meeting. In the proration of prepaid items, the seller is reimbursed by the buyer for the buyer's portion of the paid bill. In the proration of accrued items, the buyer is paid in advance for the seller's portion of a bill that will be due and payable at a future date. In all prorated items, the seller is responsible for the day of closing. Misrepresentation or omission of monies on the HUD-1 would be a violation of licensing law for a real estate licensee and could represent loan fraud with major state and federal penalties including jail time.

QUESTIONS

1. Which of the following statements is *TRUE* of real estate closings in North Carolina?
   a. Closings are usually conducted by real estate brokers.
   b. The seller usually pays the expenses for the day of closing.
   c. The buyer usually reimburses the seller for accrued but unpaid expenses.
   d. The seller usually pays the attorney for the preparation of the deed of trust.

2. Which of the following does *NOT* normally occur at closing?
   a. Seller transfers ownership to the buyer via general warranty deed.
   b. Buyer delivers certified funds for the purchase of the property.
   c. Closing agent assures that all paperwork required by the lender have been properly signed and dated.
   d. Buyer pays for the appraisal and the credit report required by the lender.

3. The RESPA Uniform Settlement Statement must be used to illustrate all settlement charges for
   a. every real estate sales transaction.
   b. only real estate transactions financed by VA and FHA loans.
   c. all residential real estate transactions financed by federally related mortgage loans.
   d. all commercial real estate transactions.

4. If annual real estate taxes of $1,800 have been paid in advance of closing, what would the HUD-1 entry for the current taxes be if closing is set for September 15?
   a. Credit seller $525; debit buyer $1,275
   b. Credit seller $1,275; debit buyer $525
   c. Credit buyer $1,275; debit seller $1,275
   d. Credit seller $525; debit buyer $525

5. A seller collected rent of $450 on June 1, payable in advance, from the tenant of the property being sold. How will the rent appear on the HUD-1 if closing is scheduled for June 23?
   a. Credit seller $345; debit buyer $105
   b. Credit buyer $105; debit seller $105
   c. Credit seller $345; debit buyer $345
   d. Rent will not appear on the HUD-1 in this situation.

6. A building was purchased for $150,000, with 10 percent down and a loan for the balance. If the lender charged the buyer two discount points and a 1 percent loan origination fee, how much cash did the buyer need to pay the down payment and loan fees?
   a. $15,450
   b. $16,620
   c. $19,050
   d. $19,500

7. At a closing, the closing attorney debited the seller and credited the buyer for certain accrued items. These included bills relating to the property that were
   I. already paid by the seller.
   II. yet to be paid by the buyer.
      a. I only
      b. II only
      c. Both I and II
      d. Neither I nor II

Questions 8 through 12 should be answered as to how certain items would normally appear on a closing statement if the standard NCAR/NCBA Offer to Purchase and Contract is used.

8. The sales price of the property is a
   a. credit to the buyer.
   b. debit to the seller.
   c. credit to the buyer; debit to the seller.
   d. credit to the seller; debit to the buyer.

9. The earnest money held in escrow by the listing broker is a
   a. credit to the buyer.
   b. debit to the seller.
   c. credit to the buyer; debit to the seller.
   d. credit to the seller; debit to the buyer.

10. The cost of the fuel oil left in a holding tank on the property is a
    a. credit to the buyer.
    b. debit to the seller.
    c. credit to the buyer; debit to the seller.
    d. credit to the seller; debit to the buyer.

11. The principal amount of the purchaser's new mortgage loan is a
    a. debit to the buyer.
    b. credit to the buyer.
    c. credit to the buyer; debit to the seller.
    d. credit to the seller; debit to the buyer.

12. Unpaid homeowners' association fees, water service charges, and waste disposal service fees are
    a. credits to the buyer.
    b. debits to the seller.
    c. credits to the buyer; debits to the seller.
    d. credits to the seller; debits to the buyer.

13. The Real Estate Settlement Procedures Act applies to the activities of
    a. brokers selling commercial and office buildings.
    b. security salespeople selling limited partnerships.
    c. Ginnie Mae or Fannie Mae when purchasing mortgages.
    d. lenders financing the purchase of a borrower's residence.

14. RESPA requires that
    I. a good faith estimate of closing costs be given to the borrower within 7 business days of loan application.
    II. a standardized settlement statement be used to reflect all charges in connection with the transaction.
       a. I only
       b. II only
       c. Both I and II
       d. Neither I nor II

15. A survey of property is usually paid for by
    a. the seller.
    b. the buyer.
    c. splitting the bill equally between the buyer and the seller.
    d. the closing attorney out of their fee.

16. Which of the following closing expenses is NOT typically paid by the seller?
    a. Excise tax
    b. Attorney's fee
    c. Deed preparation fee
    d. Brokers' commission

17. Which of the following closing expenses is NOT generally prorated between the buyer and the seller at closing?
    a. Current ad valorem real estate taxes
    b. Homeowner association dues
    c. Rent
    d. Interim interest on new loan

18. Under RESPA, the settlement agent must
    I. allow the borrower to examine the closing statement one business day before closing.
    II. keep the settlement statement for two years after closing.
       a. I only
       b. II only
       c. Both I and II
       d. Neither I nor II

19. On the HUD-1, the prorations for unpaid real estate taxes at a March 24th closing would be shown as a
    a. credit to the seller; debit to the buyer.
    b. debit to the seller; credit to the buyer.
    c. credit to both the seller and the buyer.
    d. debit to both the seller and the buyer.

20. On the HUD-1, the option fee in Alternative 2 in the NCAR/NCBA Standard Offer to Purchase and contract will always be a
    I. credit to the buyer.
    II. debit to the seller.
       a. I only
       b. II only
       c. Both I and II
       d. Neither I nor II

■ CLOSING STATEMENT PROBLEM

Answer Questions 21–24 using the following information.

Julie and Vern Marenatha are selling their home to Martha and Joe White for $110,000. The Whites made a $5,000 earnest money deposit, which is being held by the Marenathas' real estate broker in escrow until closing. The Whites are to obtain an 80 percent conventional loan at 10 percent interest and make a 20 percent down payment. The closing date is October 15. The Marenathas agreed to pay their broker a 6 percent commission.

The Marenathas' existing mortgage loan (at 10 percent interest) will have a balance of $82,750 after their October 1 payment. The sellers must also pay accrued interest on their loan payoff at closing. The loan must be paid off at closing. The property taxes for the current year are $1,100 and are unpaid; parties agreed to the double-debit method of proration.

The Whites will pay their mortgage company a $50 credit report fee and a $150 appraisal report fee at closing. The mortgage company is charging a 1 percent loan origination fee and a 1.5 percent loan discount fee. Interim interest on the new loan is to be paid by the Whites at closing. The first loan payment will be due on December 1. The Whites must pay a $345 homeowner's insurance premium, and must deposit an additional $500 into escrow at the closing for property taxes and homeowner's insurance premiums.

Other closing expenses (listed here) will be paid in accordance with custom.

> Property survey: $200
> Pest inspection report: $75
> Title insurance premium: $250
> Excise tax at the current rate
> Fee to prepare deed: $50
> Fee to record deed: $7
> Fee to record sellers' satisfaction of mortgage: $7
> Fee to record buyers' deed of trust: $7
> Buyers' lawyer's fee: $500

Use a 360-day year and 30-day month to calculate prorations. As to prorations between the buyers and sellers, the seller is responsible for the day of closing. Perform proration calculations without rounding. Final entries on the HUD-1 for the buyers and sellers should be rounded to the nearest penny.

21. What are the Line 1400 total settlement charges to the buyers?
   a. $4,675.10
   b. $4,904.14
   c. $5,546.06
   d. $7,747.96

22. What are the Line 1400 total settlement charges to the sellers?
   a. $6,876.04
   b. $7,527.04
   c. $7,747.96
   d. $7,977.00

23. How much cash will come from the buyers?
   a. $19,157.25
   b. $21,675.10
   c. $21,904.14
   d. $22,775.10

24. How much cash will go to the sellers?
   a. $19,157.25
   b. $19,386.29
   c. $21,675.10
   d. $21,904.14

CHAPTER 16

Basic Residential Construction

■ **LEARNING OBJECTIVES** *When you have finished reading this chapter, you should be able to*

- ■ **describe** basic architectural types and styles of residential construction.

- ■ **identify** the components of a house foundation and the house framing.

- ■ **describe** all components of residential construction.

- ■ **explain** provisions of North Carolina Building Codes, HUD minimum standards, and contractor licensing.

- ■ **define** these *key terms:*

baseboards	frame	sheathing
basement	frieze board	shingles
BTU	girder	siding
building code	header	sill
ceiling joists	HVAC	slab
certificate of occupancy	insulation	soffit
crawl space	pier	sole plate
eave	pitch	stud
fascia board	rafter	subfloor
floor joists	ridge board	top plate
footings	roofing felt	
foundation wall	R-value	

It is important for real estate agents to have a basic knowledge of residential construction. As agents show homes to prospective buyers, they need to be able to point out basic features and answer basic construction questions. This chapter offers a rudimentary introduction to wood-frame residential construction. Wood-frame construction is most popular because it (1) has flexibility of design, (2) costs less, (3) is easy to insulate, and (4) takes less time to build.

■ ARCHITECTURAL TYPES AND STYLES

A few basic architectural styles maintain high levels of popularity, including the one-story, or ranch-style, home; the split-level home; and several types of two-story homes, such as the Cape Cod, colonial, and French provincial.

Ranch-style homes offer easy accessibility and maintenance because everything is on one floor. Owners have no need to make frequent trips upstairs or to use high ladders to paint second-story exterior surfaces. Although ranch houses are usually moderate-sized and affordable, they are the most expensive to build per square foot because the two most expensive elements of a house, the roof and the foundation, must cover the same amount of space as the living area of the house.

The split-level home, sometimes called a tri-level, takes advantage of uneven terrain with a minimum of grading to prepare the lot. Two-story homes are the most economical to build on a cost per square foot basis because they offer twice the living area for the cost of only one foundation and roof. A story and a half (1½ story) house functions much like a two-story residence except that the upper level's ceiling is the underside of the roofline and there is no attic space above that living area. Just due to height of the construction alone, maintenance and access of multilevel homes is more difficult than a single-story home. Contemporary designs usually combine elements of one-story, two-story, or split-level homes with a lot of open space, multilevel rooflines, and skylights or windows. Contemporary designs are particularly popular in scenic areas due to the generous use of large windows.

No one design is inherently superior to another. Whether a buyer prefers a contemporary ranch-style to a colonial two-story is simply a matter of individual taste and style and how the architectural style fits in with the topography of the property. Refer to Figure 16.1 for examples of various architectural styles.

■ FOUNDATIONS

The foundation of a home must be built on firm soil with materials that are capable of supporting the weight of the house and resisting damage caused by wood-eating pests.

Basic Components

The basic components of a foundation include the following:

■ *Footings.* The foundation rests on **footings,** which are usually made of concrete that is poured into trenches or forms that have been dug or placed beneath the soil line. Footings must be wider than the structure being

FIGURE   16.1   Architectural Styles

Split Level

MULTILEVEL

GARAGE UNDER SECOND STORY

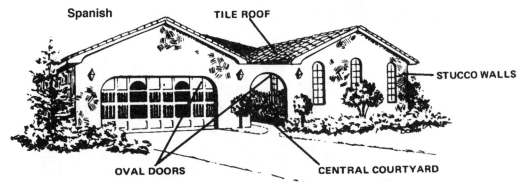

Spanish

TILE ROOF

STUCCO WALLS

OVAL DOORS

CENTRAL COURTYARD

Ranch

1 STORY - LOW TO THE GROUND

PICTURE WINDOW

Cape Cod

1½ STORIES

SHINGLES

CENTRAL ENTRANCE

FIGURE   16.1   Architectural Styles (continued)

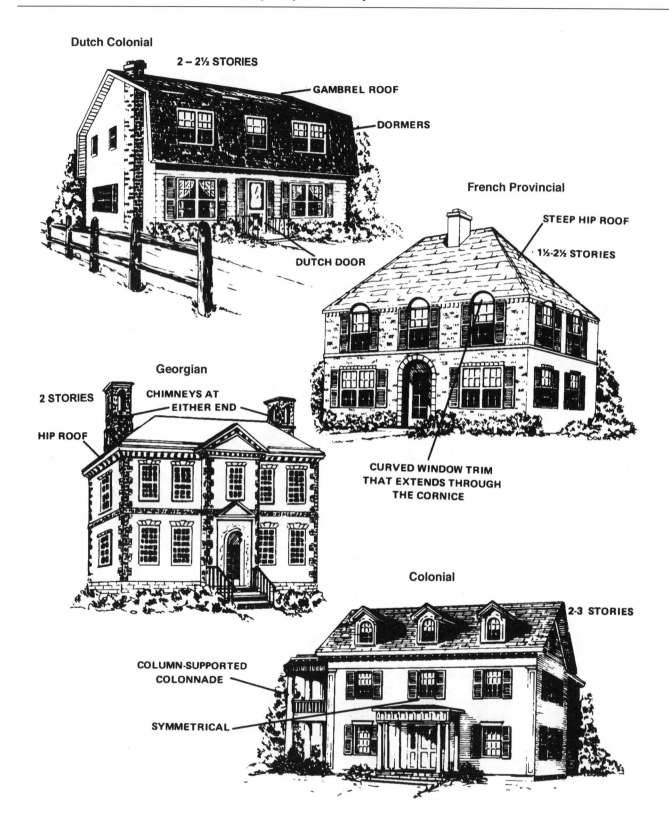

supported and are typically 16 inches wide and 6 inches to 8 inches deep. The bottom of each footing must be located below the frost line to avoid the shifting that can be caused when the ground freezes. Footings are the lowest part of construction and serve to spread the weight of the structure over the ground.

- *Foundation walls*. **Foundation walls** rest on top of the footings and provide a surface upon which the flooring is built. Foundation walls are usually made out of poured concrete, masonry block, or brick and are typically 8 inches to 12 inches thick.
- *Piers*. **Piers** (columns), usually made of masonry block, may be required to support the flooring between the foundation walls when a crawlspace or basement construction is used.

These basic components of a foundation, as well as other house components, are illustrated in Figure 16.4.

Major Types

The three major types of foundations found in North Carolina include the following:

- *Crawl space.* Foundation walls with a crawl space are very popular in North Carolina residential construction. Lifting the living space above the ground aids with ventilation, moisture control, and prevention of pest infestation. Proper ventilation of the crawl space through the adequate use of *foundation vents* works in conjunction with proper grading of the soil to drain moisture away from under the building. Additional moisture control may be accomplished by waterproofing the foundation walls and/or installing a *vapor barrier* in the crawl space.
- *Basement.* Basements are basically story-high crawl spaces that may be used for storage or living space, depending on the quality of finish used. While basement space is popular, it is also expensive to construct, especially in the central and eastern parts of North Carolina due to the high water table and the additional excavation below the frost line.
- *Concrete slab.* A flat, horizontal, reinforced with steel bars, concrete slab poured directly on the level ground to create the foundation without use of a crawlspace or basement. The two types of slab foundations are: (1) a *monolithic slab* that is poured in one large section with the thicker edges serving as the footings for the building, and (2) *a floating slab* that poured inside the outline of the footings and foundation walls.

Termite Protection

Because North Carolina is home to many wood-destroying insects, builders must be very careful to protect structures from damage from such pests. All firewood or wood materials must be removed from around the foundation construction site and the decking of the residence to discourage termites and other wood-destroying insects.

In new construction, the soil near the foundation walls and piers must be chemically treated. Any lumber used in the construction that comes in contact with the ground must be pressure-treated. Frequently, the company that treats the soil will offer a termite bond that is renewable and transferable to provide infestation protection warranty.

◼ FRAMING

Various dimensions of lumber are used to build the **frame** of a house, which is similar to the skeleton of a body. The elements of the framing consist of the floors, the walls, the ceiling, and the roof. See Figure 16.2 and Figure 16.3 for examples of various framing cross-sections.

- ◼ *Floor framing.* The floor framing consists of the **sill** (the lowest horizontal wooden part of framing), pieces of treated lumber that are placed on top of the foundation walls. **Floor joists** are then attached to the sills at 16-inch or 24-inch intervals. Because the floor joists must support the entire weight of the floor, they typically cannot span the entire width of the structure. Instead, **girders,** which rest on top of piers, are used to support the joists between sills. The **subfloor** is then attached to this system of joists and girders. The subfloor is usually made of sheets of plywood or pressboard, which are laid on top of the joists and girders. Finally, the subfloor is covered with the floor covering, such as vinyl, carpeting, tile, or hardwood strips.

- ◼ *Wall framing.* Wall framing consists of **studs,** vertical lumber spaced about 16 inches apart. The **sole plate** connects the studs to the flooring; the **top plate** connects the studs to the ceiling framing. **Headers,** two pieces of lumber joined together to form a beam, are used to give extra support to wall framing where a window or door will be positioned. This type of framing is called *platform* framing.

  Two other less typical types of framing include *balloon* framing and *post and beam* framing. With balloon framing, a single system of lengthy wall studs is used. The studs run from the foundation up to the ceiling (through both the first and second stories). With post and beam framing, extra-large framing members are used—either 4 x 4 inch or 6 x 6 inch. These large posts can be placed farther apart than the traditional 16-inch distance between wall studs.

- ◼ *Roof framing.* **Ceiling joists** are attached to the top plate of the wall and carry the weight of the roof. **Rafters,** the sloping members of the roof frame, connect the ceiling joists and the **ridge boards** (the highest part of the construction). The rafters support the decking or other roofing materials. An alternative method to using ceiling joists, rafters, and ridge boards is *truss framing.* The roof truss is a prefabricated triangular structure that serves the same functions as the ceiling joists, rafters, and ridge boards but is easier and quicker to install. The overhang of the roof is called the **eave,** which is made up of the **fascia board**, the **soffit**, and the **frieze board**. Gutters are usually attached to the fascia board. Ventilation for the attic is usually located in the soffit of the eaves. The frieze board is a sometimes decorative board at the top of the exterior wall directly under the soffit that prevents penetration of the elements through the joint between the exterior wall and roof.

FIGURE   16.2   Roof Framing Systems

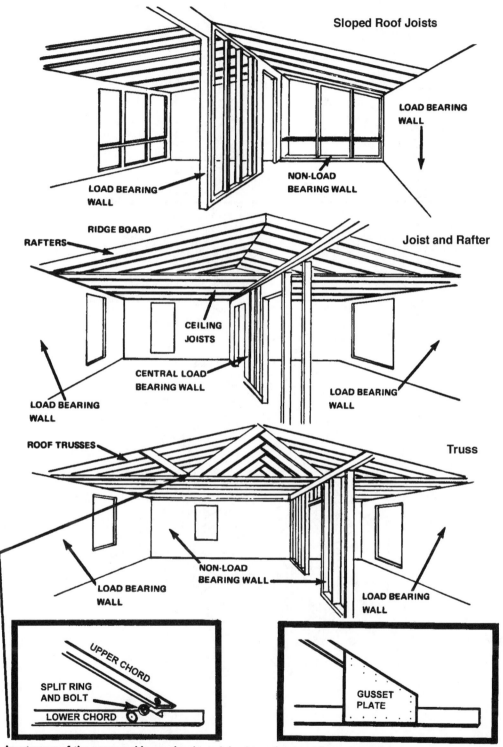

In a truss roof the upper and lower chords are joined together by either a gusset plate or a split ring and bolt.

FIGURE 16.3 **Exterior Structure Walls and Framing**

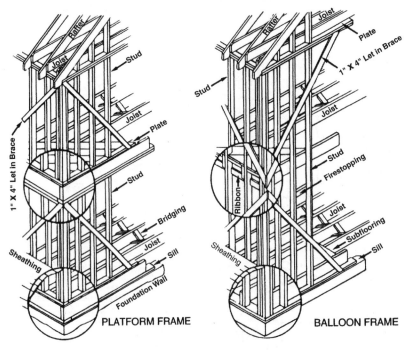

PLATFORM FRAME

BALLOON FRAME

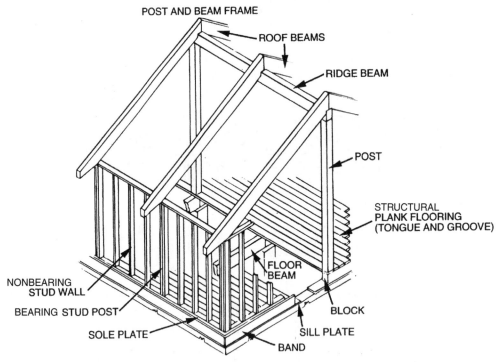

POST AND BEAM FRAME

■ ELEMENTS OF CONSTRUCTION

Refer to Figure 16.4 for a complete illustration of home construction.

Exterior Walls

To build the exterior walls, **sheathing** is added to the wall framing to insulate the house from the elements. Several types of materials are used for sheathing, including particleboard, foam sheathing, and plywood. Exterior siding is then added to the sheathing. Exterior siding may be wood-manufactured hardboard (e.g., Masonite®), brick veneer, fiber cement board, vinyl, aluminum, stucco, or synthetic stucco (e.g., EIFS). In older existing homes, wood is the most common siding material; however, in recent years most homes built in North Carolina use one of the other types of siding. **Siding** protects the home from the elements and provides a pleasing look.

Windows and Exterior Doors

Windows allow for ventilation, light, a view, and style. Today, windows are made of wood, aluminum, and some composite materials, plus they normally use multi-pane insulated glass for energy efficiency. There are three basic types of window: (1) the sliding windows that have sash units that slide either vertically (sometimes called double-hung) or horizontally past each other to open or close the window opening; (2) the swinging windows that include the casement (a sash unit is hinged on one side to fully swing outward), jalousie (glass louvers), hopper (hinged on the bottom), and awning (hinged on the top) styles; and (3) the fixed windows that do not open include bay, bow, picture, and Palladian styles.

In addition to providing access, exterior doors add to the style of a home. Exterior doors are usually made of wood, steel, or a combination of wood and glass (such as French doors) with a solid core for maximum insulation value. The major types of exterior doors include: (1) the *flush door* that is of smooth finish construction and appearance; (2) the *panel door* that has multiple raised or indented panels; (3) the *sliding glass door* that is frequently used as access to patios or decks; and (4) the *French door* that provides a more upscale decorative door with glass panels.

The major components of window and door framework are the same: the *sill* is the bottom, the *jamb* is the side, and the *header* is the top of the framing. In a window, the glass panel that moves is the *sash*. The sash used to be composed of several small rectangular windowpanes that were joined together by pieces of wood. The cross hatch of dividing wood is comprised of the *muntins* (horizontal pieces) and the *mullions* (vertical pieces).

Roofing

Roofing materials must be able to withstand the elements and provide water protection to the structure. Of course, roofing materials also add to the home's style and character. The most common types of roofing materials are composition **shingles** (made of asphalt and fiberglass), wood shingles or shakes, and layers of **roofing felt** interspersed with tar or asphalt (called a *built-up roof*). Sometimes, the same sheathing that is attached to the exterior walls for insulation purposes also is attached to the rafters and is called decking.

The gable roof is the most common roof design. Refer to Figure 16.5 for examples of popular roof designs. The slope of the roof is measured by the **pitch**, which is

F I G U R E 16.4   **Home Construction**

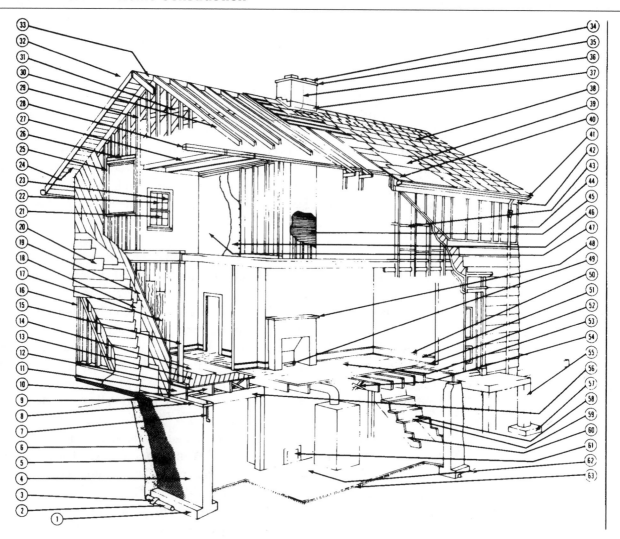

1. FOOTING	22. MUNTIN	43. FIRESTOP
2. FOUNDATION DRAIN TILE	23. WINDOW SASH	44. DOWNSPOUT
3. CRUSHED/WASHED STONE	24. EAVE (ROOF PROJECTION)	45. LATHS
4. FOUNDATION WALL	25. WINDOW JAMB TRIM	46. PLASTER BOARD
5. DAMPPROOFING OR	26. WINDOW HEADER	47. PLASTER FINISH
WEATHERPROOFING	27. CEILING JOIST	48. MANTEL
6. BACKFILL	28. TOP AND TIE PLATES	49. ASH DUMP
7. ANCHOR BOLT	29. GABLE STUD	50. BASE TOP MOLDING
8. SILL PLATE	30. RAFTERS	51. BASEBOARD
9. TERMITE SHIELD	31. COLLAR TIES	52. SHOE MOLDING
10. FLOOR JOIST	82. GABLE END OF ROOF	53. FINISH MOLDING
11. BAND OR BOX BEAM	33. RIDGE BEAM	54. CROSS BRIDGING
12. SOLE PLATE	34. CHIMNEY FLUES	55. PIER
13. SUBFLOORING	35. CHIMNEY CAP	56. GIRDER
14. BUILDING PAPER	36. CHIMNEY	57. FOOTING
15. WALL STUD	37. CHIMNEY FLASHING	58. RISER
16. CORNER STUDS	38. ROOFING SHINGLES	59. TREAD
17. INSULATION	39. ROOFING FELT/ICE AND WATER	60. STRINGER
18. HOUSE WRAP	MEMBRANE	61. CLEANOUT DOOR
19. WALL SHEATHING	40. ROOF SHEATHING	62. CONCRETE BASEMENT FLOOR
20. SIDING	41. EVE TROUGH OR GUTTER	63. CRUSHED/WASHED STONE
21. MULLION	42. FRIEZE BOARD	

FIGURE 16.5

Roof Designs

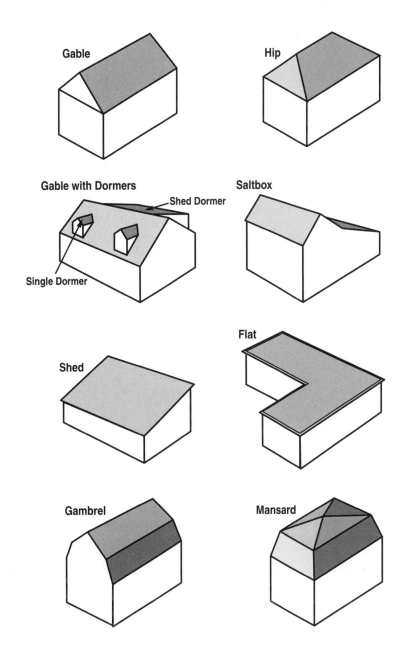

the number of inches of rise per foot of horizontal distance. The larger the rise per foot, the steeper the slope will be.

Insulation

Insulation is an important factor in any building. Today's energy-conscious consumers are anxious to buy homes that take little energy to heat and cool. Materials used to insulate homes include batts or blankets of insulating materials (which come in rolls) or loose fill insulation (which is blown into open spaces). In addition to this interior insulation, the sheathing or house wrapping materials used under the exterior covering of the building would add extra insulating value. Of course, any materials containing asbestos are prohibited.

The insulation value of materials is expressed as an **R-value.** The higher the R-value, the more resistant the material is to the transfer of heat. Building codes require different elements of each home to have different minimum R-values. For example, North Carolina building codes require R-19 insulation in floors, R-13 in walls, and R-30 in ceilings. Higher R-values are required in the colder, mountainous sections of the state.

In addition to installing the appropriate insulation throughout the building, property owners are wise to weatherstrip around exterior doors and windows. *Weatherstrips* of felt, metal, or other substance are used to block drafts between the door or window sash and the casing. *Caulking* around openings can also reduce energy loss.

Interior Finishes

Interior finishes are mostly a matter of cost and taste. There is a wide variety of interior finishes—one suited for every budget.

Drywall or gypsum board that has been textured and painted is a typical finish for interior walls, as is wood paneling. Ceilings may be finished with Sheetrock™, acoustical tiles, or tongue-and-groove boards. Floors are usually finished with hardwood strips, ceramic tiles, carpeting, or vinyl. Moldings, such as **baseboards** and casings, are used to finish the seams between the walls and the floors and the areas around doors and windows. Crown molding is used to cover the joint between the walls and the ceiling and can be quite elaborate.

■ HVAC

Several types of heating, ventilation, and air-conditioning, or **HVAC,** systems exist. The most common forms include central heating units fueled by gas, oil, or electricity; heat pumps; and forced warm air systems (which use a central blower). Some less common power sources are coal, wood, steam, and electric wire. The most efficient type of heating system is warm forced air, even though other systems can still be found, especially in older homes. Electric baseboard heating system, wood stoves, electric heaters, and kerosene heaters have all had periods of popularity that have waned. Fireplaces, while aesthetically appealing, can be a drain on the pocketbook since they usually act as an exhaust vent for the home's air. Modern air conditioning systems, much like the heating systems, are generally forced air systems powered by electricity, gas or oil. Occasionally, room-sized heating and air units are installed for small areas that may be separated from the rest of the living area, such as an office over the garage.

Solar panels, which provide energy on a year-round basis, have gained in popularity over the last few years but are still not as common as gas, oil, or electric heating systems. Solar heating systems can be either passive or active. Passive solar systems utilize the natural heating power of direct sunlight captured through the use of southern exposure windows and brick interior walls that radiate heat back into the room at night. Active systems require a system of collection, storage, and distribution throughout the house. Generally, a solar heating system will require an auxiliary system to supplement the solar power.

A very popular HVAC system in most of North Carolina, the heat pump provides a combination of heating and air conditioning. The heat pump "pulls" heat from the outside winter air and pumps it into the house and then reverses the process to remove heat from the residence during the summer months. This system functions best in temperate climates and usually has an auxiliary system to supplement when nature is too hot or too cold for efficiency.

The **BTU,** or British Thermal Unit, is a measure of heat and is used in rating the capacity of air-conditioning and heating equipment. While R-values are stated as smaller numbers, BTU numbers are in the thousands. A 4,000 BTU furnace might be called a *two-ton* unit. Many larger homes utilize a dual system (one system for the first floor and a second system for the upper floor) while some incorporate zoned heating for different "zones" of the residence.

■ GOVERNMENT REGULATION

North Carolina Uniform Building Code

North Carolina has adopted a statewide uniform **building code** that sets minimum construction standards for public safety. The state building code is under the supervision of the North Carolina Department of Insurance.

The code consists of hundreds of pages of requirements on the structure of buildings and their electrical and plumbing systems. Local municipalities may adopt more stringent building codes to raise the quality of construction in their jurisdiction. Each municipality has a building department that issues building permits and enforces the building code by inspecting buildings during construction. Before a structure can be occupied, the building department must issue a **certificate of occupancy**, which means that the construction has been completed in a safe, satisfactory manner. There appears to be a significant misunderstanding in the general population about the need for building permits. Even though a property owner does not need a general contractor's license to build or renovate their personal property, they will usually need to apply for the appropriate building permits. Although there is significant variance about what activities require a permit among county and city inspectors, there appears to be a fairly consistent agreement about three types of work that prompt the need for a permit: any electrical, plumbing, or structural work. The definition of structural work seems to be the type of work that is the most subject to interpretation. A licensee listing a property that has had additions or major improvements should verify that the work was permitted. Unapproved space is a material fact since unpermitted space may have to be taken down or pass inspection retroactively, and may not be insurable.

HUD Minimum Standards

Homes that are financed with government-backed loans (such as FHA or VA loans) must meet minimum construction standards set by HUD. Some of these standards may be stricter than the state building codes.

IN PRACTICE

North Carolina uniform building codes are subject to change periodically as are HUD minimum standards. An agent working with a buyer who wants to obtain FHA and/or VA financing should always check to ensure that the property meets both standards before an offer to purchase containing provisions for FHA or VA financing is presented to a seller.

Contractor Licensing

In North Carolina, anyone who contracts to construct a building for others that costs more than $30,000 must obtain a general contractor's license from the state. Different classifications of licenses exist for different types of construction. For example, single-family home construction requires a residential building classification.

■ RELATED WEB SITE

North Carolina Department of Insurance: *www.ncdoi.com*

■ SUMMARY

Many different architectural types and styles of homes are built in North Carolina. The most economical residence to build is the two-story because the two most expensive parts of the residence to construct—the foundation and the roof—are being utilized for twice the living space square footage on the same lot size as a ranch-style home.

The lowest member of construction is the footing, which represents the footprint of the structure. The foundation wall rests on top of the footing and provides a level surface for the flooring system.

The frame of the house forms the skeleton of the building with the basic parts comprising the floors, the walls, the ceilings, and the roof. The sill is the lowest horizontal wooden member of the house, and the ridge board is the highest piece of construction. The floor and ceiling joists are the horizontal elements that support the flooring and the roof. The wall studs are attached to the floor and ceiling by sole plates and top plates, respectively. The rafters or trusses give shape to the roof and the eaves are where they overhang the exterior wall.

State and local building codes set the minimum building standards for various types of construction. If FHA or VA financing will be used, federal HUD building codes must be observed. When there are multiple sets of codes, the stricter standards will prevail. Anyone that contracts for more than $30,000 to build or renovate a building for others in North Carolina must have a general contractor's license. Even a property owner that can improve or build their own residence without a contractor's license will need to apply for the appropriate building permits.

QUESTIONS

1. R-value refers to
   a. resistance to the transfer of heat.
   b. resistance to termite infestation.
   c. reduction in construction costs.
   d. high-end residential zoning.

2. Pressure-treated lumber is used
   a. to improve the appearance of a home.
   b. to help prevent termite infestation.
   c. to increase the R-value.
   d. for moisture resistance in bathrooms.

3. The vertical framing member of a wall is a
   a. sole plate.
   b. girder.
   c. joist.
   d. stud.

4. Based on the cost per square foot of living space, which of the following is the most economical house design?
   a. Split-level
   b. One-story
   c. Two-story
   d. Tri-level

5. The most common roof style in North Carolina is
   a. hip.
   b. gambrel.
   c. gable.
   d. mansard.

6. The foundation wall rests on top of the
   a. footing.
   b. sill.
   c. girder.
   d. floor joist.

7. A certificate of occupancy is required
   I. from the local building department.
   II. before anyone can move into a home.
      a. I only
      b. II only
      c. Both I and II
      d. Neither I nor II

8. The lowest wooden part of residential construction is the
   a. sill.
   b. foundation wall.
   c. footing.
   d. ridge board.

9. The highest part of the frame construction is the
   a. soffit.
   b. rafter.
   c. ridge board.
   d. ceiling joist.

10. The following are components of an eave *EXCEPT* the
   a. soffit.
   b. fascia board.
   c. header.
   d. frieze board.

CHAPTER

17

Real Property Valuation

■ **LEARNING OBJECTIVES** *When you have finished reading this chapter, you should be able to*

■ **explain** the concepts and types of value, how value may be used, value-in-exchange and value-in-use.

■ **give** examples of the basic economic principles of value.

■ **explain** the steps in the appraisal process and the three basic valuation approaches used by appraisers.

■ **describe** the three types of depreciation and the concepts of effective age and economic life.

■ **define** these *key terms*:

age-life method	functional obsolescence	reproduction cost
appraisal	gross rent multiplier (GRM)	sales comparison approach
arm's-length transaction		
capitalization rate	highest and best use	square-foot method
comparable (comp)	income capitalization approach	straight-line method
comparative market analysis	net operating income (NOI)	substitution
cost approach		unit-in-place method
depreciation	physical deterioration	value
economic life	quantity-survey method	
economic obsolescence	reconciliation	
effective age	replacement cost	

■ APPRAISING

An **appraisal** is an estimate or opinion of value of a specific property as of a specific date. Appraisal reports are relied on in important decisions made by mortgage lenders, investors, public utilities, government agencies, businesses, and individuals.

The highest level of appraisal activity is conducted by skilled professionals. However, everyone engaged in the real estate business, even those who are not experts in appraisal, must possess at least a fundamental knowledge of real estate valuation. In the appraisal of residential real estate, a person familiar with the market in a given neighborhood could try to make a quick judgment of market values, but this is not an appraisal and should not be considered particularly reliable and useful.

In North Carolina, to conduct a formal appraisal that can be used in federally related transactions, appraisers must be licensed by the state. *Certified residential appraisers* usually appraise residential properties; *certified general appraisers* typically appraise commercial properties. Note that appraisers are paid a fee, not a commission. The fee is based on the complexity of the appraisal and the length of time necessary to complete it. The fee never should be based on a percentage of the appraised value of the property.

The Financial Institutions Reform, Recovery and Enforcement Act of 1989 (FIRREA) was passed by Congress for the primary purpose of overhauling regulations of the thrift industry. However, a major portion of this Act was for the regulation of appraisers performing appraisals for federally related loan transactions. This Act established many federal agencies charged with the task of setting appraisal standards and minimum qualification requirements. The Appraisal Qualifications Board sets qualification standards and requirements for state-certified appraisers. The Appraisal Standards Board sets minimum standards of practice. In North Carolina, appraisers are licensed and certified through the North Carolina Appraisal Board after meeting minimum education and experience requirements and passing state examinations. The licensed appraiser need not have a real estate license to perform a real estate appraisal.

Informal estimate of value by real estate brokers.   As an exception to the North Carolina Appraisers Act, licensed real estate brokers are allowed to perform a comparative market analysis (which will be discussed later in this chapter) as long as they do not in any way represent themselves as a real estate appraiser. Brokers can be compensated only for completing a comparative market analysis (CMA) for prospective or current brokerage clients. The Act defines a CMA as "… the analysis of sales of similar recently sold properties in order to derive an indication of the probable sales price of a particular property by a licensed real estate broker." In the NC Real Estate Manual, licensees are cautioned to never refer to their estimate of value as an "appraisal" and to consider making some clarifying statement about it being an informal estimate of value and not to be confused with an appraisal.

■ VALUE

Value is an abstract word with many acceptable definitions. In a broad sense, **value** may be defined as the relationship between an object desired and a potential purchaser. It is the power of a good or service to command other goods or services in exchange. In terms of real estate appraisal, value may be described as *the present worth of future benefits arising from the ownership of real property.*

For a property to have value in the real estate market, it must have four characteristics, which can be remembered by the acronym DUST:

> The four characteristics of value may be remembered by the acronym *DUST:* Demand, Utility, Scarcity, and Transferability.

1. *Demand*—the need or desire for possession or ownership backed by the financial means to satisfy that need
2. *Utility*—the capacity to satisfy future owners' needs and desires; how future owners can make good use of the property
3. *Scarcity*—a finite supply
4. *Transferability*—the relative ease of transfer of ownership rights from one person to another; often relates to clear title and satisfactory physical condition

Market Value

Even though a given parcel of real estate may have many different kinds of value at the same time, such as insurance value, assessed value, and so on, generally the goal of an appraiser is to estimate *market value*. The market value of real estate is the most probable price that a property will bring in a competitive and open market, allowing a reasonable time to find a purchaser who buys the property with knowledge of all the uses to which it is adapted and for which it is capable of being used. Included in this definition are the following key points:

- Market value is the *most probable* price a property will bring.
- Payment must be made in *cash* or its equivalent.
- Buyer and seller must act without *undue pressure*.
- A *reasonable length of time* must be allowed for the property to be exposed in the open market.
- Both buyer and seller must be *well informed* of the property's use and potential, including its assets and defects.

> *Market value* is a reasonable opinion of a property's value; *market price* is the actual selling price of a property; *cost* may not equal either market value or market price.

Market value versus market price. Market value is an opinion of value based on an analysis of data that may include not only an analysis of comparable sales but also an analysis of potential income, expenses, and replacement costs (less depreciation). *Market price*, on the other hand, is what a property *actually* sells for—its sales price. Theoretically, the market price should be the same as the market value. Market price can be taken as accurate evidence of current market value, but only if the conditions essential to market value exist. However, the market price may not be indicative of market value. There are circumstances under which a property may be sold below market value, as when the seller is forced to sell quickly or when a sale is arranged between relatives.

Market value versus cost. An important distinction exists between market value and cost. Cost represents past expenditures on the property: what the owner has spent on the property. One of the most common misconceptions about valuing property is that cost represents market value. Cost and market value may be equal and often are when the improvements on a property are new. But more often, cost does not equal market value.

■ **FOR EXAMPLE** Two homes are identical in every respect, except that one is located on a street with heavy traffic and the other is on a quiet residential street. The value of the former may be less than that of the latter, although the cost of each may be exactly the same. Another example is a homeowner who installs a swimming pool at a cost of $15,000; however, the cost of the improvement may not add $15,000 to the value of the property.

Forces and Factors Influencing Property Value

Four forces affect property values:

1. *Social forces*. Social forces that affect property values include trends in marriage and divorce rates, family size and longevity, and desirability of social activities.
2. *Economic forces*. Economic forces include income and employment levels, the rate of property taxation, current interest rates, and general economic growth.
3. *Political forces*. Political forces include government activities such as zoning and building codes, growth management, environmental legislation, and tax structures.
4. *Physical forces*. Physical forces that affect property values include topography, location, climate, size, shape, proximity to major arterials, jobs, and public transportation.

Basic Economic Principles of Value

A number of economic principles affect the value of real estate. The most important of these principles are defined in the following paragraphs.

Highest and best use.   The most profitable single use to which a property is adapted and for which it is needed, or the use that is likely to be in demand in the reasonably near future, is its **highest and best use**. Highest and best use is noted in every appraisal but also may be the object of a more extensive analysis. For example, a highest-and-best-use study may show that a parking lot in a busy downtown area or a farm surrounded by urbanized land is not the highest and best use of the property. Note that there can be only one highest and best use at any given time. Highest and best use is subject to change—the highest and best use of a property today may not be the highest and best use of the same property five years from now.

Substitution.   The principle of **substitution** states when several items with essentially the same amenities and utilities are available, the item with the lowest price will attract the most demand. In other words, a consumer will purchase what is perceived to be the best buy for the money. This principle is the cornerstone of the sales comparison approach to value (discussed in detail later). For example, if house A and house B are equally desirable properties with similar assets and house A is selling for $160,000 and house B is selling for $170,000, virtually every buyer will choose house A.

Supply and demand.   This principle states that the value of a property will change if the supply decreases and the demand either increases or remains constant—and vice versa. For example, the last lot to be sold in a residential area where the demand for homes is high would probably be worth more than the first lot sold in that area, assuming normal economic conditions exist. Supply and demand in real estate is sometimes referenced as being in a *buyer's market* or a *seller's market*.

Conformity. *Conformity* means that maximum value is realized if the use of land conforms to existing neighborhood standards. In residential areas of single-family houses, for example, buildings should be similar in design, construction, size, and age. Subdivision protective covenants rely on the principle of conformity to ensure maximum future value. Building a home that is significantly bigger than surrounding houses violates the principle of conformity. This mistake is commonly referred to as *overbuilding the neighborhood*.

Anticipation. This principle holds that value can increase or decrease *in anticipation* of some future benefit or detriment affecting the property. For example, the value of a house could be affected by rumors that an adjacent parcel may be converted to some different use in the near future. In other words, current value is being affected by future possibilities whether based on fact or rumor.

Contribution. This principle affirms that the value of any component of a property is defined by what its addition *contributes* to the value of the whole or what its absence detracts from that value. For example, the cost of installing an air-conditioning system and remodeling an older office building may be greater than is justified by the increase in market value (a function of expected net increases) that may result from the improvement to the property. In residential properties an owner sometimes will make a super-improvement such as installing solid mahogany kitchen cabinets. While these cabinets may be quite attractive, the average buyer will not pay for the added cost of this *overimprovement*.

Competition. This principle states that profits tend to attract competition. For example, the success of a retail store may motivate investors to open similar stores in the area. This tends to mean less profit for all stores concerned unless the purchasing power in the area increases substantially. Note that excess profit tends to attract ruinous competition.

Change. No physical or economic condition remains constant. Real estate is subject to natural phenomena, such as tornadoes, fires, and routine wear and tear of the elements. The real estate business also is subject to the changing demands of its market, as is any business. It is an appraiser's job to study the past to be better able to predict the effects of natural phenomena and the behavior of the marketplace in the future. Appraisers must also be sensitive to the stage of progression within the *neighborhood life cycle*. Most residential neighborhoods go through four phases of the cycle of change: growth, stability, decline, and renewal. The area's position within the *life cycle* will affect value.

■ THE APPRAISAL PROCESS

The key to an accurate appraisal lies in the methodical collection of data. The appraisal process is an orderly set of procedures used to collect and analyze data to arrive at an ultimate value conclusion. The data are divided into two basic classes:

1. *Specific data*, covering details of the subject property (the property that is being appraised) and including comparative data relating to costs, sales, and income and expenses of properties similar to and competitive with the subject property.
2. *General data*, covering the nation, region, city, and neighborhood. Of particular importance is the neighborhood, where an appraiser finds the physical, economic, social, and political influences that directly affect the value and potential of the subject property.

The steps an appraiser takes in carrying out an appraisal assignment are as follows:

1. *State the problem.* The kind of value to be estimated must be specified, and the valuation approach(es) most valid and reliable for the kind of property under appraisal must be selected.
2. *List the data needed and the sources.* Based on the approach(es) the appraiser will be using, the types of data needed, and the sources to be consulted are listed.
3. *Gather, record, and verify the necessary data.* Specific data about the subject site and improvements must be collected and verified. Depending on the appraisal approach(es) used, comparative information relating to sales, income, expenses, and construction costs of comparable properties must be collected.
4. *Determine the highest and best use.* The appraiser analyzes market forces such as competition and current versus potential uses to determine the reasonableness of the property's present use in terms of its profitability.
5. *Estimate the land value.* The features and sales prices of comparable sites are compared with the subject property to determine the value of the land alone. Neither the cost nor the income approach can be used to estimate land value.
6. *Estimate the value by each of the three approaches.* The sales comparison, cost, and income capitalization approaches are used to estimate the value of the subject property.
7. *Reconcile the estimated values for the final value estimate.* The appraiser makes a definite statement of conclusions reached, usually in the form of a value estimate of the property. Note that the three approaches are never simply averaged.
8. *Report the final value estimate.* After the three approaches have been reconciled and an opinion of value has been reached, the appraiser prepares a formal written report for the client. All information used to estimate the value of a property should be included in this report. A complete appraisal report should

   - identify the real estate and real property interest being appraised;
   - state the purpose and intended use of the appraisal;
   - define the value to be estimated;
   - state the effective date of the value and the date of the report;
   - describe the process of collecting, confirming, and reporting the data;

■ list all assumptions and limiting conditions that affect the analysis, opinion, and conclusions of value;

■ describe the information considered, the appraisal procedures followed, and the reasoning that supports the report's conclusions (if an approach was excluded, the report should explain why);

■ describe (if necessary or appropriate) the appraiser's opinion of the highest and best use of the real estate;

■ describe any additional information that may be appropriate in order to show compliance with specific guidelines established in the Uniform Standards of Professional Appraisal Practice (USPAP) or to clearly identify and explain any departures from these guidelines; and

■ include a signed certification, as required by the Uniform Standards.

IN PRACTICE   The role of the appraiser is not to determine value. Rather, an appraiser develops a supportable and objective report about the value of the subject property. The appraiser relies on experience and expertise in valuation theories to evaluate market data. The appraiser does not establish the property's worth but instead verifies what the market indicates. This is important to remember, particularly when dealing with a property owner who may lack objectivity about the realistic value of the property. The lack of objectivity also can complicate a broker's ability to list the property within the most probable range of market value. Agents are cautioned against listing property at a price that is so unreasonably high that it is unlikely the property will be shown or sold.

Many lenders and federal agencies have their own form reports. One of the most frequently used is the Fannie Mae Form 1004, Uniform Residential Appraisal Report; only the first three pages are shown in Figure 17.1, since the rest of the form is just instructions for the form's use. This form is required by many government agencies. The major sections of this form are as follows:

■ *Subject:* identification of the property being appraised
■ *Neighborhood:* information showing boundaries, characteristics, and market conditions
■ *Site:* information on lot dimensions, utilities, topography, off-site improvements, easements, flood conditions, etc.
■ *Description of improvements:* general descriptions, exterior, interior, foundation, effective age, etc.
■ *Comments:* additional features, condition of improvements, and adverse environmental conditions
■ *Cost approach:* showing applicable estimates derived from the cost approach
■ *Sales comparison analysis:* showing three comparables and adjustments and estimated value derived from the sales comparison approach
■ *Indicated value by the income approach*
■ *Reconciliation:* showing the final estimate of value, the date of the estimate, signatures, and license numbers of the appraisers

■ APPROACHES TO VALUE (APPRAISAL METHODS)

To arrive at an accurate estimate of value, three basic approaches, or techniques, are traditionally used by appraisers:

1. The sales comparison approach
2. The cost approach
3. The income capitalization approach

Each method, when completed independently, serves as a check against the others and narrows the range within which the final estimate of value will fall. Generally, each method is considered most reliable for specific types of property.

The Sales Comparison Approach

In the **sales comparison approach,** also known as the *market data approach,* an estimate of value is obtained by comparing the subject property (the property under appraisal) with recently sold comparable properties (properties similar to the subject). This approach is most often used in valuing single-family homes and land. Because no two parcels of real estate are exactly alike, each comparable property must be compared with the subject property, and the sales prices of the comparables must be adjusted for any dissimilar features. The principal factors for which adjustments must be made fall into four basic categories:

> **The Sales Comparison Approach**
>
> 1. Date of sale
> 2. Location
> 3. Physical features
> 4. Terms and conditions of sale

1. *Date of sale.* An adjustment must be made if economic changes occur between the date of sale of a comparable property and the date of the appraisal.
2. *Location.* An adjustment may be necessary to compensate for location differences. For example, similar properties might differ in price from neighborhood to neighborhood or even within the same neighborhood.
3. *Physical features.* Physical features that may require adjustment include age of building, size of lot, landscaping, construction, number of rooms, square feet of living space, interior and exterior condition, presence or absence of a garage, a fireplace or an air conditioner, and so forth.
4. *Terms and conditions of sale.* This consideration becomes important if a sale is not financed with a standard mortgage. Be sure that the sale was an **arm's-length transaction,** which means that the property did not sell for an unusually high or low price because of a special relationship between the buyer and seller. An example would be a low-price sale between a parent and child.

Selecting Comparables

First and foremost, the **comparables,** sometimes called *comps,* selected should be as similar to the subject property as possible, and should have been recently sold (preferably within the past year) in an open and competitive market, under typical market conditions, when the seller and buyer are well informed and are not acting under undue pressure. Please note that the acceptable age of comps is greatly dependent upon the degree of change in the market condition within a particular local area. For example, in markets where prices have been very stable for a long period of time, a comparable that has closed within 12–15 months may be acceptable. However, in markets where there have been drastic increases or decreases in market conditions, a more recent comp may be more appropriate. Nontypical conditions may involve seller financing; an estate sale; a foreclosure sale; a buyer under pressure to buy quickly because of school, business, or family pressure; and

FIGURE 17.1 Uniform Residential Appraisal Report

Uniform Residential Appraisal Report

File #

The purpose of this summary appraisal report is to provide the lender/client with an accurate, and adequately supported, opinion of the market value of the subject property.

SUBJECT

Property Address 4807 Catalpa Road City Woodview State IL Zip Code 60000
Borrower Owner of Public Record County Dakota
Legal Description attached to this report
Assessor's Parcel # Tax Year R.E. Taxes $ 2,278
Neighborhood Name Map Reference Census Tract
Occupant ☒ Owner ☐ Tenant ☐ Vacant Special Assessments $ ☐ PUD HOA $ ☐ per year ☐ per month
Property Rights Appraised ☒ Fee Simple ☐ Leasehold ☐ Other (describe)
Assignment Type ☐ Purchase Transaction ☐ Refinance Transaction ☐ Other (describe)
Lender/Client Address
Is the subject property currently offered for sale or has it been offered for sale in the twelve months prior to the effective date of this appraisal? ☒ Yes ☐ No
Report data source(s) used, offering price(s), and date(s).

CONTRACT

I ☐ did ☐ did not analyze the contract for sale for the subject purchase transaction. Explain the results of the analysis of the contract for sale or why the analysis was not performed.

Contract Price $ Date of Contract Is the property seller the owner of public record? ☐ Yes ☐ No Data Source(s)
Is there any financial assistance (loan charges, sale concessions, gift or downpayment assistance, etc.) to be paid by any party on behalf of the borrower? ☐ Yes ☐ No
If Yes, report the total dollar amount and describe the items to be paid.

NEIGHBORHOOD

Note: Race and the racial composition of the neighborhood are not appraisal factors.

Neighborhood Characteristics	One-Unit Housing Trends	One-Unit Housing	Present Land Use %
Location ☐ Urban ☒ Suburban ☐ Rural	Property Values ☒ Increasing ☐ Stable ☐ Declining	PRICE $ (000) / AGE (yrs)	One-Unit 100 %
Built-Up ☒ Over 75% ☐ 25–75% ☐ Under 25%	Demand/Supply ☐ Shortage ☒ In Balance ☐ Over Supply	Low	2-4 Unit %
Growth ☐ Rapid ☒ Stable ☐ Slow	Marketing Time ☒ Under 3 mths ☐ 3–6 mths ☐ Over 6 mths	High	Multi-Family %
Neighborhood Boundaries Boundaries are shown on attached map		Pred.	Commercial %
			Other %

Neighborhood Description Subject property is located in a desirable subdivision in the Central Eastern section of the Village of Woodview. Schools, shopping, and other necessary facilities and services are within a reasonable distance.

Market Conditions (including support for the above conclusions) Steady demand for housing with a gradual uptrend in values reflects a relatively healthy local economy. Conventional financing readily available with interest rates at 6% to 8%. The desirability of this neighborhood is reflected by the fact that most homes are sold within 2 months of being put on the market.

SITE

Dimensions 65' × 130' Area 8,450 squre feet Shape rectangular View tree-lined st/typical
Specific Zoning Classification R-2 Zoning Description Single-family residence
Zoning Compliance ☒ Legal ☐ Legal Nonconforming (Grandfathered Use) ☐ No Zoning ☐ Illegal (describe)
Is the highest and best use of the subject property as improved (or as proposed per plans and specifications) the present use? ☒ Yes ☐ No If No, describe

Utilities	Public	Other (describe)		Public	Other (describe)	Off-site Improvements—Type	Public	Private
Electricity	☒	☐	Water	☒	☐	Street	☒	☐
Gas	☒	☐	Sanitary Sewer	☒	☐	Alley	☐	☐

FEMA Special Flood Hazard Area ☐ Yes ☒ No FEMA Flood Zone FEMA Map # FEMA Map Date
Are the utilities and off-site improvements typical for the market area? ☒ Yes ☐ No If No, describe
Are there any adverse site conditions or external factors (easements, encroachments, environmental conditions, land uses, etc.)? ☐ Yes ☒ No If Yes, describe
Underground electric and telephone lines; no easements or encroachments

IMPROVEMENTS

General Description	Foundation	Exterior Description materials/condition	Interior materials/condition
Units ☒ One ☐ One with Accessory Unit	☐ Concrete Slab ☒ Crawl Space	Foundation Walls Concrete/gd	Floors Vinyl/cpt/oak/gd
# of Stories 1	☐ Full Basement ☐ Partial Basement	Exterior Walls Brick veneer/gd	Walls Drywall/paint/gd
Type ☒ Det. ☐ Att. ☐ S-Det./End Unit	Basement Area sq. ft.	Roof Surface Asphlt.shingle/gd	Trim/Finish Wood/Avg
☒ Existing ☐ Proposed ☐ Under Const.	Basement Finish %	Gutters & Downspouts Galv./paint/gd	Bath Floor Ceram/gd
Design (Style) Ranch	☐ Outside Entry/Exit ☐ Sump Pump	Window Type Wood double-hung/gd	Bath Wainscot Ceram/gd
Year Built 25 years ago	Evidence of ☐ Infestation	Storm Sash/Insulated Comb.alum/gd	Car Storage ☐ None
Effective Age (Yrs) 15	☐ Dampness ☐ Settlement	Screens Comb.alum/gd	☒ Driveway # of Cars 2
Attic ☐ None	Heating ☒ FWA ☐ HWBB ☐ Radiant	Amenities ☐ Woodstove(s) #	Driveway Surface Asphalt
☒ Drop Stair ☐ Stairs	☐ Other Fuel	☐ Fireplace(s) # ☐ Fence	☒ Garage # of Cars
☐ Floor ☐ Scuttle	Cooling ☒ Central Air Conditioning	☐ Patio/Deck ☐ Porch	☐ Carport # of Cars
☐ Finished ☐ Heated	☐ Individual ☐ Other	☐ Pool ☐ Other	☐ Att. ☒ Det. ☐ Built-in

Appliances ☒ Refrigerator ☒ Range/Oven ☒ Dishwasher ☒ Disposal ☐ Microwave ☐ Washer/Dryer ☒ Other (describe) Oven fan/hood
Finished area **above** grade contains: 7 Rooms 3 Bedrooms 2.00 Bath(s) 1,950 Square Feet of Gross Living Area Above Grade
Additional features (special energy efficient items, etc.) 6" insulation above ceiling and behind drywall; 6' redwood fence around rear yard.

Describe the condition of the property (including needed repairs, deterioration, renovations, remodeling, etc.). Overall, house and garage are in good shape with normal wear and tear indicating 25% depreciation. There is no evidence of functional or external obsolescence.

Are there any physical deficiencies or adverse conditions that affect the livability, soundness, or structural integrity of the property? ☐ Yes ☒ No If Yes, describe
No detrimental influences.

Does the property generally conform to the neighborhood (functional utility, style, condition, use, construction, etc.)? ☒ Yes ☐ No If No, describe

Freddie Mac Form 70 March 2005 Page 1 of 6 Fannie Mae Form 1004 March 2005

FIGURE 17.1   **Uniform Residential Appraisal Report (continued)**

Uniform Residential Appraisal Report   File

| There are | 2 | comparable properties currently offered for sale in the subject neighborhood ranging in price from $ 178,90.00 | | to $ 184,500.00 | | . |
| There are | 5 | comparable sales in the subject neighborhood within the past twelve months ranging in sale price from $ 152,000.00 | | to $ 186,240.00 | | . |

FEATURE	SUBJECT	COMPARABLE SALE # 1		COMPARABLE SALE # 2		COMPARABLE SALE # 3	
Address	4807 Catalpa Road	4310 W. Gladys		3840 W. Monroe		316 Iowa	
Proximity to Subject							
Sale Price	$	$	177,750	$	180,000	$	186,240
Sale Price/Gross Liv. Area	$ sq. ft.	$ 90.00 sq. ft.		$ 92.31 sq. ft.		$ 96.00 sq. ft.	
Data Source(s)							
Verification Source(s)							
VALUE ADJUSTMENTS	DESCRIPTION	DESCRIPTION	+(-) $ Adjustment	DESCRIPTION	+(-) $ Adjustment	DESCRIPTION	+(-) $ Adjustment
Sale or Financing Concessions		conventional		conventional		conventional	
Date of Sale/Time		6 wks. ago		3 wks. ago		6 wks. ago	
Location	Suburban	quiet res.		quiet res.		quiet res.	
Leasehold/Fee Simple	fee simple	fee simple		fee simple		fee simple	
Site	8,450 sq. ft.	65' × 130'		65' × 130'		65' × 130'	
View	good/street	good/street		good/street		good/street	
Design (Style)	ranch	ranch		ranch		ranch	
Quality of Construction	good	good		good		good	
Actual Age	25 yrs.	25 yrs.		25 yrs.		25 yrs.	
Condition	good	good		good		good	
Above Grade	Total Bdrms. Baths	Total Bdrms. Baths		Total Bdrms. Baths		Total Bdrms. Baths	
Room Count	7 3 2	7 3 2		7 3 2		7 3 2	
Gross Living Area	1,950 sq. ft.	1,975 sq. ft.		1,950 sq. ft.		1,940 sq. ft.	
Basement & Finished Rooms Below Grade	crawlspace	crawlspace		crawlspace		finished basement	−10,000
Functional Utility	adequate	adequate		adequate		adequate	
Heating/Cooling	central h/a	central h/a		central h/a		central h/a	
Energy Efficient Items	extra insulation	equal		equal		equal	
Garage/Carport	2-car detached	2-car detached		2-car detached		2-car detached	
Porch/Patio/Deck							
Fireplace	masonry	none	+5,000	masonry		masonry	
Fence	fence	fence		fence		fence	
Net Adjustment (Total)		☒ + ☐ -	$ 5,000	☐ + ☐ -	$	☐ + ☒ -	$ −10,000
Adjusted Sale Price of Comparables		Net Adj. 2.80 % Gross Adj.2.80 %	$ 182,750	Net Adj. % Gross Adj. %	$ 180,000	Net Adj. −5.40 % Gross Adj. 5.40 %	$ 176,240

☒ did ☐ did not research the sale or transfer history of the subject property and comparable sales. If not, explain

My research ☐ did ☒ did not reveal any prior sales or transfers of the subject property for the three years prior to the effective date of this appraisal.

Data source(s)   County tax assessor

My research ☐ did ☒ did not reveal any prior sales or transfers of the comparable sales for the year prior to the date of sale of the comparable sale.

Data source(s)   County tax assessor

Report the results of the research and analysis of the prior sale or transfer history of the subject property and comparable sales (report additional prior sales on page 3).

ITEM	SUBJECT	COMPARABLE SALE # 1	COMPARABLE SALE # 2	COMPARABLE SALE # 3
Date of Prior Sale/Transfer				
Price of Prior Sale/Transfer				
Data Source(s)				
Effective Date of Data Source(s)				

Analysis of prior sale or transfer history of the subject property and comparable sales

Summary of Sales Comparison Approach

Indicated Value by Sales Comparison Approach $ 180,000

Indicated Value by: Sales Comparison Approach $ 180,000   Cost Approach (if developed) $ Income Approach (if developed) $ 169,000

This appraisal is made ☒ "as is", ☐ subject to completion per plans and specifications on the basis of a hypothetical condition that the improvements have been completed, ☐ subject to the following repairs or alterations on the basis of a hypothetical condition that the repairs or alterations have been completed, or ☐ subject to the following required inspection based on the extraordinary assumption that the condition or deficiency does not require alteration or repair:

Based on a complete visual inspection of the interior and exterior areas of the subject property, defined scope of work, statement of assumptions and limiting conditions, and appraiser's certification, my (our) opinion of the market value, as defined, of the real property that is the subject of this report is
$, as of   , which is the date of inspection and the effective date of this appraisal.

FIGURE 17.1 Uniform Residential Appraisal Report (continued)

Uniform Residential Appraisal Report

File #

ADDITIONAL COMMENTS

COST APPROACH TO VALUE (not required by Fannie Mae)

Provide adequate information for the lender/client to replicate the below cost figures and calculations.

Support for the opinion of site value (summary of comparable land sales or other methods for estimating site value)

ESTIMATED ☒ REPRODUCTION OR ☐ REPLACEMENT COST NEW	OPINION OF SITE VALUE = $	45,000
Source of cost data	Dwelling 1,950 Sq. Ft. @ $ 90 = $	175,500
Quality rating from cost service Effective date of cost data	Sq. Ft. @ $ = $	
Comments on Cost Approach (gross living area calculations, depreciation, etc.)	Extra insulation	1,200
Depreciation based on normal wear and tear for well-maintained	Garage/Carport 500 Sq. Ft. @ $ 30 = $	15,000
property with effective age of 15 years.	Total Estimate of Cost-New = $	191,700
	Less Physical Functional External	
	Depreciation 47,925 = $(	47,925)
	Depreciated Cost of Improvements = $	143,775
	"As-is" Value of Site Improvements = $	8,400
Estimated Remaining Economic Life (HUD and VA only) Years	Indicated Value By Cost Approach = $	197,175

INCOME APPROACH TO VALUE (not required by Fannie Mae)

Estimated Monthly Market Rent $ 1,300 X Gross Rent Multiplier 130 = $ 169,000 Indicated Value by Income Approach

Summary of Income Approach (including support for market rent and GRM) Comparable home sales prices/monthly rental income:

$160,000/$1,200; $166,500/$1,275; $173,500/$1,300.

PROJECT INFORMATION FOR PUDs (if applicable)

Is the developer/builder in control of the Homeowners' Association (HOA)? ☐ Yes ☐ No Unit type(s) ☐ Detached ☐ Attached

Provide the following information for PUDs ONLY if the developer/builder is in control of the HOA and the subject property is an attached dwelling unit.

Legal name of project

Total number of phases   Total number of units   Total number of units sold

Total number of units rented   Total number of units for sale   Data source(s)

Was the project created by the conversion of an existing building(s) into a PUD? ☐ Yes ☐ No If Yes, date of conversion

Does the project contain any multi-dwelling units? ☐ Yes ☐ No Data source(s)

Are the units, common elements, and recreation facilities complete? ☐ Yes ☐ No If No, describe the status of completion.

Are the common elements leased to or by the Homeowners' Association? ☐ Yes ☐ No If Yes, describe the rental terms and options.

Describe common elements and recreational facilities

Freddie Mac Form 70 March 2005   Page 3 of 6   Fannie Mae Form 1004 March 2005 so forth. An important point to remember is this: *the more similar the comparable is, the more recently sold, and the fewer adjustments that are required, the more reliable the estimate of value will be*. To have a reliable estimate of value, at least three similar comparable properties should be located.

After a careful analysis of the differences between comparable properties and the subject property, the appraiser assigns a dollar value to each of these differences. On the basis of the appraiser's knowledge and experience, the appraiser estimates dollar adjustments that reflect actual values assigned in the marketplace. The value of a feature present in the subject property but not in a comparable property is *added to the comparable property's total sales price*. This presumes that, all other features being equal, a property having a feature (such as a fireplace or wet bar) not present in a comparable property would tend to have a higher market value solely because of this feature. (The feature need not be a physical amenity; it may be locational or aesthetic.) Likewise, the value of a feature present in a comparable but not in the subject property *is subtracted from the comparable property's total sales price*. Remember, *all adjustments are made to the sales prices of the comparables, not to that of the subject property*. It must be stressed that a variable is adjusted by value in the marketplace and not by cost. For example, a fireplace may add less value to a dwelling than the actual cost of creating it. If the comparable property has a feature that is *inferior* to the subject, the appraiser will make a *positive* adjustment to the value of the comparable. Conversely, if the comparable property has a feature that is *superior* to the subject a *negative* adjustment will be made to the value of the comparable. Remember to *never* adjust the value of the subject.

The adjusted sales prices of the comparables represent the probable value range of the subject property. The appraiser then *correlates* the adjusted sales prices of the comparables to determine a single market value estimate for the subject property. The correlation is the result of a *weighted averaging process;* never use simple averaging of the adjusted sales prices. The comparable that is most similar to the subject property is given more weight than the other comparables when calculating the single estimate of value.

The sales comparison approach is essential in almost every appraisal of real estate. It is considered the most reliable of the three approaches in appraising residential property, where the amenities (intangible benefits) may be difficult to measure. The most difficult time to employ the sales comparison approach occurs when there are no comparable sales. Agents may want to use the services of a licensed appraiser for any property for which it is difficult to establish an asking price. An example of the sales comparison approach is shown in Table 17.1.

Comparative market analysis (CMA).   An informal version of the sales comparison approach is used by real estate brokers to help a seller set a realistic asking price for residential real estate or to help a buyer determine a reasonable purchase price in an active market. This informal version is called a **comparative market analysis**, or CMA. While the CMA is a form of appraisal, the licensed real estate agent need not hold an appraiser's license to perform this function while serving a client. However, the North Carolina Real Estate Commission (NCREC) will hold agents accountable for not performing a CMA in a competent manner, and it can take appropriate disciplinary action against the licensee. One major difference

TABLE 17.1 **Sales Comparison Approach to Value**

	Subject Property: 155 Potter Dr.	Comparables				
		A	B	C	D	E
Sales price		$118,000	$112,000	$121,000	$116,500	$110,000
Financing concessions	none	none	none	none	none	none
Date of sale		current	current	current	current	current
Location	good	same	poorer + 6,500	same	same	same
Age	6 years	same	same	same	same	same
Size of lot	60' × 135'	same	same	larger – 5,000	same	larger – 5,000
Landscaping	good	same	same		same	same
Construction	brick	same	same	same	same	same
Style	ranch	same	same	same	same	same
No. of rooms	6	same	same	same	same	same
No. of bedrooms	3	same	same	same	same	same
No. of baths	1½	same	same	same	same	same
Sq. ft. of living space	1,500	same	same	same	same	same
Other space (basement)	full basement	same	same	same	same	same
Condition—exterior	average	better – 1,500	poorer + 1,000	better – 1,500	same	poorer + 2,000
Condition—interior	good	same	same	better – 500	same	same
Garage	2-car attached	same	same	same	same	none + 5,000
Other improvements	none	none	none	none	none	none
Net Adjustments		– 1,500	+ 7,500	– 7,000	-0-	+ 2,000
Adjusted Value		$116,500	$119,500	$114,000	$116,500	$112,000

Note: The value of a feature that is present in the subject but not in the comparable property is added to the sales price of the comparable. Likewise, the value of a feature that is present in the comparable but not in the subject property is subtracted. The adjusted sales prices of the comparables represent the probable range of value of the subject property. From this range, a single market value estimate can be selected. Because the value range of the properties in the comparison chart (excluding comparables B and E) is close, and comparable D required no adjustment, an appraiser might conclude that the indicated market value of the subject is $116,500. However, appraisers use a complex process of evaluating adjustment percentages and may consider other objective factors or subjective judgments based on research.

between an appraisal and a CMA is that while an appraiser must declare a specific appraised value, a real estate licensee usually determines a range of value. It is common for agents preparing a CMA to reference listed properties and properties whose listings have expired as well as recently sold properties. Listed properties that have not sold generally represent the upper ceiling of value because sales prices tend to be lower than listing prices. Expired listings are useful in showing the seller how unreasonable prices affect sales (generally, listings that have expired were priced too high to sell within the listing period). Once you have listed a property, it is a good idea to update the CMA on at least a monthly basis. Make the sellers aware of the changes in listing and sales prices in their area. Have the CMA on hand when presenting an offer to purchase from any prospective buyer.

Information about these three types of properties (active listings, expired listings, and closed sales) is very helpful when putting together a CMA to help a seller set a listing price. However, bear in mind that an appraiser is allowed to use only actual closed sales when preparing a sales comparison appraisal. Do not count a listing that is under contract as a *sold* property because the contract sales price is subject to change until the transaction is closed.

The Cost Approach

The **cost approach** to value is also based on the principle of substitution, which states that the maximum value of a property tends to be set by the cost of acquiring an equally desirable and valuable substitute property. The cost approach consists of five steps:

1. Estimate the value of the land as if it were vacant and available to be put to its highest and best use, based on the sales comparison approach, because land cannot be depreciated.
2. Separate the land from the improvements, and estimate the current cost of constructing the building(s) and site improvements based, in general, on cost data and experience.
3. Estimate the amount of accrued depreciation of the improvements resulting from physical deterioration, functional obsolescence, or economic obsolescence.
4. Deduct the accrued depreciation from the estimated construction cost of the new building(s) and the contributory depreciated value of site improvements.
5. Add the estimated value of the land to the depreciated cost of the building(s) and site improvements to determine the total property value.

Land is always valued as if vacant, and land value is estimated by using the sales comparison approach (step 1); that is, the location and improvements of the subject site are compared with those of similar nearby vacant sites, and adjustments are made for significant differences in size, shape, topography, utilities available, assessments, and so on.

There are two ways to look at the construction cost of a building for appraisal purposes (step 2): reproduction cost versus replacement cost. **Reproduction cost** is the dollar amount required to construct an exact duplicate of the subject building at current prices. Reproduction cost is mainly used when appraising historical property. **Replacement cost** is the construction cost, at current prices and using modern materials and methodology, of a property that is not necessarily an exact duplicate but serves the same purpose or function as the original property. Replacement cost is most often used in appraising because it eliminates obsolete features and takes advantage of current construction materials and techniques.

An example of the cost approach to value is shown in Table 17.2.

Determining reproduction or replacement cost.   An appraiser using the cost approach computes the reproduction or replacement cost of a building using one of the following methods:

■ **Square-foot method.** The cost per square foot of a recently built comparable structure is multiplied by the number of square feet in the subject building. The **square-foot method** is the most common method of cost estimation. The example in Table 17.2 uses the square-foot method. For some property, the cost per cubic foot of a recently built comparable structure is multiplied by the number of cubic feet in the subject structure.
■ **Unit-in-place method.** The replacement cost of a structure is estimated based on the construction cost per unit of measure of individual building components, including material, labor, overhead, and builder's profit. In

TABLE 17.2			
Cost Approach to Value	**Subject Property**: 155 Potter Dr.		
	Land Valuation: Size 60' × 135' @ $450 per front foot =		$27,000
	Plus site improvements: driveway, walks, landscaping, etc. =		8,000
	Total		$35,000
	Building Valuation: Replacement Cost		
	1,500 sq. ft. @ $65 per sq. ft. =	$97,500	
	Less Depreciation:		
	Physical depreciation		
	Curable		
	(items of deferred maintenance)		
	exterior painting	$4,000	
	Incurable (structural deterioration)	9,750	
	Functional obsolescence	2,000	
	External depreciation	-0-	
	Total	−15,750	
	Depreciated Value of Building		$ 81,750
	Indicated Value by Cost Approach		$116,750

the **unit-in-place method,** most components are measured in square feet, although items like plumbing fixtures are estimated by unit cost.

- **Quantity-survey method.** An estimate is made of the quantities of raw materials needed to replace the subject structure (lumber, plaster, brick, and so on) as well as of the current price of such materials and their installation costs. These factors are added to indirect costs (building permit, survey, payroll taxes, builder's profit) to arrive at the total replacement cost of the structure. The **quantity-survey method** is similar to the approach a building contractor takes when preparing a bill for the construction of a building.

Depreciation. In a real estate appraisal, **depreciation** (a loss in value for any reason) refers to any condition that adversely affects the value of an *improvement* to real property. Land does not depreciate because it is here forever and can always be put to its highest and best use when economically and legally feasible to do so. For appraisal purposes (as opposed to depreciation for tax purposes, which will be discussed in Chapter 19), depreciation is divided into three classes according to its cause:

1. **Physical deterioration**—*curable*: Repairs that are physically possible and economically feasible and will result in an increase in appraised value equal to or exceeding their cost fall into this category. Routine maintenance, such as painting and roof replacement, is an example of curable **physical deterioration.**

   1a. **Physical deterioration**—*incurable*: Repairs to major structural components of a building, which deteriorate at different rates, may not be economically feasible and therefore fall into this category. Examples are load-bearing walls and foundations.

2. **Functional obsolescence**—*curable*: Physical or design features that are no longer considered desirable by property buyers but can be replaced or redesigned at low cost constitute this class of depreciation. For example, outmoded fixtures, such as plumbing, are usually easily replaced. Room function

might be redefined at no cost if the basic room layout allows it. A bedroom adjacent to a kitchen, for instance, may be converted to a family room.

2a. **Functional obsolescence**—*incurable*: Currently undesirable physical or design features that cannot be remedied easily are considered functionally obsolete. Many older multistory industrial buildings are considered less suitable than one-story buildings, for example. An office building that cannot be air-conditioned because of the cost of duct installation also suffers from **functional obsolescence.** A residential example might be a home with five bedrooms but only one bath.

3. **Economic (environmental or external) obsolescence**—*incurable only*: Caused by factors outside the subject property, **economic (environmental or external) obsolescence** cannot be considered curable. For instance, proximity to a nuisance, such as a polluting factory, is an unchangeable factor that cannot be cured by the owner of the subject property. Economic obsolescence also may be referred to as *locational obsolescence*.

In determining a property's depreciation, most appraisers use the *breakdown method*, in which depreciation is broken down into the three classes, with separate estimates for curable and incurable factors in each class. Depreciation is difficult to measure, and the older the building, the more difficult it is to estimate. The easiest but least precise way to determine depreciation is the **age-life method**, which uses the effective age of a building and its economic (useful) life. When the cost of an asset is depreciated evenly over its useful life, this is called **straight-line method** of depreciation, as illustrated in the example below. Depreciation is assumed to occur at an even rate over a structure's **economic life**, the period during which it is expected to remain useful for its original intended purpose. (Compare this with a property's *actual life*, the period during which the improvements are expected to remain standing.) To derive the amount of annual depreciation, the property's cost is divided by the number of years of its expected economic life.

■ **FOR EXAMPLE** A $120,000 property may have a land value of $30,000 and an improvement value of $90,000. If the improvements are expected to last 60 years, the annual straight-line depreciation would be $1,500 ($90,000 ÷ 60 years). Such depreciation can be calculated as an annual dollar amount or as a percentage of the property's replacement cost.

Likewise, you can determine a building's **effective age** by multiplying its economic life by the amount of depreciation the building has already suffered.

■ **FOR EXAMPLE** If a building has suffered 25% depreciation and it has an economic life of 25 years, its effective age is 6.25 years (25 years × 0.25 = 6.25 years). Regardless of this building's actual age, its effective age would be considered to be about 6 years. Thus it could be considered to have a remaining economic life of 18.75 years.

Much functional obsolescence and all economic obsolescence, however, can be evaluated only by considering the actions of buyers in the marketplace.

Special-purpose properties.   The cost approach is most helpful in the appraisal of special-purpose buildings such as schools, churches, and public buildings. Such properties are difficult to appraise using other methods because there are seldom any local sales to use as comparables and these properties ordinarily do not generate income.

In the appraisal of special-purpose properties, an inexperienced appraiser may complete only a cost approach analysis and may estimate market value based on the results of that approach alone. But just because a structure was originally constructed for a certain purpose does not mean that it is necessarily the highest and best use for the property. This being the case, a market analysis of other properties having the same projected highest and best use is very important in this type of appraisal. Adjustments must be made for such variables as modification costs, location, time of sale, lot sizes, and the like, to make valid comparisons between the comparables and the subject property.

The Income Capitalization Approach

The **income capitalization approach** to value, also known as the *income approach*, is based on the present worth of the future rights to income. It assumes that the income derived from a property will control the value of that property. The income approach is used for valuation of income-producing properties—apartment buildings, office buildings, shopping centers, and the like. Many properties have potential for producing income but do not because they are owner-occupied. In such cases, the appraiser projects income and expenses based on market studies of similar income-producing properties. In using the income approach to estimate value, an appraiser must work through the following steps:

1. Estimate the annual potential *gross income* using rents from comparable properties, as well as income from other sources such as concessions, laundry facilities, and vending machines.
2. Based on market experience, deduct an appropriate allowance for vacancy and rent collection losses to arrive at the *effective gross income*.
3. Based on appropriate operating standards, deduct the annual *operating expenses* of the real estate from the effective gross income to arrive at the annual **net operating income (NOI)**. Operating expenses include taxes, insurance, maintenance, repairs, and reserves for replacement. Management costs are always included as operating expenses, even if the current owner manages the property and does not show a cost for this item. Mortgage payments of principal and interest, are debt service and are not considered operating expenses. For example, if a property owner spends $35,000 a year on operating expenses and $25,000 a year on mortgage payments, the $35,000 would be subtracted from effective gross income to determine the property's net income; the $25,000 of mortgage payments (debt service) would not.
4. Estimate the price a typical investor would pay for the income produced by this particular type and class of property. This is done by estimating the rate of return (or yield) that an investor will demand for the investment of capital in this type of building. This rate of return is called the **capitalization** (or *cap*) **rate** and is determined by comparing the relationship of NOI to the sales prices of similar properties that have sold in the current market. For example, a comparable property that produces an annual NOI of $15,000 is sold for $187,500. The capitalization rate is $15,000 ÷ $187,500, or 8 percent. If other comparable properties sell at prices that yield substantially

the same rate, it may be assumed that 8 percent is the rate that the appraiser should apply to the subject property. Note that the cap rate is inversely related to the market value of the property; as one goes up, the other goes down.

5. Finally, the capitalization rate is applied to the property's annual NOI, resulting in the appraiser's estimate of the property value.

With the appropriate capitalization rate and the projected annual net operating income, the appraiser can estimate value by the income approach in the following manner:

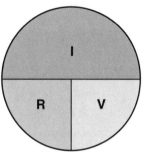

Net Operating Income ÷ Capitalization Rate = Value
Example: $18,000 NOI ÷ 9% cap rate = $200,000 value

This formula and its variations are important in estimating the value of income-producing property.

$$\frac{Income}{Rate} = Value \qquad \frac{Income}{Value} = Rate \qquad Value \times Rate = Income$$

TABLE 17.3		
Income Capitalization Approach to Value		

Potential Gross Annual Income Market rent (100% capacity)		$60,000
Income from other sources (vending machines and pay phones)		+ 600
		$60,600
Less vacancy and collection losses (estimated) @4%		– 2,424
Effective Gross Income		$58,176
Expenses:		
Real estate taxes	$9,000	
Insurance	1,000	
Heat	2,800	
Maintenance	6,400	
Utilities, electricity, water, gas	800	
Repairs	1,200	
Decorating	1,400	
Replacement of equipment	800	
Legal and accounting	600	
Advertising	300	
Management	3,000	
Total		$ – 27,300
Annual Net Operating Income		$ 30,876

Capitalization rate = 10% (overall rate)

Capitalization of annual net income: $\dfrac{\$30,876}{0.10}$

Indicated Value by Income Approach = $308,760

A very simplified version of the computations used in applying the income capitalization approach is illustrated in Table 17.3.

The most difficult step in the income approach to value is determining the appropriate capitalization rate for the property. This rate must be selected to recapture the original investment over the building's economic life, must give the owner an acceptable rate of return on investment, and must provide for the repayment of borrowed capital. An income property that carries with it a great deal of risk as an investment generally requires a higher rate of return than does a property considered a safe investment. Capitalization rates for similar properties may be different from block to block within a city owing to varying neighborhood influences.

Gross rent multipliers or gross income multipliers.   Certain properties, such as one-family or two-family homes, are not generally purchased as income properties. As a substitute for a more elaborate income analysis, the **gross rent multiplier (GRM)** method may be used in appraising such properties. The GRM relates the sales price of a property to its expected rental income. (Gross *monthly* income is used for residential property; gross *annual* income is used for commercial and industrial property.) The formula is as follows:

$$\frac{\text{Sales Price}}{\text{Rental Income}} = \text{Gross Rent Multiplier}$$

■   **FOR   EXAMPLE**   If a property recently sold for $82,000 and its monthly rental income was $650, the GRM for the property would be computed thus:

$$\frac{\$82,000}{\$650} = 126.2 \text{ GRM}$$

To establish an accurate GRM, an appraiser should have recent sales and rental data from at least three properties similar to the subject property. The most appropriate GRM can then be applied to the estimated fair market rental of the subject property to arrive at its market value. The formula would then be

$$\text{Rental Income} \times \text{GRM} = \text{Estimated Market Value}$$

Table 17.4 shows some examples of GRM comparisons.

If a property's income also comes from nonrental sources (such as sales concessions), a *gross income multiplier (GIM)* is used similarly.

Much skill is required to use multipliers accurately because no fixed multiplier exists for all areas or all types of properties. Therefore, many appraisers view the technique simply as a quick, informal way to check the validity of a property value obtained by one of the other appraisal methods. Because the gross multiplier methods are based on gross income rather than net income (they do not take into account operating expenses), the results may not be very accurate.

Reconciliation

If more than one of the three approaches to value are applied to the same property (and appraisers should apply all three methods whenever possible), they

	Comparable No.	Sales Price	Monthly Rent	GRM
TABLE 17.4	1	$93,600	$650	144
Gross Rent Multiplier	2	78,500	450	174
	3	95,500	675	141
	4	82,000	565	145
	Subject	?	625	?

Note: Based on an analysis of these comparisons, a GRM of 145 seems reasonable for homes in this area. In the opinion of an appraiser, then, the estimated value of the subject property would be $625 × 145, or $90,625.

will normally produce different indications of value. **Reconciliation** (sometimes called *final reconciliation*) is the art of analyzing and effectively weighing the findings from the different approaches used. To come up with a valid estimate, the appraiser must give more weight to the most appropriate appraisal method for that particular type of property.

Although each approach may serve as an independent guide to value, whenever possible all three approaches should be used as a check on the final estimate of value. The process of reconciliation is more complicated than simply taking the average of the derived value estimates. An average implies that the data and logic applied in each of the approaches are equally valid and reliable and should therefore be given equal weight. In fact, certain approaches are more valid and reliable with some kinds of properties than with others.

Simple averaging is considered an improper methodology. In fact, reconciliation never simply entails averaging the three value estimates. For example, in appraising a home, the income capitalization approach is rarely used, and the cost approach is of limited value unless the home is relatively new; therefore, the sales comparison approach is usually given greatest weight in valuing single-family residences. In the appraisal of income or investment property, the income capitalization approach is normally given the greatest weight. In the appraisal of churches, libraries, museums, schools, and other special-use properties that produce little or no income or sales revenue, the cost approach is usually assigned the greatest weight. From this analysis, or reconciliation, a single estimate of market value is produced.

■ THE PROFESSION OF APPRAISING

In 1932, the American Institute of Real Estate Appraisers was founded. A few years later, another organization, now known as the Society of Real Estate Appraisers, was formed. These two organizations have recently merged. Through the years, a number of other professional appraisal organizations have come into existence; they include the American Society of Appraisers, the National Association of Review Appraisers, the National Association of Independent Fee Appraisers, and the American Society of Farm Managers and Rural Appraisers. These organizations have professional designations and strict codes of ethics.

The Appraisal Institute offers two professional designations: RM (Residential Member) and MAI (Member of the Appraisal Institute). The National Association of Independent Fee Appraisers offers the designations IFA (member) and IFAS (senior member). The American Society of Appraisers designation is ASA (senior member).

Through these groups, courses have been established in universities and colleges, plus books, journals, and other publications devoted to various aspects of appraising have been published. Appraising has become the most specialized branch of real estate. Before awarding their designations, the major recognized appraisal associations require a four-year college degree or the equivalent, plus five years of full-time appraisal experience, in addition to passing an examination and writing acceptable appraisals.

Federally related appraisals must follow the guidelines stated in Uniform Standards of Professional Appraisal Practice (USPAP). To become state-licensed, appraisers must meet educational, experiential, and examination requirements. An application and information book on becoming an appraiser can be obtained by writing to the North Carolina Appraisal Board at PO Box 20500, Raleigh, NC 27619-0500 or by visiting their Web site.

■ RELATED WEB SITES

American Society of Appraisers: *www.appraisers.org*
American Society of Farm Managers and Rural Appraisers: *www.asfmra.org*
Appraisal Foundation: *www.appraisalfoundation.org*
Appraisal Institute: *www.appraisalinstitute.org*
National Association of Master Appraisers: *www.masterappraisers.org*
North Carolina Appraisal Board: *www.ncappraisalboard.org*

■ SUMMARY

To appraise real estate is to estimate its value as of a given date. Due to the possibility of change in the marketplace, an appraisal is generally considered to be *good* only for the day the appraisal is completed. If there are no significant changes in the marketplace, custom will honor an appraisal for up to 60 days to allow for closing time. Although many types of value exist, the most common objective of an appraisal is to estimate market value—the most probable sales price of a property. Basic to appraising are certain underlying economic principles, such as highest and best use, substitution, supply and demand, conformity, anticipation, contribution, competition, and change.

A professional appraiser analyzes a property through three approaches to value. In the sales comparison approach, the value of the subject property is compared with the values of at least three other closed comparable properties that have sold recently. Because no two properties are exactly alike, adjustments must be made to the comparables' sales prices to account for any differences between the comparables and the subject property. Adjustments are added to inferior comps and subtracted from superior comps; adjustments are *never* made to the subject property. Once the comps have been adjusted, the appraiser will assign weight to the comparables according to similarity to the subject property to arrive at an indication of value. Simple averaging should not be used.

Although only licensed appraisers can conduct appraisals, real estate licensees are constantly called upon by consumers to give an informal estimate of value called a competitive market analysis (CMA). Buyers and sellers generally use CMAs to guide them in determining the amounts of offering prices and listing prices. Licensees will usually utilize the economic concept of substitution to reach an indication of value in a process very similar to the sales comparison approach. Licensees should never call their estimate of value an "appraisal."

With the cost approach, an appraiser calculates the cost of building a similar structure on a similar site. The appraiser then subtracts depreciation (loss in value), which reflects the differences between new properties of this type and the present condition of the subject property. This depreciated value of the improvement is then added to value of the land that was determined by the sales comparison approach.

The income capitalization approach is an analysis based on the relationship between the rate of return that an investor requires and the net income that a property produces. The value estimate is determined by dividing the net operating income by the capitalization rate. A special, informal version of the income capitalization approach, the gross rent multiplier (GRM), is sometimes used to estimate the value of properties that are not rented but could be. The GRM is computed by dividing the sales price of a property by its gross monthly rent.

Normally, the application of the different approaches results in different estimates of value. In the process of reconciliation, the validity and reliability of each approach are weighed objectively to arrive at the single best and most supportable conclusion of value.

QUESTIONS

1. The amount of money a property commands in the marketplace is its
   I. assessed value.
   II. market value.
      a. I only
      b. II only
      c. Both I and II
      d. Neither I nor II

2. Reconciliation refers to
   a. averaging the results of the sales comparison approach.
   b. separating the value of land from the total value of property to compute depreciation.
   c. analyzing the results obtained by the three different approaches to value to determine a final estimate of value.
   d. the process by which an appraiser determines the highest and best use for a parcel of land.

3. One method to determine a building's replacement cost uses the estimated cost of the raw materials needed to build the structure, plus labor and indirect costs. This is called the
   a. square-foot method.
   b. quantity-survey method.
   c. cubic-foot method.
   d. unit-in-place method.

4. If a property's annual net income is $24,000 and it is valued at $300,000, what is its capitalization rate?
   a. 8%
   b. 10.5%
   c. 12.5%
   d. 15%

5. An appraiser needs certain financial figures in order to determine value by the income approach. Which one of the following numbers is NOT required for the income approach to value?
   a. Annual net operating income
   b. Capitalization rate
   c. Accrued depreciation
   d. Annual gross income

6. The highest and best use of a property is the
   a. sales price paid for a similar property.
   b. most return the owner can receive for the use of the property.
   c. cost of buying a lot and erecting a similar building on it.
   d. use of the land for a long-term lease.

7. The income capitalization approach is given the most weight in the valuation of a(n)
   a. single-family residence.
   b. one-bedroom condominium.
   c. office building.
   d. school.

8. Capitalization is the process by which annual net operating income is used as the basis to
   a. determine cost.
   b. estimate value.
   c. establish depreciation.
   d. determine potential tax value.

9. The depreciation that an appraiser uses in the cost approach to value represents the
   a. remaining economic life of the building.
   b. remodeling costs to increase rentals.
   c. loss of value due to any cause.
   d. costs to modernize the building.

10. Which of the following factors is NOT important in selecting comparable properties under the sales comparison approach to value?
    a. Date of sale
    b. Interior decorating
    c. Size of the property
    d. Location

11. The appraised value of a residence with four bedrooms and one bathroom would probably be reduced because of
    a. external obsolescence.
    b. functional obsolescence.
    c. physical deterioration—curable.
    d. physical deterioration—incurable.

12. The reason for loss of value that is always incurable is
    a. functional obsolescence.
    b. physical deterioration.
    c. replacement obsolescence.
    d. economic obsolescence.

13. Which appraisal approach makes use of a rate of investment return?
    a. Sales comparison
    b. Cost
    c. Income capitalization
    d. Market data

14. Which of the following is *NOT* true about market value?
    a. It is the highest price a property could bring in an open market.
    b. Buyer and seller must be knowledgeable and acting without undue pressure.
    c. It should be an arm's length transaction.
    d. A reasonable amount of time should be allowed for full exposure to the market.

15. Developers have just announced a new championship golf course community. Property values in the area will tend to increase due to this announcement. This is an example of the principle of
    a. supply and demand.
    b. anticipation.
    c. substitution.
    d. conformity.

16. Which of the following statements is *TRUE* of the income approach to value?
    a. The reproduction or replacement cost of the building must be computed.
    b. The capitalization rate must be estimated.
    c. Depreciation must be determined.
    d. Sales of similar properties must be considered.

17. In the cost approach to value, it is necessary to
    a. determine a dollar value for depreciation.
    b. estimate future expenses and operating costs.
    c. check sales prices of recently sold comparable properties in the area.
    d. reconcile differing value estimates.

18. The subject property has two bedrooms and the comparable property has three bedrooms. The estimated value of the third bedroom is $2,500. According to the sales comparison method, the appraiser should
    a. deduct $2,500 from the value of the subject property.
    b. add $2,500 to the value of the subject property.
    c. deduct $2,500 from the value of the comparable property.
    d. add $2,500 to the value of the comparable property.

19. All of the following items should be deducted from gross income to compute net operating income *EXCEPT*
    a. utility bills.
    b. mortgage payments.
    c. maintenance expenses.
    d. repair costs.

20. If the appraiser decides to increase the capitalization rate, the market value of the property will
    a. increase.
    b. decrease.
    c. stay the same.
    d. be equal to the capitalization rate.

21. The number of years a property is expected to remain useful for its original purpose is called its
    a. actual life.
    b. economic life.
    c. progressive life.
    d. depreciated life.

22. The formula for estimating value based on the gross rent multiplier is
    a. rental income × gross rent multiplier = estimated market value.
    b. rental income ÷ gross rent multiplier = estimated market value.
    c. estimated market value × rental income = gross rent multiplier.
    d. net operating income × gross rent multiplier = estimated market value.

23. In estimating the value of real estate using the cost approach, the appraiser should
   a. estimate the replacement cost of the improvements.
   b. deduct for depreciation of the land.
   c. determine the original cost and adjust for changes in capitalization rates.
   d. review the sales prices of comparable properties.

24. Under the income approach to estimating the value of real estate, the capitalization rate is the
   a. rate at which the property will increase in value.
   b. rate of return the property will earn as an investment.
   c. rate of capital required to keep the property operating efficiently.
   d. maximum rate of return allowed by usury limits.

25. An example of economic obsolescence is
   a. numerous pillars supporting the ceiling in a store.
   b. roof leaks making the premises unusable and therefore unrentable.
   c. massive cornices in an older structure.
   d. abandoned buildings in the area.

26. Mary lives in a home located in a suburban community. A new expressway is being built a few blocks away that will reduce the commute time to the urban employment center by 30 minutes. Mary's home is expected to increase in value based on the principle of
   a. anticipation.
   b. competition.
   c. contribution.
   d. highest and best use.

27. An apartment building generates a monthly gross income of $6,000. Monthly managerial expenses total $1,000. Monthly taxes total $300. Monthly debt service totals $2,675. Monthly repairs and maintenance total $1,100. What is the building's monthly net income?
   a. $925
   b. $1,225
   c. $3,600
   d. $3,900

28. The subject property is a two-story home with three bedrooms, three baths, a family room, a dining room, and an attached two-car garage. Which of the following would be a legitimate comparable sale?
   I. Two-story home with 3 bedrooms and 2.5 baths in the same neighborhood that sold 18 months ago
   II. One-story home in a different neighborhood with 3 bedrooms and 2 baths, a detached one-car garage, and no family or dining room
   a. I only
   b. II only
   c. Both I and II
   d. Neither I nor II

29. The subject property has 2,100 square feet, 4 bedrooms, a 2-car garage, no patio, no pool, 2.5 baths, and sits on 1 acre. The comparable recently sold for $140,000 and has 1,900 square feet, 3 bedrooms, a 1-car garage, a patio, a pool, 2 baths, and sits on 1.5 acres. Market cost data shows the following values: Square foot = $72, 1 bedroom = $2,000, 1-car garage = $1,500, patio = $2,000, pool = $14,000, ½ bath = $800, and 1 acre = $30,000. Using this cost data, what is the estimated value of the subject property?
   a. $113,700
   b. $125,700
   c. $127,700
   d. $129,200

30. A broker is asked to estimate the value of a property. She finds four recently sold comparables, A, B, C, and D. Comparables A, B, and D have positive features worth $3,000, $2,000, and $5,000, respectively, which are not common to the subject property. Comparable C has negative features worth $3,500 that are not common to the subject property. The comparables sold for the following prices: A, $73,000; B, $74,000; C, $62,000; and D, $71,000. What is the range of indicated values for the subject property?
   a. $58,500 to $76,000
   b. $65,500 to $66,000
   c. $65,500 to $72,000
   d. $66,000 to $72,000

31. Which of the following statements is *TRUE* of a comparative market analysis?

    a. It is another term for an appraisal.

    b. It can help the seller price the property.

    c. By law, it must be completed for each listing taken.

    d. Per Commission Rule, it must be retained by the broker for at least five years.

CHAPTER 18

Property Insurance

■ **LEARNING OBJECTIVES** *When you have finished reading this chapter, you should be able to*

- ■ **describe** the protection afforded by insurance and the characteristics of various types of standard policies.

- ■ **identify** insurance policy terms such as condition, exclusion, and endorsement.

- ■ **explain** the following legal issues: (1) insurable interest, (2) coinsurance clause, and (3) unoccupied building exclusion.

- ■ **explain** the purpose of the Federal Emergency Management Agency.

- ■ **define** these *key terms:*

broad form (HO-2)	endorsement	package insurance
casualty insurance	exclusion	premium
coinsurance clause	homeowner's insurance	property insurance
condition	policy	subrogation clause
deductible	liability insurance	

■ BASIC INSURANCE CONCEPTS

Because home ownership represents a large financial investment for most purchasers, homeowners usually protect their investment by taking out insurance on the property. If the property is mortgaged, homeowner's insurance is usually mandatory because the lender wishes to protect the collateral.

An insurance policy is an agreement between two parties: the insurer and the insured. Insurance represents the transfer of risk from the individual homeowner to the group of policyholders affiliated with the insurance company. The insurer is the insurance company, which agrees to reimburse the insured, the property owner, for losses caused by a covered event. For example, if a homeowner buys an insurance policy that protects against fire loss and the insured property burns down, the insurer must reimburse the homeowner for the loss, within the limitations of the insurance policy. Insurance companies and insurance policies are regulated by government agencies.

However, the insurance policy is also a contract, subject to all the normal rules of contract law. For example, consideration in the form of **premiums** is required for the insurance contract to be valid. Premiums are considered to be the consumer's cost of coverage. Insurance policies have definite beginning and ending dates.

A **property insurance** or **casualty insurance** policy protects the insured from losses caused by damage to the property and the improvements on that property. A **liability insurance** policy protects the insured from losses caused to third persons or their property. A **package insurance** policy protects the insured from both types of losses.

■ HOMEOWNER'S INSURANCE

Although it is possible for a homeowner to obtain an individual policy for each type of risk, most residential property owners take out insurance in the form of a packaged **homeowner's insurance policy** (also called hazard insurance) on their residence. These policies insure holders against the destruction of their property by named perils, injury to others that occurs on the property, and theft from the premises of any personal property that is owned by the insured or members of the insured's immediate family.

Coverage and Claims

The basis for most homeowner's policies is called a basic form (HO-1), and it usually provides property coverage against:

- fire and lightning,
- glass breakage,
- windstorm and hail,
- explosion,
- riot and civil commotion,
- damage by aircraft,
- damage from vehicles,
- damage from smoke,
- vandalism and malicious mischief,
- theft, and
- loss of property removed from the premises when it is endangered by fire or other perils.

The packaged homeowner's policy also includes *liability coverage* for (1) personal injuries to others resulting from the insured's acts of negligence, (2) voluntary medical payments and funeral expenses for accidents sustained by guests or resident employees on the insured's property, and (3) physical damage to the property of others caused by the insured. Voluntary medical payments cover injuries to a resident employee but do not cover benefits due under any workers' compensation or occupational disease law.

Characteristics of Homeowners' Policies

Although coverage provided may vary among policies, all homeowners' policies have three common characteristics. First, they all have *fixed ratios of coverage*. That is, each type of coverage in a policy must be maintained at a certain level. The amount of coverage on household contents and other items must be a fixed percentage of the amount of insurance on the building itself. Although the amount of contents coverage may be increased, it cannot be reduced below the standard percentage. In addition, theft coverage may be contingent on the full amount of the contents coverage.

Second, homeowners' policies have an *indivisible premium*, which means the insured receives coverage for all the perils included in the policy for a single rate and may not exclude certain perils from coverage.

Finally, *first-party and third-party insurance* is the liability coverage discussed above. It covers not only damage or loss to the insured's property or its contents but also the insured's legal liability for losses or damages to another's property as well as for injuries suffered by another party while on the insured's property.

The following basic types of insurance policies are identified by number.

- *HO-2*. This Homeowners' **Broad Form** insurance policy is a *named peril policy*, which means that if a specific peril or hazard is not named in the policy, it is not covered. HO-2 covers more perils than the basic form (including falling objects; weight of ice, snow, or sleet; collapse of buildings; malfunctioning heating systems; accidental discharge of water or steam, and electrical currents).
- *HO-3*. This Homeowners' Special Form is an *all-risk form* insurance policy that provides even greater coverage than HO-2 because loss and damage to real property caused by all perils is covered without having to be named. HO-3 remains a named peril policy regarding damage or loss to personal property. Because it provides the insured with a greater amount of protection, it is the most commonly used residential policy today.
- *HO-4*. This Homeowners' Contents Broad Form is a *tenant's policy* (renter's policy) that covers the same perils as HO-2 regarding the insured's personal property. It cannot cover the building in which the tenant lives because the tenant does not hold the required financial interest in the property. HO-4 will frequently include liability insurance for any damage that the tenant might cause to the rented property.
- *HO-6*. This Homeowners' Unit-Owners Form policy is designed for the special needs of *condominium owners*. Because condo ownership is limited to *air space*, fixture coverage is the main area of real property concern.
- *HE-7*. An extended all-risk form providing broad coverage of both real and personal property. The HE-7 is designed for and primarily sold to owners of very expensive property.

- *HO-8.* This Homeowners' Modified Coverage Form is generally used when properties have less market value than the cost to replace them. It may be used to insure older homes.

Contents of Standard HO-3 Policy

Agreement to insure.   As with all enforceable bilateral contracts, both parties promise some action in exchange for the other party's promised action. The insurer promises to financially reimburse the insured in the event of a covered loss while the insured promises to make timely payment of premiums.

Declaration page.   This section clearly states the terms of the insurance policy. The actual dates of coverage are specified; and the insurance rating is determined by the property description. The basic details of the real and personal property coverage includes the limits of liability coverage and any **deductibles** that the insured might have to personally pay before coverage can be applied. Any endorsements, or perils that have been added to the general policy, will be noted here. The declaration page will also contain the name of any mortgagee, signature of an authorized agent, and other administrative matters.

Standardized policy provisions.   All the details of coverage are contained in the various policy provisions. If it is a named peril policy, those perils that are covered will be clearly stated; whereas, if it is an all risk policy, all the exclusions will be clarified. Any conditions or added endorsements to the policy will be specified.

Insurance definitions.   A **condition** is a limitation on the coverage of a specific insured property. For example, damage to a vehicle will only be covered if the vehicle was inside the garage at the time of the damage.

An **endorsement** is coverage for specific property or perils that are not covered in the original policy and is sometimes called a rider. For example, if the homeowner owns a collection of rare books, an endorsement would probably be needed to fully insure the collection against loss.

An **exclusion** is some item, or loss due to a specific event, that is not covered by the policy. For example, most policies exclude the coverage of loss due to acts of war or terrorism.

Selected Legal Issues

Insurable interest.   The insured party must have some type of financial interest in the property to recover any losses. The insured person may be the homeowner, the lender, or even a property manager. Sometimes the conditions of the policy will limit a concurrent owner to the amount of their financial interest. The insured will, however, *never recover more than the actual loss.*

Unoccupied building exclusion.   Most policies contain provisions that state that *if the insured building is unoccupied for more than a certain length of time, the owner may not be able to recover any losses that may occur.* According to the courts in North Carolina, insurance companies may use 60 days as the vacancy time period. A property owner should make sure the building is not vacant for a longer period than that stated in the insurance policy (e.g., 60 days). The contract definition of *vacant* can vary widely from policy to policy. For example, in one policy if there is no human occupancy for the prescribed time, vacancy has occurred. A similar policy may specify that as long as one piece of furniture is present in each room of the residence, despite presence or absence of humans, the property is still classified as *occupied*. Awareness of this insurance policy exclusion is important for licensees because sellers occasionally move from their listed or under-contract property and expect their agent to look after the property in their absence.

Interpretation of Policies

The insurance policy is a contract. Most insurance policy contracts are standard forms approved by the North Carolina Department of Insurance. These standard forms have been drafted mostly in favor of the insurer, not the insured. The owner may have to ask a court to interpret any ambiguous clauses. To obtain a clear interpretation of the policies, it is necessary to read and interpret the policy as a whole in order to understand what is and is not covered.

Coinsurance. Most homeowner's insurance policies contain a **coinsurance clause**, which penalizes the policyholder for underinsuring the property. This provision usually requires that the insured maintain insurance on the property in an amount equal to at least 80 percent of the replacement cost of the dwelling (not including the price of the land). If the owner carries such a policy, a claim may be made for the cost of the repair or replacement of the damaged property without deduction for depreciation.

The formula for calculating the amount of recovery for a fully insured claim is as follows:

$$\frac{\text{Amount of insurance carried}}{80\% \text{ replacement value}} \times \text{Claim} = \text{Recovery}$$

For example, assume a homeowner's dwelling has a replacement cost of $100,000 and is damaged by fire. The estimated cost to repair the damaged portion of the dwelling is $71,000. Thus, if the homeowner carries at least $80,000 (equivalent of 80% replacement value) worth of insurance on the dwelling, the claim against the insurance company can be for the full $71,000.

If the homeowner carries coverage of less than 80 percent of the full replacement cost of the dwelling, the loss will be either settled for the actual cash value (replacement cost less depreciation) or prorated by dividing the percentage of replacement cost actually covered by the policy by the minimum coverage requirement (usually 80 percent). For example, if the building is insured for only 60 percent of its value and suffers a $71,000 loss, the insurance company will pay only $53,250 ($60,000 ÷ $80,000, or 75% of $71,000 = $53,250).

In any event, the *total settlement cannot exceed the face value of the policy*. Because of coinsurance clauses, it is important that homeowners periodically review all policies to be certain that the coverage equals at least 80 percent of the current replacement (new) cost of their home.

Most policies also have a **subrogation clause**, which provides that if the insured collects for damage from the insurance company, any rights the insured may have to sue the person who caused the damage are assigned to the insurance company. A subrogation clause allows the insurance company to pursue legal action to collect the amount paid out from the party at fault and prevents the insured from collecting twice for the same damage.

Insurability Issues

At least partially due to the excessive numbers of natural disasters and class action suits, insurance companies are reluctant to fully insure properties or policyholders that have an active history of claims. In recent years, noninsurability of a particular property or property owner due to large or multiple claims has become an issue because providing adequate homeowner insurance on the collateral property is generally a condition of financing. Insurance companies are relying more and more on policy purchasers' credit reports and property loss history reports to decide insurability issues. Insurers and property buyers are accessing the Comprehensive Loss Underwriting Exchange (CLUE) report on property addresses and on property owners to determine insurability. CLUE manages a loss history exchange primarily where insurers exchange and store claim information by address and owner. The claim/loss history stays with the property *and* goes with the property owner who filed the claim(s).

IN PRACTICE

In recent years, builders used a synthetic stucco exterior finish on some residential properties. This exterior insulating finishing system (EIFS) is a highly effective moisture barrier that also tends to seal in moisture, trapping water in the home's walls and resulting in massive wood rot. Frequently, the effects of the rotting cannot be seen until the damage is extensive and sometimes irreparable. Some insurance companies are now refusing to insure homes with EIFS exteriors, and class action lawsuits have been brought against builders by distressed homeowners.

Federal Flood Insurance Program

The National Flood Insurance Act of 1968 was authorized by Congress to help owners of property located in flood-prone areas by subsidizing flood insurance. As of 1975, such property owners must obtain flood damage insurance on properties financed by mortgages or other loans, grants, or guarantees obtained from federal agencies and federally insured or regulated lending institutions. The program also seeks to improve future management of floodplain areas through land-use and land-control measures.

The Federal Emergency Management Agency (FEMA), which administers the flood insurance program, has maps prepared by the Army Corps of Engineers that identify specific flood-prone areas throughout the country. Property owners in the designated areas who do not obtain flood insurance are unable to obtain federal and federally related financial assistance.

■ RISK MANAGEMENT FOR PROPERTY MANAGERS

Homeowners are not the only ones who should be concerned about property insurance. Because enormous dollar losses can result from certain occurrences, one of the most critical areas of responsibility for a property manager is the field of insurance. Knowing the purposes of insurance coverage and how to make best use of the many types of insurance available is part of *risk management*.

Risk management involves answering the question, "What will happen if something goes wrong?" The perils of any risk must be evaluated in terms of options.

In considering the possibility of a loss, the property manager must decide whether it is better to

- *avoid it* by removing the source of risk, such as a swimming pool;
- *retain it* to a certain extent by insuring it with a large **deductible** (loss not covered by the insurer);
- *control it* by installing sprinklers, fire doors, and other preventive measures; or
- *transfer it* by taking out an insurance policy.

When insurance is considered, a competent, reliable insurance agent should be selected to survey the property and make recommendations. Additional insurance surveys should be obtained if any questions remain. Final decisions, however, must be made by the property owner. A proper decision as to how much and what type of insurance to purchase and where to focus the insurance could save many thousands of dollars, especially in large buildings. The addition of lease requirements could contribute to risk management. Requiring tenants to purchase renter's insurance as a condition of the lease is possibly a way to minimize risk. Also, by refusing to allow certain types or breeds as pets, such as pit bull or Doberman dogs, the insurance premiums may be lowered due to the reduction in liability. Property managers often are responsible for large sums of funds held in escrow for owners and tenants. Often these funds are administered by the managers or their bookkeepers. *Bonding* should be seriously considered for employees who have such financial responsibilities. Bonding provides a form of "honesty" insurance so that any money lost or embezzled by an employee will be reimbursed by the insurance company.

Types of Insurance Coverage

Many kinds of insurance coverage are available to income-property owners and managers. Listed below are some of the more common types.

- *Fire and hazard.* Fire insurance policies provide coverage against direct loss or damage to property from a fire on the premises. Standard fire coverage can be extended to cover hazards such as windstorm, hail, smoke damage, or civil insurrection (like a typical homeowner's policy).
- *Consequential loss, use, and occupancy.* Consequential loss insurance, which can include rent loss, covers the loss of revenue to a business if the business's property cannot be used.
- *Contents and personal property.* This type of insurance covers building contents and personal property during periods when neither is actually located on the business premises, such as stolen from the company van while traveling.
- *Liability.* Public liability insurance covers the risks an owner assumes when the public enters the building. Payments under this coverage are used to settle claims for medical expenses for a person injured in the building as a result of the owner's negligence. Another liability risk is that of medical or hospital payments for injuries sustained by building employees in the course of their employment. These claims are covered by state laws known as workers' compensation acts. These laws require that a building owner who is an employer obtain a workers' compensation policy from a private insurance company.
- *Casualty.* Casualty insurance policies include coverage against theft, burglary, vandalism, and machinery damage as well as health and accident

insurance. Casualty policies are usually written on specific risks, such as theft, rather than being all-inclusive.

- *Surety bonds.* Surety bonds cover an owner against financial losses resulting from an employee's criminal acts or negligence while performing assigned duties.

Today, many insurance companies offer multi-peril policies for apartment and business buildings. These policies offer the property manager an insurance package that includes such standard types of commercial coverage as fire, hazard, public liability, and casualty.

Claims

When a claim is made under a policy insuring a building or another physical object, the amount of the claim can be determined using one of two methods: the *depreciated actual value* or *cash value* of the damaged property or the *current replacement cost.* When purchasing insurance, a manager must assess whether the property should be insured at full replacement cost or at depreciated cost. As with the homeowners' policies discussed earlier, commercial policies include *coinsurance clauses* that require that the insured carry fire coverage, usually in an amount equal to 80 percent of the building's replacement value.

IN PRACTICE

Agents must be sure that homebuyers acquire a homeowner's insurance policy on or before the day of closing. This is required if there will be a mortgage, but it is still strongly advised if it is a cash purchase. Buyers should be reminded that the typical homeowners' insurance policies do not provide coverage for termite damage, breakdown of appliances, flood damage, loss of trees, or losses incurred over an extended period of time (such as a leaking roof). Assuming the seller's policy could mean that the buyer does not have a policy that fits the buyer's needs.

■ RELATED WEB SITES

Choice Point: *www.choicepoint.com*
Choice Trust: *www.consumerdisclosure.com*
Federal Emergency Management Authority: *www.fema.gov*

■ SUMMARY

To protect their investment in real estate, most homeowners purchase property insurance. A standard homeowner's insurance policy covers fire, theft, and liability and can be extended to cover many types of less common risks. Different types of insurance are available to people who live in apartments and condominiums.

The insurance policy is a contract. Most insurance policy contracts are standard forms approved by the North Carolina Insurance Commission. These standard forms have been drafted mostly in favor of the insurer, not the insured. The most common homeowner insurance policy type in North Carolina is HO-3, the all risk form.

The insured party must have some type of financial interest in the property to recover any losses. The insured will, however, never recover more than the actual loss. Most policies contain an unoccupied property exclusion provision that states that if the insured building is unoccupied for a certain length of time, the owner may not be able to recover on any losses that may occur.

Once an insurance company pays for damages to a policyholder's property, the company may ask for a subrogation clause. A subrogation clause enables the insurance company to sue the party responsible for damage to the insured's property on the insured's behalf. Some properties and property owners are finding that they are uninsurable due to excessive claim history especially if the claims involved water damage. Insurers are relying on Comprehensive Loss Underwriting Exchange (CLUE) reports more and more before they decide to issue policies or calculate the premiums to be charged.

In addition to homeowner's insurance, the federal government makes flood insurance mandatory for people living in flood-prone areas who wish to obtain federally regulated or federally insured mortgage loans. An area must comply with FEMA standards to be eligible for flood insurance coverage. Flood insurance is a separate policy from standard homeowner's policies and may restrict construction in a FEMA flood hazard area.

Most homeowner's policies contain a coinsurance clause that requires that the policyholder maintain insurance in an amount equal to 80 percent of the replacement (new) cost of the home. If this percentage is not met, the policyholder will share in the repair costs when a loss occurs proportionate to their degree of underinsurance.

An important duty of a property manager is securing adequate insurance coverage for the premises. The basic types of coverage applicable to commercial structures include fire and hazard insurance on the property and fixtures; consequential loss, use and occupancy insurance to protect the owner against revenue losses; and casualty insurance to provide coverage against such losses as theft, vandalism, and destruction of machinery. The manager also should secure both public liability insurance to cover the owner against claims made by people injured on the premises and workers' compensation policies to cover the claims of employees injured on the job. It also is advisable to require tenants to purchase renter's insurance as a lease condition.

QUESTIONS

1. A typical homeowner's insurance policy covers all of the following *EXCEPT*
   a. personal injury claims due to property owner's negligence.
   b. theft of property.
   c. vandalism and malicious mischief.
   d. flood damage.

2. In homeowner's insurance, coinsurance refers to the
   a. specific form of policy which allows the premium to be split equitably between multiple owners.
   b. stipulation that the homeowner must purchase insurance coverage equal to at least 80 percent of the replacement cost of the structure to be able to collect the full insured amount in the event of a loss.
   c. stipulation that the homeowner must purchase insurance coverage equal to at least 75 percent of the replacement cost of the structure to be able to collect the full insured amount in the event of a loss.
   d. specific form of policy purchased when a property is owned by co-owners.

3. Federal flood insurance is
   a. required in certain areas to insure properties financed by federally backed mortgage loans against flood damage.
   b. only required on real estate purchases located on the North Carolina coast.
   c. only required in North Carolina on federally-owned lands.
   d. paid for by the federal government.

4. A subrogation clause in an insurance policy enables the
   a. insurer to sue the party responsible for damage to the insured's property.
   b. insured to receive 100 percent of replacement cost less depreciation.
   c. insurer to receive full cost of the repair or replacement of the damaged property.
   d. insured to protect the property in case of a flood.

5. When a property manager chooses an insurance policy with a $150 deductible, the risk management technique being employed is risk
   a. avoidance.
   b. abatement.
   c. control.
   d. transfer.

6. Which of the following statements is *NOT* true about homeowner insurance?
   a. Most policies exclude coverage for property that is unoccupied longer than a set time period.
   b. Most homeowners purchase an HO-3 policy for their residence.
   c. A homeowner policy can be purchased on a residence by any interested party.
   d. A property owner with an extensive history of filing insurance claims may be denied insurance.

7. Although the insurance company requires 80 percent coverage on an insured dwelling, the owner only purchased 50 percent coverage on the $175,000 dwelling. If a fire causes $82,000 of damage, how much will the insurance cover?
   a. $41,000
   b. $51,250
   c. $65,600
   d. $82,000

8. Which type of insurance coverage protects the property owner against the claims of employees injured on the job?
   a. Consequential loss
   b. Workers' compensation
   c. Casualty
   d. Surety bond

9. A tenant slips on an icy apartment building stair and is hospitalized. A claim for medical expenses may be paid under which of the following policies held by the owner?
   a. Workers' compensation
   b. Casualty
   c. Liability
   d. Fire and hazard

10. Which clause in a standard homeowner's insurance policy literally makes the insured share in the loss?

    a. Exclusion clause

    b. Coinsurance clause

    c. Conditions clause

    d. Casualty clause

CHAPTER 19

Federal Income Taxation of Real Property Ownership

■ **LEARNING OBJECTIVES** *When you have finished reading this chapter, you should be able to*

■ **identify** the tax benefits of home ownership, including itemized deductions and adjustments that reduce gain.

■ **explain** basic tax concepts as they relate to home ownership and when gains may or may not be taxable.

■ **explain** the differences in taxation on personal residences and on investment property.

■ **calculate** the basis, adjusted basis, amount realized, and gains on factual situations.

■ **define** these *key terms*:

adjusted basis	cost basis	long-term capital gain
basis	depreciation	short-term capital gain
boot	gain	tax-deferred exchange
capital gain	installment sale	
capital loss	like-kind properties	

■ INTRODUCTION

All real estate agents should have a general understanding of the tax implications of owning a home. The tax advantages available to homeowners can significantly reduce the out-of-pocket cost of owning a home, and this should be explained to homebuyers, especially first-time homebuyers. However, the discussion and examples used in this chapter are designed to introduce the reader to only general tax concepts—a tax lawyer or certified public accountant (CPA) should be consulted for further details on specific regulations. Real estate agents should never try to give their clients or customers tax advice. Instead, they should indicate that all real estate transactions have tax implications that should be discussed with a competent adviser.

TAX BENEFITS FOR HOMEOWNERS

To encourage home ownership, the federal government allows homeowners certain income tax advantages. Even though the Tax Reform Act of 1986 greatly restricted or eliminated tax deductions in other areas, benefits for homeowners were kept largely intact.

Tax-Deductible Loan Expenses

Homeowners may be able to deduct from their taxable income

- *mortgage interest payments* on first and second homes. For a principal residence, a second residence, or both, the total amount of acquisition debt for which interest can be deducted cannot exceed a total of $1 million. *Acquisition indebtedness* is defined as the debt incurred in acquiring, constructing, or substantially improving a principal residence or second residence (or both) of the taxpayer, where the debt is secured by such property. Home equity loans—loans secured by the property and in amounts less than the difference between fair market value and outstanding mortgage loan balance—cannot exceed $100,000. *Home equity indebtedness* is defined as the debt secured by the taxpayer's residence(s) that does not exceed the fair market value of such a residence(s) less the amount of acquisition indebtedness.
- *loan discount points* (those that are prepaid interest to reduce the loan interest rate when acquiring a residence, not a refinance, are deductible in the year of purchase).
- *mortgage prepayment penalties* (rare in North Carolina).
- *some loan origination fees*, if they are quoted as a percent of the loan amount and if paid to obtain the loan. (*Agents and buyers should check with their tax advisers before stating that such fees may or may not be deductible.*)

Real Property Taxes

Real property taxes paid by a homeowner also are deductible in the year paid. Note that the interest paid on overdue taxes is not deductible. The mortgage interest deduction combined with the real property tax deduction can mean a substantial annual tax savings for the homeowner.

TAX BENEFITS OF SELLING REAL PROPERTY

While the two tax benefits discussed above are available to those who currently own real estate, other tax benefits are available to those selling their property. However, before discussing these tax advantages, some basic tax concepts must be explained.

Basic Tax Concepts

Because the government taxes income, it is worth quickly noting the definition of income. Obviously, income includes wages from employment, interest on savings, dividends on stock, pension payments, and other commonly accepted forms of income. However, income also includes the gain that a person recognizes when he or she sells a capital asset. If a person sells a painting for $10,000 that was acquired for $6,000, that person has recognized a **gain,** that is, income, of $4,000, and that income is taxable (unless specifically excluded by the tax code). So it is with the buying and selling of real property.

When a person sells real property for more than its cost, that person has received a **capital gain.** Capital gains, the profits realized from the sale or exchange of property, are taxed as ordinary income if it is a **short-term capital gain** (held 12 months or less). However, the maximum tax rate that applies to **long-term capital gain** (held longer than 12 months) is currently 15 percent (not the ordinary 39.6 percent). Because capital gain laws change often, check with a tax specialist before quoting any rates.

The amount of the gain realized from a sale of real property depends on that property's **basis.** The **cost basis** of property is the owner's initial cost for the real estate (purchase price plus allowable closing expenses). The owner of a property can add to the cost basis the cost of any physical capital improvements that add value to the property or prolong its life. This is the property's **adjusted basis.** (Note that the cost of ordinary repairs or maintenance does not increase the adjusted basis.) When the owner sells the property, the amount by which the amount realized (sales price minus allowable closing expenses) exceeds the property's adjusted basis is the capital gain subject to taxation. If the amount realized is less than the adjusted basis, a **capital loss** has occurred. Capital loss is not currently recognized on the sale of a personal residence, but can frequently be used to off-set capital gain in other situations. As noted before, a tax specialist should be consulted on this matter."

The basis can be adjusted by adding
- allowable closing costs
- capital improvements

Essentially, a property owner determines the adjusted basis by adding:

Purchase price
Allowable closing costs
+ Capital improvements
———————————————
Adjusted basis

■ **FOR EXAMPLE** Suppose Johnson buys a home for $85,000. The closing costs that can be allocated to purchasing the property (but not to obtaining financing) include the lawyer's fees and recording fee, which equal $250. One year later, Johnson spends $2,000 pressure washing and treating her roof. Two years later, Johnson spends $10,000 on a room addition to the house. Johnson will calculate her adjusted basis as follows:

$85,000	purchase price
250	allowable closing costs
+10,000	capital improvements
$95,250	adjusted basis

Notice that the $2,000 spent maintaining the roof is not added to the basis. This is a normal maintenance expense whereas roof replacement might be an acceptable capital expense.

To determine the gain that is realized from the sale of a property, the property owner takes the sales price and deducts the allowable closing costs from that.

Sales price
— Allowable closing costs
_____
Amount realized

■ **FOR EXAMPLE** Let's continue our previous example. Johnson sells the house for $110,000. Her selling expenses are $5,300. To calculate the amount she realized on the sale, subtract her allowable closing costs from the sales price.

$110,000   sales price
— $5,300   allowable closing costs
_____
$104,700   amount realized

To calculate an owner's gain on the sale of a property, simply subtract the adjusted basis from the amount realized on the sale.

Amount realized
— Adjusted basis
_____
Capital gain (or loss)

■ **FOR EXAMPLE** Once again, let's return to Johnson's situation. To calculate her gain on the sale, take the amount realized and subtract her adjusted basis.

$104,700   amount realized
— 95,250   adjusted basis
_____
$ 9,450   capital gain

Johnson's taxable capital gain on the sale of her house is $9,450.

Tax-Free Gains from Sale of Principal Residence

Taxpayers who sell their principal residences can take advantage of tax laws that took effect in May 1997. Under current tax law, capital gains—up to $500,000 for a married couple filing jointly and up to $250,000 for a single person or a married person filing singly—from the sale of a principal residence are excluded from taxation.

There are a few restrictions on this tax benefit: (1) the seller must have occupied the property as a primary residence for two of the previous five years (residency does not have to be continuous) and (2) the exclusion is available only once every two years. Because of the first restriction, this exclusion of gain does not apply to vacation properties or second homes.

Under these tax provisions, homeowners with substantial capital gains can downsize into smaller, less-expensive homes without a tax penalty (in most cases). If a seller has gains that exceed the $500,000 or $250,000 limit, those gains will be currently taxed at the maximum 15 percent long-term capital gains rate.

■ **FOR EXAMPLE** Suppose the Bowers sold their principal residence, where they have lived for the previous 20 years. They originally purchased the house for $98,000, paying $550 in closing costs. They sold it for $879,000, having $54,600 in selling expenses. The gain on the sale can be calculated as follows:

$98,000   purchase price
+   550   original closing costs
$98,550   adjusted basis

$879,000   sales price
− 54,600   allowable closing costs
$824,400   amount realized

$824,400   amount realized
− 98,550   adjusted basis
$725,850   capital gain

Because the Bowers are married/filing jointly and have occupied the primary residence far in excess of the two-year minimum requirement, they will be able to take the full $500,000 tax exemption. The amount of capital gain in excess of the exemption is taxable at the long-term capital gains rate of 15 percent (owned longer than 12 months). The Bowers will only owe capital gains tax in the amount of $33,877.50 on a total gain of over $700,000.

$725,850   capital gain
− 500,000   tax exemption
$225,850   taxable capital gain

$225,850 (taxable capital gain) × 15% (tax rate) = $33,877.50 (tax bill)

Office in the Home

To qualify for tax deductions for an office in the home, that portion of the home must be used *exclusively* for business purposes; it must be the taxpayer's principal place of business; it must be where clients, customers, or patients are met in the normal course of business; or it must be a separate structure not attached to the dwelling. Consult with a tax expert for more details.

■ TAX BENEFITS OF REAL ESTATE INVESTMENT

One of the main reasons real estate investments were popular—and profitable—in the past was that federal law allowed investors to use losses generated by the investments to shelter income from other sources. The Tax Reform Act of 1986 eliminated some important tax advantages of owning investment real estate, but with professional tax advice investors still may be able to make wise real estate investment purchases.

Adjusted Basis

As discussed earlier, the adjusted basis in a property is roughly equivalent to the owner's investment in the property. The adjusted basis affects the amount of gain that is realized from the sale of real property. The owner of an investment property calculates the owner's basis in that property a little differently from the homeowner. The owner of income property can also add to the cost basis the cost of any physical capital improvements (as opposed to repairs that may be expensed annually) subsequently made to the property. He must subtract from the basis any payment received for the sale of an easement on the property and/or the amount of any depreciation claimed as a tax deduction (discussed later) to arrive at the property's adjusted basis.

Installment Sales

When a seller finances the sale of the seller's property, or when the seller is to receive all or some portion of the sales price in a year or years other than the year of sale, the sale qualifies as an **installment sale**. For instance, a seller may agree to personally finance the sale of the property, receiving a 5 percent down payment, with the balance of the purchase price to be received in monthly payments over a ten-year term. The seller benefits tax-wise from this type of sale by being able to spread taxation of any gain over the term of the loan.

> Tax benefits of owning a home:
> - Tax-deductible interest payments
> - Tax-deductible property taxes
> - Adjustments to reduce capital gain liability

With an installment sale, the taxpayer is taxed on a pro rata portion of the total gain as each installment actually is received. For example, if a taxpayer received a gain of $10,000 on a $100,000 contract price, her profit percentage would be 10 percent. If during the tax year she received $5,000 in principal payments, 10 percent of those payments would be taxable that year. Ten percent of $5,000 is $500. She would have to report a taxable gain of $500 in that tax year.

Note that if a homeowner sells a principal residence and the gain will exceed the statutory limits of exclusion discussed previously, the homeowner may also benefit by selling the principal residence on an installment basis.

Vacation Homes

If a property owner has a vacation home and if it is in full use by others, certain expenses may be deductible for tax purposes. But if the owner personally uses the property for more than 14 days per year, or for more than 10 percent of the number of days for which the property is rented, whichever is greater, certain deductions will be disallowed.

Tax-Deferred Exchanges

Real estate investors can *defer* taxation of capital gains by exchanging property versus selling it and receiving taxable profit. A **tax-deferred exchange** offers significant tax advantages because no matter how much a property has appreciated since its initial purchase, it may be exchanged for another property and the taxpayer may be able to defer taxes on the entire gain. Note that the tax is deferred, not eliminated, so whenever the investor actually sells the newly acquired property without the use of an exchange, the capital gain will be taxable.

The requirements for a tax-deferred exchange, sometimes called a Section 1031 Exchange based on the federal tax code, are fairly straightforward. First of all, there must be a property transferred (*the relinquished property*) and a property received (*the replacement property*). These properties must be *exchanged*—they cannot be sold. Both the property transferred and the property received must be held for productive use in a trade or business or for investment. (An exchange of principal residences will not qualify for tax-deferral.) Finally, the properties must be **like-kind properties**. Essentially, the like-kind requirement is met when real estate is exchanged for real estate. An apartment building can be exchanged for an office building or gas station, and the exchange will still qualify as like-kind.

The apartment building real estate does not have to be exchanged for an apartment building to qualify.

Sometimes, a property is exchanged for another property that is worth substantially more or less money. When this happens, cash or personal property may be included in the transaction to even out the value of the exchange. This cash or personal property is called **boot**. The party receiving boot is taxed on the value of the boot at the time of the exchange. Direct, equal-value property swaps are very rare, so most Section 1031 exchanges are *delayed exchanges* where the relinquished property and the replacement property are disposed of and acquired at different times. The rules for a delayed exchange are very clear and strict with deadlines that cannot be missed (time is of the essence).

The North Carolina Real Estate Commission (NCREC) cautions licensees not to give advice about tax-deferred exchanges or the eligibility of property for such an exchange. Clients should be counseled to consult a tax adviser or attorney who has experience with such exchanges.

Depreciation

Depreciation, or *cost recovery*, allows an investor to recover the cost of an income-producing asset by taking tax deductions over the period of the asset's useful life. Even though investors usually expect the value of the property to appreciate over time, according to the tax laws all physical structures deteriorate and lose value over time. Cost recovery deductions may be taken only on personal property and improvements to land and only if they are used in a trade or business or for the production of income. Cost recovery deductions cannot be claimed on a principal residence or on land (technically, land never wears out or becomes obsolete).

When depreciation is taken in equal amounts over an asset's useful life, the method used is called *straight-line depreciation*. For certain property purchased before 1987, it was also possible to use an *accelerated cost recovery* system to claim greater deductions in the early years of ownership, gradually reducing the amount deducted in each year of the useful life.

For residential rental property placed in service as of January 1, 1987, the recovery period is set at 27.5 years; for nonresidential property placed in service after May 12, 1993, the recovery period is set at 31.5 years, using only the straight-line depreciation method. The accelerated depreciation schedule is not allowed on property purchased after 1987.

Deducting Losses

In addition to tax deductions for depreciation, investors may be able to deduct losses from their real estate investments. The tax laws are very complex, particularly as a result of the Tax Reform Act of 1986. The amount of loss that may be deducted depends on the following factors:

- Whether an investor actively participates in the day-to-day management of the rental property or makes management decisions
- The amount of the loss
- The source of the income against which the loss is to be deducted

Investors who do not actively participate in the management or operation of the real estate are considered *passive investors,* which prevents them from using a loss to offset *active income.* Active income is considered to be wages, income generated from active participation in real estate management, or income from stocks, bonds, and the like. The tax code cites specific rules for active and passive income and losses and is subject to changes in the law.

■ RELATED WEB SITE

Internal Revenue Service: *www.irs.gov*

■ SUMMARY

All real estate agents should have a general understanding of the tax implications of owning and investing in real property. Agents should refrain, however, from giving their clients and customers tax advice.

One of the income tax benefits available to homeowners is the ability to annually deduct property taxes and mortgage interest payments (with certain limitations) on their federal income tax returns. There are also federal tax deductions for certain closing expenses available to both the buyer and the seller in the year in which they transfer or acquire property. Some expenses of a vacation home may be tax deductible if the property also is used as rental property. There is limit on the amount of personal use before tax deductions are allowed.

Capital gains on the sale of a primary, or principal, residence may be excluded from taxation if the homeowner occupied the home for two of the previous five years. Single homeowners and married homeowners filing separate tax returns may exempt up to $250,000 of capital gain while married couples filing joint returns are eligible for a $500,000 tax exemption. Any gain in excess of the allowed exemption will be taxed at the current long-term capital gain tax rate. Homeowners also may take advantage of an owner-financed installment sale to spread tax liabilities across several years. Once again, licensees are cautioned against giving specific tax advice. Consumers should be referred to an appropriate tax expert.

Real estate investors can utilize a tax-deferred exchange to delay the payment of tax on capital gain by exchanging investment property for like-kind property. The definition of "like-kind" is very broad but is basically investment property for investment property. A primary residence cannot be used in a tax-deferred exchange. Federal regulations are very strict for Section 1031 exchanges and licensees should advise clients to get adequate tax advice before attempting such an exchange.

QUESTIONS

1. In June of 2009, the Smiths sold their principal residence that they have lived in since they purchased it in February, 2008. They received capital gains of $22,000. The gain will most probably be
   a. tax exempt since it is their principal residence.
   b. taxed at the Smiths' regular tax rate.
   c. taxed as ordinary income, but at a lower rate.
   d. subject to the purchase price rule.

2. For tax purposes, the initial cost of an investment property plus the cost of any subsequent improvements to the property less depreciation represents the investment's
   a. adjusted basis.
   b. capital gain.
   c. basis.
   d. market value.

3. Which of the following statements is *TRUE* of capital gains?
   a. They may be realized only from the sale of improvements to real estate, not from the sale of the land itself.
   b. They may be realized only from the sale of the land itself, not from the sale of improvements to the real estate.
   c. They will be taxed at the taxpayer's regular tax rate if the property was owned for one year or less.
   d. They must be paid only by property owners under the age of 65.

4. Federal income tax law allows for
   I. a tax on all capital gains over $250,000.
   II. a possible exclusion of gain up to $500,000 from the sale of a personal residence by a married couple filing jointly.
       a. I only
       b. II only
       c. Both I and II
       d. Neither I nor II

5. Federal income tax laws do *NOT* currently allow a homeowner to deduct which of the following expenses from taxable income?
   a. Mortgage interest
   b. Real estate taxes
   c. Discount points
   d. Repairs or maintenance

6. The profit a homeowner receives from the sale of their principal residence may be
   a. rolled over into the purchase of a more expensive property without any tax liability, once every 24 months.
   b. subject to long-term federal income tax if the profit exceeds the excluded limits.
   c. excluded from taxation every year up to a statutory limit of $500,000 per married couple filing jointly.
   d. taxed at a lower rate because depreciation is deductible from each annual income tax return.

7. Mike Tyler, unmarried, age 38, sells his home of eight years and realizes a $25,000 gain from the sale. Income tax on this gain may be
   a. excluded from taxation.
   b. excluded from taxation if Tyler purchases a property with a value equal to or exceeding the adjusted basis of the previous residence.
   c. reduced by subtracting the depreciation of the property when compared to the reproduction cost of a like-kind improvement.
   d. reduced by the amount of mortgage interest paid over the life of the property's owner.

8. Ada Ryan, age 62, sells the home she has occupied for 18 months of the previous five years and realizes a $52,000 gain from the sale. Income tax on the profit from this sale may be

   a. taxed as long-term capital gains.
   b. postponed by purchasing another residence of equal or greater value within 12 months before or after the sale.
   c. eliminated if she donates at least 50 percent of the profit to a charity.
   d. reduced by the amount of mortgage interest paid over the property's economic life.

9. A homeowner sold his principal residence for $127,500. Selling expenses were $750. The house had been purchased new three years earlier for $75,000. What is the homeowner's gain on this transaction?

   a. $51,750
   b. $52,500
   c. $53,250
   d. $75,000

10. In question 9, if the property were an investment property, how much of the gain would be subject to income tax?

   a. $21,000
   b. $42,300
   c. $51,750
   d. $52,500

11. A homeowner bought her house for $72,000. She spent $15,000 on an addition, $3,000 on a new deck, $5,000 on repairs, and $2,000 on interior painting. Her adjusted basis is

   a. $87,000.
   b. $90,000.
   c. $95,000.
   d. $97,000.

12. Which of the following statements is TRUE about tax-deferred exchanges?

   a. The properties being exchanged must be of equal value.
   b. A taxpayer's personal home can be used as an exchange property.
   c. A retail property must be exchanged for another retail property.
   d. Any boot that is received will be taxable.

13. Which of the following statements is/are TRUE?

   I. Some of the expenses of a vacation home, that is also a rental property, may be tax deductible if the taxpayer/owner limits their private use of the home.
   II. An installment sales contract may provide tax benefits to the seller by spreading the sales income over several tax years.

   a. I only
   b. II only
   c. Both I and II
   d. Neither I nor II

20

CHAPTER

Fair Housing and Ethical Practices

■ **LEARNING OBJECTIVES** *When you have finished reading this chapter, you should be able to*

■ **describe** the purpose of federal and state fair housing laws, how they are enforced, and their impact on real estate brokers.

■ **list** and define the classes of people who are protected against discrimination by various federal and state laws.

■ **explain** the purposes of the Americans with Disabilities Act.

■ **define** what constitutes sexual harassment.

■ **define** these *key terms:*

Americans with Disabilities Act (ADA)	Equal Credit Opportunity Act (ECOA)	Office of Fair Housing and Equal Opportunity (OFHEO)
blockbusting	Federal Fair Housing Act	
channeling	North Carolina Fair Housing Act of 1983	panic peddling
Civil Rights Act of 1866		protected classes
code of ethics	North Carolina Human Relations Commission	redlining
Department of Housing and Urban Development (HUD)		steering

■ EQUAL OPPORTUNITY IN HOUSING

The purpose of civil rights laws that affect the real estate industry is to create a marketplace in which all persons of similar financial means have a similar range of housing choices. The goal is to ensure that everyone has the opportunity to live where he or she chooses. Owners, real estate licensees, apartment management companies, real estate organizations, lending agencies, builders, and developers must all take a part in creating this single housing market. Federal, state, and local fair housing or equal opportunity laws affect every phase of a real estate transaction, from listing to closing.

The U.S. Congress and the Supreme Court have created a legal framework that preserves the Constitutional rights of all citizens. However, while the passage of laws may establish a code for public conduct, centuries of discriminatory practices and attitudes are not so easily changed. Real estate licensees cannot allow their own prejudices to interfere with the ethical and legal conduct of their profession. Similarly, the discriminatory attitudes of property owners or property seekers must not be allowed to affect compliance with the fair housing laws. This is not always easy, and the pressure to avoid offending the person who pays the commission can be intense. However, just remember: *Failure to comply with fair housing laws is both a civil and criminal violation, and it is grounds for disciplinary action against a licensee* (see Rule A.1601).

> "All citizens of the United States shall have the same right in every state and territory as is enjoyed by white citizens thereof to inherit, purchase, lease, sell, hold, and convey real and personal property."
> —Civil Rights Act of 1866

The federal government's effort to guarantee equal housing opportunities to all U.S. citizens began with the passage of the **Civil Rights Act of 1866**. This law prohibited any type of discrimination based on race. Unlike many laws, there are no exceptions to the Civil Rights Act of 1866.

The U.S. Supreme Court's 1896 decision in *Plessy v. Ferguson* established the *separate but equal* doctrine of legalized racial segregation. A series of court decisions and federal laws in the 20 years between 1948 and 1968 attempted to address the inequities in housing that were results of *Plessy*. Those efforts, however, tended to address only certain aspects of the housing market (such as federally funded housing programs). As a result, their impact was limited.

FEDERAL FAIR HOUSING ACT

In 1968, the federal government began to address specific discriminatory practices throughout the real estate industry. Title VIII of the Civil Rights Act of 1968 (called the *Federal Fair Housing Act*) prohibited discrimination in housing based on race, color, religion, or national origin. In 1974, the Housing and Community Development Act added sex to the list of **protected classes.** In 1988, the Fair Housing Amendments Act included handicapping condition and familial status. Today, these laws are known as the **Federal Fair Housing Act** (see Figure 20.1). The Federal Fair Housing Act, as amended, prohibits discrimination on the basis of the following protected classes:

- *Race*: a group of people that an individual was born into or has affiliated with all of their lives;
- *Color*: the actual color of the skin's pigmentation including the degree of darkness;
- *Religion*: the spiritual beliefs of an individual;
- *National origin*: the country in which an individual was born or from which they derive their direct ancestry (not related to citizenship);

FIGURE   20.1   Federal Fair Housing Laws

Legislation	Race	Color	Religion	National Origin	Sex	Age	Marital Status	Disability	Discrimination	Familial Status	Public Assistance Income
Civil Rights Act of 1866	✔										
Federal Fair Housing Act of 1968 (Title VIII)	✔	✔	✔	✔					✔		
Housing and Community Development Act of 1974					✔				✔		
Fair Housing Amendments Act of 1988								✔	✔	✔	
Equal Credit Opportunity Act of 1974 (lending)	✔	✔	✔	✔	✔	✔	✔		✔		✔

- *Sex:* strictly male or female gender (does not include sexual orientation);
- *Handicapping condition:* defined by HUD as "any physical or mental impairment that substantially limits one or more major life activities, or being regarded as having such an impairment;" which includes persons with AIDS and HIV; and
- *Familial status:* any type of family unit with at least one dependent child (under the age of 18), includes pregnant women.

The Act also prohibits discrimination against individuals because of their *association* with persons in the protected classes. This law is administered by the **Department of Housing and Urban Development (HUD).** HUD has established rules and regulations that further interpret the practices affected by the law. In addition, HUD distributes an *equal housing opportunity poster* (see Figure 20.2). The poster declares that the office in which it is displayed promises to adhere to the Federal Fair Housing Act and pledges support for affirmative marketing and advertising programs.

IN   PRACTICE

When HUD investigates a broker for discriminatory practices, it may consider failure to prominently display the equal housing opportunity poster in the broker's place of business as evidence of discrimination.

Table 20.1 describes the activities prohibited by the Federal Fair Housing Act.

Expanded Definitions

HUD's regulations provide specific definitions that clarify the scope and application of the Federal Fair Housing Act.

Housing.   The regulations define *housing* as a *dwelling,* which includes any building or part of a building designed for occupancy as a residence by one or more families. This includes any residence, such as a single-family house, a condominium,

F I G U R E   20.2   Equal Housing Opportunity Poster

U.S. Department of Housing and Urban Development

EQUAL HOUSING
OPPORTUNITY

We Do Business in Accordance With the Federal Fair Housing Law

(The Fair Housing Amendments Act of 1988)

It is Illegal to Discriminate Against Any Person Because of Race, Color, Religion, Sex, Handicap, Familial Status, or National Origin

---

■ In the sale or rental of housing or residential lots

■ In advertising the sale or rental of housing

■ In the financing of housing

■ In the provision of real estate brokerage services

■ In the appraisal of housing

■ Blockbusting is also illegal

Anyone who feels he or she has been discriminated against may file a complaint of housing discrimination:
   1-800-669-9777 (Toll Free)
   1-800-927-9275 (TDD)

**U.S. Department of Housing and Urban Development
Assistant Secretary for Fair Housing and Equal Opportunity
Washington, D.C. 20410**

Previous editions are obsolete

form HUD-928.1A (2/2003)

---

a cooperative, or manufactured housing, as well as vacant land on which any of these structures will be built.

Familial status. *Familial status* refers to the presence of one or more individuals who have not reached the age of 18 and who live with either a parent or legal guardian. The term also includes a woman who is pregnant. Unless a property qualifies as housing for older persons, all properties must be made available to families with children under the same terms and conditions as to anyone else. It is illegal to advertise properties as being for adults only or to indicate a preference for a certain number of children. The number of persons permitted to reside in a property (the occupancy standards) must be based on objective factors such

T A B L E   20.1   **Federal Fair Housing Act Restrictions**

Prohibited by Federal Fair Housing Act	Example
Refusing to sell, rent, or negotiate the sale or rental of housing	Kate owns an apartment building with several vacant units. When an Asian family asks to see one of the units, she tells them to go away.
Changing terms, conditions, or services for different individuals as a means of discriminating	Sarah, a Roman Catholic, calls on a duplex, and the landlord tells her the rent is $400 per month. When she talks to the other tenants, she learns that all the Lutherans in the complex pay only $325 per month.
Advertising any discriminatory preference or limitation in housing or making any inquiry or reference that is discriminatory in nature	A real estate agent places the following advertisement in a newspaper: "Just Listed! Perfect home for white family, near excellent parochial school!" A developer places this ad in an urban newspaper: "Sunset River Hollow—Dream Homes Just for You!" The ad is accompanied by a photo of several African American families.
Representing that a property is not available for sale or rent when in fact it is	Jason, who uses a wheelchair, is told that the house he wants to rent is no longer available. The next day, however, the For Rent sign is still in the window.
Profiting by inducing property owners to sell or rent on the basis of the prospective entry into the neighborhood of persons of a protected class	Nancy, a real estate agent, sends brochures to homeowners in the predominantly white Ridgewood neighborhood. The brochures, which feature her past success selling homes, include photos of racial minorities, population statistics, and the caption, "The Changing Face of Ridgewood."
Altering the terms or conditions of a home loan, or denying a loan, as a means of discrimination	A lender requires Maria, a divorced mother of two young children, to pay for a credit report. In addition, her father must cosign her application. After talking to a single male friend, Maria learns that he was not required to do either of those things, despite his lower income and poor credit history.
Denying membership or participation in a multiple listing service, a real estate organization, or another facility related to the sale or rental of housing as a means of discrimination	The Topper County Real Estate Practitioners' Association meets every week to discuss available properties and buyers. None of Topper County's African American or female agents are allowed to be members of the association.

as sanitation or safety. HUD's general standard of occupancy is "two heartbeats per bedroom." Landlords cannot restrict the number of occupants to eliminate families with children. Complaints about discrimination based on familial status account for a major portion of fair housing violations. Consistency and documentation of applied standards are crucial to compliance with the laws.

■ **F O R   E X A M P L E**   Greg owned an apartment building. One of his elderly tenants, Paul, was terminally ill. Paul requested that no children be allowed in the vacant apartment next door because the noise would be difficult for him to bear. Greg agreed and refused to rent to families with children. Even though Greg only wanted to make things easier for a dying tenant, he was nonetheless found to have violated the Federal Fair Housing Act by discriminating on the basis of familial status. Intentions, whether good or bad, are irrelevant in determining the violation of the Act.

A *handicapping condition* is an impairment that substantially limits one or more of a person's major life activities.

Handicapping condition. It is unlawful to discriminate against prospective buyers or tenants on the basis of a handicapping condition. Landlords must make reasonable accommodations to existing policies, practices, or services to permit persons with disabilities to have equal enjoyment of the premises. For instance, it would be reasonable for a landlord to permit service animals (such as guide dogs) in a normally no-pets building or to provide a designated handicapped parking space in a generally unreserved lot.

IN PRACTICE

The Federal Fair Housing Act's protection of disabled persons does not include those who are current users of illegal or controlled substances. Nor are individuals who have been convicted of the illegal manufacture or distribution of a controlled substance protected under this law. However, the law does prohibit discrimination against those who are participating in addiction recovery programs. For instance, a landlord could lawfully discriminate against a cocaine user but not against a rehabilitated member of Narcotics Anonymous.

People with handicapping conditions must be permitted to make reasonable modifications to the premises at their own expense. Such modifications might include lowering countertops or installing bath rails to accommodate a person in a wheelchair. Failure to permit reasonable modification constitutes discrimination. However, the law recognizes that some reasonable modifications might make a rental property undesirable to the general population. In such a case, the landlord is allowed to require that the property be restored to its previous condition by the tenant when the lease period ends.

The law does not prohibit restricting occupancy exclusively to persons with handicaps in dwellings that are designed specifically for their accommodation.

For new construction of certain multifamily properties, a number of accessibility and usability requirements must be met under the **Americans with Disabilities Act (ADA)**. Access is specified for public and common-use portions of the buildings, and adaptive and accessible design must be implemented for the interior of the dwelling units. Some states have their own accessibility laws as well.

Exemptions to the Federal Fair Housing Act

The Federal Fair Housing Act provides for certain exemptions. It is important for licensees to know in what situations the exemptions apply. However, licensees should be aware that *no exceptions apply when a real estate licensee is involved in a transaction*.

The sale or rental of a single-family home is exempt when

- the home is owned by an individual who does not own more than three such homes at one time (and who does not sell more than one every two years);
- a real estate broker is *not* involved in the transaction; and
- discriminatory advertising is not used.

The rental of rooms or units is exempt in an *owner-occupied* one-family to four-family dwelling.

Dwelling units owned by religious organizations may be restricted to people of the same religion if membership in the organization is not restricted on the basis of protected class. A private club that is not open to the public may restrict the rental or occupancy of lodgings that it owns to its members as long as the lodgings are not operated commercially.

The Federal Fair Housing Act does not require that housing be made available to any individual whose tenancy would constitute a direct threat to the health or safety of other individuals or that would result in substantial physical damage to the property of others.

Housing for older persons.   While the Federal Fair Housing Act protects families with children, certain properties can be restricted to occupancy by elderly persons. The Housing for Older Persons Act of 1995 (HOPA) allows certain exemptions from the familial status protection. Housing intended solely for occupancy by persons age 62 or older or housing occupied by at least one person 55 years of age or older per unit (where 80 percent of the units are occupied by individuals 55 or older) is exempt.

Jones v. Mayer

In 1968, the Supreme Court heard the case of *Jones v. Alfred H. Mayer Company*, 392 U.S. 409 (1968). In its decision, the Court upheld the Civil Rights Act of 1866. This decision is important because although the federal law exempts individual homeowners and certain groups, the 1866 law *prohibits all racial discrimination without exception*. A person who is discriminated against on the basis of race may still recover damages under the 1866 law. *Where race is involved, no exceptions apply.*

The U.S. Supreme Court has expanded the definition of the term *race* to include ancestral and ethnic characteristics, including certain physical, cultural, or linguistic characteristics that are commonly shared by a national origin group. These rulings are significant because discrimination on the basis of race, as it is now defined, affords due process of complaints under the provisions of the Civil Rights Act of 1866.

Enforcement of the Federal Fair Housing Act

The Federal Fair Housing Act is administered by the **Office of Fair Housing and Equal Opportunity (OFHEO)** under the direction of the Secretary of HUD. Any aggrieved person who believes illegal discrimination has occurred may file a complaint with HUD within one year of the alleged act. HUD may also initiate its own complaint. Complaints may be reported to the Office of Fair Housing and Equal Opportunity, Department of Housing and Urban Development, Washington, DC 20410, or to the Office of Fair Housing and Equal Opportunity in care of the nearest HUD regional office. Complaints also may be submitted directly to HUD using an online form.

Upon receiving a complaint, HUD initiates an investigation. Within 100 days of the filing of the complaint, HUD either determines that reasonable cause exists to bring a charge of illegal discrimination or dismisses the complaint. During this investigation period, HUD can attempt to resolve the dispute informally through conciliation. *Conciliation* is the resolution of a complaint by obtaining assurance that the person against whom the complaint was filed (the respondent) will remedy any violation that may have occurred. The respondent further agrees to take steps to eliminate or prevent discriminatory practices in the future. If necessary, these agreements can be enforced through civil action.

The aggrieved person has the right to seek relief through administrative proceedings. Administrative proceedings are hearings held before *administrative law judges (ALJs)*. An ALJ has the authority to award actual damages to the aggrieved person or persons and, if it is believed the public interest will be served, to impose monetary penalties. The penalties range can be up to $10,000 for the first offense, up to $25,000 for a second violation within five years, and up to $50,000 for further violations within seven years. The ALJ also has the authority to issue an injunction to order the offender to either do something (such as rent an apartment to the complaining party) or refrain from doing something (such as acting in a discriminatory manner).

The parties may elect civil action in federal court at any time within two years of the discriminatory act. For cases heard in federal court, unlimited punitive damages can be awarded in addition to actual damages. The court can also issue injunctions. As noted in Chapter 7, errors and omissions insurance carried by licensees normally does not cover losses caused by violations of the fair housing laws.

Whenever the attorney general has reasonable cause to believe that any person or group is engaged in a pattern or practice of resistance to the full enjoyment of any of the rights granted by the federal fair housing laws, the attorney general may file a civil action in any federal district court. Civil penalties may result in an amount not to exceed $50,000 for a first violation and an amount not to exceed $100,000 for second and subsequent violations.

Complaints brought under the Civil Rights Act of 1866 are taken directly to federal courts. The only time limit for bringing legal action is a state's statute of limitations for *torts*—injuries one individual inflicts on another.

■ EQUAL CREDIT OPPORTUNITY ACT

The Equal Credit Opportunity Act prohibits discrimination in granting credit based on
- race,
- color,
- religion,
- national origin,
- sex,
- marital status,
- age, and
- receipt of public assistance.

The federal **Equal Credit Opportunity Act (ECOA)** guarantees nondiscrimination in the granting of credit by protecting classes of persons similar to the Federal Fair Housing Act. It prohibits discrimination based on race, color, religion, national origin, sex, marital status, or age in the granting of credit. Marital status and age are classes that are unique to ECOA. It also prevents lenders from discriminating against recipients of public assistance programs such as food stamps and Social Security. As in the Federal Fair Housing Act, the ECOA requires that credit applications be considered only on the basis of income, net worth, job stability, and credit rating. More information about the ECOA is available at the Federal Trade Commission's Web site.

■ NORTH CAROLINA FAIR HOUSING ACT OF 1983

In 1983, North Carolina passed a fair housing law that is almost identical to the Federal Fair Housing Act of 1968. The North Carolina list of protected classes is the same as the list used under the federal Act. The major difference between the state and federal discrimination laws is the differences in exemptions.

Prohibited Acts

The **North Carolina Fair Housing Act of 1983** prohibits the same activities as the federal law (refer to the list of prohibited activities discussed under the Federal Fair Housing Act). Thus, one discriminatory act violates both federal and state laws and subjects the violator to both federal and state penalties.

Exemptions

While the state law's prohibited activities are identical to those of the federal law, the exemptions to the state Act contain substantial differences.

> There are substantial differences in exemptions under federal and state laws; the stricter law rules.

- ■ The Federal Fair Housing Act exempts private owners who sell their own homes without the use of a real estate broker. There is no similar exemption to the state Fair Housing Act. *Note that when there is a conflict between state and federal law, the most restrictive law applies:* persons selling their own homes must not resort to discriminatory practices even though they are exempted by federal law. The state does, however, exempt the rental of rooms in a private home occupied by the owner.
- ■ The state Act exempts the rental of a unit in a one- to four-unit residential building if the owner or one of the owner's family members lives in one of the units. The federal law exempts such a unit only if the owner lives in one of the units.
- ■ The state Act exempts the rental of rooms in a single-sex dormitory. The federal law does not include this exemption (although it is doubtful that such a practice would be prosecuted as a violation of the federal law).

The other exemptions in the federal Act are mirrored in the state Act. Again, if there is disagreement between the state and federal fair housing legislation, the stricter of the two will rule.

Enforcement of North Carolina Fair Housing Act

The first place to file a complaint by those who have been injured by discriminatory housing acts is the **North Carolina Human Relations Commission.** The Commission then begins investigating the complaint and simultaneously tries to resolve the conflict through conference, conciliation, or persuasion. If the Commission finds there are no reasonable grounds for the complaint, it is dismissed, but the injured party may still bring a discrimination suit in state court. However, if there are reasonable grounds to believe unlawful discrimination took place and the Commission's informal negotiation process does not work, the Commission must then

- ■ dismiss the complaint and issue a right-to-sue letter to the injured party (which entitles the party to bring a court case against the accused at the complainant's own expense) or
- ■ file a lawsuit in state court against the accused.

■ SEXUAL HARASSMENT

North Carolina has a law (G.S. 14-395) pertaining to sexual harassment of a prospective tenant by a landlord (lessor) or a lessor's agent. This statute defines sexual harassment as *unsolicited overt requests or demands for sexual acts* when (1) submission to such conduct is made a term of the execution or continuation of the lease agreement or (2) submission to or rejection of such conduct by an individual is used to determine whether rights under the lease are accorded.

Sexual harassment has been further defined as any type of sexual behavior that creates an intimidating, hostile, or offensive environment. Examples of sexual harassment include

- *verbal harassment*—sexual innuendo, suggestive comments, insults, jokes about sex or gender, sexual propositions, and threats;
- *nonverbal harassment*—suggestive or insulting sounds, leering, whistling, and obscene gestures; and
- *physical harassment*—inappropriate touching, pinching, brushing the body, fondling the body, coerced sexual intercourse, and sexual assault.

IN PRACTICE   The North Carolina Real Estate Commission can take disciplinary measures against licensees for violating state fair housing laws. Rule A.1601 Fair Housing states: "Conduct by a licensee which violates the provisions of the State Fair Housing Act constitutes improper conduct in violation of G.S. 93A-6(a)(10)."

■ IMPLICATIONS FOR BROKERS

To a large extent, the laws place the burden of responsibility for effecting and maintaining fair housing on real estate brokers. Licensees must comply with the laws, which are clear and widely known. The complainant does not have to prove that the accused was guilty of actual knowledge or specific intent—only the fact that discrimination occurred. In other words, if a licensee violated a fair housing law, that licensee could be found guilty of discrimination even if there was no intent to discriminate.

How does a broker go about complying with the laws and making that policy known? HUD offers guidelines for nondiscriminatory language and illustrations for use in real estate advertising. The agency further requires that every broker take affirmative marketing action in the choice of advertising media and in individual canvassing to ensure that all interested individuals have the same range of housing options.

In addition, the National Association of REALTORS® affirms that a broker's position can be emphasized and problems avoided by the prominent display of a sign stating that it is against company policy as well as state and federal laws to offer any information on the protected class composition of a neighborhood or to place restrictions on listing, showing, or providing information on the availability of homes for any of these reasons. If a prospect still expresses a locational preference for housing based on presence or absence of a protected class, the NAR's guidelines suggest the following response: "I cannot give you that kind of advice. I will show you several homes that meet your specifications. You will have to decide which one you want."

There is more to fair housing practices than just following the letter of the law, however. Discrimination involves a sensitive area of human emotions—specifically, fear and the drive for self-preservation based on considerable prejudice and misconception. The broker who complies with the law still must interact, in many cases, with a general public whose attitudes cannot be altered by legislation alone. Therefore, a licensee who wishes to comply with the fair housing laws and also succeed in the real estate business must work to educate the public.

For every broker, a sincere, positive attitude toward fair housing laws is a good start in dealing with this sensitive issue. It provides an effective model for all who come in contact with the licensee. Active cooperation with local real estate board programs and community committees is also an excellent idea. This shows the licensee's willingness to serve the community and observe the laws, and it helps to change public attitudes. Both factors can result in good public relations and, ultimately, more business for the licensee.

IN PRACTICE　Agents encounter clients and customers who may want to discriminate on purpose or who may not realize their intentions are actually forms of discrimination. Following are some typical situations with suggested responses.

Situation: A seller-client wants an agent to discriminate against a protected class.

Response: The agent should advise the seller that the Act prohibits sellers, when using a broker, to discriminate. Suggested response: "Under the North Carolina Fair Housing Act, you have a right to sell to anyone as long as you do not discriminate on the basis of race, color, religion, sex, handicap, national origin, or familial status."

Situation: A buyer (client or customer) doesn't want to be shown dwellings in a neighborhood occupied by persons in a protected class.

Response: Collect all information on all properties in all areas that meet the buyer's needs. Have the information available and allow the buyer to choose which properties to see.

Situation: A buyer wants information about the racial and/or ethnic makeup of a neighborhood in which the buyer is interested.

Response: "We do not keep records or statistics on racial or ethnic population in particular areas since distribution of that information would be a violation of state and federal fair housing laws."

■ AMERICANS WITH DISABILITIES ACT

Although the Americans with Disabilities Act (ADA) is not a housing or credit law, it has a significant effect on the real estate industry. The ADA is important to licensees because it addresses the rights of individuals with disabilities in employment and public accommodations. Real estate brokers are often employers, and real estate brokerage offices are public spaces. The ADA's goal is to enable individuals with disabilities to become part of the economic and social mainstream of society.

> The Americans with Disabilities Act requires reasonable accommodations in employment and access to goods, services, and public buildings.

Title I of the ADA requires that employers (including real estate brokers) make *reasonable accommodations* that enable an individual with a disability to perform essential job functions. Reasonable accommodations include making the work site accessible, restructuring a job, providing part-time or flexible work schedules, and modifying equipment that is used on the job. The provisions of the ADA apply to any employer with 15 or more employees.

Title III of the ADA provides for accessibility to goods and services for individuals with disabilities. While the federal civil rights laws have traditionally been viewed in the real estate industry as housing-related, the practices of licensees who deal with nonresidential property are significantly affected by the ADA. Because people with disabilities have the right to full and equal access to businesses and public services under the ADA, building owners and managers must ensure that any obstacle restricting this right is eliminated. The Americans with Disabilities Act Accessibility Guidelines (ADAAG) contain detailed specifications for designing parking spaces, curb ramps, elevators, drinking fountains, toilet facilities, and directional signs to ensure maximum accessibility.

ADA and the Federal Fair Housing Act

The ADA exempts two types of property from its requirements:

1. Property that is covered by the Federal Fair Housing Act
2. Property that is exempt from coverage by the Federal Fair Housing Act

Some properties, however, are subject to both laws. For example, in an apartment complex, the rental office is a *place of public accommodation*. As such, the rental office is covered by the ADA, and must be accessible to persons with disabilities at the owner's expense. The Federal Fair Housing Act would cover individual rental units. A tenant who wishes to modify the unit to make it accessible would be responsible for the cost.

IN PRACTICE

Real estate agents need a general knowledge of the ADA's provisions. It is necessary that a broker's workplace and employment policies comply with the law. Also, licensees who are building managers must ensure that the properties are legally accessible. However, ADA compliance questions may arise with regard to a client's property too. Unless the agent is a qualified ADA expert, it is best to advise commercial clients to seek the services of an attorney, an architect, or a consultant who specializes in ADA issues. It is possible that an appraiser may be liable for failing to identify and account for a property's noncompliance.

■ FAIR HOUSING PROHIBITED PRACTICES

For the civil rights laws to accomplish their goal of eliminating discrimination, licensees must apply them routinely. Of course, compliance also means that licensees avoid violating both the laws and the ethical standards of the profession. The following discussion examines the ethical and legal issues that confront real estate licensees.

Blockbusting

> *Blockbusting*: Encouraging the sale or renting of property by claiming that the entry of a protected class into the neighborhood will negatively affect property values.

Blockbusting (also known as **panic peddling**) is the act of encouraging people to sell or rent their homes by claiming that the entry of a protected class into the neighborhood will have some negative impact on property values. Blockbusting was a common practice during the 1950s and 1960s, as unscrupulous real estate agents profited by fueling *white flight* from cities to suburbs. Any message, however subtle, that property should be sold or rented because the neighborhood is *undergoing changes* is considered blockbusting. It is illegal to assert that the presence of members of a certain protected class will cause property values to decline, crime or antisocial behavior to increase, and the quality of schools to suffer.

A critical element in blockbusting, according to HUD, is the profit motive. A property owner may be intimidated into selling a property at a depressed price to the blockbuster, who in turn sells the property to another person at a higher price. Another term for this activity is *panic selling*. To avoid accusations of blockbusting, licensees should use good judgment when choosing locations and methods for marketing their services and soliciting listings.

Steering

> *Steering*: Channeling home seekers toward or away from particular neighborhoods based on presence or absence of a protected class.

Steering is the **channeling** of home seekers to particular neighborhoods based on the presence or absence of a protected class. It also includes discouraging potential buyers from considering some areas. In either case, it is an illegal limitation of a purchaser's options.

The intent of steering may be either to preserve the character of a neighborhood or to change its character intentionally. Many cases of steering are subtle, motivated by assumptions or perceptions about a home seeker's preferences, based on some stereotype. Assumptions are not only dangerous—they are often *wrong*. The licensee cannot *assume* that a prospective home seeker expects to be directed to certain neighborhoods or properties. Steering anyone is illegal. Licensees should always allow the client to select which properties or neighborhoods are viewed.

■ **FOR EXAMPLE**
- An agent lists a home in a predominantly Hispanic neighborhood. He places an ad in a publication primarily aimed at Hispanic readers and does not advertise the property in any other publications.
- An agent showing property to a black couple in a predominantly white neighborhood does not use his best efforts to present the offer and get it accepted.
- A broker is marketing homes in a new subdivision and in pictorial ads shows only adults enjoying the amenities.

Advertising

No advertisement of property for sale or rent may include language indicating a preference or limitation for the protected class status of the prospective buyer or tenant. No exception to this rule exists, regardless of how subtle the choice of words. HUD's regulations cite examples that are considered discriminatory (see Figure 20.3).

The media used for promoting property or real estate services cannot target one protected class population to the exclusion of others. The selective use of media, whether by language or geography, may have discriminatory impact. For instance, advertising property only in a Korean-language newspaper tends to discriminate against non-Koreans. Similarly, limiting advertising to a magazine targeted to female subscribers may be construed as a discriminatory act. However, if an advertisement also appears in general-circulation media, it may be legal.

Appraising

Those who prepare appraisals or any statements of valuation, whether they are formal or informal, oral or written (including a competitive market analysis), may consider any factors that affect value. However, race, color, religion, national origin, sex, handicap, and familial status are not factors that may be considered.

Redlining

Redlining is an illegal practice by lending institutions to deny or discourage loan applications in an area based on its racial composition or deterioration.

The practice of refusing to make mortgage loans or issue insurance policies in specific areas for reasons other than the economic qualifications of the applicants or the collateral value of the property offered is known as **redlining.** Redlining refers to literally drawing a line around particular areas. This practice is often a major contributor to the deterioration of older neighborhoods. Redlining is frequently based on racial or ethnic grounds rather than on any real objection to an applicant's creditworthiness. For example, the lender makes a policy decision that no property in a certain area is qualified for a loan, no matter who wants to buy it, because of the neighborhood's ethnic character. The Federal Fair Housing Act prohibits discrimination in mortgage lending and covers not only the actions of primary lenders but also activities in the secondary mortgage market. A lending institution can refuse a loan, but solely on *sound* economic grounds. Charging different loan fees or interest rates based on protected class membership by the proposed borrower also would constitute redlining.

The Home Mortgage Disclosure Act requires that all institutional mortgage lenders with assets in excess of $10 million and one or more offices in a given geographic area make annual reports. The reports must detail all mortgage loans the institution has made or purchased, broken down by census tract. This law enables

F I G U R E   20.3   HUD's Advertising Guidelines

Category	Rule	Permitted	Not Permitted
Race Color National Origin	No discriminatory limitation or preference may be expressed	"master bedroom" "good neighborhood"	"white neighborhood" "no French"
Religion	No religious preference or limitation	"chapel on premises" "kosher meals available" "Merry Christmas"	"no Muslims" "nice Christian family" "near great Catholic school"
Sex	No explicit preference based on gender	"mother-in-law suite" "master bedroom" "bachelor apartment"	"great house for a man" "wife's dream kitchen" "only female tenants allowed"
Handicap	No exclusions or limitations based on disability	"wheelchair ramp" "walk to shopping" "walk-in closet"	"no wheelchairs" "able-bodied tenants only"
Familial Status	No preference or limitation based on family size or composition	"two-bedroom" "family room" "quiet neighborhood"	"no more than two children" "adults only"
Photographs Illustrations of People	People should be clearly representative and nonexclusive	Illustrations showing ethnic races, family groups, singles, etc.	Illustrations showing groups of all-adult people, people of a single ethnicity, elderly white adults, etc.

the government to detect patterns of lending behavior that might constitute redlining.

Intent and Effect

If a property owner or real estate licensee *purposely* sets out to engage in blockbusting, steering, or other unfair activities, the intent to discriminate is obvious. However, owners and licensees must examine their activities and policies carefully to determine whether they have *unintentional discriminatory effects*. Whenever policies or practices result in unequal treatment of persons in the protected classes, they are considered discriminatory regardless of any innocent intent. This *effects* test is applied by regulatory agencies to determine whether an individual has been subjected to discrimination.

Threats or Acts of Violence

Being a real estate agent is not generally considered a dangerous occupation. However, some licensees may find themselves the targets of threats or violence merely for complying with fair housing laws. The Federal Fair Housing Act of 1968 protects the rights of those who seek the benefits of the open housing law. It also protects property owners and brokers who aid or encourage the enjoyment of open housing rights. Threats, coercion, and intimidation are punishable by criminal action. In such a case, the victim should report the incident immediately to the local police and to the nearest office of the Federal Bureau of Investigation.

■ PROFESSIONAL ETHICS

Professional conduct involves more than just complying with the law. In real estate, state licensing laws establish those activities that are illegal and therefore prohibited. However, merely complying with the letter of the law may not be enough: licensees may perform *legally*, yet not *ethically*. *Ethics* refers to a system of *moral* principles, rules, and standards of conduct. The ethical system of a profession establishes conduct that goes beyond merely complying with the law. These moral principles address two sides of a profession:

1. They establish standards for integrity and competence in dealing with consumers of an industry's services.
2. They define a code of conduct for relations within the industry, among its professionals.

Code of Ethics

One way that many organizations address ethics among their members or in their respective businesses is by adopting codes of professional conduct. A **code of ethics** is a written system of standards for ethical conduct. The code contains statements designed to advise, guide, and regulate job behavior. To be effective, a code of ethics must be specific by dictating rules that either prohibit or demand certain behavior. Lofty statements of positive goals are not especially helpful. By including sanctions for violators, a code of ethics becomes more effective.

The National Association of REALTORS® (NAR), the largest trade association in the country, adopted a Code of Ethics for its members in 1913. REALTORS® are expected to subscribe to this strict code of conduct. NAR has established procedures for professional standards committees at the local, state, and national levels of the organization to administer compliance. Interpretations of the code are known as *Standards of Practice*. NAR has instituted a quadrennial ethics refresher course requirement for all REALTORS®. The NAR Code of Ethics has proved helpful because it contains practical applications of business ethics. Many other professional organizations in the real estate industry have codes of ethics as well. In addition, many state real estate regulatory commissions are required by law to establish codes or canons of ethical behavior for their states' licensees.

■ RELATED WEB SITES

Federal Trade Commission: *www.ftc.gov*
National Association of REALTORS®: *www.realtor.org*
National Fair Housing Advocate Online: *www.fairhousing.com*
Office of Fair Housing and Equal Opportunity:
    www.hud.gov/offices/fheo/index.cfm

■ SUMMARY

The federal regulations regarding equal opportunity in housing are contained principally in two laws. The Civil Rights Act of 1866 prohibits all racial discrimination in the sale or leasing of all real and personal property; there is no exception to this law. The Federal Fair Housing Act (Title VIII of the Civil Rights Act of 1968), as amended, prohibits discrimination on the basis of race, color, religion, sex, handicap, familial status, or national origin in the sale, rental, or financing of residential property. Discriminatory actions include refusing to deal with an individual or a specific group, changing any terms of a real estate or loan transaction, changing the services offered for any individual or group, creating statements or advertisements that indicate discriminatory restrictions, or otherwise attempting to make a dwelling unavailable to any person or group because of membership in a protected class. The law also prohibits steering, blockbusting, and redlining.

Complaints under the Federal Fair Housing Act may be reported to and investigated by the Department of Housing and Urban Development (HUD) through the Office of Fair Housing and Equal Opportunity (OFHEO). Such complaints may also be taken directly to U.S. district courts. In states and localities that have enacted fair housing legislation that is substantially equivalent to the federal law, complaints are handled by state and local agencies and state courts. Complaints under the Civil Rights Act of 1866 must be taken to federal courts.

Equal Credit Opportunity Act (ECOA) prohibits discrimination in the granting of credit. The protected classes of ECOA are slightly different from the classes under Fair Housing because they include income source, age, and marital status instead of familial status.

State equal opportunity housing laws are found in the North Carolina Fair Housing Act of 1983. Its provisions are substantially identical to the Federal Fair Housing Act, except in the area of allowable exemptions. Whereas a for-sale-by-owner is exempt under the federal law, the North Carolina law does not exempt private sellers even if they are not using a real estate licensee or discriminatory ads.

Although the state law allows discrimination with a one-family to four-family unit rental if the owner or a family member occupies one of the units, the federal law requires owner-occupancy for exemption. North Carolina also allows same sex dormitories that are not federally acceptable. The first place to file a complaint of discrimination in North Carolina is with the North Carolina Human Relations Commission. If there is a conflict between the state and federal fair housing laws, the stricter law will prevail.

The Americans with Disabilities Act (ADA) affects the real estate industry somewhat indirectly. Because a real estate brokerage office is a place of employment as well as a place of public accommodation, the real estate office must be in compliance with the ADA requirements. Handicapping condition is any physical or mental impairment that seriously impacts at least one major life function.

A real estate business is only as good as its reputation. Real estate licensees can maintain good reputations by demonstrating good business ability and adhering to ethical standards of business practices. Many licensees subscribe to a code of ethics as members of professional real estate organizations.

QUESTIONS

1. Which of the following actions is permitted under the Federal Fair Housing Act?
   a. Advertising property for sale only to a particular ethnic group
   b. Altering the terms of a loan for a member of a minority group
   c. Refusing to sell a home to an individual because of a poor credit history
   d. Telling a wheelchair-bound individual that an available apartment has been rented because the property owner does not want to allow reasonable accommodations by the applicant

2. What will happen if there is conflict between the federal and state fair housing legislation?
   a. The federal law will prevail over the state law.
   b. The state law will prevail over the federal law.
   c. The more recent law will prevail.
   d. The stricter law will prevail.

3. The Civil Rights Act of 1866 is unique because it
   a. has been broadened to protect the aged.
   b. adds welfare recipients as a protected class.
   c. contains *choose your neighbor* provisions.
   d. provides no exceptions to racial discrimination.

4. "They are the first of their kind to move into the neighborhood. Better list with me today before the property values start to drop!" is an example of
   a. steering.
   b. blockbusting.
   c. redlining.
   d. testing.

5. The act of channeling home seekers to a particular area either to maintain or to change the character of the neighborhood is
   a. blockbusting.
   b. redlining.
   c. steering.
   d. permitted under the Federal Fair Housing Act of 1968.

6. Under the provisions of the Federal Fair Housing Act, if a lender refuses to make loans in certain areas because the population is made up of more than 25 percent African-Americans, the lender is probably practicing
   a. redlining.
   b. blockbusting.
   c. steering.
   d. borrower qualifying.

7. Which practice is *NOT* permitted under the Federal Fair Housing Act as amended?
   I. Preference in the rental of rooms by a private club to its members
   II. An owner of a 20-unit apartment building renting exclusively to females
   a. I only
   b. II only
   c. Both I and II
   d. Neither I nor II

8. Under federal law, families with children may be refused rental or purchase in buildings where strict conditions are met and occupancy is reserved exclusively for those at least how many years old?
   a. 55
   b. 60
   c. 62
   d. 65

9. A newspaper ad reads: "For sale: 4 BR brick home; Redwood School District; excellent location; short walk to St. John's Catholic Church; and right on the bus line. Move-in conditions. Priced to sell." Which of the following statements is *TRUE*?
   a. The ad describes the property for sale and is very appropriate.
   b. The fair housing laws do not apply to newspaper advertising.
   c. The ad should state that the property is available to families with children.
   d. The ad should not mention St. John's Catholic Church.

10. An African American real estate broker's practice of offering a special discount to African American clients is
    a. legally acceptable.
    b. illegal.
    c. legal but ill-advised.
    d. of no consequence.

11. Protection from discrimination against a single father with a child under 18 in the sale or rental of real estate is provided by the
    a. Fair Housing Amendments Act of 1988.
    b. Civil Rights Act of 1866.
    c. Americans with Disabilities Act.
    d. Equal Credit Opportunity Act of 1974.

12. The Federal Fair Housing Amendments Act of 1988 added which of the following as protected classes?
    a. Occupation and source of income
    b. Handicap and familial status
    c. Political affiliation and country of origin
    d. Age and marital status

13. A real estate agent told a single man with two small children that units for sale in a condominium complex are available only to married couples with no children. Which of the following statements is *TRUE*?
    a. The condominium complex is permitted to restrict buyers in any way as long as it is uniform in applying the restrictions.
    b. Multi-family complexes are exempt from the fair housing laws.
    c. The man may file a fair housing complaint alleging discrimination on the basis of familial status.
    d. The man may file a fair housing complaint alleging discrimination on the basis of marital status.

14. The seller requests that showings be restricted to buyers of a particular race and national origin. The listing agent
    a. must obey the seller-client regardless of the agent's personal beliefs.
    b. should terminate the listing if the seller will not reconsider the instructions.
    c. may obey the client as long as the agent is not obvious in the restriction.
    d. should ignore the seller's instructions and show to all buyers.

15. In North Carolina, a person who feels she has been discriminated against in housing by a property owner should file a complaint with the
    a. local sheriff.
    b. North Carolina Human Relations Commission.
    c. North Carolina Board of REALTORS®.
    d. North Carolina Real Estate Commission.

16. After a broker takes a residential listing, the owner states that he does not want his home shown or sold to a Mexican buyer. The broker should
    a. advertise the property exclusively in Spanish-language newspapers.
    b. explain that the broker cannot knowingly comply with any instruction that violates federal law.
    c. abide by the client's directions since the agency's duty of obedience overrides fair housing laws.
    d. require that the owner sign a separate legal document stating the additional instruction as an amendment to the listing agreements.

17. All of the following are in violation of the Federal Fair Housing Act of 1968 *EXCEPT* the
    a. refusal of a property manager to rent an apartment to a Catholic couple who are otherwise qualified.
    b. general policy of a loan company to avoid granting home loans in an ethnically transitional neighborhoods.
    c. intentional neglect of a broker to show an Asian family property listings in all-white neighborhoods.
    d. insistence of a widowed woman on renting her spare bedroom only to another widow.

18. A real estate broker wants to end racial segregation. As an office policy, the broker requires that agents show prospective buyers from racial or ethnic minority groups only properties that are in certain areas of town in order to create more diversity in residential areas. The broker has prepared a map illustrating the appropriate neighborhoods for each racial or ethnic group. Which of the following statements is true regarding this broker's policy?

a. The broker's policy constitutes blockbusting only because of the use of the prepared area map.

b. It constitutes illegal steering, regardless of the broker's intentions.

c. The broker's policy clearly shows the intent to improve community diversity and is therefore legal.

d. The broker's policy constitutes steering because the broker requires policy compliance by his agents.

19. All of the following are protected classes under the Equal Credit Opportunity Act EXCEPT

a. national origin.

b. familial status.

c. religion.

d. age.

CHAPTER 21

Environmental Issues and the Real Estate Transaction

■ **LEARNING OBJECTIVES** *When you have finished reading this chapter, you should be able to*

■ **identify** the basic environmental hazards of which an agent should be aware in order to protect the interests of clients.

■ **describe** the warning signs, characteristics, causes, and solutions of the most common environmental hazards found in real estate transactions.

■ **understand** the disclosure requirements of the Lead-Based Paint Hazard Reduction Act.

■ **recognize** North Carolina environmental laws and their relevance to specific transactions.

■ **explain** the liability issues arising under environmental protection laws.

■ **name** the agencies that administer and enforce environmental laws.

■ **define** these *key terms:*

asbestos	landfill	NC Leaking Petroleum
carbon monoxide	Lead-Based Paint Hazard	Underground Storage
Comprehensive	Reduction Act	Tank Cleanup Act
Environmental	lead poisoning	NC Sediment Pollution
Response,	mitigation	Control Act
Compensation, and	NC Coastal Area	radon
Liability Act (CERCLA)	Management Act	underground storage tank
electromagnetic fields	(CAMA)	(UST)
(EMFs)	NC Dredge and Fill Act	urea-formaldehyde foam
encapsulation		insulation (UFFI)
groundwater		water table

ENVIRONMENTAL ISSUES

Most states have recognized the need to balance the legitimate commercial use of land with the needs to preserve vital resources and protect the quality of their air, water, and soil. A growing number of homebuyers base their decisions in part on the desire for fresh air, clean water, and outdoor recreational opportunities. Preservation of a state's environment both enhances the quality of life and helps strengthen property values. The prevention and cleanup of pollutants and toxic wastes not only revitalize the land but also create greater opportunities for responsible development.

Environmental issues have become an important factor in the practice of real estate. Consumers are becoming more health-conscious and safety-concerned and are enforcing their rights to make informed decisions. Scientists are learning more about our environment, and consumers are reacting by demanding that their surroundings be free of chemical hazards. These developments affect not only participants in sales transactions, but also appraisers, developers, lending institutions, and property managers.

Real estate licensees must be alert to the existence of environmental hazards. Although it is important to ensure the health and safety of property users, the burden of disclosure or elimination of hazards is heaviest at the time ownership of property transfers. This creates added liability for real estate practitioners if the presence of a toxic substance causes a health problem. If a property buyer suffers physical harm because of the substance, the licensee can be vulnerable to a personal injury suit in addition to other legal liability. Environmental issues are health issues, and health issues based on environmental hazards have become real estate issues. For this reason, it is extremely important that licensees not only make property disclosures but also see that prospective purchasers get authoritative information about and inspections for hazardous substances so that they can make informed decisions.

Licensees should be familiar with state and federal environmental laws and the regulatory agencies that enforce them. Licensees are not expected to have the technical expertise necessary to determine whether a hazardous substance is present. However, they must be aware of environmental issues and take steps to ensure that the interests of all parties involved in real estate transactions are protected.

HAZARDOUS SUBSTANCES

Pollution and hazardous substances in the environment are of interest to real estate brokers because they affect the attractiveness, desirability, and market value of cities, neighborhoods, and backyards. A toxic environment is not a place where anyone would want to live (see Figure 21.1).

Asbestos

Asbestos is a mineral that was once used as insulation because it is resistant to fire and contains heat effectively. Until the use of asbestos insulation was banned in 1978, asbestos was found in most residential construction. It was a component

FIGURE 21.1 Environmental Hazards

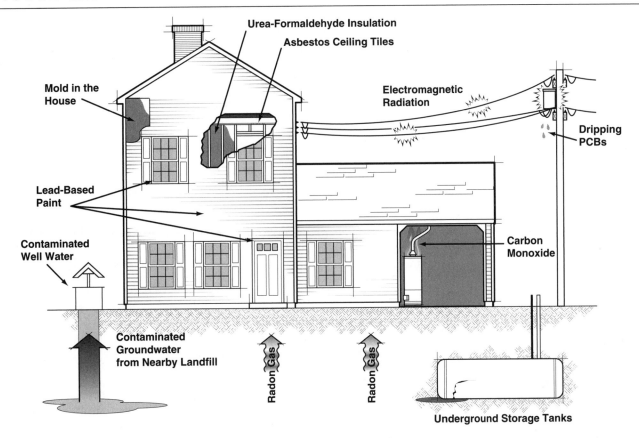

Asbestos insulation can create airborne contaminants that may result in respiratory diseases and cancer.

of more than 3,000 types of building materials, including appliances, ceiling and floor tiles, exterior siding, and roofing. The Environmental Protection Agency (EPA) estimates that about 20 percent of the nation's commercial and public buildings contain asbestos.

Today, we know that inhaling microscopic asbestos fibers may result in a variety of respiratory diseases as well as lung and stomach cancer. The mere presence of asbestos insulation is not necessarily a health hazard if the asbestos-laden item is intact. Asbestos is harmful only if it is disturbed or exposed, as often occurs during renovation or remodeling. Asbestos is highly *friable;* that is, as it ages, asbestos fibers break down easily into tiny filaments and particles. When these particles become airborne, they pose a health risk to humans. Airborne asbestos contamination is most prevalent in public and commercial buildings, including schools. If the asbestos fibers in the indoor air of a building reach a dangerous level, the building becomes almost impossible to lease, finance, or insure since no safe level of asbestos exposure has been determined.

Asbestos contamination also can be found in residential properties. Asbestos was used to cover pipes, ducts, plus heating and hot water units. Its fire-resistant properties made it a popular material for use in floor tile, exterior siding, and roofing products. Though it may be easy to identify asbestos when it is visible (for instance, when it is wrapped around heating units and water pipes), identification may be more difficult when it is behind walls or under floors.

Asbestos is costly to remove because the process requires state-licensed asbestos abatement contractors and specially sealed environments. In addition, removal itself may be dangerous: improper removal procedures may further contaminate the air within the structure. The waste generated should be disposed of at a licensed facility, which further adds to the expense of removal. **Encapsulation**, or the sealing off of disintegrating asbestos, is an alternate method of asbestos control that may be preferable to removal in certain circumstances. However, an owner must periodically monitor the condition of the encapsulated asbestos to make sure it is not disintegrating.

Tests can be conducted to determine the level of airborne asbestos to provide an accurate disclosure in a sales transaction. An engineer skilled in identifying the presence of materials that contain asbestos can perform a thorough analysis of a building. An asbestos report is now required in North Carolina before a permit will be issued for the reconstruction, renovation, or demolition of any residential or commercial structure. Either of these approaches can satisfy the concerns of a consumer. Appraisers also should be aware of the possible presence of asbestos.

More information on asbestos-related issues is available from the EPA (telephone: 202-554-1404). In addition, the EPA has numerous publications that provide guidance, information, and assistance with asbestos issues.

Lead-Based Paint and Other Lead Hazards

Lead was used as a pigment and drying agent in alkyd oil-based paint prior to 1978. Lead-based paint may be on any interior or exterior surface, but it is particularly common on doors, windows, and other woodwork. The federal government estimates that lead is present in about 75 percent of all private housing built before 1978; that involves approximately 57 million homes, ranging from low-income apartments to million-dollar mansions.

Lead poisoning from paint or other sources can result in damage to the brain, nervous system, kidneys, and blood.

An elevated level of lead in the human body causes **lead poisoning** that can lead to serious damage to the brain, kidneys, nervous system, and red blood cells. The degree of harm is related to the amount of exposure and the age at which a person is exposed. Children are most at risk, and it is estimated that as many as one in every six children may have dangerously high amounts of lead in the blood that may first manifest as learning disabilities. Lead dust can be ingested from the hands by a crawling infant, inhaled by any occupant of a structure, or ingested from the water supply because of lead pipes or lead solder. In fact, lead particles can be present elsewhere, too. Soil and groundwater may be contaminated by everything from lead plumbing in leaking landfills to discarded skeet and bullets from an old shooting range. High levels of lead have been found in the soil near waste-to-energy incinerators.

The residential use of lead-based paint was banned in 1978. Licensees who are involved in the sale, management, financing, or appraisal of properties constructed before 1978 face potential liability for any personal injury that might be suffered by an occupant. Numerous legislative efforts affect licensees, sellers, and landlords. There is considerable controversy about practical approaches for handling the presence of lead-based paint. Some suggest that it should be removed; others argue that it should be encapsulated; still others advocate testing to determine the amount of lead present, which then would be disclosed to a prospective owner or resident. In many states, only licensed lead inspectors, abatement contractors, risk assessors, abatement project designers, and abatement workers may deal with the removal or encapsulation of lead in a structure.

No federal law requires that homeowners test for the presence of lead-based paint. However, known lead-based paint hazards must be disclosed. In 1996, the EPA and the Department of Housing and Urban Development (HUD) issued final regulations requiring disclosure of the presence of any known lead-based paint hazards to potential buyers or renters. Under the Residential **Lead-Based Paint Hazard Reduction Act**, persons selling or leasing residential housing constructed before 1978 must disclose the presence of known lead-based paint and provide purchasers or lessees with any relevant records or reports. A lead-based paint disclosure statement must be attached to all sales contracts and leases regarding residential properties built before 1978, and a lead hazard informational pamphlet must be distributed to all prospective buyers and tenants. Purchasers and tenants must be given ten days in which to conduct risk assessments or inspections for lead-based paint or lead-based paint hazards. Purchasers are not bound by any real estate contract until the ten-day period has expired. A tenant's right to rescind a lease under this Act terminate when the tenant begins occupancy of the rental unit. The regulations specifically require that real estate agents ensure that all parties comply with the law. The purpose of the rule is to ensure that buyers and renters of housing built prior to 1978 receive proper disclosures. The North Carolina law, the Lead-Based Paint Poisoning Act of 1971 (NCGS §130A-131.5), is a statute that targets the elimination of lead-based paint in houses connected with HUD-assisted projects. Note that lead poisoning may also result from plumbing systems that contain lead pipes. Systems that use lead pipes should be tested frequently. EPA guidance pamphlets and other information about lead-based hazards are available from the National Lead Information Center, 800-424-5323, or online.

Radon

Radon is a radioactive gas produced as a by-product of the natural decay of other radioactive substances. Although radon can occur anywhere, some areas are known to have abnormally high amounts. Radon is found in every state, with the highest concentrations in the plains states, the upper Midwest, and northeastern United States (see Figure 21.2). Radon has been found in every county in North Carolina, with the heaviest concentration in the mountainous areas of the state. If radon dissipates into the atmosphere, it is not likely to cause harm. However, when radon enters buildings and is trapped in high concentrations (usually in basements with inadequate ventilation), it can cause health problems.

Opinions differ as to minimum safe levels, but the EPA has established guidelines that concentrations of 4.0 picocuries or higher are undesirable. Exposure to radon does not usually cause immediate symptoms, but prolonged contact with elevated levels has been linked to increased risk of lung cancer. Growing evidence suggests that radon may be the most underestimated cause of lung cancer, particularly for children, individuals who smoke, and those who spend considerable time indoors.

Because radon is clear, odorless and tasteless, it is impossible to detect without testing. Care should be exercised in the manner in which tests are conducted to ensure that the results are accurate. Radon levels vary, depending on the amount

FIGURE 21.2 **Radon Concentration in the United States**

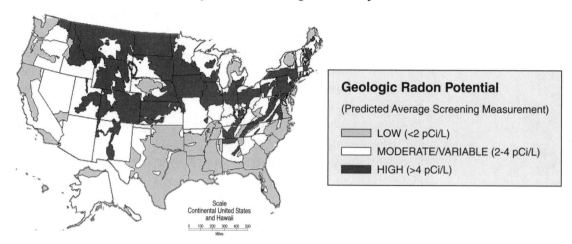

GENERALIZED GEOLOGIC RADON POTENTIAL OF THE UNITED STATES
by the U.S. Geological Survey

of fresh air that circulates through a house, the weather conditions, and the time of year. It is relatively easy to reduce levels of radon by installing a **mitigation** system using ventilation systems or exhaust fans.

> *Radon* is a naturally occurring radioactive gas that is a suspected cause of lung cancer.

Interestingly, the modern practice of creating energy-efficient homes and buildings with practically airtight walls and windows may increase the potential for radon gas accumulation. Once radon enters a building through tiny openings in the foundation or around openings for pipes or drains and accumulates in a low area like a basement, efficient heating and ventilation systems can rapidly spread the gas throughout the building.

Home radon-detection kits are available, although radon-detection professionals can conduct more accurate testing. It is estimated that about one-third of all radon testing is done in connection with a real estate transaction. The EPA's pamphlet "A Citizen's Guide to Radon" is available from your local EPA office or on the EPA Web site. North Carolina also has a radon-specific Web site listed at the end of the chapter.

Urea-Formaldehyde

Urea-formaldehyde was first used in building materials, particularly insulation, in the 1970s. Gases leak out of the **urea-formaldehyde foam insulation (UFFI),** as it hardens, and they become trapped in the interior of a building. In 1982, the Consumer Product Safety Commission originally banned the use of UFFI; but the ban was reduced to a warning after courts determined that there was insufficient evidence to support a ban. Urea-formaldehyde is known to cause cancer in animals, though the evidence of its effect on humans is inconclusive.

Formaldehyde does cause some individuals to suffer respiratory problems or asthma attacks as well as eye and skin irritations. Consumers are becoming increasingly wary of the presence of formaldehyde, particularly if they are sensitive to it.

UFFI is an insulating foam that can release harmful formaldehyde gases.

Tests can be conducted to determine the level of formaldehyde gas in a house. Again, however, care should be exercised to ensure that the results of the tests are accurate and that the source of the gases is properly identified. Elevated levels could be due to a source other than the insulation such as glues or bonding agents found in furniture or other home furnishings. Licensees should be careful that any conditions in an agreement of sale that require tests for formaldehyde are worded properly to identify the purpose for which the tests are being conducted, such as to determine the presence of the insulation or some other source. Appraisers should also be aware of the presence of UFFI.

Carbon Monoxide

Carbon monoxide is a by-product of incomplete fuel combustion that may result in deathly concentrations in poorly ventilated areas.

Carbon monoxide (CO) is a colorless, odorless gas that occurs as a by-product of burning such fuels as wood, oil, and natural gas if combustion is incomplete. Furnaces, water heaters, space heaters, fireplaces, and wood stoves all produce CO as a natural result of their combustion of fuel. When these appliances function properly and are properly ventilated, their CO emissions are not a problem. When improper ventilation or equipment malfunctions permit large quantities of CO to be released into a residence or commercial structure, it poses a significant health hazard. Its effects are compounded by the fact that CO is so difficult to detect. Carbon monoxide is quickly absorbed by the human body where it inhibits the blood's ability to transport oxygen, resulting in dizziness and nausea. As the concentrations of CO increase, the symptoms become more severe. More than 200 deaths from CO poisoning occur each year.

Carbon monoxide detectors are available, and their use is mandatory in some areas. Annual maintenance of heating systems also helps avoid CO exposure. Buyers should have an inspection of the HVAC system that includes CO monitoring prior to purchase.

Electromagnetic Fields

EMFs are produced by electrical currents and may be related to a variety of health complaints.

Electromagnetic fields (EMFs) are generated by the movement of electrical currents. The use of any electrical appliance creates a small field of electromagnetic radiation: clock radios, blow dryers, televisions, and computers all produce EMFs. The major concern regarding electromagnetic fields involves high-tension power lines. The EMFs produced by these high-voltage lines, as well as by secondary distribution lines and transformers, are suspected of causing cancer, hormonal changes, and behavioral abnormalities. There is considerable controversy (and much conflicting evidence) about whether EMFs pose a health hazard. In a May 1999 report to the U.S. Congress, the National Institute of Environmental Health Science reported that there is no evidence of a correlation between EMFs and adverse health effects. Buyers who are aware of the controversy may, however, be unwilling to purchase property near power lines or transformers. As research into EMFs continues, real estate licensees should stay informed about current findings. At the time of this publication, Progress Energy's Web site states that they will address questions about EMFs through their customer service number (800-700-8744).

Groundwater Contamination

Groundwater is the water that exists under the earth's surface within the tiny spaces or crevices in geological formations. Groundwater forms the water table, the natural level at which the ground is saturated. This may be near the surface in areas where the water table is very high or several hundred feet underground. Surface water also can be absorbed into the groundwater.

Any contamination of the underground water can threaten the supply of pure, clean water for private wells or public water systems. If groundwater is not protected from contamination, the earth's natural filtering systems may be inadequate to ensure the availability of pure water. Numerous state and federal laws have been enacted to preserve and protect the water supply including the amended Safe Drinking Water Act of 1974.

Water can be contaminated from a number of sources. Runoff from waste disposal sites, leaking underground storage tanks, improperly discarded commercial byproducts, and pesticides and herbicides are some of the main culprits. Because water flows quickly from one place to another, contamination can spread far from its source. As an example of the far reaching effects of leakage, it is estimated that one gallon of gasoline can contaminate one million gallons of drinking water. Once contamination has been identified, its source can be eliminated and the water may eventually become clean. However, the process can be time consuming and extremely expensive.

IN PRACTICE

Real estate agents need to be on the alert for potential groundwater contamination sources both on and off a property. These include underground storage tanks, septic systems, holding ponds, dry wells, buried materials, and surface spills. Remember, because groundwater flows over wide areas, the source of contamination may not be nearby.

Underground Storage Tanks

Approximately 3 million to 5 million **underground storage tanks (USTs)** exist in the United States. According to the EPA, an underground storage tank system is a tank and any underground piping connected to the tank that has at least 10 percent of its combined volume underground. As of the end of the EPA September 2008 reporting period, almost a half million of those USTs have experienced confirmed leaks. The increase in reports of leaks can be partially attributed to the fact that until the mid-1980s, most USTs were made of bare steel, which will corrode over time. Underground storage tanks are commonly found on sites where petroleum products are used or where gas stations and auto repair shops are located. They also may be found in a number of other commercial and industrial establishments—including printing and chemical plants, wood treatment plants, paper mills, paint manufacturers, dry cleaners, and food processing plants—for storing chemical or other process waste. Military bases and airports also are common sites for underground tanks. Many, if not most, of the residential UST tanks that were used to store heating oil have been abandoned when newer heating systems were installed.

Some tanks are currently in use, but many are long forgotten. It is an unfortunate fact that it was once common to dispose of toxic wastes by simple burial: *out of sight, out of mind.* Over time, however, neglected tanks may leak hazardous substances into the environment. This permits contaminants to pollute not only the soil around the tank but also adjacent parcels and groundwater. Licensees should be particularly alert to the presence of fill pipes, vent lines, stained soil, oil sheens in wet areas, and fumes or odors, any of which may indicate the presence of a UST. Detection, removal, and cleanup of surrounding contaminated soil can be an expensive operation.

■ **FOR EXAMPLE** In the 1940s, a gas station in a rural town went out of business. The building fell into disrepair and was torn down. The site was vacant for several years, and its former use was forgotten. A series of commercial ventures were built on the land: a grocery store, a drive-in restaurant, and a convenience store. In the late 1980s, residents of the town began noticing strong gasoline fumes in their basements, particularly after a rainstorm. Government investigators concluded that the gasoline tanks buried beneath the former gas station had broken down with age and leaked their contents into the soil. Because the town was located over a large subsurface rock slab, the gasoline could not leach down into the soil, but rather it was forced to spread out under the entire town and surrounding farmland. Because the water table floated on the rock slab and the gasoline floated on the water, rains that raised the water table forced the gasoline into the soil near the residents' basements and crawlspaces, resulting in the unpleasant and potentially unhealthy fumes. When the gasoline fumes ignited and destroyed a local manufacturing plant, the residents learned that the problem was not only unpleasant but dangerous, as well.

State and federal laws impose very strict requirements on landowners on which underground storage tanks are located to detect and correct leaks in an effort to protect the groundwater. The EPA under the Resource Conservation and Recovery Act of CERCLA created the Office of Underground Storage Tanks in 1985 to regulate the federal UST program. The federal UST regulations apply to only underground tanks and piping storing either petroleum or certain hazardous substances. Commercial UST owners are required to register their tanks and adhere to strict technical and administrative requirements that govern installation, maintenance, corrosion prevention, overspill prevention, monitoring, and record keeping. Owners also are required to demonstrate that they have sufficient financial resources to cover any damage that might result from leaks.

The following types of tanks are among those that are exempt from federal regulations:

- Tanks that hold less than 110 gallons
- Farm and residential tanks that hold 1,100 gallons or less of motor fuel used for noncommercial purposes
- Tanks that store heating oil burned on the premises
- Tanks on or above the floor of underground areas, such as basements or tunnels
- Septic tanks and systems for collecting stormwater and wastewater

North Carolina, like many states, has adopted laws regulating underground storage tanks that are sometimes more stringent than the federal laws. North Carolina has maintained an EPA-approved UST program since 1999 under the NC Department of Environment and Natural Resources (DENR). According to the 2007-2008 DENR report to the EPA, North Carolina has over 28,000 active regulated tanks that accounted for just over 200 confirmed releases plus over 500 confirmed leaks from non-regulated USTs, primarily for heating oil.

In addition to being aware of possible noncompliance with state and federal regulations, the parties to a real estate transaction should be aware that many older tanks have never been registered or fall into the exempt category. There may be no visible sign of their presence. If a leaking UST cannot be removed and the contamination totally remediated, the leak will become a cloud on the title of the property.

Waste Disposal Sites

Americans produce vast quantities of garbage every day. Despite public and private recycling and composting efforts, huge piles of waste materials—from beer cans, junk mail, and diapers to food, paint, and toxic chemicals—require disposal. Landfill operations have become the main receptacles for garbage and refuse. Special hazardous-waste disposal sites have been established to contain radioactive waste from nuclear power plants, toxic chemicals, and waste materials produced by medical, scientific, and industrial processes.

Perhaps the most prevalent method of common waste disposal is simply to bury it. A **landfill** is an enormous hole, either excavated for the purpose of waste disposal or left over from surface mining operations. The hole is lined with clay or a synthetic liner to prevent leakage of waste material into the water supply. A system of underground drainage pipes permits monitoring of leaks and leaching. Waste is laid on the liner at the bottom of the excavation, and a layer of topsoil is then compacted onto the waste. The layering procedure is repeated again and again until the landfill is full, the layers mounded up sometimes as high as several hundred feet over the surrounding landscape. *Capping* is the process of laying two to four feet of soil over the top of the site and then planting grass or some other vegetation to enhance the landfill's aesthetic value and to prevent erosion. A ventilation pipe runs from the landfill's base through the cap to vent off accumulated natural gases created by the decomposing waste.

Federal, state, and local regulations govern the location, construction, content, and maintenance of landfill sites. Test wells around landfill operations are installed to constantly monitor the groundwater in the surrounding area, and soil analyses can be used to test for contamination. Completed landfills have been used for such purposes as parks and golf courses. Rapid suburban growth has resulted in many housing developments and office campuses being built on landfill sites. However, buildings constructed on landfills may have problems caused by settling.

■ **FOR EXAMPLE** A suburban office building constructed on an old landfill site was very popular until its parking lot began to sink. While the structure itself was supported by pylons driven deep into the ground, the parking lot was unsupported. As the landfill beneath it compacted, the wide concrete lot sank lower and lower around the building. Each year, the building's management had to re-landscape to cover the exposed foundations. The sinking parking lot eventually severed underground phone and power lines and water mains, causing the tenants considerable inconvenience. Computers were offline for hours, and flooding was frequent on the ground floor. Finally, leaking gases from the landfill began causing unpleasant odors. The tenants moved out, and the building was left vacant, a victim of a poorly conceived landfill design.

Hazardous and radioactive waste disposal sites are subject to strict state and federal regulation to prevent the escape of toxic substances into the surrounding environment. Some materials, such as radioactive waste, are sealed in containers and placed in *tombs* buried deep underground. The tombs are designed to last thousands of years and are built according to strict federal and state regulations.

IN PRACTICE

Environmental issues have a significant impact on the real estate industry. In 1995, a jury awarded $6.7 million to homeowners whose property values had been lowered because of the defendant tire company's negligent operation and maintenance of a 'hazardous waste dumpsite. The 1,713 plaintiffs relied on testimony from economists and a real estate appraiser to demonstrate how news stories about the site had lowered the market values of their homes. Nationwide, some landfill operators now offer price guarantees to purchasers of homes near waste disposal sites. A recent university study found that a home's value increases by more than $6,000 for each mile of its distance from a garbage incinerator.

Mold

Mold is the latest environmental issue of concern in the last decade due in large part to massive exposure in the media to extraordinary situations of excessive amounts of *toxic* mold in some homes around the country. Perhaps the major real estate industry issue related to mold is how the surge in insurance claims has affected the insurability of properties with previous water claims. The mere presence of mold in a residence is not a material fact according to NCREC unless there is an excessive amount of mold in *unusual* locations. Numerous online sites can be visited to garner information about mold and its treatment.

■ CERCLA AND ENVIRONMENTAL PROTECTION

The majority of legislation dealing with environmental problems has been instituted within the past two decades. Although the EPA was created at the federal level to oversee such problems, several other federal agencies' areas of concern generally overlap. The federal laws were created to encourage state and local governments to enact their own legislation.

Comprehensive Environmental Response, Compensation, and Liability Act

The **Comprehensive Environmental Response, Compensation, and Liability Act (CERCLA)** was created in 1980. It established a fund of $9 billion, called the *Superfund*, to clean up uncontrolled hazardous waste sites and to respond to spills. It created a process for identifying potentially responsible parties (PRPs) and ordering them to take responsibility for the cleanup action. CERCLA is administered and enforced by the EPA.

Liability.   A landowner is liable under CERCLA when a release or a threat of release of a hazardous substance has occurred on the landowner's property. Regardless of whether the contamination is the result of the landowner's actions or those of others, the owner can be held responsible for the cleanup. This liability includes the cleanup not only of the landowner's property but also of any neighboring property that has been contaminated. A landowner who is not responsible for the contamination can seek reimbursement for the cleanup cost from previous landowners, any other responsible party, or the Superfund. However, if other parties are not available, even a landowner who did not cause the problem could be solely responsible for the cleanup costs.

Once the EPA determines that hazardous material has been released into the environment, it is authorized to begin remedial action. First, it attempts to identify the PRPs. If the PRPs agree to cooperate in the cleanup, they must agree about how to divide the cost. If the PRPs do not voluntarily undertake the cleanup, the EPA may hire its own contractors to do the necessary work. The EPA then bills the PRPs for the cost. If the PRPs refuse to pay, the EPA can seek damages in court for up to three times the actual cost of the cleanup.

Liability under the Superfund is considered to be strict, joint and several, and retroactive. *Strict liability* means that the owner is responsible to the injured party without excuse. *Joint and several liability* means that each of the individual owners is personally responsible for the total damages. If only one of the owners is financially able to handle the total damages, that owner must pay the total and collect the proportionate shares from the other owners whenever possible. *Retroactive liability* means that the liability is not limited to the current owner but includes people who have owned the site in the past.

Superfund Amendments and Reauthorization Act.   In 1986, the U.S. Congress reauthorized the Superfund. The amended statute contains stronger cleanup standards for contaminated sites and five times the funding of the original Superfund, which expired in September 1985.

The amended Act also sought to clarify the obligations of lenders. As mentioned, liability under the Superfund extends to both the present and all previous owners of the contaminated site. Real estate lenders found themselves either as present owners or somewhere in the chain of ownership through foreclosure proceedings.

The amendments created a concept called *innocent landowner immunity*. It was recognized that in certain cases, a landowner in the chain of ownership was completely innocent of all wrongdoing and therefore should not be held liable. The innocent landowner immunity clause established the criteria by which to judge whether a person or business could be exempted from liability. The criteria included the following:

■ The pollution was caused by a third party.
■ The property was acquired after the fact.
■ The landowner had no knowledge of the damage.
■ Due care was exercised when the property was purchased (the landowner made a reasonable search, called an *environmental site assessment*) to determine that no damage to the property existed.
■ Reasonable precautions were taken in the exercise of ownership rights.

■ NORTH CAROLINA ENVIRONMENTAL ISSUES

NC Leaking Petroleum Underground Storage Tank Cleanup Act

The purpose of the **Leaking Petroleum Underground Storage Tank Cleanup Act** (NCGS §143-215.94A) is to regulate underground storage tanks' discharge of any hazardous substance, including gas and oil. Owners of properties with tanks that may be leaking face the heavy financial burden of cleanup costs, *even though they themselves did not install the tanks or cause the leak*. This Act covers both residential and commercial properties.

NC Coastal Area Management Act

The **North Carolina Coastal Area Management Act (CAMA)** (NCGS §113A-100) is designed to protect, preserve, and give management guidelines in coastal areas of the state. It places a severe limitation on developments in the coastal estuarine system. A majority of coastal areas in North Carolina, such as wetlands and marshes, have been declared *areas of environmental concern*. Any proposed development or changes in these areas, such as building, dredging, filling or digging, clearing or bulkheading, must first be approved through a permit process. Property owners in violation of CAMA will face serious legal problems including the probability of a court order mandating that they finance the repair of any damage done to the estuarine system. Brokers practicing in the eastern third of the state should consider CAMA compliance a material fact in transactions that might involve land development.

Mountain Ridge Protection Act

The Mountain Ridge Protection Act (NCGS §113A-208) was the first comprehensive law in the nation passed by a state to regulate construction on protected mountain ridges. The construction of a 10-story condominium project on Little Sugar Mountain in Avery County sparked public outrage locally at what was perceived as a "blight" upon the scenic views of the Blue Ridge Mountains. The Act allows a municipality to adopt and enforce "…any ordinance that regulates the construction of tall buildings or structures on protected mountain ridges…"

NC Dredge and Fill Act

Under the **NC Dredge and Fill Act** (NCGS §113-229), a property owner must obtain a permit from the Coastal Resources Commission before participating in any dredging or filling that may affect vegetation or aquatic conditions in North Carolina waters or marshlands. This Act is part of compliance with the federal Clean Water Acts that protect wetlands and other waters of the United States. The federal government defines *wetlands* as "areas periodically inundated or saturated to the extent that they can or do support vegetation adapted to aquatic conditions."

NC Sediment Pollution Control Act

The **NC Sediment Pollution Control Act** (NCGS §113A-50) was enacted to handle problems that occur as a result of sedimentation in state waters. Sedimentation may have natural causes, such as erosion, or human-made causes that result in a deposit of soil or other materials into water. Such deposits may have an adverse effect on the aquatic life in the area. Any type of development, construction, or any other activity that may disturb vegetation or topography in a way that may cause sedimentation is illegal and subject to the Act. The Act calls for erosion control devices, the development of sedimentation plans, and the creation of natural buffer zones. The law is enforced by the North Carolina Department of Environment, Natural Resources.

■ LIABILITY OF REAL ESTATE PROFESSIONALS

Environmental law is a relatively new phenomenon. Although federal and state laws have defined many of the liabilities involved, common law is being used for further interpretation. The real estate professional and all others involved in a real estate transaction must be aware of both actual and potential liability.

Sellers, as mentioned earlier, often carry the most legal exposure. Innocent landowners might be held responsible, even though they did not know about the presence of environmental hazards. Purchasers may be held liable, even if they did not cause the contamination. Lenders may end up owning worthless assets if owners default on the loans rather than undertake expensive cleanup efforts. Real estate licensees could be held liable for improper disclosure; therefore, it is necessary to be aware of the potential environmental risks from neighboring properties such as gas stations, manufacturing plants, or even funeral homes.

Additional exposure is created for individuals involved in other aspects of real estate transactions. For example, real estate appraisers must identify and adjust for environmental problems. Adjustments to market value typically reflect the cleanup cost plus an adjustment for the degree of panic and suspicion that exist in the current market. Although the sales price can be affected dramatically, it is possible that the underlying market value would remain relatively equal to others in the neighborhood. The real estate appraiser's greatest responsibility is to the lender, who depends on the appraiser to identify environmental hazards. Although the lender may be protected under certain conditions through the 1986 amendments to the Superfund Act, the lender must be aware of any potential problems and may require additional environmental reports.

Insurance carriers also might be affected in the transactions. Mortgage insurance companies protect lenders' mortgage investments and might be required to carry part of the ultimate responsibility in cases of loss. More importantly, hazard insurance carriers might be directly responsible for damages if such coverage was included in the initial policy.

Discovery of Environmental Hazards

Real estate licensees are not expected to have the technical expertise necessary to discover the presence of environmental hazards. However, because they are presumed by the public to have special knowledge about real estate, licensees must be aware both of possible hazards and of where to seek professional help.

Obviously, the first step for a licensee is to ask the owner. The owner already may have conducted tests for carbon monoxide or radon. He or she also may be aware of a potentially hazardous condition. A previous environmental hazard can actually be turned into a marketing plus if the owner has already completed the detection and abatement work. The most appropriate people on whom a licensee can rely for sound environmental information are scientific or technical experts. Environmental auditors can provide the most comprehensive studies; frequently beginning with a *Phase I Environmental Site Assessment* which may prompt further testing. Developers and purchasers of commercial and industrial properties usually rely on these expert services. An environmental audit includes the property's history of use and the results of extensive and complex tests of the soil, water, air, and structures. Trained inspectors conduct air-sampling tests to detect radon, asbestos, or EMFs. They can test soil and water quality and can inspect for lead-based paints. While environmental auditors may be called at any stage in a transaction, they are most frequently brought in as a condition of closing. Not only can such experts detect environmental problems, they can usually offer guidance about how best to resolve the conditions.

Disclosure of Environmental Hazards

State laws address the issue of disclosure of known material facts regarding a property's condition. These same rules apply to the known presence of environmental hazards. A real estate licensee may be liable if he or she should have known of a condition, even if the seller neglected to disclose it. Property condition disclosures are discussed in Chapter 9.

■ RELATED WEB SITES

Environmental Protection Agency (EPA):   *www.epa.gov*
EPA: asbestos: *www.epa.gov/asbestos/insulation.html*
EPA: mold: *www.epa.gov/mold/moldresources.html*
EPA Office of Underground Storage Tanks: *www.epa.gov/OUST.html*
Mold Help Organization: *www.mold-help.com*
National Institute of Environmental Health Sciences: Electromagnetic Fields:
     www.niehs.nih.gov/health/topics/agents/emf/
NC Dept. of Coastal Management: CAMA:
     www.nccoastalmanagement.net/index.htm
NC Dept. of Environment and Natural Resources: Radon Program:
     www.ncradon.org
NC Dept. of Environment and Natural Resources: Underground storage tanks:
     http://ust.ehnr.state.nc.us/
Safe Drinking Water Act: *www.epa.gov/safewater/sdwa/index.html*

■ SUMMARY

Environmental issues are important to real estate licensees because they are material facts that may affect real estate transactions by raising issues of health risk or cleanup costs. Some of the principal environmental toxins include asbestos, lead, radon, mold, and urea-formaldehyde insulation.

Licensees who are involved with the sale, management, financing, or appraisal of residential properties constructed before 1978 should be aware of potential lead-based paint in the structures. Under the Residential Lead-based Paint Hazard Reduction Act, residential property owners wishing to sell or lease their property must provide potential buyers or tenants a federal pamphlet on lead poisoning and a form disclosing what the owner knows about the presence of lead paint in the property. The owner does not have to test for or remove lead paint from the property. The law applies even if there is no real estate agent involved in the transaction. Purchaser has a 10-day risk assessment period during which they are not bound by a sales contract.

Other environmental concerns that can potentially affect a real estate transaction include carbon monoxide, electromagnetic fields, contaminated groundwater, underground storage tanks, waste disposal, and mold. Landfills are the most common method of disposing of solid waste materials by layering them between several feet of soil. Improperly constructed or maintained landfills may present a danger to groundwater.

CERCLA established the Superfund to finance the cleanup of hazardous waste disposal sites. Under the Superfund, liability for cleanup costs of unlawful hazardous waste sites can be assigned to the property owner even if not personally responsible for the contamination. North Carolina has several environmental protection laws, including the Leaking Petroleum Underground Storage Tank Cleanup Act, the Coastal Area Management Act, the Mountain Ridge Protection Act, the Dredge and Fill Act, and the Sediment Pollution Control Act.

QUESTIONS

1. Asbestos is most dangerous when it
   a. is used as insulation.
   b. becomes airborne.
   c. gets wet.
   d. is around water pipes.

2. Encapsulation refers to the
   a. process of sealing a landfill with three to four feet of topsoil.
   b. way to apply asbestos insulation to pipes and wiring systems.
   c. method of sealing disintegrating asbestos.
   d. way in which asbestos becomes friable.

3. Broker Jerry shows a pre-World War I house to Tom, a prospective buyer. Tom has two toddlers and is worried about potential health hazards. Which of the following is *TRUE*?
   a. There is a risk that urea-foam insulation was used in the original construction.
   b. Because Jerry is a licensed real estate broker, he can offer to inspect for and remove any environmental hazards.
   c. There is a good likelihood of the presence of lead-based paint.
   d. Radon should not be a concern due to the age of the property.

4. Which of the following is true regarding asbestos?
   a. The improper removal of asbestos can cause further contamination of a building.
   b. Asbestos causes health problems only when it is eaten.
   c. Asbestos was only used in various types of insulation.
   d. HUD requires asbestos to be removed from all residential buildings prior to transfer of title.

5. Underground storage tanks
   a. are found only on commercial properties.
   b. that leak and can not be removed may create a cloud on the title of the property.
   c. are currently regulated only by local laws.
   d. are easily detected by a vent pipe.

6. All of the following are true of electromagnetic fields *EXCEPT* that electromagnetic fields are
   a. a suspected but unproven cause of cancer, hormonal abnormalities, and behavioral disorders.
   b. generated by all electrical appliances.
   c. present only near high-tension wires or large electrical transformers.
   d. caused by the movement of electricity.

7. Which of the following describes the process of creating a landfill site?
   a. Waste is liquefied, treated, and pumped through pipes to *tombs* under the water table.
   b. Waste and topsoil are layered in a pit, mounded up, then covered with dirt and plants.
   c. Waste is compacted and sealed into a container, then placed in a *tomb* designed to last several thousand years.
   d. Waste is buried in an underground concrete vault.

8. Liability under the Superfund is
   a. limited to the current owner of record.
   b. joint and several, retroactive, but not strict.
   c. voluntary.
   d. strict, joint and several, and retroactive.

9. All of the following have been proven to pose health hazards *EXCEPT*
   a. asbestos fibers.
   b. carbon monoxide.
   c. electromagnetic fields.
   d. urea-formaldehyde.

10. Which of the following is/are *TRUE* about radon?
    I. Radon is easily detected by its strong fruity odor.
    II. Radon can be remediated by encapsulation.
       a. I only
       b. II only
       c. Both I and II
       d. Neither I nor II

11. Under the Federal Lead-Based Paint Hazard and Reduction Act, which of the following statements is *TRUE*?

    a. All residential housing built prior to 1978 must be tested for the presence of lead-based paint before being listed for sale or rent.

    b. A disclosure statement must be provided to all purchasers and lessees involving residential properties built prior to 1978.

    c. A lead hazard pamphlet must be distributed to all prospective buyers but not to tenants.

    d. Purchasers of housing built before 1978 must be given five days to test the property for the presence of lead-based paint.

12. Radon poses the greatest potential health risk to humans when it is

    a. contained in insulation material used during the 1970s.

    b. found in high concentrations of unimproved land.

    c. trapped and concentrated in inadequately ventilated areas.

    d. emitted by malfunctioning or inadequately ventilated appliances.

CHAPTER 22

Real Estate Mathematics

■ **LEARNING OBJECTIVES** *When you have finished reading this chapter, you should be able to*

- **apply** formulas used to compute area, percentages, and fractions, and be able to make necessary conversions.

- **calculate** loan-to-value ratio, interest rate on a loan, prorations, and PITI.

- **determine** different commission amounts.

- **explain** the difference between gross and net profit.

- **define** these *key terms:*

amortization	percentage	prorations

■ INTRODUCTION

Real estate involves working with numbers, from calculating commissions to determining loan payments to prorating property taxes. Therefore, a real estate professional must have a working knowledge of math. This chapter focuses on the basic principles of math that a residential real estate licensee will use when working with a client or customer. The North Carolina Real Estate Commission's published syllabus on the Broker Prelicensing course lists the particular subject areas of real estate math in which the prelicensing state exam applicant must be able to demonstrate a high level of proficiency. Even though there are many math examples and working solutions throughout this textbook, this chapter is designed to provide some basic math applications and give the student practice in problem solving through mathematical calculation. There are numerous practice problems for students to sharpen their skills for applied real estate math.

■ MATH BASICS

Most real estate professionals use calculators or computers to assist them with math computations. Additionally, calculators are permitted when taking the state licensing exam. (See *Real Estate Licensing in North Carolina*, published by the North Carolina Real Estate Commission, for detailed information on calculators.) A basic calculator that adds, subtracts, multiplies, and divides is sufficient for most purposes. Financial calculators can offer additional functions, such as determining monthly loan payment amounts. Because each brand of calculator tends to be slightly different, be sure to refer to the user's manual for your calculator to understand how to use it properly. Calculators that have the ability to store words are *not* approved for use on the state licensing exam.

Decimals

Calculators state numbers in decimal form. Therefore, to use a calculator, all numbers must be expressed in the same way. The use of a calculator will often result in numerous digits following a decimal point.

■ **FOR EXAMPLE**   100 divided by 30 = 3.3333333

Use normal rounding off at 3 decimal places before going to the next calculation: 3.3333333 would round down to 3.333.

> *Example:*   800 divided by 30 = 26.666666, which
> rounds up to 26.667

If the fourth digit is less than 5, drop the fourth and any following digits. If the fourth digit is 5 or more, round up the third digit.

Converting Fractions to Decimals

To convert a fraction to a decimal, divide the numerator (top number) by the denominator (bottom number).

> *Examples:*
> $\frac{1}{2} = 1 \div 2 = 0.5$
> $\frac{3}{4} = 3 \div 4 = 0.75$
> $\frac{5}{8} = 5 \div 8 = 0.625$
> $\frac{9}{3} = 9 \div 3 = 3$
> 5 and $\frac{1}{4} = 5 + (1 \div 4) = 5 + 0.25 = 5.25$

■ WORKING WITH PERCENTAGES

Many real estate calculations use percentages. For example, a real estate broker's commission is usually stated as a percentage of the sales price. A **percentage** is a portion of a whole amount. The whole or total always represents 100 percent. For instance, 20 percent means 20 parts of the possible 100 parts that comprise the whole.

> *Example:*   20% = 20 parts of 100

Working with Percentages

When working with percentages, the percent must first be converted to a decimal. To do this, move the decimal two places to the *left* and *drop* the percent sign.

Another way to convert a percent to a decimal is to *divide* the percent by 100 and *drop* the percent sign.

Example: 20% → 20 ÷ 100 → 0.20

Most calculators will automatically change a number stated as a percent into a decimal (usually by entering the percentage number and then pressing the percent key), so that it can be used in a calculation.

Working with Decimals

Percents are sometimes stated as decimals. To find the percent, you need to do the reverse of what was just explained above. To do this, move the decimal two places to the right and add the percent sign.

Example: 0.20 → 20%

Another way to convert a decimal to a percent is to *multiply* the decimal by 100 and add the percent sign.

Example: 0.20 → 0.20 × 100 → 20%

Approaching a Percentage Problem

Keep in mind that a percentage problem always has three components. The first is the rate, or percentage. The second is the whole amount, or the number from which you will determine a percentage. And the third is the part of the whole number. If you have two of these components, you can calculate the third.

Rate = Part ÷ Whole

Whole = Part ÷ Rate   Part = Rate × Whole

Calculating the Part of a Whole

To calculate the part of a whole number, you multiply the whole by the rate, or the percent stated as a decimal.

Example: A broker is going to receive a commission of 20% of the sales price on a parcel of land. If the land sells for $230,000, what commission will the broker receive?

(Note that 20% is the rate, expressed as a percent; $230,000 is the whole. We are trying to find the commission, which is the part.)

Step 1. Convert the percent to a decimal.
20% → 20 ÷ 100 → 0.20
Step 2. Multiply the whole (here, sales price) by the decimal.
$230,000 × 0.20 = $46,000

The broker will receive a $46,000 commission.

Calculating the Rate

Just as the part of a whole number can be calculated if we know the whole and the rate, the rate can be calculated if we know the part and the whole. To calculate the rate, you divide the part by the whole.

> *Example:* Suppose that a broker received a $46,000 commission on the sale of land for which the sales price was $230,000. What percentage rate of the whole did the broker receive?

(Note that $230,000 is the whole, and $46,000 is the part; we are trying to find the rate.)

> Step 1. Divide the part by the whole.
> $$\$46{,}000 \div \$230{,}000 = \$0.200$$
> Step 2. Convert the decimal to a percent.
> $$0.20 \rightarrow 0.20 \times 100 \rightarrow 20\%$$

The broker received a 20% commission.

Calculating the Whole or Total Amount

The whole or total amount can be found when we know the part and the rate. To calculate the whole amount, you divide the part by the rate.

> *Example:* Suppose that a broker received a $46,000 commission on the sale of land, and that the commission rate was 20 percent. What was the sales price of the land?

(Note that $46,000 is the part and 20% is the rate, expressed as a percent; we are trying to find the whole.)

> Step 1. Convert the percentage to a decimal.
> $$20\% \rightarrow 20 \div 100 \rightarrow 0.20$$
> Step 2. Divide the part by the rate.
> $$\$46{,}000 \div 0.20 = \$230{,}000$$

The land sold for $230,000.

Summary

The following formulas summarize the concept of working with percentage problems.

$$\text{Part} = \text{Whole} \times \text{Rate}$$
$$\text{Rate} = \text{Part} \div \text{Whole}$$
$$\text{Whole} = \text{Part} \div \text{Rate}$$

■ PERCENTAGE CALCULATIONS

The following is a summary of some of the most common uses of percentages in real estate.

Broker's Commission

A broker's commission is usually set as a percentage of the sales price. Further, a subagent's share of the commission is usually set as a percentage of the broker's commission.

Example: A seller listed a home for $200,000 and agreed to pay the broker a commission of 5 percent. The home sold four weeks later for 90 percent of the list price. The listing broker paid the listing agent 50 percent of her share of the commission. How much commission did the listing agent receive?

Sales price = $200,000 × 90% = $200,000 × 0.90 = $180,000
Broker's commission = $180,000 × 5% = $180,000 × 0.05 = $9,000
Listing agent's commission = $9,000 × 50% = $9,000 × 0.50 = $4,500

Loan-to-Value Ratio

Lenders typically are concerned about the amount of money they are lending for the purchase of property, compared with the value of the property. They obviously would like the value to be greater than the loan amount, in case they need to foreclose on the property to pay off the outstanding loan amount. In analyzing the relationship between the loan amount and the value of the property, lenders compute a percentage that is referred to as the *loan-to-value (LTV) ratio*. This ratio is calculated by dividing the loan amount by the value of the property.

Example 1: A borrower is obtaining a $150,000 loan to buy an $187,500 property. What is the LTV ratio? (The part [loan amount] and the whole [property value] are given, and we are trying to find the rate.)

LTV (rate) = part ÷ whole = $150,000 ÷ $187,500 = 0.80 = 80%

Example 2: A buyer wants to purchase a $200,000 home, and the lender tells the buyer he can get a 90 percent LTV (sales price × LTV = loan amount).

$200,000 × 0.90 = $180,000 loan amount; $200,000 purchase price − $180,000 loan amount = $20,000 down payment

Interest

Interest is the cost associated with borrowing money. It is usually stated as a percentage of the amount of money borrowed. The percentage is referred to as the *interest rate*, which is an annual rate. The amount of interest paid (a part) is determined by multiplying the loan amount (whole) by the interest rate.

Example 1:   A lender charges 7.5 percent simple interest a year. If a borrower takes out a loan for $335,000, how much interest will the borrower pay in the first year?

Interest = $335,000 × 7.5% = $335,000 × 0.075 = $25,125 annual interest.

Example 2:   The annual interest on a loan of $100,000 is $9,000. What is the interest rate?

$9,000 interest ÷ $100,000 loan amount = 0.09 = 9% rate

Example 3:   If the annual interest is $7,200 and the interest rate is 9%, what is the loan amount?

$7,200 interest ÷ 0.09 rate = $80,000 loan amount

Loan Discount Points   Points are monies charged by a lender for making a loan at a rate lower than the current market rate. It takes approximately 1 discount point to effectively increase the yield by one-eighth of 1 percent. This is known as the lender's *rule of thumb*. For each one-eighth percent increase in yield, the lender charges one discount point. The cost to the borrower of one point equals 1 percent of the loan amount.

Example 1:   The market interest rate is 7.5%, but the buyer wants to get a 7% loan. How many points would the lender have to charge on the 7% loan to equal return of the 7.5% loan?

7.5% – 7.0% = 0.5% difference in rate
50% = 1/2% = 4/8% = 4 points to be charged

Example 2:   A lender charges 4 points to make a mortgage loan. The buyer plans on buying a $200,000 house and needs to take out a loan for 80 percent of the purchase price. How many points will the buyer have to pay?

Loan Amount = $200,000 × 80% = $200,000 × 0.80 = $160,000
Points = $160,000 × 4% = $160,000 × 0.04 = $6,400

Example 3:   Market rates are 7½ percent; the borrower wants a 7 percent loan. Enough points will be charged to increase the yield by one-half percent.

½% = ⅘% = 4 points charged

■ MEASUREMENT CALCULATIONS

To determine the area of a parcel of land or space in a house, real estate professionals must know how to use and calculate measurements.

Linear Measurements

Linear measurement is a measurement along a straight line. It is usually used to determine the length of something, such as the length of a lot line or width of a room. To convert an inch into a decimal part of a foot, divide the inches by 12.

Example: A measurement of 10 feet (') 7 inches (") would be converted to 10' + (7" ÷ 12" = 0.583) = 10.583'.

Common Types of Linear Measurements
Inch
Foot (12 inches)
Yard (3 feet)
Rod (16.5 feet)
Mile (5,280 feet)

Area Measurements

Area is the two-dimensional surface of an object. Area is quoted in square units, or in acres.

Common Types of Area Measurements
Square foot (144 square inches)
Square yard (9 square feet)
Acre (43,560 square feet)
Square mile (640 square acres)

Memorize
43,560 sq. ft. = 1 acre
1 acre = 43,560 square feet

Converting one unit of measurement to another.   One unit of measurement can easily be converted to another unit of measurement (known to an unknown). If the known unit is smaller than the unknown unit (for instance, when you know the number of feet and are trying to calculate the number of yards), you divide the known unit by how many known units there are in the unknown unit (such as 3 feet in a yard). If the known unit is larger than the unknown unit (for instance, when you know the number of inches and are trying to calculate the number of feet), you multiply the known unit by how many known units there are in the unknown unit (such as 12 inches to a foot).

Example 1: A lot contains 45,000 square feet. How many acres are in the lot?

45,000 sq. ft. ÷ 43,560 sq. ft. in an acre = 1.033 acres

Example 2: A room consists of 18 square yards. How many square feet is that?

Number of sq. yd. × number of sq. ft. per yd. = 18 × 9 = 162 sq. ft.

Conversion of square feet and acres.   To convert square feet into acreage, divide the number of square feet by 43,560. To convert acreage into square feet, multiply the number of acres by 43,560.

Example 1:   A lot contains 217,800 square feet. How many acres in the lot?

217,800 sq. ft. ÷ 43,560 sq. ft. in an acre = 5 acres

Example 2:   There are 7.2 acres in a parcel. How many square feet does the parcel contain?

7.2 acres × 43,560 = 313,632 sq. ft.

Conversion of measurements into value.   Divide the value or dollar amount by the unit of measurement.

Example: A parcel of land containing 62,500 square feet just sold for $100,000. How much did it sell for per square foot? ($100,000 ÷ 62,500 = $1.60 per square foot) How much did it sell for per acre? (62,500 ÷ 43,560 = 1.43 acres; $100,000 ÷ 1.43 = $69,930.07 per acre)

Calculating the area of a square or rectangle.   Squares and rectangles are four-sided objects. All four sides of a square are the same length. Opposite sides of a rectangle are the same length.

To determine the area of a square or a rectangle, *multiply the length by the width.*

Example 1:   A room is 10 feet wide and 13 feet long (rectangle). How many square feet?

length × width = 10' × 13' = 130 sq. ft.

Example 2:   A lot is 120 feet wide and 175 feet deep (rectangle). How many square feet? How many acres?

length × width = 120' × 175' = 21,000 sq. ft.
21,000 sq. ft. ÷ 43,560 sq. ft. in an acre = 0.4821 acre

Calculating the area of a triangle.   A triangle is a three-sided object. The three sides of a triangle can be the same length or different lengths. If a triangle has a right angle at one corner (90 degrees, known as a *right triangle*), one side of the right angle is referred to as the base, and the other side is referred to as the height. Calculating the area of this type of triangle involves *multiplying the base times the height and then dividing by two. A right triangle is really nothing more than half of a square or rectangle.*

Example: A right-angle triangle has a base of 50 feet and a height of 20 feet. What is the square footage?

(base × height) ÷ 2 = (50' × 20') ÷ 2 = 1,000 sq. ft. ÷ 2 = 500 sq. ft.

Calculating the area of an irregular shape.   To calculate the area of an irregular shape, divide the shape into regular shapes such as squares, rectangles, and triangles. Calculate the area of each regular shape and add the areas together.

Using Measurements

Square footage of a room.   Very often, a real estate professional will be asked about the square footage or area of a room. The best way to approach this is by thinking of a room as the area of a rectangle or square. Therefore, to find the square footage, multiply the length in feet by the width in feet.

Example: A room is 20 feet wide and 14 feet long (rectangle). How many square feet is the room?

length × width = 20' × 14' = 280 sq. ft.

Size of a lot.   To calculate the area of a lot shaped like a rectangle or square, simply multiply the measure of the front lot line in feet by that of the depth of the lot in feet (length × width). For irregularly shaped lots, divide the lot into regular shapes, calculate the area of each shape, and add the area totals together. The area of a lot is typically expressed in acres, or for smaller lots in square feet. The first measurement quoted would be considered the front footage, especially if the lot fronts a road, lake or ocean.

Example: John Farmer has a piece of land that is 110 feet wide and 420 feet long. He is interested in subdividing it into four equal lots. If he can do this, how many acres will there be per lot?

area of parcel = length × width = 110' wide × 420' long = 46,200 sq. ft.
46,200 sq. ft. ÷ 43,560 sq. ft. in an acre = 1.06 acres
1.06 acres ÷ 4 lots = 0.2652 acre or *about one-fourth of an acre each*

■ SPECIFIC MATH APPLICATIONS

Real Property Taxation (Chapter 2)

Owners of real property in North Carolina are required to pay annual property taxes based on an assessed value of the property and an annual tax rate.

Parts of the problem:

1. The annual tax rate
2. The assessed value
3. The annual taxes

Formulas:

1. Annual taxes = tax rate × assessed value
2. Assessed value = annual taxes ÷ tax rate
3. Tax rate = annual taxes ÷ assessed value

Note: The tax rate is expressed as a dollar amount per $100 of assessed value. If the tax rate is $1.67/$100, the property owner will pay $1.67 for each $100 of assessed value. The assessed value can be divided by 100, and the result multiplied by $1.67 to get the annual taxes. Or divide the $1.67 by $100 (1.67 ÷ 100 = 0.0167) and multiply by the assessed value (0.0167 × assessed value).

Example 1: If the tax rate is $1.67/$100 and the assessed value is $120,000, what are the annual taxes?

$1.67 ÷ $100 = 0.0167 × $120,000 = $2,004 annual taxes, or $120,000 ÷ 100 = $1,200 × $1.67 = $2,004.

Example 2: If the annual taxes are $1,800 and the assessed value is $110,000. What is the annual tax rate?

$1,800 ÷ $110,000 = 0.0163636, rounded to 0.0164 × 100 = $1.64/$100

Example 3: If the tax rate is $1.20/$100 and the annual taxes are $1,200, what is the assessed value?

$1,200 ÷ 0.012 (rate ÷ $100) = $100,000 assessed value.

Excise Tax (Chapter 5)

This was discussed previously in Chapter 5, page 76. There will be some practice math questions on this subject at the end of this chapter.

Brokerage Commissions, Commission Splits: In-House and Cooperating (Chapter 9)

Even though previously mentioned as part of the section on percentages, commissions and commission splits need to be further discussed. Agents and their clients agree on a commission in the employment agreement. It is normally determined as a percentage of the final accepted gross sales price.

Parts of commission math problems include: (1) the sales price, (2) the commission rate, (3) commission earned, (4) in-house splits, and (5) splits with cooperating brokers.

Formulas: Earned commission = sales price × commission rate
Rate = commission ÷ sales price
Sales price = commission ÷ rate

In-house commission splits. The sales agents work for the brokerage firm. Their employment agreements establish commission splits.

Example: Two agents working for ABC Realty are on an in-house 50/50 split with the firm. One sells a listing for $120,000 at a 6% commission. The gross commission is $7,200 ($120,000 × 0.06 = $7,200). If one agent listed and the other sold the property, their combined earned commission is $3,600, and ABC Realty's share is $3,600. That is, if Lucy listed the property and Sam sold it, $3,600 would go to ABC Realty, Lucy would earn $1,800, and Sam would earn $1,800.

Cooperating brokerage splits. If one company lists the property and another firm sells the property, normally through a multiple-listing service (MLS), the gross commission will be split between the two firms, based on a previous agreement. The commission will be split between the two firms and then between the firms and their individual agents.

Example: Sharon, the listing agent with ABC Realty, listed a home for $200,000 at a commission rate of 6 percent. Harold, an agent working for XYZ Realty, sold the home for the listed price. The co-op split is 50/50 ($200,000 × 0.06 = $12,000 gross commission × 0.50 = $6,000; $6,000 goes to ABC and $6,000 goes to XYZ). If Sharon is on an in-house 50/50 split, she earns $3,000, her firm earns $3,000. If Harold is on a 70/30 in-house split, that is, 70 percent to Harold and 30 percent to the firm, he earns $4,200 ($6,000 × 0.70) and XYZ earns $1,800 ($6,000 × 0.30).

Profit and Loss Math; Percent of Gross and Net Profit; Seller's Net (Chapter 9)

Profit and loss. When real property is sold, a profit or a loss may occur. Many times sellers are concerned about the profit they may earn or, if a low price is accepted, a loss they may incur. The agent must understand the concepts of profit and loss math and how it applies to real estate transactions.

If the problem gives the value (present or original) and asks for a percent of loss or a percent of profit, the math is quite simple. Divide the amount of profit (or loss) by the original value, and that gives the percent of profit or loss.

Example 1: A house recently sold for $120,000 and was originally purchased for $100,000. The profit is 20 percent ($120,000 present value – $100,000 original value = $20,000 amount of profit ÷ original value of $100,000 = 0.20, or 20%).

Example 2:   A house was purchased for $100,000 a few
                      years ago and just sold at $90,000. The loss of
                      10 percent ($100,000 present value – $90,000
                      original value = $10,000 loss ÷ original value of
                      $100,000 = 0.10, or 10%).

If a problem gives the original or present value, gives the percentage of profit or
loss in the problem, then asks for the present or original value, the math becomes
a bit more complicated. Following are three rules to remember:

1. When a problem gives the *original value* and asks for *present value*, you *multiply* by the percentage of profit or loss.
2. When the problem gives the *present value* and asks for the *original value*, you *divide* by the percentage of profit or loss.
3. If a profit occurs, add; if a loss occurs, subtract. Treat the original value given in the problem as the 100 percent figure.

Example 1:   A house recently sold for $120,000 at a 13
                      percent profit. What was the original value?

$120,000 present value = 100% original value + 13% gain = 113% =
            1.13 ratio between present and original value
        $120,000 ÷ 1.13 = $106,194.69 original value

Example 2:   A house recently sold for $96,000 at a 10
                      percent loss. What was the original value?

$96,000 present value = 100% original value – 10% loss = 90% =
            0.90 ratio between present and original value
        $96,000 ÷ 0.90 = $106,666.66 original value

Example 3:   A house cost $230,000 four years ago and
                      just sold at a 9 percent profit. What was the
                      sales price?

$230,000 original value = 100% original value + 9% profit = 109% =
            1.09 ratio between present and original value
        $230,000 × 1.09 = $250,700 sales price (present value)

Example 4:   A house cost $180,000 four years ago and
                      just sold at an 11 percent loss. What did it
                      sell for?

$180,000 original value = 100% original value – 11% loss = 89% =
            0.89 ratio between present and original value
        $180,000 × 0.89 = $160,200 sales price (present value)

Gross profit versus net profit.   *Gross profit* is nothing more than the present
value less the original value, and the difference equals the amount of gross profit.
The amount of gross profit divided by the original value equals the percent of gross
profit.

Example: The original value of a house was $80,000, and it recently sold for $100,000. The gross profit is 25 percent ($100,000 present value – $80,000 original value = $20,000 gross profit ÷ $80,000 original value = 0.25 = 25%).

To find *net profit,* take into consideration the closing costs the buyer had to pay when the house was purchased and the selling expenses that had to be paid when it was sold.

Example: (using the figures in the preceding example) When the owners bought the house for $80,000, they had to pay $1,000 in closing costs, making the original cost $81,000. When they later sold for $100,000, they had to pay $7,000 in selling expenses. Their net profit is 14.8 percent ($80,000 + $1,000 = $81,000 original net value; $100,000 – $7,000 = $93,000 present net value; $93,000 – $81,000 = $12,000 net profit; $12,000 net profit ÷ $81,000 original value = 0.148 = 14.8% net profit).

Determining minimum sales price to net the seller a specific amount. Often the seller will want to know what the house must sell for in order to *net* (realize a profit of) a certain amount. The agent should be able to calculate a probable sales price. This is also known as a *net to seller problem.* This question asks what the minimum projected sales price should be. Students can check their work by taking one of the answers giving the proposed sales price and deducting the sales expenses. The resulting amount should equal the amount that the seller wishes to net.

Parts of the problem: (1) seller's desired net; (2) the commission to be paid; (3) closing costs to be paid by the seller.

Step 1.   Add the seller's net to all closing costs, including any loan payoff.
Step 2.   Subtract the given commission rate from 100 percent.
Step 3.   Divide Step 1 by Step 2.

Example: A seller wants to net $120,000 from the sale of his home. The closing costs are estimated to be $1,200 and the agreed-on commission is 7 percent. There is an existing loan of $40,000 that must be paid off at closing. What must the house sell for if the seller is to receive his $120,000 *net?*

Step 1. $120,000 net + $1,200 closing costs + $40,000 loan payoff = $161,200.

Step 2.   100% – 7% = 93% = 0.93

Step 3. $161,200 ÷ 0.93 = $173,333.33 is the lowest acceptable sales price needed to get the desired net for the seller.

Real Estate Financing Calculations (Chapters 13 and 14)

Agents must be familiar with calculations involving principal and interest, computation of monthly payments (PITI), mortgage debt reduction (amortization), total interest paid over the life of the loan, loan origination fees, discount points, loan-to-value ratios, and computation of total loan fees. Agents also must be able to give buyers a general idea of about how much they will be able to borrow based on standard qualifying ratios.

Amortization (debt liquidation).   **Amortization** is the process of paying off a home loan by making periodic (usually monthly) payments of principal (P) and interest (I), called debt service. *Amortization* literally means to *kill the debt*. A monthly PI payment can be easily computed by using a mortgage payment constant chart (amortization chart). The chart is based on a $1,000 loan. The interest rate and the term dictate the loan factor, which is the monthly P&I amount in dollars needed to amortize a $1,000 loan. Looking at the chart (see Table 22.1), if a person borrowed $1,000 for 30 years at 7 percent annual interest rate, the monthly payment would be $6.65. To compute a monthly PI payment: You want to borrow $75,000 at 7 percent for 30 years: $75,000 ÷ $1,000 = 75 thousand × $6.65 payment per thousand = $498.75 monthly PI.

Principal, interest, taxes, insurance (PITI).   The borrower will probably be required by the lender to place into escrow one-twelfth of the annual property taxes and one-twelfth of the homeowner's annual insurance premium each month, along with the PI (debt service) payment. The PITI can be computed by adding monthly debt service to the tax and insurance monthly escrow payments.

Example: The borrower wants to borrow $130,000 at 7.5% for 30 years. The loan factor is 6.99 per thousand borrowed. The estimated annual taxes are $1,200, and the estimated annual insurance premium is $360. What is the monthly PITI payment?

$130,000 ÷ 1,000 = 130 thousands borrowed × 6.99 factor = $908.70 monthly PI

$1,200 annual tax ÷ 12 months = $100 monthly T

$360 annual insurance ÷ 12 months = $30.00 monthly I

$908.70 PI + $100 T + $30 I = $1,038.70 PITI

Total interest paid over the life of the loan.   On a fixed-rate mortgage loan the monthly PI payment remains constant. Multiply the monthly PI payment by the number of payments made over the life of the loan and subtract the original principal to find the total interest paid. If the monthly PI is $498.75 on the 30-year $75,500 loan, total interest paid over the life of the loan is $104,050; ($498.75 PI × 360 payments = $179,550 total PI – $75,500 original P = $104,050 total I).

Mortgage debt reduction (amortization).   The monthly PI payment will do two things. The principal portion will reduce the debt by the amount of monthly principal paid, and the interest portion will supply the lender's yield on the loan.

Example: The monthly PI payment is $498.75 with the loan amount of $75,500 at 7 percent. After the first month's payment, what is the new loan balance?

$75,500 loan balance × 0.07 annual interest rate = $5,285 annual interest ÷ 12 months = $440.42 monthly I; $498.75 PI – $440.42 I = $58.33 P; $75,500 beginning loan balance – $58.33 P payment = $75,441.67 loan balance after one month's payment

Loan origination fees, discount points, and assumption fees.   Lenders charge various fees to the borrower when processing a loan application. The origination fee is normally 1 percent of the loan amount, and discount points (previously discussed) may be charged to increase the yield. In the event of a loan assumption, the lender normally will charge an assumption fee, quoted as a percentage of the amount to be assumed.

Example: The loan amount is $90,500. The lender will charge a 1 percent loan origination fee. Market interest rates are 7.25 percent, but the buyer wants to get a rate of 7 percent, which the lender has approved with payment of appropriate discount points. What is the total amount of fees to be paid by the buyer?

$90,500 loan amount × 0.01 = $905 origination fee; 7.25% – 7% = 0.25% = $\frac{2}{8}$% = 2 points; $90,500 × 0.02 = $1,810 discount points; $905 origination fee + $1,810 points = $2,715 total loan fees

Equity.   Equity is defined as the difference between the value of the property and the debts on the property. As time goes by, the value increases and the debt is reduced, which creates an increase in equity over a period of time.

Value – Debt = Equity

Example: A buyer purchases a home for $100,000 and receives an $80,000 loan ($100,000 value – $80,000 debt = $20,000 original equity).

To find the percent of equity increase, divide the amount of increase in equity by the original equity.

TABLE 22.1   **Mortgage Factor Chart**

	Equal Monthly Debt Service (PI) Payment to Amortize a Loan of $1,000				
Rate	Term 10 Years	Term 15 Years	Term 20 Years	Term 25 Years	Term 30 Years
4	10.13	7.40	6.06	5.28	4.78
4⅛	10.19	7.46	6.13	5.35	4.85
4¼	10.25	7.53	6.20	5.42	4.92
4⅜	10.31	7.59	6.26	5.49	5.00
4½	10.37	7.65	6.33	5.56	5.07
4⅝	10.43	7.72	6.40	5.63	5.15
4¾	10.49	7.78	6.47	5.71	5.22
4⅞	10.55	7.85	6.54	5.78	5.30
5	10.61	7.91	6.60	5.85	5.37
5⅛	10.67	7.98	6.67	5.92	5.45
5¼	10.73	8.04	6.74	6.00	5.53
5⅜	10.80	8.11	6.81	6.07	5.60
5½	10.86	8.18	6.88	6.15	5.68
5⅝	10.92	8.24	6.95	6.22	5.76
5¾	10.98	8.31	7.03	6.30	5.84
5⅞	11.04	8.38	7.10	6.37	5.92
6	11.10	8.44	7.16	6.44	6.00
6⅛	11.16	8.51	7.24	6.52	6.08
6¼	11.23	8.57	7.31	6.60	6.16
6⅜	11.29	8.64	7.38	6.67	6.24
6½	11.35	8.71	7.46	6.75	6.32
6⅝	11.42	8.78	7.53	6.83	6.40
6¾	11.48	8.85	7.60	6.91	6.49
6⅞	11.55	8.92	7.68	6.99	6.57
7	11.61	8.98	7.75	7.06	6.65
7⅛	11.68	9.06	7.83	7.15	6.74
7¼	11.74	9.12	7.90	7.22	6.82
7⅜	11.81	9.20	7.98	7.31	6.91
7½	11.87	9.27	8.05	7.38	6.99
7⅝	11.94	9.34	8.13	7.47	7.08
7¾	12.00	9.41	8.20	7.55	7.16
7⅞	12.07	9.48	8.29	7.64	7.25
8	12.14	9.56	8.37	7.72	7.34
8⅛	12.20	9.63	8.45	7.81	7.43
8¼	12.27	9.71	8.53	7.89	7.52
8⅜	12.34	9.78	8.60	7.97	7.61
8½	12.40	9.85	8.68	8.06	7.69
8⅝	12.47	9.93	8.76	8.14	7.78
8¾	12.54	10.00	8.84	8.23	7.87
8⅞	12.61	10.07	8.92	8.31	7.96
9	12.67	10.15	9.00	8.40	8.05
9⅛	12.74	10.22	9.08	8.48	8.14
9¼	12.81	10.30	9.16	8.57	8.23
9⅜	12.88	10.37	9.24	8.66	8.32
9½	12.94	10.45	9.33	8.74	8.41
9⅝	13.01	10.52	9.41	8.83	8.50
9¾	13.08	10.60	9.49	8.92	8.60
9⅞	13.15	10.67	9.57	9.00	8.69
10	13.22	10.75	9.66	9.09	8.78
10⅛	13.29	10.83	9.74	9.18	8.87
10¼	13.36	10.90	9.82	9.27	8.97
10⅜	13.43	10.98	9.90	9.36	9.06
10½	13.50	11.06	9.99	9.45	9.15
10⅝	13.57	11.14	10.07	9.54	9.25
10¾	13.64	11.21	10.16	9.63	9.34

How To Use This Chart

To use this chart, find the appropriate interest rate. Then follow that row over to the column for the appropriate loan term. This number is the interest rate factor required each month to amortize a $1,000 loan. To calculate the principal and interest (PI) payment, multiply the interest rate factor by the number of 1,000s in the total loan.

For example, if the interest rate is 10% for a term of 30 years, the interest rate factor is 8.78. If the total loan is $100,000, the loan contains 100 1,000s. Therefore,

100 × 8.78 = $878 PI

To estimate a mortgage loan amount using the amortization chart, divide the PI payment by the appropriate interest rate factor. Using the same facts as in the first example:

$878 ÷ 8.78 = $100 1,000s, or $100,000 LV

Example: The value of the above home increases to $130,000 and the debt is reduced to $70,000. What is the percent of equity increase?

$130,000 value – $70,000 debt = $60,000 new equity; $60,000 new equity – $20,000 original equity = $40,000 increase in equity; $40,000 increase in equity ÷ $20,000 original equity = 2.00 = 200% percentage increase in equity

Qualifying the buyer.   This was discussed previously in Chapter 14, page 269. There will be some practice math questions on this subject at the end of this chapter.

Closing Calculations (Chapter 15)

Completing a HUD-1 Closing Statement.   Closing statement preparation was previously discussed in depth in Chapter 15, starting on page 288. There is a practice closing problem at the end of that chapter.

Prorations.   *Prorate* means *to divide proportionately*. In real estate, **prorations** are used to divide income and expenses of a property between buyer and seller at closing. Refer to Chapter 15 for an introduction of when and how prorations are used at closing and for math examples. Remember to use a *banker's calendar* where every month has 30 days and each year has 360 days, and remember that the seller owns the day of closing.

Calculating prorations.   In most cases when calculating prorations there are three steps to follow.

Step 1.   Find the daily amount.

Real estate taxes: annual taxes are $1,080 ÷ 360 days = $3 per day

Step 2.   Count the number of days the seller has owned the property for the proration period, including the day of closing.

Closing is April 15: Jan. 1 to Apr. 15 = 105 days

Step 3.   Multiply Step 1 by Step 2

$3 per day × 105 days = $315 debit seller/credit buyer

Note: If a prorated item has been prepaid by the seller prior to closing, a fourth step must be added in which the seller must be credited for the overpaid amount, which will be debited to the buyer. Subtract the seller's actual liability from what seller has prepaid and credit the seller, debit the buyer.

Closing is November 19, annual real estate taxes are $1,080, and seller has paid the taxes prior to closing ($1,080 ÷ 360 days = $3 per day; Jan. 1 – Nov. 19 = 319 days × $3 = $957 *seller share* of taxes; seller paid $1,080 – $957 = $123 credit seller/debit buyer).

These same steps will be followed when prorating rents, interest on an assumed loan, and insurance premiums.

Difference between debit and credit. To calculate a proration problem, you need to know how expenses and income are posted on the closing statement. A *debit takes money* from a person. A *credit gives money* to a person. When the pro-rated item involves both the buyer and seller, there always will be a double entry. If the seller owes the buyer, the prorated amount will be debited to the seller and credited to the buyer. If the buyer owes the seller, the prorated item will be debited to the buyer and credited to the seller.

A word of caution! *If the math application is done correctly and the student is not knowledgeable about the proper entries to be made on the closing statement, the math question will probably be missed. You must know when items will be debited and credited to the parties!*

Seller net calculations. To calculate the amount of the proceeds with which the seller should leave the closing table, requires knowledge of the closing expenses for which the seller will be responsible. From the gross sales price, the seller must pay all seller expenses, usually including commission, with the balance representing the net proceeds. The licensee should be able to calculate the minimum sales price that will achieve the seller's net proceeds goal by adding all estimated expenses to the net goal amount. Frequently, all expenses are presented as dollar amounts except for the brokerage commission that is normally represented as a percentage of gross sales price; therefore, the licensee must understand how to use the dollar amounts and the commission percentage together to project minimum acceptable selling price.

To calculate the minimum sales price required: (1) add all closing expenses expressed as dollar amounts; (2) add the minimum net proceeds amount that the seller wishes to net; and (3) divide this total by 100 percent minus the percentage of the brokerage commission.

Example: Seller wishes to net $50,000 from the sell of his house after paying off his mortgage loan balance of $124,000 and closing expenses that equal $3,190. Seller has also agreed to pay a 6 percent listing commission to the real estate firm. What is the minimum sales price that will net the required amount?

1. $124,000 loan balance + $3190 closing expenses = $127,190 total dollar expenses
2. $127,190 + $50,000 required net = $177,190 (minimum sales price without commission)
3. 100% total sales price − 6% commission rate = 94% (portion of sales price that step 2 represents
4. $177,190 ÷ 94% = $188,500 minimum sales price

Appraisal Calculations (Chapter 17)

Appraisal math calculations were discussed in Chapter 17, page 333, to the extent required. There are some practice problems on this subject at the end of this chapter.

Income Tax Calculations Related to Home Ownership (Chapter 19)

Tax math calculations were previously discussed in Chapter 19, page 361, to the extent required. There are some practice problems on this subject at the end of this chapter.

■ SUMMARY

Real estate professionals can expect to encounter math-type problems in their day-to-day activities. Because calculators and computers greatly help with any needed computations, licensees should become familiar with operating a calculator and/or computer. When using a calculator, all numbers must first be converted to decimal form.

The three most common types of math computations that come up in residential real estate are (1) working with percentages, (2) figuring measurements, and (3) estimating prorations.

A percentage is a portion of a whole number stated as a percent. The whole or total always represents 100 percent. To calculate the part of the whole number, you multiply the whole by the percent rate stated as a decimal. Percents are used in calculating commissions, property and conveyance taxes, financing points and interest, and appreciation and depreciation.

Measurements are used to determine the area of a parcel of land or space in a house. Linear measurements, such as feet, are single-dimension measurements that are used to measure the length of the perimeter of a room or lot. Area measurements, such as square feet, are two-dimension measurements that can be used to measure the floor area of a room or acreage of a lot. Licensee should know that there are 43,560 square feet in an acre.

Prorations are used to equitably divide income and expenses of a property between buyer and seller at closing. The manner and process of proration depends on local customs. In general, when calculating prorations, you need to know to whom the proration is to be debited and credited, the number of days owed, and the amount of the expense or income per day. Items such as property taxes, rent, insurance, and fuel oil are typically prorated, along with interest on an assumed loan and homeowners' association dues. In North Carolina, the seller always owns the day of closing in a proration situation. The only time the buyer will pay for the day of closing is when calculating interim interest on the buyer's new loan.

QUESTIONS

1. Bob is buying a house for $123,000. His lender will give him a mortgage loan for 95 percent of the purchase price. How much down payment must Bob pay?
   a. $1,230
   b. $6,150
   c. $12,300
   d. $116,850

2. Two firms split a 6 percent commission equally on a $73,000 home. The selling licensee, Joe, was paid 70 percent of his broker's share. The listing licensee, Janice, was paid 30 percent of her broker's share. How much did Janice receive?
   a. $657
   b. $1,314
   c. $1,533
   d. $4,380

3. Carly is taking out a $356,000 loan to buy a property that is appraised for $1,200,000. What is the loan-to-value ratio?
   a. 3.37%
   b. 29.67%
   c. 29.8%
   d. 30.23%

4. A house recently sold for $135,000 at a commission rate of 6.5 percent. The MLS service got 5 percent of the commission as a listing fee. The listing broker got 40 percent of the commission with 55 percent going to the selling broker. You, the selling agent, have an in-house split of 60 percent to you, 40 percent to your broker. What was your earned commission?
   a. $1,930.50
   b. $2,106.00
   c. $2,750.96
   d. $2,895.75

5. A recent sale generated a gross commission of $2,000. Agent Al received 2 percent of the sales price, the broker received 5 percent of the sales price and agent Betty received 3 percent of the sales price. How much in dollars did Al, the broker, and Betty, respectively, receive for this transaction?
   a. $200, $800, $1,000
   b. $400, $1,000, $600
   c. $500, $1,000, $500
   d. None of the above

6. A residential lot in Mecklenburg County is presently assessed by the county tax assessor's office at $75,000, and the tax rate is $1.678/$100 of assessed value. If the property owner constructs a house on the lot that is assessed at $250,000 upon completion, what is the property owner's new monthly tax liability?
   a. $454.46
   b. $2,261.20
   c. $4,195.33
   d. $5,453.50

7. Sam bought a rectangular parcel of land containing 350 acres with 1,300 feet of road frontage. Margaret wants to buy the neighboring rectangular tract that has the same depth but has 6,000 feet of road frontage. How many acres are in the tract of land that Margaret wants to buy?
   a. 1,430 acres
   b. 1,615.4 acres
   c. 1,815.3 acres
   d. 1,840 acres

8. A parcel of land is 660 ft. by 660 ft., and a small stream equally divides the parcel into two lots. How many acres are contained in each lot?
   a. 0.5
   b. 2.5
   c. 5
   d. 10

9. Charles bought a cabin in the mountains five years ago for $20,000. Today he sold it for $25,000. What percent profit did he make on his investment?
   a. 20%
   b. 25%
   c. 33%
   d. 80%

10. Tom bought five lots several months ago for $20,000 each. During the next few months, he had the lots surveyed and redivided the land into nine lots that he sold for $17,000 each. What was his percent profit?
    a. 33%
    b. 47%
    c. 53%
    d. 65%

11. The sellers tell you they would like to net $135,000 from the sale of their home. You estimate they will have to pay $950 in miscellaneous closing costs. You will charge them a 6.5 percent commission to sell the property. They also have a loan payoff of $53,500. What must the property sell for to ensure they receive their desired net?
    a. $145,401.06
    b. $201,604.27
    c. $201,764.25
    d. $202,620.32

Based on the following scenario, answer questions 12 through 14.

Gary bought a house for $180,000 with an 85 percent LTV ratio. The term of the loan is 30 years at a 7 percent rate of interest. It will take a loan factor of 6.65 to amortize the loan. The annual real property taxes are estimated to be $996. The annual premium for the homeowner's policy is estimated at $480.

12. What is the monthly PITI?
    a. $1,017.45
    b. $1,100.45
    c. $1,140.45
    d. $1,320.00

13. What will be the total amount of interest paid over the life of the loan if payments are made for the full 30-year term?
    a. $153,000
    b. $213,282
    c. $321,300
    d. $366,282

14. What will be the principal amount owed after the first monthly payment has been made?
    a. $152,775.05
    b. $152,875.05
    c. $153.000.00
    d. $152,323.33

15. Bill and Betty in the process of buying a new home for $185,500 with an 80 percent LTV ratio. The lender is charging a 1% loan origination fee and is lending the money with 2 discount points. Bill and Betty must pay an attorney $400 to handle the closing. How much money will the lender be paid in fees?
    a. $1,484
    b. $2,226
    c. $3,710
    d. $ 4,452

16. Using the same information as in question 15, how much cash do Bill and Betty need to close the transaction?
    a. $1,484
    b. $4,452
    c. $41,552
    d. $41,952

17. Lynn bought a home five years ago for $105,000 with a 90 percent LTV ratio. She is now selling the home for 20 percent more than it cost. Her loan balance has been reduced by 8 percent. What is her percent of equity increase?
    a. 2.72%
    b. 27.2%
    c. 272%
    d. 372%

18. A husband and wife apply for an $80,000 conventional mortgage loan on a house valued at $85,000. The lender estimates that the couple's housing expenses will be $895 per month, and they have other recurring debts of $425 per month. The couple's combined annual gross income is $40,800. Under which of the following expense-to-income ratios will the lender find the couple to be qualified, based on the 28:36 ratio?

I. Housing-expense-to-gross-income ratio
II. Recurring-obligations-to-gross-income ratio
   a. I only
   b. II only
   c. Both I and II
   d. Neither I nor II

19. Using the 28:36 ratios, how much annual income must the borrower have to qualify for a $98,000 loan at 8 percent for 30 years if the proposed PI payment will be $719.32, taxes and insurance will be $135 per month, and the borrower's other monthly recurring debts total $500?

   a. $28,478.32
   b. $36,613.71
   c. $45,144.00
   d. $58,042.00

20. What is the maximum amount a buyer can borrow using the 28:36 ratio if her annual income is $53,000, her monthly taxes and insurance are estimated to be $150 per month, the mortgage factor is 8.0462, and her non-housing recurring debts total $650?

   a. $54,270.04
   b. $98,182.99
   c. $153,695.85
   d. $197,608.95

21. Joan wants to buy a house for $96,000. Her annual income is $38,500. The amount she wishes to borrow will generate a monthly PITI payment of $700. What are the maximum non-housing debts she can have to qualify under the 28:36 ratios?

   a. $455
   b. $480
   c. $557
   d. $700

22. You are purchasing a four-unit apartment building and will close on November 14. Each apartment rents for $575 per month. On November 1, one apartment is vacant and the other tenants have paid the November rent. Compute the rent proration through the day of closing, and indicate proper entries on a closing statement.

   a. $805 credit seller/debit buyer
   b. $805 debit seller/credit buyer
   c. $920 credit seller/debit buyer
   d. $920 debit seller/credit buyer

23. The buyer is going to assume the seller's 7 percent loan with a loan balance of $82,000 as of the day of closing, which will be August 11. Which would be the correct closing statement entries for the interest proration?

   a. $175.38 debit seller/credit buyer
   b. $175.38 credit seller/debit buyer
   c. $302.94 credit seller/debit buyer
   d. $302.91 debit seller/credit buyer

24. Closing will take place on November 15. Annual real estate taxes are $1,260 and have been paid by the seller. Which would be the appropriate closing statement entries for the taxes?

   a. $157.50 debit seller/credit buyer
   b. $157.50 credit seller/debit buyer
   c. $1,102.50 credit seller/debit buyer
   d. $1,102.50 debit seller/credit buyer

Use the following information to answer questions 25 through 28.

Closing will take place on February 15. The following items have been agreed on by both buyer and seller in the accepted offer to purchase and contract. Determine the net due the seller and the cash needed by the buyer. (Use the 360-day year/30-day month method of prorations and round to the third decimal place.)

Sales price:	$150,000
Commission:	7.5%
Buyer's new loan:	$90,000 at 7%
Buyer to pay interim interest:	
Buyer's earnest money deposit:	$3,000
Buyer's origination fee:	1%
Buyer's discount points:	1%
Seller's loan payoff:	$50,000
Unpaid real estate taxes:	$1,260
Other miscellaneous closing costs:	

Deed preparation:	$150
Excise tax:	Standard rate
Title insurance premium:	$185
New homeowner's policy:	$380
Attorney fees:	$550

25. What are the total settlement charges to the buyer (line 1400)?
   a. $1,485
   b. $2,385
   c. $2,535
   d. $3,195

26. What are the total settlement charges to the seller (line 1400)?
   a. $450.00
   b. $11,550.00
   c. $11,700.00
   d. $11,857.50

27. How much cash is due from buyer (line 303)?
   a. $59,137.50
   b. $60,020.00
   c. $60,037.50
   d. $60,195.00

28. How much cash is due to seller (line 603)?
   a. $60,037.50
   b. $88,142.50
   c. $88,300.00
   d. $88,442.50

29. The subject property to be appraised is a 3-bedroom brick ranch with 3,000 square feet. It does not have a garage but does have a patio. Comparable 1 is a 3-bedroom brick ranch that recently sold for $100,000. It has 2,800 square feet, a garage, and a patio. Comparable 2, a 3-bedroom brick ranch, recently sold for $110,000. It also has a garage and a patio and 3,000 square feet. Comparable 3, a 3-bedroom brick ranch, recently sold for $86,000, has 2,600 square feet, no garage, but does have a patio. Using the sales comparison approach, estimate the value of the subject property.
   a. $94,000
   b. $106,000
   c. $109,000
   d. $114,000

Use the following information to answer questions 30 through 33.

When you bought your home, you paid $120,000 for it plus $2,600 in closing costs. You added $16,000 worth of capital improvements. When you sold the home for $165,000, you paid a 7 percent commission and other closing costs of $1,300. Answer the following questions.

30. What was your cost basis?
   a. $120,000
   b. $122,600
   c. $138,600
   d. $152,150

31. What was your adjusted basis?
   a. $120,000
   b. $122,600
   c. $138,600
   d. $152,150

32. What was your amount realized?
   a. $120,000
   b. $122,600
   c. $138,600
   d. $152,150

33. What was your capital gain?
    a. $13,550
    b. $29,000
    c. $45,000
    d. $165,000

34. Frank Farmer sold his 120 acres for $2,000 per acre. What was the price for which the total acreage sold?
    a. $24,000
    b. $240,000
    c. $360,000
    d. $630,000

35. George Grower sold his vacant lot to Ollie for $200 per front foot. The lot depth was 1,200 feet. The total area was 120,000 square feet. For how much did George sell his lot?
    a. $20,000
    b. $24,000
    c. $200,000
    d. $240,000

36. Ollie then sold the 120,000-square-foot lot to Sawyer for $10,000 per acre. For how much did Sawyer purchase the lot?
    a. $2,548.20
    b. $2,754.82
    c. $27,448.21
    d. $27,548.21

Use the following information to answer questions 37 through 39.

Savvy Seller has a 4-acre property. Sam plans to subdivide the acreage into 150 ft. × 150 ft. lots.

37. Into how many lots could Sam carve the acreage?
    a. 4
    b. 6
    c. 7
    d. 8

38. Expressed in acreage, what would be the size of each of those lots?
    a. 0.384
    b. 0.517
    c. 7.0
    d. 8.0

39. Expressed in acreage, what would be the size of the remaining land?
    a. 38.4
    b. 0.384
    c. 0.517
    d. 384

Use the following information to answer questions 40 through 42.

Peggy purchased a property for $115,000 in 1994 obtaining an 80 percent loan. When Peggy sold the property in 2004 for $205,000 her remaining principal on the loan was $51,000.

40. What was the dollar amount of Peggy's profit or loss at the time of sale?
    a. $51,000 loss
    b. $51,000 profit
    c. $90,000 loss
    d. $90,000 profit

41. What was the percent of profit Peggy realized at the time of sale?
    a. 0.078%
    b. 0.783%
    c. 7.83%
    d. 78.26%

42. What was Peggy's percent change in equity?
    a. 350%
    b. 470%
    c. 570%
    d. 670%

43. How much did Mieke net from a sale of $205,000? Her expenses included commission at a rate of 4.6%, $51,000 loan payoff, excise tax at the standard rate, recording fee of $15 for the release of the mortgage, and courier fee of $40 for her lender to overnight her payoff documentation.
    a. $144,105
    b. $144,301
    c. $144,311
    d. $145,712

44. Seller sold his property for $285,000. He purchased it three years ago for $249,000. What percentage of profit or loss did the seller have?
   a. 14% profit
   b. 14% loss
   c. 24% profit
   d. 24% loss

45. Seller sold his property for $149,000. He purchased it three years ago for $185,000. What percentage of profit or loss did the seller have?
   a. 19% loss
   b. 19% profit
   c. 119% loss
   d. 119% profit

46. Seller sold his property for $97,000. He made a 321.74 percent profit. What was the price for which he purchased the property?
   a. $13,000
   b. $23,000
   c. $74,000
   d. $97,000

47. Don and Donna have a combined annual income of $64,090. They have a $400 car payment that will continue for two years, credit card payments totaling $125 per month, and monthly payments on a dishwasher at $50 per month. What is the maximum PITI for which they can qualify using a 29:41 ratio?
   a. $1,485.84
   b. $1,548.84
   c. $1,614.74
   d. $2,189.74

48. Jan has a gross monthly income of $1,900. Jan has a $150 per month student loan payment that will continue for five more years. What is the maximum PITI for which she can qualify using a 29:41 ratio?
   a. $551
   b. $629
   c. $779
   d. $876

49. Determine the principal balance after the first payment has been made on the following fixed rate-level payment loan: $120,000 at 9.5 percent annual interest for 30 years with monthly principal and interest payments of $1,009.20.
   a. $118,999.08
   b. $119,050.00
   c. $119,109.20
   d. $119,940.80

50. Determine the amount of excise tax charged at closing if the purchase price is $273,750. and the buyer is assuming the seller's loan for $175,000.
   a. $197.50
   b. $350.00
   c. $547.50
   d. $548.00

A P P E N D I X **A**

Study Tips and Comprehensive Practice Examination

■ PREPARING FOR THE EXAM

Mental and Physical Preparation.   An excellent method of preparing for an exam is to take practice tests prior to the actual exam. You can gain important points simply by being an experienced test taker. That is the strategy behind the end of chapter quizzes and the practice exam that follows this discussion. It is also critical to know your vocabulary; it is very difficult to answer a question when you do not understand the word used in the question!

You will also earn a better score if you are in top physical and mental shape the day of the exam. Get your normal amount of sleep the night before the exam; it is *NOT* wise to pull an "all-nighter" in a panic-stricken attempt to cram. Eat normally, but do not have a heavy meal before taking the test. If you tend to be easily distracted, you might consider bringing and using ear plugs during the exam to tune out random noise in the testing site.

Your attitude is at least as important as your metabolic state. A small amount of anxiety is natural and can even help you do your best; too much anxiety is a handicap. You should be prepared, determined, and positive. That positive attitude is much easier to possess if you feel prepared; that requires a game plan to maximize your study benefits. Short regular study sessions are usually better than lengthy cram sessions. Schedule your study periods in a quiet place during a time of the day when you function best. Utilize acronyms to help with memorization. Consider making flashcards of difficult terms to increase your retention. Coordinate a study group . . . but only after you have done some studying on your own.

Taking the Exam.   Most of the computer-administered exam software programs provide a tutorial on how to effectively use the testing program. Take the time to review this tutorial because it will show how to utilize all the features during the exam, such as marking items for later review. The time to use the tutorial does not count toward your four hours for the exam. When you actually begin taking the exam, read directions and questions carefully, not quickly. Be sure you understand each question before answering. Read each question twice to make sure of the question being asked. A major cause of test errors is carelessness. Always try to choose the *BEST* answer to a question; more than one answer alternative may be partially correct. Do not look for trick questions; choose the most logical answer to the premise of each question. Statistically, your first answer is likely to be the correct answer, so do not change it unless you are absolutely sure you have marked an incorrect answer.

Work through the exam at a comfortable rate. You are allowed ample time to finish the exam; however, you should work as rapidly as you can without sacrificing accuracy. Budget your time before you begin the exam. Plan on having more than half the questions answered before half the exam time has elapsed. You may want to take a short break halfway through the exam. You can at least stretch your legs and relax in your seat for a minute or two; this breaks the tension and helps prevent mistakes.

As you work through the exam, consider answering the easy questions first—they are worth as much as the hard questions and they build your confidence! On the exam, you can mark and return to difficult or time-consuming calculations later. Do not give hurried answers just because you are intimidated by the number of questions.

431

Remember that on multiple-choice tests they always give you the correct answer! Most objective questions are not very time consuming. Do not become discouraged if the exam seems difficult. No one is expected to get a perfect score. If you do not know the correct answer immediately, rule out the answer choices that you know are wrong and see if you can narrow your choice down to two . . . then may a reasonable guess. The only sure way to increase your odds of a correct answer is to *study and learn the material*.

In the multiple-choice test format, the question is in the last line of the stem before the answer choices. Exam questions frequently have superfluous information to distract you, so you must determine which information is necessary to answer the question. It is still very important to read every single word in the question. If the terms used in the question are very legalistic, translate to everyday language . . . and the question becomes clearer and easier; *seller* is a lot clearer than *grantor*. Reading the questions too quickly might cause you to skim over an important clue in the wording; slow down! Make sure that the right person is performing the action in the answer choice or the correct number of days is noted.

On multiple-choice exams, the math problems are word problems in paragraph format that intimidate some people. Take the facts out of the paragraph format and just write the facts as a list. Also, use a good, easy to read calculator that you are comfortable using. Arithmetic problems frequently require multi-step calculations. The incorrect answer options are often numbers created on the way to the right answer; so make sure you answered the question. Math problems also tend to have units that need to be converted or standardized, such as converting square feet to acres or making sure everything is standardized to a monthly amount. Sometimes, you can work a math problem backwards using the answer options. If you do have to guess blindly on an arithmetic problem, the odds favor the discard of the two extreme answers and picking one of the remaining choices.

The last suggestion about tackling the math section of the exam is to *NOT* do the math last. On the North Carolina licensing exam, the arithmetic section is the last section on the exam. If you are confident about the math calculations, consider doing that section first while your brain is freshest. If you are not comfortable with arithmetic, you probably should not start with the math section. Work on the other part of the exam for 20-30 minutes and then venture into the math section and pick out the math problems that you recognize and feel rather confident about working; find the commission calculation, because you know you can do that one! If you begin to get overwhelmed by the math, go back to the other part of the exam and keep working. Unless you get very competent with closing statements, you might leave the closing problem until last since those problems are so time-consuming and only count for four answers.

So consider the following test-taking game plan:

1. Read the items carefully to determine the general subject that the item is testing and exactly what is being asked.
2. Reread the question for essential facts and qualifiers.
3. Eliminate answers that you know are incorrect.
4. Rephrase the problem (often helpful).
5. Determine what principles or formulas are necessary and how to solve the problem.
6. Apply relevant information to arrive at a solution.
7. Reread the question and check the answer.

Good luck and successful testing!

The following comprehensive practice exam contains questions on topics examinees might find on the North Carolina licensing examination. These questions are meant to provide prospective licensees with additional practice in preparing for the examination. Note that proration calculations are based on a 30-day month/360-day year unless otherwise stated.

■ REAL ESTATE LAW AND BROKERAGE PRACTICE

1. Which method of describing land is *NOT* used in North Carolina?
   a. Metes and bounds
   b. Rectangular survey
   c. Lot and block
   d. Reference to a recorded deed

2. The last day that real estate taxes for the current year may be paid without penalty is
   a. at any time.
   b. by September 1 of the current tax year.
   c. by January 5th of the next year.
   d. by December 31st of the current tax year.

3. A description of property that reads "Beginning at the large oak tree on the northern line of State Road 18, approximately one mile west to the intersection of State Road and the Great Southern Railroad right-of-way, north approximately 15' along the old drainage ditch . . ." is
   I. a legal description that could be used in North Carolina.
   II. a metes-and-bounds description.
      a. I only
      b. II only
      c. Both I and II
      d. Neither I nor II

4. To be valid in North Carolina, a deed must include
   a. the grantor's seal.
   b. the grantee's signature.
   c. consideration amount.
   d. words of conveyance.

5. All these freehold estates can pass by inheritance *EXCEPT* a(n)
   a. fee simple estate.
   b. defeasible fee estate.
   c. estate for the life of another.
   d. conventional life estate.

6. Which of the following contains no warranties at all and may convey no title at all, depending on the grantor's interest in the property when the deed is executed?
   a. Sheriff's deed
   b. Quitclaim deed
   c. Trustee's deed
   d. Deed of trust

7. Which of the following statements is *TRUE* about manufactured homes?
   I. It is regulated by North Carolina building codes.
   II. Permanently attaching the unit to a permanent foundation is all that is required to convert the unit from personal property to real property for legal and tax purposes.
      a. I only
      b. II only
      c. Both I and II
      d. Neither I nor II

8. The North Carolina law that provides that a contract to sell land is not protected against a third party unless recorded is called the
   a. Statute of Frauds.
   b. Conner Act.
   c. Machinery Act.
   d. Marketable Title Act.

9. The deed that contains covenants against all encumbrances that would affect the title conveyed and assures quiet enjoyment is the
   a. general warranty deed.
   b. quitclaim deed.
   c. special warranty deed.
   d. grant deed.

10. Hannah grants a life estate to her grandson and stipulates that on the grandson's death, the title to the property will pass to her son-in-law. This second estate is known as an estate

    a. in remainder.
    b. in reversion.
    c. pur autrie vie.
    d. at sufferance.

11. A tenancy for years is a tenancy that

    a. renews automatically.
    b. expires on a specific date.
    c. requires notice to terminate.
    d. is only used to lease land.

12. Kristopher built a structure with six stories. Several years later, an ordinance was passed in that area banning any building higher than four stories. Kristopher is probably being allowed to keep his property in its existing state because of a

    a. nonconforming use.
    b. conditional use.
    c. variance.
    d. zoning amendment.

13. Under the Statute of Frauds, an oral lease for longer than three years is

    a. not assignable.
    b. renewable.
    c. illegal.
    d. unenforceable.

14. Police power does NOT include

    a. zoning.
    b. deed restrictions.
    c. building codes.
    d. subdivision statutes and regulations.

15. A cloud on title to a property may be cured by

    a. obtaining quitclaim deeds from the party or parties with possible interests in the property.
    b. recording the new owner's title as per the Conner Act.
    c. paying cash for the property at closing to avoid RESPA compliance.
    d. bringing an action to repudiate the title.

16. Which of the following is/are true regarding liens?

    I. A specific lien is enforceable for three years, while a general lien good for five years.
    II. A specific lien is a lien against a particular parcel of real estate, while a general lien may apply to all of the debtor's property.

    a. I only
    b. II only
    c. Both I and II
    d. Neither I nor II

17. Someone seeking to be excused from the dictates of a zoning ordinance because of hardship should request a

    a. building permit.
    b. certificate of alternative usage.
    c. variance.
    d. certificate of nonconforming use.

18. Under the concept of riparian rights, the owners of property adjacent to navigable rivers or streams have the right to use the water and

    a. may erect a dam across the navigable river or stream.
    b. are considered to own the submerged land to the center point of the waterway.
    c. are considered owners of the water adjacent to the land.
    d. are considered to own the land to the edge of the water.

19. A leasehold estate that automatically renews itself at each expiration is a

    a. tenancy for years.
    b. periodic tenancy.
    c. tenancy at will.
    d. tenancy at sufferance.

20. In the typical real estate sales transaction in North Carolina, the buyer is responsible for the cost of

    a. title insurance.
    b. deed preparation.
    c. excise tax.
    d. clearing a title defect.

21. Which of the following does *NOT* terminate an offer?

    a. Revocation of the offer before its acceptance
    b. The death of the offeror before acceptance
    c. A counteroffer by the offeree
    d. An offer from a third party

22. Fred and Karen enter into a contract wherein Karen will purchase Fred's vacation lot for $50,000. Shortly thereafter, Karen changes her mind. Valerie, Karen's friend, would like to buy Fred's lot on the same terms as Karen. Fred agrees and enters into a new contract with Valerie. Fred and Karen tear up their original contract. This is known as a(n)

    a. assignment.
    b. novation.
    c. substitution.
    d. rescission.

23. An offer to purchase real estate is a binding contract after it has been signed, communicated, and accepted by whom?

    a. Buyer
    b. Seller
    c. Both a and b
    d. Neither a nor b

24. A broker enters into a listing agreement with a seller wherein the seller will receive $120,000 from the sale of a vacant lot and the broker will receive any sales proceeds exceeding that amount as commission. This type of agreement is called a(n)

    a. exclusive-agency listing.
    b. exclusive-right-to-sell listing.
    c. net listing.
    d. illegal listing.

25. While using the NCAR/NCBA Standard 2-T Offer to Purchase and Contract Form, buyer and seller agree upon Alternative 2. Which of the following is *TRUE*?

    a. Buyer must purchase the property but may do so only during the option period.
    b. Buyer is entitled to a refund of all monies if buyer notifies seller of cancellation within ten days of entering into the contract.
    c. Buyer can cancel the contract and receive all monies back until after the option period has expired.
    d. Buyer has no obligation to purchase the property during the option period and may be entitled to a full refund of any earnest money deposit paid.

26. On Monday, Tom makes a written offer to buy Kyle's vacant lot for $32,000. On Tuesday, Kyle counteroffers by raising the purchase price to $33,500. Tom does not reply, so on Friday, Kyle changes his mind and accepts Tom's original price of $32,000. Under these circumstances, there is

    a. a valid agreement because Kyle accepted Tom's offer exactly as it was made.
    b. a valid agreement because Kyle accepted before Tom withdrew his original offer.
    c. no valid agreement because Tom's offer was not accepted within 72 hours of its having been made.
    d. no valid agreement because Kyle's counteroffer was a rejection of Tom's offer.

27. Which of the following situations present at signing would result in a void contract?

    a. The seller has been declared incompetent by a court.
    b. The buyer is 17 years old.
    c. The buyer is very drunk.
    d. The seller was under anesthesia for surgery less than 24 hours earlier.

28. Which of the following items are *NOT* usually prorated between the seller and buyer at closing?

    a. Tenant security deposits
    b. Real estate taxes
    c. Prepaid rents
    d. Owner association dues

29. The Fairfields agree to an open listing for their house with only ABC Realty and Homes Realty. Open listings are not allowed to be entered into the local multiple listing service. The house is sold by Nancy, a licensee with XYZ Realty. Which statement is *TRUE* regarding the Fairfields' obligation to pay commission?
    a. ABC Realty and Homes Realty will share the commission.
    b. Only XYZ Realty is entitled to the commission.
    c. ABC Realty, Homes Realty, and XYZ Realty are all entitled to share the commission.
    d. The Fairfields are not obligated to pay the commission to anyone.

30. Broker Dickerson found a buyer for Presser's house. The buyer put down an earnest money deposit with the broker, and the parties signed a sales contract. Before the sale was closed, a title search revealed a defect in the seller's title, making it impossible for Presser to deliver good title. Which statement is *TRUE*?
    a. The buyer was entitled to cancel the sale without penalty.
    b. The seller was entitled to keep the buyer's deposit if the buyer canceled the sale.
    c. The buyer must accept a non-warranty deed at closing.
    d. The buyer must complete the transaction if the seller reduces the sales price appropriately.

31. Which type of listing provides the strongest protection of the broker's interests?
    a. Net
    b. Exclusive agency
    c. Exclusive right to sell
    d. Open

32. Which contract does *NOT* have to be in writing to be enforceable?
    a. Contract to sell real estate
    b. Listing agreement
    c. Three-year lease
    d. Agreement creating an easement

33. On the settlement statement, the earnest money deposit appears as a
    a. credit to the seller and a debit to the buyer.
    b. debit to the seller and a credit to the buyer.
    c. credit to the seller.
    d. credit to the buyer.

34. A seller's agent must disclose the agency status to a prospective buyer no later than
    a. before closing the transaction.
    b. before presenting the buyer's offer to the seller.
    c. at first substantial contact.
    d. before the seller accepts the buyer's offer.

35. A property manager should make efforts to do all the following *EXCEPT*
    a. maximize the property owner's net profit.
    b. maintain or increase the value of the property.
    c. perform the landlord's duties under the lease.
    d. reinvest the profits by making capital improvements on the property.

36. A broker receives an earnest money deposit with a written offer that indicates that Buyer Bill will leave the offer open for the seller's acceptance for ten days. On the fifth day, and prior to acceptance by the seller, Buyer Bill notifies the broker that he is withdrawing his offer and demands the return of the deposit. In this situation, which statement is true?
    a. The offeror cannot withdraw the offer; it must be held open for the full ten-day period.
    b. The offeror has the right to withdraw the offer and have the deposit returned any time before contract acceptance.
    c. The offeror can withdraw the offer, but the seller and the broker will each retain one-half of the forfeited deposit.
    d. The offeror can withdraw the offer, but the broker will declare the deposit forfeited and retain all of it in lieu of a commission.

37. Which of the following items would normally be considered to be a fixture that would transfer to the buyer with the purchase of a residential property?
    a. A basketball goal that is cemented into the driveway extension
    b. Curtains in the master bedroom that match the wallpaper
    c. A dining room chandelier that is a family heirloom
    d. A security system that is leased by the seller

38. When the subdivision developer built the roads and installed the utilities throughout the neighborhood, what type of easement was given to the utility providers?
    a. Implied easement
    b. Easement in gross
    c. Appurtenant easement
    d. Prescriptive easement

39. Which of the following statements about subdivisions is/are *TRUE*?
    I. There must be at least five separate parcels or lots to be called a subdivision.
    II. No sales contracts can be accepted on subdivision lots until the final plat has been recorded.
    a. I only
    b. II only
    c. Both I and II
    d. Neither I nor II

40. Which of the following statements is/are correct about the NC Real Estate Commission's *Working with Real Estate Agents* publication?
    I. The licensee must provide and review the publication with consumers in all real estate transactions upon initial contact.
    II. The consumer must sign the acknowledgment panel to create an agency relationship with the broker.
    a. I only
    b. II only
    c. Both I and II
    d. Neither I nor II

41. The buyer agent has found a property that meets his client's detailed list of required features. The listing firm is offering the selling agent a $1500 bonus for a signed contract by the end of the month. Does the buyer agent have to disclose the bonus to his buyer-client before writing an offer?
    a. No, because the buyer will want to share part of the bonus.
    b. Yes, because all compensation must be disclosed to a broker's client is a timely manner.
    c. No, because disclosure of the bonus on the closing statement will be adequate.
    d. Yes, because the buyer will find out about the bonus eventually anyway.

42. The legal practice of oral buyer agency in North Carolina requires
    a. the relationship be put in writing before presenting an offer.
    b. that the consumer go under contract to buy a property within 30 days.
    c. a definite time period for the agency relationship.
    d. the buyer to agree to oral dual agency as well.

■ MISCELLANEOUS TOPICS

43. Which tax advantage is *NOT* associated with owner-occupied personal dwellings?
    a. Ability to depreciate the property
    b. Capital gains treatment of resale profits
    c. Possibility of tax-free capital gains
    d. Deductibility of mortgage interest

44. Which of the following statements is/are *TRUE* about the sale of property that has been the owner's principal residence for the last ten years?
    I. If the seller is single, capital gains up to $500,000 is tax-free.
    II. Any capital gain in excess of the tax-exempt amount will be subject to long-term capital gains tax.
    a. I only
    b. II only
    c. Both I and II
    d. Neither I nor II

45. Steering is the practice of
    a. leading prospective buyers to or away from certain areas based on protected class.
    b. refusing to make loans to people of a protected class.
    c. requiring brokers to join a multiple-listing service.
    d. illegally setting standard commission rates in an area.

46. A Chinese buyer-client has instructed his buyer agent to show him properties that are in predominantly Chinese neighborhoods. If the agent were to comply with this client's instructions, the agent would
    a. violate the Civil Rights Act of 1866.
    b. be in compliance with the NC Fair Housing Act.
    c. violate the Federal Fair Housing Act of 1968.
    d. be in compliance with the NC Real Estate License Law because he must obey his client.

47. Broker Green calls several property owners in a neighborhood. He states that several minority homebuyers are moving into the area and that this will decrease property values. Then Broker Green tries to solicit listings from these owners. Under the Federal Fair Housing Act of 1968, this would be considered
    a. blockbusting.
    b. redlining.
    c. steering.
    d. channeling.

48. All the following are parts of the flooring system *EXCEPT*
    a. sill.
    b. girders.
    c. joists.
    d. header.

49. Which of the following statements is/are *TRUE*?
    I. The sale of a house built prior to 1978 will require the seller to disclose what the seller knows about the presence of lead-based paint in the property.
    II. Radon gas is easily detected by its sickly sweet smell.
    a. I only
    b. II only
    c. Both I and II
    d. Neither I nor II

50. Which of the following statements is/are *TRUE* about the Residential Property Disclosure Act?
    I. Seller must disclose property condition in the mandatory form to the buyer prior to first offer unless the property is exempted from the Act.
    II. If the buyer does not receive the information required by the Act in a timely manner, the buyer will have a ten-day rescission period after contract.
    a. I only
    b. II only
    c. Both I and II
    d. Neither I nor II

51. If property owners underinsure their property, what concept of homeowner's insurance should concern them most?

    a. Endorsement
    b. Coinsurance
    c. Exclusions
    d. Insurable interest

■ NORTH CAROLINA REAL ESTATE LAW

52. The North Carolina Real Estate Commission has the power to

    a. regulate the brokerage activities of licensees.
    b. determine the maximum commission a broker may charge on any one transaction.
    c. fine licensees that do not comply with licensing law and/or Commission Rules.
    d. interpret the legality of a real estate contract between consumers.

53. If a person is being compensated, which of the following activities does *NOT* require an active North Carolina real estate license?

    a. Managing apartments in several different complexes for family members
    b. Negotiating exchanges of property
    c. Listing property for sale
    d. Negotiating the sale of personally owned real estate

54. Which statement is *TRUE* of advertising regulations?

    a. A broker must have the owner's permission before placing a For Sale sign on any property.
    b. A provisional broker may advertise another person's property so long as the firm's office phone number is given in the ad.
    c. A provisional broker can place ads on her own initiative as long as she personally pays for the advertising.
    d. Advertising cannot include any financing information.

55. Which statement is true regarding trust account records?

    a. The North Carolina Real Estate Commission requires that records be kept for a period of three years.
    b. Office records are considered trade secrets and not subject to inspection by the North Carolina Real Estate Commission.
    c. A broker-in-charge is responsible for trust funds and cannot delegate daily trust account activities to anyone else.
    d. Trust funds cannot be held in interest-bearing accounts.

56. Rental payments received by a broker must be deposited into a trust or an escrow account

    a. no later than three banking days following receipt of the money.
    b. no later than five calendar days following receipt.
    c. no later than 24 hours after receipt.
    d. per landlord's instructions regardless of other time limits.

57. A broker-in-charge is responsible for all the following *EXCEPT*

    a. all advertising done in the name of the firm.
    b. supervision of all provisional brokers in the firm even if there are multiple office locations.
    c. retention of current pocket cards by all brokers affiliated with the firm.
    d. proper maintenance and record retention of trust funds.

58. In North Carolina, the annual license pocket renewal card
    a. must be carried by the licensee at all times when conducting real estate activities.
    b. expires on June 30th unless the licensee has met all continuing education requirements.
    c. shows whether the license status is active or inactive.
    d. expires on June 10th unless the licensee has paid the renewal fee.

59. A real estate firm may establish one or more branch offices, provided that
    a. each office has a broker-in-charge.
    b. each office has at least five licensees.
    c. the qualifying broker personally supervises the provisional brokers at each office.
    d. the firm uses a different trade name for each branch office.

60. The license status of a licensee who completed all continuing education and post licensing education in a timely manner but forgot to pay the license renewal fee on time is
    a. active.
    b. canceled.
    c. expired.
    d. inactive.

61. The license status of a provisional broker who paid the license renewal fee on time and completed all continuing education in a timely manner but did not complete at least one of the post-licensing courses by the first required deadline is
    a. active.
    b. canceled.
    c. expired.
    d. inactive.

62. The license status of a provisional broker who paid the license renewal fee on time and completed all continuing education in a timely manner but did not complete all three of the post-licensing courses by the required deadline is
    a. active.
    b. canceled.
    c. expired.
    d. inactive.

63. A provisional broker must successfully complete all three of the post-licensing courses
    I. even if the license is on inactive status.
    II. prior to the second renewal of the license.
       a. I only
       b. II only
       c. Both I and II
       d. Neither I nor II

64. Which of the following statements about the Time Share Act is/are true?
    I. An active real estate license is required to sell time shares in North Carolina.
    II. If a public offering statement is not given to the buyer prior to contract, the buyer has a seven-day contract rescission period.
       a. I only
       b. II only
       c. Both I and II
       d. Neither I nor II

■ REAL ESTATE FINANCE

65. A mortgage requires monthly payments of $875.70 for 20 years and a final payment of $24,095. The final payment is known as what type of payment?
    a. Wraparound
    b. Variable
    c. Balloon
    d. Accelerated

66. In North Carolina, a trustee is the conditional holder of title to mortgaged real estate. North Carolina is considered what type of state?
    a. Title theory
    b. Lien theory
    c. Statutory share
    d. Strict forfeiture

67. Wilma purchased a condominium unit and obtained financing from a local savings association. In this situation, which best identifies Wilma's role under a deed of trust?
    a. Mortgagee
    b. Grantor
    c. Trustee
    d. Beneficiary

68. A typical promissory note for an FHA-insured loan may contain all the following EXCEPT a(n)
    a. acceleration clause.
    b. alienation clause.
    c. prepayment penalty.
    d. mortgage insurance requirement.

69. Which statement is TRUE of an adjustable rate mortgage loan?
    a. The monthly payment is usually fixed for the life of the loan.
    b. The interest rate always adjusts to the prevalent market interest rate on the date of adjustment.
    c. Negative amortization is possible if there is a payment cap.
    d. The original interest rate is usually slightly higher than comparable fixed rate loans.

70. The effect of discount points is
    a. an increase in the lender's yield.
    b. a decrease in the borrower's interest rate.
    c. both a and b.
    d. neither a nor b.

71. Gerald is purchasing a home under a land contract. Until the contract is paid in full, Gerald has
    a. legal title to the premises.
    b. no interest in the property.
    c. a legal life estate in the premises.
    d. equitable title to the property.

72. Jim has just made the final payment on his mortgage loan to his bank. Jim will regain his full legal title once what is recorded?
    a. Satisfaction of mortgage
    b. Mortgage novation
    c. Deed of trust
    d. Promissory note

73. Discount points on a real estate loan are usually a closing cost to the buyer. The value of points is
    a. set by the FHA and VA for their loan programs.
    b. charged only on conventional loans.
    c. limited by government regulations.
    d. determined by the market.

74. Acceleration is a loan provision that says
    a. the borrower can make extra payments at any time.
    b. the lender can call the loan due and payable in full if the borrower defaults.
    c. the trustee can speed up the foreclosure procedure due to the amount of the loan.
    d. the lender can charge additional interest if the payment is late.

75. Anne's real estate loan indicates that if she transfers title to the property, the lender must be paid in full immediately. This is known as
    a. acceleration.
    b. alienation.
    c. subordination.
    d. satisfaction.

76. Paul defaulted on his mortgage loan payments, and the lender foreclosed. At the foreclosure sale, Paul's property sold for $64,000; the unpaid loan balance at the time of foreclosure was $78,000. What must the lender do in an attempt to recover the $14,000 that Paul still owes?

    a. Sue for specific performance
    b. Sue for damages
    c. Seek a deficiency judgment
    d. Seek a judgment by default

77. Which is *TRUE* of a term mortgage loan?

    a. All of the interest is paid at the end of the term.
    b. The debt is partially amortized over the life of the loan.
    c. The length of the term is limited by state statutes.
    d. The entire principal amount is due at the end of the term.

78. A real estate loan that uses both real estate and personal property as collateral is known as a

    a. blanket mortgage.
    b. package mortgage.
    c. growing equity mortgage.
    d. graduated payment mortgage.

79. Which of the following loan terms will *NOT* be considered a trigger term under Regulation Z?

    a. Annual percentage rate
    b. Monthly payment amount
    c. Annual interest rate
    d. Number of payments

80. In funding a loan that is secured by a residence, the lender is required to disclose all costs involved in obtaining the financing. This consumer protection is provided by the

    a. Fair Credit Reporting Act.
    b. Truth-in-Lending Act.
    c. Sherman Anti-trust Act.
    d. Equal Credit Opportunity Act.

■ REAL ESTATE VALUATION

81. A residence with leaky plumbing is suffering from

    a. functional obsolescence.
    b. curable physical deterioration.
    c. incurable physical deterioration.
    d. external obsolescence.

82. The market value of a parcel of land is

    a. an estimate of the present worth of future benefits.
    b. a measure of past expenditures.
    c. the price the seller wants for the property.
    d. equal to assessed value.

83. Each legitimate comparable should be as similar as possible in all the following *EXCEPT*

    a. location.
    b. sale price.
    c. date of sale.
    d. square footage.

84. If the annual net income of a commercial property remains constant and the capitalization rate increases, the value of the property will

    a. be unaffected.
    b. increase.
    c. increase the tax basis only.
    d. decrease.

85. Paul has just been hired to appraise a property for loan purposes. The property is an elegant old mansion that has been converted into three apartments. Which approach to value is Paul most likely to use?

    a. Reproduction cost approach
    b. Sales comparison approach
    c. Replacement cost approach
    d. Income capitalization approach

86. Mary built a $125,000 home in a residential neighborhood. The block next to hers is going to be rezoned to allow a mix of residential and retail uses. Because of this future zoning change, the value of her home dropped to $100,000. This is due to the principle of
    a. substitution.
    b. competition.
    c. anticipation.
    d. supply and demand.

87. An appraiser is using the cost approach to value. After determining the replacement cost of the building, she will
    a. estimate depreciation on the building.
    b. add the land value that was determined by the sales comparison approach.
    c. do both a and b.
    d. do neither a nor b.

88. All the following are elements of value EXCEPT
    a. scarcity.
    b. demand.
    c. utility.
    d. uniqueness.

89. The principle that is the basis for the sales comparison approach is the principle of
    a. replacement.
    b. competition.
    c. substitution.
    d. highest and best use.

90. Sharon is appraising an owner-occupied, single-family residence. The method that is the most reliable in estimating its value is the
    a. sales comparison approach.
    b. cost approach.
    c. income capitalization approach.
    d. gross rent multiplier method.

91. Steve's house is three blocks away from an international airport. This is an example of
    a. functional obsolescence.
    b. economic obsolescence.
    c. physical deterioration.
    d. deferred maintenance.

92. The art of analyzing and effectively weighing the findings from the different appraisal methods is called
    a. averaging.
    b. capitalization.
    c. final estimating.
    d. reconciliation.

93. When determining net income, which of the following are NOT deducted from gross income?
    a. Mortgage payments
    b. Management costs
    c. Utility costs
    d. Insurance expenses

■ REAL ESTATE MATHEMATICS

Use a 30-day month/360-day year for all calculations.

94. The principal balance on Zach's loan is $98,763 and his monthly debt service payment is $584.00. The interest rate on the loan is 5.75%. How much money will Zach still owe on his principal after the next monthly payment has been made?
    a. $98,179.00
    b. $98,289.76
    c. $98,652.24
    d. $98,729.42

95. A purchaser buys a home for $143,900 and assumes the seller's loan balance of $109,700. How much excise tax will be paid at closing?
    a. $69.00
    b. $220.00
    c. $287.80
    d. $288.00

96. A property owner is selling a rectangular lot that has 150' of road frontage and is 375' deep. If the owner sells the lot for $50,000 per acre, what would be the sales price per front foot?
    a. $333.33
    b. $430.43
    c. $50,000
    d. $64,565

97. A borrower computed the interest he was charged for the previous month on his $60,000 loan balance as $412.50. What is his annual interest rate?

    a. 6.875%
    b. 7.75%
    c. 8.25%
    d. 8.5%

98. Assuming that the listing broker and the selling broker in a transaction split the commission equally, what was the sales price of the property if the commission rate was 6.5 percent and the listing broker received $2,593.50?

    a. $39,900
    b. $56,200
    c. $79,800
    d. $88,400

99. A seller wants to net $65,000 from the sale of her house after paying the broker's 6% fee based on gross sales price. Her gross sales price needs to be

    a. $61,100.
    b. $61,321.
    c. $68,900.
    d. $69,149.

100. The commission rate is 7¾ percent on a sale of $50,000. What is the dollar amount of the commission?

    a. $3,500
    b. $3,875
    c. $4,085
    d. $6,452

101. Margaret is purchasing a $107,000 home with an 80 percent loan. The lender is charging two and one-half discount points. Margaret's loan discount expense will total

    a. $1,980.
    b. $2,140.
    c. $2,575.
    d. $2,675.

102. The assessed value of a parcel of land is $64,000 and the local ad valorem tax rate is $.72 per $100. Which of the following is the correct tax proration in accordance with customary practice if the closing is April 28?

    a. Seller will be debited $151.04 and buyer will be credited $151.04.
    b. Seller will be credited $151.04 and buyer will be debited $151.04.
    c. Seller will be debited $151.04 and buyer will be debited $309.76.
    d. Seller will be debited $309.76 and buyer will be credited $309.76.

103. Assume a house is sold for $84,500 and the commission rate is 7 percent. The commission is split so that 60 percent goes to the selling broker and 40 percent goes to the listing broker. Each broker splits her share of the commission evenly with the provisional broker responsible for procuring the sale. How much will the provisional broker who personally listed the property receive from this sale?

    a. $1,183
    b. $1,775
    c. $2,366
    d. $3,549

104. A borrower has been approved for a 6.5 percent fixed rate 30-year mortgage loan for $138,000. He will be closing on September 27. What will be the HUD-1 interim interest entry?

    a. $847.17
    b. $672.75
    c. $99.67
    d. $74.75

105. A subject property is a 1,800 square foot house with 3 bedrooms, 1½ baths, a 2-car garage and a deck that is listed for $163,500. A very good comparable for the subject property sold for $166,200 and has 1850 square feet, 3 bedrooms, 2 baths, a 1-car garage and a deck. The comparable property closed 2 months ago and appreciation in the area has averaged 6 percent per year. Estimate a market value for the subject property, if the following market values are used: a full bathroom = $2000; a 2-car garage = $5000; additional square footage = $55 per square foot.

   a. $164,750
   b. $163,500
   c. $166,612
   d. $166,549

106. Joseph wants to net $72,000 on the sale of his home. He has agreed to pay a brokerage commission of 6 percent. What is the minimum sales price that will ensure that Joseph will get his $72,000?

   a. $75,935
   b. $76,320
   c. $76,596
   d. $77,890

107. The buyers enter into a purchase contract with the sellers to buy the sellers' house for $84,500. The buyers deposit $2,000 as earnest money and obtain a new mortgage loan for $67,600. The purchase contract provides for a March 15 settlement. The buyers and sellers prorate the year's estimated real estate taxes (using the 360-day method) of $880.96. The taxes are unpaid and will be paid later in the year by the buyers. The buyers have additional closing costs of $1,250, and the sellers have other closing costs of $850. How much cash must the buyers bring to the settlement?

   a. $15,966
   b. $16,238
   c. $16,338
   d. $16,638

108. Ben sold his house to Marsha for $105,000. He owned the house for five years and made a profit of 25 percent on the sale over his previous purchase price. What did Ben originally pay for the house?

   a. $78,750
   b. $80,000
   c. $84,000
   d. $95,000

109. A buyer wants to purchase a house for $185,000 and applies to a lender for a $166,500 conventional mortgage loan to finance the purchase. The buyer's mortgage PITI payment on this loan would be $1386 per month. Recurring monthly obligations for a car payment and a school loan payment total $725 per month. What is the minimum monthly income, rounded to the nearest dollar, needed by the buyer to qualify for this loan if the qualifying ratios are 28:36?

   a. $7,539
   b. $5,864
   c. $4,950
   d. $3,850

110. Gerta is financing her new house with a fixed rate mortgage for $394,000 for 30 years at a 6 percent interest rate. Her monthly principal and interest payment will be $2,364.00. If Gerta takes all 30 years to pay off this loan, what will be the total interest paid over the life of her loan?

   a. $425,520
   b. $457,040
   c. $709,200
   d. $851,040

APPENDIX B

Residential Square Footage Guidelines

INTRODUCTION

It is often said that the three most important factors in making a homebuying decision are "location," "location," and "location." Other than "location," the single most-important factor is probably the size or "square footage" of the home. Not only is it an indicator of whether a particular home will meet a homebuyer's space needs, but it also affords a convenient (though not always accurate) method for the buyer to estimate the value of the home and compare it with other properties.

Although real estate agents are not required by the Real Estate License Law or Real Estate Commission rules to report the square footage of properties offered for sale (or rent), when they do report square footage, it is essential that the information they give prospective purchasers be accurate. At a minimum, information concerning square footage should include the amount of *living area* in the dwelling. The following guidelines and accompanying illustrations are designed to assist real estate brokers and salespersons in measuring, calculating and reporting (both orally and in writing) the *living area* contained in detached and attached single-family residential buildings. When reporting square footage, real estate agents should carefully follow these *Guidelines* or any other standards that are comparable to them, including those approved by the American National Standards Institute, Inc. (ANSI) which are recognized by the

North Carolina Real Estate Commission as comparable standards.* Agents should be prepared to identify, when requested, the standard used.

LIVING AREA CRITERIA

Living area (sometimes referred to as "heated living area" or "heated square footage") is space that is intended for human occupancy and is:

1. Heated by a conventional heating system or systems (forced air, radiant, solar, etc.) that are permanently installed in the dwelling—not a portable heater—which generates heat sufficient to make the space suitable for year-round occupancy;

2. Finished, with walls, floors and ceilings of materials generally accepted for interior construction (e.g., painted drywall/sheet rock or panelled walls, carpeted or hardwood flooring, etc.) and with a ceiling height of at least seven feet, except under beams, ducts, etc. where the height must be at least six feet four inches *[Note: In rooms with sloped ceilings (e.g., finished attics, bonus rooms, etc.) you may also include as living area the portion of the room with a ceiling height of at least five feet if at least one-half of the finished area of the room has a ceiling height of at least seven feet.];* and

3. Directly accessible from other living area (through a door or by a heated hallway or stairway).

---

*The following materials were consulted in the development of these *Guidelines*:
The *American National Standard for Single-Family Residential Buildings:
Square Footage-Method for Calculating* approved by the American National Standards Institute, Inc.;
House Measuring & Square Footage published by the Carolina Multiple Listing Services, Inc.; and
materials compiled by Bart T. Bryson, MAI, SRA, and Mary L. D'Angelo.

Real estate appraisers and lenders generally adhere to more detailed criteria in arriving at the *living area* or "gross living area" of residential dwellings. This normally includes distinguishing "above-grade" from "below-grade" area, which is also required by many multiple listing services. "Above-Grade" is defined as space on any level of a dwelling which has *living area* and no earth adjacent to any exterior wall on that level. "Below-Grade" is space on any level which has *living area*, is accessible by interior stairs, and has earth adjacent to any exterior wall on that level. If earth is adjacent to any portion of a wall, the entire level is considered "below-grade." Space that is "at" or "on grade" is considered "above-grade."

While real estate agents are encouraged to provide the most complete information available about properties offered for sale, the *Guidelines* recognize that the separate reporting of "above-grade" and "below-grade" area can be impractical in the advertising and marketing of homes. For this reason, *real estate agents are permitted under these Guidelines to report square footage of the dwelling as the total "living area" without a separate distinction between "above-grade" and "below-grade" areas.* However, to help avoid confusion and concern, agents should alert purchasers and sellers that the appraisal report may reflect differences in the way *living area* is defined and described by the lender, appraiser, and the *North Carolina Building Code* which could affect the amount of *living area* reported.

Determining whether an area is considered *living area* can sometimes be confusing. Finished rooms used for general living (living room, dining room, kitchen, den, bedrooms, etc.) are normally included in *living area*. For other areas in the dwelling, the determination may not be so easy. *For example, the following areas are considered **living area** if they meet the criteria (i.e., heated, finished, directly accessible from living area):*

- *Attic*, but note in the listing data that the space is located in an attic (Fig. 2). *[Note: If the ceiling is sloped, remember to apply the "ceiling height" criteria.]*

- *Basement (or "Below-Grade")*, but note in the listing data that the space is located in a basement or "below-grade" (Fig. 1). *[Note: For reporting purposes, a "basement" is defined as an area below the entry level of the dwelling which is accessible by a **full** flight of stairs and has earth adjacent to some portion of at least one wall above the floor level.]*

- *Bay Window*, if it has a floor, a ceiling height of at least seven feet, and otherwise meets the criteria for living area (Fig. 2).

- *Bonus Room (e.g., Finished Room over Garage)* (Fig. 3). *[Note: If the ceiling is sloped, remember to apply the "ceiling height" criteria.]*

- *Breezeway* (enclosed).

- *Chimney*, if the chimney base is inside *living area*. If the chimney base is outside the *living area* but the hearth is in the *living area*, include the hearth in the *living area* but not the chimney base (Fig. 1).

- *Closets*, if they are a functional part of the *living area*.

- *Dormers* (Fig. 6).

- *Furnace (Mechanical) Room* Also, in order to avoid excessive detail, if the furnace, water heater, etc. is located in a small closet in the *living area*, include it in *living area* even if it does not meet other *living area* criteria (Fig. 4).

- *Hallways*, if they are a functional part of the *living area*.

- *Laundry Room/Area* (Fig. 6).

- *Office* (Fig. 1).

- *Stairs*, if they meet the criteria and connect to *living area* (Fig. 1, 2, 3, 4, 5, 6). Include the stairway with the area from which it descends, **not to exceed the area of the opening in the floor.** If the opening for the stairway exceeds the length and width of the stairway, deduct the excess open space from the upper level area. Include as part of the lower level area the space beneath the stairway, regardless of its ceiling height.

- *Storage Room* (Fig. 6).

OTHER AREA

Note in the listing data and advise purchasers of any space that does not meet the criteria for *living area* but which contributes to the value of the dwelling; for example, unfinished basements, unfinished attics (with permanent stairs), unfinished bonus rooms, shops, decks, balconies, porches, garages and carports.

HELPFUL HINTS

Concealed in the walls of nearly all residential construction are pipes, ducts, chases, returns, etc. necessary to support the structure's mechanical systems. Although they may occupy *living area*, to avoid excessive detail, do **not** deduct the space from the *living area.*

When measuring and reporting the *living area* of homes, be alert to any remodeling, room additions (e.g., an enclosed porch) or other structural modifications to assure that the space meets all the criteria for *living area*. **Pay particular attention to the heating criteria, because the heating system for the original structure may not be adequate for the increased square footage.** Although agents are not required to determine the adequacy of heating systems, they should at least note whether there are heat vents, radiators or other heat outlets in the room before deciding whether to include space as *living area*.

When an area that is not part of the *living area* (e.g., a garage) shares a common wall with the *living area*, treat the common wall as the exterior wall for the *living area*; therefore, the measurements for the *living area* will include the thickness of the common wall, and the measurements for the other area will not.

Interior space that is open from the floor of one level to the ceiling of the next higher level is included in the square footage for the lower level only. However, any area occupied by interior balconies, lofts, etc. on the upper level or stairs that extend to the upper level is included in the square footage for the upper level.

MEASURING

The amount of *living area* and "other area" in dwellings is based upon **exterior measurements**. A one-hundred-foot-long tape measure is recommended for use in measuring the exterior of dwellings, and a thirty-foot retractable tape for measuring interior and hard-to-reach spaces. A tape measure that indicates linear footage in "tenths of a foot" will greatly simplify your calculations. For best results, take a partner to assist you in measuring. But if you do not have someone to assist you, a screwdriver or other sharp tool can be used to secure the tape measure to the ground.

Begin at one corner of the dwelling and proceed with measuring each exterior wall. **Round off your measurements to the nearest inch** (or tenth-of-a-foot if your tape indicates footage in that manner). Make a sketch of the structure. Write down each measurement as you go, and record it on your sketch. A clipboard and graph paper are helpful in sketching the dwelling and recording the measurements. Measure *living area* and "other area," but identify them separately on your sketch. Look for offsets (portions of walls that "jut out"), and adjust for any "overlap" of exterior walls (Fig. 3) or "overhang" in upper levels (Fig. 5).

When you cannot measure an exterior surface (such as in the case of attics and below-grade areas), measure the perimeter walls of the area from the inside of the dwelling. Remember to add **six inches** for each exterior wall and interior wall that you encounter in order to arrive at the exterior dimensions (Fig. 2, 3, 4, 6).

Measure all sides of the dwelling, making sure that the overall lengths of the front and rear sides are equal, as well as the ends. Then inspect the interior of the dwelling to identify spaces which cannot be included in *living area*. You may also find it helpful

to take several photographs of the dwelling for later use when you return to your office.

CALCULATING SQUARE FOOTAGE

From your sketch of the dwelling, identify and separate *living area* from "other area." If your measurements are in inches (rather than tenths-of-a-foot), convert your figures to a decimal as follows:

1" = .10 ft.	7" = .60 ft.
2" = .20 ft.	8" = .70 ft.
3" = .25 ft.	9" = .75 ft.
4" = .30 ft	10" = .80 ft.
5" = .40 ft.	11" = .90 ft.
6" = .50 ft.	12" = 1.00 ft.

Calculate the *living area* (and other area) by multiplying the length times the width of each rectangular space. Then add your subtotals and round off your figure for total square footage to the nearest **square foot**. Double-check your calculations. When in doubt, re-check them and, if necessary, re-measure the house.

ATTACHED DWELLINGS

When measuring an "attached" single-family home (e.g., townhouse, duplex, condominium, etc.), use the same techniques just described. If there is a common wall, measure to the inside surface of the wall and add **six inches**. [*Note: In the case of condominiums, do not include the thickness of exterior or common walls.*] Do not include any "common areas" (exterior hallways, stairways, etc.) in your calculations.

PROPOSED CONSTRUCTION

For proposed construction, your square footage calculations will be based upon dimensions described in blueprints and building plans. When reporting the projected square footage, be careful to disclose that you have calculated the square footage based upon plan dimensions. Therefore, the square footage may differ in the completed structure. Do not rely on any calculations printed on the plans.

AGENTS' RESPONSIBILITIES
(Effective May 9, 2001)

Real estate agents are expected to be able to accurately calculate the square footage of most dwellings. When reporting square footage, whether to a party to a real estate transaction, another real estate agent, or others, a real estate agent is expected to provide accurate square footage information that was compiled using these *Guidelines* or comparable standards. While an agent is expected to use reasonable skill, care and diligence when calculating square footage, it should be noted that the Commission does not expect absolute perfection. Because all properties are unique and no guidelines can anticipate every possibility, minor discrepancies in deriving square footage are not considered by the Commission to constitute negligence on the part of the agent. Minor variations in tape readings and small differences in rounding off or conversion from inches to decimals, when multiplied over distances, will cause reasonable discrepancies between two competent measurements of the same dwelling. In addition to differences due to minor variations in measurement and calculation, discrepancies between measurements may also be attributable to reasonable differences in interpretation. For instance, two agents might reasonably differ about whether an addition to a dwelling is sufficiently finished under these *Guidelines* to be included within the measured living area. Differences

which are based upon an agent's thoughtful judgment reasonably founded on these or other similar guidelines will not be considered by the Commission to constitute error on the agent's part. Deviations in calculated square footage of less than five percent will seldom be cause for concern.

As a general rule, the most reliable way for an agent to obtain accurate square footage data is by personally measuring the dwelling unit and calculating the square footage. It is especially recommended that *listing agents* use this approach for dwellings that are not particularly unusual or complex in their design.

As an alternative to personally measuring a dwelling and calculating its square footage, an agent may rely on the square footage reported by other persons when it is reasonable under the circumstances to do so. Generally speaking, an agent working with a buyer (either as a buyer's agent or as a seller's agent) may rely on the listing agent's square footage representations except in those unusual instances when there is an error in the reported square footage that should be obvious to a reasonably prudent agent. For example, a buyer's agent would not be expected to notice that a house advertised as containing 2200 square feet of living area in fact contained only 2000 square feet. On the other hand, that same agent, under most circumstances, would be expected to realize that a house described as containing 3200 square feet really contained only 2300 square feet of living area. If there is such a "red flag" regarding the reported square footage, the agent working with the buyer should promptly point out the suspected error to the buyer and the listing agent. The listing agent should then verify the square footage and correct any error in the information reported.

It is also appropriate for an agent to rely upon measurements and calculations performed by other professionals with greater expertise in determining square footage. A new agent who may be unsure of his or her own calculations should seek guidance from a more experienced agent. As the new agent gains experience and confidence, he or she will become less reliant on the assistance of others. In order to ensure accuracy of the square footage they report, even experienced agents may wish to rely upon a competent state-licensed or state-certified appraiser or another agent with greater expertise in determining square footage. For example, an agent might be confronted with an unusual measurement problem or a dwelling of complex design. The house described in Figure 8 in these *Guidelines* is such a property. When an agent relies upon measurements and calculations personally performed by a competent appraiser or a more expert agent, the appraiser or agent must use these *Guidelines* or other comparable standards and the square footage reported must be specifically determined in connection with the current transaction. An agent who relies on another's measurement would still be expected to recognize an obvious error in the reported square footage and to alert any interested parties.

Some sources of square footage information are by their very nature unreliable. For example, an agent should **not** rely on square footage information determined by the property owner or included in property tax records. An agent should also **not** rely on square footage information included in a listing, appraisal report or survey prepared in connection with an earlier transaction.

In areas where the prevailing practice is to report square footage in the advertising and marketing of homes, agents whose policy is **not** to calculate and report square footage must disclose this fact to prospective buyer and seller clients before entering into agency agreements with them.

ILLUSTRATIONS

For assistance in calculating and reporting the area of homes, refer to the following illustrations showing the *living area* shaded. To test your knowledge, an illustration and blank "Worksheet" for a home with a more challenging floor plan has also been included. (A completed "Worksheet" for the Practice Floor Plan can be found on page 23.) In reviewing the illustrations, assume that for those homes with basements, attics, etc., the exterior measurements shown have been derived from interior measurements taking into account walls and partitions. (*see page 4*). Where there is a common wall between *living area* and other area (*see page 3*) the measurements shown in the illustrations include the thickness of the common wall in *living area* except in the condominium example where wall thickness is not included.

ONE STORY WITH BASEMENT AND CARPORT

(Figure 1)

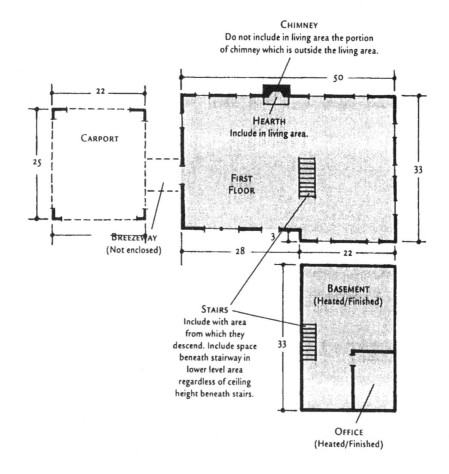

CHIMNEY
Do not include in living area the portion
of chimney which is outside the living area.

50

22

CARPORT

HEARTH
Include in living area.

25

33

**FIRST
FLOOR**

BREEZEWAY
(Not enclosed)

28

3

22

BASEMENT
(Heated/Finished)

STAIRS
Include with area
from which they
descend. Include space
beneath stairway in
lower level area
regardless of ceiling
height beneath stairs.

33

OFFICE
(Heated/Finished)

One Story With Basement and Carport Worksheet

LIVING AREA			
AREA	DIMENSIONS	SUBTOTAL	TOTAL
1st Floor	50 x 30	1,500	
	3 x 22	+ 66	1,566
Basement	22 x 33		<u>726</u>
Total			2,292

OTHER AREA			
AREA	DIMENSIONS	SUBTOTAL	TOTAL
Carport	22 x 25		550

REPORT: ONE-STORY DETACHED HOUSE WITH 2,292 SQUARE FEET OF LIVING AREA OF WHICH 726 SQUARE FEET ARE IN A FINISHED BASEMENT, PLUS A 550-SQUARE-FOOT CARPORT.

Two Story With Open Foyer and Finished Attic

(Figure 2)

Attic
Add 1 ft. (6" for each exterior side wall) to inside measurements. Thus, 19' inside measurement equals 20' exterior measurement. In this example, do NOT add for front and rear walls since the allowable square footage (5' ceiling height) does not extend to the kneewalls.

3RD FLOOR ATTIC
(Heated/Finished)

3 Ft. Kneewall
In rooms with sloped ceilings, do not include any area with a ceiling height of less than 5 ft.

Stairway with Open Area
1. Calculate area of open space (10' x 12' = 120 sf).
2. Subtract from second floor area (1,200-120=1,080 sf).
3. Add stairway (6' x 4' = 24 + 1,080 = 1,104 sf).

Bay Window
(Floored)
Include in living area if it is floored and has ceiling height of at least 7 ft.
1. Calculate area of triangles (3' x 4'÷ 2 = 6 sf x 2 = 12 sf).
2. Add area of triangles (12 sf) to remaining area of bay window (6' x 4' = 24 sf) = 36 sf.

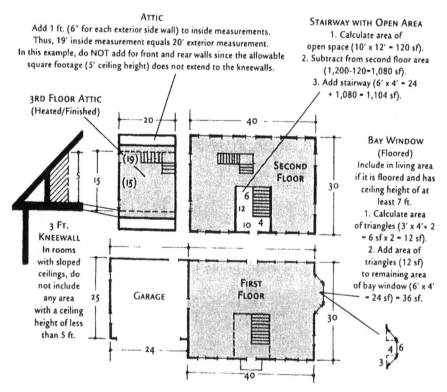

Two Story With Open Foyer and Finished Attic Worksheet

LIVING AREA			
AREA	DIMENSIONS	SUBTOTAL	TOTAL
1st Floor	40 x 30	1,200	
Bay Window		36	1,236
2nd Floor	40 x 30	1,200	
	10 x 12	– 120	
	4 x 6	+ 24	1,104
Fin. Attic	20 x 15		300
Total			2,640
OTHER AREA			
AREA	DIMENSIONS	SUBTOTAL	TOTAL
Garage	25 x 24		600

REPORT: TWO-STORY DETACHED HOUSE WITH 2,640 SQUARE FEET OF LIVING AREA OF WHICH 300 SQUARE FEET ARE IN A FINISHED ATTIC, PLUS A 600-SQUARE-FOOT GARAGE.

TWO STORY WITH "BONUS ROOM" OVER GARAGE

(Figure 3)

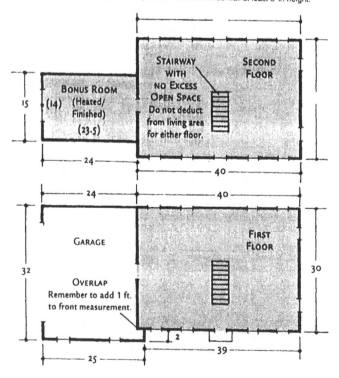

BONUS ROOM
If the "Bonus Room" is accessible from living area through a door,
hallway or stairway, include in living area; otherwise, report as other area.

In rooms with sloped ceilings, add 6" for each knee wall at least 5' in height.

Two Story With "Bonus Room" Over Garage Worksheet

LIVING AREA			
AREA	DIMENSIONS	SUBTOTAL	TOTAL
1st Floor	40 x 30		1,200
2nd Floor	40 x 30		1,200
Bonus Room	15 x 24		<u>360</u>
Total			2,760
OTHER AREA			
AREA	DIMENSIONS	SUBTOTAL	TOTAL
Garage	24 x 32	768	
	1 x 2	+ 2	770

REPORT: TWO-STORY DETACHED HOUSE WITH 2,760 SQUARE FEET OF LIVING AREA OF WHICH 360 SQUARE FEET ARE IN A "BONUS ROOM" OVER THE GARAGE, PLUS A 770-SQUARE-FOOT GARAGE.

SPLIT FOYER

(Figure 4)

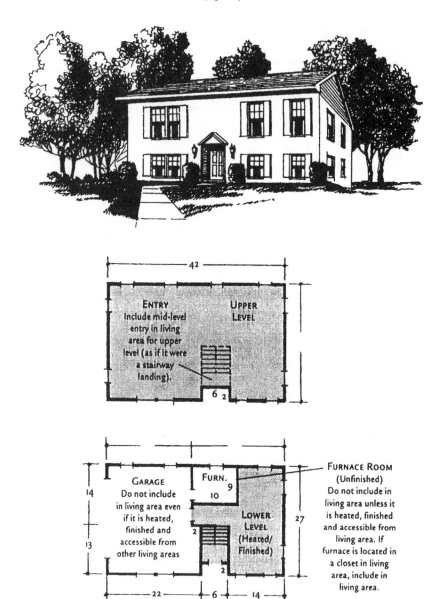

SPLIT FOYER WORKSHEET

LIVING AREA			
AREA	DIMENSIONS	SUBTOTAL	TOTAL
Upper Level	27 x 42	1,134	
	6 x 2	– 12	1,122
Lower Level	22 x 27	594	
	6 x 2	– 12	
	13 x 2	– 26	
	9 x 10	– 90	466
Total			1,588
OTHER AREA			
AREA	DIMENSIONS	SUBTOTAL	TOTAL
Garage	27 x 20	540	
	2 x 13	+ 26	566
Furnace Room	9 x 10		90

REPORT: SPLIT-FOYER DETACHED HOUSE WITH 1,588 SQUARE FEET OF LIVING AREA,
PLUS A 566-SQAURE-FOOT GARAGE AND 90-SQUARE-FOOT FURNACE ROOM.

SPLIT (TRI-) LEVEL WITH OVERHANG

(Figure 5)

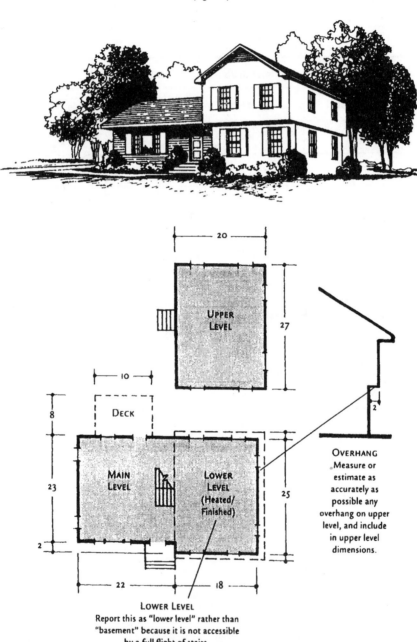

LOWER LEVEL
Report this as "lower level" rather than
"basement" because it is not accessible
by a full flight of stairs.

Split (Tri-) Level With Overhang Worksheet

LIVING AREA			
AREA	DIMENSIONS	SUBTOTAL	TOTAL
Main Level	22 x 23		506
Lower Level	18 x 25		450
Upper Level	27 x 20		<u>540</u>
Total			1,496
OTHER AREA			
AREA	DIMENSIONS	SUBTOTAL	TOTAL
Deck	8 x 10		80

REPORT: SPLIT-LEVEL DETACHED HOUSE WITH 1,496 SQUARE FEET OF LIVING AREA, PLUS AN 80-SQUARE-FOOT DECK.

ONE AND ONE-HALF STORY

(Figure 6)

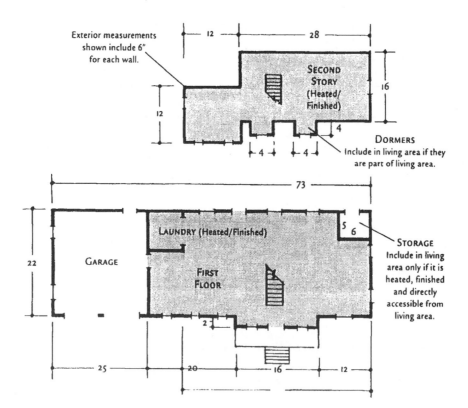

ONE AND ONE-HALF STORY WORKSHEET

LIVING AREA			
AREA	DIMENSIONS	SUBTOTAL	TOTAL
1st Floor	48 x 22	1,056	
	16 x 2	+ 32	
	5 x 6	− 30	1,058
2nd Floor	16 x 28	448	
	4 x 4	+ 16	
	4 x 4	+ 16	
	12 x 12	+ 144	<u>624</u>
Total			1,682
OTHER AREA			
AREA	DIMENSIONS	SUBTOTAL	TOTAL
Garage	22 x 25		550
Storage	5 x 6		30

REPORT: ONE AND ONE-HALF STORY DETACHED HOUSE WITH 1,682 SQUARE FEET OF LIVING AREA,
PLUS A 550-SQUARE-FOOT GARAGE.

CONDOMINIUM

(Figure 7)

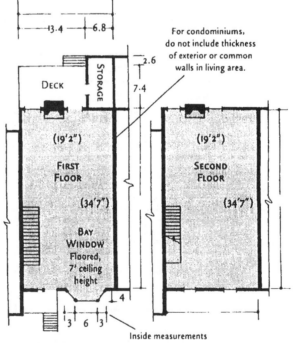

For condominiums, do not include thickness of exterior or common walls in living area.

Inside measurements

CONDOMINIUM WORKSHEET

LIVING AREA			
AREA	DIMENSIONS	SUBTOTAL	TOTAL
1st Floor	34.6 x 19.2	664.3	
Bay Window		36.0	700
2nd Floor	34.6 x 19.2	664.3	664
Total			1,364
OTHER AREA			
AREA	DIMENSIONS	SUBTOTAL	TOTAL
Deck	13.4 x 7.4	99.2	99
Storage	10 x 6.8		68

REPORT: TWO-STORY CONDOMINIUM WITH 1,364 SQUARE FEET OF LIVING AREA, PLUS A 99 SQUARE FOOT DECK.

PRACTICE FLOOR PLAN

(Figure 8)

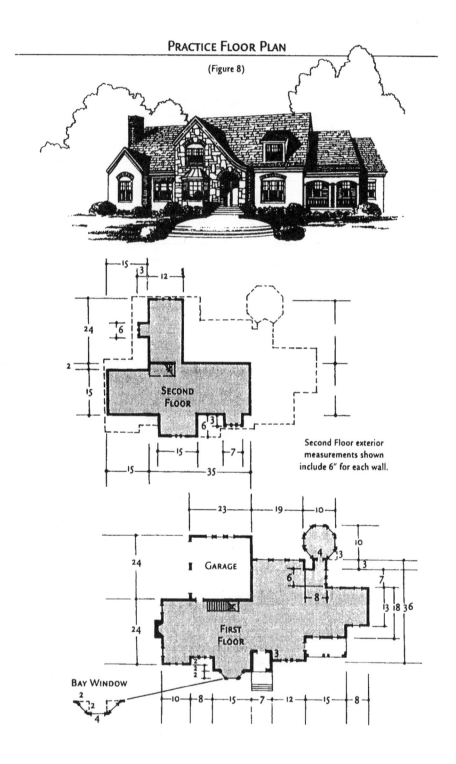

Second Floor exterior measurements shown include 6" for each wall.

PRACTICE FLOOR PLAN WORKSHEET

LIVING AREA			
AREA	DIMENSIONS	SUBTOTAL	TOTAL
OTHER AREA			
AREA	DIMENSIONS	SUBTOTAL	TOTAL

REPORT:

PRACTICE FLOOR PLAN

(Zoned to facilitate calculations)

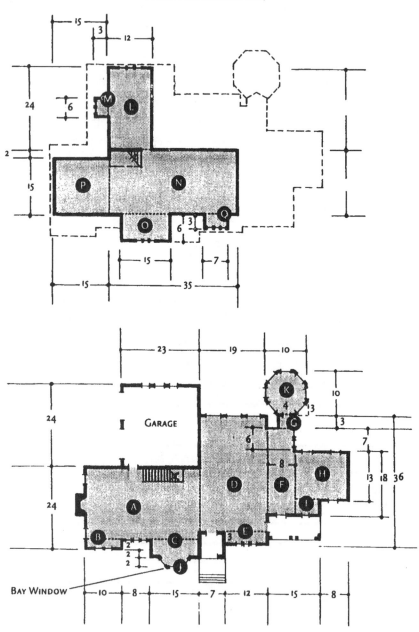

BAY WINDOW

PRACTICE FLOOR PLAN

(Zoned to facilitate calculations)

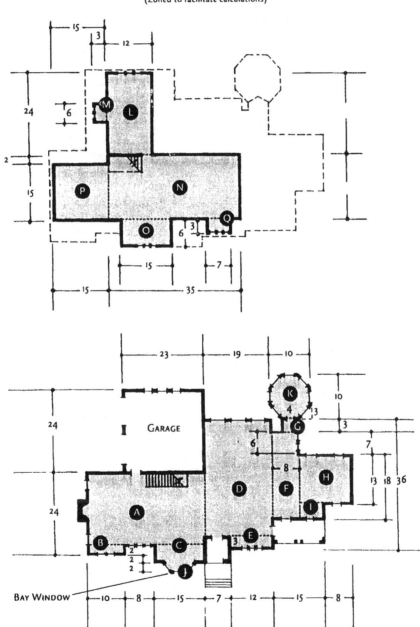

PRACTICE FLOOR PLAN WORKSHEET

LIVING AREA			
AREA	DIMENSIONS	SUBTOTAL	TOTAL
1st Floor A	22 x 33	726	
1st Floor B	2 x 10	20	
1st Floor C	4 x 15	60	
1st Floor D	19 x 33	627	
1st Floor E	3 x 12	36	
1st Floor F	8 x 25	200	
1st Floor G	4 x 3	12	
1st Floor H	15 x 13	195	
1st Floor I	7 x 5	35	
Bay Window J		12	
Oct. Window K		82	2,005
2nd Floor L	24 x 12	288	
2nd Floor M	3 x 6	18	
2nd Floor N	17 x 35	595	
2nd Floor O	15 x 6	90	
2nd Floor P	15 x 15	225	
2nd Floor Q	3 x 7	21	1,237
Total			3,242

OTHER AREA			
AREA	DIMENSIONS	SUBTOTAL	TOTAL
Garage	24 x 23		552

REPORT: ONE AND ONE-HALF STORY DETACHED HOUSE WITH 3,242 SQUARE FEET OF LIVING AREA, PLUS A 552-SQUARE-FOOT GARAGE.

APPENDIX C

Real Estate License Law and Commission Rules

In 1957, the North Carolina General Assembly enacted into law, to be effective July 1, 1957, the Real Estate Licensing Act, codified as Chapter 93A of the General Statutes of North Carolina. This law created the North Carolina Real Estate Commission (NCREC) and empowered it to write and enforce reasonable rules and regulations concerning the business activities of real estate licensees. The Commission has the authority to approve real estate prelicensing schools and also publishes prelicensing course syllabi. The Real Estate Commission also publishes and updates as required a booklet entitled *Real Estate Licensing in North Carolina*. The real estate licensing applicant is required to be knowledgeable about the portions of General Statute 93A and Commission Rules, which are contained in this appendix. The study of this material should take place directly from the materials in this appendix. The NCREC has provided clarifying comments and examples for some of the more complex sections of the law and rules in the *License Law and Rule Comments* beginning on page 524. In an effort to further clarify some of the remaining sections of the law and rules, the publisher has added a *Key Point Review* at the end of the appendix.

NORTH CAROLINA REAL ESTATE LICENSE LAW
Codified as Chapter 93A of the General Statutes of North Carolina

Please note: Certain "gender neutral" terms used in the Real Estate License Law as reprinted in this booklet are subject to final revision by the Revisor of Statutes.

Source: Reprinted with permission of the North Carolina Real Estate Commission

Real Estate License Law
[Codified as Chapter 93A of the General Statutes of North Carolina]

ARTICLE 1.
REAL ESTATE BROKERS.

93A-1. License required of real estate brokers.

From and after July 1, 1957, it shall be unlawful for any person, partnership, corporation, limited liability company, association, or other business entity in this State to act as a real estate broker, or directly or indirectly to engage or assume to engage in the business of real estate broker or to advertise or hold himself or herself or themselves out as engaging in or conducting such business without first obtaining a license issued by the North Carolina Real Estate Commission (hereinafter referred to as the Commission), under the provisions of this Chapter. A license shall be obtained from the Commission even if the person, partnership, corporation, limited liability company, association, or business entity is licensed in another state and is affiliated or otherwise associated with a licensed real estate broker in this State.

93A-2. Definitions and exceptions.

(a) A real estate broker within the meaning of this Chapter is any person, partnership, corporation, limited liability company, association, or other business entity who for a compensation or valuable consideration or promise thereof lists or offers to list, sells or offers to sell, buys or offers to buy, auctions or offers to auction (specifically not including a mere crier of sales), or negotiates the purchase or sale or exchange of real estate, or who leases or offers to lease, or who sells or offers to sell leases of whatever character, or rents or offers to rent any real estate or the improvement thereon, for others.

(a1) The term broker-in-charge within the meaning of this Chapter shall mean a real estate broker who has been designated as the broker having responsibility for the supervision of real estate salespersons engaged in real estate brokerage at a particular real estate office and for other administrative and supervisory duties as the Commission shall prescribe by rule.

(a2) The term provisional broker within the meaning of this Chapter means a real estate broker who, pending acquisition and documentation to the Commission of the education or experience prescribed by either G.S. 93A-4(a1) or G.S. 93A-4.3, must be supervised by a broker-in-charge when performing any act for which a real estate license is required.

(b) The term real estate salesperson within the meaning of this Chapter shall mean and include any person who was formerly licensed by the Commission as a real estate salesperson before April 1, 2006.

(c) The provisions of this Chapter shall not apply to and shall not include:

(1) Any person, partnership, corporation, limited liability company, association, or other business entity who, as owner or lessor, shall perform any of the acts aforesaid with reference to property owned or leased by them, where the acts are performed in the regular course of or as incident to the management of that property and the investment therein.

(2) Any person acting as an attorney-in-fact under a duly executed power of attorney from the owner authorizing the final consummation of performance of any contract for the sale, lease or exchange of real estate.

(3) The acts or services of an attorney-at-law.

(4) Any person, while acting as a receiver, trustee in bankruptcy, guardian, administrator or executor or any person acting under order of any court.

(5) Any person, while acting as a trustee under a trust agreement, deed of trust or will, or his or her regular salaried employees.

(6) Any salaried person employed by a licensed real estate broker, for and on behalf of the owner of any real estate or the improvements thereon, which the licensed broker has contracted to manage for the owner, if the salaried employee is limited in his or her employment to: exhibiting units on the real estate to prospective tenants; providing the prospective tenants with information about the lease of the units; accepting applications for lease of the units; completing and executing preprinted form leases; and accepting security deposits and rental payments for the units only when the deposits and rental payments are made payable to the owner or the broker employed by the owner. The salaried employee shall not negotiate the amount of security deposits or rental payments and shall not negotiate leases or any rental agreements on behalf of the owner or broker.

(7) Any owner who personally leases or sells his or her own property.

(8) Any housing authority organized in accordance with the provisions of Chapter 157 of the General Statutes and any regular salaried employees of the housing authority when performing acts authorized in this Chapter as to any property owned or leased by the housing authority. This exception shall not apply to any person, partnership, corporation, limited liability company, association, or other business entity that contracts with a housing authority to sell or manage property owned or leased by the housing authority.

93A-3. Commission created; compensation; organization.

(a) There is hereby created the North Carolina Real Estate Commission, hereinafter called the Commission. The Commission shall consist of nine members, seven members to be appointed by the Governor, one member to be appointed by the General Assembly upon the recommendation of the President Pro Tempore of the Senate in accordance with G.S. 120-121, and one member to be appointed by the General Assembly upon the recommendation of the Speaker of the House of Representatives in accordance with G.S. 120-121. At least three members of the Commission shall be licensed real estate brokers. At least two members of the Commission shall be persons who are not involved directly or indirectly in the real estate or real estate appraisal business. Members of the Commission shall serve three-year terms so staggered that the terms of three members expire in one year, the terms of three members expire in the next year, and the terms of three members expire in the third year of each three-year period. The members of the Commission shall elect one of their members to serve as chairman of the Commission for a term of one year. The Governor may remove any member of the Commission for misconduct, incompetency, or willful neglect of duty. The Governor shall have the power to fill all vacancies occurring on the Commission, except vacancies in legislative appointments shall be filled under G.S. 120-122.

(b) The provisions of G.S. 93B-5 notwithstanding, members of the Commission shall receive as compensation for each day spent on work for the Commission a per diem in an amount established by the Commission by rule, and mileage reimbursement for transportation by privately owned automobile at the business standard mileage rate set by the Internal Revenue Service per mile of travel along with actual cost of tolls paid. The total expense of the administration of this Chapter shall not exceed the total income therefrom; and none of the expenses of said Commission or the compensation or expenses of any office thereof or any employee shall ever be paid or payable out of the treasury of the State of North Carolina; and neither the Commission nor any officer or employee thereof shall have any power or authority to make or incur any expense, debt or other financial obligation binding upon the State of North Carolina. After all expenses of operation, the Commission may set aside an expense reserve each year not to exceed ten percent (10%) of the previous year's gross income; then any surplus shall go to the general fund of the State of North Carolina. The Commission may deposit moneys in accounts, certificates of deposit, or time deposits as the Commission may approve, in any bank, savings and loan association, or trust company. Moneys also may be invested in the same classes of securities referenced in G.S. 159-30(c).

(c) The Commission shall have power to make reasonable bylaws, rules and regulations that are not inconsistent with the provisions of this Chapter and the General Statutes; provided, however, the Commission shall not make rules or regulations regulating commissions, salaries, or fees to be charged by licensees under this Chapter.

(c1) The provisions of G.S. 93A-1 and G.S. 93A-2 notwithstanding, the Commission may adopt rules to permit a real estate broker to pay a fee or other valuable consideration to a travel agent for the introduction or procurement of tenants or potential tenants in vacation rentals as defined in G.S. 42A-4. Rules adopted pursuant to this subsection may include a definition of the term 'travel agent', may regulate the conduct of permitted transactions, and may limit the amount of the fee or the value of the consideration that may be paid to the travel agent. However, the Commission may not authorize a person or entity not licensed as a broker to negotiate any real estate transaction on behalf of another.

(c2) The Commission shall adopt a seal for its use, which shall bear thereon the words "North Carolina Real Estate Commission." Copies of all records and papers in the office of the Commission duly certified and authenticated by the seal of the Commission shall be received in evidence in all courts and with like effect as the originals.

(d) The Commission may employ an Executive Director and professional and clerical staff as may be necessary to carry out the provisions of this Chapter and to put into effect the rules and regulations that the Commission may promulgate. The Commission shall fix salaries and shall require employees to make good and sufficient surety bond for the faithful performance of their duties. The Commission shall reimburse its employees for travel on official business. Mileage expenses for transportation by privately owned automobile shall be reimbursed at the business standard mileage set by the Internal Revenue Service per mile of travel along with the actual tolls paid. Other travel expenses shall be reimbursed in accordance with G.S. 138-6. The Commission may, when it deems it necessary or convenient, delegate to the Executive Director, legal counsel for the Commission, or other Commission staff, professional or clerical, the Commission's authority and duties under this Chapter, but the Commission may not delegate its authority to make rules or its duty to act as a hearing panel in accordance with the provisions of G.S. 150B-40(b).

(e) The Commission shall be entitled to the services of the Attorney General of North Carolina, in connection with the affairs of the Commission or may on approval of the Attorney General, employ an attorney to assist or represent it in the enforcement of this Chapter, as to specific matters, but the fee paid for such service shall be approved by the Attorney General. The Commission may prefer a complaint for violation of this Chapter before any court of competent jurisdiction, and it may take the necessary legal steps through the proper legal offices of the State to enforce the provisions of this Chapter and collect the penalties provided therein.

(f) The Commission is authorized to acquire, hold, convey, rent, encumber, alienate, and otherwise deal with real property in the same manner as a private person or corporation, subject only to the approval of the Governor and Council of State. The rents, proceeds, and other revenues and benefits of the ownership of real property shall inure to the Commission. Collateral pledged by the Commission for any encumbrance of real property shall be limited to the assets, income, and revenues of the Commission. Leases, deeds, and other instruments relating to the Commission's interest in real property shall be valid when executed by the executive director of the Commission. The Commission may create and conduct education and information programs relating to the real estate business for the information, education, guidance and protection of the general public, licensees, and applicants for license. The education and information programs may include preparation, printing and distribution of publications and articles and the conduct of conferences, seminars, and lectures. The Commission may claim the copyright to written materials it creates and may charge fees for publications and programs.

93A-4. Applications for licenses; fees; qualifications; examinations; privilege licenses; renewal or reinstatement of license; power to enforce provisions.

(a) Any person, partnership, corporation, limited liability company, association, or other business entity hereafter desiring to enter into business of and obtain a license as a real estate broker shall make written application for such license to the Commission in the form and manner prescribed by the Commission. Each applicant for a license as a real estate broker shall be at least 18 years of age. Each applicant for a license as a real estate broker shall, within three years preceding the date the application is made, have satisfactorily completed, at a school approved by the Commission, an education program consisting of at least 75 hours of classroom instruction in subjects determined by the Commission, or shall possess real estate education or experience in real estate transactions which the Commission shall find equivalent to the education program. Each applicant for a license as a real estate broker shall be required to pay a fee, fixed by the Commission but not to exceed thirty dollars ($30.00).

(a1) Each person who is issued a real estate broker license on or after April 1, 2006, shall initially be classified as a provisional broker and shall, within three years follow-ing initial licensure, satisfactorily complete, at a school approved by the Commission, a postlicensing education program consisting of 90 hours of classroom instruction in subjects determined by the Commission or shall possess real estate education or experience in real estate transactions which the Commission shall find equivalent to the education program. The Commission may, by rule, establish a schedule for completion of the prescribed postlicensing education that requires provisional brokers to complete portions of the 90-hour postlicensing education program in less than three years, and provisional brokers must comply with this schedule in order to be entitled to actively engage in real estate brokerage. Upon completion of the postlicensing education program, the provisional status of the broker's license shall be terminated. When a provisional broker fails to complete all 90 hours of required postlicensing education within three years following initial licensure, the broker's license shall be cancelled, and the Commission may, in its discretion, require the person whose license was cancelled to satisfy the postlicensing education program and the requirements for original licensure prescribed in this Chapter as a condition of license reinstatement, including the examination requirements and the license reinstatement fee prescribed by subsection (c) of this section.

(a2) An approved school shall pay a fee of ten dollars ($10.00) per licensee to the Commission for each licensee completing a postlicensing education course conducted by the school, provided that these fees shall not be charged to a community college, junior college, college, or university located in this State and accredited by the Southern Association of Colleges and Schools.

(b) Except as otherwise provided in this Chapter, any person who submits an application to the Commission in proper manner for a license as real estate broker shall be required to take an examination. The examination may be administered orally, by computer, or by any other method the Commission deems appropriate. The Commission may require the applicant to pay the Commission or a provider contracted by the Commission the actual cost of the examination and its administration. The cost of the examination and its administration shall be in addition to any other fees the applicant is required to pay under subsection (a) of this section. The examination shall determine the applicant's qualifications with due regard to the paramount interests of the public as to the applicant's competency. A person who fails the license examination shall be entitled to know the result and score. A person who passes the exam shall be notified only that the person passed the examination. Whether a person passed or failed the examination shall be a matter of public record; however, the scores for license examinations shall not be considered public records. Nothing in this subsection shall limit the rights granted to any person under G.S. 93B-8.

An applicant for licensure under this Chapter shall satisfy the Commission that he or she possesses the competency, honesty, truthfulness, integrity, and general moral character necessary to protect the public interest and promote public confidence in the real estate brokerage business. The Commission may investigate the moral character of each applicant for licensure and require an applicant to provide the Commission with a criminal record report. All applicants shall obtain criminal record reports from one or more reporting services designated by the Commission to provide criminal record reports. Applicants are required to pay the designated reporting service for the cost of these reports. If the results of any required competency examination and investigation of the applicant's moral character shall be satisfactory to the Commission, then the Commission shall issue to the applicant a license, authorizing the applicant to act as a real estate broker in the State of North Carolina, upon the payment of privilege taxes now required by law or that may hereafter be required by law. Notwithstanding G.S. 150B-38(c), in a contested case commenced upon the request of a party applying for licensure regarding the question of the moral character or fitness of the applicant, if notice has been reasonably attempted, but cannot be given to the applicant personally or by certified mail in accordance with G.S. 150B-38(c), the notice of hearing shall be deemed given to the applicant when a copy of the notice is deposited in an official depository of the United States Postal Service addressed to the applicant at the latest mailing address provided by the applicant to the Commission or by any other means reasonably designed to achieve actual notice to the applicant.

(b1) The Department of Justice may provide a criminal record check to the Commission for a person who has applied for a license through the Commission. The Commission shall provide to the Department of Justice, along with the request, the fingerprints of the applicant, any additional information required by the Department of Justice, and a form signed by the applicant consenting to the check of the criminal record and to the use of the fingerprints and other identifying information required by the State or national repositories. The applicant's fingerprints shall be forwarded to the State Bureau of Investigation for a search of the State's criminal history record file, and the State Bureau of Investigation shall forward a set of the fingerprints to the Federal Bureau of Investigation for a national criminal history check. The Commission shall keep all information pursuant to this subsection privileged, in accordance with applicable State law and federal guidelines, and the information shall be confidential and shall not be a public record under Chapter 132 of the General Statutes.

The Department of Justice may charge each applicant a fee for conducting the checks of criminal history records authorized by this subsection.

(c) All licenses issued by the Commission under the provisions of this Chapter shall expire on the 30th day of June following issuance or on any other date that the Commission may determine and shall become invalid after that date unless reinstated. A license may be renewed 45 days prior to the expiration date by filing an application with and paying to the Executive Director of the Commission the license renewal fee. The license renewal fee is thirty dollars ($30.00) unless the Commission sets the fee at a higher amount. The Commission may set the license renewal fee at an amount that does not exceed fifty dollars ($50.00). The license renewal fee may not increase by more than five dollars ($5.00) during a 12-month period. The Commission may adopt rules establishing a system of license renewal in which the licenses expire annually with varying expiration dates. These rules shall provide for prorating the annual fee to cover the initial renewal period so that no licensee shall be charged an amount greater than the annual fee for any 12-month period. The fee for reinstatement of an expired license shall be fifty-five dollars ($55.00). In the event a licensee fails to obtain a reinstatement of such license within six months after the expiration date thereof, the Commission may, in its discretion, consider such person as not having been previously licensed, and thereby subject to the provisions of this Chapter relating to the issuance of an original license, including the examination requirements set forth herein. Duplicate licenses may be issued by the Commission upon payment of a fee of five dollars ($5.00) by the licensee. Commission certification of a licensee's license history shall be made only after the payment of a fee of ten dollars ($10.00).

(d) The Commission is expressly vested with the power and authority to make and enforce any and all reasonable rules and regulations connected with license application, examination, renewal, and reinstatement as shall be deemed necessary to administer and enforce the provisions of this Chapter. The Commission is further authorized to adopt reasonable rules and regulations necessary for the approval of real estate schools, instructors, and textbooks and rules that prescribe specific requirements pertaining to instruction, administration, and content of required education courses and programs.

(e) Nothing contained in this Chapter shall be construed as giving any authority to the Commission nor any licensee of the Commission as authorizing any licensee to engage in the practice of law or to render any legal service as specifically set out in G.S. 84-2.1 or any other legal service not specifically referred to in said section.

93A-4.1. Continuing education.

(a) The Commission shall establish a program of continuing education for real estate brokers. An individual licensed as a real estate broker is required to complete continuing education requirements in an amount not to exceed eight classroom hours of instruction a year during any license renewal period in subjects and at times the Commission deems appropriate. Any licensee who fails to complete continuing education requirements pursuant to this section shall not actively engage in the business of real estate broker.

(a1) The Commission may, as part of the broker continuing education requirements, require real estate brokers-in-charge to complete during each annual license period a special continuing education course consisting of not more than four classroom hours of instruction in subjects prescribed by the Commission.

(b) The Commission shall establish procedures allowing for a deferral of continuing education for brokers while they are not actively engaged in real estate brokerage.

(c) The Commission may adopt any reasonable rules not inconsistent with this Chapter to give purpose and effect to the continuing education requirement, including rules that govern:

(1) The content and subject matter of continuing education courses.

(2) The curriculum of courses required.

(3) The criteria, standards, and procedures for the approval of courses, course sponsors, and course instructors.

(4) The methods of instruction.

(5) The computation of course credit.

(6) The ability to carry forward course credit from one year to another.

(7) The deferral of continuing education for brokers and salespersons not engaged in brokerage.

(8) The waiver of or variance from the continuing education requirement for hardship or other reasons.

(9) The procedures for compliance and sanctions for noncompliance.

(d) The Commission may establish a nonrefundable course application fee to be charged to a course sponsor for the review and approval of a proposed continuing education course. The fee shall not exceed one hundred twenty-five dollars ($125.00) per course. The Commission may charge the sponsor of an approved course a nonrefundable fee not to exceed seventy-five dollars ($75.00) for the annual renewal of course approval. An approved course sponsor shall pay a fee of ten dollars ($10.00) per licensee to the Commission for each licensee completing an approved continuing education course conducted by the sponsor. The Commission shall not charge a course application fee, a course renewal fee, or any other fee for a continuing education course sponsored by a community college, junior college, college, or university located in this State and accredited by the Southern Association of Colleges and Schools.

(e) The Commission may award continuing education credit for an unapproved course or related educational activity. The Commission may prescribe procedures for a licensee to submit information on an unapproved course or related educational activity for continuing education credit. The Commission may charge a fee to the licensee for each course or activity submitted. The fee shall not exceed fifty dollars ($50.00).

93A-4.2. Broker-in-charge qualification.

To be qualified to serve as a broker-in-charge of a real estate office, a real estate broker shall possess at least two years of full-time real estate brokerage experience or equivalent part-time real estate brokerage experience within the previous five years or real estate education or experience in real estate transactions that the Commission finds equivalent to such experience and shall complete, within a time prescribed by the Commission, a course of study prescribed by the Commission for brokers-in-charge not to exceed 12 classroom hours of instruction. A provisional broker may not be designated as a broker-in-charge.

93A-4.3. Elimination of salesperson license; conversion of salesperson licenses to broker licenses.

(a) Effective April 1, 2006, the Commission shall discontinue issuing real estate salesperson licenses. Also effective April 1, 2006, all salesperson licenses shall become broker licenses, and each person holding a broker license that was changed from salesperson to broker on that date shall be classified as a provisional broker as defined in G.S. 93A-2(a2).

(b) A provisional broker as contemplated in subsection (a) of this section who was issued a salesperson license prior to October 1, 2005, shall, not later than April 1, 2008, complete a broker transition course prescribed by the Commission, not to exceed 24 classroom hours of instruction, or shall demonstrate to the Commission that he or she possesses four years' full-time real estate brokerage experience or equivalent part-time real estate brokerage experience within the previous six years. If the provisional broker satisfies this requirement by April 1, 2008, the provisional status of his or her broker license will be terminated, and the broker will not be required to complete the 90-classroom-hour broker postlicensing education program prescribed by G.S. 93A-4(a1). If the provisional broker fails to satisfy this requirement by April 1, 2008, his or her license will be placed on inactive status, if not already on inactive status, and he or she must complete the 90-classroom-hour broker postlicensing education program prescribed by G.S. 93A-4(a1) in order to terminate the provisional status of the broker license and to be eligible to return his or her license to active status.

(c) An approved school or sponsor shall pay a fee of ten dollars ($10.00) per licensee to the Commission for each licensee completing a broker transition course conducted by the school or sponsor, provided that these fees shall not be charged to a community college, junior college, college, or university located in this State and accredited by the Southern Association of Colleges and Schools.

(d) A provisional broker as contemplated in subsection (a) of this section, who was issued a salesperson license between October 1, 2005, and March 31, 2006, shall, not later than April 1, 2009, satisfy the requirements of G.S. 93A-4(a1). Upon satisfaction of the requirements of G.S. 93A-4(a1), the provisional status of the broker's license will be terminated. If the provisional broker fails to satisfy the requirements of G.S. 93A-4(a1) by April 1, 2009, the broker's license shall be cancelled, and the person will be subject to the requirements for licensure reinstatement prescribed by G.S. 93A-4(a1).

(e) A broker who was issued a broker license prior to April 1, 2006, shall not be required to complete either the 90-classroom-hour broker postlicensing education program prescribed by G.S. 93A-4(a1) or the broker transition course prescribed by subsection (b) of this section.

(f) For the purpose of determining a licensee's status, rights, and obligations under this section, the Commission may treat a person who is issued a license on or after the October 1, 2005, or April 1, 2006, dates cited in subsections (a), (b), (d), or (e) of this section as though the person had been issued a license prior to those dates if the only reason the person's license was not issued prior to those dates was that the person's application was pending a determination by the Commission as to whether the applicant possessed the requisite moral character for licensure. If a license application is pending on April 1, 2006, for any reason other than a determination by the Commission as to the applicant's moral character for licensure, and if the applicant has not satisfied all education and examination requirements for licensing in effect on April 1, 2006, the applicant's application shall be cancelled and the application fee refunded.

(g) No applications for a real estate salesperson license shall be accepted by the Commission between September 1, 2005, and September 30, 2005.

93A-5. Register of applicants; roster of brokers; financial report to Secretary of State.

(a) The Executive Director of the Commission shall keep a register of all applicants for license, showing for each the date of application, name, place of residence, and whether the license was granted or refused. Said register shall be prima facie evidence of all matters recorded therein.

(b) The Executive Director of the Commission shall also keep a current roster showing the names and places of business of all licensed real estate brokers, which roster shall be kept on file in the office of the Commission and be open to public inspection.

(c) On or before the first day of September of each year, the Commission shall file with the Secretary of State a copy of the roster of real estate brokers holding certificates of license, and at the same time shall also file with the Secretary of State a report containing a complete statement of receipts and disbursements of the Commission for the preceding fiscal year ending June 30 attested by the affidavit of the Executive Director of the Commission.

93A-6. Disciplinary action by Commission.

(a) The Commission has the power to take disciplinary action. Upon its own initiative, or on the complaint of any person, the Commission may investigate the actions of any person or entity licensed under this Chapter, or any other person or entity who shall assume to act in such capacity. If the Commission finds probable cause that a licensee has violated any of the provisions of this Chapter, the Commission may hold a hearing on the allegations of misconduct.

The Commission has the power to suspend or revoke at any time a license issued under the provisions of this Chapter, or to reprimand or censure any licensee, if, following a hearing, the Commission adjudges the licensee to be guilty of:

(1) Making any willful or negligent misrepresentation or any willful or negligent omission of material fact.

(2) Making any false promises of a character likely to influence, persuade, or induce.

(3) Pursuing a course of misrepresentation or making of false promises through agents, advertising or otherwise.

(4) Acting for more than one party in a transaction without the knowledge of all parties for whom he or she acts.

(5) Accepting a commission or valuable consideration as a real estate salesperson for the performance of any of the acts specified in this Article or Article 4 of this Chapter, from any person except his or her broker-in-charge or licensed broker by whom he or she is employed.

(6) Representing or attempting to represent a real estate broker other than the broker by whom he or she is engaged or associated, without the express knowledge and consent of the broker with whom he or she is associated.

(7) Failing, within a reasonable time, to account for or to remit any moneys coming into his or her possession which belong to others.

(8) Being unworthy or incompetent to act as a real estate broker in a manner as to endanger the interest of the public.

(9) Paying a commission or valuable consideration to

any person for acts or services performed in violation of this Chapter.

(10) Any other conduct which constitutes improper, fraudulent or dishonest dealing.

(11) Performing or undertaking to perform any legal service, as set forth in G.S. 84-2.1, or any other acts constituting the practice of law.

(12) Commingling the money or other property of his or her principals with his or her own or failure to maintain and deposit in a trust or escrow account in an insured bank or savings and loan association in North Carolina all money received by him or her as a real estate licensee acting in that capacity, or an escrow agent, or the custodian or manager of the funds of another person or entity which relate to or concern that person's or entity's interest or investment in real property, provided, these accounts shall not bear interest unless the principals authorize in writing the deposit be made in an interest bearing account and also provide for the disbursement of the interest accrued.

(13) Failing to deliver, within a reasonable time, a completed copy of any purchase agreement or offer to buy and sell real estate to the buyer and to the seller.

(14) Failing, at the time the transaction is consummated, to deliver to the seller in every real estate transaction, a complete detailed closing statement showing all of the receipts and disbursements handled by him or her for the seller or failing to deliver to the buyer a complete statement showing all money received in the transaction from the buyer and how and for what it was disbursed.

(15) Violating any rule or regulation promulgated by the Commission.

The Executive Director shall transmit a certified copy of all final orders of the Commission suspending or revoking licenses issued under this Chapter to the clerk of superior court of the county in which the licensee maintains his or her principal place of business. The clerk shall enter these orders upon the judgment docket of the county.

(b) Following a hearing, the Commission shall also have power to suspend or revoke any license issued under the provisions of this Chapter or to reprimand or censure any licensee when:

(1) The licensee has obtained a license by false or fraudulent representation;

(2) The licensee has been convicted or has entered a plea of guilty or no contest upon which final judgment is entered by a court of competent jurisdiction in this State, or any other state, of the criminal offenses of: embezzlement, obtaining money under false pretense, fraud, forgery, conspiracy to defraud, or any other offense involving moral turpitude which would reasonably affect the licensee's performance in the real estate business;

(3) The licensee has violated any of the provisions of G.S. 93A-6(a) when selling, leasing, or buying his or her own property;

(4) The broker's unlicensed employee, who is exempt from the provisions of this Chapter under G.S. 93A-2(c)(6), has committed, in the regular course of business, any act which, if committed by the broker, would constitute a violation of G.S. 93A-6(a) for which the broker could be disciplined; or

(5) The licensee, who is also a State-licensed or State-certified real estate appraiser pursuant to Chapter 93E of the General Statutes, has violated any provisions of Chapter 93E of the General Statutes and has been reprimanded or has had his or her appraiser license or certificate suspended or revoked by the Appraisal Board.

(c) The Commission may appear in its own name in superior court in actions for injunctive relief to prevent any person from violating the provisions of this Chapter or rules promulgated by the Commission. The superior court shall have the power to grant these injunctions even if criminal prosecution has been or may be instituted as a result of the violations, or whether the person is a licensee of the Commission.

(d) Each broker shall maintain complete records showing the deposit, maintenance, and withdrawal of money or other property owned by his or her principals or held in escrow or in trust for his or her principals. The Commission may inspect these records periodically, without prior notice and may also inspect these records whenever the Commission determines that they are pertinent to an investigation of any specific complaint against a licensee.

(e) When a person or entity licensed under this Chapter is accused of any act, omission, or misconduct which would subject the licensee to disciplinary action, the licensee, with the consent and approval of the Commission, may surrender his or her or its license and all the rights and privileges pertaining to it for a period of time established by the Commission. A person or entity who surrenders his or her or its license shall not thereafter be eligible for or submit any application for licensure as a real estate broker or salesperson during the period of license surrender.

(f) In any contested case in which the Commission takes disciplinary action authorized by any provision of this Chapter, the Commission may also impose reasonable conditions, restrictions, and limitations upon the license, registration, or approval issued to the disciplined person or entity. In any contested case concerning an application for licensure, time share project registration, or school, sponsor, instructor, or course approval, the

Commission may impose reasonable conditions, restrictions, and limitations on any license, registration, or approval it may issue as a part of its final decision.

93A-6.1. Commission may subpoena witnesses, records, documents, or other materials.

(a) The Commission, Executive Director, or other representative designated by the Commission may issue a subpoena for the appearance of witnesses deemed necessary to testify concerning any matter to be heard before or investigated by the Commission. The Commission may issue a subpoena ordering any person in possession of records, documents, or other materials, however maintained, that concern any matter to be heard before or investigated by the Commission to produce the records, documents, or other materials for inspection or deliver the same into the custody of the Commission's authorized representatives. Upon written request, the Commission shall revoke a subpoena if it finds that the evidence, the production of which is required, does not relate to a matter in issue, or if the subpoena does not describe with sufficient particularity the evidence, the production of which is required, or if for any other reason in law the subpoena is invalid. If any person shall fail to fully and promptly comply with a subpoena issued under this section, the Commission may apply to any judge of the superior court resident in any county where the person to whom the subpoena is issued maintains a residence or place of business for an order compelling the person to show cause why he or she should not be held in contempt of the Commission and its processes. The court shall have the power to impose punishment for acts that would constitute direct or indirect contempt if the acts occurred in an action pending in superior court.

(b) The Commission shall be exempt from the requirements of Chapter 53B of the General Statutes with regard to subpoenas issued to compel the production of a licensee's trust account records held by any financial institution. Notwithstanding that exemption, the Commission shall serve, pursuant to G.S. 1A-1, Rule 4(j) of the N.C. Rules of Civil Procedure or by certified mail to the licensee's last known address, a copy of the subpoena and notice that the subpoena has been served upon the financial institution. Service of the subpoena and notice on the licensee shall be made within 10 days following service of the subpoena on the financial institution holding the trust account records.

93A-7. Power of courts to revoke.

Whenever any person, partnership, association or corporation claiming to have been injured or damaged by the gross negligence, incompetency, fraud, dishonesty or misconduct on the part of any licensee following the calling or engaging in the business herein described and shall file suit upon such claim against such licensee in any court of record in this State and shall recover judgment thereon, such court may as part of its judgment or decree in such case, if it deem it a proper case in which so to do, order a written copy of the transcript of record in said case to be forwarded by the clerk of court to the chairman of the said Commission with a recommendation that the licensee's certificate of license be revoked.

93A-8. Penalty for violation of Chapter.

Any person violating the provisions of this Chapter shall upon conviction thereof be deemed guilty of a Class 1 misdemeanor.

93A-9. Licensing nonresidents.

(a) An applicant from another state, which offers licensing privileges to residents of North Carolina, may be licensed by conforming to all the provisions of this Chapter and, in the discretion of the Commission, such other terms and conditions as are required of North Carolina residents applying for license in such other state; provided that the Commission may exempt from the examination prescribed in G.S. 93A-4 a broker or salesperson duly licensed in another state if a similar exemption is extended to licensed brokers from North Carolina. A license applicant who has been a resident of North Carolina for not more than 90 days may be considered by the Commission as a nonresident for the purposes of this subsection.

(b) The Commission may issue a limited broker's license to a person or an entity from another state or territory of the United States without regard to whether that state or territory offers similar licensing privileges to residents in North Carolina if the person or entity satisfies all of the following:

(1) Is of good moral character and licensed as a real estate broker or salesperson in good standing in another state or territory of the United States.

(2) Only engages in business as a real estate broker in North Carolina in transactions involving commercial real estate and while the person or entity is affiliated with a resident North Carolina real estate broker.

(3) Complies with the laws of this State regulating real estate brokers and rules adopted by the Commission.

The Commission may require an applicant for licensure under this subsection to pay a fee not to exceed three hundred dollars ($300.00). All licenses issued under this subsection shall expire on June 30 of each year following issuance or on a date that the Commission deems appropriate unless the license is renewed pursuant to the requirements of G.S. 93A-4. A person or entity licensed under this subsection may be disciplined by the Commission for violations of this Chapter as provided in G.S. 93A-6 and G.S. 93A-54.

Any person or entity licensed under this subsection shall be affiliated with a resident North Carolina real estate broker, and the resident North Carolina real estate broker shall actively and personally supervise the licensee in a manner that reasonably assures that the licensee complies with the requirements of this Chapter and rules adopted by the Commission. A person or entity licensed under this subsection shall not, however, be affiliated with a resident North Carolina real estate provisional broker. The Commission may exempt applicants for licensure under this subsection from examination and the other licensing requirements under G.S. 93A-4. The Commission may adopt rules as it deems necessary to give effect to this subsection, including rules establishing: (i) qualifications for licensure; (ii) licensure and renewal procedures; (iii) requirements for continuing education; (iv) conduct of persons and entities licensed under this subsection and their affiliated resident real estate brokers; (v) a definition of commercial real estate; and (vi) any requirements or limitations on affiliation between resident real estate brokers and persons or entities seeking licensure under this subsection.

93A-10. Nonresident licensees; filing of consent as to service of process and pleadings.

Every nonresident applicant shall file an irrevocable consent that suits and actions may be commenced against such applicant in any of the courts of record of this State, by the service of any process or pleading authorized by the laws of this State in any county in which the plaintiff may reside, by serving the same on the Executive Director of the Commission, said consent stipulating and agreeing that such service of such process or pleadings on said Executive Director shall be taken and held in all courts to be valid and binding as if due service had been made personally upon the applicant in this State. This consent shall be duly acknowledged, and, if made by a corporation, shall be executed by an officer of the corporation. The signature of the officer on the consent to service instrument shall be sufficient to bind the corporation and no further authentication is necessary. An application from a corporation or other business entity shall be signed by an officer of the corporation or entity or by an individual designated by the Commission.

In all cases where process or pleadings shall be served, under the provisions of this Chapter, upon the Executive Director of the Commission, such process or pleadings shall be served in duplicate, one of which shall be filed in the office of the Commission and the other shall be forwarded immediately by the Executive Director of the Commission, by registered mail, to the last known business address of the nonresident licensee against which such process or pleadings are directed.

93A-11. Reimbursement by real estate independent

contractor of brokers' workers' compensation.

(a) Notwithstanding the provisions of G.S. 97-21 or any other provision of law, a real estate broker may include in the governing contract with a real estate salesperson whose nonemployee status is recognized pursuant to section 3508 of the United States Internal Revenue Code, 26 U.S.C. § 3508, an agreement for the salesperson to reimburse the broker for the cost of covering that salesperson under the broker's workers' compensation coverage of the broker's business.

(b) Nothing in this section shall affect a requirement under any other law to provide workers' compensation coverage or in any manner exclude from coverage any person, firm, or corporation otherwise subject to the provisions of Article 1 of Chapter 97 of the General Statutes.

93A-12. Disputed monies.

(a) A real estate broker licensed under this Chapter may deposit with the clerk of court in accordance with this section monies, other than a residential security deposit, the ownership of which are in dispute and that the real estate broker received while acting in a fiduciary capacity.

(b) The disputed monies shall be deposited with the clerk of court in the county in which the property for which the disputed monies are being held is located. At the time of depositing the disputed monies, the real estate broker shall certify to the clerk of court that the persons who are claiming ownership of the disputed monies have been notified in accordance with subsection (c) of this section that the disputed monies are to be deposited with the clerk of court and that the persons may initiate a special proceeding with the clerk of court to recover the disputed monies.

(c) Notice to the persons who are claiming ownership to the disputed monies required under subsection (b) of this section shall be provided by delivering a copy of the notice to the person or by mailing it to the person by first-class mail, postpaid, properly addressed to the person at the person's last known address.

(d) A real estate broker shall not deposit disputed monies with the clerk of court until 90 days following notification of the persons claiming ownership of the disputed monies.

(e) Upon the filing of a special proceeding to recover the disputed monies, the clerk shall determine the rightful ownership of the monies and distribute the disputed monies accordingly. If no special proceeding is filed with the clerk of court within one year of the disputed monies being deposited with the clerk of court, the disputed monies shall be deemed unclaimed and shall be delivered by the clerk of court to the State Treasurer in accordance with the provisions of Article 4 of Chapter 116B of the General Statutes.

Sections 93A-13 through 93A-15: Reserved for future codification purposes.

ARTICLE 2.
REAL ESTATE RECOVERY FUND.

93A-16. Real Estate Recovery Fund created; payment to fund; management.

(a) There is hereby created a special fund to be known as the "Real Estate Recovery Fund" which shall be set aside and maintained by the North Carolina Real Estate Commission. Said fund shall be used in the manner provided under this Article for the payment of unsatisfied judgments where the aggrieved person has suffered a direct monetary loss by reason of certain acts committed by any real estate salesperson licensed before April 1, 2006, or by any real estate broker.

(b) On September 1, 1979, the Commission shall transfer the sum of one hundred thousand dollars ($100,000) from its expense reserve fund to the Real Estate Recovery Fund. Thereafter, the Commission may transfer to the Real Estate Recovery Fund additional sums of money from whatever funds the Commission may have, provided that, if on December 31 of any year the amount remaining in the fund is less than fifty thousand dollars ($50,000), the Commission may determine that each person or entity licensed under this Chapter, when renewing his or her or its license, shall pay in addition to his or her license renewal fee, a fee not to exceed ten dollars ($10.00) per broker and five dollars ($5.00) per salesperson as shall be determined by the Commission for the purpose of replenishing the fund.

(c) The Commission shall invest and reinvest the moneys in the Real Estate Recovery Fund in the same manner as provided by law for the investment of funds by the clerk of superior court. The proceeds from such investments shall be deposited to the credit of the fund.

(d) The Commission shall have the authority to adopt reasonable rules and procedures not inconsistent with the provisions of this Article, to provide for the orderly, fair and efficient administration and payment of monies held in the Real Estate Recovery Fund.

93A-17. Grounds for payment; notice and application to Commission.

(a) An aggrieved person who has suffered a direct monetary loss by reason of the conversion of trust funds by a real estate salesperson licensed before April 1, 2006, or by any licensed real estate broker shall be eligible to recover, subject to the limitations of this Article, the amount of trust funds converted and which is otherwise unrecoverable provided that:

(1) The act or acts of conversion which form the basis of the claim for recovery occurred on or after September 1, 1979;

(2) The aggrieved person has sued the real estate broker or salesperson in a court of competent jurisdiction and has filed with the Commission written notice of such lawsuit within 60 days after its commencement unless the claim against the Real Estate Recovery Fund is for an amount less than three thousand dollars ($3,000), excluding attorneys fees, in which case the notice may be filed within 60 days after the termination of all judicial proceedings including appeals;

(3) The aggrieved person has obtained final judgment in a court of competent jurisdiction against the real estate broker or salesperson on grounds of conversion of trust funds arising out of a transaction which occurred when such broker or salesperson was licensed and acting in a capacity for which a license is required; and

(4) Execution of the judgment has been attempted and has been returned unsatisfied in whole or in part.

Upon the termination of all judicial proceedings including appeals, and for a period of one year thereafter, a person eligible for recovery may file a verified application with the Commission for payment out of the Real Estate Recovery Fund of the amount remaining unpaid upon the judgment which represents the actual and direct loss sustained by reason of conversion of trust funds. A copy of the judgment and return of execution shall be attached to the application and filed with the Commission. The applicant shall serve upon the judgment debtor a copy of the application and shall file with the Commission an affidavit or certificate of such service.

(b) For the purposes of this Article, the term "trust funds" shall include all earnest money deposits, down payments, sales proceeds, tenant security deposits, undisbursed rents and other such monies which belong to another or others and are held by a real estate broker or salesperson acting in that capacity. Trust funds shall also include all time share purchase monies which are required to be held in trust by G.S. 93A-45(c) during the time they are, in fact, so held. Trust funds shall not include, however, any funds held by an independent escrow agent under G.S. 93A-42 or any funds which the court may find to be subject to an implied, constructive or resulting trust.

(c) For the purposes of this Article, the terms "licensee", "broker", and "salesperson" shall include only individual persons licensed under this Chapter as brokers or individual persons who were licensed under this Chapter as salespersons prior to April 1, 2006. The terms "licensee", "broker", and "salesperson" shall not include a time share developer, time share project, independent escrow agent, corporation or other entity licensed under this Chapter.

93A-18. Hearing; required showing.

Upon such application by an aggrieved person, the Commission shall conduct a hearing and the aggrieved person shall be required to show:

(1) He or she is not a spouse of the judgment debtor or a person representing such spouse; and

(2) He or she is making application not more than one year after termination of all judicial proceedings, including appeals, in connection with the judgment;

(3) He or she has complied with all requirements of this Article;

(4) He or she has obtained a judgment as described in G.S. 93A-17, stating the amount owing thereon at the date of application;

(5) He or she has made all reasonable searches and inquiries to ascertain whether the judgment debtor is possessed of real or personal property or other assets liable to be sold or applied in satisfaction of the judgment;

(6) That by such search he or she has discovered no real or personal property or other assets liable to be sold or applied, or that he or she has discovered certain of them, describing them, but that the amount so realized was insufficient to satisfy the judgment, stating the amount realized and the balance remaining due on the judgment after application of the amount realized; and

(7) He or she has diligently pursued his or her remedies including attempted execution on the judgment against all the judgment debtors which execution has been returned unsatisfied. In addition to that, he or she knows of no assets of the judgment debtor and that he or she has attempted collection from all other persons who may be liable to him or her in the transaction for which he or she seeks payment from the Real Estate Recovery Fund if there be any such other persons.

93A-19. Response and defense by Commission and judgment debtor; proof of conversion.

(a) Whenever the Commission proceeds upon an application as set forth in this Article, counsel for the Commission may defend such action on behalf of the fund and shall have recourse to all appropriate means of defense, including the examination of witnesses. The judgment debtor may defend such action on his or her own behalf and shall have recourse to all appropriate means of defense, including the examination of witnesses. Counsel for the Commission and the judgment debtor may file responses to the application, setting forth answers and defenses. Responses shall be filed with the Commission and copies shall be served upon every party by the filing party. If at any time it appears there are no triable issues of fact and the application for payment from the fund is without merit, the Commission shall dismiss the application. A motion to dismiss may be supported by affidavit of

any person or persons having knowledge of the facts and may be made on the basis that the application or the judgment referred to therein do not form a basis for meritorious recovery within the purview of G.S. 93A-17, that the applicant has not complied with the provisions of this Article, or that the liability of the fund with regard to the particular licensee or transaction has been exhausted; provided, however, notice of such motion shall be given at least 10 days prior to the time fixed for hearing. If the applicant or judgment debtor fails to appear at the hearing after receiving notice of the hearing, the applicant or judgment debtor shall waive his or her rights unless the absence is excused by the Commission.

(b) Whenever the judgment obtained by an applicant is by default, stipulation, or consent, or whenever the action against the licensee was defended by a trustee in bankruptcy, the applicant, for purposes of this Article, shall have the burden of proving his or her cause of action for conversion of trust funds. Otherwise, the judgment shall create a rebuttable presumption of the conversion of trust funds. This presumption is a presumption affecting the burden of producing evidence.

93A-20. Order directing payment out of fund; compromise of claims.

Applications for payment from the Real Estate Recovery Fund shall be heard and decided by a majority of the members of the Commission. If, after a hearing, the Commission finds the claim should be paid from the fund, the Commission shall enter an order requiring payment from the fund of whatever sum the Commission shall find to be payable upon the claim in accordance with the limitations contained in this Article.

Subject to Commission approval, a claim based upon the application of an aggrieved person may be compromised; however, the Commission shall not be bound in any way by any compromise or stipulation of the judgment debtor. If a claim appears to be otherwise meritorious, the Commission may waive procedural defects in the application for payment.

93A-21. Limitations; pro rata distribution; attorney fees.

(a) Payments from the Real Estate Recovery Fund shall be subject to the following limitations:

(1) The right to recovery under this Article shall be forever barred unless application is made within one year after termination of all proceedings including appeals, in connection with the judgment;

(2) The fund shall not be liable for more than twenty-five thousand dollars ($25,000) per transaction regardless of the number of persons aggrieved or parcels of real estate involved in such transaction; and

(3) The liability of the fund shall not exceed in the aggregate twenty-five thousand dollars ($25,000) for any one licensee within a single calendar year, and in no event shall it exceed in the aggregate fifty thousand dollars ($50,000) for any one licensee.

(4) The fund shall not be liable for payment of any judgment awards of consequential damages, multiple or punitive damages, civil penalties, incidental damages, special damages, interest, costs of court or action or other similar awards.

(b) If the maximum liability of the fund is insufficient to pay in full the valid claims of all aggrieved persons whose claims relate to the same transaction or to the same licensee, the amount for which the fund is liable shall be distributed among the claimants in a ratio that their respective claims bear to the total of such valid claims or in such manner as the Commission, in its discretion, deems equitable. Upon petition of counsel for the Commission, the Commission may require all claimants and prospective claimants to be joined in one proceeding to the end that the respective rights of all such claimants to the Real Estate Recovery Fund may be equitably resolved. A person who files an application for payment after the maximum liability of the fund for the licensee or transaction has been exhausted shall not be entitled to payment and may not seek judicial review of the Commission's award of payment to any party except upon a showing that the Commission abused its discretion.

(c) In the event an aggrieved person is entitled to payment from the fund in an amount of one thousand five hundred dollars ($1,500) or less, the Commission may allow such person to recover from the fund reasonable attorney's fees incurred in effecting such recovery. Reimbursement for attorney's fees shall be limited to those fees incurred in effecting recovery from the fund and shall not include any fee incurred in obtaining judgment against the licensee.

93A-22. Repayment to fund; automatic suspension of license.

Should the Commission pay from the Real Estate Recovery Fund any amount in settlement of a claim or toward satisfaction of a judgment against a licensed real estate broker or salesperson, any license issued to the broker or salesperson shall be automatically suspended upon the effective date of the order authorizing payment from the fund. No such broker or salesperson shall be granted a reinstatement until the fund has been repaid in full, including interest at the legal rate as provided for in G.S. 24-1.

93A-23. Subrogation of rights.

When the Commission has paid from the Real Estate Recovery Fund any sum to the judgment creditor, the Commission shall be subrogated to all of the rights of the judgment creditor to the extent of the amount so paid and the judgment creditor shall assign all his or her right, title, and interest in the judgment to the extent of the amount so paid to the Commission and any amount and interest so recovered by the Commission on the judgment shall be deposited in the Real Estate Recovery Fund.

93A-24. Waiver of rights.

The failure of an aggrieved person to comply with this Article shall constitute a waiver of any rights hereunder.

93A-25. Persons ineligible to recover from fund.

No real estate broker or real estate salesperson who suffers the loss of any commission from any transaction in which he or she was acting in the capacity of a real estate broker or real estate salesperson shall be entitled to make application for payment from the Real Estate Recovery Fund for such loss.

93A-26. Disciplinary action against licensee.

Nothing contained in this Article shall limit the authority of the Commission to take disciplinary action against any licensee under this Chapter, nor shall the repayment in full of all obligations to the fund by any licensee nullify or modify the effect of any other disciplinary proceeding brought under this Chapter.

Sections 93A-27 through 93A-31: Reserved for future codification purposes.

ARTICLE 3.
PRIVATE REAL ESTATE SCHOOLS.

Interested persons may obtain a copy of Article 3 by making written request to the North Carolina Real Estate Commission.

ARTICLE 4.
TIME SHARES.

93A-39. Title.

This Article shall be known and may be cited as the "North Carolina Time Share Act."

93A-40. Registration required of time share projects; real estate license required.

(a) It shall be unlawful for any person in this State to engage or assume to engage in the business of a time share salesperson without first obtaining a real estate broker license issued by the North Carolina Real Estate Commission under the provisions of Article I of this Chapter, and it shall be unlawful for a time share developer to sell or offer to sell a time share located in this State without first obtaining a certificate of registration for the time share project to be offered for sale issued by the North Carolina Real Estate Commission under the provisions of this Article.

(b) A person responsible as general partner, corporate officer, joint venturer or sole proprietor who intentionally acts as a time share developer, allowing the offering of sale or the sale of time shares to a purchaser, without first obtaining registration of the time share project under this Article shall be guilty of a Class I felony.

93A-41. Definitions.

When used in this Article, unless the context otherwise requires, the term:

(1) "Commission" means the North Carolina Real Estate Commission;

(2) "Developer" means any person or entity which creates a time share or a time share project or program, purchases a time share for purpose of resale, or is engaged in the business of selling its own time shares and shall include any person or entity who controls, is controlled by, or is in common control with the developer which is engaged in creating or selling time shares for the developer, but a person who purchases a time share for his or her occupancy, use, and enjoyment shall not be deemed a developer;

(3) "Enrolled" means paid membership in exchange programs or membership in an exchange program evidenced by written acceptance or confirmation of membership;

(4) "Exchange company" means any person operating an exchange program;

(5) "Exchange program" means any opportunity or procedure for the assignment or exchange of time shares among purchasers in the same or other time share project;

(5a) "Independent escrow agent" means a licensed attorney located in this State or a financial institution located in this State;

(6) "Managing agent" means a person who undertakes the duties, responsibilities, and obligations of the management of a time share program;

(7) Person" means one or more natural persons, corporations, partnerships, associations, trusts, other entities, or any combination thereof;

(7a) "Project broker" means a natural person licensed as a real estate broker and designated by the developer to supervise brokers at the time share project;

(8) "Purchaser" means any person other than a developer or lender who owns or acquires an interest or proposes to acquire an interest in a time share;

(9) "Time share" means a right to occupy a unit or any of several units during five or more separated time periods over a period of at least five years, including renewal options, whether or not coupled with a freehold estate or an estate for years in a time share project or a specified portion thereof, including, but not limited to, a vacation license, prepaid hotel reservation, club membership, limited partnership, vacation bond, or a plan or system where the right to use is awarded or apportioned on the basis of points, vouchers, split, divided, or floating use;

(9a) "Time share instrument" means an instrument transferring a time share or any interest, legal or beneficial, in a time share to a purchaser, including a contract, installment contract, lease, deed, or other instrument;

(10) "Time share program" means any arrangement for time shares whereby real property has been made subject to a time share;

(11) "Time share project" means any real property that is subject to a time share program;

(11a) "Time share registrar" means a natural person who is designated by the developer to record or cause time share instruments and lien releases to be recorded and to fulfill the other duties imposed by this Article;

(12) "Time share salesperson" means a person who sells or offers to sell on behalf of a developer a time share to a purchaser; and

(13) "Time share unit" or "unit" means the real property or real property improvement in a project which is divided into time shares and designated for separate occupancy and use.

93A-42. Time shares deemed real estate.

(a) A time share is deemed to be an interest in real estate, and shall be governed by the law of this State relating to real estate.

(b) A purchaser of a time share may in accordance with G.S. 47-18 register the time share instrument by which he or she acquired his or her interest and upon such registration shall be entitled to the protection provided by Chapter 47 of the General Statutes for the recordation of other real property instruments. A time share instrument transferring or encumbering a time share shall not be rejected for recordation because of the nature or duration of that estate, provided all other requirements necessary to make an instrument recordable are complied with.

(c) The developer shall record or cause to be recorded a time share instrument:

(1) Not less than six days nor more than 45 days following the execution of the contract of sale by the purchaser; or

(2) Not later than 180 days following the execution of the contract of sale by the purchaser, provided that all payments made by the purchaser shall be placed by the developer with an independent escrow agent upon the expiration of the 10-day escrow period provided by G.S. 93A-45(c).

(d) The independent escrow agent provided by G.S. 93A-42(c)(2) shall deposit and maintain the purchaser's payments in an insured trust or escrow account in a bank or savings and loan association located in this State. The trust or escrow account may be interest-bearing and the interest earned shall belong to the developer, if agreed upon in writing by the purchaser; provided, however, if the time share instrument is not recorded within the time periods specified in this section, then the interest earned shall belong to the purchaser. The independent escrow agent shall return all payments to the purchaser at the expiration of 180 days following the execution of the contract of sale by the purchaser, unless prior to that time the time share instrument has been recorded. However, if prior to the expiration of 180 days following the execution of the contract of sale, the developer and the purchaser provide their written consent to the independent escrow agent, the developer's obligation to record the time share instrument and the escrow period may be extended for an additional period of 120 days. Upon recordation of the time share instrument, the independent escrow agent shall pay the purchaser's funds to the developer. Upon request by the Commission, the independent escrow agent shall promptly make available to the Commission inspection of records of money held by him or her.

(e) In no event shall the developer be required to record a time share instrument if the purchaser is in default of his or her obligations.

(f) Recordation under the provisions of this section of the time share instrument shall constitute delivery of that instrument from the developer to the purchaser.

93A-43. Partition.

When a time share is owned by two or more persons as tenants in common or as joint tenants either may seek a partition by sale of that interest but no purchaser of a time share may maintain an action for partition by sale or in kind of the unit in which such time share is held.

93A-44. Public offering statement.

Each developer shall fully and conspicuously disclose in a public offering statement:

(1) The total financial obligation of the purchaser, which shall include the initial purchase price and any additional charges to which the purchaser may be subject;

(2) Any person who has or may have the right to alter, amend or add to charges to which the purchaser may be subject and the terms and conditions under which such charges may be imposed;

(3) The nature and duration of each agreement between the developer and the person managing the time share program or its facilities;

(4) The date of availability of each amenity and facility of the time share program when they are not completed at the time of sale of a time share;

(5) The specific term of the time share;

(6) The purchaser's right to cancel within five days of execution of the contract and how that right may be exercised under G.S. 93A-45;

(7) A statement that under North Carolina law an instrument conveying a time share must be recorded in the Register of Deeds Office to protect that interest; and

(8) Any other information which the Commission may by rule require.

The public offering statement shall also contain a one page cover containing a summary of the text of the statement.

93A-45. Purchaser's right to cancel; escrow; violation.

(a) A developer shall, before transfer of a time share and no later than the date of any contract of sale, provide a prospective purchaser with a copy of a public offering statement containing the information required by G.S. 93A-44. The contract of sale is voidable by the purchaser for five days after the execution of the contract. The contract shall conspicuously disclose the purchaser's right to cancel under this subsection and how that right may be exercised. The purchaser may not waive this right of cancellation. Any oral or written declaration or instrument that purports to waive this right of cancellation is void.

(b) A purchaser may elect to cancel within the time period set out in subsection (a) by hand delivering or by mailing notice to the developer or the time share salesperson. Cancellation under this section is without penalty and upon receipt of the notice all payments made prior to cancellation must be refunded immediately.

(c) Any payments received by a time share developer or time share salesperson in connection with the sale of the time share shall be immediately deposited by such developer or salesperson in a trust or escrow account in an insured bank or savings and loan association in North Carolina and shall remain in such account for 10 days or cancellation by the purchaser, whichever occurs first. Payments held in such trust or escrow accounts shall be deemed to belong to the purchaser and not the developer. In lieu of such escrow requirements, the Commission shall have the authority to accept, in its discretion, alternative financial assurances adequate to protect the purchaser's interest during the contract cancellation period, including but not limited to a surety bond, corporate bond, cash deposit or irrevocable letter of credit in an amount equal to the escrow requirements.

(d) If a developer fails to provide a purchaser to whom a time share is transferred with the statement as required by subsection (a), the purchaser, in addition to any rights to damages or other relief, is entitled to receive from the developer an amount equal to ten percent (10%) of the sales price of the time share not to exceed three thousand dollars ($3,000). A receipt signed by the purchaser stating that he or she has received the statement required by subsection (a) is prima facie evidence of delivery of such statement.

93A-46. Prizes.

An advertisement of a time share which includes the offer of a prize or other inducement shall fully comply with the provisions of Chapter 75 of the General Statutes.

93A-47. Time shares proxies.

No proxy, power of attorney or similar device given by the purchaser of a time share regarding the management of the time share program or its facilities shall exceed one year in duration, but the same may be renewed from year to year.

93A-48. Exchange programs.

(a) If a purchaser is offered the opportunity to subscribe to any exchange program, the developer shall, except as provided in subsection (b), deliver to the purchaser, prior to the execution of (i) any contract between the purchaser and the exchange company, and (ii) the sales contract, at least the following information regarding such exchange program:

(1) The name and address of the exchange company;

(2) The names of all officers, directors, and shareholders owning five percent (5%) or more of the outstanding stock of the exchange company;

(3) Whether the exchange company or any of its officers or directors has any legal or beneficial interest in any developer or managing agent for any time share project participating in the exchange program and, if so, the name and location of the time share project and the nature of the interest;

(4) Unless the exchange company is also the developer a statement that the purchaser's contract with the exchange company is a contract separate and distinct from the sales contract;

(5) Whether the purchaser's participation in the exchange program is dependent upon the continued affiliation of the time share project with the exchange program;

(6) Whether the purchaser's membership or participation, or both, in the exchange program is voluntary or mandatory;

(7) A complete and accurate description of the terms and conditions of the purchaser's contractual relationship with the exchange company and the procedure by which changes thereto may be made;

(8) A complete and accurate description of the procedure to qualify for and effectuate exchanges;

(9) A complete and accurate description of all limitations, restrictions, or priorities employed in the operation of the exchange program, including, but not limited to, limitations on exchanges based on seasonality, unit size, or levels of occupancy, expressed in boldfaced type, and, in the event that such limitations, restrictions, or priorities are not uniformly applied by the exchange program, a clear description of the manner in which they are applied;

(10) Whether exchanges are arranged on a space available basis and whether any guarantees of fulfillment of specific requests for exchanges are made by the exchange program;

(11) Whether and under what circumstances an owner, in dealing with the exchange company, may lose the use and occupancy of his or her time share in any properly applied for exchange without his or her being provided with substitute accommodations by the exchange company;

(12) The expenses, fees or range of fees for participation by owners in the exchange program, a statement whether any such fees may be altered by the exchange company, and the circumstances under which alterations may be made;

(13) The name and address of the site of each time share project or other property which is participating in the exchange program;

(14) The number of units in each project or other property participating in the exchange program which are available for occupancy and which qualify for participation in the exchange program, expressed within the following numerical groupings, 1-5, 6-10, 11-20, 21-50 and 51, and over;

(15) The number of owners with respect to each time share project or other property which are eligible to participate in the exchange program expressed within the following numerical groupings, 1-100, 101-249, 250-499, 500-999, and 1,000 and over, and a statement of the criteria used to determine those owners who are currently eligible to participate in the exchange program;

(16) The disposition made by the exchange company of time shares deposited with the exchange program by owners eligible to participate in the exchange program and not used by the exchange company in effecting exchanges;

(17) The following information which, except as provided in subsection (b) below, shall be independently audited by a certified public accountant in accordance with the standards of the Accounting Standards Board of the American Institute of Certified Public Accountants and reported for each year no later than July 1, of the succeeding year:

a. The number of owners enrolled in the exchange program and such numbers shall disclose the relationship between the exchange company and owners as being either fee paying or gratuitous in nature;

b. The number of time share projects or other properties eligible to participate in the exchange program categorized by those having a contractual relationship between the developer or the association and the exchange company and those having solely a contractual relationship between the exchange company and owners directly;

c. The percentage of confirmed exchanges, which shall be the number of exchanges confirmed by the exchange company divided by the number of exchanges properly applied for, together with a complete and accurate statement of the criteria used to determine whether an exchange requested was properly applied for;

d. The number of time shares or other intervals for which the exchange company has an outstanding obligation to provide an exchange to an owner who relinquished a time share or interval during the year in exchange for a time share or interval in any future year; and

e. The number of exchanges confirmed by the exchange company during the year; and

(18) A statement in boldfaced type to the effect that the percentage described in subparagraph (17)c. of subsection (a) is a summary of the exchange requests entered with the exchange company in the period reported and that the percentage does not indicate a purchaser's/owner's probabilities of being confirmed to any specific choice or range of choices, since availability at individual locations may vary.

The purchaser shall certify in writing to the receipt of the information required by this subsection and any other information which the Commissioners may by rule require.

(b) The information required by subdivisions (a), (2), (3), (13), (14), (15), and (17) shall be accurate as of December 31 of the year preceding the year in which the information is delivered, except for information delivered within the first 180 days of any calendar year which shall be accurate as of December 31 of the year two years preceding the year in which the information is delivered to the purchaser. The remaining information required by subsection (a) shall be accurate as of a date which is no more than 30 days prior to the date on which the information is delivered to the purchaser.

(c) In the event an exchange company offers an exchange program directly to the purchaser or owner, the exchange company shall deliver to each purchaser or owner, concurrently with the offering and prior to the execution of any contract between the purchaser or owner and the exchange company the information set forth in subsection (a) above. The requirements of this paragraph shall not apply to any renew-

al of a contract between an owner and an exchange company.

(d) All promotional brochures, pamphlets, advertisements, or other materials disseminated by the exchange company to purchasers in this State which contain the percentage of confirmed exchanges described in (a)(17)c. must include the statement set forth in (a)(18).

93A-49. Service of process on exchange company.

Any exchange company offering an exchange program to a purchaser shall be deemed to have made an irrevocable appointment of the Commission to receive service of lawful process in any proceeding against the exchange company arising under this Article.

93A-50. Securities laws apply.

The North Carolina Securities Act, Chapter 78A, shall also apply, in addition to the laws relating to real estate, to time shares deemed to be investment contracts or to other securities offered with or incident to a time share; provided, in the event of such applicability of the North Carolina Securities Act, any offer or sale of time shares registered under this Article shall not be subject to the provisions of G.S. 78A-24 and any real estate broker registered under Article 1 of this Chapter shall not be subject to the provisions of G.S. 78A-36.

93A-51. Rule-making authority.

The Commission shall have the authority to adopt rules and regulations that are not inconsistent with the provisions of this Article and the General Statutes of North Carolina. The Commission may prescribe forms and procedures for submitting information to the Commission.

93A-52. Application for registration of time share project; denial of registration; renewal; reinstatement; and termination of developer's interest.

(a) Prior to the offering in this State of any time share located in this State, the developer of the time share project shall make written application to the Commission for the registration of the project. The application shall be accompanied by a fee in an amount fixed by the Commission but not to exceed one thousand five hundred dollars ($1,500), and shall include a description of the project, copies of proposed time share instruments including public offering statements, sale contracts, deeds, and other documents referred to therein, information pertaining to any marketing or managing entity to be employed by the developer for the sale of time shares in a time share project or the management of the project, information regarding any exchange program available to the purchaser, an irrevocable appointment of the Commission to receive service of any lawful process in any proceeding against the developer or the developer's time share salespersons arising under this Article, and such other information as the Commission may by rule require.

Upon receipt of a properly completed application and fee and upon a determination by the Commission that the sale and management of the time shares in the time share project will be directed and conducted by persons of good moral character, the Commission shall issue to the developer a certificate of registration authorizing the developer to offer time shares in the project for sale. The Commission shall within 15 days after receipt of an incomplete application, notify the developer by mail that the Commission has found specified deficiencies, and shall, within 45 days after the receipt of a properly completed application, either issue the certificate of registration or notify the developer by mail of any specific objections to the registration of the project. The certificate shall be prominently displayed in the office of the developer on the site of the project.

The developer shall promptly report to the Commission any and all changes in the information required to be submitted for the purpose of the registration. The developer shall also immediately furnish the Commission complete information regarding any change in its interest in a registered time share project. In the event a developer disposes of, or otherwise terminates its interest in a time share project, the developer shall certify to the Commission in writing that its interest in the time share project is terminated and shall return to the Commission for cancellation the certificate of registration.

(b) In the event the Commission finds that there is substantial reason to deny the application for registration as a time share project, the Commission shall notify the applicant that such application has been denied and shall afford the applicant an opportunity for a hearing before the Commission to show cause why the application should not be denied. In all proceedings to deny a certificate of registration, the provisions of Chapter 150B of the General Statutes shall be applicable.

(c) The acceptance by the Commission of an application for registration shall not constitute the approval of its contents or waive the authority of the Commission to take disciplinary action as provided by this Article.

(d) All certificates of registration granted and issued by the Commission under the provisions of this Article shall expire on the 30th day of June following issuance thereof, and shall become invalid after such date unless reinstated. Renewal of such certificate may be effected at any time during the month of June preceding the date of expiration of such registration upon proper application to the Commission and by the payment of a renewal fee fixed by the Commission but not to exceed one thousand five hundred dollars ($1,500) for each time share project. The developer shall, when making application for renewal, also provide a copy of the report required in G.S. 93A-48. Each certificate reinstated after the expiration date thereof shall be subject to a fee of fifty dollars ($50.00) in addition to the required renewal fee. In the event a time share developer fails to reinstate the registration within 12 months after the expiration date thereof, the Commission may, in its discretion, consider the time share project as not having been previously registered, and thereby subject to the provisions of this Article relating to the issuance of an original certificate. Duplicate certificates may be issued by the Commission upon payment of a fee of one dollar ($1.00) by the registrant developer. Except as prescribed by Commission rules, all fees paid pursuant to this Article shall be nonrefundable.

93A-53. Register of applicants; roster of registrants; registered projects; financial report to Secretary of State.

(a) The Executive Director of the Commission shall keep a register of all applicants for certificates of registration, showing for each the date of application, name, business address, and whether the certificate was granted or refused.

(b) The Executive Director of the Commission shall also keep a current roster showing the name and address of all time share projects registered with the Commission. The roster shall be kept on file in the office of the Commission and be open to public inspection.

(c) On or before the first day of September of each year, the Commission shall file with the Secretary of State a copy of the roster of time share projects registered with the Commission and a report containing a complete statement of income received by the Commission in connection with the registration of time share projects for the preceding fiscal year ending June 30th attested by the affidavit of the Executive Director of the Commission. The report shall be made a part of those annual reports required under the provisions of G.S. 93A- 5.

93A-54. Disciplinary action by Commission.

(a) The Commission shall have power to take disciplinary action. Upon its own motion, or on the verified complaint of any person, the Commission may investigate the actions of any time share salesperson, developer, or project broker of a time share project registered under this Article, or any other person or entity who shall assume to act in such capacity. If the Commission finds probable cause that a time share salesperson, developer, or project broker has violated any of the provisions of this Article, the Commission may hold a hearing on the allegations of misconduct.

The Commission shall have the power to suspend or revoke at any time a real estate license issued to a time share salesperson or project broker, or a certificate of registration of a time share project issued to a developer; or to reprimand or censure such salesperson, developer, or project broker; or to fine such developer in the amount of five hundred dollars ($500.00) for each violation of this Article, if, after a hearing, the Commission adjudges either the salesperson, developer, or project broker to be guilty of:

(1) Making any willful or negligent misrepresentation or any willful or negligent omission of material fact about any time share or time share project;

(2) Making any false promises of a character likely to influence, persuade, or induce;

(3) Pursuing a course of misrepresentation or making of false promises through agents, salespersons, advertising or otherwise;

(4) Failing, within a reasonable time, to account for all money received from others in a time share transaction, and failing to remit such monies as may be required in G.S. 93A-45 of this Article;

(5) Acting as a time share salesperson or time share developer in a manner as to endanger the interest of the public;

(6) Paying a commission, salary, or other valuable consideration to any person for acts or services performed in violation of this Article;

(7) Any other conduct which constitutes improper, fraudulent, or dishonest dealing;

(8) Performing or undertaking to perform any legal service as set forth in G.S. 84-2.1, or any other acts not specifically set forth in that section;

(9) Failing to deposit and maintain in a trust or escrow account in an insured bank or savings and loan association in North Carolina all money received from others in a time share transaction as may be required in G.S. 93A-45 of this Article or failing to place with an independent escrow agent the funds of a time share purchaser when required by G.S. 93A-42(c);

(10) Failing to deliver to a purchaser a public offering statement containing the information required by G.S. 93A-44 and any other disclosures that the Commission may by regulation require;

(11) Failing to comply with the provisions of Chapter 75 of the General Statutes in the advertising or promotion of time shares for sale, or failing to assure such compliance by persons engaged on behalf of a developer;

(12) Failing to comply with the provisions of G.S. 93A-48 in furnishing complete and accurate information to purchasers concerning any exchange program which may be offered to such purchaser;

(13) Making any false or fraudulent representation on an application for registration;

(14) Violating any rule or regulation promulgated by the Commission;

(15) Failing to record or cause to be recorded a time share instrument as required by G.S. 93A-42(c), or failing to provide a purchaser the protection against liens required by G.S. 93A-57(a); or

(16) Failing as a time share project broker to exercise reasonable and adequate supervision of the conduct of sales at his or her project or location by the brokers and salespersons under his or her control.

(a1) The clear proceeds of fines collected pursuant to subsection (a) of this section shall be remitted to the Civil Penalty and Forfeiture Fund in accordance with G.S. 115C-457.2.

(b) Following a hearing, the Commission shall also have power to suspend or revoke any certificate of registration issued under the provisions of this Article or to reprimand or censure any developer when the registrant has been convicted or has entered a plea of guilty or no contest upon which final judgment is entered by a court of competent jurisdiction in this State, or any other state, of the criminal offenses of: embezzlement, obtaining money under false pretense, fraud, forgery, conspiracy to defraud, or any other offense involving moral turpitude which would reasonably affect the developer's performance in the time share business.

(c) The Commission may appear in its own name in superior court in actions for injunctive relief to prevent any person or entity from violating the provisions of this Article or rules promulgated by the Commission. The superior court shall have the power to grant these injunctions even if criminal prosecution has been or may be instituted as a result of the violations, or regardless of whether the person or entity has been registered by the Commission.

(d) Each developer shall maintain or cause to be maintained complete records of every time share transaction including records pertaining to the deposit, maintenance, and withdrawal of money required to be held in a trust or escrow account, or as otherwise required by the Commission, under G.S. 93A-45 of this Article. The Commission may inspect these records periodically without prior notice and may also inspect these records whenever the Commission determines that they are pertinent to an investigation of any specific complaint against a registrant.

(e) When a licensee is accused of any act, omission, or misconduct under this Article which would subject the licensee to disciplinary action, the licensee may, with the consent and approval of the Commission, surrender his or her or its license and all the rights and privileges pertaining to it for a period of time to be established by the Commission. A licensee who surrenders his or her or its license shall not be eligible for, or submit any application for, licensure as a real estate broker or registration of a time share project during the period of license surrender. For the purposes of this section, the term licensee shall include a time share developer.

93A-55. Private enforcement.

The provisions of the Article shall not be construed to limit in any manner the right of a purchaser or other person injured by a violation of this Article to bring a private action.

93A-56. Penalty for violation of Article.

Except as provided in G.S. 93A-40(b) and G.S. 93A-58, any person violating the provisions of this Article shall be guilty of a Class 1 misdemeanor.

93A-57. Release of liens.

(a) Prior to any recordation of the instrument transferring a time share, the developer shall record and furnish notice to the purchaser of a release or subordination of all liens affecting that time share, or shall provide a surety bond or insurance against the lien from a company acceptable to the Commission as provided for liens on real estate in this State, or such underlying lien document shall contain a provision wherein the lienholder subordinates its rights to that of a time share purchaser who fully complies with all of the provisions and terms of the contract of sale.

(b) Unless a time share owner or a time share owner who is his or her predecessor in title agree otherwise with the lienor, if a lien other than a mortgage or deed of trust becomes effective against more than one time share in a time share project, any time share owner is entitled to a release of his or her time share from a lien upon payment of the amount of the lien attributable to his or her time share. The amount of the payment must be proportionate to the ratio that the time share owner's liability bears to the liabilities of all time share owners whose interests are subject to the lien. Upon receipt of payment, the lien holder shall promptly deliver to the time share owner a release of the lien covering that time share. After payment, the managing agent may not assess or have a lien against that time share for any portion of the expenses incurred in connection with that lien.

93A-58. Registrar required; criminal penalties; project broker.

(a) Every developer of a registered project shall, by affidavit filed with the Commission, designate a natural person to serve as time share registrar for its registered projects. The registrar shall be responsible for the recordation of time share instruments and the release of liens required by G.S. 93A-42(c) and G.S. 93A-57(a). A developer may, from time to time, change the designated time share registrar by proper filing with the Commission and by otherwise complying with this subsection. No sales or offers to sell shall be made until the registrar is designated for a time share project.

The registrar has the duty to ensure that the provisions of this Article are complied with in a time share project for which he or she is registrar. No registrar shall record a time share instrument except as provided by this Article.

(b) A time share registrar shall be guilty of a Class I felony if he or she knowingly or recklessly fails to record or cause to be recorded a time share instrument as required by this Article.

A person responsible as general partner, corporate officer, joint venturer or sole proprietor of the developer of a time share project shall be guilty of a Class I felony if he or she intentionally allows the offering for sale or the sale of time share to purchasers without first designating a time share registrar.

(c) The developer shall designate for each project and other locations where time shares are sold or offered for sale a project broker. The project broker shall act as supervising broker for all time share salespersons at the project or other location and shall directly, personally, and actively supervise all such persons at the project or other location in a manner to reasonably ensure that the sale of time shares will be conducted in accordance with the provisions of this Chapter.

93A-59. Preservation of time share purchaser's claims and defenses.

(a) For one year following the execution of an instrument of indebtedness for the purchase of a time share, the purchaser of a time share may assert against the seller, assignee of the seller, or other holder of the instrument of indebtedness, any claims or defenses available against the developer or the original seller, and the purchaser may not waive the right to assert these claims or defenses in connection with a time share purchase. Any recovery by the purchaser on a claim asserted against an assignee of the seller or other holder of the instrument of indebtedness shall not exceed the amount paid by the purchaser under the instrument. A holder shall be the person or entity with the rights of a holder as set forth in G.S. 25-3-301.

(b) Every instrument of indebtedness for the purchase of a time share shall set forth the following provision in a clear and conspicuous manner:

"NOTICE: FOR A PERIOD OF ONE YEAR FOLLOWING THE EXECUTION OF THIS INSTRUMENT OF INDEBTEDNESS, ANY HOLDER OF THIS INSTRUMENT OF INDEBTEDNESS IS SUBJECT TO ALL CLAIMS AND DEFENSES WHICH THE PURCHASER COULD ASSERT AGAINST THE SELLER OF THE TIME SHARE. RECOVERY BY THE PURCHASER SHALL NOT EXCEED AMOUNTS PAID BY THE PURCHASER UNDER THIS INSTRUMENT."

Sections 93A-60 through 93A-69: Reserved for future codification purposes.

Article 5.
Real Estate Appraisers.
[Repealed]

NORTH CAROLINA REAL ESTATE COMMISSION RULES

CHAPTER 93A

Statutory Authority: Sections 93A-3(c), 93A-4(d), 93A-33, and 93A-51 of the
North Carolina Real Estate License Law; and the North Carolina Administrative Procedures Act.

NORTH CAROLINA ADMINISTRATIVE CODE
TITLE 21
OCCUPATIONAL LICENSING BOARDS
CHAPTER 58
REAL ESTATE COMMISSION

CHAPTER 58
REAL ESTATE COMMISSION
Subchapter 58A
Real Estate Brokers

SECTION A.0100
GENERAL BROKERAGE

A.0101 Proof of Licensure

(a) The annual license renewal pocket card issued by the Commission to each licensee shall be retained by the licensee as evidence of licensure. Each licensee shall carry his or her pocket card on his or her person at all times while engaging in real estate brokerage and shall produce the card as proof of licensure whenever requested.

(b) The qualifying broker of a firm shall retain the firm's renewal pocket card at the firm and shall produce it upon request as proof of firm licensure as required by Rule .0502.

(c) Every licensed real estate business entity or firm shall prominently display its license certificate or facsimile thereof in each office maintained by the entity or firm. A broker-in-charge shall also prominently display his or her license certificate in the office where he or she is broker-in-charge.

(d) Every licensee shall include his or her license number in agency contracts and disclosures as provided in Rule .0104 of this subchapter.

A.0102 Branch Office   (Repealed)

A.0103 Licensee Name and Address

Upon initial licensure and at all times thereafter, every licensee shall assure that the Commission has on record the licensee's current personal name, firm name, trade name, residence address and firm address. Every licensee shall notify the Commission in writing of each change of personal name, firm name, trade name, residence address and firm address within ten days of said change. All addresses shall be sufficiently descriptive to enable the Commission to correspond with and locate the licensee.

A .0104 Agency Agreements and Disclosure

(a) Every agreement for brokerage services in a real estate transaction and every agreement for services connected with the management of a property owners association shall be in writing and signed by the parties thereto. Every agreement for brokerage services between a broker and an owner of the property to be the subject of a transaction must be in writing and signed by the parties from the time of its formation. Every agreement for brokerage services between a broker and a buyer or tenant shall be express and shall be reduced to writing and signed by the parties thereto not later than the time one of the parties makes an offer to purchase, sell, rent, lease, or exchange real estate to another. However, every agreement between a broker and a buyer or tenant which seeks to bind the buyer or tenant for a period of time or to restrict the buyer's or tenant's right to work with other agents or without an agent shall be in writing and signed by the parties thereto from its formation. A broker shall not continue to represent a buyer or tenant without a written, signed agreement when such agreement is required by this Rule. Every written agreement for brokerage services of any kind in a real estate transaction shall provide for its existence for a definite period of time, shall include the licensee's license number, and shall provide for its termination without prior notice at the expiration of that period, except that an agency agreement between a landlord and broker to procure tenants or receive rents for the landlord's property may allow for automatic renewal so long as the landlord may terminate with notice at the end of any contract period and any subsequent renewals. For the purposes of this rule, an agreement between licensees to cooperate or share compensation shall not be considered an agreement for brokerage services and, except as required by Rule .1807 of this Subchapter, need not be memorialized in writing.

(b) Every listing agreement, written buyer agency agreement or other written agreement for brokerage services in a real estate transaction shall contain the following provision: The broker shall conduct all brokerage activities in regard to this agreement without respect to the race, color, religion, sex, national origin, handicap or familial status of any party or prospective party. The provision shall be set forth in a clear and conspicuous manner which shall distinguish it from other provisions of the agreement. For the purposes of this Rule, the term, familial status, shall be defined as it is in G.S. 41A-3(1b).

(c) In every real estate sales transaction, a broker shall, at first substantial contact directly with a prospective buyer or seller, provide the prospective buyer or seller with a copy of the publication "Working with Real Estate Agents," set forth the broker's name and license number thereon, review the publication with the buyer or seller, and determine whether the agent will act as the agent of the buyer or seller in the transaction. If the first substantial contact with a prospective buyer or seller occurs by telephone or other electronic means of communication where it is not practical to provide the "Working with Real Estate Agents" publication, the broker shall at the earliest opportunity thereafter, but in no event later than three days from the date of first substantial contact, mail or otherwise transmit a copy of the publication to the prospective buyer or seller and review it with him or her at the earliest practicable opportunity thereafter. For the purposes of this Rule, "first substantial contact" shall include contacts between a broker and a consumer where the consumer or broker begins to act as though an agency relationship exists and the consumer begins to disclose to the broker personal or confidential information.

(d) A real estate broker representing one party in a transaction shall not undertake to represent another party in the transaction without the written authority of each party. The written authority must be obtained upon the formation of the relationship except when a buyer or tenant is represented by a broker without a written agreement in conformity with the requirements of Paragraph (a) of this Rule. Under such circumstances, the written authority for dual agency must be reduced to writing not later than the time that one of the parties represented by the broker makes an offer to purchase, sell, rent, lease, or exchange real estate to another party.

(e) In every real estate sales transaction, a broker working directly with a prospective buyer as a seller's agent or subagent shall disclose in writing to the prospective buyer at the first substantial contact with the prospective buyer that the broker represents the interests of the seller. The written disclosure shall include the broker's license number. If the first substantial contact occurs by telephone or by means of other electronic communication where it is not practical to provide written disclosure, the broker shall immediately disclose by similar means whom he represents and shall immediately mail or otherwise transmit a copy of the written disclosure to the buyer. In no event shall the broker mail or transmit a copy of the written disclosure to the buyer later than three days from the date of first substantial contact with the buyer.

(f) In every real estate sales transaction, a broker representing a buyer shall, at the initial contact with the seller or seller's agent, disclose to the seller or seller's agent that the broker represents the buyer's interests. In addition, in every real estate sales transaction other than auctions, the broker shall, no later than the time of delivery of an offer to the seller or seller's agent, provide the seller or seller's agent with a written confirmation disclosing that he represents the interests of the buyer. The written confirmation may be made in the buyer's offer to purchase and shall include the broker's license number.

(g) The provisions of Paragraphs (c), (d) and (e) of this Rule do not apply to real estate licensees representing sellers in auction sales transactions.

(h) A broker representing a buyer in an auction sale transaction shall, no later than the time of execution of a written agreement memorializing the buyer's contract to purchase, provide the seller or seller's agent with a written confirmation disclosing that he represents the interests of the buyer. The written confirmation may be made in the written agreement.

(i) A firm which represents more than one party in the same real estate transaction is a dual agent and, through the brokers associated with the firm, shall disclose its dual agency to the parties.

(j) When a firm represents both the buyer and seller in the same real estate transaction, the firm may, with the prior express approval of its buyer and seller clients, designate one or more individual brokers associated with the firm to represent only the interests of the seller and one or more other individual brokers associated with the firm to represent only the interests of the buyer in the transaction. The authority for designated agency must be reduced to writing not later than the time that the parties are required to reduce their dual agency agreement to writing in accordance with Paragraph (d) of this Rule. An individual broker shall not be so designated and shall not undertake to represent only the interests of one party if the broker has actually received confidential information concerning the other party in connection with the transaction. A broker-in-charge shall not act as a designated broker for a party in a real estate sales transaction when a provisional broker under his or her supervision will act as a designated broker for another party with a competing interest.

(k) When a firm acting as a dual agent designates an individual broker to represent the seller, the broker so designated shall represent only the interest of the seller and shall not, without the seller's permission, disclose to the buyer or a broker designated to represent the buyer:

(1) that the seller may agree to a price, terms, or any conditions of sale other than those established by the seller;

(2) the seller's motivation for engaging in the transaction unless disclosure is otherwise required by statute or rule; and

(3) any information about the seller which the seller has identified as confidential unless disclosure of the information is otherwise required by statute or rule.

(l) When a firm acting as a dual agent designates an individual broker to represent the buyer, the broker so designated shall represent only the interest of the buyer and shall not, without the buyer's permission, disclose to the seller or a broker designated to represent the seller:

(1) that the buyer may agree to a price, terms, or any conditions of sale other than those established by the seller;

(2) the buyer's motivation for engaging in the transaction unless disclosure is otherwise required by statute or rule; and

(3) any information about the buyer which the buyer has identified as confidential unless disclosure of the information is otherwise required by statute or rule.

(m) A broker designated to represent a buyer or seller in accordance with Paragraph (j) of this Rule shall disclose the identity of all of the brokers so designated to both the buyer and the seller. The disclosure shall take place no later than the presentation of the first offer to purchase or sell.

(n) When an individual broker represents both the buyer and seller in the same real estate sales transaction pursuant to a written agreement authorizing dual agency, the parties may provide in the written agreement that the broker shall not disclose the following information about one party to the other without permission from the party about whom the information pertains:

    (1) that a party may agree to a price, terms or any conditions of sale other than those offered;

    (2) the motivation of a party for engaging in the transaction, unless disclosure is otherwise required by statute or rule; and

    (3) any information about a party which that party has identified as confidential, unless disclosure is otherwise required by statute or rule.

A.0105 Advertising

(a) Blind Ads. A licensee shall not advertise the sale, purchase, exchange, rent or lease of real estate, for another or others, in a manner indicating the offer to sell, purchase, exchange, rent, or lease is being made by the licensee's principal only. Every such advertisement shall conspicuously indicate that it is the advertisement of a broker or brokerage firm and shall not be confined to publication of only a post office box number, telephone number, street address, internet web address or e-mail address.

(b) Registration of Assumed Name. In the event that any licensee shall advertise in any manner using a firm name or an assumed name which does not set forth the surname of the licensee, the licensee shall first file the appropriate certificate with the office of the county register of deeds in compliance with G.S. 66-68 and notify the Commission in writing of the use of such a firm name or assumed name.

(c) Authority to Advertise.

    (1) A provisional broker shall not advertise any brokerage service or the sale, purchase, exchange, rent or lease of real estate for another or others without the consent of his or her broker-in-charge and without including in the advertisement the name of the broker or firm with whom the provisional broker is associated.

    (2) A licensee shall not advertise or display a "for sale" or "for rent" sign on any real estate without the consent of the owner or his or her authorized agent.

(d) Business names. A licensee shall not include the name of a provisional broker or an unlicensed person in the name of a sole proprietorship, partnership or non-corporate business formed for the purpose of real estate brokerage.

(e) A person licensed as a limited nonresident commercial broker shall comply with the provisions of Rule .1809 of this Subchapter in connection with all advertising concerning or relating to his or her status as a North Carolina licensee.

A.0106 Delivery of Instruments

(a) Except as provided in Paragraph (b) of this Rule, every broker shall immediately, but in no event later than five days from the date of execution, deliver to the parties thereto copies of any required written agency agreement, contract, offer, lease, or option affecting real property.

(b) A broker may be relieved of his or her duty under Paragraph (a) of this Rule to deliver copies of leases or rental agreements to the property owner, if the broker:

    (1) obtains the express written authority of the property owner to enter into and retain copies of leases or rental agreements on behalf of the property owner;

    (2) executes the lease or rental agreement on a pre-printed form, the material terms of which may not be changed by the broker without prior approval by the property owner except as may be required by law;

    (3) promptly provides a copy of the lease or rental agreement to the property owner upon reasonable request; and

    (4) delivers to the property owner within 45 days following the date of execution of the lease or rental agreement, an accounting which identifies the leased property and which sets forth the names of the tenants, the rental rates and rents collected.

A.0107 Handling and Accounting of Funds

(a) Except as provided herein, all monies received by a licensee acting in his or her fiduciary capacity shall be deposited in a trust or escrow account maintained by a broker not later than three banking days following receipt of such monies except that earnest money deposits paid by means other than currency which are received on offers to purchase real estate and tenant security deposits paid by means other than currency which are received in connection with real estate leases shall be deposited in a trust or escrow account not later than three banking days following acceptance of such offer to purchase or lease; the date of acceptance of such offer to purchase or lease shall be set forth in the purchase or lease agreement. All monies received by a provisional broker shall be delivered immediately to the broker by whom he or she is employed, except that all monies received by nonresident commercial licensees shall be delivered as required by Rule .1808 of this Subchapter. A licensee may accept custody of a check or other negotiable instrument made payable to the seller of real property as option money only for the purpose of delivering the instrument to the optionor-seller. While the instrument is in the custody of the licensee, the licensee shall, according to the instructions of the buyer-optionee, either deliver it to the seller-optionor or return it to the buyer-optionee. The licensee shall safeguard the instrument and shall be responsible to the parties on the instrument for its prompt and safe delivery. In no event shall a licensee retain such an instrument for more than three business days after the acceptance of the option contract.

(b) In the event monies received by a licensee while acting in a fiduciary capacity are deposited in a trust or escrow account which bears interest, the licensee having custody over such monies shall first secure from all parties having an interest in the monies written authorization for the deposit of the monies in an interest-bearing account. Such authorization shall specify how and to whom the interest will be disbursed, and, if contained in an offer, contract, lease, or other transaction instrument, such authorization shall be set forth in a conspicuous manner which shall distinguish it from other provisions of the instrument.

(c) Closing statements shall be furnished to the buyer and the seller in the transaction not more than five days after closing.

(d) Trust or escrow accounts shall be so designated by the bank or savings and loan association in which the account is located, and all deposit tickets and checks drawn on said account as well as the monthly bank statement for the account shall bear the words "Trust Account" or "Escrow Account."

(e) A licensee shall maintain and retain records sufficient to identify the ownership of all funds belonging to others. Such records shall be sufficient to show proper deposit of such funds in a trust or escrow account and to verify the accuracy and proper use of the trust or escrow account. The required records shall include:

(1) bank statements.

(2) canceled checks which shall be referenced to the corresponding journal entry or check stub entries and to the corresponding sales transaction ledger sheets or for rental transactions, the corresponding property or owner ledger sheets. Checks shall conspicuously identify the payee and shall bear a notation identifying the purpose of the disbursement. When a check is used to disburse funds for more than one sales transaction, owner, or property, the check shall bear a notation identifying each sales transaction, owner, or property for which disbursement is made, including the amount disbursed for each, and the corresponding sales transaction, property, or owner ledger entries. When necessary, the check notation may refer to the required information recorded on a supplemental disbursement worksheet which shall be cross-referenced to the corresponding check. In lieu of retaining canceled checks, a licensee may retain digitally imaged copies of the canceled checks or substitute checks provided that such images are legible reproductions of the front and back of such instruments with no smaller images than 1.1875 x 3.0 inches and provided that the licensee's bank retains for a period of at least six years the original checks, "substitute checks" as described in 12 C.F.R. 229.51 or the capacity to provide substitute checks as described in 12 C.F.R. 229.51 and makes the original or substitute checks available to the licensee and the Commission upon request.

(3) deposit tickets. For a sales transaction, the deposit ticket shall identify the purpose and remitter of the funds deposited, the property, the parties involved, and a reference to the corresponding sales transaction ledger entry. For a rental transaction, the deposit ticket shall identify the purpose and remitter of the funds deposited, the tenant, and the corresponding property or owner ledger entry. For deposits of funds belonging to or collected on behalf of a property owner association, the deposit ticket shall identify the property or property interest for which the payment is made, the property or interest owner, the remitter, and the purpose of the payment. When a single deposit ticket is used to deposit funds collected for more than one sales transaction, property owner, or property, the required information shall be recorded on the ticket for each sales transaction, owner, or property, or the ticket may refer to the same information recorded on a supplemental deposit worksheet which shall be cross-referenced to the corresponding deposit ticket.

(4) a payment record sheet for each property or interest for which funds are collected and deposited into a property owner association trust account as required by Subsection (i) of this Rule. Payment record sheets shall identify the amount, date, remitter, and purpose of payments received, the amount and nature of the obligation for which payments are made, and the amount of any balance due or delinquency.

(5) a separate ledger sheet for each sales transaction and for each property or owner of property managed by the licensee identifying the property, the parties to the transaction, the amount, date, and purpose of the deposits and from whom received, the amount, date, check number, and purpose of disbursements and to whom paid, and the running balance of funds on deposit for the particular sales transaction or, in a rental transaction, the particular property or owner of property. Monies held as tenant security deposits in connection with rental transactions may be accounted for on a separate tenant security deposit ledger for each property or owner of property managed by the licensee. For each security deposit the tenant security deposit ledger shall identify the remitter, the date the deposit was paid, the amount, the tenant, landlord, and subject property. For each disbursement of tenant security deposit monies, the ledger shall identify the check number, amount, payee, date, and purpose of the disbursement. The ledger shall also show a running balance. When tenant security deposit monies are accounted for on a separate ledger as provided herein, deposit tickets, canceled checks and supplemental worksheets shall reference the corresponding tenant security deposit ledger entries when appropriate.

(6) a journal or check stubs identifying in chronological sequence each bank deposit and disbursement of monies to and from the trust or escrow account, including the amount and date of each deposit and a reference to the corresponding deposit ticket and any supplemental deposit worksheet, and the amount, date, check number, and purpose of disbursements and to whom paid. The journal or check stubs shall also show a running balance for all funds in the account.

(7) copies of contracts, leases and management agreements.

(8) closing statements and property management statements.

(9) covenants, bylaws, minutes, management agree-

ments and periodic statements relating to the management of a property owner association.

(10) invoices, bills, and contracts paid from the trust account, and any documents not otherwise described herein necessary and sufficient to verify and explain record entries.

Records of all receipts and disbursements of trust or escrow monies shall be maintained in such a manner as to create an audit trail from deposit tickets and canceled checks to check stubs or journals and to the ledger sheets. Ledger sheets and journals or check stubs must be reconciled to the trust or escrow account bank statements on a monthly basis. To be sufficient, records of trust or escrow monies must include a worksheet for each such monthly reconciliation showing the ledger sheets, journals or check stubs, and bank statements to be in agreement and balance.

(f) All trust or escrow account records shall be made available for inspection by the Commission or its authorized representatives in accordance with Rule 58A .0108.

(g) In the event of a dispute between the seller and buyer or landlord and tenant over the return or forfeiture of any deposit other than a residential tenant security deposit held by a licensee, the licensee shall retain said deposit in a trust or escrow account until the licensee has obtained a written release from the parties consenting to its disposition or until disbursement is ordered by a court of competent jurisdiction. Alternatively, the licensee may deposit the disputed monies with the appropriate clerk of court in accordance with the provision of G.S. 93A-12. If it appears to a licensee holding a disputed deposit that a party has abandoned his or her claim, the licensee may disburse the money to the other claiming parties according to their written agreement provided that the licensee first makes a reasonable effort to notify the party who has apparently abandoned his or her claim and provides that party with an opportunity to renew his or her claim to the disputed funds. Tenant security deposit monies shall be disposed of in accordance with the requirements of N.C.G.S. 42-50 through 56 and N.C.G.S. 42A-18.

(h) A licensee may transfer earnest money deposits in his or her possession collected in connection with a sales transaction from his or her trust account to the closing attorney or other settlement agent not more than ten days prior to the anticipated settlement date. A licensee shall not disburse prior to settlement any earnest money in his or her possession for any other purpose without the written consent of the parties.

(i) The funds of a property owner association, when collected, maintained, disbursed or otherwise controlled by a licensee, are trust monies and shall be treated as such in the manner required by this Rule. Such funds must be deposited into and maintained in a trust or escrow account dedicated exclusively for funds belonging to a single property owners association and may not be commingled with funds belonging to other property owner associations or other persons or parties. A licensee who undertakes to act as manager of a property owner association or as the custodian of funds belonging to a property own-

er association shall provide the association with periodic statements which report the balance of association funds in the licensee's possession or control and which account for the funds the licensee has received and disbursed on behalf of the association. Such statements must be made in accordance with the licensee's agreement with the association, but in no event shall the statements be made less frequently than every 90 days.

(j) Every licensee shall safeguard the money or property of others coming into his or her possession in a manner consistent with the requirements of the Real Estate License Law and the rules adopted by the Commission. A licensee shall not convert the money or property of others to his or her own use, apply such money or property to a purpose other than that for which it was paid or entrusted to him or her, or permit or assist any other person in the conversion or misapplication of such money or property.

(k) In addition to the records required by paragraph (e) of this rule, a licensee acting as agent for the landlord of a residential property used for vacation rentals shall create and maintain a subsidiary ledger sheet for each property or owner of such properties onto which all funds collected and disbursed are identified in categories by purpose. On a monthly basis, the licensee shall reconcile the subsidiary ledger sheets to the corresponding property or property owner ledger sheet.

(l) In lieu of maintaining a subsidiary ledger sheet, the licensee may maintain an accounts payable ledger sheet for each owner or property and each vendor to whom trust monies are due for monies collected on behalf of the owner or property identifying the date of receipt of the trust monies, from whom the monies were received, rental dates, and the corresponding property or owner ledger sheet entry including the amount to be disbursed for each and the purpose of the disbursement. The licensee may also maintain an accounts payable ledger sheet in the format described in paragraph (k) above for vacation rental tenant security deposit monies and vacation rental advance payments.

A.0108 Retention of Records

Licensees shall retain records of all sales, rental, and other transactions conducted in such capacity, whether the transaction is pending, completed or terminated prior to its successful conclusion. The licensee shall retain such records for three years after all funds held by the licensee in connection with the transaction have been disbursed to the proper party or parties or until the successful or unsuccessful conclusion of the transaction, whichever occurs later. Such records shall include contracts of sale, written leases, agency contracts, options, offers to purchase, trust or escrow records, earnest money receipts, disclosure documents, closing statements, brokerage cooperation agreements, declarations of affiliation, and any other records pertaining to real estate transactions. All such records shall be made available for inspection and reproduction by the Commission or its authorized representatives without prior notice.

A.0109 Brokerage Fees and Compensation

(a) A licensee shall not receive, either directly or indirectly, any commission, rebate or other valuable consideration of more than nominal value from a vendor or a supplier of goods and services for an expenditure made on behalf of the licensee's principal in a real estate transaction without the written consent of the licensee's principal.

(b) A licensee shall not receive, either directly or indirectly, any commission, rebate, or other valuable consideration of more than nominal value for services which the licensee recommends, procures, or arranges relating to a real estate transaction for a party, without full and timely disclosure to such party.

(c) In a real estate sales transaction, a broker shall not receive any compensation, incentive, bonus, rebate, or other consideration of more than nominal value:

(1) from his principal unless the compensation, incentive, bonus, rebate, or other consideration is provided for in a written agency contract prepared in conformity with the requirements of 21 NCAC 58A .0104.

(2) from any other party or person unless the broker provides full and timely disclosure of the incentive, bonus, rebate, or other consideration, or the promise or expectation thereof to the broker's principal. The disclosure may be made orally, but must be confirmed in writing before the principal makes or accepts an offer to buy or sell.

(d) Full disclosure shall include a description of the compensation, incentive, bonus, rebate, or other consideration including its value and the identity of the person or party by whom it will or may be paid. A disclosure is timely when it is made in sufficient time to aid a reasonable person's decision-making.

(e) Nothing in this rule shall be construed to require a broker to disclose to a person not his principal the compensation the broker expects to receive from his principal or to disclose to his principal the compensation the broker expects to receive from the broker's employing broker. For the purpose of this Rule, nominal value means of insignificant, token, or merely symbolic worth.

(f) The Commission shall not act as a board of arbitration and shall not compel parties to settle disputes concerning such matters as the rate of commissions, the division of commissions, pay of brokers, and similar matters.

(g) Except as provided in (h) of this rule, a licensee shall not undertake in any manner, any arrangement, contract, plan or other course of conduct, to compensate or share compensation with unlicensed persons or entities for any acts performed in North Carolina for which licensure by the Commission is required.

(h) A broker may pay or promise to pay consideration to a travel agent in return for procuring a tenant for a vacation rental as defined by the Vacation Rental Act if:

(1) the travel agent only introduces the tenant to the broker, but does not otherwise engage in any activity which would require a real estate license;

(2) the introduction by the travel agent is made in the regular course of the travel agent's business; and

(3) the travel agent has not solicited, handled or received any monies in connection with the vacation rental.

For the purpose of this Rule, a travel agent is any person or entity who is primarily engaged in the business of acting as an intermediary between persons who purchase air, land, and ocean travel services and the providers of such services. A travel agent is also any other person or entity who is permitted to handle and sell tickets for air travel by the Airlines Reporting Corporation (ARC). Payments authorized hereunder shall be made only after the conclusion of the vacation rental tenancy. Prior to the creation of a binding vacation rental agreement, the broker shall provide a tenant introduced by a travel agent a written statement advising him or her to rely only upon the agreement and the broker's representations about the transaction. The broker shall keep for a period of three years records of a payment made to a travel agent including records identifying the tenant, the travel agent and their addresses, the property and dates of the tenancy, and the amount paid.

(i) Nothing in this Rule shall be construed to permit a licensee to accept any fee, kickback or other valuable consideration that is prohibited by the Real Estate Settlement Procedures Act (12 USC 2601 et. seq.) or any rules and regulations promulgated by the United States Department of Housing and Urban Development pursuant to said Act or to fail to make any disclosure required by said Act or rules.

A.0110 Broker-in-Charge

(a) Every real estate firm shall designate a broker to serve as the broker-in-charge at its principal office and a broker to serve as broker-in-charge at any branch office. No broker shall be broker-in-charge of more than one office at a time. If a firm shares office space with one or more other firms, one broker may serve as broker-in-charge of each firm at that location. No office or branch office of a firm shall have more than one designated broker-in-charge. A broker who is a sole proprietor shall designate himself or herself as a broker-in-charge if the broker engages in any transaction where the broker is required to deposit and maintain monies belonging to others in a trust account, engages in advertising or promoting his or her services as a broker in any manner, or has one or more other brokers affiliated with him or her in the real estate business. Maintenance of a trust or escrow account by a broker solely for holding residential tenant security deposits received by the broker on properties owned by the broker in compliance with N.C.G.S. 42-50 shall not, standing alone, subject the broker to the requirement to designate himself or herself as a broker-in-charge. A broker desiring to be a broker-in-charge shall declare in writing his or her designation as broker-in-charge of an office to the Commission on a form prescribed by the Commission within 10 days following the broker's designation as broker-in-charge of any office. The broker-in-charge shall, in accordance with the requirements of G.S. 93A and the rules adopted by the Commission, assume the responsibility at his or her office for:

(1) the retention of current license renewal pocket cards by all brokers employed at the office for which he or she is broker-in-charge; the proper display of licenses at such office in accordance with Rule .0101 of this Section; and assuring that each licensee employed at the office has complied with Rules .0503, .0504 and .0506 of this Subchapter;

(2) the proper notification to the Commission of any change of business address or trade name of the firm and the registration of any assumed business name adopted by the firm for its use;

(3) the proper conduct of advertising by or in the name of the firm at such office;

(4) the proper maintenance at such office of the trust or escrow account of the firm and the records pertaining thereto;

(5) the proper retention and maintenance of records relating to transactions conducted by or on behalf of the firm at such office, including those required to be retained pursuant to Rule .0108 of this Section;

(6) the proper supervision of provisional brokers associated with or engaged on behalf of the firm at such office in accordance with the requirements of Rule .0506 of this Subchapter;

(7) the proper supervision of all licensees employed at the office for which he or she is broker-in-charge with respect to adherence to agency agreement and disclosure requirements.

(b) When used in this Rule, the term:

(1) "Branch Office" means any office in addition to the principal office of a broker which is operated in connection with the broker's real estate business; and

(2) "Office" means any place of business where acts are performed for which a real estate license is required or where monies received by a licensee acting in a fiduciary capacity are handled or records for such trust monies are maintained.

(c) To qualify to become as a broker-in-charge, a broker shall:

(1) have a license on active status, but not on provisional status;

(2) possess at least two years of full-time real estate brokerage experience or equivalent part-time real estate brokerage experience within the previous five years or real estate education or experience in real estate transactions that the Commission finds equivalent to such experience; and

(3) complete the Commission's 12 classroom hour broker-in-charge course either within three years prior to designation as a broker-in-charge or within 120

days following designation as a broker-in-charge.

By submission of a broker-in-charge declaration to the Commission, a broker certifies that he or she possesses the experience required to become a broker-in-charge and upon acknowledgement by the Commission of a completed declaration, the broker shall receive his or her broker-in-charge designation and be authorized to act as a broker-in-charge. Upon his or her designation as broker-in-charge and completion of the broker-in-charge course within the time period prescribed in Subparagraph (b)(3) of this Rule, the designated broker-in-charge acquires the eligibility to be re-designated as a broker-in-charge at any time in the future after a period of not actively serving as a broker-in-charge without having to again satisfy the qualification requirements for initial designation stated in this Paragraph so long as the broker continuously satisfies the requirements to retain such eligibility described in Paragraph (e) of this Rule. A broker-in-charge designation shall be immediately terminated if a broker-in-charge fails to complete the broker-in-charge course during the required time period or if the Commission finds the broker-in-charge does not possess the required experience. Upon the request of the Commission, a broker shall provide to the Commission evidence that he or she possesses the required experience. A broker who is removed as broker-in-charge for failure to timely complete the Commission's 12 hour broker-in-charge course must first complete the 12 hour broker-in-charge course before he or she may again be designated as broker-in-charge. A broker-in-charge, upon written request of the Commission or a broker who has been affiliated with the broker-in-charge within the previous five years, shall provide the Commission or broker an accurate written statement regarding the broker's work at the office of the broker-in-charge, including the dates of affiliation, average number of hours worked per week, and the number and type of properties listed, sold, bought, leased, or rented for others by the licensee during his or her affiliation with the broker-in-charge.

(d) A broker who was the broker-in-charge of a real estate office on April 1, 2006, whose broker-in-charge declaration was received by the Commission prior to that date, and who completed the Commission's broker-in-charge course prior to April 1, 2006 or within 120 days following designation as a broker-in-charge, may continue to serve as a broker-in-charge thereafter until his or her eligibility to serve as a broker-in-charge is terminated as provided in paragraph (f) of this Rule.

(e) Once a broker has been designated as a broker-in-charge and completed the 12 hour broker-in-charge course as prescribed by Paragraph (c) of this Rule, the broker may maintain broker-in-charge eligibility by timely annual renewal of his or her broker license, completion each license year of the four hour mandatory continuing education update course prescribed for all licensees and known as the "Real Estate Update Course," and completion each license year of the four hour special continuing education course prescribed by the Commission only for brokers-in-charge and known as the "Broker-In-Charge Annual Review Course." The Broker-In-Charge Annual Review Course must be taken initially by a broker-in-charge during the first full license year following the license year in which the broker was designated as a broker-in-charge and must be taken each license year thereafter in order for the broker to maintain broker-in-charge eligibility. The Broker-In-Charge Annual Review Course shall satisfy the broker's general continuing education elective course requirement, but the broker must also take the mandatory continuing education Real Estate Update Course each license year. The Broker-In-Charge Annual Review Course is reserved exclusively for current brokers-in-charge, and brokers who are not currently acting as a broker-in-charge but who desire to retain their broker-in-charge eligibility. Only these brokers shall receive continuing education elective credit for taking the course.

(f) A broker's broker-in-charge eligibility and, if currently designated as a broker-in-charge, his or her broker-in-charge designation shall be terminated upon the occurrence of any of the following events:

(1) The broker's license expires or the broker's license is suspended, revoked or surrendered;

(2) the broker's license is made inactive for any reason, including failure to satisfy the continuing education requirements described in Rule .1702 of this Subchapter;

(3) the broker fails to complete the Broker-In-Charge Annual Review Course described in Paragraph (e) of this Rule; or

(4) the broker is found by the Commission to have not possessed the experience required in Paragraph (c) of this Rule at the time of either initial designation as a broker-in-charge or re-designation as a broker-in-charge.

When a broker who is a former broker-in-charge desires to be re-designated as a broker-in-charge following termination of his or her broker-in-charge designation or eligibility, he or she must first have a license on active status. The broker then must satisfy the experience requirements for initial designation set forth in Paragraph (c) of this Rule, and the broker must complete the 12 hour broker-in-charge course within 120 days following re-designation, except that if the broker has taken the 12 hour broker-in-charge course within the preceding three years, he or she has the option to complete the Broker-In-Charge Annual Review Course for the current license year within 120 days following re-designation as a broker-in-charge in lieu of repeating the 12 hour broker-in-charge course. If a broker who has been re-designated as a broker-in-charge and then removed as a broker-in-charge due to failure to satisfy his education requirement within 120 days following re-designation subsequently seeks another re-designation as broker-in-charge, the broker must first complete the 12 hour broker-in-charge course before he or she may again be designated as a broker-in-charge, even if the broker has completed the 12 hour broker-in-charge course within the preceding three years.

(g) A broker-in-charge shall notify the Commission in writing that he or she no longer is serving as broker-in-charge of a particular office within 10 days following any such change.

(h) A licensed real estate firm is not required to designate a broker-in-charge if it:

(1) has been organized for the sole purpose of receiving compensation for brokerage services furnished by its qualifying broker through another firm or broker;

(2) is treated for tax purposes as a Subchapter S corporation by the United States Internal Revenue Service;

(3) has no branch office; and

(4) has no person associated with it other than its qualifying broker.

(i) A broker-in-charge residing outside of North Carolina who is the broker-in-charge of a principal or branch office not located in North Carolina is not required to complete the broker-in-charge course or the special continuing education course prescribed for brokers-in-charge under paragraph (e) of this Rule. However, if such broker-in-charge either becomes a resident of North Carolina or becomes broker-in-charge of an office located within North Carolina, then he or she must take the 12 hour broker-in-charge course within 120 days of such change, unless he or she has taken the 12 hour course within the preceding three years. Such broker-in-charge shall take the special broker-in-charge continuing education course prescribed in paragraph (e) of this Rule during the first full license year following the change and each license year thereafter so long as the broker-in-charge remains a resident of North Carolina or continues to manage an office located in North Carolina.

(j) A nonresident commercial real estate broker licensed under the provisions of Section .1800 of this Subchapter shall not act as or serve in the capacity of a broker-in-charge of a firm or office in North Carolina.

A.0111 Drafting Legal Instruments

(a) A broker acting as an agent in a real estate transaction shall not draft offers, sales contracts, options, leases, promissory notes, deeds, deeds of trust or other legal instruments by which the rights of others are secured; however, a broker may complete preprinted offer, option contract, sales contract and lease forms in real estate transactions when authorized or directed to do so by the parties.

(b) A broker may use electronic, computer, or word processing equipment to store preprinted offer and sales contract forms which comply with Rule .0112, as well as preprinted option and lease forms, and may use such equipment to complete and print offer, contract and lease documents. Provided, however, a broker may not alter the form before it is presented to the parties. If the parties propose to delete or change any word or provision in the form, the form must be marked to indicate the change or deletion made. The language of the form shall

STATE OF NORTH CAROLINA
RESIDENTIAL PROPERTY DISCLOSURE STATEMENT
INSTRUCTIONS TO PROPERTY OWNERS

1.   G.S. 47E requires owners of residential real estate (single-family homes and buildings with up to four dwelling units) to furnish purchasers a property disclosure statement. This form is the only one approved for this purpose. A disclosure statement must be furnished in connection with the sale, exchange, option and sale under a lease with option to purchase (unless the tenant is already occupying or intends to occupy the dwelling). A disclosure statement is not required for some transactions, including the first sale of a dwelling which has never been inhabited and transactions of residential property made pursuant to a lease with option to purchase where the lessee occupies or intends to occupy the dwelling. For a complete list of exemptions, see G.S. 47E-2.

2.   You must check one of the boxes for each of the 21 questions on the reverse side of this form.

   a.   If you check "Yes" for any question, you must explain your answer and either describe any problem or attach a report from an engineer, contractor, pest control operator or other expert or public agency describing it. If you attach a report, you will not be liable for any inaccurate or incomplete information contained in it so long as you were not grossly negligent in obtaining or transmitting the information.

   b.   If you check "No", you are stating that you have no actual knowledge of any problem. If you check "No" and you know there is a problem, you may be liable for making an intentional misstatement.

   c.   If you check "No Representation", you have no duty to disclose the conditions or characteristics of the property, even if you should have known of them.

   *   If you check "Yes" or "No" and something happens to the property to make your Statement incorrect or inaccurate (for example, the roof begins to leak), you must promptly give the purchaser a corrected Statement or correct the problem.

3.   If you are assisted in the sale of your property by a licensed real estate broker, you are still responsible for completing and delivering the Statement to the purchasers; and the broker must disclose any material facts about your property which they know or reasonably should know, regardless of your responses on the Statement.

4.   You must give the completed Statement to the purchaser no later than the time the purchaser makes an offer to purchase your property. If you do not, the purchaser can, under certain conditions, cancel any resulting contract (See **"Note to Purchasers"** below). You should give the purchaser a copy of the Statement containing your signature and keep a copy signed by the purchaser for your records.

   Note to Purchasers: If the owner does not give you a Residential Property Disclosure Statement by the time you make your offer to purchase the property, you may under certain conditions cancel any resulting contract and be entitled to a refund of any deposit monies you may have paid. To cancel the contract, you must personally deliver or mail written notice of your decision to cancel to the owner or the owner's agent within three calendar days following your receipt of the Statement, or three calendar days following the date of the contract, whichever occurs first. However, in no event does the Disclosure Act permit you to cancel a contract after settlement of the transaction or (in the case of a sale or exchange) after you have occupied the property, whichever occurs first.

---

5.   In the space below, type or print in ink the address of the property (sufficient to identify it) and your name. Then sign and date.

   Property Address: _____

   Owner's Name(s): _____

   Owner(s) acknowledge having examined this Statement before signing and that all information is true and correct as of the date signed.

   Owner Signature: _____ Date _____

   Owner Signature: _____ Date _____

   Purchaser(s) acknowledge receipt of a copy of this disclosure statement; that they have examined it before signing; that they understand that this is not a warranty by owner or owner's agent; that it is not a substitute for any inspections they may wish to obtain; and that the representations are made by the owner and not the owner's agent(s) or subagent(s). Purchaser(s) are encouraged to obtain their own inspection from a licensed home inspector or other professional.

   Purchaser Signature: _____ Date _____

   Purchaser Signature: _____ Date _____

Property Address/Description: _____

[Note: In this form, "property" refers only to dwelling unit(s) and not sheds, detached garages or other buildings.]
Regarding the property identified above, do you know of any problem (malfunction or defect) with any of the following:

	Yes*	No	No Representation

1. FOUNDATION, SLAB, FIREPLACES/CHIMNEYS, FLOORS, WINDOWS (INCLUDING STORM WINDOWS AND SCREENS), DOORS, CEILINGS, INTERIOR AND EXTERIOR WALLS, ATTACHED GARAGE, PATIO, DECK OR OTHER STRUCTURAL COMPONENTS including any modifications to them?......... ☐ ☐ ☐
   a. Siding is ☐ Masonry ☐ Wood ☐ Composition/Hardboard ☐ Vinyl ☐ Synthetic Stucco ☐ Other _____ .... ☐
   b. Approximate age of structure? _____ .... ☐

2. ROOF (leakage or other problem)?.. ☐ ☐ ☐
   a. Approximate age of roof covering? _____ .... ☐

3. WATER SEEPAGE, LEAKAGE, DAMPNESS OR STANDING WATER in the basement, crawl space or slab?......... ☐ ☐ ☐

4. ELECTRICAL SYSTEM (outlets, wiring, panel, switches, fixtures etc.)?.................................. ☐ ☐ ☐

5. PLUMBING SYSTEM (pipes, fixtures, water heater, etc.)?.. ☐ ☐ ☐

6. HEATING AND/OR AIR CONDITIONING?... ☐ ☐ ☐
   a. Heat Source is: ☐ Furnace ☐ Heat Pump ☐ Baseboard ☐ Other_____ .... ☐
   b. Cooling Source is: ☐ Central Forced Air ☐ Wall/Window Unit(s) ☐ Other_____ .... ☐
   c. Fuel Source is: ☐ Electricity ☐ Natural Gas ☐ Propane ☐ Oil ☐ Other _____ .... ☐

7. WATER SUPPLY (including water quality, quantity and water pressure)?.............................. ☐ ☐ ☐
   a. Water supply is: ☐ City/County ☐ Community System ☐ Private Well ☐ Other _____ .... ☐
   b. Water pipes are: ☐ Copper ☐ Galvanized ☐ Plastic ☐ Other _____ ☐ Unknown............... ☐

8. SEWER AND/OR SEPTIC SYSTEM?.. ☐ ☐ ☐
   a. Sewage disposal system is: ☐ Septic Tank ☐ Septic Tank with Pump ☐ Community System ☐ Connected to City/County System ☐ City/County System available ☐ Straight pipe (wastewater does not go into a septic or other sewer system [note: use of this type of system violates state law]) ☐ Other _____ .... ☐

9. BUILT-IN APPLIANCES (RANGE/OVEN, ATTACHED MICROWAVE, HOOD/FAN, DISHWASHER, DISPOSAL, etc.)?.. ☐ ☐ ☐

10. PRESENT INFESTATION, OR DAMAGE FROM PAST INFESTATION OF WOOD DESTROYING INSECTS OR ORGANISMS which has not been repaired?.. ☐ ☐ ☐

11. DRAINAGE, GRADING OR SOIL STABILITY OF LOT?.. ☐ ☐ ☐

12. OTHER SYSTEMS AND FIXTURES: CENTRAL VACUUM, POOL, HOT TUB, SPA, ATTIC FAN, EXHAUST FAN, CEILING FAN, SUMP PUMP, IRRIGATION SYSTEM, TV CABLE WIRING OR SATELLITE DISH, OR OTHER SYSTEMS?.. ☐ ☐ ☐

Also regarding the property identified above, including the lot, other improvements, and fixtures located thereon, do you know of any:

13. ROOM ADDITIONS OR OTHER STRUCTURAL CHANGES ?.. ☐ ☐ ☐

14. ENVIRONMENTAL HAZARDS (substances, materials or products) including asbestos, formaldehyde, radon gas, methane gas, lead-based paint, underground storage tank, or other hazardous or toxic material (whether buried or covered), contaminated soil or water, or other environmental contamination? .... ☐ ☐ ☐

15. COMMERCIAL OR INDUSTRIAL NUISANCES (noise, odor, smoke, etc.) affecting the property?.................... ☐ ☐ ☐

16. VIOLATIONS OF ZONING ORDINANCES, RESTRICTIVE COVENANTS OR OTHER LAND-USE RESTRICTIONS OR BUILDING CODES INCLUDING THE FAILURE TO OBTAIN PROPER PERMITS FOR ROOM ADDITIONS OR OTHER STRUCTURAL CHANGES?....................................... ☐ ☐ ☐

17. UTILITY OR OTHER EASEMENTS, SHARED DRIVEWAYS, PARTY WALLS OR ENCROACHMENTS FROM OR ON ADJACENT PROPERTY?.. ☐ ☐ ☐

18. LAWSUITS, FORECLOSURES, BANKRUPTCY, TENANCIES, JUDGMENTS, TAX LIENS, PROPOSED ASSESSMENTS, MECHANICS' LIENS, MATERIALMENS' LIENS, OR NOTICE FROM ANY GOVERNMENTAL AGENCY that could affect title to the property? .... ☐ ☐ ☐

19. OWNERS' ASSOCIATION OR "COMMON AREA" EXPENSES OR ASSESSMENTS?.................... ☐ ☐ ☐

20. FLOOD HAZARD or that the property is in a FEDERALLY-DESIGNATED FLOOD PLAIN?.................. ☐ ☐ ☐

21. PRIVATE ROAD(S) OR STREETS adjoining the property?.. ☐ ☐ ☐
    a. If yes, do you know of an existing owners association or maintenance agreement to maintain the road or street?....... ☐ ☐ ☐

* If you answered "Yes" to any of the above 21 questions, please explain (Attach additional sheets, if necessary): _____

Owner Initials and Date	Owner Initials and Date
Purchaser Initials and Date	Purchaser Initials and Date

not be modified, rewritten, or changed by the broker or their clerical employees unless directed to do so by the parties.

(c) Nothing contained in this rule shall be construed to prohibit a broker from making written notes, memoranda or correspondence recording the negotiations of the parties to a real estate transaction when such notes, memoranda or correspondence do not themselves constitute binding agreements or other legal instruments.

A.0112 Offers and Sales Contracts

(a) A broker acting as an agent in a real estate transaction shall not use a preprinted offer or sales contract form unless the form describes or expressly requires the entry of the following information:

(1) the names of the buyer and seller;

(2) a legal description of the real property sufficient to identify and distinguish it from all other property;

(3) an itemization of any personal property to be included in the transaction;

(4) the purchase price and manner of payment;

(5) any portion of the purchase price that is to be paid by a promissory note, including the amount, interest rate, payment terms, whether or not the note is to be secured, and other material terms;

(6) any portion of the purchase price that is to be paid by the assumption of an existing loan, including the amount of such loan, costs to be paid by the buyer or seller, the interest rate and number of discount points and a condition that the buyer must be able to qualify for the assumption of the loan and must make every reasonable effort to quality for the assumption of the loan;

(7) the amount of earnest money, if any, the method of payment, the name of the broker or firm that will serve as escrow agent, an acknowledgment of earnest money receipt by the escrow agent, and the criteria for determining disposition of the earnest money, including disputed earnest money, consistent with Rule .0107 of this Subchapter;

(8) any loan that must be obtained by the buyer as a condition of the contract, including the amount and type of loan, interest rate and number of discount points, loan term, and who shall pay loan closing costs; and a condition that the buyer shall make every reasonable effort to obtain the loan;

(9) a general statement of the buyer's intended use of the property and a condition that such use must not be prohibited by private restriction or governmental regulation;

(10) the amount and purpose of any special assessment to which the property is subject and the responsibility of the parties for any unpaid charges;

(11) the date for closing and transfer of possession;

(12) the signatures of the buyer and seller;

(13) the date of offer and acceptance;

(14) a provision that title to the property must be delivered at closing by general warranty deed and must be fee simple marketable title, free of all encumbrances except ad valorem taxes for the current year, utility easements, and any other encumbrances approved by the buyer, or a provision otherwise describing the estate to be conveyed, and encumbrances, and the form of conveyance;

(15) the items to be prorated or adjusted at closing;

(16) who shall pay closing expenses;

(17) the buyer's right to inspect the property prior to closing and who shall pay for repairs and improvements, if any;

(18) a provision that the property shall at closing be in substantially the same condition as on the date of the offer (reasonable wear and tear excepted), or a descdription of the required property condition at closing: and

(19) a provision setting forth the identity of each real estate agent and firm involved in the transaction and disclosing the party each agent and firm represents.

(b) The provisions of this Rule apply only to preprinted offer and sales contract forms which a broker acting as an agent in a real estate transaction proposes for use by the buyer and seller. Nothing contained in this Rule shall be construed to prohibit the buyer and seller in a real estate transaction from altering, amending or deleting any provision in a form offer to purchase or contract; nor shall this Rule be construed to limit the rights of the buyer and seller to draft their own offers or contracts or to have the same drafted by an attorney at law.

(c) A broker acting as an agent in a real estate transaction shall not use a preprinted offer or sales contract form containing the provisions or terms listed in Subparagraphs (b)(1) and (2) of this Rule. A broker or anyone acting for or at the direction of the broker shall not insert or cause to be inserted into any such preprinted form, even at the direction of the parties or their attorneys, the following provisions and terms:

(1) any provision concerning the payment of a commission or compensation, including the forfeiture of earnest money, to any broker or firm; or

(2) any provision that attempts to disclaim the liability of a broker for his or her representations in connection with the transaction.

A.0113 Reporting Criminal Convictions and Disciplinary Actions

Any broker who is convicted of any felony or misdemeanor or who is disciplined by any governmental agency in connection with any other occupational license, or whose notarial commission is restricted, suspended, or revoked, shall file with the Commission a written report of such conviction or action within 60 days of the final judgment, order, or disposition in the case. A form for this report is available from the Commission.

A.0114 Residential Property Disclosure Statement

(a) Every owner of real property subject to a transfer of the type contemplated by Chapter 47E of the General Statutes, shall complete the ... residential property disclosure statement and furnish a copy of the complete statement to a purchaser in accordance with the requirements of G.S. 47E-4. The form shall bear the seal of the North Carolina Real Estate Commission and shall read as [approved and published by the Commission].

(b) The form described in Paragraph (a) of this Rule may be reproduced, but the form shall not be altered or amended in any way.

A.0115 Disclosure of Offers Prohibited

A broker shall not disclose the price or other material terms contained in a party's offer to purchase, sell, lease, rent, or to option real property to a competing party without the express authority of the offering party.

SECTION A.0200
GENERAL PROVISIONS
(Repealed)

SECTION A.0300
APPLICATION FOR LICENSE

A.0301 Form

An individual or business entity who wishes to file an application for a broker license shall make application on a form prescribed by the Commission and can obtain the required form upon request to the Commission. In general, the application form for an individual calls for information such as the applicant's name and address, the applicant's social security number, satisfactory proof of the applicant's identity, places of residence, education, prior real estate licenses, and such other information necessary to identify the applicant and determine the applicant's qualifications and fitness for licensure. The application form for a business entity is described in Rule .0502 of this Section.

A.0302 Filing and Fees

(a) Applications for a real estate license shall be complete and, except as provided by Rule .0403 of this Subchapter, shall be submitted to the Commission's office accompanied by the application fee. Examination scheduling of applicants who are required to pass the real estate licensing examination shall be accomplished in accordance with Rule .0401 of this Subchapter.

(b) Except for persons applying for licensure under the provisions of Section .1800 of this Subchapter, the license application fee shall be $30.00. In addition to the license application fee, applicants for licensure who are required to take the license examination must pay the examination fee charged by the Commission's authorized testing service in the form and manner acceptable to the testing service. Persons applying for licensure under Section .1800 of this Subchapter shall pay the application fee set forth in Rule .1803 of this Subchapter.

(c) An applicant shall update information provided in connection with an application or submit a newly completed application form without request by the Commission to assure that the information provided in the application is current and accurate. Failure to submit updated information prior to the issuance of a license may result in disciplinary action against a licensee in accordance with G.S. §93A-6(b)(1). In the event that the Commission requests an applicant to submit updated information or to provide additional information necessary to complete the application and the applicant fails to submit such information within 90 days following the Commission's request, the Commission shall cancel the applicant's application. The license application of an individual found by the Commission to be qualified for the licensing examination shall be immediately canceled if the applicant fails to pass a scheduled licensing examination, fails to appear for and take any examination for which the applicant has been scheduled without having the applicant's examination postponed or absence excused in accordance with Rule .0401(b) and (c) of this Section, or fails to take and pass the examination within 180 days of filing a complete application as described in Rule .0301 of this Section and having the application entered into the Commission's examination applicant file. Except as permitted otherwise in Rule .0403 of this Subchapter, an applicant whose license application has been canceled and who wishes to obtain a real estate license must start the licensing process over by filing a complete application to the Commission and paying all required fees.

A.0303 Payment of Application Fees

Payment of application fees shall be made to the Commission by bank check, certified check, money order, debit card, or credit card. Once an application has been filed and processed, the application fee may not be refunded.

A.0304 Equivalent Experience Qualifications for Applicants

Experience obtained by a broker applicant in violation of law or rule may not be recognized by the Commission as fulfilling the requirements for licensure when the applicant is requesting the Commission to waive the prescribed education requirement based wholly or in part on equivalent experience obtained by the applicant.

SECTION A.0400
EXAMINATIONS

A.0401 Scheduling Examinations

(a) An applicant who is required and qualified to take the licensing examination shall be provided a notice of examination eligibility that shall be valid for a period of 180 days and for a single administration of the licensing examination. Upon receipt of the notice of examination eligibility, the applicant shall contact the Commission's authorized testing service to pay for and schedule the examinations in accordance with procedures established by the testing service. The testing service will schedule applicants for examination by computer at their choice of one of the testing locations and will notify applicants of the time and place of their examinations.

(b) An applicant may postpone a scheduled examination provided the applicant makes the request for postponement directly to the Commission's authorized testing service in accordance with procedures established by the testing service. An applicant's examination shall not be postponed beyond the 180 day period allowed for taking the examination without first refiling another complete application with the Commission.

A request to postpone a scheduled licensing examination without complying with the procedures for re-applying for examination described in Rule .0403 of this Subchapter shall be granted only once unless the applicant satisfies the requirements for obtaining an excused absence stated in Paragraph (c) of this Rule.

(c) An applicant may be granted an excused absence from a scheduled examination if the applicant provides evidence that the absence was the direct result of an emergency situation or condition which was beyond the applicant's control and which could not have been reasonably foreseen by the applicant. A request for an excused absence must be promptly made in writing and must be supported by documentation verifying the reason for the absence.

The request must be submitted directly to the testing service in accordance with procedures established by the testing service. A request for an excused absence from an examination shall be denied if the applicant cannot be rescheduled and examined prior to expiration of the 180 day period allowed for taking the examination without first refiling another complete application with the Commission.

A.0402 Subject Matter and Passing Scores

(a) The real estate licensing examination shall test applicants on the following general subject areas:
(1) real estate law;
(2) real estate brokerage law and practices;
(3) the Real Estate License Law, rules of the Commission, and the Commission's trust account guidelines;
(4) real estate finance;
(5) real estate valuation (appraisal);
(6) real estate mathematics; and
(7) related subject areas.

(b) In order to pass the real estate licensing examination, an applicant must attain a score at least equal to the passing score established by the Commission in compliance with psychometric standards for establishing passing scores for occu-

pational licensing examinations as set forth in the "Standards for Educational and Psychological Testing" jointly promulgated by the American Educational Research Association, the American Psychological Association, and the National Council on Measurement in Education. Passing applicants will receive only a score of "pass"; however, failing applicants will be informed of their actual score. A passing examination score obtained by a license applicant shall be recognized as valid for a period of one year from the date of examination, during which time the applicant must fully satisfy any remaining requirements for licensure that were pending at the time of examination; provided that the running of the one-year period shall be tolled upon mailing the applicant the letter contemplated in 21 NCAC 58A .0616(b) informing the applicant that his or her moral character is in question, and shall resume running when the applicant's application is either approved for license issuance, denied or withdrawn. The application of an applicant with a passing examination score who fails to satisfy all remaining requirements for licensure within one year shall be canceled and the applicant shall be required to reapply and satisfy all requirements for licensure, including retaking and passing the license examination, in order to be eligible for licensure.

A.0403 Re-applying for Examination

(a) An individual whose license application has been canceled and whose 180 day examination eligibility period has expired who wishes to be rescheduled for the real estate license examination must re-apply to the Commission by filing a complete license application as described in Rule .0301 of this Subchapter and paying the prescribed application fee. Subsequent examinations shall be scheduled in accordance with Rule .0401 of this Section.

(b) An individual whose license application has been canceled who wishes to be rescheduled for the license examination before the expiration of his or her 180 day examination eligibility period may utilize an abbreviated electronic license application and examination rescheduling procedure by directly contacting the Commission's authorized testing service, paying both the license application fee and the examination fee to the testing service, and following the testing service's established procedures.

(c) An applicant who fails the license examination shall not be allowed to retake the examination for at least 10 calendar days.

A.0404 Cheating and Related Misconduct

Applicants shall not cheat or attempt to cheat on an examination by any means, including both giving and receiving assistance, and shall not communicate in any manner for any purpose with any person other than an examination supervisor during an examination. Applicants shall not disrupt the quiet and orderly administration of an examination in any manner. Violation of this Rule shall be grounds for dismissal from an examination, invalidation of examination scores, and denial of a real estate license, as well as for disciplinary action if the applicant has been issued a license.

A.0405 Confidentiality of Examinations

Licensing examinations are the exclusive property of the Commission and are confidential. No applicant or licensee shall obtain, attempt to obtain, receive or communicate to other persons examination questions or answers. Violation of this Rule is grounds for denial of a real estate license if the violator is an applicant and disciplinary action if the violator is a licensee or becomes a licensee prior to the discovery of the violation by the Commission.

A.0406 Examination Review

An applicant who fails the license examination may review the examination at the testing center immediately following completion of the examination and receipt of the applicant's examination results but prior to leaving the testing center. An applicant who fails the examination and who declines the opportunity to immediately review the examination prior to leaving the testing center will be deemed to have waived the right to review the examination. An applicant who is reviewing his or her failed examination may not have any other person present during his or her review, nor may any other person review an examination on behalf of an applicant. An applicant who passes the license examination may not review the examination.

SECTION A.0500 LICENSING

A.0501 Character (Repealed)

A.0502 Business Entities

(a) Every business entity other than a sole proprietorship shall apply for and obtain from the Commission a firm license prior to engaging in business as a real estate broker. An entity that changes its business form other than by conversion shall submit a new license application immediately upon making the change and obtain a new firm license. An entity which converts to a different business entity in conformity with and pursuant to applicable North Carolina General Statutes is not required to apply for a new license. However, such converted entity shall provide the information required by this paragraph in writing to the Commission within ten (10) days of said conversion and shall include the applicable fee to have the firm license reissued in the legal name of the converted entity. Incomplete applications shall not be acted upon by the Commission. Application forms for partnerships, corporations, limited liability companies, associations and other business entities required to be licensed as brokers shall be available upon request to the Commission and shall require the applicant to set forth:

(1) the name of the entity;

(2) the name under which the entity will do business;

(3) the type of business entity;

(4) the address of its principal office;

(5) the entity's North Carolina Secretary of State Identification Number if required to be registered with the Office of the North Carolina Secretary of State;

(6) the name, real estate license number and signature of the proposed qualifying broker for the proposed firm;

(7) the address of and name of the proposed broker-in-charge for each office as defined in Rule .0110(b) of this subchapter, along with a completed broker-in-charge declaration form for each proposed broker-in-charge;

(8) any past criminal conviction of and any pending criminal charge against any principal in the company or any proposed broker-in-charge;

(9) any past revocation, suspension or denial of a business or professional license of any principal in the company or any proposed broker-in-charge;

(10) if a general partnership, a full description of the applicant entity, including a copy of its written partnership agreement or if no written agreement exists, a written description of the rights and duties of the several partners;

(11) if a business entity other than a corporation, limited liability company or partnership, a full description of the organization of the applicant entity, including a copy of its organizational documents evidencing its authority to engage in real estate brokerage;

(12) if a foreign business entity, a certificate of authority to transact business in North Carolina and an executed consent to service of process and pleadings; and

(13) any other information required by this rule.

When the authority of a business entity to engage in the real estate business is unclear in the application or in law, the Commission shall require the applicant to declare in the license application that the applicant's organizational documents authorize the firm to engage in the real estate business and to submit organizational documents, addresses of affiliated persons and similar information. For purposes of this Rule, the term principal, when it refers to a person or entity, means any person or entity owning ten percent or more of the business entity, or who is an officer, director, manager, member, partner or who holds any other comparable position.

(b) After filing a written application with the Commission and upon a showing that at least one principal of the business entity holds a broker license on active status and in good standing and will serve as qualifying broker of the entity, the entity shall be licensed provided it appears that the applicant entity employs and is directed by personnel possessed of the requisite truthfulness, honesty, and integrity. The qualifying broker of a partnership of any kind must be a general partner of the partnership; the qualifying broker of a limited liability company must be a manager of the company; and the qualifying broker of a corporation must be an officer of the corporation. A licensed business entity may serve as the qualifying broker of another licensed business entity if the qualifying broker-entity has as its qualifying broker a natural person who is licensed as a broker. The natural person who is qualifying broker shall assure the performance of the qualifying broker's duties with regard to both entities. A provisional broker may not serve as a qualifying broker.

(c) The licensing of a business entity shall not be construed to extend to the licensing of its partners, managers, members, directors, officers, employees or other persons acting for the entity in their individual capacities regardless of whether they are engaged in furthering the business of the licensed entity.

(d) The qualifying broker of a business entity shall assume responsibility for:

(1) designating and assuring that there is at all times a broker-in-charge for each office and branch office of the entity as office and branch office are defined in Rule .0110(b) of this Subchapter;

(2) renewing the real estate broker license of the entity;

(3) retaining the firm's renewal pocket card at the firm and producing it as proof of firm licensure upon request and maintaining a photocopy of the firm license certificate and pocket card at each branch office thereof;

(4) notifying the Commission of any change of business address or trade name of the entity and the registration of any assumed business name adopted by the entity for its use;

(5) notifying the Commission in writing of any change of his or her status as qualifying broker within ten days following the change;

(6) securing and preserving the transaction and trust account records of the firm whenever there is a change of broker-in-charge at the firm or any office thereof and notifying the Commission if the trust account records are out of balance or have not been reconciled as required by rule .0107 of this Subchapter;

(7) retaining and preserving the transaction and trust account records of the firm upon termination of his or her status as qualifying broker until a new qualifying broker has been designated with the Commission or, if no new qualifying broker is designated, for the period of time for which said records are required to be retained by Rule .0108 of this Subchapter; and

(8) notifying the Commission if, upon the termination of his or her status as qualifying broker, the firm's transaction and trust account records cannot be retained or preserved or if the trust account records are out of balance or have not been reconciled as required by Rule .0107(e) of this Subchapter.

(e) Every licensed business entity and every entity applying for licensure shall conform to all the requirements imposed upon it by the North Carolina General Statutes for its continued existence and authority to do business in North Carolina. Failure to conform to such requirements is grounds for disciplinary action or denial of the entity's application for licensure. Upon receipt of notice from an entity or agency of this state that a licensed entity has ceased to exist or that its authority to engage in business in this state has been terminated by operation of law, the Commission shall cancel the license of the entity.

A.0503 License Renewal; Penalty for Operating While License Expired

(a) All real estate licenses issued by the Commission under G.S. 93A, Article 1 shall expire on the 30th day of June following issuance. Any licensee desiring renewal of a license shall apply for renewal within 45 days prior to license expiration by submitting a renewal application on a form provided by the Commission and submitting with the application the required renewal fee of forty dollars ($40.00).

(b) Any person desiring to renew his or her license on active status shall, upon the second renewal of such license following initial licensure, and upon each subsequent renewal, have obtained all continuing education required by G.S. 93A-4A and Rule .1702 of the Subchapter.

(c) A person renewing a license on inactive status shall not be required to have obtained any continuing education in order to renew such license; however, in order to subsequently change his or her license from inactive status to active status, the licensee must satisfy the continuing education requirement prescribed in Rule .1703 or Rule .1711 of the Subchapter.

(d) Any person or firm which engages in the business of a real estate broker while his, her, or its license is expired is subject to the penalties prescribed in G.S. 93A-6.

A.0504 Active and Inactive License Status

(a) Except for licenses that have expired or that have been canceled, revoked, suspended or surrendered, all licenses issued by the Commission shall be designated as being either on active status or inactive status. The holder of a license on active status may engage in any activity requiring a real estate license and may be compensated for the provision of any lawful real estate brokerage service. The holder of a license on inactive status may not engage in any activity requiring a real estate license, including the referral for compensation of a prospective seller, buyer, landlord or tenant to another real estate licensee or any other party. A licensee holding a license on inactive status must renew the license and pay the prescribed license renewal fee in order to continue to hold the license. The Commission may take disciplinary action against a licensee holding a license on inactive status for any violation of G.S. 93A or any rule adopted by the Commission, including the offense of engaging in an activity for which a license is required while a license is on inactive status.

(b) A license issued to a provisional broker shall, upon initial licensure, be assigned to inactive status, except that a license issued to a provisional broker based on reciprocity with another licensing jurisdiction shall be assigned to active status. A license issued to a firm or a broker other than a provisional broker shall be assigned to active status. Except for persons licensed under the provisions of Section .1800 of this Subchapter, a broker may change the status of his or her license from active to inactive status by submitting a written request to the Commission. A provisional broker's license shall be assigned by the Commission to inactive status when the provisional broker is not under the active, direct supervision of a broker-in-charge. A firm's license shall be assigned by the Commission to inactive status when the firm does not have a qualifying broker with an active license in good standing. Except for persons licensed under the provisions of Section .1800 of this Subchapter, a broker shall also be assigned to inactive status if, upon the second renewal of his or her license following initial licensure, or upon any subsequent renewal, he or she has not satisfied the continuing education requirement described in Rule .1702 of this Subchapter.

(c) A provisional broker with an inactive license who desires to have the license placed on active status must comply with the procedures prescribed in Rule .0506 of this Section.

(d) A broker, other than a provisional broker, with an inactive license who desires to have the license placed on active status shall file with the Commission a request for license activation on a form provided by the Commission containing identifying information about the broker, a statement that the broker has satisfied the continuing education requirements provided by Rule .1703 of this Subchapter, the date of the request, and the signature of the broker. Upon the mailing or delivery of this form, the broker may engage in real estate brokerage activities requiring a license; however, if the broker does not receive from the Commission a written acknowledgment of the license activation within 30 days of the date shown on the form, the broker shall immediately terminate his or her real estate brokerage activities pending receipt of the written acknowledgment from the Commission. If the broker is notified that he or she is not eligible for license activation due to a continuing education deficiency, the broker must terminate all real estate brokerage activities until such time as the continuing education deficiency is satisfied and a new request for license activation is submitted to the Commission.

(e) A firm with an inactive license which desires to have its license placed on active status shall file with the Commission a request for license activation containing identifying information about the firm and its qualifying broker and satisfy the requirements of Rule .0110 of this Subchapter. If the qualifying broker has an inactive license, he or she must satisfy the requirements of Paragraph (d) of this Rule. Upon the mail-ing or delivery of the completed form by the qualifying broker, the firm may engage in real estate brokerage activities requiring a license; however, if the firm's qualifying broker does not receive from the Commission a written acknowledgment of the license activation within 30 days of the date shown on the form, the firm shall immediately terminate its real estate brokerage activities pending receipt of the written acknowledgment from the Commission. If the qualifying broker is notified that the firm is not eligible for license activation due to a continuing education deficiency on the part of the qualifying broker, the firm must terminate all real estate brokerage activities until` such time as the continuing education deficiency is satisfied and a new request for license activation is submitted to the Commission.

(f) A person licensed as a broker under Section .1800 of this Subchapter shall maintain his or her license on active status at all times as required by Rule .1804 of this Subchapter.

A.0505 Reinstatement of Expired License, Revoked, Surrendered or Suspended License

(a) Licenses expired for not more than six (6) months may be reinstated upon the submission of payment of a fifty-five dollar ($55.00) reinstatement fee. In order to reinstate the license on active status, the person requesting reinstatement shall have obtained the continuing education as is required by Rule .1703 of this Subchapter to change an inactive license to active status. A person reinstating a license on inactive status is not required to have obtained any continuing education in order to reinstate the license; however, in order to subsequently change his or her reinstated license from inactive status to active status, the licensee must satisfy the continuing education requirement prescribed in Rule .1703 of this Subchapter, and be supervised by a broker-in-charge in compliance with the requirements of Rule .0506 of this Section.

(b) Reinstatement of licenses expired for more than six months or provisional broker licenses cancelled pursuant to G.S. 93A-4(a) shall be considered upon the submission of a complete and accurate application and payment of a fifty-five dollar ($55.00) fee. Applicants must satisfy the Commission that they possess the current knowledge, skills and competence, as well as the truthfulness, honesty and integrity, necessary to function in the real estate business in a manner that protects and serves the public interest. To demonstrate knowledge, skills and competence, the Commission may require the applicants to complete real estate education or pass the license examination or both.

(c) Reinstatement of a revoked license shall be considered upon the submission of a complete and accurate application and payment of a thirty dollar ($30.00) fee. Applicants must satisfy the same requirements as those prescribed in Paragraph (b) of this Rule for reinstatement of licenses expired for more than six (6) months.

(d) Reinstatement of a license surrendered under the

provisions of G.S. 93A-6(e) shall be considered upon termination of the period of surrender specified in the order approving the surrender and upon the submission of a complete and accurate application and payment of a thirty dollar ($30.00) fee. Applicants must satisfy the same requirements as those prescribed in Paragraph (b) of this Rule for reinstatement of licenses expired for more than six (6) months.

(e) When a license is suspended by the Commission, the suspended license shall be restored at the end of the period of active suspension provided that any applicable license renewal fees that accrued during the time of the suspension are paid by the licensee within sixty days from the end of the period of license suspension. In order for the license to be restored on active status, the licensee shall be required to demonstrate that the licensee has satisfied the continuing education requirement for license activation prescribed by Rule .1703 of this Subchapter and that the licensee is supervised by a broker-in-charge in compliance with the requirements of Rule .0506 of this Section, if applicable. Failure to pay the accrued license renewal fees within the time set forth in this paragraph shall result in expiration of the license effective the last day of the suspension period. A former licensee whose license expires under this paragraph and who thereafter seeks reinstatement must satisfy the same requirements as those prescribed in Paragraph (b) of this Rule for reinstatement of licenses expired for more than six months.

(f) Whenever a license is reinstated by the Commission following expiration for more than six months, cancellation, revocation, or voluntary surrender, the date of licensure for the licensee shall be the date of reinstatement and not the date of original licensure.

A.0506 Provisional Broker to be Supervised by Broker

(a) This Rule shall apply to all real estate provisional brokers.

(b) A provisional broker may engage in or hold himself or herself out as engaging in activities requiring a real estate license only while his or her license is on active status and he or she is supervised by the broker-in-charge of the real estate firm or office where the provisional broker is associated. A provisional broker may be supervised by only one broker-in-charge at a time.

(c) Upon a provisional broker's association with a real estate broker or brokerage firm, the provisional broker and the broker-in-charge of the office where the provisional broker will be engaged in the real estate business shall immediately file with the Commission a provisional broker supervision notification on a form provided by the Commission containing identifying information about the provisional broker and the broker-in-charge, a statement from the broker-in-charge certifying that he or she will supervise the provisional broker in the performance of all acts for which a license is required, the date that the broker-in-charge assumes responsibility for such supervision, and the signatures of the provisional broker and broker-in-charge. If the provisional broker is on inactive status at the time of associating with a broker or brokerage firm, the provisional broker and broker-in-charge shall also file, along with the provisional broker supervision notification, the provisional broker's request for license activation on a form provided by the Commission containing identifying information about the provisional broker, the provisional broker's statement that he or she has satisfied the continuing education requirements prescribed by Rule .1703 of this Subchapter, the provisional broker's statement that he or she has satisfied the postlicensing education requirements, if applicable, prescribed by Rule .1902 of this Subchapter, the date of the request, and the signatures of the provisional broker and the provisional broker's proposed broker-in-charge. Upon the mailing or delivery of the required form(s), the provisional broker may engage in real estate brokerage activities requiring a license under the supervision of the broker-in-charge; however, if the provisional broker and broker-in-charge do not receive from the Commission a written acknowledgment of the provisional broker supervision notification and, if appropriate, the request for license activation, within 30 days of the date shown on the form, the broker-in-charge shall immediately terminate the provisional broker's real estate brokerage activities pending receipt of the written acknowledgment from the Commission. If the provisional broker and broker-in-charge are notified that the provisional broker is not eligible for license activation due to a continuing education deficiency, the broker-in-charge shall cause the provisional broker to immediately cease all activities requiring a real estate license until such time as the continuing education deficiency is satisfied and a new provisional broker supervision notification and request for license activation is submitted to the Commission.

(d) A broker-in-charge who certifies to the Commission that he or she will supervise a provisional broker shall actively and directly supervise the provisional broker in a manner which reasonably assures that the provisional broker performs all acts for which a real estate license is required in accordance with the Real Estate License Law and Commission rules. A supervising broker who fails to supervise a provisional broker as prescribed in this Rule may be subject to disciplinary action by the Commission.

(e) Upon the termination of the supervisory relationship between a provisional broker and his or her broker-in-charge, the provisional broker and the broker-in-charge shall provide written notification of the date of termination to the Commission not later than 10 days following said termination.

A.0507 Payment of License Fees

Checks, credit cards, and other forms of payment given the Commission for fees due which are returned unpaid shall be considered cause for license denial, suspension, or revocation.

A.0508 Duplicate License Fee (Repealed)

A.0509 Duplicate License Fee

A licensee may, by filing a prescribed form and paying a five dollar ($5.00) fee to the Commission, obtain a duplicate real estate license or pocket card to replace an original license or pocket card which has been lost, damaged or destroyed or if the name of the licensee has been lawfully changed.

SECTION A.0600
REAL ESTATE COMMISSION HEARINGS

A.0601 Complaints/Inquiries/Motions/Other Pleadings

(a) There shall be no specific form required for complaints. To be sufficient, a complaint shall be in writing, identify the respondent licensee and shall reasonably apprise the Commission of the facts which form the basis of the complaint.

(b) When investigating a complaint, the scope of the Commission's investigation shall not be limited only to matters alleged in the complaint. In addition, a person making a complaint to the Commission may change his or her complaint by submitting the changes to the Commission in writing.

(c) When a complaint has not been submitted in conformity with this rule, the Commission's legal counsel may initiate an investigation if the available information is sufficient to create a reasonable suspicion that any licensee or other person or entity may have committed a violation of the provisions of the Real Estate License Law or the rules adopted by the Commission.

(d) There shall be no specific forms required for answers, motions, or other pleadings relating to contested cases before the Commission, except they shall be in writing. To be sufficient, the document must reasonably apprise the Commission of the matters it alleges or answers. To be considered by the Commission, every answer, motion, request or other pleading must be submitted to the Commission in writing or made during the hearing as a matter of record.

(e) During the course of an investigation of a licensee, the Commission, through its legal counsel or other staff, may send the licensee a Letter of Inquiry requesting the licensee to respond. The Letter of Inquiry, or attachments thereto, shall set forth the subject matter being investigated. Upon receipt of the Letter of Inquiry, the licensee shall respond within 14 calendar days. Such response shall include a full and fair disclosure of all information requested. Licensees shall include with their written response copies of all documents requested in the Letter of Inquiry.

(f) Hearings in contested cases before the Commission shall be conducted according to the provisions of Article 3A of Chapter 150B of the General Statutes of North Carolina.

(g) Persons who make complaints are not parties to contested cases, but may be witnesses.

A.0616 Procedures For Requesting Hearings When Applicant's Character Is In Question

(a) When the moral character of an applicant for licensure or approval is in question, the applicant shall not be licensed or approved until the applicant has affirmatively demonstrated that the applicant possesses the requisite truthfulness, honesty and integrity. For the purposes of this rule, applicant means any person or entity making application for licensure as a real estate broker or for licensure or approval as a prelicensing or continuing education instructor, director, coordinator, school, or sponsor. When the applicant is an entity, it shall be directed and controlled by persons who are truthful and honest and who possess integrity.

(b) When the character of an applicant is in question, the Commission shall defer action upon the application until the applicant is notified by letter. The letter informing the applicant that his or her moral character is in question shall be sent by certified mail, return receipt requested, to the address shown upon the application. The applicant shall have 60 days from the date of receipt of this letter to request a hearing before the Commission. If the applicant fails to request a hearing within this time or if a properly addressed letter is returned to the Commission undelivered, applicant's right to a hearing shall be considered waived and the application shall be deemed denied. If the applicant makes a timely request for a hearing in accordance with the provisions of this rule, the Commission shall provide the applicant with a Notice of Hearing and hearing as required by Article 3A of Chapter 150B of the North Carolina General Statutes.

(c) Nothing in this Rule shall be interpreted to prevent an unsuccessful applicant from reapplying for licensure or approval if such application is otherwise permitted by law.

SECTION A.0700
PETITIONS FOR RULES

SECTION A.0800
RULE MAKING

SECTION A.0900
DECLARATORY RULINGS

SECTION A.1000
SCHOOLS
(Transferred to C.0100)

SECTION A.1100
REAL ESTATE PRE-LICENSING COURSES
(Transferred/Repealed.Transfers are at C.0300 Prelicensing and Pre-certification Courses)

SECTION A.1200
CERTIFICATION OF REAL ESTATE INSTRUCTORS
(Repealed)

SECTION A.1300
PRIVATE REAL ESTATE SCHOOLS
(Transferred/Repealed. Transfers are at C.0200)

SECTION A.1400
REAL ESTATE RECOVERY FUND

SECTION A.1500 FORMS (Repealed)

Interested persons may obtain a copy of Sections A.0600 through A.1500 by making written request to the North Carolina Real Estate Commission.

SECTION A.1600
DISCRIMINATORY PRACTICES PROHIBITED

A.1601 Fair Housing

Conduct by a licensee which violates the provisions of the State Fair Housing Act constitutes improper conduct in violation of G.S. 93A-6(a)(10).

SECTION A.1700
MANDATORY CONTINUING EDUCATION

A.1701 Purpose and Applicability

This Section describes the continuing education requirement for real estate brokers authorized by G.S. 93A-4A, establishes the continuing education requirement to change a license from inactive status to active status, establishes attendance requirements for continuing education courses, establishes the criteria and procedures relating to obtaining an extension of time to complete the continuing education requirement, establishes the criteria for obtaining continuing education credit for an unapproved course or related educational activity, and addresses other similar matters.

A.1702 Continuing Education Requirement

(a) Except as provided in 21 NCAC 58A.1708 and A.1711, in order to renew a broker license on active status, the person requesting renewal of a license shall, upon the second renewal of such license following initial licensure, and upon each subsequent annual renewal, have completed, within one year preceding license expiration, eight classroom hours of real estate continuing education in courses approved by the Commission as provided in Subchapter 58E. Four of the required eight classroom hours must be obtained each license period by completing a mandatory update course developed annually by the Commission. The remaining four hours must be obtained by completing one or more Commission-approved elective courses described in Rule .0305 of Subchapter 58E. The licensee bears the responsibility for providing, upon request of the Commission, evidence of continuing education course completion satisfactory to the Commission.

(b) No continuing education shall be required to renew a broker license on inactive status; however, to change a license from inactive status to active status, the licensee must satisfy the continuing education requirement described in Rule .1703 of this Section.

(c) No continuing education shall be required for a licensee who is a member of the U. S. Congress or North Carolina General Assembly in order to renew his or her license on active status.

(d) The terms "active status" and "inactive status" are defined in Rule .0504 of this Subchapter. For continuing education purposes, the term "initial licensure" shall include the first time that a license of a particular type is issued to a person, the reinstatement of a canceled, revoked or surrendered license and any license expired for more than six months. The issuance, pursuant to G.S. 93A-4.3, of a broker license on provisional status on April 1, 2006 to licensees who held a salesperson license as of that date shall not be considered to constitute initial licensure for continuing education purposes.

A.1703 Continuing Education for License Activation

(a) A broker requesting to change an inactive license to active status on or after the licensee's second license renewal following his or her initial licensure shall be required to demonstrate completion of continuing education as described in Paragraph (b) or (c) of this Rule, whichever is appropriate.

(b) If the inactive licensee's license has properly been on active status at any time since the preceding July 1, the licensee is considered to be current with regard to continuing education and no additional continuing education is required to activate the license.

(c) If the inactive licensee's license has not properly been on active status since the preceding July 1 and the licensee has a deficiency in his or her continuing education record for the previous license period, the licensee must make up the deficiency and fully satisfy the continuing education requirement for the current license period in order to activate the license. Any deficiency may be made up by completing, during the current license period or previous license period, approved continuing education elective courses; however, such courses will not be credited toward the continuing education requirement for the current license period. When crediting elective courses for purposes of making up a continuing education deficiency, the maximum number of credit hours that will be awarded for any course is four hours. When evaluating the continuing education record of a licensee with a deficiency for the previous license period to determine the licensee's eligibility for active status, the licensee shall be deemed eligible for active status if the licensee has fully satisfied the continuing education requirement for the current license period and has taken any two additional continuing education courses since the beginning of the previous license period, even if the licensee had a continuing education deficiency prior to the beginning of the previous license period.

A.1704 No Credit for Prelicensing or Postlicensing Courses

No credit toward the continuing education requirement shall be awarded for completing a real estate prelicensing or postlicensing course.

A.1705 Attendance and Participation Requirements

In order to receive any credit for satisfactorily completing an approved continuing education course, a licensee must attend at least 90 percent of the scheduled classroom hours for the course, regardless of the length of the course, and must comply with student participation standards described in Rule .0511 of Subchapter 58E. No credit shall be awarded for attending less than 90 percent of the scheduled classroom hours.

A.1706 Repetition of Courses

A continuing education course may be taken only once for continuing education credit within a single license period.

A.1707 Elective Course Carry-Over Credit

A maximum of four hours of continuing education credit for an approved elective course taken during the current license period may be carried over to satisfy the continuing education elective requirement for the next following license period if the licensee receives no continuing education elective credit for the course toward the elective requirement for the current license period or the previous license period. However, if a continuing education elective course is used to wholly or partially satisfy the elective requirement for the current or previous license period, then any excess hours completed in such course which are not needed to satisfy the four-hour elective requirement for that license period may not be carried forward and applied toward the elective requirement for the next following license period.

A.1708 Equivalent Credit

(a) A licensee may request that the Commission award continuing education credit for a course taken by the licensee that is not approved by the Commission, or for some other real estate education activity, by making such request on a form prescribed by the Commission and submitting a nonrefundable evaluation fee of thirty dollars ($30.00) for each request for evaluation of a course or real estate education activity. In order for requests for equivalent credit to be considered and credits to be entered into a licensee's continuing education record prior to the June 30 license expiration date, such requests and all supporting documents must be received by the Commission on or before June 10 preceding expiration of the licensee's current license, with the exception that requests from instructors desiring equivalent credit for teaching Commission-approved continuing education courses must be received by June 30. Any equivalent continuing education credit awarded under this Rule shall be applied first to make up any continuing education deficiency for the previous license period and then to satisfy the continuing education requirement for the current license period; however, credit for an unapproved course or educational activity, other than teaching an approved elective course, that was completed during a previous license period may not be applied to a subsequent license period.

(b) The Commission may award continuing education elective credit for completion of an unapproved course which the Commission finds equivalent to the elective course component of the continuing education requirement set forth in Section .0300 of Subchapter 58E. Completion of an unapproved course may serve only to satisfy the elective requirement and cannot be substituted for completion of the mandatory update course.

(c) Real estate education activities, other than teaching a Commission-approved course, which may be eligible for credit include, but are not limited to: developing a Commission-approved elective continuing education course, authorship of a published real estate textbook; and authorship of a scholarly article, on a topic acceptable for continuing education purposes, which has been published in a professional journal such as a law journal or professional college or university journal or periodical. The Commission may award continuing education elective credit for activities which the Commission finds equivalent to the elective course component of the continuing education requirement set forth in Section .0300 of Subchapter 58E. No activity other than teaching a Commission-developed mandatory update course shall be considered equivalent to completing the mandatory update course.

(d) The Commission may award credit for teaching the Commission-developed mandatory update course and for teaching an approved elective course. Credit for teaching an approved elective course shall be awarded only for teaching a course for the first time. Credit for teaching a Commission-developed mandatory update course may be awarded for each licensing period in which the instructor teaches the course. The amount of credit awarded to the instructor of an approved continuing education course shall be the same as the amount of credit earned by a licensee who completes the course. Licensees who are instructors of continuing education courses approved by the Commission shall not be subject to the thirty dollar ($30.00) evaluation fee when applying for continuing education credit for teaching an approved course. No credit toward the continuing education requirement shall be awarded for teaching a real estate prelicensing or postlicensing course.

(e) A licensee completing a real estate appraisal prelicensing, precertification or continuing education course approved by the North Carolina Appraisal Board may obtain real estate continuing education elective credit for such course by submitting to the Commission a written request for equivalent continuing education elective credit accompanied by a nonrefundable processing fee of twenty dollars ($20.00) and a copy of the certificate of course completion issued by the course sponsor for submission to the North Carolina Appraisal Board.

A.1709 Extensions of Time to Complete Continuing Education

A licensee on active status may request and be granted an extension of time to satisfy the continuing education requirement for a particular license period if the licensee provides evidence satisfactory to the Commission that he or she was unable to obtain the necessary education due to an incapacitating illness or other circumstance which existed for a substantial portion of the license period and which constituted a severe and verifiable hardship such that to comply with the continuing education requirement would have been impossible or unreasonably burdensome. The Commission shall in no case grant an extension of time to satisfy the continuing education requirement for reasons of business or personal conflicts. The Commission also shall not grant such an extension of time when, in the opinion of the Commission, the principal reason for the licensee's inability to obtain the required education in a timely manner was unreasonable delay on the part of the licensee in obtaining such education. If an extension of time is granted, the licensee shall be permitted to renew his or her license on active status but the license shall be automatically changed to inactive status at the end of the extension period unless the licensee satisfies the continuing education requirement prior to that time. If an extension of time is not granted, the licensee may either satisfy the continuing education requirement prior to expiration of the license period or renew his or her license on inactive status. The length of any extension of time granted and the determination of the specific courses which shall be accepted by the Commission as equivalent to the continuing education the licensee would have been required to have completed had the licensee not been granted the extension is wholly discretionary on the part of the Commission. The licensee's request for an extension of time must be submitted on a form prescribed by the Commission.

A.1710 Denial or Withdrawal of Continuing Education Credit

(a) The Commission may deny continuing education credit claimed by a licensee or reported by a course sponsor for a licensee, and may withdraw continuing education credit previously awarded by the Commission to a licensee upon finding that:

(1) The licensee or course sponsor provided incorrect or incomplete information to the Commission concerning continuing education completed by the licensee;

(2) The licensee failed to comply with either the attendance requirement established by Rule .1705 of this Section or the student participation standards set forth in Rule .0511 of Subchapter 58E; or

(3) The licensee was mistakenly awarded continuing education credit due to an administrative error.

(b) When continuing education credit is denied or withdrawn by the Commission under Paragraph (a) of this Rule, the licensee remains responsible for satisfying the continuing education requirement. However, when an administrative error or an incorrect report by a course sponsor results in the denial or withdrawal of continuing education credit for a licensee, the Commission may, upon request of the licensee, grant the licensee an extension of time to satisfy the continuing education requirement.

(c) A licensee who obtains or attempts to obtain continuing education credit through misrepresentation of fact, dishonesty or other improper conduct shall be subject to disciplinary action pursuant to G.S. 93A-6.

A.1711 Continuing Education Required of Nonresident Licensees

(a) To be considered a nonresident for continuing education purposes, a real estate broker licensed in North Carolina shall not have a North Carolina business address, mailing address or residence address at the time he or she applies for license renewal if he or she seeks to renew his or her license on active status. A nonresident North Carolina broker who wishes to renew his or her license on active status may fully satisfy the continuing education requirement by any one of the following means:

(1) A nonresident licensee may, at the time of license renewal, hold a real estate license on active status in another state and certify on a form prescribed by the Commission that the licensee holds such license.

(2) A nonresident licensee may, within one year preceding license expiration, complete the Commission-prescribed Update course plus one Commission-approved continuing education elective course, or complete two Commission-approved continuing education elective courses.

(3) A nonresident licensee may, within one year preceding license expiration, complete eight classroom hours in courses approved for continuing education credit by the real estate licensing agency in the licensee's state of residence or in the state where the course was taken. To obtain credit for a continuing education course completed in another state and not approved by the Commission, the licensee must submit a writ-

ten request for continuing education credit accompanied by a nonrefundable processing fee of twenty dollars ($20.00) per request and evidence satisfactory to the Commission that the course was completed and that the course was approved for continuing education credit by the real estate licensing agency in the licensee's state of residence or in the state where the course was taken.

(4) A nonresident licensee may obtain eight hours equivalent credit for a course or courses not approved by the Commission or for related educational activities as provided in Rule .1708 of this Section. The maximum amount of continuing education credit the Commission will award a nonresident licensee for an unapproved course or educational activity is eight hours.

(b) When requesting to change an inactive license to active status, or when applying for reinstatement of a license expired for not more than six months, a nonresident broker may fully satisfy the continuing education requirements described in Rules .0505 and .1703 of this Subchapter by complying with any of the options described in Paragraph (a) of this Rule, except that the requirements in (a)(2) and (a)(3) restricting the taking of courses to one year preceding license expiration shall not be applicable.

(c) No carry-over credit to a subsequent license period shall be awarded for a course taken in another state that has not been approved by the North Carolina Real Estate Commission as an elective course.

SECTION A .1800
LIMITED NONRESIDENT COMMERCIAL LICENSING

A.1801 General Provisions

(a) Any person resident in a state or territory of the United States other than North Carolina may perform the acts or services of a real estate broker in North Carolina in transactions involving commercial real estate if said person first applies for and obtains a limited nonresident commercial real estate broker license as provided in this Section.

(b) Corporations, business associations and entities shall be ineligible for licensure under this Section.

(c) Nothing in this Section shall be construed to limit the rights of any person duly licensed as a real estate broker in North Carolina under the provisions of N.C.G.S.§§ 93A-4 or 93A-9(a).

A.1802 Definitions

For the purposes of this Section:

(1) "Commercial Real Estate" means any real property or interest therein, whether freehold or non-freehold, which at the time the property or interest is made the subject of an agreement for brokerage services:

(a) is lawfully used primarily for sales, office, research, institutional, warehouse, manufacturing, industrial or mining purposes or for multifamily residential purposes involving five or more dwelling units;

(b) may lawfully be used for any of the purposes listed in (1) above by a zoning ordinance adopted pursuant to the provisions of Article 18 of Chapter 153A or Article 19 of Chapter 160A of the General Statutes or which is the subject of an official application or petition to amend the applicable zoning ordinance to permit any of the uses listed in (1) above which is under consideration by the government agency with authority to approve the amendment; or

(c) is in good faith intended to be immediately used for any of the purposes listed in (1) above by the parties to any contract, lease, option, or offer to make any contract, lease, or option.

(2) "Qualifying state" means the state or territory of the United States where an applicant for, and the holder of, a limited nonresident commercial license issued under this Section is licensed in good standing as a real estate broker or salesperson. The qualifying state must be the state or territory where the applicant or limited nonresident commercial licensee maintains his or her primary place of business as a real estate broker or salesperson. Under no circumstances may North Carolina be a qualifying state.

A.1803 Requirements For Licensure; Application And Fee

(a) A person desiring to obtain a broker license under this Section shall demonstrate to the Real Estate Commission that:

(1) he or she is a resident of a state or territory of the United States other than North Carolina;

(2) he or she is licensed as a real estate broker in a qualifying state and that said license is on active status and not in abeyance for any reason. If licensed as a salesperson, he or she shall also demonstrate that he or she is acting under the supervision of a broker in accordance with the applicable governing statutes or regulations in the qualifying state; and

(3) he or she possesses the requisite honesty, truthfulness, integrity, and moral character for licensure as a broker in North Carolina.

A person applying for licensure under this Section shall not be required to show that the state or territory where he or she is currently licensed offers reciprocal licensing privileges to North Carolina brokers.

(b) A person desiring to be licensed under this Section shall submit an application on a form prescribed by the Commission and shall show the Commission that he or she has satisfied the requirements set forth in (a) of this rule. In connection with his or her application a person applying for licensure under this rule shall provide the Commission with a certification of license history from the qualifying state where he or she is licensed. He or she shall also provide the Commission with a report of his or her criminal history from the service designated by the Commission. An applicant for licensure under this Section shall be required to update his or her application as required by Rule .0302(c) of this Subchapter.

(c) The fee for persons applying for licensure under this Section shall be $100 and shall be paid in the form of a certified check, bank check, cashier's check, money order, or by credit card. Once paid, the application fee shall be non-refundable.

(d) If the Commission has received a complete application and the required application fee and if the Commission is satisfied that the applicant possesses the moral character necessary for licensure, the Commission shall issue to the applicant a limited nonresident commercial real estate broker license.

A.1804 Active Status

Broker licenses issued under this Section shall be issued on active status and shall remain valid only so long as the licensee's license in the qualifying state remains valid and on active status. In addition, a license issued to a salesperson under this Section shall remain valid only while the salesperson is acting under the supervision of a real estate broker in accordance with the applicable laws and rules in the qualifying state. Individuals licensed under this Section shall immediately notify the Commission if his or her license in the qualifying state lapses or expires, is suspended or revoked, made inactive, or is placed in abeyance for any reason.

A.1805 Renewal

(a) A license issued under this Section shall expire on June 30 following issuance unless it is renewed in accordance with the provisions of Rule .0503 and Rule .1711 of this Subchapter.

(b) The Commission shall not renew a license issued under this Section unless the licensee has demonstrated that he or she has complied with the requirements of paragraph (a) of this rule and that his or her license in the qualifying state is on active status in good standing and is not lapsed, expired, suspended, revoked, or in abeyance for any reason.

A.1806 Limitations

(a) A person licensed under this Section may act as a real estate broker in this state only if:

(1) he or she does not reside in North Carolina;

(2) the real property interest which is the subject of any transaction in connection with which he or she acts as a broker in this state is commercial real estate as that term is defined in Rule .1802 of this Section; and

(3) he or she is affiliated with a resident North Carolina real estate broker as required in rule .1807 of this Section.

(b) A nonresident commercial real estate broker licensed under the provisions of Section .1800 of this Subchapter shall not act as or serve in the capacity of a broker-in-charge

of a firm or office in North Carolina.

A.1807 Affiliation With Resident Broker

(a) No person licensed under N.C.G.S. 93A-9(b) shall enter North Carolina to perform any act or service for which licensure as a real broker is required unless he or she has first entered into a brokerage cooperation agreement and declaration of affiliation with an individual who is a resident in North Carolina licensed as a North Carolina real estate broker.

(b) A brokerage cooperation agreement as contemplated by this rule shall be in writing and signed by the resident North Carolina broker and the non-resident commercial licensee. It shall contain:

(1) the material terms of the agreement between the signatory licenses;

(2) a description of the agency relationships, if any, which are created by the agreement among the nonresident commercial licensee, the resident North Carolina broker, and the parties each represents;

(3) a description of the property or the identity of the parties and other information sufficient to identify the transaction which is the subject of the affiliation agreement; and

(4) a definite expiration date.

(c) A declaration of affiliation shall be written and on the form provided by the Commission and shall identify the nonresident commercial licensee and the affiliated resident North Carolina licensee. It shall also contain a description of the duties and obligations of each as required by the North Carolina Real Estate License Law and rules duly adopted by the Commission. The declaration of affiliation may be a part of the brokerage cooperation agreement or separate from it.

(d) A nonresident commercial licensee may affiliate with more than one resident North Carolina broker at any time. However, a nonresident commercial licensee may be affiliated with only one resident North Carolina broker in a single transaction.

(e) A resident North Carolina broker who enters into a brokerage cooperation agreement and declaration of affiliation with a nonresident commercial licensee shall:

(1) verify that the nonresident commercial licensee is licensed in North Carolina;

(2) actively and directly supervise the nonresident commercial licensee in a manner which reasonably insures that the nonresident commercial licensee complies with the North Carolina Real Estate License Law and rules adopted by the Commission; and

(3) promptly notify the Commission if the nonresident commercial licensee violates the Real Estate License Law or rules adopted by the Commission; and

(4) insure that records are retained in accordance with the requirements of the Real Estate License Law and rules adopted by the Commission; and

(5) maintain his or her license on active status continuously for the duration of the brokerage cooperation agreement and the declaration of affiliation.

(f) The nonresident commercial licensee and the affiliated resident North Carolina broker shall each retain in his or her records a copy of brokerage cooperation agreements and declarations of affiliation from the time of their creation and for at least three years following their expiration. Such records shall be made available for inspection and reproduction by the Commission or its authorized representatives without prior notice.

A.1808 Trust Monies

A nonresident commercial licensee acting as real estate broker in North Carolina shall immediately deliver to the North Carolina resident broker with whom he or she is affiliated all money belonging to others received in connection with the nonresident commercial licensee's acts or services as a broker. Upon receipt of said money, the resident North Carolina broker shall cause said money to be deposited in a trust account in accordance with the provisions of Rule .0107 of this Subchapter.

A.1809 Advertising

In all advertising involving a nonresident commercial licensee's conduct as a North Carolina real estate broker and in any representation of such person's licensure in North Carolina, the advertising or representation shall conspicuously identify the nonresident commercial licensee as a "Limited Nonresident Commercial Real Estate Broker."

A.1810 Payment Of Fees

Commissions, fees, or other compensation earned by a nonresident commercial licensee shall not be paid directly to the licensee if said licensee is employed by or working for a real estate broker or firm. Instead, such fees or compensation shall be paid to the licensee's employing broker or firm.

SECTION A .1900
POSTLICENSING EDUCATION

A.1901 Purpose and Applicability

This section prescribes specific procedures relating to the postlicensing education requirement for real estate brokers as prescribed by G.S. 93A-4(a1).

A.1902 Postlicensing Education Requirement

(a) The 90 classroom hour postlicensing education program shall consist of three 30 classroom hour courses prescribed by the Commission which may be taken in any sequence. A provisional broker as described in G.S. 93A-4(a1) or G.S. 93A-4.3(d) must satisfactorily complete at least one of the 30-hour courses during each of the first three years following the date of his or her initial licensure as a broker in order to retain his or her eligibility to actively engage in real estate brokerage. Upon completion of all three courses by a provisional broker, the provisional status of the broker's license shall be terminated by the Commission. The three courses shall be devoted to:

(1) real estate brokerage relationships and responsibilities;

(2) real estate contracts and transactions; and

(3) specialized topics, including commercial real estate, rental management, real estate finance, real estate appraisal, real estate development, and real estate regulation.

(b) If a provisional broker as described in G.S. 93A-4(a1) or G.S. 93A-4.3(d) fails to complete the required postlicensing education described in paragraph (a) of this Rule by the end of either the first or second year following the date of his or her initial licensure as a broker, his or her license shall be placed on inactive status. Between the end of the first year after initial licensure and the end of the third year after initial licensure, a provisional broker who is subject to the postlicensing education requirement and who desires to activate a license that is on inactive status shall make up any postlicensing education deficiency as well as satisfy the continuing education requirements for license activation described in Rule .1703 of this Subchapter, satisfy the requirement for supervision by a broker-in-charge described in Rule .0506 of this Subchapter and file with the Commission a request for license activation as described in Rule .0504 of this Subchapter.

(c) If a provisional broker as described in G.S. 93A-4(a1) or G.S. 93A-4.3(d) fails to complete all three postlicensing courses within three years following the date of his or her initial licensure, his or her license shall be cancelled and, in order to reinstate such license, the former broker must satisfy the requirements described in G.S. 93A-4(a1) and Rule .0505 of this Subchapter.

A.1903 Extensions Of Time To Complete Postlicensing Education

A provisional broker as described in G.S. 93A-4(a1) or G.S. 93A-4.3(d) may request and be granted an extension of time to satisfy the postlicensing education requirement for the first and second years following the date of his or her initial licensure as a broker if the licensee provides evidence satisfactory to the Commission that he or she was unable to obtain the necessary education due to an incapacitating illness or other circumstance which existed for a substantial portion of the year in question and which constituted a severe and verifiable hardship such that to comply with the education requirement would have been impossible or unreasonably burdensome. The Commission shall in no case grant an extension of time to satisfy the postlicensing education requirement that extends beyond the end of the third year after initial licensure as a broker. The Commission also shall not grant an extension of time when the reason for the request is a business or personal conflict or when, in the opinion of the Commission, the principal reason for the provisional broker's failure to obtain the required education in a timely manner was unreasonable delay on the part of the provisional broker in obtaining such education. If an extension of time is granted, the provisional broker may retain his or her license on active status until expiration of the extension period, but the license shall be automatically changed to inactive status at the end of the extension period unless the licensee obtains the required postlicensing education prior to that time. If an extension of time is not granted, the provisional broker's license shall be treated as described in Rule .1902(b) of this Section. A request for an extension of time must be submitted on a form prescribed by the Commission.

A .1904 Denial Or Withdrawal Of Postlicensing Education Credit

(a) The Commission may deny postlicensing education credit claimed by a provisional broker or reported by a school for a provisional broker, and may withdraw postlicensing education credit previously awarded by the Commission to a provisional broker and make appropriate license status changes for that licensee upon finding that:

(1) The provisional broker or school provided incorrect or incomplete information to the Commission concerning postlicensing education completed by the provisional broker;

(2) the provisional broker was mistakenly awarded postlicensing education credit due to an administrative error; or

(3) the provisional broker attended a postlicensing course while concurrently attending a different postlicensing course at the same school or a different school if such concurrent attendance in the two courses resulted in the provisional broker participating in postlicensing course sessions for more than 21 classroom hours in any given seven-day period.

(b) When postlicensing education credit is denied or withdrawn by the Commission under Paragraph (a) of this Rule, the provisional broker remains responsible for satisfying the postlicensing education requirement in a timely manner.

(c) A licensee who obtains or attempts to obtain postlicensing education credit through misrepresentation of fact, dishonesty or other improper conduct is subject to disciplinary action pursuant to G.S. 93A-6.

Subchapter 58B
Time Shares

SECTION B.0100
TIME SHARE PROJECT REGISTRATION

B.0101 Application for Registration

(a) Every application for time share project registration shall be filed at the Commission's office upon a form prescribed by the Commission. Every such application shall contain or have appended thereto:

(1) information concerning the developer's title or right to use the real property on which the project is located, including a title opinion provided by an independent attorney performed within 30 days preceding the date of application;

(2) information concerning owners of time shares at the project other than the developer;

(3) a description of the improvements and amenities located at the project, including a description of the number and type of time share units;

(4) a description of the time share estate to be sold or conveyed to purchasers;

(5) information concerning the developer and his or her financial ability to develop the project (including the developer's most recent audited financial statement, any loan commitments for completion of the proposed time share project, a projected budget for the construction, marketing and operation of the time share project until control by purchasers is asserted, and details of any source of funding for the time share project other than consumer sales proceeds), and information concerning the marketing and managing entities and their relationship to the developer;

(6) the developer's name and address, past real estate development experience and such other information necessary to determine the moral character of those selling and managing the project;

(7) copies of all documents to be distributed to time share purchasers at the point of sale or immediately thereafter; and

(8) such information as may be required by G.S. 93A-52.

The form shall also describe the standards for its proper completion and submission.

(b) In accordance with G.S. 93A-52, an application for time share registration shall be considered to be properly completed when it is wholly and accurately filled out and when all required documents are appended to it and appear to be in compliance with the provisions of the Time Share Act, and, where the project is a condominium, the Condominium Act or Unit Ownership Act.

(c) An entity which owns time shares at a time share project where there are one or more existing registered developers may also apply to the Commission for registration of its time shares, provided that the entity does not control a registered developer, is not controlled by a registered developer, and is not in common control of the project with a registered developer.

B.0102 Registration Fee

(a) Every application for time share project registration must be accompanied by a certified check made payable to the North Carolina Real Estate Commission. For the initial registration of any time share project, or for a subsequent registration of a time share project by a developer proposing to sell or develop time shares equivalent to at least 20 per cent of the original time share project, the fee is $1,000.00. For a subsequent registration of a previously or presently registered time share project by a developer proposing to sell or develop time shares equivalent to less than 20 per cent of the original time share project, the fee is $800.00. For an initial or subsequent time share project consisting of a single family dwelling unit or a single dwelling unit in a multiple dwelling unit property and in which 10 or less time shares will be or have been created, the fee is $600.00. For any time share registration by a homeowner association for the purpose of re-selling time shares in its own project which it has acquired in satisfaction of unpaid assessments by prior owners, the fee is $400.00.

(b) Applications for registration not accompanied by the appropriate fee shall not be considered by the Commission.

(c) In the event a properly completed application filed with the Commission is denied for any reason, or if an incomplete application is denied by the Commission or abandoned by the developer prior to a final decision by the Commission, the amount of two hundred fifty dollars ($250.00) shall be retained by the Commission from the application fee and the balance refunded to the applicant developer.

B.0103 Renewal of Time Share Project Registration

(a) Every developer desiring the renewal of a time share project registration shall apply for the same in writing upon a form prescribed by the Commission during the month of June. Every such renewal application shall be accompanied by a certified check made payable to the North Carolina Real Estate Commission in the amount of seven hundred fifty dollars ($750.00). To renew the time share project registration, the properly completed renewal application accompanied by the prescribed fee must be received at the Commission's office prior to the expiration of the certificate of registration.

(b) Applications for the renewal of a time share project registration shall be signed by the developer, by two executive officers of the developer, or by the developer's attorney at law and shall certify that the information contained in the registration filed with the Commission is accurate and current on the date of the renewal application. Making a false certification on a time share project registration renewal application shall be grounds for disciplinary action by the Commission.

B.0104 Amendments to Time Share Project Registration

(a) A developer shall notify the Commission immediately, but in no event later than 15 days, after any material change in the information contained in the time share project registration.

(b) A material change shall be any change which reflects a difference in:

(1) the nature, quality or availability of the purchaser's ownership or right to use the time share;

(2) the nature, quality or availability of any amenity at the project;

(3) the developer's title, control or right to use the real property on which the project is located;

(4) the information concerning the developer, the managing or marketing entities, or persons connected therewith, previously filed with the Commission;

(5) the purchaser's right to exchange his or her unit; however, a change in the information required to be disclosed to a purchaser by G.S. 93A-48 shall not be a material change; or

(6) the project or time share as originally registered which would be significant to a reasonable purchaser.

(c) Amendments to time share project registrations shall be submitted in the form of substitute pages for material previously filed with the Commission. New or changed information shall be conspicuously indicated by underlining in red ink. Every amendment submitted shall be accompanied by a cover letter signed by the developer or the developer's attorney containing a summary of the amendment and a statement of reasons for which the amendment has been made. The cover letter shall state:

(1) the name and address of the project and its registration number;

(2) the name and address of the developer;

(3) the document or documents to which the amendment applies;

(4) whether or not the changes represented by the amendment required the assent of the time share owners and, if so, how the assent of the time share owners was obtained; and

(5) the recording reference in the office of the register of deeds for the changes, if applicable.

Developers of multiple projects must submit separate amendments and cover letters for each project for which amendments are submitted.

(d) The Commission may, in its discretion, require the developer to file a new time share project registration application in the place of an amendment form. Such refiling shall be without fee.

B.0105 Notice of Termination

(a) A developer of a registered time share project which, for any reason, terminates its interest, rights, ownership or control of the project or any significant part thereof shall immediately notify the Commission in writing on a form prescribed by the Commission for that purpose. Notice of termination to the Commission shall include the date of termination, the reasons therefor, the identity of the developer's successor, if any, and a report on the status of time share sales to purchasers on the date of termination.

(b) Upon receipt of a properly executed notice of termination of the developer's interest in a time share project, the Commission shall enter a notation of cancellation of registration in the file of the project, and shall notify the developer of cancellation. A developer's failure to give notice of termination as provided herein shall not prevent cancellation of the project's registration under G.S. 93A-52

SECTION B.0200
PUBLIC OFFERING STATEMENT

B.0201 General Provisions

(a) Information contained in a public offering statement shall be accurate on the day it is supplied to a purchaser. Before any public offering statement is supplied to a purchaser, the developer shall file a copy of the statement with the Commission.

(b) In addition to the information required to be contained in a public offering statement by G.S. 93A-44, every public offering statement shall disclose to the purchaser of a time share complete and accurate information concerning:

(1) the real property type of the time share program, whether tenancy-in-common, condominium or other, and a description of the estate the purchaser will own, the term of that estate and the remainder interest, if any, once the term has expired;

(2) the document creating the time share program, a statement that it is the document which governs the program and a reference to the location where the purchaser may obtain or examine a copy of the document;

(3) whether or not the property is being converted to a time share from some other use and, if so, a statement to that effect and disclosure of the prior use of the property;

(4) the maximum number of time shares in the project, each recreational and other commonly used facility offered, and who or what will own each facility, if the project is to be completed in one development or construction phase;

(5) if the project is planned in phased construction or development, the complete plan of phased offerings, including the maximum number of time shares which may be in the project, each recreational and other commonly used facility, who or what will own each facility, and the developer's representations regarding his or her commitment to build out the project;

(6) the association of owners or other entity which will ultimately be responsible for managing the time share program, the first date or event when the entity will convene or commence to conduct business, each owner's voting right, if any, and whether and for how long the developer, as time share owner, will control the entity;

(7) the location where owners may inspect the articles and bylaws of the owners association, or other organizational documents of the entity and the books and records it produces;

(8) whether the entity has lien rights against time share owners for failure to pay assessments;

(9) whether or not the developer has entered into a management contract on behalf of the managing entity, the extent to which the managing entity's powers are delegated to the manager and the location where a copy of the management contract may be examined;

(10) whether or not the developer will pay assessments for time shares which it owns and a statement that the amount of assessments due the managing entity from owners will change over time, as circumstances may change;

(11) whether or not the developer sponsors or will sponsor a rental or resale program and, if so, a summary of the program or programs; and

(12) the developer's role at the project, if the developer is a separate entity from any other registered developer of the time share project.

(c) The inclusion of false or misleading statements in a public offering statement shall be grounds for disciplinary action by the Commission.

B.0202 Public Offering Statement Summary

Every public offering statement shall contain a one page cover prescribed by the Commission and completed by the developer entitled Public Offering Statement Summary. The Public Offering Statement Summary shall read as follows:

PUBLIC OFFERING STATEMENT SUMMARY

NAME OF PROJECT:
NAME AND REAL ESTATE LICENSE NUMBER OF BROKER:

This Public Offering Statement contains information which deserves your careful study, as you decide whether or not to purchase a time share.

The Public Offering Statement includes general informa-

tion about the real estate type, the term, and the size of this time share project. It also includes a general description of the recreational and other facilities existing now, or to be provided in the future. The Public Offering Statement will tell you how maintenance and management of the project will be provided and how the costs of these services will be charged to purchasers. From the Public Offering Statement, you will also learn how the project will be governed and whether purchasers will have a voice in that government. You will also learn that a time share instrument will be recorded to protect your real estate interest in your time share.

The Public Offering Statement contains important information, but is not a substitute for the detailed information contained in the contract of purchase and the legal documents which create and affect the time share program at this project.

Please study this Public Offering Statement carefully. Satisfy yourself that any questions you may have are answered before you decide to purchase. If a salesperson or other representative of the developer has made a representation which concerns you, and you cannot find that representation in writing, ask that it be pointed out to you.

NOTICE

UNDER NORTH CAROLINA LAW, YOU MAY CANCEL YOUR TIME SHARE PURCHASE WITHOUT PENALTY WITHIN FIVE DAYS AFTER SIGNING YOUR CONTRACT. TO CANCEL YOUR TIME SHARE PURCHASE, YOU MUST MAIL OR HAND DELIVER WRITTEN NOTICE OF YOUR DESIRE TO CANCEL YOUR PURCHASE TO (name and address of project). IF YOU CHOOSE TO MAIL YOUR CANCELLATION NOTICE, THE NORTH CAROLINA REAL ESTATE COMMISSION RECOMMENDS THAT YOU USE REGISTERED OR CERTIFIED MAIL AND THAT YOU RETAIN YOUR POSTAL RECEIPT AS PROOF OF THE DATE YOUR NOTICE WAS MAILED. UPON CANCELLATION, ALL PAYMENTS WILL BE REFUNDED TO YOU.

B.0203 Receipt for Public Offering Statement

(a) Prior to the execution of any contract to purchase a time share, a time share developer or a time share salesperson shall obtain from the purchaser a written receipt for the public offering statement, which shall display, directly over the buyer signature line in type in all capital letters, no smaller than the largest type on the page on which it appears, the following statement: DO NOT SIGN THIS RECEIPT UNLESS YOU HAVE RECEIVED A COMPLETE COPY OF THE PUBLIC OFFERING STATEMENT TO TAKE WITH YOU.

(b) Receipts for public offering statements shall be maintained as part of the records of the sales transaction.

SECTION B.0300
CANCELLATION

B.0301 Proof of Cancellation

(a) The postmark date affixed to any written notice of a purchaser's intent to cancel his or her time share purchase shall be presumed by the Commission to be the date the notice was mailed to the developer. Evidence tending to rebut this presumption shall be admissible at a hearing before the Commission.

(b) Upon receipt of a purchaser's written notice of his or her intent to cancel his or her time share purchase, the developer, or his or her agent or representative, shall retain the notice and any enclosure, envelope or other cover in the developer's files at the project, and shall produce the file upon the Commission's request.

(c) When there is more than one registered developer at a time share project and a purchaser gives written notice of his or her intent to cancel his or her time share purchase that is received by a developer or sales staff other than the one from whom his or her time share was purchased, the developer or sales staff receiving such notice shall promptly deliver it to the proper developer who shall then honor the notice if it was timely sent by the purchaser.

SECTION B.0400
TIME SHARE SALES OPERATIONS

B.0401 Retention of Time Share Records

A time share developer and a time share salesperson shall retain or cause to be retained for a period of three years complete records of every time share sale, rental, or exchange transaction made by or on behalf of the developer. Records required to be retained shall include but not be limited to offers, applications and contracts to purchase, rent or exchange time shares; records of the deposit, maintenance and disbursement of funds required to be held in trust; receipts; notices of cancellation and their covers if mailed; records regarding compensation of salespersons; public offering statements; and any other records pertaining to time share transactions. Such records shall be made available to the Commission and its representatives upon request.

B.0402 Time Share Agency Agreements and Disclosure

Time share sales transactions conducted by licensees on behalf of a time share developer are subject to 21 NCAC 58A .0104.

SECTION B.0500
HANDLING AND ACCOUNTING OF FUNDS

B.0501 Time Share Trust Funds

(a) Except as otherwise permitted by G.S. 93A-45(c), all monies received by a time share developer or a time share broker in connection with a time share sales transaction shall be deposited into a trust or escrow account not later than three banking days following receipt and shall remain in such account for ten days from the date of sale or until cancellation by the purchaser, whichever first occurs.

(b) All monies received by a person licensed as a broker in connection with a time share transaction shall be delivered immediately to his or her project broker.

(c) When a time share purchaser timely cancels his or her time share purchase, the developer shall refund to the purchaser all monies paid by the purchaser in connection with the purchase. The refund shall be made no later than 30 days following the date of execution of the contract. Amounts paid by the purchaser with a bank card or a credit card shall be refunded by a cash payment or by issuing a credit voucher to the purchaser within the 30-day period.

(d) Every project broker shall obtain and keep a written representation from the developer as to whether or not lien-free or lien-subordinated time share instruments can be recorded within 45 days of the purchaser's execution of the time share purchase agreement. When a lien-free or lien-subordinated instrument cannot be recorded within said time period, on the business day following the expiration of the ten day time share payment escrow period, a project broker shall transfer from his or her trust account all purchase deposit funds or other payments received from a purchaser who has not canceled his or her purchase agreement, to the independent escrow agent in a check made payable to the independent escrow agent. Alternatively, the check may be made payable to the developer with a restrictive endorsement placed on the back of the check providing "For deposit to the account of the independent escrow agent for the (name of time share project) only."

SECTION B.0600
PROJECT BROKER

B.0601 Designation of Project Broker

The developer of a registered time share project shall designate for each project subject to the developer's control a project broker by filing with the Commission an affidavit on the form prescribed. The developer may from time to time change the designated project broker by filing a new designation form with the Commission within ten days following the change. A broker licensed under the provisions of Section .1800 of Subchapter 58A shall not be designated as a project broker. Provisional brokers shall not be designated as a project broker.

B.0602 Duties of the Project Broker

(a) The broker designated by the developer of a time share project to be project broker shall assume responsibility for:

(1) The display of the time share project certificate registration and the license certificates of the real estate brokers associated with or engaged on behalf of the developer at the project;

(2) The determination of whether each licensee employed has complied with Rules .0503 and .0506 of Subchapter 58A;

(3) The notification to the Commission of any change in the identity or address of the project or in the identity or address of the developer or marketing or managing entities at the project;

(4) The deposit and maintenance of time share purchase or rental monies in a trust or escrow account until proper disbursement is made; and

(5) The proper maintenance of accurate records at the project including all records relating to the handling of trust monies at the project, records relating to time share sales and rental transactions and the project registration and renewal.

(b) The project broker shall review all contracts, public offering statements and other documents distributed to the purchasers of time shares at the project to ensure that the documents comport with the requirements of the Time Share Act and the rules adopted by the Commission, and to ensure that true and accurate documents have been given to the purchasers.

(c) The project broker shall not permit time share sales to be conducted by any person not licensed as a broker, and shall not delegate or assign his or her supervisory responsibilities to any other person, nor accept control of his or her supervisory responsibilities by any other person.

(d) The project broker shall notify the Commission in writing of any change in his or her status as project broker within ten days following the change.

SECTION B.0700—
TIME SHARE FORMS

B.0701 Forms for Time Share Projects

The following forms are required by the Commission for use in filing and submitting information with respect to applications for time share project registration, renewal and termination:

(1) Application for Time Share Project Registration;

(2) Affidavit of Time Share Project Broker;

(3) Affidavit of Time Share Registrar;

(4) Affidavit of Independent Escrow Agent;

(5) Developer Designation of Time Share Project Broker, Registrar and Independent Escrow Agent;

(6) Application for Time Share Project Renewal;

(7) Notice of Developer Termination of Time Share Project Registration;

(8) Consent to Service of Process and Pleadings.

Subchapter 58C
Real Estate Prelicensing Education

Rules for Subchapter 58C are not reprinted in this booklet but are available upon written request to the North Carolina Real Estate Commission.

Subchapter 58D
Real Estate Appraisers
(Repealed)
Subchapter 58E
Real Estate Continuing Education

Rules for Subchapter 58E are not reprinted in this booklet but are available upon written request to the North Carolina Real Estate Commission.

Subchapter 58F
Broker Transition Course

SECTION .0100 – REQUIREMENTS

F .0101 Basic Requirement

A provisional broker who was issued a real estate salesperson license prior to October 1, 2005 that was changed to a broker license on provisional status on April 1, 2006 in accordance with G.S. 93A-4.3(a), shall, as prescribed in G.S. 93A-4.3(b), complete a broker transition course consisting of 24 classroom hours of instruction prescribed by the Commission not later than April 1, 2008, unless the provisional broker can demonstrate to the Commission not later than April 1, 2008 that he or she possesses four years' full-time real estate brokerage experience or equivalent part-time real estate brokerage experience within the previous six years.

The remaining rules in this section are not reprinted, but are available upon written request to the NCREC.

LICENSE LAW AND RULE COMMENTS

Comments on Selected Provisions of the
North Carolina Real Estate License Law
and Real Estate Commission Rules

INTRODUCTION

These comments on selected North Carolina Real Estate License Law and Real Estate Commission Rules provisions are intended to assist real estate licensees, prelicensing course students and others in understanding the License Law and Commission rules. The comments are organized in a topic format that often differs from the sequence in which the topics are addressed in the License Law and Commission rules. The topics selected for comment here are not only of particular importance in real estate brokerage practice but also are likely to be tested on the real estate license examination. The appropriate references to the License Law and Commission rules are provided beside each listed topic.

REQUIREMENT FOR A LICENSE
General [G.S. 93A-1 and 93A-2]

Any person or business entity who directly or indirectly engages in the business of a real estate broker for compensation or the promise thereof while physically in the state of North Carolina must have a North Carolina real estate broker license. In North Carolina, a real estate licensee may only engage in brokerage as an "agent" for a party to a transaction. Thus, a real estate licensee is commonly and appropriately referred to as a real estate "agent" even though the latter term does not actually appear in the License Law. Note that a real estate "licensee" is NOT automatically a "REALTOR®." A licensed real estate agent is a REALTOR® **only** if he/she belongs to the National Association of REALTORS®, a private trade association. Thus, the term REALTOR® should not be used to generally refer to all real estate licensees.

License Categories [G.S. 93A-2]

There is only one "type" of license, a **broker** license; however, there are several license status categories as described below:

Provisional Broker – This is the "entry level" license status category. A person who has met all the license qualification requirements (including a *75-hour prelicensing course and passing the Commission's license examination*) is initially issued **a broker license on "provisional" status** and is referred to as a **"provisional broker."** A provisional broker generally may perform the same acts as a broker whose license is NOT on provisional status so long as he or she is supervised by a broker who is a designated **broker-in-charge**. A provisional broker may not operate independently in any way. G.S. 93A-2(a2) defines a **"provisional broker"** as "...a real estate broker who, pending acquisition and documentation

to the Commission of the education or experience prescribed by either G.S. 93A-4(a1) or G. S. 93A-4.3, must be supervised by a broker-in-charge when performing any act for which a real estate license is required." This license status category is comparable to a "salesperson" license in most other states except that it is a **temporary license status category**. Provisional brokers may not retain this status indefinitely – they must complete required **postlicensing education** (one 30-hour course each year for the three years following initial licensure – total of 90 hours) to avoid cancellation of their licenses and to remove the "provisional" status of their licenses.

Broker – A "provisional broker" who satisfies all postlicensing education requirements to terminate the "provisional" status of such license becomes simply a **"broker"** and is NOT required to be supervised by a broker-in-charge in order to hold an "active" license. Applicants qualifying for licensure in NC based on **broker** licensure in another state (both applicants who qualify for direct licensure by reciprocity and applicants from non-reciprocal states who qualify by taking the NC license examination) may be licensed directly as a **broker NOT on provisional status**. All others must first be licensed in NC as a **provisional broker** and then satisfy the postlicensing education requirement to become a non-provisional broker.

Most frequently, brokers elect to work for another broker or brokerage firm. Brokers may also elect to operate independently as a sole proprietor; however, with limited exceptions, such broker will have to qualify for and designate himself or herself as a **broker-in-charge** in order to operate independently and perform most brokerage activities (discussed further below under "broker-in-charge" and also in a subsequent section on brokers-in-charge that appears near the end of this appendix).

Broker-In-Charge – G.S. 93A-2(a1) defines a **"broker-in-charge"** as "...*a real estate broker who has been designated as the broker having responsibility for the supervision of real estate provisional brokers engaged in real estate brokerage at a particular real estate office and for other administrative and supervisory duties as the Commission shall prescribe by rule.*" Commission Rule A.0110 requires that each real estate office must have a broker who meets the qualification requirements to serve as "broker-in-charge" of the office and who has designated himself or herself as the broker-in-charge of that office. As is the case with "provisional broker," *broker-in-charge" is not a separate license, but only a **separate license status category**. A broker who is to serve as the broker-in-charge (BIC) of an office (including working independently) must be designated as a BIC with the Commission.

To qualify for designation as a broker-in-charge, a broker's license must be on "active" status but NOT on "provisional" status, the broker must have **two years full-time or part-time equivalent ACTUAL brokerage experience within the previous five years**, and the broker must complete a 12-hour **Broker-In-Charge Course** within 120 days after designation. Broker-in-charge requirements are addressed in detail in a separate subsequent section.

Limited Nonresident Commercial Broker – A broker or salesperson residing in a state other than North Carolina who holds an active broker or salesperson license in the state where his or her primary place of real estate business is located may apply for and obtain a North Carolina **"limited nonresident commercial broker license"** that entitles such licensee to engage in transactions for compensation involving "commercial real estate" in North Carolina, but the licensee must enter into a "declaration of affiliation" and a "brokerage cooperation agreement" with a resident North Carolina broker and the licensee must be supervised by the North Carolina broker while performing commercial real estate brokerage in North Carolina. Like a "firm" license, a limited nonresident commercial broker license is a separate license.

Licensing of Business Entities [G.S. 93A-1 and 2; Rule A.0502]

In addition to individuals (persons), "business entities" also must be licensed in order to engage in the real estate business. Any corporation, partnership, limited liability company, association or other business entity (other than a sole proprietorship) must obtain a separate real estate **firm** broker license.

Activities Requiring a License [G.S. 93A-2]

Persons and business entities who for compensation or the promise thereof perform the activities listed below as an agent for others are considered to be performing brokerage activities and must have a real estate license. There is no exemption for engaging in a limited number of transactions. A person or entity who performs a brokerage service in even one transaction must be licensed. Similarly, no fee or other compensation is so small as to exempt one from the application of the statute when acting for another in a real estate transaction. Brokerage activities include:

1. Listing (or offering to list) real estate for sale or rent, including any act performed by a real estate licensee in connection with obtaining and servicing a listing agreement. Examples of such acts include, but are not limited to, soliciting listings, providing information to the property owner, and preparing listing agreements or property management agreements.
2. Selling or buying (or offering to sell or buy) real estate, including any act performed by a real estate licensee in connection with assisting others in selling or buying real estate. Examples of such acts include, but are not limited to, advertising listed property for sale, "showing" listed property to prospective buyers, providing information about listed property to prospective buyers (other than basic property facts that might commonly appear in an advertisement in a newspaper, real estate publication or internet website), negotiating a sale or purchase of real estate, and assisting with the completion of contract offers and counteroffers using preprinted forms and communication of offers and acceptances.
3. Leasing or renting (or offering to lease or rent) real estate, including any act performed by real estate licensees in connection with assisting others in leasing or renting real estate. Examples of such acts include, but are not limited to, advertising listed property for rent, "showing" listed rental property to prospective tenants, providing information about listed rental property to prospective tenants (other than basic property facts that might commonly appear in an advertisement in a newspaper, real estate publication or internet website), negotiating lease terms, and assisting with the completion of lease offers and counteroffers using preprinted forms and communication of offers and acceptances.
4. Conducting (or offering to conduct) a real estate auction. (Mere criers of sale are excluded.) NOTE: An auctioneer's license is also required to auction real estate.
5. Selling, buying, leasing, assigning or exchanging any interest in real estate, including a leasehold interest, in connection with the sale or purchase of a business.
6. Referring a party to a real estate licensee, if done for compensation. Any arrangement or agreement between a licensee and an unlicensed person that calls for the licensee to compensate the unlicensed person in any way for finding, introducing or referring a party to the licensee has been determined by North Carolina's courts to be prohibited under the License Law. Therefore, *no licensee may pay a finder's fee, referral fee, "bird dog" fee or similar compensation to an unlicensed person.*

Unlicensed Employees — Permitted Activities

The use of unlicensed assistants and other unlicensed office personnel in the real estate industry is very widespread and the Commission is frequently asked by licensees what acts such persons may lawfully perform. To provide guidance to licensees regarding this matter, the Commission has prepared the following list of acts that an unlicensed assistant or employee may lawfully perform so long as the assistant or employee is salaried or hourly paid and is not paid on a per-transaction basis.

An unlicensed, salaried employee MAY:
1. Receive and forward phone calls and electronic messages to licensees.
2. Submit listings and changes to a multiple listing service, but only if the listing data or changes are compiled and provided by a licensee.
3. Secure copies of public records from public reposi-

tories (i.e., register of deeds office, county tax office, etc.).

4. Place "for sale" or "for rent" signs and lock boxes on property at the direction of a licensee.

5. Order and supervise routine and minor repairs to listed property at the direction of a licensee.

6. Act as a courier to deliver or pick up documents.

7. Provide to prospects basic factual information on listed property that might commonly appear in advertisements in a newspaper, real estate publication or internet website.

8. Schedule appointments for showing property listed for sale or rent.

9. Communicate with licensees, property owners, prospects, inspectors, etc. to coordinate or confirm appointments.

10. Show rental properties managed by the employee's employing broker to prospective tenants and complete and execute preprinted form leases for the rental of such properties.

11. Type offers, contracts and leases from drafts of preprinted forms completed by a licensee.

12. Record and deposit earnest money deposits, tenant security deposits and other trust monies, and otherwise maintain records of trust account receipts and disbursements, under the close supervision of the office broker-in-charge, who is legally responsible for handling trust funds and maintaining trust accounts.

13. Assist a licensee in assembling documents for closing.

14. Compute commission checks for licensees affiliated with a broker or firm and act as bookkeeper for the firm's bank operating accounts.

Exemptions [G.S. 93A-2]

The following persons and organizations are specifically exempted from the requirement for real estate licensure:

1. **Property owners** when selling or leasing their own property. This includes both individual property owners personally selling or leasing their property and business entities selling or leasing real estate owned by the business entity. To qualify under this exemption, the person or entity must be the actual title holder or share title with an undivided interest.

Note: The Commission takes the position that the *bona fide* **officers and employees of a corporation need not be licensed to sell or lease real estate belonging to the corporation. This is because corporations have a separate legal identity and can only function through its officers and employees, thus such officers and employees must be exempt when selling or leasing the corporation's property in order to give effect to the corporation exemption. However, the officers and employees of other business entities are considered to be exempt only if they personally are title owners of the property to be sold or leased. Thus, a partner in a general partnership is exempt as an owner when selling or leasing partnership-owned real estate, but an officer or employee of the partnership who is not also a partner is not exempt.**

---

2. Persons acting as attorneys-in-fact under a power of attorney in consummating performance under a contract for the sale, lease or exchange of real estate. (Note: This limited exemption applies only to the final completion of a transaction already commenced. The licensing requirement may not be circumvented by obtaining a power of attorney.)

3. Attorneys-at-law when performing real estate activities in the normal course of providing legal services to their clients, such as when administering an estate or trust. Attorneys may NOT otherwise engage in real estate brokerage practice without a real estate license.

4. Persons acting under court order (e.g., receivers, trustees in bankruptcy, guardians or personal representatives)

5. Trustees acting under a trust agreement, deed of trust or will.

6. Certain salaried employees of broker-property managers. (See G.S. 93A-2(c)(6) for details.)

NOTE: Although there is no specific statutory exemption for real estate appraisers, persons who appraise real estate for compensation are not required to have a real estate license to conduct such appraisals. However, such persons are required to be licensed or certified as a real estate appraiser by the North Carolina Appraisal Board.

THE REAL ESTATE COMMISSION
Composition [G.S. 93A-3(a)]

The Real Estate Commission consists of nine (9) members who serve three-year terms. Seven members are appointed by the Governor and two are appointed by the General Assembly upon the recommendations of the Speaker of the House of Representatives and the President Pro Tempore of the Senate. At least three (3) members must be licensed brokers. At least two (2) members must be "public members" who are NOT involved directly or indirectly in the real estate brokerage or appraisal businesses.

Purpose and Powers [G.S. 93A-3(a), (c) and (f); G.S. 93A-6(a) and (b);G.S. 93A-4(d) and 93A-4A]

The principal purpose of the Real Estate Commission is to protect the interests of members of the general public in their dealings with real estate brokers. This is accomplished through the exercise of the following statutory powers granted to the Commission:

1. Licensing real estate brokers and brokerage firms, and registering time share projects.
2. Establishing and administering prelicensing and postlicensing education programs for prospective licensees and a continuing education program for licensees.
3. Providing education and information relating to the real estate brokerage business for licensees and the general public.
4. Regulating the business activities of brokers and brokerage firms, including disciplining licensees who violate the License Law or Commission rules.

It should be noted that the Commission is specifically prohibited, however, from regulating commissions, salaries or fees charged by real estate licensees and from arbitrating disputes between parties regarding matters of contract such as the rate and/or division of commissions, pay of salespersons or similar matters. [See G.S. 93A-3(c) and Rule A.0109.]

Disciplinary Authority [G.S. 93A-6(a)-(c)]

The Real Estate Commission is authorized to take a variety of disciplinary actions against licensees who the Commission finds guilty of violating the License Law or Commission rules while acting as real estate licensees. These are: reprimand, censure, license suspension and license revocation. The License Law also permits a licensee under certain circumstances to surrender his/her license with the consent of the Commission. Disciplinary actions taken against licensees are regularly reported in the Commission's quarterly newsletter which is distributed to all licensees and also may be reported in local and regional newspapers.

It should be noted that licensees may be disciplined by the Commission for committing acts prohibited by the License Law when selling, leasing, or buying real estate for themselves, as well as for committing such acts in transactions handled as agents for others. [G.S. 93A-6(b)(3)]

The Commission also has the power to seek in its own name injunctive relief in superior court to prevent any person (licensees and others) from violating the License Law or Commission rules. A typical example of where the Commission might pursue injunctive relief in the courts is where a person engages in real estate activity without a license or during a period when the person's license is suspended, revoked or expired. [G.S. 93A-6(c)]

Any violation of the License Law or Commission rules is a criminal offense (misdemeanor) and may be prosecuted in a court of law. However, a finding by the Commission that a licensee has violated the License Law or Commission rules does not constitute a criminal conviction. [G.S. 93-8]

PROHIBITED ACTS BY LICENSEES

G.S. 93A-6 provides a list of prohibited acts which may result in disciplinary action against licensees. Discussed below are the various prohibited acts, except for those related to handling and accounting for trust funds, which are discussed in the Commission's "Trust Account Guidelines," and the failure to deliver certain instruments to parties in a transaction, which is discussed in the subsequent section on "General Brokerage Provisions."

Important Note

The provisions of the License Law relating to misrepresentation or omission of a material fact, conflict of interest, licensee competence, handling of trust funds, and improper, fraudulent or dishonest dealing generally apply independently of other statutory law or case law such as the law of agency. Nevertheless, another law may have an effect on the application of a License Law provision. For example, the requirements of the N.C. Tenant Security Deposit Act relating to the accounting to a tenant for a residential security deposit within 30 days after termination of a tenancy amplify the general License Law provisions (and Commission rules) requiring licensees to account for such funds within a reasonable time. Thus, in this instance, a violation of the Tenant Security Deposit Act's provisions would also be considered by the Commission to be a violation of the License Law.

Similarly, the law of agency and the law of contracts, which are derived from case law, may be taken into consideration when applying the provisions of the License Law. Thus, a licensee's agency status and role in a transaction might affect the licensee's duties under the license law. Examples of how an agent's duties under the License Law may be affected by the application of other laws are included at various points in this section on "Prohibited Acts by Licensees."

Misrepresentation or Omission [G.S. 93A-6(a)(1)]

Misrepresentation or omission of a material fact by brokers or salespersons is prohibited, and this prohibition includes both "willful" and "negligent" acts. A "willful" act is one that is done intentionally and deliberately, while a "negligent" act is one that is done unintentionally. A "misrepresentation" is communicating false information, while an "omission" is failing to provide or disclose information where there is a duty to provide or disclose such information.

For purposes of applying G.S. 93A-6(a)(1), whether a fact is "material" depends on the facts and circumstances of a particular transaction and the application of statutory and/or case law. The Commission has historically interpreted **"material facts"** under the Real Estate License Law to at least include:

Facts about the property itself (such as a structural defect or defective mechanical systems);

Facts relating directly to the property (such as a pending zoning change or planned highway construction in the immediate vicinity); and

Facts relating directly to the ability of the agent's principal to complete the transaction (such as a pending foreclosure sale).

Regardless of which party in a transaction a real estate agent represents, the facts described above must be disclosed to both

the agent's principal and to third parties the agent deals with on the principal's behalf. In addition, an agent has a duty to disclose to his or her principal any information that may affect the principal's rights and interests or influence the principal's decision in the transaction.

Note, however, that G.S. 39-50 and 42-14.2 specifically provide that the fact that a property was occupied by a person who died or had a serious illness while occupying the property is NOT a material fact. Thus, agents do not need to voluntarily disclose such a fact. If a prospective buyer or tenant specifically asks about such a matter, the agent may either decline to answer or respond honestly. If, however, a prospective buyer or tenant inquires as to whether a previous owner or occupant had AIDS, the agent is prohibited by fair housing laws from answering such an inquiry because persons with AIDS are considered to be "handicapped" under such laws and disclosure of the information may have the effect of discriminating against the property owner based on the handicapping condition.

This introductory information should assist in understanding G.S. 93A-6(a)(1), which establishes four separate (although closely related) categories of conduct which are prohibited. These are discussed below, and a few examples of prohibited conduct are provided for each category.

Willful Misrepresentation — This occurs when an agent who has "actual knowledge" of a material fact deliberately misinforms a buyer, seller, tenant or landlord concerning such fact. A misrepresentation is also considered to be "willful" when an agent who does NOT have actual knowledge of a matter material to the transaction provides incorrect information concerning such matter to a buyer, seller, tenant or landlord without regard for the actual truth of the matter (i.e., when an agent intentionally provides information without knowing whether or not it is true and the information provided is in fact not true).

Note: The following examples of willful misrepresentation apply regardless of the agent's status (seller's agent or buyer's agent) or role (listing agent or selling agent).

> **Example:** An agent knows that a listed house has a severe problem with water intrusion in the crawl space during heavy rains. In response to a question from a prospective buyer who is being shown the house during dry weather, the agent states that there is no water drainage problem.

> **Example:** An agent knows that the heat pump at a listed house does not function properly, but tells a prospective buyer that all mechanical systems and appliances are in good condition.

> **Example:** An agent knows that the approximate market value of a house is $225,000, but tells the property owner that the house is worth $250,000 in order to obtain a listing.

> **Example:** An agent is completely unfamiliar with the features or condition of a listed property; however, the agent informs a prospective buyer that the

plumbing is in good working order without first checking with the owner. (The agent in such instance is acting without regard for the truth of the matter being represented. If the plumbing in fact needs significant repair, then the agent may be guilty of willful misrepresentation.)

> **Example:** Without checking with the owner, an agent tells a prospective buyer of a listed house that heating and cooling costs are "very reasonable." (Because the agent acted without regard for the truth of the matter, he may be guilty of willful misrepresentation if heating and cooling costs are in fact extraordinarily high.)

Negligent Misrepresentation — This occurs when an agent unintentionally misinforms a buyer, seller, tenant or landlord concerning a material fact either because the agent does not have actual knowledge of the fact, because the agent has incorrect information, or because of a mistake by the agent. If a reasonably prudent agent "should reasonably have known" the truth of the matter that was misrepresented, then the agent may be guilty of "negligent misrepresentation" even though the agent was acting in good faith.

Negligent misrepresentation by real estate agents occurs frequently in real estate transactions. A very common situation is the recording of incorrect information in an MLS® computer or book due to the negligence of the listing agent. When a prospective buyer is subsequently provided the incorrect information from the MLS® by the agent working with the buyer, a negligent misrepresentation by the listing agent occurs.

A listing agent is generally held to a higher standard with regard to negligent misrepresentation of material facts about a listed property to a buyer than is a selling agent who is acting as a seller's subagent. This is because (1) The listing agent is in the best position to ascertain facts about the property, (2) the listing agent is expected to take reasonable steps to assure that property data included with the listing is correct and (3) it is generally considered reasonable for a selling agent to rely on the accuracy of the listing data except in those situations where it should be obvious to a reasonably prudent agent that the listing information is incorrect. However, a buyer's agent may in some cases be held to a higher standard than a seller's subagent because of the buyer's agent's duties to the buyer under the law of agency and the buyer's agent's special knowledge of the buyer's particular situation and needs.

> **Example:** An agent has previously sold several lots in a subdivision under development and all those lots passed a soil suitability test for an on-site septic system. The agent then sells Lot 35 without checking as to whether this lot satisfies the soil test; however, the agent informs the buyer that Lot 35 will support an on-site septic system when in fact the contrary is true. (While the agent's conduct may not rise to the level of willful disregard for the truth of the matter,

the agent was at least negligent in not checking the soil test result on Lot 35 and is therefore guilty of negligent misrepresentation. This result is not affected by the agent's agency status or role in the transaction.)

Example: An owner tells a listing agent with ABC Realty that his house has 1850 heated square feet. Without verifying the square footage, the agent records 1850 square feet on the listing form and in the listing information published in the local MLS. The house is subsequently sold by a sales agent with XYZ Realty who tells the buyer that according to the MLS data, the house has 1850 square feet. The buyer later discovers that the house actually has only 1750 square feet. (In this situation, the listing agent did not make a direct misrepresentation to the buyer; however, he/she initiated the chain of communication which led to the buyer being misinformed, and thus indirectly misrepresented a material fact. Further, the listing agent's failure to verify the square footage constituted negligence. Therefore, the listing agent is guilty of a negligent misrepresentation. Although the selling agent directly communicated the incorrect information to the buyer, he/she probably acted reasonably in relying on the data in the MLS book. In this case, if the selling agent had no reason to doubt the MLS data, the selling agent is not guilty of a negligent misrepresentation. Note, however, that if the square footage discrepancy had been sufficiently large that a reasonably prudent selling agent should have known the listed data was incorrect, then the selling agent would also have been guilty of negligent misrepresentation. The result in this particular example is not affected by the selling agent's agency status (seller's subagent or buyer's agent), although this might be a factor in other situations.

Willful Omission — This occurs when the agent has "actual knowledge" of a material fact and a duty to disclose such fact to a buyer, seller, tenant, or landlord, but he deliberately fails to disclose such fact.

Example: An agent knows that a zoning change is pending which would adversely affect the value of a listed property, but fails to disclose such information to a prospective buyer. The agent has committed a willful omission and this result is not affected by the agent's agency status or role in the transaction.

[Note: Information about a zoning change (or planned highway) that would enhance the value of a seller's property must also be disclosed to the seller, even if the agent is a buyer's agent.]

Example: An agent knows that the city has just decided to extend water and sewer lines to a subdivision that has been plagued for years by serious water quality and sewage disposal problems. This will result in a substantial increase in the value of homes in the subdivision. The agent, who is working with a buyer to purchase a house in the subdivision, does not inform the seller of the city's recent decision. The agent has committed a willful omission and this result is not affected by the agent's agency status or role in the transaction.

Example: An agent knows that a listed house has a major defect (e.g., crumbling foundation, no insulation, malfunctioning septic tank, leaking roof, termite infestation, or some other problem) but fails to disclose such information to a prospective buyer. The agent has committed a willful omission and this result is not affected by the agent's agency status or role in the transaction.

Example: A selling agent working with a buyer as a subagent of the seller learns that the buyer is willing to pay more than the price in the buyer's offer, but fails to disclose this information to the seller (or listing agent) when presenting the offer. The selling agent has committed a willful omission. If, however, the selling agent were acting as a buyer's agent, then the result would be different because the agent does not represent the seller.

Example: A buyer's agent becomes aware that the seller with whom his buyer is negotiating is under pressure to sell quickly and may accept much less than the listing price. Believing such information should always be kept confidential, the buyer's agent does not provide the buyer with this information. The buyer's agent is guilty of a willful omission. An agent must disclose to his/her principal any information that might affect the principal's decision in the transaction.

Example: Suppose in the immediately preceding example that the seller's property is listed with the firm of the buyer's agent and the firm's policy is to practice dual agency in in-house sales situations where it represents both the seller and the buyer. In this situation, the buyer's agent would not be considered to have committed a willful omission under the License Law by not disclosing the information about the seller's personal situation to the buyer. NOTE: This assumes however that the buyer's agent properly disclosed his/her status as a buyer's agent to the seller or seller's agent upon "initial contact," that dual agency was properly authorized in writing by both the seller and buyer prior to showing the seller's property to the buyer and that the agency agreements provided for this limitation on disclosure of information in dual agency situations (as is the case with the agency agreement forms provided by the North Carolina Association of REALTORS® for use by its members).

Negligent Omission — This occurs when an agent does NOT have actual knowledge of a material fact, but a reasonably prudent agent "should reasonably have known" of such fact. In this case, the agent may be guilty of "negligent omission" if he/she fails to disclose this fact to a buyer, seller, tenant or landlord, even though the agent acted in good faith in the transaction.

The prohibition against negligent omission creates a *"duty to discover and disclose" material facts* which a reasonably prudent agent would typically have discovered in the course of the transaction. A listing agent is typically in a much better position than a selling agent to discover material facts relating to a listed property and thus, will be held to a higher standard than will a selling agent acting as a seller's subagent. On the other hand, a buyer's agent in some circumstances may be held to a higher standard than a seller's subagent because of the buyer's agent's duties to the buyer under the law of agency, particularly if the buyer's agent is aware of a buyer's special needs with regard to a property. Again we see how the agency relationships between agents and principals to a transaction and the agent's role in the transaction can affect a licensee's duties and responsibilities under the License Law.

Instances of negligent omission occur much less frequently than instances of negligent misrepresentation. This is because most facts about a listed property are recorded on a detailed property data sheet from which information is taken for inclusion in MLS computer files/books. If incorrect information taken from an MLS computer file/book is passed on to a prospective purchaser, then a "misrepresentation," rather than an "omission," has occurred. Nevertheless, there are examples of negligent omission which can be cited.

Example: A listing agent lists for sale a house located adjacent to a street that is about to be widened into a major thoroughfare. The thoroughfare project has been very controversial and highly publicized. The city recently finalized its decision to proceed with the project and the plans for the street widening are recorded in the city planner's office. A buyer, working with a selling agent, makes an offer to buy the house. The listing agent does not disclose the street widening plans to the buyer or selling agent and claims later that he/she was not aware of the plans. In this situation, both the listing and selling agents are probably guilty of a negligent omission because each "should reasonably have known" of the street widening plans, clearly a material fact, and should have disclosed this fact to the buyer. This result is not affected by whether the selling agent is a buyer agent or seller's subagent.

Example: A seller has a 30,000 square foot commercial property for sale which cannot be expanded under local zoning laws. The buyer is looking for property in the 25,000 - 30,000 square foot range, but has told his buyer's agent that he needs a property where

he can expand to 50,000 square feet or more in the future. The seller does not think to advise the buyer's agent that the property cannot be expanded, and the buyer's agent makes no inquiry about it although he is aware of the buyer's special needs. If the buyer purchases the property without knowing about the restriction on expansion, the buyer's agent is guilty of a negligent omission for failing to discover and disclose a special circumstance that the agent knew was especially important to his/her client.

Example: When listing a house, a listing agent is told by the seller that one area of the roof leaks badly when it rains, but the moisture so far is being contained in the attic. The listing agent forgets to note this on the MLS data sheet and forgets to disclose the leaking roof problem to prospective buyers and selling agents. The listing agent is guilty of a negligent omission. Because the agent's failure to disclose the leaking roof problem was unintentional, the listing agent is not guilty of a willful omission; however, his/her forgetfulness resulting in his/her failure to disclose the defect constitutes a negligent omission.

Making False Promises [G.S. 93A-6(a)(2)]

Real estate brokers are prohibited from "making any false promises of a character likely to influence, persuade or induce." It is unimportant whether or not the broker originally intended to honor his/her promise – failure to honor a promise is sufficient to constitute a violation of this provision. The promise may relate to any matter which might influence, persuade or induce a person to perform some act which he/she might not otherwise perform.

Example: An agent promises a prospective apartment tenant that the apartment the prospect is considering renting will be repainted before the tenant moves in. The agent then fails to have the work done after the lease is signed.

Example: An agent promises a property owner that if he/she lists his/her house for sale with the agent's firm, then the firm will steam-clean all the carpets and wash all the windows. The firm then fails to have the work done after the listing contract is signed.

Other Misrepresentations [G.S. 93A-6(a)(3)]

Real estate brokers are prohibited from pursuing a course of misrepresentation (or making of false promises) through other agents or salespersons or through advertising or other means.

Example: In marketing subdivision lots for a developer, a broker regularly advertises that the lots for sale are suitable for residential use when in fact the lots will not pass a soil suitability test for on-site sewage systems.

Example: A broker is marketing a new condominium complex which is under construction. Acting with the full knowledge and consent of the broker, the broker's agents regularly inform prospective buyers that units will be available for occupancy on June 1, when in fact the units won't be available until at least September 1.

Conflict of Interest [G.S. 93A-6(a)(4) and (6); Rule A.0104(d)]

G.S. 93A-6(a)(4) prohibits a real estate agent from "acting for more than one party in a transaction without the knowledge of all parties for whom he or she acts." Commission Rule A.0104(d) takes this a step further by providing that a broker or brokerage firm representing one party in a transaction shall not undertake to represent another party in the transaction without the express written authority (i.e., authorization of dual agency) of each party (subject to one exception, explained in the dual agency section). A typical violation of this provision occurs when the agent has only one principal in a transaction but acts in a manner which benefits another party without the principal's knowledge. In such a situation, the agent violates the duty of loyalty and consent owed to his principal.

> **Example:** A house is listed with Firm X. When showing the house to a prospective buyer not represented by Firm X, an agent of Firm X advises the buyer to offer substantially less than the listing price because the seller must move soon and is very anxious to sell the property fast. The agent and Firm X are contractually obligated to represent only the seller. By advising the prospective buyer as indicated in this example, the agent is acting to benefit the buyer without the seller's knowledge and consent. This act violates both the License Law and the Law of Agency.

> **Example:** An agent with Firm Y assists her sister in purchasing a house listed with Firm X without advising Firm X or the seller of her relationship with the buyer. The agent is "officially" acting as a subagent of the seller in the transaction. In this situation, there is an inherent conflict of interest on the part of the agent. If the agent does not disclose her relationships to both parties, then the agent violates both the License Law and Law of Agency. In fact, since her allegiance lies with her sister, the agent should instead act as a buyer's agent from the outset. The same would be true if the buyer were a close friend or business associate of the agent, or in any way enjoyed a special relationship to the agent which would clearly influence the agent to act in behalf of the buyer rather than the seller.

G.S. 93A-6(a)(4) also prohibits any **"self-dealing"** on the part of an agent. For example, if an agent attempts to make a secret profit in a transaction where he is supposed to be representing a principal, then the agent violates this "conflict of interest" provision.

> **Example:** An agent lists a parcel of undeveloped property which is zoned for single-family residential use. The agent knows that this property is about to be rezoned for multi-family residential use, which will greatly in-

crease the property's value. Rather than informing the seller of this fact, the agent offers to buy the property at the listed price, telling the seller that he wants to acquire the property as a long-term investment. The deal closes. Several months later, after the rezoning has been accomplished, the agent sells the property at a substantial profit.

G.S. 93A-6(a)(6) prohibits a licensee from "representing or attempting to represent a real estate broker other than the broker by whom he or she is engaged or associated, without the express knowledge and consent of the broker with whom he or she is associated." While brokers may work for or be associated with more than one real estate company, so long as they have the express consent of all brokers-in-charge, provisional brokers may never engage in brokerage activities for more than one company at a time.

Improper Brokerage Commission [G.S. 93A-6(a)(5) and (9)]

A broker may NOT pay a commission or valuable consideration to any person for acts or services performed in violation of the License Law. [G.S. 93A-6(a)(9)] This provision flatly prohibits a broker or salesperson from paying an *unlicensed* person for acts which require a real estate license. Following are examples of prohibited payments:

> **Example:** The payment by brokers of commissions to previously licensed sales associates who failed to properly renew their licenses for any acts performed after their licenses had expired. [Note that payment could properly be made for commissions earned while the license was on active status, even if the license is inactive or expired at time of payment. The determining factor is whether the license was on active status at the time all services were rendered which generated the commission?]

> **Example:** The payment of a commission, salary or fee by brokers to unlicensed employees or independent contractors (e.g., secretaries, "trainees" who haven't passed the license examination, etc.) for performing acts or services requiring a real estate license.

> **Example:** The payment by licensees of a "finder's fee," "referral fee," "bird dog fee," or any other valuable consideration to unlicensed persons who find, introduce, or bring together parties to a real estate transaction. This is true even if the ultimate consummation of the transaction is accomplished by a licensee and even if the act is performed without expectation of compensation. Thus, a licensee may NOT compensate a friend, relative, former client or any other unlicensed person for "referring" a prospective buyer, seller, landlord or tenant to such licensee. This prohibition extends to "owner referral" programs at condominium or time share complexes and "tenant referral" programs at apartment complexes.

In addition, a *provisional* broker may NOT accept any compensation for brokerage services from anyone other than his employing broker or brokerage firm. Consequently, a broker may not pay a commission or fee directly to a provisional broker of another broker or firm. Any such payment must be made through the provisional broker's employing broker or firm. [G.S. 93A-6(a)(5)]

Note: *See also the discussion of Rule A.0109 on "Brokerage Fees and Compensation" under the subsequent section titled "General Brokerage Provisions."*

Unworthiness and Incompetence [G.S. 93A-6(a)(8)]

This broad provision authorizes the Real Estate Commission to discipline any licensee who, based on his or her conduct and consideration of the public interest, is found to be unworthy or incompetent to work in the real estate business. A wide range of conduct may serve as the basis for a finding of unworthiness or incompetence, including conduct which violates other specific provisions of the License Law or Commission rules. Here are a few examples of improper conduct which do not specifically violate another License Law provision but which might support a finding of unworthiness or incompetence.

1. Failure to properly complete (fill in) real estate contracts or to use contract forms which are legally adequate.
2. Failure to diligently perform the services required under listing contracts or property management contracts.
3. Failure to provide accurate closing statements to sellers and buyers or accurate income/expense reports to property owners.

Improper Dealing [G.S. 93A-6(a)(10)]

This broad provision prohibits a real estate licensee from engaging in "any other conduct [not specifically prohibited elsewhere in the License Law] which constitutes **improper, fraudulent or dishonest dealing**." The determination as to whether particular conduct constitutes "improper, fraudulent or dishonest dealing" is made by the Real Estate Commission on a case-by-case basis. Therefore, a broad range of conduct might be found objectionable under this provision, depending on the facts in a case.

One category of conduct which violates this provision is any breach of the duty to exercise skill, care, and diligence in behalf of a client under the Law of Agency. (Note that other breaches of Agency Law duties constituting either a "misrepresentation or omission," a "conflict of interest" or a "failure to properly account for trust funds" are covered by other specific statutory provisions.)

Another category of conduct which violates this provision is any violation of the State Fair Housing Act. This is mentioned separately under the "Discriminatory Practices" heading.

Example: A broker is personally conducting the closing of a real estate sale he has negotiated. The seller does not show up for the closing. In order to avoid a delay in closing the transaction, the broker forges the seller's signature on a deed to the property and proceeds with the closing in the seller's absence.

Example: An agent assists a prospective buyer in perpetrating a fraud in connection with a mortgage loan application by preparing two contracts — one with false information for submission to the lending institution, and another which represents the actual agreement between seller and buyer. (This practice is commonly referred to as "dual contracting" or "contract kiting.")

Example: A broker lists a property for sale and agrees in the listing contract to place the listing in the local MLS, to advertise the property for sale, and to use his best efforts in good faith to find a buyer. The broker places a "For Sale" sign on the property, but fails to place the property in the MLS for more than 30 days and fails to otherwise advertise the property during the listing period. (The broker has failed to exercise reasonable skill, care and diligence in behalf of his client as required by the listing contract and the Law of Agency.)

Example: An agent is aware that the owners of a house listed with his company are out of town for the weekend, yet the agent gives a prospective buyer the house keys and allows such prospect to look at the listed house without accompanying the prospect. (The agent has failed to exercise reasonable skill, care and diligence in behalf of his client.)

Discriminatory Practices [G.S. 93A-6(a)(10); Rule A.1601]

Any conduct by a licensee which violates the provisions of the State Fair Housing Act is considered by the Commission to constitute "improper conduct" and to be a violation of the License Law.

Practice of Law [G.S. 93A-4(e); G.S. 93A-6(a)(11); Rule A.0111]

Real estate licensees may not perform for others any legal service described in G.S. 84-2.1 or any other legal service. Following are several examples of real estate-related legal services which licensees may NOT provide.

1. Drafting legal documents such as deeds, deeds of trust, leases and real estate sales contracts for others. Although licensees may "fill in" or "complete" pre-printed real estate contract forms which have been drafted by an attorney, they may NOT under any circumstances complete or fill in deed or deed of trust forms.
2. Abstracting or rendering an opinion on legal title to real property.
3. Providing "legal advice" of any nature to clients and customers, including advice concerning the nature of any interest in real estate or the means of holding title to real estate. (Note: Although providing advice concerning the legal ramifications of a real estate sales contract is prohibited, merely "explaining" the provisions of such a contract is not only acceptable, but highly recommended.)

Other Prohibited Acts [G.S. 93A-6(b)]

In addition to those prohibited acts previously discussed, G.S. 93A-6(b) prescribes several other specific grounds for disciplinary action by the Commission, including:

1. Where a licensee has obtained a license by false or fraudulent representation (e.g., falsifying documentation of prelicensing education, failing to disclose prior criminal convictions, etc.).
2. Where a licensee has been convicted of, or pled guilty or no contest to, certain types of criminal offenses.
3. Where a broker's unlicensed employee, who is exempt from licensing under G.S. 93A-2(c)(6) (property management exception), has committed an act which, if committed by the broker, would have constituted a violation of the License Law.
4. Where a licensee who is also a State-licensed or State-certified real estate appraiser has violated any of the provisions of the North Carolina Real Estate Appraisers Act and been disciplined by the N.C. Appraisal Board.

Lastly, be aware that under (b)(3), licensees may be disciplined for violating any of the 15 provisions under subsection (a) when selling, buying, or leasing their own property.

GENERAL BROKERAGE PROVISIONS

Discussed below are selected Commission rules related to general brokerage.

Agency Agreements and Disclosure [Rule A.0104]

Provided below is a brief summary of the various provisions of the Commission's rule regarding agency agreements and disclosure. For a much more in-depth discussion of this rule and its application, the reader is referred to the Commission's *North Carolina Real Estate Manual.*

Agency Agreements: Rule A.0104(a) requires all agency agreements for brokerage services (in both sales and lease transactions) to be in writing and signed by the parties thereto. Paragraph (a):

- Requires agency agreements with property owners (both sellers and lessors) of any type of property to be in writing from the time the agreement is initially made;
- Allows an express **oral buyer/tenant** agency agreement from the outset of the relationship, *but the agreement must be reduced to writing no later than the time any party to the transaction wants to extend an offer.* As a practical matter, this oral agreement needs to address all key aspects of the relationship, including agent compensation, authorization for dual agency, etc.

(**Note:** A buyer/tenant agency agreement must be in writing from the outset if it seeks to limit the buyer/tenant's right to work with other agents or binds the client to the agent for any definite time period. In other words, an oral buyer/tenant agency agreement must be "non-exclusive" and must be for an indefinite period and terminable by the client at any time.)

Further, every *written* agency agreement of any kind must also:

- Provide for its existence for a definite period of time and terminate without prior notice at the expiration of that period. [Exception: an agency agreement between a broker and a landlord to procure tenants for the landlord's property may allow for automatic renewal so long as the landlord may terminate with notice at the end of any contract or renewal period.]
- Contain the Rule A.0104(b) non-discrimination (fair housing) provision, namely: "The broker shall conduct all his brokerage activities in regard to this agreement without respect to the race, color, religion, sex, national origin, handicap or familial status of any party or prospective party to the agreement." (This provision must be set forth in a clear and conspicuous manner which shall distinguish it from other provisions of the agency agreement.)
- Include the license number of the individual licensee who signs the agreement.

Allowing an agent to work with a buyer under an express *oral* buyer agency agreement is intended to address the problem of buyers being reluctant to sign a written buyer agency agreement at the outset of their relationship with a buyer agent. The idea underlying this approach is to allow an agent to work temporarily with a prospective buyer as a buyer's agent under an oral agreement while the agent establishes a rapport with the buyer that makes the buyer feel more comfortable with signing a written buyer agency agreement.

Although the rule allows oral buyer/tenant agency agreements until the point in time when any party is ready to make an offer, it nevertheless is highly advisable that agents have such agreements reduced to writing and signed by the buyer/tenant at the earliest possible time in order to avoid misunderstanding and conflict between the buyer/ tenant and agent. Recall also that the agent must obtain a written buyer agency agreement from the buyer not later than the time either party to the transaction extends an offer to the other. If the buyer will not sign a written buyer agency agreement prior to making or receiving an offer, then the agent may not continue to work with the buyer as a buyer's agent. Moreover, the agent may not begin at this point to work with the buyer as a seller's subagent unless the agent (1) fully advises the buyer of the consequences of the agent switching from buyer's agent to seller's agent (including the fact that the agent would have to disclose to the seller any information, including "confidential" information about the buyer, that might influence the seller's decision in the transaction), (2) obtains the buyer's consent, and (3) obtains the consent of the seller and listing firm, which is the seller's agent.

Agency Disclosure Requirement: While Rule A.0104(a) requires all agency agreements, whether for lease or sales transactions, to be in writing, the *Rule A.0104(c) agency disclosure requirement applies only to sales transactions.* It requires licensees to provide prospective buyers and sellers, at "first substantial contact," with a copy of the *Working with Real Estate Agents* brochure, to review the brochure with them and then reach an agreement regarding their agency relationship. The licensee providing the brochure should also include his/her name and license number on the brochure. Note that the obligation under this rule is not satisfied merely by handing the prospective seller or buyer the brochure to read. The agent is required to review the contents of the brochure with the prospective buyer or seller and then reach agreement with the prospective buyer or seller as to whether the agent will work with the buyer or seller as his/her agent or as the agent of the other party. In the case of a prospective **seller**, the agent may either (1) act as the seller's agent, which is the typical situation and which requires a written agreement from the outset of their relationship, or (2) work with the seller as a buyer's agent if the agent already represents a prospective buyer. In the case of a prospective **buyer**, the agent may either (1) act as the buyer's agent under either an oral or written agreement as addressed in Rule A.0104(a), or (2) work with the buyer as a seller's agent, disclosure of which must be in writing from the outset.

Disclosure of Agency Status by Sellers' Agents and Subagents to Prospective Buyers: Paragraph (e) of Rule A.0104, like paragraph (c), requires a seller's agent or subagent in sales transactions to disclose his/her agency status in writing to a prospective buyer at the "first substantial contact" with the buyer. It is recommended that sellers' agents make this required written disclosure using the form provided for this purpose in the *Working with Real Estate Agents* brochure that must be provided to buyers (as well as to sellers) at first substantial contact. This form has a place for the buyer to acknowledge receipt of the brochure and disclosure of agency status, thereby providing the agent with written evidence of having provided the brochure and disclosure. The disclosure may, however, be made using a different form — the most important point is that the disclosure be made in writing in a timely manner. The reason for this requirement is that buyers tend to assume that an agent they contact to work with them in locating a property for purchase is "their" agent and working primarily in their interest. This may or may not be the case in reality. The purpose of the disclosure requirement is to place prospective buyers on notice that the agent they are dealing with is NOT "their" agent before the prospective buyer discloses to the agent information which the buyer would not want a seller to know because it might compromise the buyer's bargaining position.

Most frequently, **"first substantial contact"** will occur at the first "face-to-face" meeting with a prospective buyer. However, the point in time that "first substantial contact" with a prospective buyer occurs will vary depending on the particular situation and may or may not be at the time of the first or initial contact with the prospective buyer. Many first contacts are by telephone and do not involve discussions which reach the level that would require disclosure,

although some initial phone contacts, especially those with out-of-town buyers, could reach this level. *"First substantial contact" occurs at the point in time when a discussion with a prospective buyer begins to focus on the buyer's specific property needs and desires or on the buyer's financial situation.* Typically, that point in time is reached when the agent is ready to solicit information from the prospective buyer that is needed to identify prospective properties to show the buyer. Therefore, an agent planning to work with a prospective buyer as a seller's agent or subagent should assure that disclosure of his/her agency status is made in writing to the prospective buyer prior to obtaining from the prospective buyer any personal or confidential information that the buyer would not want a seller to know. A few examples of such personal or confidential information include: The maximum price a buyer is willing to pay for a property; the buyer's ability to pay more than the price offered by the buyer; or the fact that a buyer has a special interest in purchasing the seller's property rather than some other similar property. In any event, the disclosure must be made prior to discussing with the prospective buyer his/her specific needs or desires regarding the purchase of a property. As a practical matter, this means the *disclosure will always need to be made prior to showing a property to a prospective buyer.* The best policy is to simply make the disclosure at the earliest possible time.

If first substantial contact occurs by telephone or by means of other electronic communication where it is not practical to provide written disclosure, the agent shall immediately disclose by similar means whom he/she represents and shall immediately, but in no event later than three days from the date of first substantial contact, mail or otherwise transmit a copy of the written disclosure to the buyer.

Disclosure of Agency Status by Buyers' Agents to Sellers or Sellers' Agents: Paragraph (f) of Rule A.0104 requires a buyer's agent to disclose his/her agency status to a seller or seller's agent at the "initial contact" with the seller or seller's agent. "Initial contact" will typically occur when a buyer's agent telephones or otherwise contacts the listing firm to schedule a showing. The initial disclosure may be oral, but a written confirmation of the previous oral disclosure must be made (except in auction sale transactions) no later than the time of delivery of an offer to purchase. The written confirmation may be (and usually is) included in the offer to purchase. In fact, Commission Rule A.0112(a)(19) requires that any preprinted offer to purchase and contract form used by an agent include a provision providing for confirmation of agency status by each real estate agent (and firm) involved in the transaction.

Consent to Dual Agency: Paragraph (d) of Rule A.0104 requires generally that an agent must obtain the written authority of all parties prior to undertaking to represent those parties as a dual agent. It is important to note that this requirement applies to all real estate transactions (sales and lease/rentals), not just sales transactions. [In sales transactions, this written authority to act as a dual agent is usually limited to "in-house" sales transactions and is usually included in the listing and buyer agency contracts. If those contracts do not grant such authority, then the agent must have both the seller and buyer consent to the dual agency prior to beginning to act as a dual agent for both parties.]

Paragraph (d) of Rule A.0104 currently *requires written authority for dual agency from the formation of the relationship except situations where a buyer/tenant is represented by an agent working under an oral agency agreement as permitted by A.0104(a), in which case written authority for dual agency must be obtained no later than the time one of the parties represented by the agent working as a dual agent makes an offer to purchase, sell, rent, lease, or exchange real estate to the other party.* Thus, it is permissible for the agent to operate for a limited period of time under an oral dual agency agreement. It is very important to remember that G.S. 93A-6(a)(4) still requires agents to obtain the consent of all parties prior to beginning to act as a dual agent for those parties. Therefore, it is essential that agents electing to operate as a dual agent for a limited period of time without obtaining this authority in writing still explain fully the consequences of their acting as a dual agent and obtain the parties' oral consent.

As a practical matter in sales transactions, agents will frequently have already obtained written authority to act as a dual agent for in-house sales transactions at the time the initial written listing or buyer agency agreement is executed. However, under Paragraph (a) of Rule A.0104, many buyer's agents may elect to work with their buyer clients for a period of time under an oral buyer agency agreement. Paragraph (d) permits such buyer's agents to also operate for a limited period of time as a dual agent under an oral agreement in order to deal with situations where a buyer client is interested in a property listed with the agent's firm. Note that, although an oral dual agency agreement for a limited period of time is permitted by Commission rules, it is strongly recommended that agents have any dual agency agreement in writing from the outset of the dual agency arrangement. This will provide the agent with some evidence that the matter of dual agency was discussed with the parties and that they consented to it. Such evidence could prove quite useful if a party later asserts that the agent did not obtain their consent for dual agency in a timely manner.

Auction Sales: Paragraph (g) of Rule A.0104 provides that the provisions of Paragraphs (c), (d) and (e) of the Rule shall not apply to real estate licensees representing sellers in auction sales transactions. Note that in auction sales, the real estate agents involved almost invariably work only as seller's agents and this fact is considered to be self-evident. Thus, there is no need for agents to distribute and review the *Working with Real Estate Agents* brochure, no need for disclosure of agency status by the seller's agents, and no dual agency. For the unusual situation where a buyer may be represented by an agent in an auction sale transaction, Paragraph (h) of Rule A.0104 provides that such a buyer's agent shall, no later than the time of execution of a written agree-ment memorializing the buyer's contract to purchase, provide the seller or seller's agent with a written confirmation that he/she represents the buyer.

Dual Agency Status of Firm: Paragraph (i) of Rule A.0104 codifies in the Commission's rules the common law rule that a firm which represents more than one party in the same real estate sales transaction is a dual agent, and further states that the firm, through the brokers and salespersons affiliated with the firm, shall disclose its dual agency to the parties. This rule provision does not establish any additional requirement for licensees and is intended merely to clarify that the Commission follows the common law rule. In other words, dual agency is not limited to those situations where an individual agent is working with both a buyer client and seller client (or lessor and commercial tenant) in the same transaction. If one agent of a firm is working with a buyer client of the firm and another agent of the same firm is working with a seller client of the firm in a transaction involving the sale of the seller client's property to the buyer client, then the firm is a dual agent (as it also holds the agency agreements). However, a firm functions through its employees, namely, its associated agents; thus, under the common law, whenever the firm is a dual agent of certain parties in a transaction, all licensees affiliated with that firm are also dual agents of those parties in that transaction.

Designated Agency: Paragraphs (j) - (m) of Rule A.0104 authorize real estate firms to engage in a form of dual agency practice referred to in the rule as "designated agency" in certain sales transactions involving in-house dual agency. *"Designated agency" is an optional method of practicing dual agency that may be adopted by a real estate firm if the firm establishes a policy consistent with the Commission's designated agency rules. Designated agency involves appointing or "designating" an individual agent(s) in a firm to represent only the interests of the seller and another individual agent(s) to represent only the interests of the buyer when a firm has an in-house dual agency situation.*

The principal advantage of the designated agency approach over the "standard" dual agency approach is that each of a firm's clients (seller and buyer) receive fuller representation by their designated agent. In the typical dual agency situation, client advocacy is essentially lost because the dual agent may not seek an advantage for (i.e, "advocate" for) one client to the detriment of the other client. The dual agent must remain completely neutral and impartial at all times. Designated agency returns "advocacy" to the services provided by the respective designated agents and allows them to more fully represent their respective clients.

Authority to practice designated agency must be in writing no later than the time a written dual agency agreement is required under A.0104(d). Additional required procedures for practicing designated agency are clearly spelled out in Paragraphs (j) - (m) and are not discussed further here. For more detailed coverage of dual and designated agency, the reader is once again referred to the Commission's *North Carolina Real Estate Manual.*

Dual Agency by Individual Agent: Paragraph (n) of Rule A.0104 authorizes individual agents representing both the buyer and seller in the same real estate sales transaction pursuant to a written dual agency agreement to include in the agreement a provision authorizing the agent not to disclose certain "confidential" information about one party to the other party without permission from the party about whom the information pertains. This provision is intended to allow individual dual agents to treat confidential information about their clients in a manner similar to that allowed for firms practicing designated agency.

Advertising [Rule A.0105]

The rule prohibits any advertisement by a licensee that indicates an offer to sell, buy, exchange, rent or lease real property is being made by the licensee's principal without the involvement of a broker – i.e., a **"blind ad."** All advertising by a licensee must indicate that it is the advertisement of a broker or brokerage firm. The rule prohibits a provisional broker from advertising "without the consent of his or her broker-in-charge" and requires that any such advertisement include the name of the broker or firm with which the provisional broker is associated. The rule further requires that brokers obtain the consent of a property owner to display a "for sale" or "for rent" sign on the owner's property.

Licensees may not advertise under an **assumed name** without registering the assumed name with the applicable County Register of Deeds office in accordance with the requirements of G.S. 66-68 and notifying the Commission of such assumed name. For individuals and partnerships, a name is "assumed" when it does not include the surname of the licensee(s). For a firm required to be registered with the Secretary of State and licensed by the Commission, a name is "assumed" when it is different from the firm's registered and licensed name.

A licensee operating as a sole proprietorship, partnership or non-corporate business entity may NOT include in its name the name of an unlicensed person or a provisional broker.

Delivery of Instruments [G.S. 93A-6(a)(13) and (14); Rules A.0106 and A.0107(c)]

Among other things, this rule requires agents to "immediately, but in no event later than five days from the date of execution, deliver to the parties thereto copies of any ... offer..." [Emphasis added.] This does NOT mean that agents may in every case wait up to five days to present an offer to a seller. Rather, it means that an agent must immediately, as soon as possible, present to the seller any offer received by the agent. If the agent is the "selling agent," then the offer should be immediately presented to the "listing agent" who should, in turn, immediately present the offer to the seller. The "five day" provision is included only to allow for situations where the seller is not immediately available (e.g., seller is out of town), and represents an outside time limit within which offers must always be presented. In all cases where the seller is available, the offer should be presented as soon as possible.

The same rule also means that a prospective buyer who signs an offer must immediately be provided a copy of such offer. (A photocopy is acceptable for this purpose.) Do NOT wait until after the offer is accepted (or rejected) by the seller.

In addition, this rule means that an offer must be immediately presented to a seller even if there is a contract pending on the property. Of course, in this instance, it is essential that the agent also advise the seller that serious legal problems could result from the seller's acceptance of such offer and that the seller should contact an attorney if he is interested in treating the offer as a "back-up" offer or in attempting to be released from the previously signed contract.

Retention of Records [Rule A.0108]

Licensees are required to retain documents pertaining to their brokerage transactions for three years from the successful or unsuccessful conclusion of the transaction or the disbursement of all trust monies pertaining to that transaction, whichever occurs later. Documents that must be retained include sale contracts, leases, offers (even those not accepted), agency contracts, earnest money receipts, trust account records, disclosure documents, closing statements, broker cooperation agreements, and any other records relating to a transaction.

Brokerage Fees and Compensation [Rule A.0109]

This rule addresses various issues associated with the disclosure of and sharing of compensation received by a real estate licensee.

Disclosure to principal of compensation from a vendor or supplier of goods or services. Paragraph (a) prohibits a licensee from receiving any form of valuable consideration from a vendor or supplier of goods or services in connection with an expenditure made on behalf of the licensee's principal in a real estate transaction without first obtaining the written consent of the principal.

> **Example:** A broker manages several rental units for various owners and routinely employs Ajax Cleaning Service to clean the units after the tenants leave. The broker pays Ajax a $50 per unit fee for its services out of rental proceeds received and deposited in his trust account. Ajax then "refunds" to the broker $10 for each $50 fee it receives, but the property owners are not aware that the broker receives this payment from Ajax in addition to his regular brokerage fee. The broker in this situation is making a secret profit without the property owners' knowledge and is violating the rule.

Disclosure to a party of compensation for recommending, procuring or arranging services for the party. Paragraph (b) prohibits a licensee from receiving any form of valuable consideration for recommending, procuring, or arranging services for a party to a real estate transaction without full and timely disclosure to such party. The party for whom the services are recommended, procured, or arranged does not have to be the agent's principal.

Example: An agent sells a listed lot to a buyer who wants to build a house on the lot. Without the buyer's knowledge, the agent arranges with ABC Homebuilders for ABC to pay the agent a 3% referral fee if the agent recommends ABC to the buyer and the buyer employs ABC to build his house. The agent then recommends ABC to the buyer, ABC builds the buyer's house for $100,000 and ABC secretly pays the agent $3,000 for his referral of the buyer. The agent has violated this rule. (Note that the buyer in this situation likely paid $3,000 more for his house than was necessary because it is very likely the builder added the agent's referral fee to the price he charged the buyer for building the house. The main point here is that the buyer had the right to know that the agent was not providing disinterested advice when recommending the builder.)

Example: A selling agent in a real estate transaction, while acting as a subagent of the seller, recommends to a buyer who has submitted an offer that the buyer apply to Ready Cash Mortgage Company for his mortgage loan. The agent knows that Ready Cash will pay him a "referral fee" of $100 for sending him the buyer's business if the loan is made to the buyer, but the agent does not disclose this fact to the buyer. If the agent subsequently accepts the referral fee from the lender, he will have violated this rule. (The buyer has the right to know that the agent's recommendation is not a disinterested one.)

Disclosure to principal of compensation for brokerage services in sales transactions. Paragraphs (c) and (d) deal with disclosure to a licensee's principal of the licensee's compensation in a **sales** transaction from various sources other than in situations addressed in paragraphs (a) and (b). A broker may not receive any compensation, incentive, bonus, rebate or other consideration of more than nominal value (1) from his or her principal unless the compensation, etc. is provided for in a written agency contract or (2) from any other party or person unless the broker provides a full and timely disclosure of the compensation, etc., including any promise or expectation of compensation, to the broker's principal. The disclosure is "timely" when it is made in sufficient time to aid a reasonable person's decision-making. The disclosure may by made orally, but must be confirmed in writing before the principal makes or accepts an offer to buy or sell.

Example: ABC Homebuilders offers to pay any broker who procures a buyer for one of ABC's inventory homes a **bonus** of $1,000 that is in addition to any brokerage commission the broker earns under any agency contract and/or commission split agreements. Any broker working with a buyer-client who is considering the purchase of one of ABC's homes must comply with the disclosure requirement and disclose the bonus to the buyer in a timely manner. **Note:**

If ABC Homebuilders also offers a bonus of $2,000 on a second sale of one of its homes and $3,000 on a third sale, and if a buyer's broker has already sold one of ABC's homes, then the broker must disclose to his or her buyer principal the entire bonus program and that his or her bonus will be at least $2,000 if the buyer purchases an ABC home.

Compensation is considered to be "nominal" if it is of insignificant, token or merely symbolic worth. The Commission has cited gifts of a $25 bottle of wine or a $50 dinner gift certificate as being examples of "nominal" compensation.

Restrictions on compensation disclosure requirement. Paragraph (e) clarifies that a broker does NOT have to disclose to a person who is not his or her principal the compensation the broker expects to receive from his or her principal, and further clarifies that a broker does NOT have to disclose to his principal the compensation the broker expects to receive from the broker's employing broker.

Commission will not arbitrate commission disputes. G.S 93A-3(c) provides that the Commission shall not make rules or regulations regulating commission, salaries, or fees to be charged by licensees. Paragraph (f) of Rule A.0109 augments that statutory provision by providing that the Commission will not act as a board of arbitration regarding such matters as the rate of commissions, the division of commissions, pay of brokers and similar matters.

Compensation of unlicensed persons by brokers prohibited. G.S. 93A-6(a)(9) authorizes the Commission to take disciplinary action against a licensee for paying any person for acts performed in violation of the License Law. Paragraph (g) of Rule A.0109 simply augments this statutory provision by providing an affirmative statement that a licensee shall not in any manner compensate or share compensation with unlicensed persons or entities for acts performed in North Carolina for which a license is required. [Note that NC brokers may split commissions or pay referral fees to licensees of another state so long as the out-of-state licensee does not provide any brokerage services while physically in North Carolina.] One narrow, limited exception to this restriction is provided in Paragraph (h) – licensees may pay referral fees to travel agents who contact them to book vacation rentals only, so long as well-defined procedures are followed.

RESPA prohibitions control. Finally, Paragraph (i) of Rule A.0109 provides that nothing in this rule permits a licensee to accept any fee, kickback, etc. that is prohibited by the federal Real Estate Settlement Procedures Act (RESPA) or implementing rules, or to fail to make any disclosure required by that act or rules.

Broker-In-Charge [Rule A.0110].

Requirement for a Broker-In-Charge. Paragraph (a) of Rule A.0110 requires that each real estate firm designate a broker who meets the qualification requirements to serve as **"broker-in-charge"** of the firm's principal office and a different broker to serve in the same capacity at each branch office. It is important to note, as discussed previously under "License Requirement," that **"broker-in-charge"** *is not a separate license, but only a separate license status category.*

This rule specifies that the "qualifying broker" of each real estate firm is responsible for assuring that a qualified broker is designated as broker-in-charge for the firm's principal office and each branch office where the firm conducts brokerage business. The broker who is to serve as broker-in-charge of an office is responsible for officially designating himself or herself with the Commission as the broker-in-charge of that office.

Sole Proprietors. In addition to each firm having to have a broker-in-charge for each office, *most broker-sole proprietors (including sole practitioners) also must be a broker-in-charge.*

Commission Rule A.0110 (a) provides that a broker who is a **sole proprietor** shall designate himself or herself as a broker-in-charge if the broker: (1) engages in any transaction where the broker is required to deposit and maintain monies belonging to others in a trust account; (2) engages in advertising or promoting his or her services as a broker in any manner; OR (3) has one or more other brokers affiliated with him or her in the real estate business. A 2009 rule revision provided that maintenance of a trust account by a broker solely for holding residential tenant security deposits received by the broker on properties owned by the broker in compliance with G.S. 42-50 shall not, standing alone, subject the broker to the requirement to designate himself or herself as a broker-in-charge.

The most misunderstood of the three broker-in-charge triggering requirements for sole proprietors cited above is # (2): "...*engages in advertising or promoting his or her services as a broker in any manner.*" Acts of a sole proprietor that trigger the BIC requirement under # (2) include, but are not limited to: Placing an advertisement for his or her services as a broker in any form or any medium; distributing business cards indicating he or she is a real estate broker; orally soliciting the real estate business of others; or listing a property for sale (which inherently involves holding oneself out as a broker and advertising).

Therefore, *a broker-sole proprietor may lawfully provide only limited brokerage services without designating himself or herself as a BIC.* A couple of examples of *permissible* brokerage activities by a broker-sole proprietor who is NOT a designated BIC include receiving a referral fee from another broker or brokerage firm for referring business to the broker or firm or representing a relative or friend as a buyer's broker in a sales transaction provided the broker has not solicited the business, has not advertised or promoted his or her services, and does not hold earnest money beyond the time it is required to be deposited in a trust account.

The practical effect of these requirements is that a broker who will be operating independently in most cases must also designate himself or herself as a BIC. The real significance of these requirements for a sole proprietor will be better understood when the qualification requirements to serve as a BIC are subsequently discussed.

Broker-In-Charge Duties. The broker-in-charge is the person the Commission will hold responsible for the supervision and management of an office. The specific responsibilities of a broker-in-charge are enumerated in Paragraph (a) of Rule A.0110 and are not repeated here.

Requirements to Serve as Broker-In-Charge (BIC). Paragraph (c) of this rule provides that the qualifying requirements to serve as a broker-in-charge are:

- Broker license must be on "active" status but NOT on "provisional" status. A "provisional broker" is ineligible to serve as a broker-in-charge, as is an "inactive" broker.

- Broker must have at least *two (2) years full-time (or part-time equivalent) real estate brokerage experience within the preceding five (5) years, or qualifications the Commission finds equivalent to such experience.* The requirement is for *actual brokerage experience, not just having a license on "active" status.* Note that by submission of a broker-in-charge declaration to the Commission, a broker certifies that he or she possesses the required experience. The Commission may at its discretion require the broker to provide evidence of possessing the required experience. It is possible for some brokers with exceptional "equivalent" qualifications other than brokerage experience (for example, several years of experience as a real estate attorney or new homes sales representative) to obtain a full waiver of the qualifying experience requirement. Others may be able to obtain a **partial** waiver based on *substantial* non-brokerage direct experience in real estate transactions or substantial brokerage experience that is more than five years old. Experience waivers must be specially requested in accordance with guidelines available upon request from the Commission.

- After designation as a broker-in-charge, a broker must complete the Commission's 12-hour **Broker-In-Charge Course** within 120 days of designation (unless the 12-hour course has been taken within the previous three years). Failure to complete this course within 120 days will result in the BIC being removed as BIC. The broker must then take the course before he or she may again be designated as a BIC.

Retaining Broker-In-Charge Eligibility. A newly designated broker-in-charge who completes the Broker-In-Charge Course within the prescribed time period acquires the eligibility to be re-designated as a broker-in-charge at any time in the future after a period of not actively serving as a broker-in-charge without having to again satisfy the qualification requirements for initial designation so long as the broker continuously satisfies the requirements to retain such eligibility. To retain eligibility to serve as a broker-in-charge, Paragraph (e) of Rule A.0110 provides that a BIC must:

- Renew his or her broker license in a timely manner each license year and keep the license on active status at all times.
- Complete each license year the four-hour mandatory CE update course known as the *Real Estate Update Course* and also the four-hour special mandatory CE course for brokers-in-charge known as the *Broker-In-Charge Annual Review (BICAR) Course*. The *BICAR Course* must be taken initially during the first full license year following designation as a broker-in-charge and each license period thereafter. The *BICAR Course* satisfies the broker's general CE elective course requirement. Note that this special CE requirement for BICs means that a BIC does not have a CE elective option after the first renewal of his or her license following BIC designation. If a broker-in-charge fails to take the BICAR Course in any given year in which it is required, then the broker will be removed as broker-in-charge the following July 1.

Termination of Broker-In-Charge Eligibility. Paragraph (f) of Rule A.0110 provides that a broker's BIC eligibility and, if currently designated as a BIC, his or her BIC designation, shall be terminated upon the occurrence of any of the following events:

License **expiration** (licensee fails to renew license annually by June 30), suspension, revocation or surrender.

License made **inactive** for any reason, *including the failure to complete all CE required for BICs.*

Broker is found by the Commission to have not possessed the required qualifying experience at the time of either initial designation or re-designation as a BIC.

The reader is referred to Paragraph (f) for the requirements to regain BIC eligibility and be redesignated as a BIC after losing BIC eligibility for any of the above reasons.

Notice to Commission. A BIC must notify the Commission in writing within 10 days upon ceasing to serve as BIC of a particular office. [See Paragraph (g).]

Exception for certain Subchapter S corporations. See Paragraph (h).

Nonresidents. Nonresident individuals and firms holding a NC broker and/or firm license and *engaging in brokerage activity in NC* are subject to the same requirements as NC resident brokers/firms with regard to when they must designate themselves as a NC broker-in-charge. Thus, a nonresident firm engaging in brokerage in NC must designate a NC broker as broker-in-charge of the firm for purposes of its NC business. Similarly, a nonresident NC broker sole practitioner engaging in activity that triggers broker-in-charge designation for a resident NC broker sole practitioner (see previous discussion on this subject) also must designate himself or herself as a NC broker-in-charge.

Education Exception for Certain Nonresident NC Brokers-In-Charge: A nonresident NC broker who has designated himself or herself as the broker-in-charge of an office NOT located in NC (and who does not operate an office in NC) is NOT required to complete the 12-hour Broker-In-Charge Course and is NOT required to complete the Broker-In-Charge Annual Review Course. [See Paragraph (i).]

Drafting Legal Instruments [Rule A.0111]

This rule prohibits licensees from drafting legal instruments, e.g., contracts, deeds, deeds of trust, etc., but does allow them to fill in the blanks on preprinted sales contract forms, which is not construed to be the unauthorized practice of law.

Offers and Sales Contracts [Rule A.0112]

This rule specifies what minimum terms must be contained in any preprinted offer or sales contract form a licensee, acting as an agent, proposes for use by a party in a real estate transaction.

Reporting Criminal Convictions [Rule A.0113]

Licensees are required to report to the Commission any criminal convictions, any disciplinary action taken against them by any other occupational licensing board, or any restriction, suspension or revocation of a notarial commission within sixty (60) days of the final judgment or order in the case. This reporting requirement is ongoing in nature.

Residential Property Disclosure Statement [Rule A.0114]

State law (Chapter 47E of the General Statutes) requires that most residential property owners complete a disclosure form to give to prospective purchasers. The form seeks to elicit information about the condition of the property by asking various questions, to which owners may answer "yes," "no," or "no representation." Failure to provide a buyer with this form may allow the buyer to cancel the contract by notifying the seller in writing within three calendar days of contract acceptance.

Note: Licensees in residential real estate transactions have a duty under G.S. 47E-8 to inform their clients of the client's rights and obligations under the statute. The Real Estate Commission also views the Real Estate License Law as imposing on licensees working with sellers and buyers certain additional responsibilities to assure statutory compliance and serve their clients' interests. See the Commission's *North Carolina Real Estate Manual* for a full discussion of the disclosure law and an agent's duties.

HANDLING TRUST FUNDS

See the "Trust Account Guidelines" contained in this booklet for complete coverage of this important topic. Licensees and applicants should have a thorough knowledge and understanding of the "Trust Account Guidelines."

■ KEY POINT REVIEW

Types of Real Estate Licenses	■ **Broker** [93A-4.(a)] ■ **Broker on Provisional Status** (Called a PB) [93A-4.(a1)] ■ **Firm License** unless acting as a sole proprietor [A.0502] ■ **Limited Nonresident Commercial** [A.1800]
Activities Requiring a License [93A-2(a)]	■ List, lease, buy, exchange, auction, negotiate, sell for others for compensation
Exceptions to Licensure [93A-2(c)]	■ Activities done by business entity property owners ■ Acting under a power of attorney ■ Attorney ■ Person acting under court order ■ Acting as a trustee ■ Salaried employee of broker property manager—if they do not negotiate ■ For sale/lease by owner ■ Housing authority employees

License Status	■ **Current:** paid annual renewal fee (currently $40) by June 30; can renew online; must renew even if on inactive status
	■ **Expired:** did not pay annual renewal by June 30
	■ **Active:** [A.0504] must be current, plus have completed all required post-licensing and continuing education, plus all provisional brokers and most brokers must be supervised by a BIC
	■ **Inactive:** [A.0504] must be current, plus at least one of the following situations
	   — Provisional broker did not affiliate with supervising BIC
	   — Did not complete eight hours of continuing education before June 10
	   — Did not complete the first or second post-licensing course by first or second license anniversary date
	   — Chose to remain or be placed on inactive status
	■ **Canceled:** [A.1902(c)] Did not complete all three post-licensing courses by third license anniversary date

Education Requirements	■ **Pre-licensing**
	   — 75-hour course with end of course exam
	   — No residency requirement; at least 18 years of age
	   — Prerequisite for state licensing exam
	■ **Post-licensing** [A.1902]
	   — Three 30-hour courses, each with an end of course exam
	   — PB must take minimum of one course per year to remain active
	   — Must take all three courses by third license anniversary date or license is canceled, even if on inactive status
	   — Does not count toward Continuing Education requirement
	■ **Continuing Education (CE)** [A.1700]
	   — Must complete eight hours annually to remain active; can take CE while inactive but not required
	   — The eight CE hours consists of the current year's four-hour Mandatory Update Course and a NCREC-approved four-hour Elective course
	   — Must be completed by midnight on June 10

— CE is required prior to second license renewal and every active renewal afterwards
— Must make up any CE deficiency before activation; maximum hours required to be made up is 16 hours
— Credit for one four-hour elective course can be carried over to the next year
— Nonresident licensee with an active license in their resident jurisdiction is not required to take NC-specific CE to maintain their NC license
— Nonresident licensee must take CE if they have an address (business or delivery) in North Carolina

Activation of License

- Correct any educational deficiency in either CE or post-licensing
- Affiliate with a supervising BIC
- File a license activation form with the NCREC

Reinstatement of Expired (Canceled, Revoked, or Surrendered) License [A.0505]

- **Expired 6 months or less**
  — Pay $55 reinstatement fee by December 31
  — No license application necessary
  — Correct any educational deficit if wish to be on active status
- **Expired more than 6 months or canceled, revoked, or surrendered for any period of time**
  — Submit complete license application including criminal record report
  — Pay $55 reinstatement fee
  — Satisfy character requirement
  — Prove current knowledge of and competence in real estate brokerage (See following section)
- **Demonstration of Current Knowledge for former Brokers (Non-Provisional)**
  — **Expired more than 6 months but no more than 2 years (or revoked or surrendered for 2 years or less)**
    - Complete any one of the 30-hour post-licensing courses successfully within 6 months of application; OR
    - Pass current licensing exam; OR
    - Possess an active broker license in another state
  — **More than 2 years but no more than 5 years**
    - Complete all three post-licensing courses successfully within 3 years prior to application; OR
    - Pass current licensing exam; OR
    - Possess an active broker license in another state
  — **More than 5 years**
    - Start over in pre-licensing as if never licensed
- **Demonstration of Current Knowledge for former Provisional Brokers and Salespersons**
  — **Expired more than 6 months but no more than 5 years (or revoked or surrendered for 5 years or less)**
    - To be reinstated as a Non-Provisional Broker, complete successfully any of the three post-licensing courses not taken within three years prior to filing for reinstatement; OR

■ To be reinstated as a Provisional Broker, meet all the requirements for original licensure.

— **More than 5 years**

■ Start over in pre-licensing as if never licensed

Broker-in-Charge [A.0110]

■ **General Requirements**
— A BIC is required in each real estate firm and in each branch office
— Can be BIC of only one physical location
— Only one BIC per location
— Sole proprietor brokers can be BIC of themselves
— Not a different license—a designation

■ **Eligibility Requirements**
— Full broker
— At least two years of full-time real estate brokerage experience within the last five years OR equivalent experience.
— Complete the BIC course within three years prior to or within 120 days after designation as BIC
— Complete the Broker-in-Charge Annual Review (BICAR) annually as part of the eight-hour CE requirement in conjunction with the Update Course
— Maintain active status

■ **Responsibilities**
— Retention and display of all current renewal pocket cards of all brokers in the firm
— Proper notification of NCREC of changes in firm information
— Proper conduct in all advertisement affiliated with firm
— Proper maintenance of trust account and associated records
— Proper retention of all agency and transactional records
— Proper supervision of all provisional brokers associated with firm
— Supervision of all licensees associated with firm in regard compliance with agency agreements and disclosures

Trust Accounts [A.0107]

■ **General rules**
— Must be created with an insured bank or savings association physically located in North Carolina
— Checks and deposit slips must be pre-printed with the words "Trust Account" or "Escrow Account"
— Must be a separate account that only holds trust funds; no illegal commingling
— Can have up to $100 of firm's money in the trust account to cover payment of bank's service charges—not considered commingling
— Can be interest-bearing if
  ■ written permission is secured from all parties with funds in the account;
  ■ how and to whom interest will be dispersed is clearly specified;
  ■ permission contained in a transactional document must stand out so as to draw attention (i.e., bold, italics, etc.) to the information
— Firms that are entitled to receive the interest from an interest-bearing trust account must remove that earned interest within 30 days to avoid illegal commingling.
— Firms are only required to have one trust account.

— The only requirement to have multiple trust accounts is the requirement for a separate trust account for each property owner association managed.

■ **Handling of Trust Money**

— Earnest money deposit and tenant security deposit paid in the form of a check must be deposited not later than three banking days following acceptance of the offer to purchase or lease.

— Cash deposits must be deposited not later than three banking days following receipt of such deposits.

— Rents, settlement proceeds, or other trust money must be deposited not later than three banking days of receipt of the funds.

— Check or other negotiable instrument made payable to the seller of real property as option money is not required to be deposited in a trust account. Check should be handled according to the instructions of the buyer-optionee. After acceptance of the option contract, the licensee has three business days to deliver the check to the seller. In the event of a dispute between seller-optionor and the buyer-optionee over option money, handle the money according to the buyer's instructions. Option money in the form of cash must be deposited into a trust account within three banking days of receipt; and must be disbursed not later than three business days following the acceptance of the option contract.

— Provisional brokers must be immediately delivered to their BIC.

— Trust monies held as part of a sales transaction can be disbursed to the settlement agent not more than 10 days prior to the anticipated closing date.

— All monies earned by the firm that are in the trust account (i.e., interest earned, earnest money deposit that converted to commission) must be disbursed within 30 days.

— Licensee must keep **Disputed Funds** in trust account until

■ Obtain written release from the parties agreeing to disposition;

■ Disposition is ordered by a court of competent jurisdiction; or

■ Parties claiming ownership to the funds have been notified by written notice 90 days prior to depositing the funds with the Clerk of Court in the county where the property for the disputed funds are being held is located.

QUESTIONS

1. The North Carolina Real Estate Commission may, after a hearing, take disciplinary action against a North Carolina licensee who has
   I. violated any of the provisions of the North Carolina license law.
   II. been disciplined by the South Carolina Real Estate Commission.
   a. I only
   b. II only
   c. Both I and II
   d. Neither I nor II

2. A person needs an active North Carolina real estate license to rent and manage rental apartments for
   a. himself or herself.
   b. an out-of-state friend for no compensation.
   c. a corporation as part of a salaried corporate job.
   d. a relative that pays $100 per month for the help.

3. A real estate license must be renewed no later than every
   a. June 30.
   b. anniversary of licensure.
   c. June 10.
   d. December 31.

4. A licensee's North Carolina real estate license may be suspended or revoked for
   a. sharing commission with the buyer-client.
   b. advertising properties in multiple counties.
   c. buying a property for personal use that is listed by the licensee's firm.
   d. placing a For Sale sign on a property without a signed listing agreement.

5. All the following people need an active North Carolina real estate license EXCEPT
   a. a court-ordered guardian selling property owned by his charge.
   b. an attorney that serves as a relief agent on Thursdays in a new homes subdivision.
   c. a real estate assistant showing listed property to the buyer-clients of her broker-boss.
   d. an on-site leasing agent that negotiates rental amounts when requested by potential tenants.

6. If a licensee violates any of the provisions of the North Carolina Real Estate License Law, the North Carolina Real Estate Commission may do all the following EXCEPT
   a. revoke the license permanently.
   b. suspend the license for a specified period of time.
   c. allow the license to remain active if a specified fine is paid.
   d. require the licensee to take prescribed education courses before reinstatement of the license.

7. Which statement is TRUE regarding a broker license on provisional status?
   a. The licensee must satisfy a 90-hour postlicensing requirement in order to retain a real estate license.
   b. The provisional broker license is converted to a broker-in-charge license upon completion of postlicensing requirements.
   c. The licensee must complete at least one postlicensing course no later than one year from licensure in order to avoid cancellation of license.
   d. The provisional license status may be retained indefinitely if the license is never activated.

8. In North Carolina, all real estate brokers must

   a. maintain a trust account.
   b. belong to the local Board of REALTORS®.
   c. include their firm's name in advertisements of a client's property.
   d. complete continuing education each year in order to keep the license current.

9. An active nonprovisional real estate broker in North Carolina may

   a. prepare deeds for seller-clients.
   b. may interpret protective covenants for a buyer-client.
   c. place an ad today for a listing that she anticipates getting next week.
   d. split the commission with a buyer-client if it is disclosed to the lender and noted on the HUD-1.

10. According to the North Carolina Time Share Act, a certificate of registration for each time-share project must

    I. be obtained from the North Carolina Real Estate Commission.
    II. must be renewed every June.
       a. I only
       b. II only
       c. Both I and II
       d. Neither I nor II

11. According to the North Carolina Time Share Act, all the following are true *EXCEPT*

    a. a time-share salesperson must have an active real estate broker's license.
    b. a time-share salesperson must provide a public offering statement about the time-share project to a potential buyer prior to showing or sharing project information.
    c. a time-share purchaser must be given a five-day cancellation right after contract formation.
    d. a time-share purchaser that properly exercises the rescission rights under the Act will receive a refund of all monies paid to the developer or his agent.

12. All North Carolina real estate licensees are legally bound by the

    a. REALTORS® Code of Ethics.
    b. North Carolina Real Estate License Law.
    c. Both a and b.
    d. Neither a nor b.

13. An offer to purchase and contract form offered for use by a real estate broker

    I. must not include a disclaimer of liability on the part of the broker.
    II. can include any agent compensation that is being split with the buyer in the contract.
       a. I only
       b. II only
       c. Both I and II
       d. Neither I nor II

14. Appointments to the North Carolina Real Estate Commission are made

    I. by the Governor, the President Pro Tempore of the State Senate, and the Speaker of the State House of Representatives.
    II. for three-year staggered terms.
       a. I only
       b. II only
       c. Both I and II
       d. Neither I nor II

15. The members of the North Carolina Real Estate Commission

    I. must include at least three licensed real estate brokers.
    II. form an arbitration appeal board for licensees dealing with compensation disputes.
       a. I only
       b. II only
       c. Both I and II
       d. Neither I nor II

16. Each time-share developer must deposit all money received from purchasers in

    a. the developer's business account immediately on receipt.
    b. an escrow account for ten days.
    c. both accounts mentioned in a and b.
    d. neither account mentioned in a nor b.

17. In North Carolina, a real estate licensee's license expires if

    a. continuing education requirements are not met by June 10.
    b. renewal fees are not received by the North Carolina Real Estate Commission by June 30.
    c. postlicensing requirements have not been met by the license anniversary date.
    d. the licensee is no longer supervised by a broker-in-charge.

18. In North Carolina, a written complaint against a licensee should be sent to the

    a. Governor.
    b. Director of Commerce.
    c. Superintendent.
    d. North Carolina Real Estate Commission.

19. A property manager broker must deposit all rents collected for others into a trust account

    a. within three banking days after receipt.
    b. that cannot be an interest-bearing account.
    c. unless directed otherwise by a party to the transaction.
    d. that is reconciled on a quarterly basis.

20. All agency agreements for property owners

    a. may be oral for some period of time.
    b. must have a definite termination date.
    c. can automatically renew.
    d. must only allow exclusive representation.

21. Earnest money deposits other than cash must be deposited into the broker's trust account

    a. within 24 hours of their receipt.
    b. only if the seller authorizes the broker to do so.
    c. no later than three banking days following contract acceptance.
    d. no later than three banking days after their receipt.

22. All written agency agreements are required by licensing law to

    a. contain a nondiscrimination provision.
    b. describe the agent's duties and list the authorizations given by the client.
    c. include the individual broker's license number.
    d. All the above.

23. Which of the following statements is NOT true?

    a. A broker's trust account must be a separate custodial account.
    b. A property management trust account must provide for withdrawal on demand.
    c. All trust account funds must be located in an insured bank or savings association in North Carolina.
    d. Brokers responsible for property management accounts, in addition to a trust account, must be bonded as required by Commission Rule.

24. A broker has authorized his bookkeeper to withdraw funds from his trust account. The bookkeeper embezzles an amount equal to less than 10 percent of the total balance of the trust account. Which of the following statements is TRUE?

    a. Only the bookkeeper is liable for the misuse of the funds, because the broker delegated this responsibility.
    b. The broker is always responsible for the misuse of trust funds for which he maintains or is required to maintain custody.
    c. Only the bookkeeper is liable for the misuse of the funds, because the loss was for less than 10 percent of the entire balance.
    d. The Commission will issue a letter to the owner of the trust funds, explaining the problem, and relieving the broker of responsibility.

25. A broker-in-charge must have

    a. an active nonprovisional broker's license.
    b. a minimum of three years' full-time real estate brokerage experience.
    c. a bonded bookkeeper.
    d. a trust account for each office he supervises.

26. A broker-in-charge is responsible for all the following EXCEPT

    a. retention and maintenance of all records required by Commission Rule.
    b. all advertising by or on behalf of the firm.
    c. agency compliance by all licensees in the firm.
    d. supervision of all provisional brokers in the principal office and any branch offices.

North Carolina Real Estate Forms

The forms in this appendix are ordered as one might encounter them in a residential sales transaction, followed by property management forms.

EXCLUSIVE RIGHT TO SELL LISTING AGREEMENT

This EXCLUSIVE RIGHT TO SELL LISTING AGREEMENT ("Agreement") is entered into (Date)_____, between_____as Seller(s) ("Seller") of the property described below (the "Property"), and_____ as Listing Firm ("Firm"). The individual agent who signs this Agreement shall, on behalf of the Firm, be primarily responsible for ensuring that the Firm's duties hereunder are fulfilled; however, it is understood and agreed that other agents of the Firm may be assigned to fulfill such duties if deemed appropriate by the Firm. For purposes of this Agreement, the term "Firm," as the context may require, shall be deemed to include the individual agent who signs this Agreement and any other agents of the Firm.

1. **REAL PROPERTY.** The real property that is the subject of this Agreement is located in _____County, North Carolina, and is known more particularly and described as:
Address: Street_____ City_____ Zip_____
Legal Description_____
Subdivision Name:_____
Plat Reference: Lot_____, Block or Section _____ as shown on
Plat Book or Slide _____ at Page(s) _____ (Property acquired by Seller in Deed Book _____ at Page _____).

2. **FIXTURES.** The following items, if any, and if owned by the Seller, are included free of liens: any built-in appliances, light fixtures, ceiling fans, attached floor coverings, blinds, shades, drapery rods and curtain rods, brackets and all related hardware, window and door screens, storm windows, combination doors, awnings, antennas, satellite dishes and receivers, burglar/fire/smoke alarms, pool and spa equipment, solar energy systems, attached fireplace screens, gas logs, fireplace inserts, electric garage door openers with controls, outdoor plants and trees (other than in movable containers), basketball goals, storage sheds, mailboxes, wall and/or door mirrors, attached propane gas tank, invisible fencing including all related equipment, lawn irrigation systems and all related equipment, water softener/conditioner and filter equipment, and any other items attached or affixed to the Property, EXCEPT the following items:_____
_____.

3. **PERSONAL PROPERTY.** The following personal property is included in the listing price:_____
_____
_____.

4. **HOME WARRANTY.** Seller ☐ agrees ☐ does not agree to obtain and pay for at closing a one year home warranty for the Property at a cost not to exceed $_____. If Seller agrees to obtain and pay for a home warranty at any time, Firm hereby discloses that an administrative fee of _____ will be offered to Firm by the person or entity through or from which any home warranty is obtained as compensation to Firm for its assistance in obtaining the home warranty, and Seller hereby consents to Firm's receipt of such fee.

5. **HOME INSPECTION:** Seller ☐ agrees ☐ does not agree to obtain and pay for a home inspection by a licensed NC Home Inspector within _____ days after the execution of this agreement.
☐ Seller acknowledges receipt of a copy of *Questions and Answers on: Home Inspections* by the NC Real Estate Commission.

6. **LISTING PRICE.** Seller lists the Property at a price of $_____ on the following terms:
( ) Cash ( ) Loan Assumption ( ) Conventional ( ) FHA ( ) VA ( ) Seller Financing ( ) Other _____. Seller agrees to sell the Property for the Listing Price or for any other price or on any other terms acceptable to Seller.

7. **TERM.** In consideration of the Seller agreeing to list the Property for sale and in further consideration of Firm's services and efforts to find a buyer, Firm is hereby granted the exclusive right to sell the Property from (Date) _____ until midnight, (Date) _____.

8. **FIRM'S COMPENSATION.** Seller agrees to pay Firm a total fee of _____ % of the gross sales price of the Property, OR_____, which shall include the amount of any compensation paid by Firm as set forth in paragraph 9 below to any other real estate firm, including individual agents and sole proprietors ("Cooperating Real Estate Firm"). Such fee shall be deemed earned under any of the following circumstances:

Page 1 of 6

North Carolina Association of REALTORS®, Inc.

Individual agent initials _____ Seller initials _____ _____

STANDARD FORM 101
Revised 1/2009
© 1/2009

(a) If a ready, willing and able buyer is procured by Firm, a Cooperating Real Estate Firm, the Seller, or anyone else during the Term of this Agreement at the price and on the terms set forth herein, or at any price and upon any terms acceptable to the Seller;

(b) If the Property is sold, exchanged, conveyed or transferred, or the Seller agrees to sell, exchange, convey or transfer the Property at any price and upon any terms whatsoever, during the Term of this Agreement or any renewal hereof;

(c) If, within _____ days after expiration of the Term of this Agreement (the "Protection Period"), Seller either directly or indirectly sells, exchanges, conveys or transfers, or agrees to sell, exchange, convey or transfer the Property upon any terms whatsoever, to any person with whom Seller, Firm, or any Cooperating Real Estate Firm communicated regarding the Property during the Term of this Agreement or any renewal hereof, provided the names of such persons are delivered or postmarked to the Seller within 15 days from date of expiration. HOWEVER, Seller shall NOT be obligated to pay such fee if a valid listing agreement is entered into between Seller and another real estate broker and the Property is sold, exchanged, conveyed or transferred during such Protection Period.

Once earned as set forth above, Firm's compensation will be due and payable at the earlier of: (i) closing on the Property; (ii) the Seller's failure to sell the Property (including but not limited to the Seller's refusal to sign an offer to purchase the Property at the price and terms stated herein or on other terms acceptable to the Seller, the Seller's default on an executed sales contract for the Property, or the Seller's agreement with a buyer to unreasonably modify or cancel an executed sales contract for the Property); or (iii) Seller's breach of this Agreement.

If additional compensation, incentive, bonus, rebate and/or other valuable consideration ("Additional Compensation") is offered to the Firm from any other party or person in connection with a sale of the Property, Seller will permit Firm to receive it in addition to the compensation set forth above. Firm shall timely disclose the promise or expectation of receiving any such Additional Compensation and confirm the disclosure in writing before Seller makes or accepts an offer to sell. (**NOTE:** NCAR Form #770 may be used to confirm the disclosure of any such Additional Compensation)

9. **COOPERATION WITH/COMPENSATION TO OTHER FIRMS.** Firm has advised Seller of Firm's company policies regarding cooperation and the amount(s) of any compensation that will be offered to subagents, buyer agents or both. Seller authorizes Firm to (*Check ALL applicable authorizations*):

❑ Cooperate with subagents representing only the Seller and offer them the following compensation:_____ % of the gross sales price or $_____ .

❑ Cooperate with buyer agents representing only the buyer and offer them the following compensation:_____ % of the gross sales price or $_____ .

OR

❑ Cooperate with and compensate other Cooperating Real Estate Firms according to the attached policy.

Firm will promptly notify Seller if compensation offered to a Cooperating Real Estate Firm is different from that set forth above. Agents with Cooperating Real Estate Firms must orally disclose the nature of their relationship with a buyer (subagent or buyer agent) to Firm at the time of initial contact with Firm, and confirm that relationship in writing no later than the time an offer to purchase is submitted for the Seller's consideration. Seller should be careful about disclosing confidential information because agents representing buyers must disclose all relevant information to their clients.

10. **FIRM'S DUTIES**. Firm agrees to provide Seller the benefit of Firm's knowledge, experience and advice in the marketing and sale of the Property. Seller understands that Firm makes no representation or guarantee as to the sale of the Property, but Firm agrees to use its best efforts in good faith to find a buyer who is ready, willing and able to purchase the property. In accordance with the REALTORS® Code of Ethics, Firm shall, with Seller's approval, in response to inquiries from buyers or Cooperating Real Estate Firms, disclose the existence of offers on the Property. Where Seller authorizes disclosure, Firm shall also disclose whether offers were obtained by the individual agent who signs this Agreement, another agent of the Firm, or by a Cooperating Real Estate Firm. Seller acknowledges that real estate brokers are prohibited by N.C. Real Estate Commission rule from disclosing the price or other material terms contained in a party's offer to purchase, sell, lease, rent or option real property to a competing party without the express authority of the party making the offer.

Seller acknowledges that Firm is required by law to disclose to potential purchasers of the Property all material facts pertaining to the Property about which the Firm knows or reasonably should know, and that REALTORS® have an ethical responsibility to treat all parties to the transaction honestly. Seller further acknowledges that Firm is being retained solely as a real estate professional, and understands that other professional service providers are available to render advice or services to Seller, including but not limited to an attorney, insurance agent, tax advisor, surveyor, structural engineer, home inspector, environmental consultant, architect, or contractor. Although Firm may provide Seller the names of providers who claim to perform such services, Seller understands that Firm cannot guarantee the quality of service or level of expertise of any such provider. Seller agrees to pay the full amount due for all

Page 2 of 6

STANDARD FORM 101
Revised 1/2009
© 1/2009

Individual agent initials _____ Seller initials _____ _____

services directly to the service provider whether or not the transaction closes. Seller also agrees to indemnify and hold Firm harmless from and against any and all liability, claim, loss, damage, suit, or expense that Firm may incur either as a result of Seller's selection and use of any such provider or Seller's election not to have one or more of such services performed.

THE AGENT (FIRM) SHALL CONDUCT ALL BROKERAGE ACTIVITIES IN REGARD TO THIS AGREEMENT WITHOUT RESPECT TO THE RACE, COLOR, RELIGION, SEX, NATIONAL ORIGIN, HANDICAP OR FAMILIAL STATUS OF ANY PARTY OR PROSPECTIVE PARTY TO THE AGREEMENT.

11. **MARKETING.**. Seller authorizes Firm (*Check ALL applicable sections*):
   - ❑ **Signs**. To place "For Sale," "Under Contract," "Sale Pending," or other similar signs on the Property (where permitted by law and relevant covenants) and to remove other such signs.
   - ❑ **Lock/Key Boxes**. To place a lock/key box on the Property.
   - ❑ **Open Houses**. To conduct open houses of the Property at such times as Seller and Firm may subsequently agree.
   - ❑ **Listing Service**. To submit pertinent information concerning the Property to any listing service of which Firm is a member or in which any of Firm's agents participate and to furnish to such listing service notice of all changes of information concerning the Property authorized in writing by Seller. Seller authorizes Firm, upon execution of a sales contract for the Property, to notify the listing service of the pending sale, and upon closing of the sale, to disseminate sales information, including sales price, to the listing service, appraisers and real estate brokers.
   - ❑ **Advertising Other Than On The Internet**. To advertise the Property in non-Internet media, and to permit other firms to advertise the Property in non-Internet media to the extent and in such manner as Firm may decide.
   - ❑ **Internet Advertising**. To display information about the Property on the Internet either directly or through a program of any listing service of which the Firm is a member or in which any of Firm's agents participate, and authorizes other firms who belong to any listing service of which the Firm is a member or in which any of Firm's agents participate to display information about the Property on the Internet in accordance with the listing service rules and regulations. *If Seller does not authorize Internet Advertising as set forth above, Seller MUST complete an opt-out form in accordance with listing service rules.* (**NOTE**: *NCAR Form #105 may be used for this purpose.*)

   If Seller authorizes Internet Advertising as set forth above, Seller further authorizes the display of (*Check ALL applicable sections*):
   - ❑ The address of the Property
   - ❑ Automated estimates of the market value of the Property
   - ❑ Third-party comments about the Property

Seller acknowledges and understands that while the marketing services selected above will facilitate the showing and sale of the Property, there are risks associated with allowing access to and disseminating information about the Property that are not within the reasonable control of the Firm, including but not limited to:
1. unauthorized use of a lock/key box,
2. control of visitors during or after a showing or an open house,
3. inappropriate use of information about the Property placed on the Internet or furnished to any listing service in which the Firm participates.

Seller therefore agrees to indemnify and hold harmless Firm from any damages, costs, attorneys' fees and other expenses as a result of any personal injury or property loss or damage to Seller or any other person not caused by Firm's negligence arising directly or indirectly out of any such marketing services.

12. **SELLER'S DUTIES.** Seller agrees to cooperate with Firm in the marketing and sale of the Property, including but not limited to:
   (a) providing to Firm, in a timely manner, accurate information including but not limited to the Residential Property Disclosure Statement (unless exempt), and the Lead-Based Paint or Lead-Based Paint Hazard Addendum with respect to any residential dwelling built prior to 1978;
   (b) making the Property available for showing (including working, existing utilities) at reasonable times and upon reasonable notice;
   (c) providing Firm as soon as reasonably possible after the execution of this Agreement copies of restrictive covenants, if any, and copies of the bylaws, articles of incorporation, rules and regulations, and other governing documents of the owners' association and/or the subdivision, if applicable;
   (d) immediately referring to Firm all inquiries or offers it may receive regarding the Property; showing the Property only by appointment made by or through Firm; and conducting all negotiations through Firm.

If the Property is sold during the period set forth herein, the Seller agrees to execute and deliver a GENERAL WARRANTY DEED conveying fee simple marketable title to the Property, including legal access to a public right of way, free of all encumbrances except

STANDARD FORM 101
Revised 1/2009
© 1/2009

Individual agent initials _____ Seller initials _____ _____

ad valorem taxes for the current year, utility easements, rights-of-way, and unviolated restrictive covenants, if any, and those encumbrances that the buyer agrees to assume in the sales contract. Seller represents that the Seller has the right to convey the Property, and that there are currently no circumstances that would prohibit the Seller from conveying fee simple marketable title as set forth in the preceding sentence, except as follows *(insert N/A if not applicable)*: _____

_____

(**NOTE**: If any sale of the Property may be a "short sale," consideration should be given to attaching NCAR form 104 as an addendum to this Agreement.)

Seller agrees to provide Firm, in a timely manner, sufficient information to enable Firm to compute Seller's net proceeds at Closing, including but not limited to, all mortgage and equity line payoffs, tax liens, judgments, mechanics' or materialmens' liens, or other outstanding liens on the Property.

❑ Seller acknowledges receipt of a sample copy of an Offer to Purchase And Contract for review purposes.
❑ Seller acknowledges receipt of a sample copy of a Professional Services Disclosure and Election form (form #760) for review purposes.

13. **FLOOD HAZARD DISCLOSURE/INSURANCE.** To the best of Seller's knowledge, the Property ❑ is ❑ is not located partly or entirely within a designated Special Flood Hazard Area. The Seller ❑ does ❑ does not currently maintain flood hazard insurance on the Property.

14. **SYNTHETIC STUCCO.** To the best of Seller's knowledge, the Property has not been clad previously (either in whole or in part) with an "exterior insulating and finishing system," commonly known as "EIFS" or "synthetic stucco", unless disclosed as follows: *(If the Seller does not wish to disclose, put "No Representation")*: _____
_____.

15. **OWNERS' ASSOCIATION.** There ❑ is ❑ is not an owners' association. If there is an owners' association, then it is recommended that the Seller provide to Firm a completed Form 2A12-T (Owners' Association Disclosure and Addendum). The name, address and telephone number of the President of the owners' association or the Property Manager is:
_____.

16. **TERMITE BOND.** There ❑ is ❑ is not a termite bond on the Property. If there is a termite bond, the name of the bonding company is: _____.

17. **EARNEST MONEY.** Unless otherwise provided in the sales contract, earnest money deposits paid toward the purchase price shall be held by the Firm, in escrow, until the consummation or termination of the transaction. Any earnest money forfeited by reason of the buyer's default under a sales contract shall be divided equally between the Firm and Seller. In no event shall the sum paid to the Firm because of a buyer's default be in excess of the fee that would have been due if the sale had closed as contemplated in the sales contract.

18. **MEDIATION.** If a dispute arises out of or related to this Agreement or the breach thereof, and if the dispute cannot be settled through negotiation, the parties agree first to try in good faith to settle the dispute by mediation before resorting to arbitration, litigation, or some other dispute resolution procedure. If the need for mediation arises, the parties will choose a mutually acceptable mediator and will share the cost of mediation equally.

19. **ADDITIONAL TERMS AND CONDITIONS.** The following additional terms and conditions shall also be a part of this Agreement: _____
_____
_____

20. **ENTIRE AGREEMENT/CHANGES.** This Agreement constitutes the entire agreement between Seller and Firm and there are no representations, inducements, or other provisions other than those expressed herein. All changes, additions, or deletions to this Agreement must be in writing and signed by both Seller and Firm.

Page 4 of 6

Individual agent initials _____ Seller initials _____ _____

21. **DUAL AGENCY.** Seller has received a copy of the "Working With Real Estate Agents" brochure and has reviewed it with Firm. Seller understands that the potential for dual agency will arise if a buyer who has an agency relationship with Firm becomes interested in viewing the Property. Firm may represent more than one party in the same transaction only with the knowledge and informed consent of all parties for whom Firm acts.

(a) Authorization *(initial only ONE).*

_____ Seller authorizes the Firm to act as a dual agent, representing both the Seller and the buyer, subject to the terms and conditions set forth in this paragraph below.

_____ Seller desires exclusive representation at all times during this agreement and does NOT authorize Firm to act in the capacity of dual agent. *If Seller does not authorize Firm to act as a dual agent, the remainder of this paragraph shall not apply.*

(b) Disclosure of Information. In the event Firm serves as a dual agent, Seller agrees that without permission from the party about whom the information pertains, Firm shall not disclose to the other party the following information:
(1) that a party may agree to a price, terms, or any conditions of sale other than those offered;
(2) the motivation of a party for engaging in the transaction, unless disclosure is otherwise required by statute or rule; and
(3) any information about a party which that party has identified as confidential unless disclosure is otherwise required by statute or rule.

(c) Firm's Role as Dual Agent. If Firm serves as agent for both Seller and a buyer in a transaction involving the Property, Firm shall make every reasonable effort to represent Seller and buyer in a balanced and fair manner. Firm shall also make every reasonable effort to encourage and effect communication and negotiation between Seller and buyer. Seller understands and acknowledges that:
(1) Prior to the time dual agency occurs, Firm will act as Seller's exclusive agent;
(2) In its separate representation of Seller and buyer, Firm may obtain information which, if disclosed, could harm the bargaining position of the party providing such information to Firm;
(3) Firm is required by law to disclose to Seller and buyer any known or reasonably ascertainable material facts.
Seller agrees Firm shall not be liable to Seller for (i) disclosing material facts required by law to be disclosed, and (ii) refusing or failing to disclose other information the law does not require to be disclosed which could harm or compromise one party's bargaining position but could benefit the other party.

(d) Seller's Role. Should Firm become a dual agent, Seller understands and acknowledges that:
(1) Seller has the responsibility of making Seller's own decisions as to what terms are to be included in any purchase and sale agreement with a buyer client of Firm;
(2) Seller is fully aware of and understands the implications and consequences of Firm's dual agency role as expressed herein to provide balanced and fair representation of Seller and buyer and to encourage and effect communication between them rather than as an advocate or exclusive agent or representative;
(3) Seller has determined that the benefits of dual agency outweigh any disadvantages or adverse consequences;
(4) Seller may seek independent legal counsel to assist Seller with the negotiation and preparation of a purchase and sale agreement or with any matter relating to the transaction which is the subject matter of a purchase and sale agreement.

Seller agrees to indemnify and hold Firm harmless against all claims, damages, losses, expenses or liabilities, other than violations of the North Carolina Real Estate License Law and intentional wrongful acts, arising from Firm's role as a dual agent. Seller shall have a duty to protect Seller's own interests and should read any purchase and sale agreement carefully to ensure that it accurately sets forth the terms which Seller wants included in said agreement.

(e) Designated Agent Option (*Initial only if applicable*).

_____ Seller hereby authorizes the Firm to designate an agent(s) to represent the Seller, to the exclusion of any other agents associated with the Firm. The agent(s) shall not be so designated and shall not undertake to represent only the interests of the Seller if the agent(s) has actually received confidential information concerning a buyer client of the Firm in connection with the transaction. The designated agent(s) shall represent only the interests of the Seller to the extent permitted by law.

Seller and Firm each acknowledge receipt of a signed copy of this Agreement.

STANDARD FORM 101
Revised 1/2009
© 1/2009

Individual agent initials _____ Seller initials _____ _____

THE NORTH CAROLINA ASSOCIATION OF REALTORS®, INC. MAKES NO REPRESENTATION AS TO THE LEGAL VALIDITY OR ADEQUACY OF ANY PROVISION OF THIS FORM IN ANY SPECIFIC TRANSACTION.

Seller_____

Seller_____

Mailing Address _____

Home Phone_____ Work Phone _____ Cell Phone _____

Fax _____ E-mail Address _____

Firm _____ Phone_____
        Real Estate Firm Name

By: _____ Individual agent license #_____
        Individual agent signature

Fax _____ E-mail Address _____

Office Address_____

STANDARD FORM 101
Revised 1/2009
© 1/2009

EXCLUSIVE RIGHT TO SELL LISTING AGREEMENT (VACANT LAND)

This EXCLUSIVE RIGHT TO SELL LISTING AGREEMENT ("Agreement") is entered into (Date)_____,
between_____ as Seller(s) ("Seller") of
the property described below (the "Property"), and_____ as
Listing Firm ("Firm"). The individual agent who signs this Agreement on behalf of the Firm shall, on behalf of the Firm, be primarily responsible for ensuring that the Firm's duties hereunder are fulfilled; however, it is understood and agreed that other agents of the Firm may be assigned to fulfill such duties if deemed appropriate by the Firm. For purposes of this Agreement, the term "Firm," as the context may require, shall be deemed to include the individual agent who signs this Agreement and any other agents of the Firm.

1. **REAL PROPERTY**. The real property that is the subject of this Agreement is located in _____
County, North Carolina, and is known more particularly and described as:
Address: Street_____ City_____ Zip_____
Legal Description_____
Subdivision Name:_____
Plat Reference: Lot_____, Block or Section _____ as shown on
Plat Book or Slide _____ at Page(s) _____ (Property acquired by Seller in Deed Book _____ at Page _____).

2. **LISTING PRICE**. Seller lists the Property at a price of $_____ on the following terms:
( ) Cash ( ) Loan Assumption ( ) Conventional ( ) FHA ( ) VA ( ) Seller Financing ( ) Other_____. Seller agrees to sell the Property for the Listing Price or for any other price or on any other terms acceptable to Seller.

3. **TERM**. In consideration of the Seller agreeing to list the Property for sale and in further consideration of Firms's services and efforts to find a buyer, Firm is hereby granted the exclusive right to sell the Property from (Date) _____
until midnight, (Date) _____ .

4. **FIRM'S COMPENSATION**. Seller agrees to pay Firm a total fee of _____ % of the gross sales price of the Property,
OR_____, which shall
include the amount of any compensation paid by Firm as set forth in paragraph 5 below to any other real estate firm, including individual agents and sole proprietors ("Cooperating Real Estate Firm"). Such fee shall be deemed earned under any of the following circumstances:

   (a) If a ready, willing and able buyer is procured by Firm, a Cooperating Real Estate Firm, the Seller, or anyone else during the Term of this Agreement at the price and on the terms set forth herein, or at any price and upon any terms acceptable to the Seller;
   (b) If the Property is sold, exchanged, conveyed or transferred, or the Seller agrees to sell, exchange, convey or transfer the Property at any price and upon any terms whatsoever, during the Term of this Agreement or any renewal hereof;
   (c) If, within _____ days after expiration of the Term of this Agreement (the "Protection Period"), Seller either directly or indirectly sells, exchanges, conveys or transfers, or agrees to sell, exchange, convey or transfer the Property upon any terms whatsoever, to any person with whom Seller, Firm, or any Cooperating Real Estate Firm communicated regarding the Property during the Term of this Agreement or any renewal hereof, provided the names of such persons are delivered or postmarked to the Seller within 15 days from date of expiration. HOWEVER, Seller shall NOT be obligated to pay such fee if a valid listing agreement is entered into between Seller and another real estate broker and the Property is sold, exchanged, conveyed or transferred during such Protection Period.

Once earned as set forth above, Firm's compensation will be due and payable at the earlier of: (i) closing on the Property; (ii) the Seller's failure to sell the Property (including but not limited to the Seller's refusal to sign an offer to purchase the Property at the price and terms stated herein or on other terms acceptable to the Seller, the Seller's default on an executed sales contract for the Property, or the Seller's agreement with a buyer to unreasonably modify or cancel an executed sales contract for the Property); or (iii) Seller's breach of this Agreement.

If additional compensation, incentive, bonus, rebate and/or other valuable consideration ("Additional Compensation") is offered to the Firm from any other party or person in connection with a sale of the Property, Seller will permit Firm to receive it in addition to the compensation set forth above. Firm shall timely disclose the promise or expectation of receiving any such Additional Compensation and confirm the disclosure in writing before Seller makes or accepts an offer to sell. (See NCAR Form #770).

Page 1 of 5

North Carolina Association of REALTORS®, Inc.

Individual agent initials _____ Seller initials _____ _____

STANDARD FORM 103
Revised 10/2008
© 10/2008

5. **COOPERATION WITH/COMPENSATION TO OTHER FIRMS.** Firm has advised Seller of Firm's company policies regarding cooperation and the amount(s) of any compensation that will be offered to subagents, buyer agents or both. Seller authorizes Firm to (*Check ALL applicable authorizations*):

❑ Cooperate with subagents representing only the Seller and offer them the following compensation:_____% of the gross sales price or $_____.

❑ Cooperate with buyer agents representing only the buyer and offer them the following compensation:_____ % of the gross sales price or $_____.

OR

❑ Cooperate with and compensate other Cooperating Real Estate Firms according to the attached policy.

Firm will promptly notify Seller if compensation offered to a Cooperating Real Estate Firm is different from that set forth above. Agents with Cooperating Real Estate Firms must orally disclose the nature of their relationship with a buyer (subagent or buyer agent) to Firm at the time of initial contact with Firm, and confirm that relationship in writing no later than the time an offer to purchase is submitted for the Seller's consideration. Seller should be careful about disclosing confidential information because agents representing buyers must disclose all relevant information to their clients.

6. **FIRM'S DUTIES.** Firm agrees to provide Seller the benefit of Firm's knowledge, experience and advice in the marketing and sale of the Property. Seller understands that Firm makes no representation or guarantee as to the sale of the Property, but Firm agrees to use its best efforts in good faith to find a buyer who is ready, willing and able to purchase the property. In accordance with the REALTORS® Code of Ethics, Firm shall, with Seller's approval, in response to inquiries from buyers or Cooperating Real Estate Firms, disclose the existence of offers on the Property. Where Seller authorizes disclosure, Firm shall also disclose whether offers were obtained by the individual agent who signs this Agreement, another agent of the Firm, or by a Cooperating Real Estate Firm. Seller acknowledges that real estate brokers are prohibited by N.C. Real Estate Commission rule from disclosing the price or other material terms contained in a party's offer to purchase, sell, lease, rent or option real property to a competing party without the express authority of the party making the offer.

Seller acknowledges that Firm is required by law to disclose to potential purchasers of the Property all material facts pertaining to the Property about which the Firm knows or reasonably should know, and that REALTORS® have an ethical responsibility to treat all parties to the transaction honestly. Seller further acknowledges that Firm is being retained solely as a real estate professional, and understands that other professional service providers are available to render advice or services to Seller, including but not limited to an attorney, insurance agent, tax advisor, surveyor, structural engineer, home inspector, environmental consultant, architect, or contractor. Although Firm may provide Seller the names of providers who claim to perform such services, Seller understands that Firm cannot guarantee the quality of service or level of expertise of any such provider. Seller agrees to pay the full amount due for all services directly to the service provider whether or not the transaction closes. Seller also agrees to indemnify and hold Firm harmless from and against any and all liability, claim, loss, damage, suit, or expense that Firm may incur either as a result of Seller's selection and use of any such provider or Seller's election not to have one or more of such services performed.

In connection with the marketing and sale of the Property, Seller authorizes and directs Firm: (*Check ALL applicable sections*)

❑ to place "For Sale," "Under Contract," "Sale Pending," or other similar signs on the Property (where permitted by law and relevant covenants) and to remove other such signs.

❑ to place a lock/key box on the Property.

❑ to advertise the Property, including, but not limited to, placing information about the Property on the Internet either directly or through a program of any listing service of which the Firm is a member or in which any of Firm's agents participate.

❑ to permit other firms who belong to any listing service of which the Firm is a member to advertise the Property on the Internet in accordance with the listing service rules and regulations.

❑ to submit pertinent information concerning the Property to any listing service of which Firm is a member or in which any of Firm's agents participate and to furnish to such listing service notice of all changes of information concerning the Property authorized in writing by Seller. Seller authorizes Firm, upon execution of a sales contract for the Property, to notify the listing service of the pending sale, and upon closing of the sale, to disseminate sales information, including sales price, to the listing service, appraisers and real estate brokers.

In addition, the Seller ❑ authorizes ❑ does not authorize open houses of the Property at such times as Seller and Firm may subsequently agree.

Seller acknowledges and understands that while the marketing services selected above will facilitate the showing and sale of the Property, there are risks associated with allowing access to and disseminating information about the Property that are not within the reasonable control of the Firm, including but not limited to:

Page 2 of 5

Individual agent initials _____ Seller initials _____ _____

1. unauthorized use of a lock/key box,
2. control of visitors during or after a showing or an open house,
3. inappropriate use of information about the Property placed on the Internet or furnished to any listing service in which the Firm participates.

Seller therefore agrees to indemnify and hold harmless Firm from any damages, costs, attorneys' fees and other expenses as a result of any personal injury or property loss or damage to Seller or any other person not caused by Firm's negligence arising directly or indirectly out of any such marketing services.

THE AGENT (FIRM) SHALL CONDUCT ALL BROKERAGE ACTIVITIES IN REGARD TO THIS AGREEMENT WITHOUT RESPECT TO THE RACE, COLOR, RELIGION, SEX, NATIONAL ORIGIN, HANDICAP OR FAMILIAL STATUS OF ANY PARTY OR PROSPECTIVE PARTY TO THE AGREEMENT.

7. **SELLER'S DUTIES.** Seller agrees to cooperate with Firm in the marketing and sale of the Property, including but not limited to:
   (a) providing to Firm, in a timely manner, accurate information about the Property of which Seller may be aware, including but not limited to presence of or access to any water supply, sewer and/or septic system; problems with drainage, grading or soil stability; environmental hazards; commercial or industrial nuisances (noise, odor, smoke, etc.); utility or other easements, shared driveways, or encroachments from or on adjacent property; lawsuits, foreclosures, bankruptcy, tenancies, judgments, tax liens, proposed assessments, mechanics' liens, materialmens' liens, or notice from any governmental agency; flood hazard; cemetery/grave sites; or abandoned well;
   (b) making the Property available for showing (including working, existing utilities) at reasonable times and upon reasonable notice;
   (c) providing Firm as soon as reasonably possible after the execution of this Agreement copies of restrictive covenants, if any, and copies of the bylaws, articles of incorporation, rules and regulations, and other governing documents of the owners' association and/or the subdivision, if applicable;
   (d) immediately referring to Firm all inquiries or offers it may receive regarding the Property; showing the Property only by appointment made by or through Firm; and conducting all negotiations through Firm.

If the Property is sold during the period set forth herein, the Seller agrees to execute and deliver a GENERAL WARRANTY DEED conveying fee simple marketable title to the Property, including legal access to a public right of way, free of all encumbrances except ad valorem taxes for the current year, utility easements, rights-of-way, and unviolated restrictive covenants, if any, and those encumbrances that the buyer agrees to assume in the sales contract. Seller represents that the Seller has the right to convey the Property, and that there are currently no circumstances that would prohibit the Seller from conveying fee simple marketable title as set forth in the preceding sentence.

❑ Seller acknowledges receipt of a sample copy of an Offer to Purchase And Contract—Vacant Lot/Land for review purposes.
❑ Seller acknowledges receipt of a sample copy of a Professional Services Disclosure and Election form (form #760) for review purposes.

8. **FLOOD HAZARD DISCLOSURE.** To the best of Seller's knowledge, the Property ❑ is ❑ is not located partly or entirely within a designated Special Flood Hazard Area.

9. **OWNERS' ASSOCIATION.** There ❑ is ❑ is not an owners' association. If there is an owners' association, then it is recommended that the Seller provide to Firm a completed Form 2A-12T (Owners' Association Disclosure and Addendum). The name, address and telephone number of the President of the owners' association or the Property Manager is:
_____.

10. **EARNEST MONEY.** Unless otherwise provided in the sales contract, earnest money deposits paid toward the purchase price shall be held by the Firm, in escrow, until the consummation or termination of the transaction. Any earnest money forfeited by reason of the buyer's default under a sales contract shall be divided equally between the Firm and Seller. In no event shall the sum paid to the Firm because of a buyer's default be in excess of the fee that would have been due if the sale had closed as contemplated in the sales contract.

11. **MEDIATION.** If a dispute arises out of or related to this Agreement or the breach thereof, and if the dispute cannot be settled through negotiation, the parties agree first to try in good faith to settle the dispute by mediation before resorting to arbitration, litigation, or some other dispute resolution procedure. If the need for mediation arises, the parties will choose a mutually acceptable mediator and will share the cost of mediation equally.

Individual agent initials _____ Seller initials _____ _____

12. **ADDITIONAL TERMS AND CONDITIONS.** The following additional terms and conditions shall also be a part of this Agreement:_____
_____
_____
_____

13. **ENTIRE AGREEMENT/CHANGES.** This Agreement constitutes the entire agreement between Seller and Firm and there are no representations, inducements, or other provisions other than those expressed herein. All changes, additions, or deletions to this Agreement must be in writing and signed by both Seller and Firm.

14. **DUAL AGENCY.** Seller has received a copy of the "Working With Real Estate Agents" brochure and has reviewed it with Firm. Seller understands that the potential for dual agency will arise if a buyer who has an agency relationship with Firm becomes interested in viewing the Property. Firm may represent more than one party in the same transaction only with the knowledge and informed consent of all parties for whom Firm acts.

    (a) Authorization *(initial only ONE).*

_____   Seller authorizes the Firm to act as a dual agent, representing both the Seller and the buyer, subject to the terms and conditions set forth in this paragraph below.

_____   Seller desires exclusive representation at all times during this agreement and does NOT authorize Firm to act in the capacity of dual agent. *If Seller does not authorize Firm to act as a dual agent, the remainder of this paragraph shall not apply.*

    (b) Disclosure of Information. In the event Firm serves as a dual agent, Seller agrees that without permission from the party about whom the information pertains, Firm shall not disclose to the other party the following information:
        (1) that a party may agree to a price, terms, or any conditions of sale other than those offered;
        (2) the motivation of a party for engaging in the transaction, unless disclosure is otherwise required by statute or rule;   and
        (3) any information about a party which that party has identified as confidential unless disclosure is otherwise required by statute or rule.

    (c) Firm's Role as Dual Agent. If Firm serves as agent for both Seller and a buyer in a transaction involving the Property, Firm shall make every reasonable effort to represent Seller and buyer in a balanced and fair manner. Firm shall also make every reasonable effort to encourage and effect communication and negotiation between Seller and buyer. Seller understands and acknowledges that:
        (1) Prior to the time dual agency occurs, Firm will act as Seller's exclusive agent;
        (2) In its separate representation of Seller and buyer, Firm may obtain information which, if disclosed, could harm the bargaining position of the party providing such information to Firm;
        (3) Firm is required by law to disclose to Seller and buyer any known or reasonably ascertainable material facts.
Seller agrees Firm shall not be liable to Seller for (i) disclosing material facts required by law to be disclosed, and (ii) refusing or failing to disclose other information the law does not require to be disclosed which could harm or compromise one party's bargaining position but could benefit the other party.

    (d) Seller's Role. Should Firm become a dual agent, Seller understands and acknowledges that:
        (1) Seller has the responsibility of making Seller's own decisions as to what terms are to be included in any purchase and sale agreement with a buyer client of Firm;
        (2) Seller is fully aware of and understands the implications and consequences of Firm's dual agency role as expressed herein to provide balanced and fair representation of Seller and buyer and to encourage and effect communication between them rather than as an advocate or exclusive agent or representative;
        (3) Seller has determined that the benefits of dual agency outweigh any disadvantages or adverse consequences;
        (4) Seller may seek independent legal counsel to assist Seller with the negotiation and preparation of a purchase and sale agreement or with any matter relating to the transaction which is the subject matter of a purchase and sale agreement.

Seller agrees to indemnify and hold Firm harmless against all claims, damages, losses, expenses or liabilities, other than violations of the North Carolina Real Estate License Law and intentional wrongful acts, arising from Firm's role as a dual agent. Seller shall have a duty to protect Seller's own interests and should read any purchase and sale agreement carefully to ensure that it accurately sets forth the terms which Seller wants included in said agreement.

Page 4 of 5

STANDARD FORM 103
Revised 10/2008
© 10/2008

Individual agent initials _____   Seller initials _____ _____

(e) Designated Agent Option (*Initial only if applicable*).

_____ Seller hereby authorizes the Firm to designate an agent(s) to represent the Seller, to the exclusion of any other agents associated with the Firm. The agent(s) shall not be so designated and shall not undertake to represent only the interests of the Seller if the agent(s) has actually received confidential information concerning a buyer client of the Firm in connection with the transaction. The designated agent(s) shall represent only the interests of the Seller to the extent permitted by law.

Seller and Firm each acknowledge receipt of a signed copy of this Agreement.

THE NORTH CAROLINA ASSOCIATION OF REALTORS®, INC. MAKES NO REPRESENTATION AS TO THE LEGAL VALIDITY OR ADEQUACY OF ANY PROVISION OF THIS FORM IN ANY SPECIFIC TRANSACTION.

Seller _____

Seller _____

Mailing Address _____

Home Phone _____ Work Phone _____ Cell Phone _____

Fax _____ E-mail Address _____

(Firm) _____ Phone _____
      Real Estate Firm Name

By: _____ Individual agent license # _____
      Individual agent signature

Fax _____ E-mail Address _____

Office Address _____

STANDARD FORM 103
Revised 10/2008
© 10/2008

SHORT SALE ADDENDUM TO
EXCLUSIVE RIGHT TO SELL LISTING AGREEMENT
(to be used with NCAR standard form 101 or 103)

Property Address:_____

The additional provisions set forth below are hereby made a part of the Exclusive Right to Sell Listing Agreement for the Property
between Seller: _____
and Firm: _____

1. **Short Sale Defined:** For purposes of the Agreement between Seller and Firm, a "Short Sale" is a sale where:
    *   The purchase price is or may be insufficient to enable Seller to pay the costs of sale, which include but are not limited to the Seller's closing costs and payment in full of all loans or debts secured by deeds of trust on the Property due and owing to one or more lender(s) and/or other lienholders ("Lienholders")
    *   Seller does not have sufficient liquid assets to pay any deficiencies and
    *   The Lienholders agree to release or discharge their liens upon payment of an amount less than the amount owed, with or without the Seller being released from any further liability.

2. **Acknowledgement of Short Sale:** Seller acknowledges that any sale of the above Property may or would be a Short Sale. Seller further acknowledges that other options may be available to Seller, including but not limited to negotiating a modification of existing loans or liens, refinancing, bankruptcy, foreclosure, or deed in lieu of foreclosure. Nevertheless, Seller desires to make special arrangements with Firm and any potential Buyer of the Property for a Short Sale. Seller acknowledges that the ability of Firm to successfully market the Property could be limited by any need for a Short Sale.

3. **Potential Credit and Tax Consequences:** Seller understands that:
    *   A Short Sale may have a negative impact on the credit rating or credit score of Seller
    *   A Short Sale may result in taxable income to Seller, even though Seller does not receive any cash proceeds from the sale.

Seller is advised to seek advice from an attorney, a certified public accountant or other professional regarding the credit, legal and tax consequences of a Short Sale.

4. **Lienholders' Conditions:** Seller understands that the Lienholders:
    *   Are not obligated to approve a Short Sale
    *   Are not obligated to release Seller from further liability even if Lienholders approve a Short Sale
    *   May impose conditions prior to consideration or approval of a Short Sale, such as obtaining a current appraisal, requiring Seller to demonstrate financial hardship or provide income tax returns, pay stubs, evidence of financial assets or other financial information

Seller acknowledges that Firm has no control over Lienholders' approval, or any act, omission or decision by any Lienholders in the Short Sale process, and that Firm has not made any promise that a Short Sale of the Property will be successful.

5. **Duties of Seller to Close a Short Sale:** Seller understands that a Short Sale may require Seller to:
    *   Deposit with the settlement agent additional funds belonging to Seller to pay obligations of the Seller at closing, and/or
    *   Obtain approval of any contract of sale for the Property from the Lienholders, and/or
    *   Pay from Seller's other assets at closing or after the sale is completed some or all of the difference between the sales price and the costs of sale

6. **Authorization of Firm:** Seller hereby authorizes Firm to take the following additional actions with regard to the listing and sale of the Property:
    *   Market the Property as a Short Sale or "pre-foreclosure" property in the multiple listing services and other advertising or promotional materials
    *   Continue to market the Property for sale according to the rules of the multiple listing service until the Short Sale is fully approved and agreed upon by all necessary parties;

Page 1 of 2

North Carolina Association of REALTORS®, Inc.

Individual agent initials _____ Seller initials _____ _____

STANDARD FORM 104
Adopted 1/2009
© 1/2009

- Disclose or provide any requested information or documentation to the Lienholders (and to the buyer and/or buyer's agent) in order to obtain approval of a Short Sale
- Contact and communicate directly with the loss mitigation or other similar departments or divisions of Lienholders to obtain loan or lien status, account and payoff-related information and to negotiate a Short Sale
- Provide comparable sale information or broker price opinions or other data or information documenting the current fair market value of the Property to the Lienholders
- Provide any and all mortgage and/or other lien account payoff information to settlement agent, prospective buyers and/or buyer's agents
- Coordinate and allow inspection of the Property by authorized representatives of Lienholders;
- Include as a part of any contract of sale that would be a Short Sale a "Short Sale Addendum" (standard form 2A14-T), a copy of which Seller acknowledges has been provided to Seller by Firm

7. **Provision of Information by Seller:** Seller shall be obligated to:
   - Promptly furnish Firm and/or Lienholders with such information or documentation as Lienholders may deem necessary to substantiate and justify the need for a Short Sale, including but not limited to:
     - Providing copies of financial information such as pay stubs, income tax returns, bank statements, proof of Seller's assets and liabilities, homeowner or condominium association lien status letters (when applicable),
     - Composing and providing a hardship letter detailing Seller's financial difficulties.

8. **Lienholder List:** Seller hereby represents to Firm that to the best of Seller's knowledge, the attached exhibit contains an accurate list of all Lienholders having any lien or encumbrance upon the Property, including the amount now owed by Seller with respect to each such lien or encumbrance.

9. **Potential Foreclosure or Judicial Sale:** Seller understands that:
   - During a Short Sale process a foreclosure or other judicial sale of the Property could occur if Seller is in default of Seller's financial obligations
   - Seller shall remain at all times responsible to be aware of the status of any such sale and to promptly inform Firm of all information possessed by Seller about any sale
   - If a foreclosure or other judicial proceeding is filed with respect to the Property, Firm is required by law to timely disclose it to any prospective buyer
   - **If a foreclosure or other judicial proceeding is filed with respect to the Property, although Firm may continue to solicit and negotiate offers to purchase, and contact, communicate with, obtain information from and supply information to Lienholders, Firm may no longer negotiate the terms and conditions of a Short Sale with Lienholders, <u>as such negotiation would constitute the practice of law</u>**

10. **Firm's Compensation:** Seller understands and acknowledges that Firm's entitlement to the fee set forth in the Listing Agreement shall not be affected by a Short Sale or any other sale of the Property.

IN THE EVENT OF A CONFLICT BETWEEN THIS ADDENDUM AND THE EXCLUSIVE RIGHT TO SELL LISTING AGREEMENT OR THE EXCLUSIVE RIGHT TO SELL LISTING AGREEMENT (VACANT LAND), THIS ADDENDUM SHALL CONTROL.

THE NORTH CAROLINA ASSOCIATION OF REALTORS®, INC. MAKES NO REPRESENTATION AS TO THE LEGAL VALIDITY OR ADEQUACY OF ANY PROVISION OF THIS FORM IN ANY SPECIFIC TRANSACTION.

Seller_____   Date_____

Seller_____   Date_____

Firm _____
     Real Estate Firm Name

By: _____   Date_____
     Individual agent signature

STANDARD FORM 104
Adopted 1/2009
© 1/2009

INTERNET ADVERTISING ADDENDUM

This INTERNET ADVERTISING ADDENDUM hereby modifies the attached: *(Check the appropriate box)*

❑ NCAR Form #101 (Exclusive Right to Sell Listing Agreement) dated_____
❑ NCAR Form #103 (Exclusive Right to Sell Listing Agreement (Vacant Land)) dated_____
❑ NCAR Form #401 (Exclusive Property Management Agreement (Long-Term Rental)) dated_____
❑ NCAR Form #402 (Exclusive Property Management Agreement (Vacation Rental)) dated_____
❑ NCAR Form #601 (Exclusive Right to Sell Listing Agreement – Auction Sales) dated_____

Seller/Owner: _____ ("Owner")

Real Estate Firm/Agent/Broker: _____ ("Firm")

Property Address: _____ ("Property")

For an Owner who has elected to limit or not permit Internet advertising of their property, ONE of the following choices **MUST** be selected:

_____ Owner authorizes Firm to display information about the Property on the Internet but does NOT authorize participants of any listing service of which the Firm is a member or in which any of Firm's agents participate to display information about the Property on the Internet. **Owner acknowledges and understands that if Owner selects this option, the Property will not be eligible for inclusion in any listing service.**

OR

_____ Owner does NOT authorize the display of information about the Property on the Internet. **Owner acknowledges and understands that consumers who conduct searches for listings on the Internet will not see information about the Property in response to their search.**

THE NORTH CAROLINA ASSOCIATION OF REALTORS®, INC. MAKES NO REPRESENTATION AS TO THE LEGAL VALIDITY OR ADEQUACY OF ANY PROVISION OF THIS FORM IN ANY SPECIFIC TRANSACTION.

_____   _____
Owner   Date

_____   _____
Owner   Date

_____   _____
Firm   Date

BY: _____   _____
Authorized Representative   Date

 REALTOR®   **North Carolina Association of REALTORS®, Inc.**   EQUAL HOUSING OPPORTUNITY   **STANDARD FORM 105**
Adopted 1/2009
© 1/2009

STATE OF NORTH CAROLINA
RESIDENTIAL PROPERTY DISCLOSURE STATEMENT
INSTRUCTIONS TO PROPERTY OWNERS

1. G.S. 47E requires owners of residential real estate (single-family homes and buildings with up to four dwelling units) to furnish purchasers a property disclosure statement. This form is the only one approved for this purpose. A disclosure statement must be furnished in connection with the sale, exchange, option and sale under a lease with option to purchase (unless the tenant is already occupying or intends to occupy the dwelling). A disclosure statement is not required for some transactions, including the first sale of a dwelling which has never been inhabited and transactions of residential property made pursuant to a lease with option to purchase where the lessee occupies or intends to occupy the dwelling. For a complete list of exemptions, see G.S. 47E-2.

2. You must check √ one of the boxes for each of the 21 questions on the reverse side of this form.

    a. If you check "Yes" for any question, you must explain your answer and either describe any problem or attach a report from an engineer, contractor, pest control operator or other expert or public agency describing it. If you attach a report, you will not be liable for any inaccurate or incomplete information contained in it so long as you were not grossly negligent in obtaining or transmitting the information.

    b. If you check "No", you are stating that you have no actual knowledge of any problem. If you check "No" and you know there is a problem, you may be liable for making an intentional misstatement.

    c. If you check "No Representation", you have no duty to disclose the conditions or characteristics of the property, even if you should have known of them.

    * If you check "Yes" or "No" and something happens to the property to make your Statement incorrect or inaccurate (for example, the roof begins to leak), you must promptly give the purchaser a corrected Statement or correct the problem.

3. If you are assisted in the sale of your property by a licensed real estate broker, you are still responsible for completing and delivering the Statement to the purchasers; and the broker must disclose any material facts about your property which they know or reasonably should know, regardless of your responses on the Statement.

4. You must give the completed Statement to the purchaser no later than the time the purchaser makes an offer to purchase your property. If you do not, the purchaser can, under certain conditions, cancel any resulting contract (See **"Note to Purchasers"** below). You should give the purchaser a copy of the Statement containing your signature and keep a copy signed by the purchaser for your records.

Note to Purchasers: If the owner does not give you a Residential Property Disclosure Statement by the time you make your offer to purchase the property, you may under certain conditions cancel any resulting contract and be entitled to a refund of any deposit monies you may have paid. To cancel the contract, you must personally deliver or mail written notice of your decision to cancel to the owner or the owner's agent within three calendar days following your receipt of the Statement, or three calendar days following the date of the contract, whichever occurs first. However, in no event does the Disclosure Act permit you to cancel a contract after settlement of the transaction or (in the case of a sale or exchange) after you have occupied the property, whichever occurs first.

---

5. In the space below, type or print in ink the address of the property (sufficient to identify it) and your name. Then sign and date.

Property Address: _____

Owner's Name(s): _____

Owner(s) acknowledge having examined this Statement before signing and that all information is true and correct as of the date signed.

Owner Signature: _____ Date _____

Owner Signature: _____ Date _____

Purchaser(s) acknowledge receipt of a copy of this disclosure statement; that they have examined it before signing; that they understand that this is not a warranty by owner or owner's agent; that it is not a substitute for any inspections they may wish to obtain; and that the representations are made by the owner and not the owner's agent(s) or subagent(s). Purchaser(s) are encouraged to obtain their own inspection from a licensed home inspector or other professional.

Purchaser Signature: _____ Date _____

Purchaser Signature: _____ Date _____

(OVER)   Page 1 of 2

REC 4.22
REV 1/08

Property Address/Description: _____

[Note: In this form, "property" refers only to dwelling unit(s) and not sheds, detached garages or other buildings.]

Regarding the property identified above, do you know of any problem (malfunction or defect) with any of the following:

	Yes*	No	No Representation
1. FOUNDATION, SLAB, FIREPLACES/CHIMNEYS, FLOORS, WINDOWS (INCLUDING STORM WINDOWS AND SCREENS), DOORS, CEILINGS, INTERIOR AND EXTERIOR WALLS, ATTACHED GARAGE, PATIO, DECK OR OTHER STRUCTURAL COMPONENTS including any modifications to them?	☐	☐	☐
a. Siding is ☐ Masonry ☐ Wood ☐ Composition/Hardboard ☐ Vinyl ☐ Synthetic Stucco ☐ Other _____			☐
b. Approximate age of structure? _____			☐
2. ROOF (leakage or other problem)?	☐	☐	☐
a. Approximate age of roof covering? _____			☐
3. WATER SEEPAGE, LEAKAGE, DAMPNESS OR STANDING WATER in the basement, crawl space or slab?	☐	☐	☐
4. ELECTRICAL SYSTEM (outlets, wiring, panel, switches, fixtures etc.)?	☐	☐	☐
5. PLUMBING SYSTEM (pipes, fixtures, water heater, etc.)?	☐	☐	☐
6. HEATING AND/OR AIR CONDITIONING?	☐	☐	☐
a. Heat Source is: ☐ Furnace ☐ Heat Pump ☐ Baseboard ☐ Other_____			☐
b. Cooling Source is: ☐ Central Forced Air ☐ Wall/Window Unit(s) ☐ Other_____			☐
c. Fuel Source is: ☐ Electricity ☐ Natural Gas ☐ Propane ☐ Oil ☐ Other _____			☐
7. WATER SUPPLY (including water quality, quantity and water pressure)?	☐	☐	☐
a. Water supply is: ☐ City/County ☐ Community System ☐ Private Well ☐ Other _____			☐
b. Water pipes are: ☐ Copper ☐ Galvanized ☐ Plastic ☐ Other _____ ☐ Unknown			☐
8. SEWER AND/OR SEPTIC SYSTEM?	☐	☐	☐
a. Sewage disposal system is: ☐ Septic Tank ☐ Septic Tank with Pump ☐ Community System ☐ Connected to City/County System ☐ City/County System available ☐ Straight pipe (wastewater does not go into a septic or other sewer system [note: use of this type of system violates state law]) ☐ Other _____			☐
9. BUILT-IN APPLIANCES (RANGE/OVEN, ATTACHED MICROWAVE, HOOD/FAN, DISHWASHER, DISPOSAL, etc.)?	☐	☐	☐
10. PRESENT INFESTATION, OR DAMAGE FROM PAST INFESTATION OF WOOD DESTROYING INSECTS OR ORGANISMS which has not been repaired?	☐	☐	☐
11. DRAINAGE, GRADING OR SOIL STABILITY OF LOT?	☐	☐	☐
12. OTHER SYSTEMS AND FIXTURES: CENTRAL VACUUM, POOL, HOT TUB, SPA, ATTIC FAN, EXHAUST FAN, CEILING FAN, SUMP PUMP IRRIGATION SYSTEM, TV CABLE WIRING OR SATELLITE DISH, OR OTHER SYSTEMS?	☐	☐	☐

Also regarding the property identified above, including the lot, other improvements, and fixtures located thereon, do you know of any:

	Yes*	No	No Representation
13. ROOM ADDITIONS OR OTHER STRUCTURAL CHANGES?	☐	☐	☐
14. ENVIRONMENTAL HAZARDS (substances, materials or products) including asbestos, formaldehyde, radon gas, methane gas, lead-based paint, underground storage tank, or other hazardous or toxic material (whether buried or covered), contaminated soil or water, or other environmental contamination?	☐	☐	☐
15. COMMERCIAL OR INDUSTRIAL NUISANCES (noise, odor, smoke, etc.) affecting the property?	☐	☐	☐
16. VIOLATIONS OF ZONING ORDINANCES, RESTRICTIVE COVENANTS OR OTHER LAND-USE RESTRICTIONS OR BUILDING CODES INCLUDING THE FAILURE TO OBTAIN PROPER PERMITS FOR ROOM ADDITIONS OR OTHER STRUCTURAL CHANGES?	☐	☐	☐
17. UTILITY OR OTHER EASEMENTS, SHARED DRIVEWAYS, PARTY WALLS OR ENCROACHMENTS FROM OR ON ADJACENT PROPERTY?	☐	☐	☐
18. LAWSUITS, FORECLOSURES, BANKRUPTCY, TENANCIES, JUDGMENTS, TAX LIENS, PROPOSED ASSESSMENTS, MECHANICS' LIENS, MATERIALMENS' LIENS, OR NOTICE FROM ANY GOVERNMENTAL AGENCY that could affect title to the property?	☐	☐	☐
19. OWNERS' ASSOCIATION OR "COMMON AREA" EXPENSES OR ASSESSMENTS?	☐	☐	☐
20. FLOOD HAZARD or that the property is in a FEDERALLY-DESIGNATED FLOOD PLAIN?	☐	☐	☐
21. PRIVATE ROAD(S) OR STREETS adjoining the property?	☐	☐	☐
a. If yes, do you know of an existing owners association or maintenance agreement to maintain the road or street?	☐	☐	☐

* If you answered "Yes" to any of the above 21 questions, please explain (Attach additional sheets, if necessary): _____

Owner Initials and Date _____	Owner Initials and Date _____
Purchaser Initials and Date _____	Purchaser Initials and Date _____

LEAD-BASED PAINT OR LEAD-BASED PAINT HAZARD ADDENDUM

Property Address: _____

It is a condition of this contract that, until _____ or the Option Termination Date, whichever occurs first, Buyer shall have the right to obtain a risk assessment or inspection of the Property for the presence of lead-based paint and/or lead-based paint hazards* at Buyer's expense. This contingency will terminate at that time unless Buyer or Buyer's agent delivers to the Seller or Seller's agent a written inspection and/or risk assessment report listing the specific existing deficiencies and corrections needed, if any. If any corrections are necessary, Seller shall have the option of completing them or refusing to complete them. If Seller elects not to complete the corrections, then Buyer shall have the option of accepting the Property in its present condition or terminating this contract, in which case all earnest monies shall be refunded to Buyer. Buyer may waive the right to obtain a risk assessment or inspection of the Property for the presence of lead-based paint and/or lead-based paint hazards at any time without cause.

*Intact lead-based paint that is in good condition is not necessarily a hazard. See EPA pamphlet "Protect Your Family From Lead in Your Home" for more information.

Disclosure of Information on Lead-Based Paint and Lead-Based Paint Hazards

Lead Warning Statement
Every Buyer of any interest in residential real property on which a residential dwelling was built prior to 1978 is notified that such property may present exposure to lead from lead-based paint that may place young children at risk of developing lead poisoning. Lead poisoning in young children may produce permanent neurological damage, including learning disabilities, reduced intelligence quotient, behavioral problems, and impaired memory. Lead poisoning also poses a particular risk to pregnant women. The Seller of any interest in residential real property is required to provide the Buyer with any information on lead-based paint hazards from risk assessments or inspections in the Seller's possession and notify the Buyer of any known lead-based paint hazards. A risk assessment or inspection for possible lead-based hazards is recommended prior to purchase.

Seller's Disclosure (initial)

_____   (a)   Presence of lead-based paint and/or lead-based paint hazards (check one below):
❏ Known lead-based paint and/or lead-based paint hazards are present in the housing (explain).
_____
_____

❏ Seller has no knowledge of lead-based paint and/or lead-based paint hazards in the housing.

_____   (b)   Records and reports available to the Seller (check one)
❏ Seller has provided the Buyer with all available records and reports pertaining to lead-based paint and/or lead-based paint hazards in the housing (list documents below).
_____
_____

❏ Seller has no reports or records pertaining to lead-based paint and/or lead-based paint hazards in the housing.

Page 1 of 2

This form jointly approved by:
North Carolina Bar Association
North Carolina Association of REALTORS, Inc.

REALTOR®

EQUAL HOUSING OPPORTUNITY

STANDARD FORM 2A9 – T
Revised 7/2004
© 7/2008

Buyer Initials _____ _____   Seller Initials _____ _____

Buyer's Acknowledgement (initial)

_____   (c)   Buyer has received copies of all information listed above.

_____   (d)   Buyer has received the pamphlet *Protect Your Family from Lead in Your Home.*

_____   (e)   Buyer has (check one below):

           ❑ Received a 10-day opportunity (or mutually agreed upon period) to conduct a risk assessment or inspection for the presence of lead-based paint and/or lead-based paint hazards; or

           ❑ Waived the opportunity to conduct a risk assessment or inspection for the presence of lead-based paint and/or lead-based paint hazards.

Agent's Acknowledgment (initial)

_____   (f)   Agent has informed the Seller of the Seller's obligations under 42 U.S.C. 4852d and is aware of his/her responsibility to ensure compliance.

Certification of Accuracy

The following parties have reviewed the information above and certify, to the best of their knowledge, that the information provided by the signatory is true and accurate.

THE NORTH CAROLINA ASSOCIATION OF REALTORS, INC. AND THE NORTH CAROLINA BAR ASSOCIATION MAKE NO REPRESENTATION AS TO THE LEGAL VALIDITY OR ADEQUACY OF ANY PROVISION OF THIS FORM IN ANY SPECIFIC TRANSACTION. IF YOU DO NOT UNDERSTAND THIS FORM OR FEEL THAT IT DOES NOT PROVIDE FOR YOUR LEGAL NEEDS, YOU SHOULD CONSULT A NORTH CAROLINA REAL ESTATE ATTORNEY BEFORE YOU SIGN IT.

Buyer:_____(SEAL)   Date_____

Buyer:_____(SEAL)   Date_____

Agent:_____   Date_____

Seller:_____(SEAL)   Date_____

Seller:_____(SEAL)   Date_____

Agent:_____   Date_____

STANDARD FORM 2A9 - T
Revised 7/2004
© 7/2008

PROFESSIONAL SERVICES DISCLOSURE AND ELECTION
[See Guidelines (Form 760G) for instructions on completing this form]

Property Address:_____("Property")
Buyer or Seller:_____
Real Estate Firm:_____("Firm")

1. There are professional services that typically are performed in connection with the purchase and sale of real estate. Buyer or Seller understands that Firm cannot give advice in certain matters that may relate to the purchase or sale of the Property, including but not limited to matters of law, taxation, financing, surveying, wood-destroying insect infestation, structural soundness or engineering.

2. Buyer or Seller acknowledges Firm has recommended that Buyer or Seller consult with a professional for an opinion regarding each service listed below to be performed pursuant to Buyer or Seller's purchase or sale of the Property. Regarding each such service, Buyer or Seller has either selected the service provider listed or elected not to have the service performed. Although Firm may provide Buyer or Seller the names of providers who claim to perform services in one or more of the listed areas, Buyer or Seller understands that Firm cannot guarantee the quality of service or level of expertise of any such provider. Buyer or Seller agrees to pay the full amount due for all services directly to the service provider whether or not the transaction closes.

Service	Selected (initial)	Waived (initial)	Name(s) of Service Provider(s)	Who Orders
Appraisal				
Attorney/Title Exam/Closing				
Home Inspections				
Home Warranty				
Mortgage Loan				
Property Insurance				
Radon Inspection				
Septic Inspection				
Survey* (see note below)				
Title Insurance				
Well/Water Inspection				
Wood Infestation				

Page 1 of 2

North Carolina Association of REALTORS®, Inc.

Individual agent Initials _____ Buyer or Seller initials _____ _____

STANDARD FORM 760
Revised 7/2007
© 7/2008

3. Buyer or Seller hereby agrees to indemnify and hold Firm harmless from and against any and all liability, claim, loss, damage, suit, or expense that Firm may incur either as a result of Buyer or Seller's selection and use of any of the listed service providers or Buyer or Seller's election not to have one or more of the listed services performed.

*NOTE REGARDING SURVEYS: Situations arise all too often that could have been avoided if the buyer had obtained a new survey from a NC registered surveyor. A survey will normally reveal such things as encroachments on the Property from adjacent properties (fences, driveways, etc.); encroachments from the Property onto adjacent properties; road or utility easements crossing the Property; violations of set-back lines; lack of legal access to a public right-of-way; and indefinite or erroneous legal descriptions in previous deeds to the Property. Although title insurance companies may provide lender coverage without a new survey, the owner's policy contains an exception for easements, set-backs and other matters which would have been shown on a survey. Many such matters are not public record and would not be included in an attorney's title examination. In addition, if the buyer does not obtain their own survey, they would have no claim against a surveyor for inaccuracies in a prior survey.

THE NORTH CAROLINA ASSOCIATION OF REALTORS®, INC. MAKES NO REPRESENTATION AS TO THE LEGAL VALIDITY OR ADEQUACY OF ANY PROVISION OF THIS FORM IN ANY SPECIFIC TRANSACTION.

_____   _____
Buyer or Seller   Signature of individual agent

_____   _____
Buyer or Seller   Real Estate Firm (print name)

Date:_____   Date:_____

STANDARD FORM 760
Revised 7/2007
© 7/2008

EXCLUSIVE RIGHT TO REPRESENT BUYER
Buyer Agency Agreement
[Consult "Guidelines" (Form 201G) for guidance in completing this form]

STATE OF NORTH CAROLINA, County of _____ , Date _____ ,
_____ ("Buyer"),
hereby employs _____ [Firm Name] ("Firm") as the
Buyer's exclusive agent to assist the Buyer in the acquisition of real property which may include any purchase, option and/or exchange
on terms and conditions acceptable to Buyer. The individual agent who signs this Agreement on behalf of the Firm shall, on behalf of
the Firm, be primarily responsible for ensuring that the Firm's duties hereunder are fulfilled; however, it is understood and agreed that
other agents of the Firm may be assigned to fulfill such duties if deemed appropriate by the Firm. For purposes of this Agreement, the
term "Firm," as the context may require, shall be deemed to include the individual agent who signs this Agreement and any other
agents of the Firm.

**Buyer represents that, as of the commencement date of this Agreement, the Buyer is not a party to a buyer representation
agreement with any other real estate firm. Buyer has received a copy of the "Working with Real Estate Agents" brochure and
has reviewed it with Firm. Buyer further represents that Buyer has disclosed to Firm information about any properties of the
type described in paragraph 1 below that Buyer has visited at any open houses or that Buyer has been shown by any other real
estate firm.**

1. **TYPE OF PROPERTY:** ☐ Residential (improved and unimproved) ☐ Commercial (improved and unimproved)
   ☐ Other _____
   (a) General Location: _____
   (b) Other: _____

2. **DURATION OF AGENCY:** Firm's authority as Buyer's exclusive agent shall begin _____ , and subject
to paragraph 4, shall expire at midnight, _____ , or when Buyer acquires real property of the type
described in paragraph 1, whichever occurs sooner.

3. **EFFECT OF AGREEMENT:** Buyer intends to acquire real property of the type described in paragraph 1. *By employing Firm as
Buyer's exclusive agent, Buyer agrees to conduct all negotiations for such property through Firm, and to refer to Firm all inquiries
received in any form from other real estate firms, prospective sellers or any other source, during the time this Agreement is in effect.*

4. COMPENSATION OF FIRM:
(a) Firm acknowledges receipt of a non-refundable retainer fee in the amount of $_____ which
   ☐ shall ☐ shall not be credited toward any compensation due Firm under this Agreement.
(b) Buyer acknowledges and understands that Firm expects to receive a fee for Firm's services hereunder in the amount of
   _____ ("Fee") as follows:
   *(Insert dollar amount, percentage of purchase price, or other method of determining Firm's compensation for each type of
   property the Buyer may purchase. Do not insert N/A or a zero [$0]).*
   i. Firm shall seek the Fee from a cooperating listing firm (through the listing firm's offer of compensation in MLS or
      otherwise) or from the seller if there is no listing firm, and Buyer agrees that Firm shall be entitled to receive same in
      consideration for Firm's services hereunder.
   ii. If Buyer purchases property where the compensation offered by the listing firm or seller is less than the Fee, or where no
      compensation is offered by either the listing firm or the seller, Buyer and Firm agree that Buyer:
      _____ will pay the difference between the Fee and the compensation offered.
      _____ will not pay the difference between the Fee and the compensation offered.
   iii. If additional compensation, incentive, bonus, rebate and/or other valuable consideration *("Additional Compensation")* is
      offered through the MLS or otherwise, Buyer will permit the Firm to receive it in addition to the Fee. Firm shall timely
      disclose the promise or expectation of receiving any such Additional Compensation and confirm the disclosure in writing
      before Buyer makes or accepts an offer to buy. (See NCAR Form #770)
(c) The compensation shall be deemed earned under any of the following circumstances:
   i. If, during the term of this Agreement, Buyer, any assignee of Buyer or any person/legal entity acting on behalf of Buyer
      directly or indirectly enters into an agreement to purchase, option, and/or exchange any property of the type described above
      regardless of the manner in which Buyer was introduced to the property; or

Page 1 of 4

    ii. If, within _____ days after expiration of this Agreement, Buyer enters into a contract to acquire property introduced to Buyer during the term of this Agreement by Firm or any third party, unless Buyer has entered into a valid buyer agency agreement with another real estate firm; or

    iii. If, having entered into an enforceable contract to acquire property during the term of this Agreement, Buyer defaults under the terms of that contract.

(d) The compensation will be due and payable at closing or upon Buyer's default of any purchase agreement. If Buyer defaults, the total compensation that would have been due the Firm will be due and payable immediately in cash from the Buyer. No assignment of rights in real property obtained for Buyer or any assignee of Buyer or any person/legal entity acting on behalf of Buyer pursuant to this Agreement shall operate to defeat any of Firm rights under this Agreement.

Notice: Buyer understands and acknowledges that there is the potential for a conflict of interest generated by a percentage of price based fee for representing Buyer. The amount, format or rate of real estate commission is not fixed by law, but is set by each broker individually, and may be negotiable between Buyer and Firm.

5. **DISCLOSURE OF BUYER'S NAME:** Unless otherwise stated in Paragraph 12 below, Firm has Buyer's permission to disclose Buyer's name.

6. **OTHER POTENTIAL BUYERS:** Buyer understands that other prospective purchasers represented by Firm may seek property, submit offers, and contract to purchase property through Firm, including the same or similar property as Buyer seeks to purchase. Buyer acknowledges, understands and consents to such representation of other prospective purchasers by Firm through its agents.

7. **FIRM'S DUTIES:** During the term of this Agreement, Firm shall promote the interests of Buyer by: (a) performing the terms of this Agreement; (b) seeking property at a price and terms acceptable to Buyer; (c) presenting in a timely manner all written offers or counteroffers to and from Buyer; (d) disclosing to Buyer all material facts related to the property or concerning the transaction of which Firm has actual knowledge; and (e) accounting for in a timely manner all money and property received in which Buyer has or may have an interest. Unless otherwise provided by law or Buyer consents in writing to the release of the information, Firm shall maintain the confidentiality of all personal and financial information and other matters identified as confidential by Buyer, if that information is received from Buyer during the brokerage relationship. In satisfying these duties, Firm shall exercise ordinary care, comply with all applicable laws and regulations, and treat all prospective sellers honestly and not knowingly give them false information. In addition, Firm may show the same property to other buyers, represent other buyers, represent sellers relative to other properties, or provide assistance to a seller or prospective seller by performing ministerial acts that are not inconsistent with Firm's duties under this Agreement.

Upon closing of any sale of property not entered in a listing service of which Firm is a member, Buyer authorizes Firm to submit pertinent information concerning the property, including sales price, to such listing service.

8. **BUYER'S DUTIES:** Buyer shall: (a) work exclusively with Firm during the term of this Agreement; (b) pay Firm, directly or indirectly, the compensation set forth above; (c) comply with the reasonable requests of Firm to supply any pertinent financial or personal data needed to fulfill the terms of this Agreement; (d) be available for reasonable periods of time to examine properties; and (e) pay for all products and/or services required in the examination and evaluation of properties (examples: surveys, water/soil tests, title reports, property inspections, etc.).

9. **NON-DISCRIMINATION: THE AGENT (FIRM) SHALL CONDUCT ALL BROKERAGE ACTIVITIES IN REGARD TO THIS AGREEMENT WITHOUT RESPECT TO THE RACE, COLOR, RELIGION, SEX, NATIONAL ORIGIN, HANDICAP OR FAMILIAL STATUS OF ANY PARTY OR PROSPECTIVE PARTY TO THE AGREEMENT.**

10. **OTHER PROFESSIONAL ADVICE:** In addition to the services rendered to Buyer by the Firm under the terms of this Agreement, Buyer is advised to seek other professional advice in matters of law, taxation, financing, insurance, surveying, wood-destroying insect infestation, structural soundness, engineering, and other matters pertaining to any proposed transaction. Although Firm may provide Buyer the names of providers who claim to perform such services, Buyer understands that Firm cannot guarantee the quality of service or level of expertise of any such provider. Buyer agrees to pay the full amount due for all services directly to the service provider whether or not the transaction closes. Buyer also agrees to indemnify and hold Firm harmless from and against any and all liability, claim, loss, damage, suit, or expense that Firm may incur either as a result of Buyer's selection and use of any such provider or Buyer's election not to have one or more of such services performed.

Page 2 of 4

STANDARD FORM 201
Revised 10/2008
© 10/2008

Individual agent initials _____   Buyer initials _____   _____

❑ Buyer acknowledges receipt of a sample copy of an Offer to Purchase And Contract for review purposes.
❑ Buyer acknowledges receipt of a copy of the brochure *Questions and Answers on: Home Inspections.*
❑ Buyer acknowledges receipt of a sample copy of a Professional Services Disclosure and Election form (form #760) for review purposes.

11. **HOME WARRANTY:** The seller of any property Buyer may be interested in buying may or may not provide a home warranty as a part of any sale. If the seller does not provide a home warranty, Buyer may elect to purchase one. Buyer understands that although Firm will assist Buyer in identifying available home warranty products, Buyer must refer specific questions regarding coverage afforded by any such product to the provider thereof.

12. **ADDITIONAL PROVISIONS:** _____
_____
_____ .

13. **ENTIRE AGREEMENT:** This Agreement constitutes the entire agreement between the parties relating to the subject thereof, and any prior agreements pertaining thereto, whether oral or written, have been merged and integrated into this Agreement. No modification of any of the terms of this Agreement shall be valid, binding upon the parties, or entitled to enforcement unless such modification has first been reduced to writing and signed by the parties.

14. **MEDIATION:** If a dispute arises out of or related to this Agreement or the breach thereof, and if the dispute cannot be settled through negotiation, the parties agree first to try in good faith to settle the dispute by mediation before resorting to arbitration, litigation, or some other dispute resolution procedure. If the need for mediation arises, the parties will choose a mutually acceptable mediator and will share the cost of mediation equally.

15. **CONFIDENTIALITY OF OFFERS:** Real estate brokers are prohibited by N.C. Real Estate Commission rule from disclosing the price or other material terms contained in a party's offer to purchase, sell, lease, rent or option real property to a competing party without the express authority of the party making the offer. However, sellers may elect not to treat the existence, terms, or conditions of any offers Buyer may make as confidential.

16. **DUAL AGENCY:** Buyer has received a copy of the "Working With Real Estate Agents" brochure and has reviewed it with Firm. Buyer understands that the potential for dual agency will arise if Buyer becomes interested in viewing property listed with Firm. Firm may represent more than one party in the same transaction only with the knowledge and informed consent of all parties for whom Firm acts.

(a) Authorization *(initial only ONE).*

_____ Buyer authorizes the Firm to act as a dual agent, representing both the Buyer and the seller, subject to the terms and conditions set forth in this paragraph below.

_____ Buyer desires exclusive representation at all times during this agreement and does NOT authorize Firm to act in the capacity of dual agent. *If Buyer does not authorize Firm to act as a dual agent, the remainder of this paragraph shall not apply.*

(b) Disclosure of Information. In the event Firm serves as a dual agent, Buyer agrees that without permission from the party about whom the information pertains, Firm shall not disclose to the other party the following information:
(1) that a party may agree to a price, terms, or any conditions of sale other than those offered;
(2) the motivation of a party for engaging in the transaction, unless disclosure is otherwise required by statute or rule; and
(3) any information about a party which that party has identified as confidential unless disclosure is otherwise required by statute or rule.

(c) Firm's Role as Dual Agent. If Firm serves as agent for both Buyer and a seller in a transaction, Firm shall make every reasonable effort to represent Buyer and seller in a balanced and fair manner. Firm shall also make every reasonable effort to encourage and effect communication and negotiation between Buyer and seller. Buyer understands and acknowledges that:
(1) Prior to the time dual agency occurs, Firm will act as Buyer's exclusive agent;
(2) In its separate representation of Buyer and seller, Firm may obtain information which, if disclosed, could harm the bargaining position of the party providing such information to Firm;
(3) Firm is required by law to disclose to Buyer and seller any known or reasonably ascertainable material facts.

Individual agent initials _____ Buyer initials _____ _____

STANDARD FORM 201
Revised 10/2008
© 10/2008

Buyer agrees Firm shall not be liable to Buyer for (i) disclosing material facts required by law to be disclosed, and (ii) refusing or failing to disclose other information the law does not require to be disclosed which could harm or compromise one party's bargaining position but could benefit the other party.

(d) Buyer's Role. Should Firm become a dual agent, Buyer understands and acknowledges that:
  (1) Buyer has the responsibility of making Buyer's own decisions as to what terms are to be included in any purchase and sale agreement with a seller client of Firm;
  (2) Buyer is fully aware of and understands the implications and consequences of Firm's dual agency role as expressed herein to provide balanced and fair representation of Buyer and seller and to encourage and effect communication between them rather than as an advocate or exclusive agent or representative;
  (3) Buyer has determined that the benefits of dual agency outweigh any disadvantages or adverse consequences;
  (4) Buyer may seek independent legal counsel to assist Buyer with the negotiation and preparation of a purchase and sale agreement or with any matter relating to the transaction which is the subject matter of a purchase and sale agreement.

Buyer agrees to indemnify and hold Firm harmless against all claims, damages, losses, expenses or liabilities, other than violations of the North Carolina Real Estate License Law and intentional wrongful acts, arising from Firm's role as a dual agent. Buyer shall have a duty to protect Buyer's own interests and should read any purchase and sale agreement carefully to ensure that it accurately sets forth the terms which Buyer wants included in said agreement.

(e) Designated Agent Option (*Initial only if applicable*).

_____ Buyer hereby authorizes the Firm to designate an agent(s) to represent the Buyer, to the exclusion of any other agents associated with the Firm. The agent(s) shall not be so designated and shall not undertake to represent only the interests of the Buyer if the agent(s) has actually received confidential information concerning a seller client of the Firm in connection with the transaction. The designated agent(s) shall represent only the interests of the Buyer to the extent permitted by law.

(NOTE: Buyer should consult with Firm before visiting any resale or new homes or contacting any other real estate firm representing sellers, to avoid the possibility of confusion over the brokerage relationship and misunderstandings about liability for compensation.)

Buyer and Firm each hereby acknowledge receipt of a signed copy of this Agreement.

THE NORTH CAROLINA ASSOCIATION OF REALTORS®, INC. MAKES NO REPRESENTATION AS TO THE LEGAL VALIDITY OR ADEQUACY OF ANY PROVISION OF THIS FORM IN ANY SPECIFIC TRANSACTION.

Buyer _____

Buyer _____

Mailing Address _____

Phone: Home _____ Work _____ Fax _____

E-mail _____

Firm _____ Phone _____
          Real Estate Firm Name

By: _____ Individual agent license # _____
          Individual agent signature

Office Address: _____

Phone _____ Fax _____ E-mail _____

STANDARD FORM 201
Revised 10/2008
© 10/2008

UNREPRESENTED SELLER DISCLOSURE AND FEE AGREEMENT
(Selling Agent Represents the Buyer)

This Agreement is entered into on (Date) _____, by and between

_____ as "Owner(s)", and

_____ (Firm Name)

_____ (Associate) as "Broker".

RECITALS:

A. Owner is the owner/seller of property commonly known as _____

_____ (the "Property").

B. Owner is endeavoring to sell the Property without the assistance of a licensed real estate agent; however, Broker has a Buyer/Client, _____
who would like to see the Property.

C. If Owner sells the Property to Broker's Buyer/Client, Owner agrees to pay Broker a fee of _____
_____.

D. THE AGENT SHALL CONDUCT ALL BROKERAGE ACTIVITIES IN REGARD TO THIS AGREEMENT WITHOUT RESPECT TO THE RACE, COLOR, RELIGION, SEX, NATIONAL ORIGIN, HANDICAP OR FAMILIAL STATUS OF ANY PARTY OR PROSPECTIVE PARTY TO THE AGREEMENT.

Accordingly, the parties agree as follows:

1. FEE. If Owner enters into a contract to sell the Property to Broker's Buyer/Client at any time within _____ from the date of Owner's signing this Agreement, Owner shall pay the fee to the Broker at closing. HOWEVER, if, prior to the expiration of this Agreement, Owner enters into a valid listing agreement with another real estate firm, Owner shall NOT be obligated to pay such fee if the listing firm offers compensation to Broker through a multiple listing service or otherwise.

2. BUYER AGENCY. Owner acknowledges that Broker is the agent representing Buyer/Client with respect to the Property. As the agent of Buyer/Client, the Broker has the duty to act on behalf of the Buyer/Client, and will not be acting on behalf of Owner. This duty requires that all information regarding this transaction given to the Broker by Owner be disclosed to Buyer/Client. For example, if Owner discloses to Broker that Owner is compelled by outside circumstances to sell by a certain date, or that Owner is prepared to lower the price, the Broker would be required to disclose this information to Buyer/Client. Please keep this in mind when communicating with Broker. By signing this Agreement, Owner acknowledges that this Buyer/Client agency relationship has been previously orally disclosed to Owner when Broker first discussed an appointment to show Property to Buyer/Client.

> **DO NOT SIGN THIS FORM UNTIL YOU HAVE RECEIVED AND READ THE "WORKING WITH REAL ESTATE AGENTS" BROCHURE**

Owner and Broker each acknowledge receipt of a signed copy of this document.

THE NORTH CAROLINA ASSOCIATION OF REALTORS®, INC. MAKES NO REPRESENTATION AS TO THE LEGAL VALIDITY OR ADEQUACY OF ANY PROVISION OF THIS FORM IN ANY SPECIFIC TRANSACTION.

OWNER(S):   **BROKER (FIRM):**

_____   _____

_____   By: _____

Date: _____   Date: _____

North Carolina Association of REALTORS®, Inc.

STANDARD FORM 150
Revised 7/2006
© 7/2008

Source: This form is the property of the North Carolina Association of REALTORS® (NCAR) and is reproduced with the permission of NCAR.

CONFIRMATION OF ADDITIONAL COMPENSATION
See Guidelines (Standard Form 770G) on proper use of this form.

Property Address:_____("Property")

Buyer or Seller:_____("Client")

Real Estate Firm:_____("Firm")

1. Disclosure. In addition to the compensation set out in the Agency Agreement specified below, a real estate firm is required by law to timely disclose to their client the receipt of (or promise or expectation of receiving) additional compensation, incentive, bonus, rebate and/or other valuable consideration of more than nominal value ("Additional Compensation") from any other party or person in a real estate sales transaction and confirm such disclosure in writing before making or accepting any offer.

2. Agency Agreement. The parties entered into an agency agreement dated _____ (hereinafter referred to as the "Agency Agreement") of the following type (**check one box only**):
- ☐ Exclusive Right to Sell Listing Agreement (NCAR Form 101)
- ☐ Exclusive Right to Sell Listing Agreement (Vacant Land) (NCAR Form 103)
- ☐ Exclusive Right to Represent Buyer (NCAR Form 201)
- ☐ Agency Disclosure and Non-Exclusive Buyer Agency Agreement (NCAR Form 203)
- ☐ _____
  (insert name of other type of agency agreement)

3. Confirmation. Firm hereby confirms that in connection with the sale or purchase of the Property, Firm expects to receive the following Additional Compensation (**check all applicable boxes**):
- ☐ Monetary: $ _____ or _____ percent of sales price of Property received/to be received from _____
- ☐ Non-monetary: (describe) _____ received/to be received from _____ estimated value: $_____
- ☐ Other: _____
  _____
  _____

THE NORTH CAROLINA ASSOCIATION OF REALTORS, INC. MAKES NO REPRESENTATION AS TO THE LEGAL VALIDITY OR ADEQUACY OF ANY PROVISION OF THIS FORM IN ANY SPECIFIC TRANSACTION.

Firm _____
      Real Estate Firm Name

By: _____   Date: _____
      Individual agent signature

ACKNOWLEDGEMENT BY CLIENT

Client hereby acknowledges receipt of a completed copy of this form.

Client: _____   Date: _____

Client: _____   Date: _____

Page 1 of 1

North Carolina Association of REALTORS®, Inc.

EQUAL HOUSING OPPORTUNITY

STANDARD FORM 770
Adopted 10/2008
© 10/2008

OFFER TO PURCHASE AND CONTRACT
[Consult "Guidelines" (form 2G) for guidance in completing this form]

_____, as Buyer,
hereby offers to purchase and _____, as Seller,
upon acceptance of said offer, agrees to sell and convey, all of that plot, piece or parcel of land described below, together with all improvements located thereon and such fixtures and personal property as are listed below (collectively referred to as the "Property"), upon the terms and conditions set forth herein. This offer shall become a binding contract on the date that: (i) the last one of the Buyer and Seller has signed or initialed this offer or the final counteroffer, if any, and (ii) such signing or initialing is communicated to the party making the offer or counteroffer, as the case may be. Such date shall be referred to herein as the "Effective Date."

1. REAL PROPERTY: Located in _____ County, State of North Carolina, being known as and more particularly described as:
Address: Street_____
City:_____
Zip_____
NOTE: Governmental authority over taxes, zoning, school districts, utilities and mail delivery may differ from address shown.
Legal Description:_____
Subdivision Name:_____
Plat Reference: Lot_____, Block or Section _____ as shown on
Plat Book or Slide _____ at Page(s) _____ (Property acquired by Seller in Deed Book _____ at Page _____).
NOTE: Prior to signing this Offer to Purchase and Contract, Buyer is advised to review Restrictive Covenants, if any, which may limit the use of the Property, and to read the Declaration of Restrictive Covenants, By-Laws, Articles of Incorporation, Rules and Regulations, and other governing documents of the owners' association and/or the subdivision, if applicable. If the Property is subject to regulation by an owners' association, it is recommended that Buyer obtain a copy of a completed Owners' Association Disclosure And Addendum (standard form 2A12-T) prior to signing this Offer to Purchase and Contract, and include it as an addendum hereto.

2. FIXTURES: The following items, if any, and if owned by the Seller, are included in the purchase price free of liens: any built-in appliances, light fixtures, ceiling fans, attached floor coverings, blinds, shades, drapery rods and curtain rods, brackets and all related hardware, window and door screens, storm windows, combination doors, awnings, antennas, satellite dishes and receivers, burglar/fire/smoke alarms, pool and spa equipment, solar energy systems, attached fireplace screens, gas logs, fireplace inserts, electric garage door openers with controls, outdoor plants and trees (other than in movable containers), basketball goals, storage sheds, mailboxes, wall and/or door mirrors, attached propane gas tank, invisible fencing including all related equipment, lawn irrigation systems and all related equipment, water softener/conditioner and filter equipment, and any other items attached or affixed to the Property, EXCEPT any such items leased by the Seller and the following items: _____
_____
_____.

3. PERSONAL PROPERTY: The following personal property is included in the purchase price: _ _ _ _ _
_____.

4. PURCHASE PRICE: The purchase price is $_____ and shall be paid in U.S. Dollars. Should any check or other funds paid by Buyer be dishonored, for any reason, by the institution upon which the payment is drawn, Buyer shall have one (1) banking day after written notice to deliver good funds to the payee. In the event Buyer does not timely deliver good funds, the Seller shall have the right to terminate this contract upon written notice to the Buyer. The purchase price shall be paid as follows:
(a) $_____, EARNEST MONEY DEPOSIT with this offer by ☐ cash ☐ personal check ☐ bank check ☐ certified check ☐ other: _____
and held in escrow by _____ ("Escrow Agent") until the sale is closed, at which time it will be credited to Buyer, or until this contract is otherwise terminated. In the event: (1) this offer is not accepted; or (2) any of the conditions hereto are not satisfied, then all earnest monies shall be refunded to Buyer. In the event of breach of this contract by Seller, all earnest monies shall be refunded to Buyer upon Buyer's request, but such return shall not affect any other remedies available to Buyer for such breach. In the event of breach of this contract by Buyer, then all earnest

Page 1 of 8

This form jointly approved by:
North Carolina Bar Association
North Carolina Association of REALTORS, Inc.

STANDARD FORM 2-T
Revised 7/2008
© 7/2008

Buyer initials _____ Seller initials _____

monies shall be forfeited to Seller upon Seller's request, but such forfeiture shall not affect any other remedies available to Seller for such breach.

NOTE: In the event of a dispute between Seller and Buyer over the return or forfeiture of earnest money held in escrow, a licensed real estate broker ("Broker") is required by state law (and Escrow Agent, if not a Broker, hereby agrees) to retain said earnest money in the Escrow Agent's trust or escrow account until Escrow Agent has obtained a written release from the parties consenting to its disposition or until disbursement is ordered by a court of competent jurisdiction. Alternatively, if a Broker is holding the Earnest Money, the Broker may deposit the disputed monies with the appropriate clerk of court in accordance with the provisions of N.C.G.S. §93A-12.

THE PARTIES AGREE THAT A REAL ESTATE BROKERAGE FIRM ACTING AS ESCROW AGENT MAY PLACE ANY EARNEST MONIES DEPOSITED BY BUYER IN AN INTEREST BEARING TRUST ACCOUNT AND THAT ANY INTEREST EARNED THEREON SHALL BE DISBURSED TO THE ESCROW AGENT MONTHLY IN CONSIDERATION OF THE EXPENSES INCURRED BY MAINTAINING SUCH ACCOUNT AND RECORDS ASSOCIATED THEREWITH.

(b) $_____, (ADDITIONAL) EARNEST MONEY DEPOSIT to be paid to Escrow Agent no later than
_____, *TIME BEING OF THE ESSENCE* WITH REGARD TO SAID DATE.

(c) $_____, OPTION FEE in accordance with paragraph 16, Alternative 2, to be paid to Seller on the Effective Date. (NOTE: If Alternative 2 applies, then do not insert $0, N/A, or leave blank).

(d) $_____, BY ASSUMPTION of the unpaid principal balance and all obligations of Seller on the existing loan(s) secured by a deed of trust on the Property in accordance with the attached Loan Assumption Addendum.

(e) $_____, BY SELLER FINANCING in accordance with the attached Seller Financing Addendum.

(f) $_____, BALANCE of the purchase price in cash at Closing.

5. <u>LOAN CONDITION:</u>

(a) **Loan:** Buyer's performance is contingent upon Buyer's ability to obtain a ❑ FHA ❑ VA (attach FHA/VA Financing Addendum) ❑ Conventional ❑ Other: _____ loan at a ❑ Fixed Rate ❑ Adjustable Rate in the principal amount of _____ (plus any financed VA Funding Fee or FHA MIP) for a term of _____ year(s), at an initial interest rate not to exceed _____ % per annum, with mortgage loan discount points not to exceed _____ % and with loan origination fee not to exceed _____% of the loan amount ("Loan").

(b) **Loan Obligations:** The Buyer agrees to:
  (i) Make written application for the Loan, authorize any required appraisal and pay any necessary fees within _____ days after the Effective Date;
  (ii) Promptly furnish Seller written confirmation from the lender of having applied for the Loan.
  If Buyer fails to furnish Seller written confirmation from the lender of having applied for the Loan, Seller may make written demand for compliance. If Buyer does not furnish Seller written confirmation from the lender of application within five (5) days after such demand, then Seller may terminate this contract by written notice to Buyer at any time thereafter, provided Seller has not received either written evidence of the application or a waiver of the Loan Condition, and all Earnest Money shall be forfeited to Seller as liquidated damages and as Seller's sole and exclusive remedy for Buyer's failure to close, but without limiting Seller's rights under paragraph 17 for damage to the Property. Buyer further agrees to:
  (iii) Pursue qualification for and approval of the Loan diligently and in good faith;
  (iv) Continually and promptly provide requested documentation to lender.

(c) **Buyer's Right to Terminate:** If Buyer has complied with Buyer's Loan Obligations in subsection (b) above, then within _____ days after the Effective Date (or any agreed-upon written extension of this deadline) *TIME BEING OF THE ESSENCE*, Buyer shall have the right to terminate this contract by delivering to Seller written notice of termination if Buyer, in Buyer's sole discretion, is not satisfied that the Loan will be approved and funded. If Buyer has timely delivered such notice, this contract shall be terminated and all Earnest Money shall be refunded to Buyer. If Buyer fails to deliver such notice, then Buyer will be deemed to have waived this condition. Thereafter, if Buyer fails to close based upon inability to obtain the Loan, then all Earnest Money shall be forfeited to Seller. If Buyer provides Seller reasonable third-party documentation confirming Buyer's inability to obtain the Loan, then the Earnest Money shall serve as liquidated damages and as Seller's sole and exclusive remedy for Buyer's failure to close, but without limiting Seller's rights under paragraph 17 for damage to the Property. (**WARNING:** Buyer is advised to consult with Buyer's lender to assure that the number of days allowed for Buyer to obtain the Loan is sufficient to allow Buyer's lender time to take all reasonable steps necessary to provide reliable loan approval.)

STANDARD FORM 2–T
Revised 7/2008
© 7/2008

Buyer initials _____ _____ Seller initials _____ _____

6. **FLOOD HAZARD DISCLOSURE/CONDITION** (Choose ONE of the following alternatives):

❑   To the best of Seller's knowledge, the Property IS located partly or entirely within a designated Special Flood Hazard Area. Buyer understands that it may be necessary to purchase flood insurance in order to obtain any loan secured by the Property from any federally regulated institution or a loan insured or guaranteed by an agency of the U.S. Government.

❑   To the best of Seller's knowledge, the Property IS NOT located partly or entirely within a designated Special Flood Hazard Area. If, following the Effective Date of this contract, it is determined that any permanent improvements on the Property are located within a designated Special Flood Hazard Area according to the current FEMA flood map, or if this contract is subject to a Loan Condition and Buyer's lender requires Buyer to obtain flood insurance as a condition of making the Loan, then in either event Buyer shall have the right to terminate this contract upon written notice to Seller, and all earnest monies shall be refunded to Buyer.

7.   **OTHER CONDITIONS:** (State N/A in each blank that is not a condition to this contract.)

(a)   There must be no restriction, easement, zoning or other governmental regulation that would prevent the reasonable use of the Property for ___residential, Homebased bus_____ purposes.

(b)   The Property must be in substantially the same or better condition at Closing as on the date of this offer, reasonable wear and tear excepted.

(c)   The Property must appraise at a value equal to or exceeding the purchase price or, at the option of Buyer, this contract may be terminated and all earnest monies shall be refunded to Buyer, even if the Loan Condition has been waived as provided in paragraph 5.

If this contract is NOT subject to a financing contingency requiring an appraisal, Buyer shall arrange to have the appraisal completed on or before ___this Date / if cash otherwise / NA___

(d)   All deeds of trust, liens and other charges against the Property, not assumed by Buyer, must be paid and satisfied by Seller prior to or at Closing such that cancellation may be promptly obtained following Closing. Seller shall remain obligated to obtain any such cancellations following Closing.

(e)   Title must be delivered at Closing by GENERAL WARRANTY DEED unless otherwise stated herein, and must be fee simple marketable and insurable title, free of all encumbrances except: ad valorem taxes for the current year (prorated through the date of Closing); utility easements and unviolated restrictive covenants that do not materially affect the value of the Property; and such other encumbrances as may be assumed or specifically approved by Buyer. The Property must have legal access to a public right of way.

8.   **SPECIAL ASSESSMENTS: NOTE:** For purposes of this agreement, a "confirmed" special assessment is defined as an assessment that has been approved by a governmental agency or an owners' association for the purpose(s) stated, whether or not it is fully payable at time of closing. A "pending" special assessment is defined as an assessment that is under formal consideration by a governing body. Seller warrants that there are no pending or confirmed governmental special assessments for sidewalk, paving, water, sewer, or other improvements on or adjoining the Property, and no pending or confirmed owners' association special assessments, except as follows (Insert "None" or the identification of such assessments, if any): ___claim by seller_____

_____.

Unless otherwise agreed, Seller shall pay all owners' association assessments and all governmental assessments confirmed through the time of Closing, if any, and Buyer shall take title subject to all pending assessments disclosed by Seller herein, if any.

9.   **PRORATIONS AND ADJUSTMENTS:** Unless otherwise provided, the following items shall be prorated and either adjusted between the parties or paid at Closing: (a) Ad valorem taxes on real property shall be prorated on a calendar year basis through the date of Closing; (b) Ad valorem taxes on personal property for the entire year shall be paid by the Seller unless the personal property is conveyed to the Buyer, in which case, the personal property taxes shall be prorated on a calendar year basis through the date of Closing; (c) All late listing penalties, if any, shall be paid by Seller; (d) Rents, if any, for the Property shall be prorated through the date of Closing; (e) Owners' association dues and other like charges shall be prorated through the date of Closing. Seller represents that the regular owners' association dues, if any, are $_____ per _____. Unless otherwise agreed, Buyer shall pay any fees required for obtaining account payment information on owners' association dues or assessments for payment or proration and any charge made by the owners' association in connection with the disposition of the Property to Buyer, including any transfer and/or document fee imposed by the owners' association.

10. **EXPENSES:** Unless otherwise agreed, Buyer shall be responsible for all costs with respect to any loan obtained by Buyer, appraisal, title search, title insurance, recording the deed and for preparation and recording of all instruments required to secure the balance of the purchase price unpaid at Closing. Seller shall pay for preparation of a deed and all other documents necessary to perform Seller's obligations under this agreement, and for excise tax (revenue stamps) required by law. Seller shall pay at Closing

Buyer initials _____ _____   Seller initials _____ _____

STANDARD FORM 2–T
Revised 7/2008
© 7/2008

$_____ toward any of Buyer's expenses associated with the purchase of the Property, including any FHA/VA lender and inspection costs that Buyer is not permitted to pay, but excluding any portion disapproved by Buyer's lender.

11. HOME WARRANTY: If a home warranty is to be provided, select one of the following: ❑ Buyer may obtain a one-year home warranty at a cost not to exceed $_____ and Seller agrees to pay for it at Closing. ❑ Seller has obtained and will provide a one-year home warranty from _____ at a cost of $ _____ and will pay for it at Closing.

12. FUEL: Buyer agrees to purchase from Seller the fuel, if any, situated in any tank on the Property at the prevailing rate with the cost of measurement thereof, if any, being paid by Seller. *need to see if any at closing*

13. EVIDENCE OF TITLE: Seller agrees to use his best efforts to deliver to Buyer as soon as reasonably possible after the Effective Date of this contract, copies of all title information in possession of or available to Seller, including but not limited to: title insurance policies, attorney's opinions on title, surveys, covenants, deeds, notes and deeds of trust and easements relating to the Property. Seller authorizes (1) any attorney presently or previously representing Seller to release and disclose any title insurance policy in such attorney's file to Buyer and both Buyer's and Seller's agents and attorneys; and (2) the Property's title insurer or its agent to release and disclose all materials in the Property's title insurer's (or title insurer's agent's) file to Buyer and both Buyer's and Seller's agents and attorneys.

14. LABOR AND MATERIAL: Seller shall furnish at Closing an affidavit and indemnification agreement in form satisfactory to Buyer showing that all labor and materials, if any, furnished to the Property within 120 days prior to the date of Closing have been paid for and agreeing to indemnify Buyer against all loss from any cause or claim arising therefrom.

15. PROPERTY DISCLOSURE:
- ❑ Buyer has received a signed copy of the N.C. Residential Property Disclosure Statement prior to the signing of this Offer to Purchase and Contract.
- ❑ Buyer has NOT received a signed copy of the N.C. Residential Property Disclosure Statement prior to the signing of this Offer to Purchase and Contract and shall have the right to terminate or withdraw this contract without penalty prior to WHICHEVER OF THE FOLLOWING EVENTS OCCURS FIRST: (1) the end of the third calendar day following receipt of the Disclosure Statement; (2) the end of the third calendar day following the date the contract was made; or (3) Closing or occupancy by the Buyer in the case of a sale or exchange.
- ❑ Exempt from N.C. Residential Property Disclosure Statement because (SEE GUIDELINES) _____
_____.
- ❑ The Property is residential and was built prior to 1978 (Attach Lead-Based Paint or Lead-Based Paint Hazards Disclosure Addendum.)

16. PROPERTY INSPECTION/INVESTIGATION (Choose ONLY ONE of the following Alternatives):

❑ **ALTERNATIVE 1:**
(a) **Property Condition:** As to all permanent improvements except:_____
_____, it is a condition of this contract that (i) the built-in appliances, electrical system, plumbing system, heating and cooling systems, roof coverings (including flashing and gutters), doors and windows, exterior building surfaces, structural components (including foundations, retaining walls, columns, chimneys, floors, walls, ceilings and roofs), porches and decks, fireplaces and flues, crawl space and attic ventilation systems (if any), water and sewer systems (public and private), shall be performing the function for which intended and shall not be in need of immediate repair; (ii) there shall be no unusual drainage conditions or evidence of excessive moisture adversely affecting the structure(s); and (iii) there shall be no friable asbestos or existing environmental contamination.
(b) **Inspections/Repair Negotiations:** Buyer, at Buyer's expense, may inspect or obtain such inspections of the Property as Buyer deems appropriate. Only items covered by subsections (a)(i), (a)(ii), and (a)(iii) above ("Necessary Repairs") are included in repair negotiations under this contract. All inspections, including but not limited to any additional inspections recommended by Buyer's inspector(s), shall be completed and written notice of Necessary Repairs shall be given to Seller on or before _____ (the "Repair Notice Date"). Seller shall have the option of completing Necessary Repairs or refusing to complete them. Seller shall provide written notice to Buyer of Seller's response within _____ days of Buyer's notice, *TIME BEING OF THE ESSENCE.* Seller's failure to provide said notice as required shall constitute an election by the Seller not to complete Necessary Repairs. If Seller elects not to complete all Necessary Repairs, then Buyer shall have the option of (a) accepting the Property in its present condition, (b) accepting Seller's offer to make repairs to the extent and as described in the Seller's response, or (c) terminating this contract, in which case all earnest monies shall be refunded. The Buyer shall deliver the Buyer's

written decision to Seller within five (5) days after receiving the Seller's written response, or Seller's failure to respond, *TIME BEING OF THE ESSENCE*. Failure of Buyer to provide this written decision by the time stated herein shall constitute acceptance of Seller's agreement to make repairs to the extent and as described in the Seller's response. Buyer shall have the right to verify that any Necessary Repairs have been completed in a good and workmanlike manner.

(c) **Wood-Destroying Insects:** Buyer shall have the option of obtaining, at Buyer's expense, a report from a licensed pest control operator on a standard form in accordance with the regulations of the North Carolina Structural Pest Control Committee, stating that as to all structures, except _____, there was no visible evidence of wood-destroying insects and containing no indication of visible damage therefrom. The report must be obtained on or before the Repair Notice Date. If

the report indicates that there is visible evidence of wood-destroying insects or visible damage therefrom, Seller shall have the option of performing any required treatment or completing Necessary Repairs, or refusing to perform any required treatment or complete Necessary Repairs. If Seller elects not to perform required treatment or complete Necessary Repairs, Buyer shall have the option of accepting the Property without the required treatment or Necessary Repairs, or terminating the contract, in which case all earnest monies shall be refunded. Buyer and Seller shall exercise their respective rights under this subsection (c) in the same manner and within the same time limitations as set forth in subsection (b) above. The Buyer is advised that the inspection report described in this paragraph may not always reveal either structural damage or damage caused by agents or organisms other than wood-destroying insects. If new construction, Seller shall provide a standard warranty of termite soil treatment.

(d) **Radon Inspection**: Buyer shall have the option, at Buyer's expense, to have the Property tested for radon on or before the Repair Notice Date. The test result shall be deemed satisfactory to Buyer if it indicates a radon level of less than 4.0 pico curies per liter of air **(as of January 1, 1997, EPA guidelines reflect an "acceptable" level as anything less than 4.0 pico curies per liter of air).** If the test result exceeds the above-mentioned level, Seller shall have the option of: a) remediating to bring the radon level within the satisfactory range; or b) refusing to remediate. Upon the completion of remediation, Buyer may have a radon test performed at Seller's expense, and if the test result indicates a radon level less than 4.0 pico curies per liter of air, it shall be deemed satisfactory to the Buyer. If Seller elects not to remediate, or if remediation is attempted but fails to bring the radon level within the satisfactory range, Buyer shall have the option of: a) accepting the Property with its then current radon level; or b) terminating the contract, in which case all earnest monies shall be refunded. Buyer and Seller shall exercise their respective rights under this subsection (d) in the same manner and within the same time limitations as set forth in subsection (b) above.

(e) **Cost Of Repair Contingency:** In addition to the above, Buyer shall have the right to terminate this contract if a reasonable estimate obtained by Buyer of the total cost of Necessary Repairs equals or exceeds $_____. This right may be exercised by Buyer without regard to any decision by Seller to complete, or refuse to complete, Necessary Repairs. Buyer shall notify the Seller in writing of its decision to terminate this contract under this Cost of Repair Contingency no later than seven (7) days following the Repair Notice Date, *TIME BEING OF THE ESSENCE*, in which case all earnest monies shall be refunded to Buyer. Neither the cost of wood-destroying insect treatment under subsection (c) above nor the cost of radon remediation under subsection (d) above shall be included in the cost of repairs under this subsection (e).

(f) <u>**CLOSING SHALL CONSTITUTE ACCEPTANCE OF THE PROPERTY IN ITS THEN EXISTING CONDITION UNLESS PROVISION IS OTHERWISE MADE IN WRITING.**</u>

☐ **ALTERNATIVE 2:** *(This Alternative applies ONLY if Alternative 2 is checked AND Buyer has paid the Option Fee.)*

(a) **Property Investigation with Option to Terminate:** In consideration of the sum set forth in paragraph 4(c) paid by Buyer to Seller (not Escrow Agent) and other valuable consideration, the sufficiency of which is hereby acknowledged (the "Option Fee"), Buyer shall have the right to terminate this contract **for any reason or no reason, whether related to the physical condition of the Property or otherwise,** by delivering to Seller written notice of termination (the "Termination Notice") by 5:00 p.m. on _____ 20____, *TIME BEING OF THE ESSENCE* (the "Option Termination Date"). At any time prior to Closing, Buyer shall have the right to inspect the Property at Buyer's expense (Buyer is advised to have all inspections/investigations of the Property, including but not limited to those matters set forth in Alternative 1, performed prior to the Option Termination Date).

(b) **Exercise of Option:** If Buyer delivers the Termination Notice prior to the Option Termination Date, *TIME BEING OF THE ESSENCE*, this contract shall become null and void and all earnest monies received in connection herewith shall be refunded to Buyer; however, the Option Fee will not be refunded and shall be retained by Seller. If Buyer fails to deliver the Termination Notice to Seller prior to the Option Termination Date, then Buyer will be deemed to have accepted the Property in its physical condition existing as of the Option Termination Date; provided such acceptance shall not constitute a waiver of any rights Buyer has under paragraphs 5, 6 or 7 above. The Option Fee is not refundable, is not a part of any earnest monies, and will be credited to the purchase price at Closing.

(c) <u>**CLOSING SHALL CONSTITUTE ACCEPTANCE OF THE PROPERTY IN ITS THEN EXISTING CONDITION UNLESS PROVISION IS OTHERWISE MADE IN WRITING.**</u>

Page 5 of 8

Buyer initials _____ _____   Seller initials _____ _____

STANDARD FORM 2–T
Revised 7/2008
© 7/2008

17. **REASONABLE ACCESS/RESTORATION AND INDEMNITY:** Seller will provide reasonable access to the Property (including working, existing utilities) through the earlier of Closing or possession by Buyer. Buyer and Buyer's agents and contractors shall have the right to enter upon the Property for the purpose of appraising and evaluating the Property, and performing the tests and inspections permitted in this contract. Buyer shall, at Buyer's expense, promptly repair any damage to the Property resulting from any activities of Buyer and Buyer's agents and contractors, but Buyer shall not be responsible for any damage caused by accepted practices either approved by the NC Home Inspector Licensure Board or applicable to any other NC licensed professional performing the inspection that reveal Necessary Repairs as defined under Alternative 1 of paragraph 16. Buyer will indemnify and hold Seller harmless from all loss, damage, claims, suits or costs, which shall arise out of any contract, agreement, or injury to any person or property as a result of any activities of Buyer and Buyer's agents and contractors relating to the Property except for any loss, damage, claim, suit or cost arising out of pre-existing conditions of the Property and/or out of Seller's negligence or willful acts or omissions. This repair obligation and indemnity shall survive this contract and any termination hereof. Buyer may conduct a walk-through inspection of the Property prior to Closing.

18. **CLOSING:** Closing shall be defined as the date and time of recording of the deed and shall be on or before _____
(the "Closing Date"). All parties agree to execute any and all documents and papers necessary in connection with Closing and transfer of title on or before the Closing Date at a place and time designated by Buyer. The deed is to be made to _____
_____.
Absent agreement to the contrary in this contract or any subsequent modification thereto, the following terms shall apply: If either party is unable to close by the Closing Date, then provided that the party is acting in good faith and with reasonable diligence to proceed to closing, such party shall be entitled to reasonable delay of the Closing Date and shall give as much notice as possible to the non-delaying party and closing agent. In such event, however, either party for whom the Closing Date is delayed shall have a maximum of ten (10) days from the Closing Date, or any extension of the Closing Date agreed-upon in writing, in which to close without payment of interest. Following expiration of the ten-day period, the party not ready to close shall be responsible for paying to the other party (if ready, willing and able to close) interest on the purchase price at the rate of eight percent (8%) per annum accruing from the end of the ten-day period until closing occurs or the contract is terminated. Should the delay in closing continue for more than thirty (30) days from the Closing Date or the last agreed-upon extension of the Closing Date, then the non-delaying party shall have the unilateral right to terminate the contract and receive the earnest money, but the right to such receipt shall not affect any other remedies available to the non-delaying party for such breach.

19. **POSSESSION:** Unless otherwise provided herein, possession shall be delivered at Closing. In the event possession is NOT to be delivered at Closing: ❑ a Buyer Possession Before Closing Agreement is attached OR ❑ a Seller Possession After Closing Agreement is attached. Seller shall remove, by the date possession is made available to the Buyer, all personal property which is not a part of the purchase and all garbage and debris from the Property.

20. **OTHER PROVISIONS AND CONDITIONS:** CHECK ALL STANDARD ADDENDA THAT MAY BE A PART OF THIS CONTRACT, IF ANY, AND ATTACH HERETO. ITEMIZE ALL OTHER ADDENDA TO THIS CONTRACT, IF ANY, AND ATTACH HERETO. (**NOTE:** UNDER NORTH CAROLINA LAW, REAL ESTATE AGENTS ARE NOT PERMITTED TO DRAFT CONDITIONS OR CONTINGENCIES TO THIS CONTRACT.)

❑ Additional Provisions Addendum (Form 2A11-T)
❑ Back-Up Contract Addendum (Form 2A1-T)
❑ Contingent Sale Addendum (Form 2A2-T)

❑ FHA/VA Financing Addendum (Form 2A4-T)
❑ Insurance Availability/Affordability Addendum (Form 370-T) (NC Association of REALTORS form only)
❑ Lead-Based Paint Or Lead-Based Paint Hazard Addendum (Form 2A9-T)
❑ OTHER: _____

❑ Loan Assumption Addendum (Form 2A6-T)
❑ New Construction Addendum (Form 2A3-T)
❑ Owners' Association Disclosure And Addendum (Form 2A12-T)
❑ Seller Financing Addendum (Form 2A5-T)
❑ Vacation Rental Addendum (Form 2A13-T)

_____
_____
_____
_____

Page 6 of 8

Buyer initials _____ _____   Seller initials _____ _____

STANDARD FORM 2–T
Revised 7/2008
© 7/2008

21. **RISK OF LOSS:** The risk of loss or damage by fire or other casualty prior to Closing shall be upon Seller. If the improvements on the Property are destroyed or materially damaged prior to Closing, Buyer may terminate this contract by written notice delivered to Seller or Seller's agent and all deposits shall be refunded to Buyer. In the event Buyer does NOT elect to terminate this contract, Buyer shall be entitled to receive, in addition to the Property, any of the Seller's insurance proceeds payable on account of the damage or destruction applicable to the Property being purchased. Seller is advised not to cancel existing insurance on the Property until after confirming recordation of the deed.

22. **ASSIGNMENTS:** This contract may not be assigned without the written consent of all parties, but if assigned by agreement, then this contract shall be binding on the assignee and his heirs and successors.

23. **TAX-DEFERRED EXCHANGE:** In the event Buyer or Seller desires to effect a tax-deferred exchange in connection with the conveyance of the Property, Buyer and Seller agree to cooperate in effecting such exchange; provided, however, that the exchanging party shall be responsible for all additional costs associated with such exchange, and provided further, that a non-exchanging party shall not assume any additional liability with respect to such tax-deferred exchange. Seller and Buyer shall execute such additional documents, at no cost to the non-exchanging party, as shall be required to give effect to this provision. (**NOTE**: If Alternative 2 under paragraph 16 of this contract will apply, Seller should seek advice concerning the taxation of the Option Fee.)

24. **PARTIES:** This contract shall be binding upon and shall inure to the benefit of the parties, i.e., Buyer and Seller and their heirs, successors and assigns. As used herein, words in the singular include the plural and the masculine includes the feminine and neuter genders, as appropriate.

25. **SURVIVAL:** If any provision herein contained which by its nature and effect is required to be observed, kept or performed after the Closing, it shall survive the Closing and remain binding upon and for the benefit of the parties hereto until fully observed, kept or performed.

26. **ENTIRE AGREEMENT:** This contract contains the entire agreement of the parties and there are no representations, inducements or other provisions other than those expressed herein. All changes, additions or deletions hereto must be in writing and signed by all parties. Nothing contained herein shall alter any agreement between a REALTOR® or broker and Seller or Buyer as contained in any listing agreement, buyer agency agreement, or any other agency agreement between them.

27. **NOTICE AND EXECUTION:** Any notice or communication to be given to a party herein may be given to the party or to such party's agent. Any written notice or communication in connection with the transaction contemplated by this contract may be given to a party or a party's agent by sending or transmitting it to any mailing address, e-mail address or fax number set forth in the "Notice Address" section below. Seller and Buyer agree that the "Notice Information" and "Escrow Acknowledgment" sections below shall not constitute a material part of this Offer to Purchase and Contract, and that the addition or modification of any information therein shall not constitute a rejection of an offer or the creation of a counteroffer. This contract may be signed in multiple originals, all of which together constitute one and the same instrument, and the parties adopt the word "SEAL" beside their signatures below.

28. **COMPUTATION OF DAYS:** Unless otherwise provided, for purposes of this contract, the term "days" shall mean consecutive calendar days, including Saturdays, Sundays, and holidays, whether federal, state, local or religious. For the purposes of calculating days, the count of "days" shall begin on the day following the day upon which any act or notice as provided in this contract was required to be performed or made.

Buyer ❑ has ❑ has not made an on-site personal examination of the Property prior to the making of this offer.

THE NORTH CAROLINA ASSOCIATION OF REALTORS®, INC. AND THE NORTH CAROLINA BAR ASSOCIATION MAKE NO REPRESENTATION AS TO THE LEGAL VALIDITY OR ADEQUACY OF ANY PROVISION OF THIS FORM IN ANY SPECIFIC TRANSACTION. IF YOU DO NOT UNDERSTAND THIS FORM OR FEEL THAT IT DOES NOT PROVIDE FOR YOUR LEGAL NEEDS, YOU SHOULD CONSULT A NORTH CAROLINA REAL ESTATE ATTORNEY BEFORE YOU SIGN IT.

Date: _____

Buyer _____ (SEAL)

Date: _____

Buyer _____ (SEAL)

Date: _____

Seller _____ (SEAL)

Date: _____

Seller _____ (SEAL)

STANDARD FORM 2-T
Revised 7/2008
© 7/2008

NOTICE INFORMATION

NOTE: INSERT THE ADDRESS AND/OR ELECTRONIC DELIVERY ADDRESS EACH PARTY AND AGENT APPROVES FOR THE RECEIPT OF ANY NOTICE CONTEMPLATED BY THIS CONTRACT. INSERT "N/A" FOR ANY WHICH ARE NOT APPROVED.

BUYER NOTICE ADDRESS:

Mailing Address: _____

_____

Buyer Fax#: _____

Buyer E-mail Address:_____

SELLER NOTICE ADDRESS:

Mailing Address: _____

_____

Seller Fax#:_____

Seller E-mail Address:_____

SELLING AGENT NOTICE ADDRESS:

Individual Selling Agent: _____

License #:_____

Firm Name:_____
Acting as ❏ Buyer's Agent ❏ Seller's (sub)Agent ❏ Dual Agent

Mailing Address: _____

_____

Selling Agent Fax#:

_____

Selling Agent E-mail Address:_____

Selling Agent Phone#:_____

LISTING AGENT NOTICE ADDRESS:

Individual Listing Agent:_____

License #:_____

Firm Name:_____
Acting as ❏ Seller's (sub)Agent ❏ Dual Agent

Mailing Address: _____

_____

Listing Agent
fax#:_____

Listing Agent E-mail Address:_____

Listing Agent Phone#:_____

ESCROW ACKNOWLEDGMENT

Escrow Agent acknowledges receipt of the earnest money and agrees to hold and disburse the same in accordance with the terms hereof.

Date_____   Firm:_____

By:_____
(Signature)

STANDARD FORM 2-T
Revised 7/2008
© 7/2008

SHORT SALE ADDENDUM

Property Address: _____

The additional provisions set forth below are hereby made a part of the Offer to Purchase and Contract ("Contract") for the Property between Buyer: _____

and Seller: _____ .

1. **Short Sale Defined**. For purposes of this Contract, a "Short Sale" is a sale where: (i) the Purchase Price is or may be insufficient to enable Seller to pay the costs of sale, which include but are not limited to the Seller's closing costs and payment in full of all loans or debts secured by deeds of trust on the Property due and owing to one or more lender(s) and/or other lienholders ("Lienholders"), (ii) Seller does not have sufficient liquid assets to pay the costs of sale, and (iii) the Lienholders agree to release or discharge their liens upon payment of an amount less than the amount secured by their liens with or without the Seller being released from any further liability.

2. **Contingency**. This Contract is contingent upon Seller obtaining Short Sale approval from Lienholders effective through Closing ("Lienholders' Approval") in an amount which will enable Seller to close and convey title in accordance with the Contract. Seller shall use best efforts to obtain Lienholders' Approval and shall reasonably cooperate in the Short Sale process by providing such documentation as may be required. Buyer and Seller understand that Lienholders' Approval may take several weeks or months to obtain, and neither the Seller nor any real estate agent representing Seller or Buyer can guarantee the timeliness of Lienholders' review, approval or rejection. If Lienholders reject the Short Sale, then either party may terminate this Contract by written notice to the other party and all Earnest Money shall be returned to Buyer.

3. **Notice of Lienholders' Approval and Buyer's Right to Terminate**. Seller agrees to provide Buyer with written notice of Lienholders' Approval. Buyer may terminate the Contract at any time prior to receipt of the Lienholders Approval by written notice to Seller, and, in such event all Earnest Money shall be returned to Buyer.

4. **No Guarantee of Lienholders' Approval**. Buyer and Seller understand that:
   - No Lienholder is required or obligated to accept a Short Sale
   - Lienholders may require some terms of the Contract be amended in exchange for approval of a Short Sale
   - Buyer and Seller are not obligated to agree to any of Lienholders' proposed terms
   - **NEITHER THE BUYER, THE SELLER, THE SETTLEMENT AGENT NOR THE BROKERS IN THIS TRANSACTION HAVE ANY CONTROL OVER LIENHOLDERS' APPROVAL, OR ANY ACT, OMISSION OR DECISION BY ANY LIENHOLDERS IN THE SHORT SALE PROCESS.**

5. **No Repairs**. Buyer acknowledges that Seller may not be financially able to make any repairs to the Property that Buyer may request. This acknowledgement shall not affect any rights that Buyer may have under the Contract to terminate the Contract as a result of any election Seller may make not to make repairs.

6. **Other Offers**. Buyer and Seller understand that additional offers may be received by the Seller's Agent, which must be presented to the Seller pursuant to North Carolina law. Such offers may be accepted by the Seller as backup contracts and forwarded to Lienholders for review and approval. Buyer and Seller are advised to seek advice from an attorney to determine their rights and obligations.

7. **Foreclosure**. Seller represents that to the best of Seller's knowledge, a foreclosure proceeding ❑ has not ❑ has been filed with respect to the Property. Further, if during the Short Sale process a foreclosure proceeding is filed, the Seller shall disclose such foreclosure filing to the Buyer. Buyer and Seller understand that if Closing does not occur before the completion of a foreclosure of the Property, Seller will lose all rights and interest in the Property. In such event, the Contract shall be void, and all Earnest Money shall be returned to Buyer. Seller and Buyer acknowledge that if a real estate agent involved in the transaction contemplated by the Contract knows or reasonably should know that a foreclosure proceeding with respect to the Property has been filed, the agent is required by law to disclose it to the Buyer as a material fact.

Page 1 of 2

This form jointly approved by:
North Carolina Bar Association
North Carolina Association of REALTORS®, Inc.

STANDARD FORM 2A14-T
Adopted 1/2009
© 1/2009

Buyer initials _____ _____   Seller initials _____ _____

8. **Tax Consequences and Advice.** Seller is advised to seek advice from an attorney, a certified public accountant or other professional regarding the credit, legal and tax consequences of a Short Sale.

IN THE EVENT OF A CONFLICT BETWEEN THIS ADDENDUM AND THE OFFER TO PURCHASE AND CONTRACT OR THE VACANT LOT OFFER TO PURCHASE AND CONTRACT, THIS ADDENDUM SHALL CONTROL.

THE NORTH CAROLINA ASSOCIATION OF REALTORS®, INC. AND THE NORTH CAROLINA BAR ASSOCIATION MAKE NO REPRESENTATION AS TO THE LEGAL VALIDITY OR ADEQUACY OF ANY PROVISION OF THIS FORM IN ANY SPECIFIC TRANSACTION. IF YOU DO NOT UNDERSTAND THIS FORM OR FEEL THAT IT DOES NOT PROVIDE FOR YOUR LEGAL NEEDS, YOU SHOULD CONSULT A NORTH CAROLINA REAL ESTATE ATTORNEY BEFORE YOU SIGN IT.

Buyer:_____(SEAL)   Date_____

Buyer:_____(SEAL)   Date_____

Seller:_____(SEAL)   Date_____

Seller:_____(SEAL)   Date_____

SAMPLE

STANDARD FORM 2A14-T
Adopted 1/2009
© 1/2009

RESPONSE TO BUYER'S OFFER

TO:_____

RE: OFFER TO PURCHASE_____
Property Address

_____

Dated:_____

Thank you for your offer to purchase the above property (the "Property"). I/we cannot accept the offer as written and hereby reject it. However, while this is not a counter offer, I/we would favorably consider the following changes:

_____
_____
_____
_____
_____
_____
_____

If the above changes are acceptable to you, please submit another offer with the noted changes.

It is further understood that until an offer has been accepted, I/we are free to consider and may accept any other offers to purchase presented that contain terms and conditions satisfactory to me/us in my/our sole discretion.

THE NORTH CAROLINA ASSOCIATION OF REALTORS, INC. MAKES NO REPRESENTATION AS TO THE LEGAL VALIDITY OR ADEQUACY OF ANY PROVISION OF THIS FORM IN ANY SPECIFIC TRANSACTION.

_____   _____   _____
Seller   Date   Time

_____   _____   _____
Seller   Date   Time

Page 1 of 1

North Carolina Association of REALTORS, Inc.

STANDARD FORM 340-T
Revised 7/2008
© **7/2008**

REPAIR REQUEST AND AGREEMENT
[See Guidelines for completing this form (Standard form # 310G)]

_____ , as Buyer,

and _____ , as Seller,

have entered into an Offer to Purchase and Contract ("Contract") regarding the purchase and sale of the following property (insert

property address): _____

_____ ("Property").

1. **Requested Repairs/Remediation/Treatment.** Buyer hereby requests Seller to complete the following repairs to the Property and/or radon remediation and/or treatment for wood-destroying insects (*attach additional page(s) if needed*):

_____

_____

_____

_____

_____

_____

_____

_____

_____

_____

_____

_____

_____

_____

_____

_____

2. **Agreement**. At such time as Buyer and Seller agree which of the repairs/remediation/treatment set forth in paragraph 1 above will be completed, Seller shall complete, prior to Closing, the agreed-upon repairs/remediation/treatment at Seller's expense and in a good and workmanlike manner.

3. **Notification, Verification.** Seller shall notify Buyer upon completion of the repairs/remediation/treatment and provide Buyer with documentation thereof. Buyer shall have the right to verify that the repairs/remediation/treatment have been completed in a good and workmanlike manner. Unless otherwise indicated in the Contract or this Agreement, such verification shall be at Buyer's expense.

4. **Additional Inspections of Hidden Defects.** (*applicable only if Alternative 1 of paragraph 16 of the Contract is in effect*) Buyer reserves the right to obtain inspections of any hidden defects covered under subsection (a) of Alternative 1 that may be revealed by the performance of the repairs/remediation/treatment. Any additional repairs that Buyer may request and Seller may agree to complete as a result of any such additional inspections will be added to paragraph 1 above and shall become a part of this Agreement.

5. **Release of Inspection Reports.** Buyer ❑ does ❑ does not agree to release any inspection reports to Seller.

North Carolina Association of REALTORS, Inc.

Buyer initials _____ _____ Seller initials _____ _____

STANDARD FORM 310-T
Revised 7/2008
© 7/2008

Page 1 of 2

6. **Agreement not to terminate Contract**.

 IF ALTERNATIVE 1 OF PARAGRAPH 16 OF THE CONTRACT IS IN EFFECT: In consideration for Seller's agreement to complete the repairs/remediation/treatment, Buyer agrees to otherwise accept the Property in its current condition and without regard to the estimated cost of any repairs, provided that the repairs/remediation/treatment are completed as agreed. This agreement is subject to buyer's rights under paragraph 4 above as well as any rights Buyer may have under paragraph 7(b) of the Contract.

 IF ALTERNATIVE 2 OF PARAGRAPH 16 OF THE CONTRACT IS IN EFFECT: In consideration for Seller's agreement to make the Repairs, Buyer agrees not to terminate the contract under subsection (a) of Alternative 2. This agreement is subject to any rights Buyer may have under paragraph 7(b) of the Contract .

7. **Effective Date; Entire Agreement.** This Agreement shall become effective on the date it has been signed by both parties. Prior to the effective date, a party's signature hereunder shall not constitute a waiver of any right or option that such party may have under paragraph 16 of the Contract. This Agreement contains the entire agreement of the parties regarding repairs/remediation/treatment and there are no representations, inducements or other provisions other than those expressed herein. All changes, additions or deletions hereto must be in writing and signed by all parties.

THE NORTH CAROLINA ASSOCIATION OF REALTORS, INC. MAKES NO REPRESENTATION AS TO THE LEGAL VALIDITY OR ADEQUACY OF ANY PROVISION OF THIS FORM IN ANY SPECIFIC TRANSACTION.

Buyer: _____ Date _____ Seller: _____ Date _____

Buyer: _____ Date _____ Seller: _____ Date _____

Page 2 of 2

STANDARD FORM 310-T
Revised 7/2008
© 7/2008

NOTICE TO SELLER THAT BUYER IS EXERCISING THEIR RIGHT TO TERMINATE
THE OFFER TO PURCHASE AND CONTRACT (FORM 2-T)

Buyer: _____("Buyer")

Seller: _____("Seller")

Property Address: _____("Property")

1. **Contract**. Buyer and Seller entered into a contract for the purchase and sale of the Property on the Offer to Purchase and Contract (form 2-T) ("Contract"). The Effective Date of the Contract is _____.

2. **Termination by Buyer**. Buyer hereby terminates the contract between Buyer and Seller for the Property for the following reason(s) (check all applicable boxes):

❑ Non-receipt of a signed copy of the N.C. Residential Property Disclosure Statement prior to the signing of this Offer to Purchase and Contract (see paragraph 15 of Contract)

❑ Seller's election not to complete Necessary Repairs requested by Buyer (see Subsection (b) of Alternative 1 of paragraph 16 of Contract)

❑ Seller's election not to remediate or failure of attempted remediation to bring radon level within satisfactory range (see Subsection (d) of Alternative 1 of paragraph 16 of the Contract)

❑ Reasonable estimate of total cost of Necessary Repairs equals or exceeds agreed-upon amount (see Subsection (e) of Alternative 1 of paragraph 16 of the Contract)

❑ Property does not appraise at a value equal to or exceeding the purchase price (see paragraph 7(c) of the Contract)

❑ Exercise by Buyer of option to terminate under Alternative 2 of the Contract (see Subsections (a) and (b) of Alternative 2 of paragraph 16 of the Contract)

❑ Buyer is not satisfied that the Loan will be approved and funded (see paragraph 5(c) of the Contract).

❑ (applicable ONLY if second check box in paragraph 6 is checked) Exercise by Buyer of option to terminate under paragraph 6 of the Contract because, *without disclosure from Seller*, permanent improvements on the Property are located within a designated Special Flood Hazard Area according to the current FEMA flood map, *or* the Contract is subject to a Loan Condition and Buyer's lender requires Buyer to obtain flood insurance as a condition of making the Loan

❑ Seller's delay in closing for more than thirty (30) days from the Closing Date or any extension of the Closing Date agreed upon in writing (see paragraph 18 of the Contract)

❑ Inability to obtain Improvement Permit or written evaluation described in provision 2 of Additional Provisions Addendum (form 2A11-T)

❑ Seller's failure to provide a copy of each vacation rental agreement covering time periods set forth in Vacation Rental Addendum (see paragraph 2 of form 2A13-T)

❑ Exercise by Buyer of right to terminate under paragraph 7 of Back-Up Contract Addendum (form 2A1-T) prior to receipt by Buyer of written notice from Seller that Back-Up Contract has become primary

❑ Seller's refusal to complete corrections described in written inspection and/or risk assessment report (see Lead-Based Paint or Lead-Based Hazard Addendum (form 2A9-T))

Page 1of 2

North Carolina Association of REALTORS , Inc.

EQUAL HOUSING
OPPORTUNITY

STANDARD FORM 350-T
Revised 7/2008
© 7/2008

❏ Exercise by Buyer of right to terminate under paragraph 1 of Contingent Sale Addendum (form 2A2-T) because Buyer has not closed on the sale of Buyer's Property by the Closing Date and the Contingency has not been waived

❏ Exercise by Buyer of right to terminate under paragraph 5 of Contingent Sale Addendum (form 2A2-T) based on Buyer's receipt of Notice of Back-Up Contract from Seller

THE NORTH CAROLINA ASSOCIATION OF REALTORS, INC. MAKES NO REPRESENTATION AS TO THE LEGAL VALIDITY OR ADEQUACY OF ANY PROVISION OF THIS FORM IN ANY SPECIFIC TRANSACTION.

Buyer	Date	Time

Buyer	Date	Time

RELEASE OF EARNEST MONEY BY SELLER*

Seller acknowledges that Buyer is entitled to a refund of any earnest monies received in connection with the contract as a result of Buyer's termination of the contract for the reason(s) set forth above, and hereby agrees that Escrow Agent may disburse any such earnest monies to Buyer.

Seller	Date

Seller	Date

*As set forth in paragraph 4(a) of the Contract, in the event of a dispute between Seller and Buyer over the return or forfeiture of earnest money held in escrow by a broker, the broker is required by state law to retain said earnest money in the broker's trust or escrow account until a written release from the parties consenting to its disposition has been obtained or until disbursement is ordered by a court of competent jurisdiction. Alternatively, if the broker is holding the earnest money, the broker may deposit the disputed monies with the appropriate clerk of court in accordance with the provisions of N.C.G.S. §93A-12.

STANDARD FORM 350-T
Revised 7/2008
© 7/2008

EXCLUSIVE PROPERTY MANAGEMENT AGREEMENT
Long-term Rental Property

This Exclusive Property Management Agreement is entered into by and between _____
_____ ("Owner")
and _____ ("Agent").

IN CONSIDERATION of the mutual covenants and promises set forth herein, Owner hereby contracts with Agent, and Agent hereby contracts with Owner, to lease and manage the property described below, as well as any other property Owner and Agent may from time to time agree in writing will be subject to this Agreement (the "Property"), in accordance with all applicable laws and regulations, upon the terms and conditions contained herein.

1. Property. City:_____ County:_____, NC
Street Address:_____
Other Description:_____
_____

2. Duration of Agreement. This Agreement shall be binding when it has been signed and dated below by Owner and Agent. It shall become effective on _____, _____, and shall be for an initial term of _____. NOT LESS THAN _____ DAYS PRIOR TO THE CONCLUSION OF THE INITIAL TERM, EITHER PARTY MAY NOTIFY THE OTHER PARTY IN WRITING OF ITS DESIRE TO TERMINATE THIS AGREEMENT, IN WHICH CASE IT SHALL TERMINATE AT THE CONCLUSION OF THE INITIAL TERM. IF NOT SO TERMINATED, THIS AGREEMENT SHALL AUTOMATICALLY RENEW FOR SUCCESSIVE TERMS OF _____ EACH UNLESS EITHER PARTY GIVES THE OTHER PARTY WRITTEN NOTICE OF ITS DESIRE TO TERMINATE THIS AGREEMENT AT LEAST _____ DAYS PRIOR TO THE CONCLUSION OF ANY SUCH RENEWAL TERM, IN WHICH CASE THIS AGREEMENT SHALL TERMINATE AT THE CONCLUSION OF SUCH TERM. If Owner terminates this Agreement within _____ days of its effective date, Owner shall pay Agent a termination fee of _____
_____.

3. Agent's Fee. For services performed hereunder, Owner shall compensate Agent in the following manner:
  ☐ A fee equal to _____ percent (_____ %) of gross rental income received on all rental agreements, or
  $ _____ per month, whichever is greater.
  ☐ Other *(describe method of compensation)*: _____
  _____.

Agent may deduct Agent's Fee from gross receipts and collections received before remitting the balance of the receipts and collections to Owner. *Note:* No fees may be deducted from any tenant security deposit until the termination of the tenancy. Thereafter, any fees due Agent from Owner may be deducted from any portion of the security deposit due to Owner.

4. Other Fees: Agent may charge tenants reasonable administrative fees permitted by law and retain any such fees, including but not limited to, fees to cover the costs of processing tenant rental applications. If, in Agent's discretion, tenant leases provide for late payment fees and/or returned check fees, such fees, when collected by Agent, shall belong to _____
_____ (Owner or Agent). Fees for purposes covered under the Tenant Security Deposit Act will be collected, held and disbursed in accordance with paragraphs 7 and 8 of this Agreement.

5. Authority and Responsibilities of Agent: During the time this Agreement is in effect, Agent shall:
  (a) Manage the Property to the best of Agent's ability, devoting thereto such time and attention as may be necessary;
  (b) OFFER THE PROPERTY TO THE PUBLIC FOR LEASING IN COMPLIANCE WITH ALL STATE AND FEDERAL HOUSING LAWS, INCLUDING BUT NOT LIMITED TO, ANY STATE AND FEDERAL LAWS PROHIBITING DISCRIMINATION ON THE BASIS OF RACE, COLOR, RELIGION, SEX, NATIONAL ORIGIN, HANDICAP OR FAMILIAL STATUS;
  (c) Use Agent's best efforts to solicit, secure and maintain tenants, including the authority to negotiate, execute, extend and renew leases in Owner's name for terms not in excess of _____;

Page 1 of 6

(d) Collect all rentals and other charges and amounts due under tenant leases and give receipts for amounts so collected;

(e) Deliver to Owner within 45 days following the date of execution of any rental agreement an accounting which sets forth the name of the tenant, the rental rate and rents collected, and promptly provide a copy of any rental agreement to Owner upon reasonable request;

(f) Provide Owner monthly statements of all monies received and disbursed in connection with Agent's management of the Property, and remit to Owner rental proceeds collected, less any deductions authorized hereunder; provided: (1) this shall not constitute a guarantee by Agent for rental payments that Agent is unable to collect in the exercise of reasonable diligence; and (2) if, pursuant to this Agreement or required by law, Agent either has refunded or will refund in whole or in part any rental payments made by a tenant and previously remitted to Owner, Owner agrees to return same to Agent promptly upon Agent's demand;

(g) Make or cause to be made any repairs which, in Agent's opinion, may be necessary to preserve, maintain and protect the Property; provided, Agent may not make any repairs that exceed $_____ without prior approval of Owner, except that in the case of an emergency, Agent may, without prior approval, make whatever expenditures on behalf of Owner that are reasonably necessary to preserve the Property or prevent further damage from occurring;

(h) Answer tenant requests and complaints and perform the duties imposed upon Owner by tenant leases or any local, state or federal law or regulations, including the authority to purchase such supplies and hire such labor as may be necessary in Agent's opinion to accomplish any necessary repairs;

(i) Retain such amounts from Owner's rental proceeds as may be necessary from time to time to establish and maintain a fund on behalf of Owner in the amount of $_____, from which Agent may pay expenses associated with the management and operation of the Property for which Owner is responsible hereunder;

(j) Negotiate partial refunds with tenants if, in Agent's reasonable opinion, the tenant's use and enjoyment of the Property has been or will be materially and adversely affected as a result of a defect in the condition of the Property (such as a repair to the electrical, plumbing, sanitary, heating or ventilating facilities or a major appliance that cannot be made reasonably and promptly);

(k) Institute and prosecute such proceedings in small claims court as may be necessary and advisable, in Agent's opinion, to recover rents and other sums due the Owner from tenants or to evict tenants and regain possession, including the authority, in Agent's discretion, to settle, compromise and release any and all such small claims proceedings; and

(l) _____
_____
_____
_____
_____
_____

6. Cooperation With/Compensation To Other Agents: Agent has advised Owner of Agent's company policies regarding cooperation and the amount(s) of any compensation, if any, that will be offered to subagents, tenant agents or both. Owner authorizes Agent to (*Check ALL applicable authorizations*):

❑ Cooperate with subagents representing only the Owner and offer them the following compensation: _____
_____

❑ Cooperate with tenant agents representing only the tenant and offer them the following compensation:_____
_____

❑ Cooperate with and compensate agents from other firms according to the attached company policy.

Agent will promptly notify Owner if Agent offers compensation to a cooperating agent(s) that is different from that set forth above.

7. Marketing. Owner authorizes Agent to advertise the Property in such manner as may be appropriate in Agent's opinion, including the authority to: (*Check ALL applicable sections*)

❑ place "For Rent" signs on the Property (where permitted by law and relevant covenants) and to remove other such signs.

❑ place information about the Property on the Internet either directly or through a program of any listing service of which the Agent is a member or in which any of Agent's associates participates.

❑ permit other firms who belong to any listing service in which the Agent participates to advertise the Property on the Internet in accordance with the listing service rules and regulations.

❑ submit pertinent information concerning the Property to any listing service of which Agent is a member or in which any of Agent's associates participates and to furnish to such listing service notice of all changes of information concerning the Property authorized in writing by Owner. Owner authorizes Agent, upon execution of a rental contract for the Property, to notify the listing service of the rental, and to disseminate rental information, including rental price, to the listing service, appraisers and real estate brokers.

Page 2 of 6

Owner Initials _____ _____ Agent Initials _____

STANDARD FORM 401
Revised 1/2008
© 1/2008

8. **Responsibilities of Owner:** During the time this Agreement is in effect, Owner shall:

(a) Be responsible for all costs and expenses associated with the maintenance and operation of the Property in accordance with the requirements of tenant leases or any local, state or federal law or regulations, including but not limited to NC General Statutes Section 42-42, and advance to Agent such sums as may be necessary from time to time to pay such costs and expenses;

(b) Provide funds to Agent promptly upon Agent's request for any cost or expense for which Owner is responsible that Agent, in Agent's discretion, incurs on Owner's behalf, including but not limited to, the costs of advertising, emergency maintenance and repairs, utilities, property taxes, owners' association dues and assessments, court costs and attorney's fees; and further, pay interest at the rate of _____ percent (%) per month on the amount of any outstanding balance thereof not paid to Agent within _____ days of Agent's written request therefore;

(c) NOT TAKE ANY ACTION OR ADOPT ANY POLICY THE EFFECT OF WHICH WOULD BE TO PREVENT AGENT FROM OFFERING THE PROPERTY FOR RENT IN COMPLIANCE WITH ALL APPLICABLE FEDERAL AND STATE LAWS AND REGULATIONS, INCLUDING BUT NOT LIMITED TO, THOSE LAWS AND REGULATIONS PROHIBITING DISCRIMINATION ON THE BASIS OF RACE, COLOR, RELIGION, SEX, NATIONAL ORIGIN, HANDICAP OR FAMILIAL STATUS IN THE LEASING OF THE PROPERTY;

(d) Carry, at Owner's expense, commercial general liability insurance (including products and completed operations coverage) against any and all claims or demands whatever arising out of, or in any way connected with, the operation, leasing and maintenance of the Property, which policies shall be written to the extent allowable so as to protect Agent in the same manner as Owner and which shall be in the minimum amounts of $_____ for each injury or death of one person in each accident or occurrence, and $_____ for property damage in each accident or occurrence; and provide at least annually a copy of such insurance policy or policies to Agent upon Agent's request; (Name of insurance agent:_____; telephone no.:_____)

(e) Indemnify and hold Agent harmless to the extent allowable by law from any and all costs, expenses, attorneys' fees, suits, liabilities, damages or claims for damages, including but not limited to, those arising out of any injury or death to any person or loss or damage to any property of any kind whatsoever and to whomsoever belonging, including Owner, in any way relating to the management of the Property by Agent or the performance or exercise of any duty, obligation or authority set forth herein or hereafter granted to Agent, except to the extent that such may be the result of gross negligence or willful or intentional misconduct by Agent; and

(f) _____
_____
_____
_____
_____
_____
_____
_____

9. Tenant Security Deposits. Agent may, in Agent's discretion, require tenants to make security deposits in an amount permitted by law to secure tenants' lease obligations (such security deposits shall hereinafter be referred to as "Tenant Security Deposits"). If the Agent requires Tenant Security Deposits, they shall be placed in a trust account in Agent's name in a North Carolina bank or savings and loan association. Upon the commencement of this Agreement, Owner shall deliver to Agent a list of any current tenants who previously made Tenant Security Deposits under existing leases and the amounts thereof. Simultaneously therewith, any such Tenant Security Deposits shall be placed in a trust account in Agent's name in a North Carolina bank or savings and loan association, and shall thereafter be administered in accordance with this Agreement.

10. Trust Account Interest. Agent may, in Agent's discretion, place gross receipts and collections, including Tenant Security Deposits, in an interest bearing trust account in the name of Agent in an insured bank or savings and loan association in North Carolina. Interest on any such amounts shall belong to _____ (Owner or Agent), except that with respect to any Tenant Security Deposits, tenant leases shall specify, in Agent's discretion, whether such interest shall be payable to Owner or to the tenant. If the lease provides that such interest is payable to the tenant, Agent shall account for the interest in the manner set forth in such lease. If the lease provides that such interest is payable to Owner or as Owner directs, then such interest shall be paid to Owner or Agent as set forth above. Agent may remove any interest payable to Agent from the account at all times and with such frequency as is permitted under the terms of the account and as the law may require.

11. Entry by Owner. Owner agrees that neither Owner nor any third party acting at Owner's direction, shall enter the Property for any purpose whatsoever during any time that it is occupied by a tenant in the absence of reasonable notice to Agent or tenant and scheduling by Agent or tenant of an appropriate time for any such entry.

Page 3 of 6

Owner Initials _____ _____ Agent Initials _____

STANDARD FORM 401
Revised 1/2008
© 1/2008

12. Lead-Based Paint/Hazard Disclosure. If the Property was built prior to 1978, Landlord understands that Landlord is required under 42 U.S.C. 4852(d) to disclose information about lead-based paint and lead-based paint hazards, and that Agent is required to ensure Landlord's compliance with said law. Landlord agrees to complete and sign a "Disclosure Of Information On Lead-Based Paint And Lead-Based Paint Hazards" form (NCAR form #430-T), photocopies of which will be provided by Agent to prospective tenants. In the alternative, Landlord authorizes Agent, in Agent's discretion, to fulfill Landlord's disclosure obligations by completing and signing said form on Landlord's behalf based on information provided by Landlord to Agent.

13. Duties on Termination. Upon termination of this Agreement by either party, each shall take such steps as are necessary to settle all accounts between them, including, but not limited to, the following:

(a) Agent shall promptly render to Owner all rents then on hand after having deducted therefrom any Agent's fees then due and amounts sufficient to cover all other outstanding expenditures of Agent incurred in connection with operating the Property;

(b) Agent shall transfer any security deposits held by Agent to Owner or such other person or entity as Owner may designate in writing; provided, Owner understands and acknowledges that the Tenant Security Deposit Act requires Owner to either deposit any such deposits in a trust account with a licensed and insured bank or savings institution located in North Carolina, or furnish a bond from an insurance company licensed to do business in North Carolina;

(c) Owner shall promptly pay to Agent any fees or amounts due the Agent under the Agreement and shall reimburse Agent for any expenditures made and outstanding at the time of termination;

(d) Agent shall deliver to Owner copies of all tenant leases and other instruments entered into on behalf of Owner (Agent may retain copies of such leases and instruments for Agent's records); and

(e) Owner shall notify all current tenants of the termination of this Agreement and transfer of any advance rents and security deposits to Owner.

14. Sale of Property. In the event Owner desires to sell the Property through Owner's own efforts or those of a firm other than Agent, Owner shall: (a) promptly notify Agent that the Property is for sale and, if applicable, disclose to Agent the name of the listing firm; and (b) promptly notify Agent if the Property goes under contract and disclose to Agent the agreed-upon closing date.

15. Entire Agreement; Modification. This Agreement contains the entire agreement of the parties and supersedes all prior written and oral proposals, understandings, agreements and representations, all of which are merged herein. No amendment or modification to this Agreement shall be effective unless it is in writing and executed by all parties hereto.

16. Non-Waiver of Default. The failure of either party to insist, in any one or more instances, on the performance of any term or condition of this Agreement shall not be construed as a waiver or relinquishment of any rights granted hereunder or of the future performance of any such term or condition, and the obligations of the non-performing party with respect thereto shall continue in full force and effect.

17. Governing Law; Venue. The parties agree that this Agreement shall be governed by and construed in accordance with the laws of the State of North Carolina, and that in the event of a dispute, any legal action may only be instituted in the county where the Property is located.

18. Relationship of Parties. Although Owner and Agent agree that they will actively and materially participate with each other on a regular basis in fulfilling their respective obligations hereunder, the parties intend for their relationship to be that of independent contractors, and nothing contained in this Agreement shall be construed to create a partnership or joint venture of any kind.

19. Exclusivity. Owner agrees that Agent shall be the exclusive rental agent for the Property, and that no other party, including Owner, shall offer the Property for rent during the time this Agreement is in effect. Any rent nevertheless received by Owner or any third party will be transferred to Agent and thereafter accounted for as if originally received by Agent, including the deduction therefrom of any fee due Agent hereunder.

20. Default. If either party defaults in the performance of any of its obligations hereunder, in addition to any other remedies provided herein or by applicable law, the non-defaulting party shall have the right to terminate this Agreement if, within thirty days after providing the defaulting party with written notice of the default and the intent to terminate, the default remains uncured.

21. Costs in Event of Default. If legal proceedings are brought by a party to enforce the terms, conditions or provisions of this Agreement, the prevailing party shall be entitled to recover all expenses (including, but not limited to, reasonable attorney fees, legal expenses and reasonable costs of collection) paid or incurred by such prevailing party in endeavoring to enforce the terms, conditions, or provisions of this Agreement and/or collect any amount owing in accordance with this Agreement.

Page 4 of 6

Owner Initials _____ _____ Agent Initials _____

STANDARD FORM 401
Revised 1/2008
© 1/2008

22. **Authority to Enter into Agreement; Principal Contact.** Owner represents and warrants to Agent that Owner has full authority to enter into this Agreement, and that there is no other party with an interest in the Property whose joinder in this Agreement is necessary. Either _____ or _____ shall serve as Owner's principal contact for purposes of making all decisions and receiving all notices and rental payments contemplated by this Agreement, and all persons signing this Agreement as Owner hereby appoint either of said persons as Owner's agent and attorney-in-fact for the purposes set forth in this section.

23. **Notices.** Any notices required or permitted to be given hereunder shall be in writing and mailed by certified mail to the appropriate party at the party's address set forth below.

24. **Binding Nature of Agreement.** This Agreement shall be binding upon and inure to the benefit of the heirs, legal and personal representatives, successors and permitted assigns of the parties.

25. **Assignments by Agent; Change of Ownership.** Owner agrees that at any time during the term of this Agreement, Agent may either assign Agent's rights and responsibilities hereunder to another real estate agency, or transfer to another person or entity all or part of the ownership of Agent's real estate agency, and that in the event of any such assignment or transfer, this Agreement shall continue in full force and effect; provided, that any assignee or transferee must be licensed to engage in the business of real estate brokerage in the State of North Carolina. In the event of any such assignment or transfer, Owner may, in addition to all other termination rights hereunder, terminate this Agreement without cause on sixty (60) days' prior written notice to the assignee or transferee of Owner's intent to terminate this Agreement.

26. **Other Professional Services.** Owner acknowledges that Agent is being retained solely as a real estate professional, and understands that other professional service providers are available to render advice or services to Owner at Owner's expense, including but not limited to an attorney, insurance agent, tax advisor, engineer, home inspector, environmental consultant, architect, or contractor. If Agent procures any such services at the request of Owner, Owner agrees that Agent shall incur no liability or responsibility in connection therewith.

27. **Addenda.** Any addenda to this Agreement are described in the following space and attached hereto:_____
_____
_____
_____.

The parties agree that any such addenda shall constitute an integral part of this Agreement. In the event of a conflict between this Agreement and any such addenda, the terms of such addenda shall control.

THE AGENT SHALL CONDUCT ALL BROKERAGE ACTIVITIES IN REGARD TO THIS AGREEMENT WITHOUT RESPECT TO THE RACE, COLOR, RELIGION, SEX, NATIONAL ORIGIN, HANDICAP OR FAMILIAL STATUS OF ANY PARTY OR PROSPECTIVE PARTY TO THE AGREEMENT.

THE NORTH CAROLINA ASSOCIATION OF REALTORS®, INC. MAKES NO REPRESENTATION AS TO THE LEGAL VALIDITY OR ADEQUACY OF ANY PROVISION OF THIS FORM IN ANY SPECIFIC TRANSACTION.

OWNER:

_____(SEAL)   DATE:_____

_____(SEAL)   DATE:_____

_____(SEAL)   DATE:_____

_____(SEAL)   DATE:_____

STANDARD FORM 401
Revised 1/2008
© 1/2008

AGENT: _____
       [Name of real estate firm]

BY:_____ Individual license #_____ DATE:_____
    [Authorized Representative]

Real Estate Agency:_____

Address:_____

Telephone: _____ Fax:_____ E-mail:_____

Owner:_____

Address:_____

Telephone: _____ Fax:_____ E-mail:_____

Social Security/Tax ID#:_____

Owner:_____

Address:_____

Telephone: _____ Fax:_____ E-mail:_____

Social Security/Tax ID#:_____

Owner:_____

Address:_____

Telephone: _____ Fax:_____ E-mail:_____

Social Security/Tax ID#:_____

Owner:_____

Address:_____

Telephone: _____ Fax:_____ E-mail:_____

Social Security/Tax ID#:_____

STANDARD FORM 401
Revised 1/2008
© 1/2008

RESIDENTIAL RENTAL CONTRACT

RESIDENT: _____ ("Tenant")

OWNER: _____ ("Landlord")

REAL ESTATE MANAGEMENT FIRM: _____ ("Agent")

PREMISES: City:_____ County: _____ State of North Carolina
   ❏ Street Address:_____
   ❏ Apartment Complex:_____Apartment No. _____
   ❏ Other Description (Room, portion of above address, etc.):_____
_____

INITIAL TERM: Beginning Date of Lease: _____ Ending Date of Lease: _____

RENT: $ _____ PAYMENT PERIOD: ❏ monthly ❏ weekly ❏ yearly ❏ other:_____

LATE PAYMENT FEE: $_____ OR _____% of rental payment, whichever is greater
(State law provides that the late fee may not exceed $15.00 or five percent (5%) of the rental payment, whichever is greater.)

SECURITY DEPOSIT: $ _____ to be deposited with: (check one) ❏ Landlord ❏ Agent
LOCATION OF DEPOSIT: (insert name of bank): _____
BANK ADDRESS: _____

RETURNED CHECK FEE: $ _____ *(The maximum processing fee allowed under State law is $25.00.)*
SUMMARY EJECTMENT ADMINISTRATIVE FEE (see paragraph 16): $ _____

PETS: ❏ PETS NOT ALLOWED ❏ PETS ALLOWED   NONREFUNDABLE PET FEE (if pets allowed): $_____
TYPE OF PET PERMITTED (if pets allowed): _____

PERMITTED OCCUPANTS (in addition to Tenant):_____
_____

   IN CONSIDERATION of the promises contained in this Agreement, Landlord, by and through Agent, hereby agrees to lease the Premises to Tenant on the following terms and conditions:

   1. **Termination and Renewal:** EITHER LANDLORD OR TENANT MAY TERMINATE THE TENANCY AT THE EXPIRATION OF THE INITIAL TERM BY GIVING WRITTEN NOTICE TO THE OTHER AT LEAST _____ DAYS PRIOR TO THE EXPIRATION DATE OF THE INITIAL TERM. IN THE EVENT SUCH WRITTEN NOTICE IS NOT GIVEN OR IF THE TENANT HOLDS OVER BEYOND THE INITIAL TERM, THE TENANCY SHALL AUTOMATICALLY BECOME A _____ (PERIOD) TO _____ (PERIOD) TENANCY UPON THE SAME TERMS AND CONDITIONS CONTAINED HEREIN AND MAY THEREAFTER BE TERMINATED BY EITHER LANDLORD OR TENANT GIVING THE OTHER _____ DAYS WRITTEN NOTICE PRIOR TO THE LAST DAY OF THE THEN CURRENT PERIOD OF THE TENANCY.

   2. **Rent:** Tenant shall pay the Rent, without notice, demand or deduction, to Landlord or as Landlord directs. The first Rent payment, which shall be prorated if the Initial Term commences on a day other than the first day of the Payment Period, shall be due on _____(date). Thereafter, all rentals shall be paid in advance on or before the **FIRST** day of each subsequent Payment Period for the duration of the tenancy.

   3. **Late Payment Fees and Returned Check Fees:** Tenant shall pay the Late Payment Fee if any rental payment is not received by midnight on the fifth (5th) day after it is due. *This late payment fee shall be due immediately without demand therefor and shall be added to and paid with the late rental payment. Tenant also agrees to pay the Returned Check Fee for each check of Tenant that is returned by the financial institution because of insufficient funds or because the Tenant did not have an account at the financial institution.*

Page 1 of 6

North Carolina Association of REALTORS®, Inc.
Tenant Initials _____ _____

STANDARD FORM 410–T
Revised 1/2008
© 1/2008

4. **Tenant Security Deposit:** The Security Deposit shall be administered in accordance with the North Carolina Tenant Security Deposit Act (N.C.G.S. § 42-50 et. seq.). IT MAY, IN THE DISCRETION OF EITHER THE LANDLORD OR THE AGENT, BE DEPOSITED IN AN INTEREST-BEARING ACCOUNT WITH THE BANK OR SAVINGS INSTITUTION NAMED ABOVE. ANY INTEREST EARNED UPON THE TENANT SECURITY DEPOSIT SHALL ACCRUE FOR THE BENEFIT OF, AND SHALL BE PAID TO, THE LANDLORD, OR AS THE LANDLORD DIRECTS. SUCH INTEREST, IF ANY, MAY BE WITHDRAWN BY LANDLORD OR AGENT FROM SUCH ACCOUNT AS IT ACCRUES AS OFTEN AS IS PERMITTED BY THE TERMS OF THE ACCOUNT.

Upon any termination of the tenancy herein created, the Landlord may deduct from the Tenant Security Deposit amounts sufficient to pay: (1) any damages sustained by the Landlord as a result of the Tenant's nonpayment of rent or nonfulfillment of the Initial Term or any renewal periods, including the Tenant's failure to enter into possession; (2) any damages to the Premises for which the Tenant is responsible; (3) any unpaid bills which become a lien against the Premises due to the Tenant's occupancy; (4) any costs of re-renting the Premises after a breach of this lease by the Tenant; (5) any court costs incurred by the Landlord in connection with terminating the tenancy; and (6) any other damages of the Landlord which may then be a permitted use of the Tenant Security Deposit under the laws of this State. No fees may be deducted from the Tenant Security Deposit until the termination of the tenancy. After having deducted the above amounts, the Landlord shall, if the Tenant's address is known to him, refund to the Tenant, within thirty (30) days after the termination of the tenancy and delivery of possession, the balance of the Tenant Security Deposit along with an itemized statement of any deductions. If there is more than one person listed above as Tenant, Agent may, in Agent's discretion, pay said balance to any such person, and the other person(s) agree to hold Agent harmless for such action. If the Tenant's address is unknown to the Landlord, the Landlord may deduct the above amounts and shall then hold the balance of the Tenant Security Deposit for the Tenant's collection for a six-month period beginning upon the termination of the tenancy and delivery of possession by the Tenant. If the Tenant fails to make demand for the balance of the Tenant Security Deposit within the six-month period, the Landlord shall not thereafter be liable to the Tenant for a refund of the Tenant Security Deposit or any part thereof.

If the Landlord removes Agent or Agent resigns, the Tenant agrees that Agent may transfer any Tenant Security Deposit held by Agent hereunder to the Landlord or the Landlord's designee and thereafter notify the Tenant by mail of such transfer and of the transferee's name and address. The Tenant agrees that such action by Agent shall relieve Agent of further liability with respect to the Tenant Security Deposit. If Landlord's interest in the Premises terminates (whether by sale, assignment, death, appointment of receiver or otherwise), Agent shall transfer the Tenant Security Deposit in accordance with the provisions of North Carolina General Statutes § 42-54.

5. **Tenant's Obligations:** Unless otherwise agreed upon, the Tenant shall:
(a) use the Premises for residential purposes only and in a manner so as not to disturb the other tenants;
(b) not use the Premises for any unlawful or immoral purposes or occupy them in such a way as to constitute a nuisance;
(c) keep the Premises, including but not limited to all plumbing fixtures, facilities and appliances, in a clean and safe condition;
(d) cause no unsafe or unsanitary condition in the common areas and remainder of the Premises used by him;
(e) comply with any and all obligations imposed upon tenants by applicable building and housing codes;
(f) dispose of all ashes, rubbish, garbage, and other waste in a clean and safe manner and comply with all applicable ordinances concerning garbage collection, waste and other refuse;
(g) use in a proper and reasonable manner all electrical, plumbing, sanitary, heating, ventilating, air conditioning, and other facilities and appliances, if any, furnished as a part of the Premises;
(h) not deliberately or negligently destroy, deface, damage or remove any part of the Premises (including all facilities, appliances and fixtures) or permit any person, known or unknown to the Tenant, to do so;
(i) pay the costs of all utility services to the Premises which are billed directly to the Tenant and not included as a part of the rentals, including, but not limited to, water, electric, telephone, and gas services;
(j) conduct himself and require all other persons on the Premises with his consent to conduct themselves in a reasonable manner and so as not to disturb other tenants' peaceful enjoyment of the Premises; and
(k) not abandon or vacate the Premises during the Initial Term or any renewals or extensions thereof. Tenant shall be deemed to have abandoned or vacated the Premises if Tenant removes substantially all of his possessions from the Premises.
(l) _____

_____

6. **Landlord's Obligations:** Unless otherwise agreed upon, the Landlord shall:
(a) comply with the applicable building and housing codes to the extent required by such building and housing codes;
(b) make all repairs to the Premises as may be necessary to keep the Premises in a fit and habitable condition; provided, however, in accordance with paragraph 10, the Tenant shall be liable to the Landlord for any repairs necessitated by the Tenant's intentional or negligent misuse of the Premises;

Tenant Initials _____ _____

STANDARD FORM 410 – T
Revised 1/2008
© 1/2008

(c) keep all common areas, if any, used in conjunction with the Premises in a clean and safe condition; and

(d) promptly repair all facilities and appliances, if any, as may be furnished by the Landlord as part of the Premises, including electrical, plumbing, sanitary, heating, ventilating, and air conditioning systems, provided that the Landlord, except in emergency situations, actually receives notification from the Tenant in writing of the needed repairs.

7. **Smoke Detectors:** Pursuant to North Carolina General Statutes § 42-42 and 42-43, the Landlord shall provide and install operable smoke detectors, either battery-operated or electrical, having an Underwriters' Laboratories, Inc., listing or other equivalent national testing laboratory approval. The Tenant shall notify the Landlord, in writing, of the need for replacement of or repairs to a smoke detector. The Landlord shall replace or repair the smoke detectors within 15 days of receipt of notification if the Landlord is notified of needed replacement or repairs in writing by the Tenant. The Landlord shall ensure that a smoke detector is operable and in good repair at the beginning of the Initial Term of the Tenancy. The Landlord shall place new batteries in any battery-operated smoke detectors at the beginning of the Initial Term of the tenancy; **the Tenant shall replace the batteries as needed during the tenancy.**

8. **Rules and Regulations:** The Tenant, his family, servants, guests and agents shall comply with and abide by all the Landlord's existing rules and regulations and such future reasonable rules and regulations as the Landlord may, at Landlord's discretion, from time to time, adopt governing the use and occupancy of the Premises and any common areas used in connection with them (the "Rules and Regulations"). Landlord reserves the right to make changes to the existing Rules and Regulations and to adopt additional reasonable rules and regulations from time to time; provided however, such changes and additions shall not alter the essential terms of this lease or any substantive rights granted hereunder and shall not become effective until thirty (30) days' written notice thereof shall have been furnished to Tenant. Tenant also agrees to abide by any applicable homeowners' association regulations as they now exist or may be amended. A copy of the existing Rules and Regulations, and any applicable homeowners' association regulations, are attached hereto and the Tenant acknowledges that he has read them. The Rules and Regulations shall be deemed to be a part of this lease giving to the Landlord all the rights and remedies herein provided.

9. **Right of Entry:** Landlord hereby reserves the right to enter the Premises during reasonable hours for the purpose of (1) inspecting the Premises and the Tenant's compliance with the terms of this lease; (2) making such repairs, alterations, improvements or additions thereto as the Landlord may deem appropriate; and (3) showing the Premises to prospective purchasers or tenants. Landlord shall also have the right to display "For Sale" or "For Rent" signs in a reasonable manner upon the Premises.

10. **Damages:** Tenant shall be responsible for and liable to the Landlord for all damage to, defacement of, or removal of property from the Premises whatever the cause, except such damage, defacement or removal caused by ordinary wear and tear, acts of the Landlord, his agent, or of third parties not invitees of the Tenant, and natural forces. Tenant agrees to pay Landlord for the cost of repairing any damage for which Tenant is responsible upon receipt of Landlord's demand therefor, and to pay the Rent during the period the Premises may not be habitable as a result of any such damage.

11. **Pets:** If pets are not allowed, Tenant agrees not to keep or allow anywhere on or about the Property any animals or pets of any kind, including but not limited to, dogs, cats, birds, rodents, reptiles or marine animals. If pets are allowed, Tenant acknowledges that the amount of the Pet Fee is reasonable and agrees that the Landlord shall not be required to refund the Pet Fee in whole or in part. If pets are allowed, Tenant agrees to reimburse Landlord for any primary or secondary damages caused thereby whether the damage is to the Premises or to any common areas used in conjunction with them, and to indemnify Landlord from any liability to third parties which may result from Tenant's keeping of such pet or pets.

The Tenant shall remove any pet previously permitted within_____ hours of written notification from the Landlord that the pet, in the Landlord's sole judgment, creates a nuisance or disturbance or is, in the Landlord's opinion, undesirable. If the pet is caused to be removed pursuant to this paragraph, the Landlord shall not be required to refund the Pet Fee; however, the Tenant shall be entitled to acquire and keep another pet of the type previously authorized.

12. **Alterations**: The Tenant shall not paint, mark, drive nails or screws into, or otherwise deface or alter walls, ceilings, floors, windows, cabinets, woodwork, stone, ironwork or any other part of the Premises or decorate the Premises or make any alterations, additions, or improvements in or to the Premises without the Landlord's prior written consent and then only in a workmanlike manner using materials and contractors approved by the Landlord. All such work shall be done at the Tenant's expense and at such times and in such manner as the Landlord may approve. All alterations, additions, and improvements upon the Premises, made by either the Landlord or Tenant, shall become the property of the Landlord and shall remain upon and become a part of the Premises at the end of the tenancy hereby created.

13. **Occupants:** The Tenant shall not allow or permit the Premises to be occupied or used as a residence by any person other than Tenant and the Permitted Occupants.

14. **Rental Application:** In the event the Tenant has submitted a Rental Application in connection with this lease, Tenant acknowledges that the Landlord has relied upon the Application as an inducement for entering into this Lease and Tenant warrants to Landlord that the facts stated in the Application are true to the best of Tenant's knowledge. If any facts stated in the Rental Application prove to be untrue, the Landlord shall have the right to terminate the tenancy and to collect from Tenant any damages resulting therefrom.

STANDARD FORM 410 – T
Revised 1/2008
© 1/2008

Tenant Initials _____ _____

15. **Tenant's Duties Upon Termination:** Upon any termination of the Tenancy created hereby, whether by the Landlord or the Tenant and whether for breach or otherwise, the Tenant shall: (1) pay all utility bills due for services to the Premises for which he is responsible and have all such utility services discontinued; (2) vacate the Premises removing therefrom all Tenant's personal

property of whatever nature; (3) properly sweep and clean the Premises, including plumbing fixtures, refrigerators, stoves and sinks, removing therefrom all rubbish, trash, garbage and refuse; (4) make such repairs and perform such other acts as are necessary to return the Premises, and any appliances or fixtures furnished in connection therewith, in the same condition as when Tenant took possession of the Premises; provided, however, Tenant shall not be responsible for ordinary wear and tear or for repairs required by law or by paragraph 6 above to be performed by Landlord; (5) fasten and lock all doors and windows; (6) return to the Landlord all keys to the Premises; and (7) notify the Landlord of the address to which the balance of the Security Deposit may be returned. If the Tenant fails to sweep out and clean the Premises, appliances and fixtures as herein provided, Tenant shall become liable, without notice or demand, to the Landlord for the actual costs of cleaning (over and above ordinary wear and tear), which may be deducted from the Security Deposit as provided in paragraph 4 above.

16. **Tenant's Default:** In the event the Tenant shall fail to:

(a) pay the rentals herein reserved as and when they shall become due hereunder; or

(b) perform any other promise, duty or obligation herein agreed to by him or imposed upon him by law and such failure shall continue for a period of five (5) days from the date the Landlord provides Tenant with written notice of such failure,

then in either of such events and as often as either of them may occur, the Landlord, in addition to all other rights and remedies provided by law, may, at its option and with or without notice to Tenant, either (i) terminate this lease or (ii) terminate the Tenant's right to possession of the Premises without terminating this lease. Regardless of whether Landlord terminates this lease or only terminates the Tenant's right of possession without terminating this lease, Landlord shall be immediately entitled to possession of the Premises and the Tenant shall peacefully surrender possession of the Premises to Landlord immediately upon Landlord's demand. In the event Tenant shall fail or refuse to surrender possession of the Premises, Landlord shall, in compliance with Article 2A of Chapter 42 of the General Statutes of North Carolina, reenter and retake possession of the Premises only through a summary ejectment proceeding. If a summary ejectment proceeding is instituted against Tenant, in addition to any court costs and past-due rent that may be awarded, Tenant shall be responsible for paying Landlord the Summary Ejectment Administrative Fee, the amount of which shall be reasonably related to the additional expense in filing the proceeding. In the event Landlord terminates this lease, all further rights and duties hereunder shall terminate and Landlord shall be entitled to collect from Tenant all accrued but unpaid rents and any damages resulting from the Tenant's breach. In the event Landlord terminates the Tenant's right of possession without terminating this lease, Tenant shall remain liable for the full performance of all the covenants hereof, and Landlord shall use reasonable efforts to re-let the Premises on Tenant's behalf. Any such rentals reserved from such re-letting shall be applied first to the costs of re-letting the Premises and then to the rentals due hereunder. In the event the rentals from such re-letting are insufficient to pay the rentals due hereunder in full, Tenant shall be liable to the Landlord for any deficiency. In the event Landlord institutes a legal action against the Tenant to enforce the lease or to recover any sums due hereunder, Tenant agrees to pay Landlord reasonable attorney's fees in addition to all other damages. No fees may be deducted from the Tenant Security Deposit until the termination of the tenancy.

17. **Landlord's Default; Limitation of Remedies and Damages:** Until the Tenant notifies the Landlord in writing of an alleged default and affords the Landlord a reasonable time within which to cure, no default by the Landlord in the performance of any of the promises or obligations herein agreed to by him or imposed upon him by law shall constitute a material breach of this lease and the Tenant shall have no right to terminate this lease for any such default or suspend his performance hereunder. In no event and regardless of their duration shall any defective condition of or failure to repair, maintain, or provide any area, fixture or facility used in connection with recreation or recreational activities, including but not limited to swimming pools, club houses, and tennis courts, constitute a material breach of this lease and the Tenant shall have no right to terminate this lease or to suspend his performance hereunder. In any legal action instituted by the Tenant against the Landlord, the Tenant's damages shall be limited to the difference, if any, between the rent reserved in this lease and the reasonable rental value of the Premises, taking into account the Landlord's breach or breaches, and in no event, except in the case of the Landlord's willful or wanton negligence, shall the Tenant collect any consequential or secondary damages resulting from the breach or breaches, including but not limited to the following items: damage or destruction of furniture or other personal property of any kind located in or about the Premises, moving expenses, storage expenses, alternative interim housing expenses, and expenses of locating and procuring alternative housing.

18. **Removal, Storage and Disposition of Tenant's Personal Property:**

(a) Ten days after being placed in lawful possession by execution of a writ of possession, the Landlord may throw away, dispose of, or sell all items of personal property remaining on the Premises. During the 10-day period after being placed in lawful possession by execution of a writ of possession, the Landlord may move for storage purposes, but shall not throw away, dispose of, or sell any items of personal property remaining on the Premises unless otherwise provided for in Chapter 42 of the North Carolina General Statutes. Upon the Tenant's request prior to the expiration of the 10-day period, the Landlord shall release possession of the property to the Tenant during regular business hours or at a time agreed upon. If the Landlord elects to sell the property at public or private sale, the Landlord shall give written notice to the Tenant by first-class mail to the Tenant's last known address at least seven

Page 4 of 6

Tenant Initials _____ _____

STANDARD FORM 410 – T
Revised 1/2008
© 1/2008

days prior to the day of the sale. The seven-day notice of sale may run concurrently with the 10-day period which allows the Tenant to request possession of the property. The written notice shall state the date, time, and place of the sale, and that any surplus of proceeds from the sale, after payment of unpaid rents, damages, storage fees, and sale costs, shall be disbursed to the Tenant, upon request, within 10 days after the sale, and will thereafter be delivered to the government of the county in which the rental property is located. Upon the Tenant's request prior to the day of sale, the Landlord shall release possession of the property to the Tenant during regular business hours or at a time agreed upon. The Landlord may apply the proceeds of the sale to the unpaid rents, damages, storage fees, and sale costs. Any surplus from the sale shall be disbursed to the Tenant, upon request, within 10 days of the sale and shall thereafter be delivered to the government of the county in which the rental property is located.

(b) If the total value of all property remaining on the Premises at the time of execution of a writ of possession in an action for summary ejectment is less than one hundred dollars ($100.00), then the property shall be deemed abandoned five days after the time of execution, and the Landlord may throw away or dispose of the property. Upon the Tenant's request prior to the expiration of the five-day period, the Landlord shall release possession of the property to the Tenant during regular business hours or at a time agreed upon.

19. **Bankruptcy:** If any bankruptcy or insolvency proceedings are filed by or against the Tenant or if the Tenant makes any assignment for the benefit of creditors, the Landlord may, at his option, immediately terminate this Tenancy, and reenter and repossess the Premises, subject to the provisions of the Bankruptcy Code (11 USC Section 101, et. seq.) and the order of any court having jurisdiction thereunder.

20. **Tenant's Insurance; Release and Indemnity Provisions:** The Tenant shall be solely responsible for insuring any of his personal property located or stored upon the Premises upon the risks of damage, destruction, or loss resulting from theft, fire, storm and all other hazards and casualties. Regardless of whether the Tenant secures such insurance, the Landlord and his agents shall not be liable for any damage to, or destruction or loss of, any of the Tenant's personal property located or stored upon the Premises regardless of the cause or causes of such damage, destruction, or loss, unless such loss or destruction is attributable to the intentional acts or willful or wanton negligence of the Landlord. The Tenant agrees to release and indemnify the Landlord and his agents from and against liability for injury to the person of the Tenant or to any members of his household resulting from any cause whatsoever except only such personal injury caused by the negligent, or intentional acts of the Landlord or his agents.

21. **Agent:** The Landlord and the Tenant acknowledge that the Landlord may, from time to time in his discretion, engage a third party ("the Agent") to manage, supervise and operate the Premises or the complex, if any, of which they are a part. If such an Agent is managing, supervising and operating the Premises at the time this lease is executed, his name will be shown as "Agent" on the first page hereof. With respect to any Agent engaged pursuant to this paragraph, the Landlord and the Tenant hereby agree that: (1) Agent acts for and represents Landlord in this transaction; (2) Agent shall have only such authority as provided in the management contract existing between the Landlord and Agent; (3) Agent may perform without objection from the Tenant, any obligation or exercise any right of the Landlord imposed or given herein or by law and such performance shall be valid and binding, if authorized by the Landlord, as if performed by the Landlord; (4) the Tenant shall pay all rentals to the Agent if directed to do so by the Landlord; (5) except as otherwise provided by law, the Agent shall not be liable to the Tenant for the nonperformance of the obligations or promises of the Landlord contained herein; (6) nothing contained herein shall modify the management contract existing between the Landlord and the Agent; however, the Landlord and the Agent may from time to time modify the management agreement in any manner which they deem appropriate; (7) the Landlord, may, in his discretion and in accordance with any management agreement, remove without replacing or remove and replace any agent engaged to manage, supervise and operate the Premises.

22. **Form:** The Landlord and Tenant hereby acknowledge that their agreement is evidenced by this form contract which may contain some minor inaccuracies when applied to the particular factual setting of the parties. The Landlord and Tenant agree that the courts shall liberally and broadly interpret this lease, ignoring minor inconsistencies and inaccuracies, and that the courts shall apply the lease to determine all disputes between the parties in the manner which most effectuates their intent as expressed herein. The following rules of construction shall apply: (1) handwritten and typed additions or alterations shall control over the preprinted language when there is an inconsistency between them; (2) the lease shall not be strictly construed against either the Landlord or the Tenant; (3) paragraph headings are used only for convenience of reference and shall not be considered as a substantive part of this lease; (4) words in the singular shall include the plural and the masculine shall include the feminine and neuter genders, as appropriate; and (5) the invalidity of one or more provisions of this lease shall not affect the validity of any other provisions hereof and this lease shall be construed and enforced as if such invalid provision(s) were not included.

23. **Amendment of Laws:** In the event that subsequent to the execution of this lease any state statute regulating or affecting any duty or obligation imposed upon the Landlord pursuant to this lease is enacted, amended, or repealed, the Landlord may, at his option, elect to perform in accordance with such statute, amendment, or act of repeal in lieu of complying with the analogous provision of this lease.

24. **Eminent Domain and Casualties:** The Landlord shall have the option to terminate this lease if the Premises, or any part thereof, are condemned or sold in lieu of condemnation or damaged by fire or other casualty.

25. **Assignment:** The Tenant shall not assign this lease or sublet the Premises in whole or part.

Page 5 of 6

Tenant Initials _____ _____

26. **Waiver:** No waiver of any breach of any obligation or promise contained herein shall be regarded as a waiver of any future breach of the same or any other obligation or promise.

27. **Other Terms and Conditions:**

(a) ❑ (Check if applicable) The Premises were built prior to 1978. (Attach Standard Form # 430 - T, "Disclosure of Information on Lead-Based Paint and Lead-Based Paint Hazards.")

(b) If there is an Agent involved in this transaction, Agent hereby discloses to Tenant that Agent is acting for and represents Landlord.

(c) The following additional terms and conditions shall also be a part of this lease:

_____
_____
_____

(d) Itemize all addenda to this Contract and attach hereto: _____
_____

28. **Inspection of Premises:** Within _____ days of occupying the Premises, Tenant has the right to inspect the Premises and complete a Move-in Inspection Form.

29. **Notice:** Any notices required or authorized to be given hereunder or pursuant to applicable law shall be mailed or hand delivered to the following addresses:

Tenant: the address of the Premises

Landlord: the address to which rental payments are sent.

30. **Execution; Counterparts:** When Tenant signs this lease, he acknowledges he has read and agrees to the provisions of this lease. This lease is executed in_____ (number) counterparts with an executed counterpart being retained by each party.

31. **Entire Agreement:** This Agreement contains the entire agreement of the parties and there are no representations, inducements or other provisions other than those expressed in writing. All changes, additions or deletions hereto must be in writing and signed by all parties.

THE NORTH CAROLINA ASSOCIATION OF REALTORS®, INC. MAKES NO REPRESENTATION AS TO THE LEGAL VALIDITY OR ADEQUACY OF ANY PROVISION OF THIS FORM IN ANY SPECIFIC TRANSACTION.

TENANT: LANDLORD:

_____(SEAL)   _____(SEAL)

_____(SEAL)   _____(SEAL)

Date: _____   By:_____, AGENT

                                        _____(SEAL)

                                        Date: _____

STANDARD FORM 410–T
Revised 1/2008
© 1/2008

Glossary

abstract of title The condensed history of a title to a particular parcel of real estate, consisting of a summary of the original grant and all subsequent conveyances and encumbrances affecting the property and a certification by the abstractor that the history is complete and accurate.

acceleration clause The clause in a mortgage or deed of trust that can be enforced to make the entire debt due immediately if the borrower defaults on an installment payment or another covenant.

acceptance Expression of intent by the offeree to be bound by the terms of the offer; must be in writing if the contract pertains to real property. Acceptance must be communicated to the opposite party to create a contract.

accession Acquiring title to additions or improvements to real property as a result of the annexation of fixtures or the accretion of alluvial deposits along the banks of streams.

accretion The increase or addition of land by the deposit of sand or soil washed up naturally from a river, lake, or sea.

accrued items On a closing statement, items of expense that are incurred but not yet payable, such as interest on a mortgage loan or taxes on real property.

acre A measure of land equal to 43,560 square feet, 4,840 square yards, 4,047 square meters, 160 square rods, or 0.4047 hectare.

actual eviction The legal process that results in the tenant's being physically removed from the leased premises; summary ejectment.

adjustable rate mortgage (ARM) A loan characterized by a fluctuating interest rate, usually one tied to a published index. Caps for adjustments on periodic interest, lifetime interest, and payment amounts are normal.

adjusted basis *See* basis.

ad valorem tax A tax levied according to value, generally used to refer to real estate tax.

adverse possession The open, continuous, exclusive, adverse, notorious, (OCEAN) possession of another's land under a claim of title. Possession for a statutory period of 20 years in North Carolina may be a means of acquiring title.

aesthetic zoning Zoning ordinances that regulate the appearance of real property, such as exterior color, exterior construction material, required screening and fencing.

age-life method A method of depreciation computed by dividing the replacement cost of a property by the number of years of remaining useful life; also called the straight-line method.

agency The relationship between a principal and an agent wherein the agent is authorized to represent the principal in certain transactions.

agent One who acts or has the power to act for another. A fiduciary relationship is created under the law of agency when a property owner, as the principal, executes a listing agreement or management contract authorizing a licensed real estate broker to be the property owner's agent. *See* LOADS.

agricultural fixture In North Carolina, a fixture attached to leased property by a tenant farmer is considered the landowner's real property rather than the tenant's personal property.

air rights The right to use the open space above a property, usually allowing the surface to be used for another purpose.

alienation The act of transferring property to another. Alienation may be voluntary, such as by gift or sale, or involuntary, as through eminent domain or adverse possession.

alienation clause This clause prevents the borrower from letting someone else assume the debt without the lender's approval. *See* due-on-sale clause.

Americans with Disabilities Act (ADA) Federal act implementing regulations that protect citizens with mental or physical disabilities. Does not apply to residential housing but to commercial facilities and places of public accommodation.

American Land Title Association (ALTA) policy A title insurance policy that protects the interest in a collateral property of a mortgage lender that originates a new real estate loan.

amortized loan A loan in which principal as well as interest is payable in periodic installments over the term of the loan.

annual percentage rate (APR) The relationship of the total finance charges associated with a loan. This must be disclosed to borrowers by lenders under the Truth-in-Lending Act.

anticipation The appraisal principle that value can increase or decrease based on the expectation of some future benefit or detriment affecting the property.

antitrust laws   Laws designed to preserve the free enterprise of the open marketplace by making illegal certain private conspiracies and combinations formed to minimize competition. Most violations of antitrust laws in the real estate business involve either price fixing (brokers conspiring to set fixed compensation rates) or allocation of customers or markets (brokers agreeing to limit their areas of trade or dealing to certain areas or properties).

appraisal   An estimate of the quantity, quality, or value of something. The process through which conclusions of property value are obtained; also refers to the report that sets forth the process of estimation and conclusion of value.

appreciation   An increase in the worth or value of a property due to economic or related causes, which may prove to be either temporary or permanent; opposite of depreciation.

appurtenance   A right, a privilege, or an improvement belonging to, and passing with, the land.

arm's-length transaction   A transaction where the parties are dealing from equal bargaining positions.

asbestos   A fire-resistant mineral fiber used in a wide variety of building supplies prior to 1978; environmental health hazard, when friable, that can cause respiratory diseases and cancer.

assessment   (1) The imposition of a tax, charge, or levy, usually according to established rates. (2) Official valuation of property for the purpose of establishing assessed value for tax purposes.

assignment   The transfer to another party in writing of rights or interest in a bond, a mortgage, a lease, or another instrument.

assumption of mortgage   Acquiring title to property on which there is an existing mortgage and agreeing to be personally liable for the terms and conditions of the mortgage, including payments.

auction   A form of selling property where oral bids are taken and the property is sold to the highest bidder.

avulsion   The sudden tearing away of land, as by earthquake, flood, volcanic action, or the sudden change in the course of a stream. The loss of land may not result in loss of title to the property.

backup offer   An offer submitted to the property owner with knowledge that the owner is already under contract; a secondary offer.

balloon payment   A final payment of a mortgage loan that is larger than the required periodic payments because the loan amount was not fully amortized.

baseboard   A board around the bottom of a wall perpendicular to the floor. Sometimes called wains, baseboards cover the gap between the floor and the wall, protecting the wall from scuffs and providing a decorative accent.

basement   Story-high space below the first floor that is totally or partially below the exterior grade; floor is usually concrete slab.

basis   The financial interest that the IRS attributes to an owner of an investment property for the purpose of determining annual depreciation and gain or loss on the sale of the asset. If a property was acquired by purchase, the owner's basis is the cost of the property plus allowable closing costs plus the value of any capital expenditures for improvements to the property, minus any depreciation allowable or actually taken. This new basis is called the adjusted basis.

beneficiary   (1) The person for whom a trust operates or in whose behalf the income from a trust estate is drawn. (2) A lender in a deed of trust loan transaction. (3) The recipient of personal property (a bequest or legacy) in a will.

bilateral contract   *See* contract.

blanket loan   A mortgage covering more than one parcel of real estate, providing for each parcel's partial release from the mortgage lien upon repayment of a definite portion of the debt.

blockbusting   The illegal practice of inducing homeowners to sell their properties by making representations regarding the entry or prospective entry of persons of a particular protected class into the neighborhood.

boot   Money or property given to make up any difference in value or equity between two properties in a 1031 exchange.

branch office   A secondary place of business apart from the principal or main office from which real estate business is conducted. A branch office usually must be run by a broker-in-charge working on behalf of the broker.

breach of contract   The violation of any terms or conditions in a contract without legal excuse; for example, failure to make a payment when it is due.

broad form (HO-2)   An insurance policy covering buildings and personal property against loss or damage from fire, lightning, removal, windstorm, hail, explosion, riot, smoke, vandalism, and theft. This form also covers falling objects; weight of snow, ice, or sleet; collapse of buildings; malfunctioning heating systems; accidental discharge of water or steam; and electrical currents that are artificially generated.

broker   (1) One who acts as an intermediary on behalf of others for a fee or commission. (2) One who is licensed to list, lease, buy, exchange, auction, negotiate or sell interest in real estate for others for a fee.

brokerage   The bringing together of buyers and sellers in the marketplace.

broker-in-charge   Required for each brokerage firm and each branch office, the full broker responsible for displaying all licenses properly, notifying the North Carolina Real Estate Commission of any change of business address or trade name, ensuring that all advertising is done properly, maintaining the trust account and trust account records properly, retaining and maintaining all real estate transaction records properly, and supervising all provisional brokers associated with the firm or office.

BTU (British Thermal Unit)   A measure of heat used in rating the capacity of heating and cooling systems.

buffer zone   A strip of land, usually used as a park or designated for a similar use, separating and screening land dedicated to one use from land dedicated to another use (e.g., residential from commercial).

building code   An ordinance that specifies minimum standards of construction for buildings to protect public safety and health.

building permit   Written governmental permission for the construction, alteration, or demolition of an improvement, showing compliance with building codes and zoning ordinances. *See* certificate of occupancy.

bulk transfer   *See* Uniform Commercial Code.

bundle of legal rights   The concept of land ownership that includes ownership of all legal rights to the land—i.e. disposition, exclusion, enjoyment, possession and control.

business cycle   The upward and downward fluctuations in business activities generally characterized by four stages: expansion, recession, depression, and revival.

buydown   A financing technique used to reduce the monthly payments for the first few years of a loan. Funds in the form of discount points are given to the lender to buy down or lower the effective interest rate paid by the buyer, thus reducing the monthly payments for a set time.

buyer-agency agreement   A principal-agent relationship in which the broker is the agent for the buyer, with fiduciary responsibilities to the buyer. The broker represents the buyer under the law of agency.

call   In surveying, a reference to a course, distance, or monument when a describing a boundary.

capital gain   The taxable profit earned from the sale of a capital asset such as real property. Profits from assets owned for 12 months or less are treated as short-term capital gain, which is taxable as ordinary income. Profits from assets owned longer than 12 months are treated as long-term capital gain that is usually taxed at a much lower rate than ordinary income.

capital loss   A loss derived from the sale of a capital asset such as real property that may be deductible from ordinary taxable income.

capitalization   A mathematical process for estimating the value of a property using a proper rate of return on the investment and the annual net operating income expected to be produced by the property. The formula is Income ÷ Rate = Value.

capitalization rate   The rate of return a property will produce on the owner's investment.

carbon monoxide   A colorless, odorless gas produced as a byproduct of inefficient burning of fuel such as gas, oil or wood; poor ventilation can lead to deadly concentration of gas.

cash flow   The net spendable income from an investment, determined by deducting all operating and fixed expenses from the gross income. When expenses exceed income, a negative cash flow results.

casualty insurance   *See* property insurance.

caveat emptor   A Latin phrase meaning "Let the buyer beware." In a caveat emptor state, sellers do not have to disclose any facts about their property when selling.

ceiling joist   Attached to the top plate of a wall, these joists carry the weight of the roof.

certificate of occupancy (CO)   A certificate issued by a government authority stating that a building is fit for occupancy and there are no building code violations; the end result of a successful building permit.

certificate of reasonable value (CRV)   A form indicating the appraised value of a property being financed with a VA loan.

certificate of title   A statement of attorney's opinion on the status of the title to a parcel of real property based on a title search of specified public records.

chain of title   The succession of title conveyances, from some accepted starting point, whereby the present holder of real property derives title.

change   The appraisal principle that no physical or economic condition remains constant.

channeling   *See* steering.

chattel   *See* personal property.

Civil Rights Act of 1866   A federal act that prohibits racial discrimination in the sale and rental of all real and personal property.

client   *See* principal.

closing   The consummation of a real estate transaction; seller delivers clear title and buyer delivers payment of the purchase price; occurs at the recordation of the deed per the standard residential sales contract.

closing agent A third party that conducts the closing of the transaction, usually an attorney in North Carolina.

closing statement A detailed cash accounting of a real estate transaction showing all cash received, all charges and credits made, and all cash paid out in the transaction.

cloud on the title Any document, claim, unreleased lien, or encumbrance that may impair the title to real property or make the title doubtful; usually revealed by a title search and removed by either a quitclaim deed or suit to quiet title.

clustering The grouping of homesites within a subdivision on smaller lots than normal, with the remaining land used as common area.

code of ethics A written system of standards for ethical conduct.

codicil A supplement or an addition to a will, executed with the same formalities as a will, that normally does not revoke the entire will.

coinsurance clause A clause in insurance policies covering real property that requires that the policyholder maintain fire insurance coverage generally equal to at least 80 percent of the property's actual replacement cost.

commingling The illegal act by a real estate broker of placing consumer funds with personal funds. By law, brokers are required to maintain a separate trust or escrow account for other parties' funds held temporarily by the broker.

commission Payment to a broker for services rendered, as in the sale or purchase of real property; traditionally, a percentage of the gross sales price of the property but can be a flat fee or some other calculation.

common elements Parts of a property that are necessary or convenient to the existence, maintenance, and safety of a condominium or are normally in common use by all of the condominium residents. Each condominium owner has an undivided ownership interest in the common elements.

common law The body of law based on custom, usage, and court decisions.

comparable Property used in an appraisal report that is substantially equivalent to the subject property.

comparative market analysis (CMA) A comparison of the prices of recently sold homes that are similar to a listing seller's home in terms of location, style, and amenities; an estimate of market value.

compensatory damages Money damages awarded to the injured party to compensate them for the breach of contract, but not to punish the breaching party.

competition The appraisal principle that states that excess profits generate competition.

comprehensive plan *See* master plan.

condemnation A judicial or an administrative proceeding to exercise the power of eminent domain, through which a government agency takes private property for public use and justly compensates the owner.

condition It limits coverage of a specified property in an insurance policy.

conditional-use permit Written governmental permission allowing a use inconsistent with zoning but in the public interest, such as locating an emergency medical facility in a predominantly residential area: special-use permit.

condition subsequent A defeasible fee simple estate that dictates some action or activity that the new owner must not perform. The former owner retains a right of reentry, so if the condition is broken, the former owner can take repossession of the property.

condominium The absolute ownership of a unit in a multiunit building based on a legal description of the airspace the unit actually occupies, plus an undivided interest in the ownership of the common elements, which are owned jointly with the other condominium unit owners.

conforming loan A standardized conventional loan that meets Fannie Mae's or Freddie Mac's purchase requirements.

conformity The appraisal principle that holds that the greater the similarity among properties in an area, the better they will hold their value.

Conner Act A North Carolina law that requires many types of real estate documents to be recorded for protection against claims from third parties. These documents include deeds, mortgages, purchase contracts, installment land contracts, assignments, options, leases exceeding three years, easements, and restrictive covenants; a pure race statute.

consequential damages Award of special damages if the breaching party entered the contract with plans to breach; injured party may sue for lost profits.

consideration (1) That received by the grantor in exchange for a deed. (2) Something of value that induces a person to enter into a legally enforceable contract.

construction loan *See* interim financing.

constructive eviction The actions of a landlord that so materially disturb or impair a tenant's enjoyment of the leased premises that the tenant is effectively forced to move out and terminate the lease without liability for any further rent.

constructive notice The notice given to the world by recorded documents. All people are charged with knowledge of such documents and their contents, whether or not they have actually examined them. Possession of property is also considered constructive notice that the person in possession has an interest in the property.

contingency A provision in a contract that requires a certain act to be done or a certain event to occur before the contract becomes binding; a condition of the contract.

contract A legally enforceable promise or set of promises between legally competent parties that must be performed for consideration. If a breach of the promise occurs, the law provides a remedy. A contract may be either unilateral, by which only one party is bound to act, or bilateral, by which all parties to the instrument are legally bound to act as prescribed.

contribution The appraisal principle that states that the value of any component of a property is what it gives to the value of the whole or what its absence detracts from that value.

conventional loan A loan from private investors that requires no government insurance nor guarantee.

conveyance A term used to refer to any document that transfers title to real property. The term is also used in describing the act of transferring.

cooperating broker/firm *See* listing broker.

cooperative ownership A residential multiunit building whose title is held by a trust or corporation that is owned by and operated for the benefit of persons living within the building, who are the beneficial owners of the trust or stockholders of the corporation, each possessing a proprietary lease to a specific apartment in the building.

co-ownership Title ownership held by two or more persons or entities.

corporation An entity or organization, created by operation of law, whose rights of doing business are essentially the same as those of an individual. The entity has continuous existence until it is dissolved according to legal procedures.

cost approach The process of estimating the value of a property by adding the appraiser's estimate of the reproduction or replacement cost of the building, less depreciation to the estimated land value.

counteroffer A new offer made in response to an offer received. It has the effect of rejecting the original offer.

covenant A written agreement between two or more parties in which a party or parties pledge to perform or not perform specified acts with regard to property; usually found in such real estate documents as deeds, mortgages, leases, and contracts for deed.

covenant of quiet enjoyment The covenant implied by law by which a landlord guarantees that a tenant may take possession of leased premises and that the landlord will not interfere in the tenant's possession or use of the property.

crawl space The space between the ground surface and the first floor; frequently found in houses without basements that are not built on a slab foundation.

credit On a closing statement, an amount entered in a person's favor—an amount the party has paid or an amount received from another party.

curtesy A life estate, usually a fractional interest, given by some states to the surviving husband in real estate owned by his deceased wife. Most states, including North Carolina, have abolished curtesy.

customer A third party to whom is owed honesty and fairness; not a fiduciary relationship.

debit On a closing statement, an amount charged; an amount the party must pay at settlement.

debt service The principle and interest payment on a loan.

decedent A person who has died.

declaration of restrictive covenants A statement of all covenant, conditions and restrictions (CC&Rs) affecting a parcel of land; sometimes noted on the plat map or in a separate document. Restrictions are appurtenant and aim to protect property values.

dedication The voluntary transfer of private property by its owner to the public for some public use, such as for streets or schools.

deductible Loss not covered by the insurer.

deed A written instrument that, when executed and delivered, conveys title to or interest in real estate; evidence of title.

deed in lieu of foreclosure A deed given by the mortgagor to the mortgagee when the mortgagor is in default under the terms of the mortgage. This avoids foreclosure but does not remove liens from the property; "friendly foreclosure."

deed of trust An instrument used to create a mortgage lien by which the borrower conveys title to a trustee, who holds it as security for the benefit of the note holder (the lender); also called a trust deed.

deed restriction Clause placed in a deed by the owner to control the future uses of the property. *See* restrictive covenants.

default The nonperformance of a duty, whether arising under a contract or otherwise; failure to meet an obligation when due.

defeasance clause A clause used in leases and mortgages that cancels a specified right upon the occurrence of a certain condition, such as cancellation of a mortgage upon repayment of the mortgage loan.

defeasible fee estate   An estate in which the holder has a fee simple title that may be terminated upon the occurrence or nonoccurrence of a specified event. Two categories of defeasible fee estates exist: fee simple determinable and fee simple on condition subsequent.

deficiency judgment   A personal judgment levied against the borrower when a foreclosure sale does not produce sufficient funds to pay the mortgage debt in full; a general lien.

delivery and acceptance   The actual delivery of a deed by a grantor and the actual or implied acceptance of the deed by the grantee; recordation of the deed is viewed as acceptance.

demand   The amount of goods people are willing and able to buy at a given price; often coupled with supply.

Department of Housing and Urban Development (HUD)   A federal cabinet department active in national housing programs. Among its many programs are urban renewal, public housing, model cities, rehabilitation loans, FHA subsidies, fair housing enforcement, and water and sewer grants.

depreciation   (1) In appraisal, a loss of value in property due to any cause, including physical deterioration, functional obsolescence, and external obsolescence. (2) In real estate investment, an expense deduction for tax purposes taken over the period of ownership of income property.

descent   The acquisition of an estate by inheritance in which an heir succeeds to the property by intestate succession.

designated dual agency   An agency option under dual agency that allows the firm, with both clients' permission, to appoint one or more licensees to exclusively represent the seller-client and one or more licensees to exclusively represent the buyer-client; also called designated agency.

developer   A person or company that attempts to put land to its most profitable use through the construction of improvements.

devise   A gift of real property by will. The donor is the devisor, and the recipient is the devisee.

direct reduction loan   A mortgage loan that requires a fixed amount of principal payment in each period; the total debt service payment starts higher than with a level payment loan since interest portion will reduce with each payment.

discount point   Interest paid in advance; one point equals 1 percent of the loan amount for the borrower and increases the yield for the investor approximately 1/8%.

dominant tenement   A property that includes in its ownership the appurtenant right to use an easement over another person's adjacent property (called the servient tenement) for a specific purpose; ownership of the easement runs with the land.

dormer   A projection built out from the slope of a roof, used to house windows on the upper floor and to provide additional headroom. Common types of dormers are the gable dormer and the shed dormer.

dower   The legal right or interest, recognized in some states, that a wife acquires in the property her husband held or acquired during their marriage. During the husband's lifetime, the right is only a possibility of an interest; upon his death, it can become an interest in land.

dual agency   Representing both parties to a transaction; must be consensual and reduced to writing prior to presentation of first offer.

due-on-sale clause   A provision in a mortgage that states that the entire balance of the note is immediately due and payable if the mortgagor transfers (sells) the property. *See* alienation clause.

duress   The unlawful constraint or action exercised on a person whereby the person is forced to perform an act against that person's will. A contract entered into under duress is voidable.

earnest money   Money deposited by a buyer under the terms of a contract, to be forfeited if the buyer defaults but applied to the purchase price if the sale is closed.

easement   A right to limited use and enjoyment of the land of another for a specific purpose without ownership; a nonpossessory interest in real estate. Two types of easements are easement appurtenant and easement in gross.

easement appurtenant   An easement that runs with the land; the easement is part of both the dominant and the servient tracts and conveys with the title to either tenement.

easement by condemnation   An easement created by the government or a government agency that has exercised its right under eminent domain.

easement by necessity   An easement allowed by law as necessary for the full enjoyment of a parcel of real estate; i.e., to allow a landlocked owner a right of ingress and egress over a grantor's land.

easement by prescription   An easement acquired through adverse use of another's property for a period of 20 or more years in North Carolina.

easement in gross   An easement that is not created for the benefit of any land owned by the owner of the easement but that attaches personally to the easement owner. There is no dominant tract; the easement attaches to the servient tract. Personal easement in gross is not assignable; a commercial easement in gross is assignable.

eave   The overhang of a sloping roof that extends beyond the walls of the house.

economic life   The number of years during which an improvement will add value to the land.

economic obsolescence   *See* obsolescence.

effective age   The apparent age of a building based on observed condition rather than chronological age.

electromagnetic fields (EMFs)   Naturally occurring energy fields near power lines and electrical appliance thought to be linked with adverse health effect but research is inconclusive.

emblements   Growing crops, such as grapes and corn, that are produced annually through labor and industry; also called fructus industriales. Usually considered to be personal property.

eminent domain   The right of a government or municipal quasi-public body to acquire property for public use through a court action called condemnation, in which the court decides that the use is a public use and determines fair compensation to be paid to the owner.

employee   Someone who works as a direct employee of an employer and has employee status. The employer is obligated to withhold income taxes and Social Security taxes from the compensation of the employee.

employment contract   A document evidencing formal employment between employer and employee or between principal and agent. In real estate, this is generally a listing agreement, a buyer agency agreement or a management agreement.

enabling acts   State legislation that confers zoning powers on municipal governments.

encapsulation   Sealing off environmental hazards instead of removal.

encroachment   An unauthorized intrusion of an improvement, or any part of an improvement, on the real property of another party; can make title to both parcels unmarketable. Best discovered by survey.

encumbrance   Any charge, claim, lien, or liability held by someone other than the owner of property that may diminish the value or use and enjoyment of a property. May not prevent the transfer of title.

endorsement   In an insurance policy, coverage added to the general policy; a rider.

Equal Credit Opportunity Act (ECOA)   The federal law that prohibits discrimination in the extension of credit because of race, color, religion, national origin, sex, age, or marital status.

equitable title   (1) The interest held by the grantor in a deed of trust that allows possession and use of the pledged property. (2) The interest held by a vendee under a contract for deed or an installment contract; the equitable right to obtain absolute ownership to property when legal title is held in another's name.

equity   The interest or value that an owner has in property over and above any indebtedness.

equity of redemption   The right of a borrower in default on a mortgage loan to reclaim the forfeited property prior to the foreclosure sale through payment in full of all debt and associated costs.

erosion   The gradual wearing away of land by water, wind, or other natural forces; the diminishing of property by the elements may cause loss of ownership.

escheat   The reversion of property to the state, as provided by state law, in cases where a decedent dies intestate without heirs capable of inheriting or when the property is abandoned.

escrow   The closing of a transaction through a third party called an escrow agent who receives certain funds and documents to be delivered upon the performance of certain conditions outlined in the escrow instructions.

escrow account   The trust account established by a broker under the provisions of the license law for the purpose of holding funds on behalf of the broker's principal or some other person until the consummation or termination of a transaction.

estate taxes   Federal taxes on a decedent's real and personal property.

estate (tenancy) at sufferance   The tenancy of a lessee who lawfully comes into possession of a landlord's real estate but who continues to occupy the premises after the lease has expired against the landlord's wishes.

estate (tenancy) at will   An estate that gives the lessee the right to possession until the estate is terminated by either party; the term of this estate is indefinite and no prior notice to terminate is needed.

estate (tenancy) for years   A possessory interest in property for a definite period of time leased for a specified consideration.

estate (tenancy) from period to period   A possessory interest in leased property that automatically renews from period to period—week to week, month to month, or year to year; notice is necessary to terminate. Also called periodic tenancy.

estoppel   A method of creating an agency relationship in which a person states incorrectly that a second person is the first person's agent and a third person relies on that representation.

estover   A necessity allowed by law; for example, the right of a life tenant to use some of the property's resources to provide for needed repairs.

ethics   The system of moral principles and rules that becomes the standard for conduct.

eviction   A legal process to oust a person from possession of real estate.

evidence of title   Proof of ownership of property; commonly a certificate of title, an abstract of title with lawyer's opinion, or a Torrens registration certificate.

excise tax   Deed transfer tax paid by the seller and required to be noted on a deed by state law; the rate is $1 per $500 of sales price.

exchange   A transaction in which all or part of the consideration is the transfer of like-kind property (such as investment real estate for investment real estate).

exclusion   Something that is not covered for loss in an insurance policy.

exclusive-agency listing   A listing contract under which the owner appoints a real estate broker as the exclusive agent for a designated period of time to sell the property, on the owner's stated terms, for a commission. The owner reserves the right to sell without paying anyone a commission if the owner sells to a prospect who has not been introduced or claimed by the broker.

exclusive-right-to-sell listing   A listing contract under which the owner appoints a real estate broker as the exclusive agent for a designated period of time to sell the property, on the owner's stated terms, and agrees to pay the broker a commission when the property is sold, regardless of who sells the property.

executed contract   A contract in which all parties have fulfilled their promises in the contract.

execution   The signing and delivery of an instrument. Also, a legal order directing an official to enforce a judgment against the property of a debtor.

executory contract   A contract under which something remains to be done by one or more of the parties.

express agreement/contract   An oral or written contract in which the parties state the contract's terms and express their intentions in words.

extender clause   A carry-over or protection clause in a listing contract that says the listing broker is entitled to commission for a time period after expiration of the listing term if the property is transferred to a prospect that the broker introduced to the property during the listing term; override clause. This clause is void if the property is listed with a broker.

external depreciation   The reduction in a property's value caused by outside factors (those that are off the property).

external obsolescence   See obsolescence.

extra-territorial jurisdictions (ETJs)   A municipality's right to regulate development in areas adjacent to but not part of the city's corporate limits. Population determines if the power extends for 1 to 3 miles from the corporate limits.

Fannie Mae (FNMA)   A quasi-government agency established to purchase any kind of mortgage loans in the secondary mortgage market from the primary lenders.

fascia board   A flat strip of wood or metal that encloses the ends of the rafters; gutters are usually attached to the fascia board.

Federal Emergency Management Agency (FEMA)   A federal agency responsible for disaster preparedness, response and recovery. Now under Department of Homeland Security.

Federal Fair Housing Act   The federal law that prohibits discrimination in housing based on race, color, religion, sex, handicap, familial status, or national origin.

Federal Reserve System   The country's central banking system, which controls the nation's monetary policy by regulating the supply of money and interest rates.

fee-for-service   Arrangement where consumer asks licensee to perform specific real estate services for a set fee; unbundling of services.

fee simple absolute   The maximum possible estate in real property; most complete and absolute ownership; indefinite in duration, freely transferable and inheritable.

fee simple defeasible   See defeasible fee estate.

fee simple determinable   An estate in real estate that continues "so long as" a prescribed land use continues. Estate ends automatically upon the termination of the prescribed use; no lawsuit is necessary for reversion.

fee simple subject to a condition subsequent   An estate in real estate that prohibits a specific condition on the property. Grantor has the right to re-enter the property and reclaim ownership through legal proceedings.

FHA loan   A loan insured by the Federal Housing Administration and made by an approved private lender in accordance with the FHA's regulations.

fiduciary   One in whom trust and confidence are placed; a reference to a principal-agent relationship.

financing statement   See Uniform Commercial Code.

first substantial contact   A flexible moment in time when conversation between a licensee and a consumer begins to address confidential needs, desires and abilities; latest moment to legally disclose agency choices to a consumer.

fixed rental lease   See gross lease.

fixture   An item of personal property that has been converted to real property by being permanently affixed to the realty.

flood hazard area   Property identified by flood certification to be in a flood-prone area with a likelihood that a flood may occur once every 100 years therefore usually requiring flood insurance if federally related financing is involved.

floor joist   A horizontal board laid on edge, resting on the beams that provide the main support for the floor. The subflooring is nailed directly to the joists.

footing   A concrete support under a foundation, chimney, or column that usually rests on solid ground and is wider than the structure being supported. Footings are designed to distribute the weight of the structure over the ground.

foreclosure   A legal procedure whereby property used as security for a debt is sold to satisfy the debt in the event of default in payment of the mortgage note or default of other terms in the mortgage document. The foreclosure procedure brings the rights of all parties to a conclusion and passes the title in the mortgaged property to either the holder of the mortgage or a third party who may purchase the realty at the foreclosure sale, free of all liens affecting the property subsequent to the mortgage.

foreshore   Land at the coast between average high tide and average low tide this is owned by the state of North Carolina.

foundation wall   The masonry or concrete wall below ground level that serves as the main support for the frame structure. Foundation walls form the side walls of the basement or crawlspace.

frame   The wooden skeleton of the house consisting of the floors, walls, ceilings, and roof.

fraud   An intentional misrepresentation of material fact so as to harm or take advantage of another person.

Freddie Mac   A corporation established to purchase primarily conventional mortgage loans in the secondary mortgage market.

freehold estate   An estate in land in which ownership is for an indeterminate length of time, in contrast to a leasehold estate.

frieze board   A wooden board fastened at the top of the exterior wall under the eave soffit to prevent penetration of weather elements; frequently the base for additional exterior decorative trim.

front footage   The measurement of a parcel of land by the number of feet of street or road frontage, or water frontage.

fructus industriales   *See* emblements.

fructus naturales   Plants that do not require annual cultivation and are considered real property.

functional obsolescence   A loss of value to an improvement to real estate arising from functional problems, often caused by age or poor design.

future interest   A person's present right to an interest in real property that will not result in possession or enjoyment until sometime in the future, such as a reversion or right of reentry.

gable   The triangular portion of an end wall rising from the level top wall under the inverted V of a sloping roof that aids water drainage. A gable can be made of weatherboard, tile, or masonry and can extend above the rafters.

gambrel   A curb roof, having a steep slope and a flatter one above, as seen in Dutch colonial architecture.

gap   A defect in the chain of title of a particular parcel of real estate; a missing document or conveyance that raises doubt as to the present ownership of the land.

general agent   One who is authorized to represent the principal in a broad range of matters related to a specific business or activity; a property manager might have this power.

general lien   The right of a creditor to have all of a debtor's current and future property for the next 10 years—both real and personal—sold to satisfy a debt; i.e. judgment lien.

general partnership   *See* partnership.

general warranty deed   A deed in which the grantor fully warrants good clear title to the premises through four covenants in the deed. Used in most real estate deed transfers, a general warranty deed offers the greatest protection to the grantee of any deed.

Ginnie Mae   A government agency under HUD that plays an important role in the secondary mortgage market. It sells mortgage-backed securities that are backed by pools of FHA and VA loans.

girder   A heavy wooden or steel beam supporting the floor joists and providing the main horizontal support for the floor.

graduated lease   A commercial lease that contracts for pre-set rental increases over the lease period.

graduated payment mortgage (GPM)   A loan in which the monthly principal and interest payments increase by a set amount each year for a certain number of years and then level off for the remaining loan term; probable negative amortization in early years.

grantee   A person who receives a conveyance of real property from a grantor.

granting clause Words in a deed of conveyance that state the grantor's intention to convey the property at the present time. This clause is generally worded as convey and warrant, grant, grant, bargain and sell, or the like.

grantor (1) The property owner that is transferring title to or an interest in real property to a grantee. (2) A borrower in a deed of trust loan transaction; also called trustor.

gross income multiplier (GIM) A figure used as a multiplier of the gross annual income of a property to produce an estimate of the property's value.

gross lease A lease of property under which a landlord pays all property charges regularly incurred through ownership, such as repairs, taxes, insurance, and operating expenses. Most residential leases are gross leases; also called flat or fixed rental lease.

gross rent multiplier (GRM) The figure used as a multiplier of the gross monthly income of a property to produce an estimate of the property's value.

ground lease A lease of land only, on which the tenant usually is required to build as specified in the lease. Such leases are usually long-term net leases.

groundwater Water under the surface of the earth.

growing-equity mortgage (GEM) A loan in which the monthly payments increase annually, with the increased amount being used to reduce directly the principal balance outstanding and thus shorten the overall term of the loan.

header The extra thick framing over doors and windows to bear the weight of the building above the opening.

heir One who might inherit or succeed to an interest in land under the state law of descent when the owner dies without leaving a valid will.

highest and best use The possible use of a property that would produce the greatest net income and thereby develop the highest value.

hip roof A pitched roof with sloping sides and ends.

historic preservation zoning Zoning to preserve the historic nature of a particular property or neighborhood. Change will require a certificate of appropriateness from the necessary regulatory power.

holdover tenant A person who retains possession of leased property after the lease has expired; the landlord may continue to accept rent or make start eviction procedures.

home equity loan A loan (sometimes called a line of credit) under which a property owners use their residence as collateral and can then draw funds up to a prearranged amount against the property.

homeowner's insurance policy A standardized package insurance policy that covers a residential real estate owner against financial loss from fire, theft, public liability, and other common risks.

Housing and Community Development Act of 1974 An act that added gender as a protected class under the Federal Fair Housing Act.

HUD *See* Department of Housing and Urban Development

HUD-1 *See* Uniform Settlement Statement

HVAC An acronym for heating, ventilation, and air-conditioning.

hypothecation The pledging of property as security for an obligation or a loan without losing possession of it.

implied agreement/contract A contract under which the agreement of the parties is demonstrated by their conduct.

implied warranty of habitability A theory in landlord/tenant law in which the landlord renting residential property implies that the property is habitable and fit for its intended use.

improvement (1) Any structure, usually privately owned, erected on a site to enhance the value of the property—for example, a fence or a driveway. (2) A publicly owned structure added to or benefiting land, such as a curb, sidewalk, street, or sewer.

income capitalization approach The process of estimating the value of an income-producing property through capitalization of the annual net income expected to be produced by the property during its remaining useful life.

independent contractor Someone who is retained to perform a certain act but who is subject to the control and direction of another only as to the end result and not as to the way in which the act is performed. Unlike an employee, an independent contractor pays all expenses and Social Security and income taxes and receives no employee benefits. Most real estate licensees are independent contractors.

index lease A commercial lease that allows the periodic adjustment of rent based on a named index such as consumer price index.

inflation The gradual reduction of the purchasing power of the dollar, usually related directly to the increases in the money supply by the federal government.

inheritance taxes State-imposed taxes on a decedent's real and personal property.

in-house sale A real estate transaction where the listing firm actually produces the buyer for their listing, as opposed to a co-brokered or cross sale that involves two firms.

installment land contract A contract for the sale of real estate financed by the seller whereby the purchase price is paid in periodic installments by the purchaser, who is in possession of the property even though legal title is retained by the seller until a future date, which may not be until final payment. Also called a contract for deed or land contract.

insulation Pieces of plasterboard, asbestos sheeting, compressed wood-wool, fiberboard, or other material placed between inner and outer surfaces, such as walls and ceilings, to protect the interior from heat loss. Insulation works by breaking up and dissipating air currents.

interest A charge made by a lender for the use of money.

interim financing A short-term loan usually made during the construction phase of a building project (in this case, often referred to as a construction loan).

Interstate Land Sales Full Disclosure Act A federal law regulating the interstate advertising and sale or lease of lots in subdivisions with 25 or more lots. Developer must be provide a property report and register the subdivision with HUD.

intestate The condition of a property owner who dies without leaving a valid will. Title to the property will pass to the decedent's heirs as provided in the state law of descent.

intrinsic value An appraisal term referring to the value created by a person's personal preferences for a particular type of property.

investment Money directed toward the purchase, improvement, and development of an asset in expectation of income or profits.

involuntary lien A lien placed on property without the consent of the property owner; such as a judgment lien.

joint tenancy A concurrent form of ownership of real estate between two or more parties who have been named in one conveyance as joint tenants. Ownership interest must be equal. Right of survivorship is not automatic in North Carolina but can be added by an attorney.

joint venture The joining of two or more people to conduct a specific business enterprise. A joint venture is similar to a partnership in that it must be created by agreement between the parties to share in the losses and profits of the venture. It is unlike a partnership in that the venture is for one specific project only, rather than for a continuing business relationship.

judgment The formal decision of a court upon the respective rights and claims of the parties to an action or a suit. After a judgment has been entered and recorded with the county recorder, it becomes a general involuntary lien on the current and future real and personal property of the debtor in the county where recorded for the next 10 years.

judicial foreclosure The form of foreclosure used in lien theory states. *See* foreclosure.

jumbo loan A residential mortgage loan in excess of acceptable loan amounts for purchase by Fannie Mae or Freddie Mac; also called nonconforming loans.

junior mortgage A mortgage that is subordinate in right or lien priority to an existing lien on the same realty.

laches A legal doctrine to bar a legal claim or prevent the assertion of a right because of undue delay or failure to assert the claim or right.

land The earth's surface, extending downward to the center of the earth and upward infinitely into space, including things permanently attached by nature, such as trees and water.

land contract *See* installment land contract.

landfill An enormous burial hole for various types of waste disposal.

lateral support The support a parcel of land receives from adjacent land; a neighbor's duty to support adjoining land in its natural state.

law of negligence If a tenant or guest is injured on the landlord's rental property, the landlord, and his/her agent, may be held liable due to their responsibility to maintain common areas and comply with the Residential Rental Agreement Act.

Lead-Based Paint Hazard Reduction Act A federal law that requires sellers/landlords to disclose the known presence of lead-based paint in residential property to potential buyers/tenants via a required disclosure addendum to sales contracts or leases; delivery of a mandatory EPA pamphlet about lead poisoning is also required. Buyer/tenant is allowed a 10-day assessment period.

lease A written or an oral contract between a landlord (the lessor) and a tenant (the lessee) that transfers the right to exclusive possession and use of the landlord's real property to the lessee for a specified period of time and for a stated consideration (rent).

leasehold estate A tenant's right to occupy real estate during the term of a lease, generally considered a personal property interest; nonfreehold estate.

lease option A lease under which the tenant has the right to purchase the property either during the lease term or at its end.

lease purchase The purchase of real property, the consummation of which is preceded by a lease, usually long-term; typically done for tax or financing purposes.

legal description A description of a specific parcel of real estate complete enough for an independent surveyor to locate and identify it.

legality of object   The purpose of a legally enforceable contract cannot be for illegal actions or acts against public policy.

legally competent parties   People who are recognized by law as being able to contract with others; those of legal age and sound mind; a requirement of a legally enforceable contract.

lessee/lessor   *See* lease.

leverage   The use of borrowed money to finance an investment.

levy   To assess; to seize or collect. To levy a tax is to assess a property and set the rate of taxation. To levy an execution is to officially seize the property of a person to satisfy an obligation.

liability insurance   Insurance providing protection of the property owner against financial claims of others.

license   (1) A privilege or right granted to a person by a state to operate as a real estate broker. (2) The revocable permission for a temporary use of land—a personal right that cannot be sold.

lien   A right given by law to certain creditors to have their debts paid out of the property of a defaulting debtor, usually by means of a court sale. An encumbrance on real property that can be general or specific.

lien theory   Some states interpret a mortgage as being purely a lien on real property. The mortgagee thus has no right of possession but must foreclose the lien and sell the property if the mortgagor defaults.

life estate   An interest in real or personal property that is limited in duration to the lifetime of its owner or some other designated person or persons.

life tenant   A person in possession of a life estate.

limited partnership   *See* partnership.

liquidated damages   An amount predetermined by the parties to a contract as compensation to an injured party if the other party breaches the contract.

liquidity   The ability to sell an asset and convert it into cash, at a price close to its true value, in a short period of time.

lis pendens   A recorded legal document giving constructive notice that an action potentially affecting title to a particular property has been filed in either a state or a federal court; title is effectively unmarketable during the litigation.

listing agreement   An employment contract between a property owner (as principal) and a real estate firm/broker (as agent) by which the broker is employed to find a ready, willing and able buyer for the owner's real estate on the owner's terms, for which service the owner agrees to pay a commission.

listing broker   The broker/firm in a multiple-listing situation representing the seller, as opposed to the cooperating broker/firm, that brings the buyer to the transaction. The listing broker and the cooperating broker may be the same person/firm.

littoral rights   (1) A landowner's claim to use water in large navigable lakes and oceans adjacent to the property. (2) The ownership rights to land bordering these bodies of water up to the average high-water mark.

LOADS   A mneumonic to remember the fiduciary duties of an agent to the principal: Loyalty, Obedience, Accountability, Disclosure of information, Skill, care and diligence.

loan origination fee   An administrative fee charged to the borrower by the lender for making a mortgage loan; usually computed as a percentage of the loan amount.

loan-to-value (LTV) ratio   The relationship between the amount of the mortgage loan and the value of the real estate being pledged as collateral.

lot-and-block (recorded plat) system   A method of describing real property that identifies a parcel of land by reference to lot and block numbers within a subdivision, as specified on a recorded subdivision plat.

Machinery Act   The North Carolina General Statutes that govern the ad valorem taxation of property.

mailbox rule   A rule of law stating that once written acceptance is placed in control of the mailing service, and out of the control of the offeree, it is considered accepted—not when the acceptance is actually received by the offeror.

mansard roof   An architectural style in which the top floor or floors of a structure are designed to appear to be the roof. Such a roof has two slopes on each of the four sides of the building, with the upper slope less steeply inclined.

manufactured home   A dwelling, also known as a mobile home or house trailer; built under HUD regulations with a permanent chassis. It is considered personal property until the moving hitch, wheels and axles are removed, the unit is attached to a permanent foundation on land owned by the owner of the manufactured home, and an affidavit attesting to these actions has been filed with the Dept. of Motor Vehicles.

market   A place where goods can be bought and sold and value established.

marketable title   A good or clear title, reasonably free from the risk of litigation over possible defects.

Marketable Title Act   The act is designed to eliminate obsolete defects in a chain of title. If a chain of title can be traced back for 30 years without a problem, it becomes a marketable title.

market value The most probable price property will bring in an arm's-length transaction under normal conditions on the open market.

mass appraisal A valuation technique sometimes used for tax assessment purposes that applies a standard percentage increase or decrease to all property in a given location; sometimes referred to as horizontal adjustments.

master plan A comprehensive plan to guide the long-term physical development of a particular area.

material fact Any fact that is important or relevant to the issue at hand; mandatory disclosure by all agents in a transaction to all parties of the transaction.

mechanic's lien A specific, involuntary lien secured by interest in real property to give security to contractors, laborers, and materialmen who have performed work or furnished materials in the erection or repair of a building.

"meeting of the minds" *See* mutual assent.

metes-and-bounds description A legal description of a parcel of land that begins at a well-marked point and follows the boundaries, using directions and distances around the tract, back to the place of beginning.

mill One-tenth of one cent. Some states use a mill rate to compute real estate taxes; for example, a rate of 52 mills would be $0.052 tax for each dollar of assessed valuation of a property.

minor Someone who has not reached the age of majority and therefore does not have legal capacity to transfer title to real property; under 18 years of age in North Carolina.

mitigation Systems to limit the source of environmental hazards and reduce their effect on humans and the surrounding environment.

modular home A dwelling consisting of a series of rooms or units built off-site according to the NC State Building Code; is considered real property as soon as it is assembled on the land. May be multi-storied.

monetary policy Governmental regulation of the amount of money in circulation through such institutions as the Federal Reserve Board.

monument A fixed natural or artificial object used to establish real estate boundaries for a metes-and-bounds description.

mortgage A conditional transfer or pledge of real estate as security for the payment of a debt. Also, the document creating a mortgage lien in a lien theory state.

mortgage banker A mortgage loan company that originates, services, and sells loans to investors.

mortgage broker An agent of a lender who brings the lender and borrower together for a fee. A broker may represent several lenders.

mortgagee/mortgagor A mortgagee is the lender in a mortgage loan transaction; a mortgagor is the borrower in a mortgage loan transaction.

mortgage lien A lien or charge on the property of a mortgagor that secures the underlying debt obligations.

multiperil policy An insurance policy that offers protection from a range of potential perils, such as those of fire, hazard, public liability, and casualty.

multiple listing service (MLS) A marketing organization composed of member brokers who agree to share their listing agreements with one another in the hope of procuring ready, willing, and able buyers for their properties more quickly than they could on their own. Most MLSs accept only exclusive-right-to-sell or exclusive-agency listings from their member brokers.

mutual assent A deliberate agreement between parties; offer and acceptance; "meeting of the minds." A requirement of a legally enforceable contract.

National Do Not Call Registry A national registry, managed by the Federal Trade Commission, that lists the phone numbers of consumers who prefer to limit the telemarketing calls they receive.

negative amortization When the debt service payment on a loan is not large enough to pay the interest due; the principal balance actually grows with each payment.

negligent misrepresentation Unintentionally misinforming any party involved in a transaction about a material fact.

negligent omission Unintentionally failing to disclose a material fact to any party involved in a transaction.

negotiable instrument A written promise or order to pay a specific sum of money that may be transferred by endorsement or delivery. The transferee then has the original payee's right to payment.

net lease A lease requiring that the tenant pay rent plus some or all of the property charges, such as taxes, insurance, utilities, and repairs.

net listing A listing based on the net price the seller will receive if the property is sold. Under a net listing, the broker can offer the property for sale at the highest price obtainable to increase the commission. While this type of listing is illegal in many states, it is legal but not encouraged in North Carolina.

net operating income (NOI) The income projected for an income-producing property after deducting losses for vacancy and collection and operating expenses.

nonconforming use An existing use of property that is permitted to continue after a zoning ordinance prohibiting it has been established for the area; a grandfathered use. Illegal nonconforming use occurs when zoning in place before the prohibited use.

nonfreehold estate *See* leasehold estate.

nonhomogeneity A lack of uniformity; dissimilarity; heterogeneity. Because no two parcels of land are exactly alike, real estate is said to be nonhomogeneic.

North Carolina Condominium Act of 1986 Specifies that a condominium is created and established when the developer of the property executes and records a declaration of its creation in the county where the property is located. The declaration must include any covenants, conditions, or restrictions on the use of the property. Other requirements include disclosure and other consumer protection measures in connection with new residential condominium unit sales.

North Carolina Fair Housing Act of 1983 State fair housing law containing similar prohibitions to those of the federal fair housing law. Unlike the federal law, however, the North Carolina law does not exempt owners who are selling their own property, and it does exempt the rental of a unit in a one-unit to four-unit residential building if the owner or one of the owner's family members lives in one of the units.

North Carolina Human Relations Council The state agency responsible for enforcing the North Carolina Fair Housing Act.

North Carolina Intestate Succession Act The state law of descent that dictates distribution of the real and personal property of the deceased that died without a will (intestate).

North Carolina Real Estate Commission The state governmental agency whose primary duties include making rules and regulations to protect the general public involved in real estate transactions, granting licenses to real estate brokers, and suspending or revoking licenses for cause.

North Carolina Time Share Act The portion of North Carolina real estate law that defines time-shares and regulates their development and sales.

note *See* promissory note.

novation Substituting a new contract for an old one or substituting new parties to an existing contract.

obsolescence The loss of value due to factors that are outmoded or less useful. Obsolescence may be functional or economic.

occupancy permit A permit issued by the appropriate local governing body to establish that the property is suitable for habitation by meeting certain safety and health standards.

octennial reappraisal In North Carolina, the statutory reappraisal of all real property in every county every eight years for tax purposes.

offer The promise by one party to act or perform in a certain manner if the other party agrees to act or perform as requested; shows an intention to enter into a contract.

offer and acceptance Two essential components of a valid contract; *See* mutual assent and acceptance.

offeror/offeree The person who makes the offer is the offeror. The person receiving the offer is the offeree.

Office of Equal Opportunity (OEO) The federal agency under the direction of the secretary of the Department of Housing and Urban Development, which is in charge of administering the Federal Fair Housing Act.

Office of Thrift Supervision (OTS) Monitors and regulates the savings and loan industry. OTS was created by the Financial Institutions Reform, Recovery, and Enforcement Act (FIRREA).

open-end loan A mortgage loan that is expandable by increments up to a maximum dollar amount, the full loan being secured by the same original mortgage; an equity line mortgage.

open listing A listing agreement under which the broker's commission is contingent on the broker personally producing a ready, willing, and able buyer before the property is sold by the seller or another broker.

opinion of title An abstract of title that a lawyer has examined and has certified to be, in the lawyer's opinion, an accurate statement of the facts concerning the property ownership.

option An agreement between the property owner (optionor) and the possible buyer (optionee), secured by the payment of an option fee, to buy or not buy property within a specific time period at terms that have been negotiated in the underlying contract; also called option to purchase or option contract.

oral buyer agency A non-exclusive verbal agency agreement between a firm and a buyer-client. There can be no time limit on oral agency, but it must be reduced to writing prior to presentation of first offer.

override clause *See* extender clause.

package insurance An insurance policy that combines the coverage of property insurance and liability insurance.

package loan A real estate loan used to finance the purchase of both real property and personal property, such as in the purchase of a furnished home that includes window coverings and major appliances.

panic peddling *See* blockbusting.

parol evidence rule A rule of evidence providing that a written agreement is the final expression of the agreement of the parties, not to be varied or contradicted by prior or contemporaneous oral or written negotiations.

partition The division of cotenants' interests in real property when all parties do not voluntarily agree to terminate the co-ownership; takes place through court procedures.

partnership An association of two or more individuals who carry on a continuing business for profit as co-owners. Under the law, a partnership is regarded as a group of individuals rather than as a single entity. A general partnership is a typical form of joint venture in which each general partner shares in the administration, profits, and losses of the operation. A limited partnership is a business arrangement whereby the operation is administered by one or more general partners and funded, by and large, by limited or silent partners, who are by law responsible for losses only to the extent of their investments.

party wall A wall that is located on or at a boundary line between two adjoining parcels of land and is used or is intended to be used by the owners of both properties; walls shared between townhouses.

payment cap The limit on the amount the monthly payment can be increased on an adjustable-rate mortgage when the interest rate is adjusted.

percentage lease A commercial lease, commonly used for retail tenants; rent is based on the tenant's gross sales at the premises. There is usually a small base monthly rental plus a percentage of any gross sales above a certain amount.

percolation test A test of the soil to determine whether it will absorb and drain water adequately to use a septic system for sewage disposal; a soil evaluation test.

periodic estate (tenancy) *See* estate (tenancy) from period to period.

personal property Items, called chattels or personalty, that do not fit into the definition of real property; movable objects. Examples would include furniture, clothing, jewelry, money, vehicles, etc.

physical deterioration A reduction in a property's value resulting from a decline in physical condition; can be caused by action of the elements or by ordinary wear and tear.

pier A column, usually of masonry block or steel-reinforced concrete. Piers are evenly spaced under a structure to support the weight. May also refer to the part of the wall between the windows or other openings that bears the wall weight.

pitch The slope of a roof measured as the vertical distance in inches (rise) divided by the horizontal distance in feet (run).

planned unit development (PUD) A planned combination of diverse land uses, such as housing, recreation, and shopping, in one contained development or subdivision.

plat map A map of a subdivision indicating the location and boundaries of individual properties. Generally shows lots, blocks, easements, streets, floodplains, etc. Usually requires official approval before recordation.

point of beginning (POB) In a metes-and-bounds legal description, the starting point of the survey, situated at one corner of the parcel. All metes-and-bounds descriptions must follow the boundaries of the parcel back to the point of beginning.

police power The government's right to impose laws, statutes, and ordinances, including zoning ordinances and building codes, to protect the public health, safety, and welfare.

power of attorney A written instrument authorizing a person, the attorney-in-fact, to act as agent for another person to the extent indicated in the instrument.

power of sale foreclosure The form of foreclosure used in a title theory state, such as North Carolina; also called nonjudicial foreclosure.

predatory lending Unscrupulous, sometimes fraudulent, lending practices usually intending to make repayment impossible; designed to take advantage of unwary borrowers that are frequently the low-income, uninformed, elderly, or non-English-speaking.

premium The consideration for an insurance policy.

prepaid item On a closing statement, (1) expenses paid before they are due, such as hazard insurance or rent; also called prepaids; (2) a lump-sum payment to set up a reserve account, such as deposits of taxes and insurance to set up the borrower's mortgage loan escrow account.

prepayment penalty A charge imposed on a borrower who pays off the loan principal early. This penalty compensates the lender for interest and other charges that would otherwise be lost due to payments made ahead of schedule.

price fixing *See* antitrust laws.

primary mortgage insurance (PMI) Insurance coverage used for obtaining conventional loans with loan-to-value ratios exceeding 80%.

primary mortgage market The mortgage market in which loans are originated, consisting of lenders such as commercial banks, savings associations, and mortgage brokers.

principal (1) A sum loaned or employed as a fund or an investment, as distinguished from its income or profits. (2) The original amount (as in a loan) of the total balance due and payable at a certain date. (3) A main party to a transaction—the person for whom the agent works; the client.

priority The order of position or time. The priority of liens is generally determined by the chronological order in which the lien documents are recorded. Property tax and assessment liens have priority even over previously recorded liens.

privity of contract Rights arising from the contract itself. *See* privity of estate.

privity of estate Rights arising from traditional property law. *See* privity of contract.

private mortgage insurance (PMI) Insurance provided by a private carrier that protects a lender against a loss in the event of a foreclosure and deficiency.

probate A legal process by which a court determines who will inherit a decedent's property and what the estate's assets are.

procuring cause The effort that began a chain of events that brings about the desired result. Under an open listing, the broker who is the procuring cause of the sale receives the commission.

promissory note A financing instrument that states the terms of the underlying obligation, is signed by its maker, and is negotiable (transferable to a third party); a personal IOU.

property insurance A policy that provides property owner coverage for the basic structure on that property.

property management agreement An agency contract between the owner of income property and a management firm or an individual property manager that outlines the scope of the manager's authority.

property manager Broker who for compensation preserves the value of an investment property while generating income as an agent for the owner. Duties include collecting rents, maintaining the property, and keeping up all accounting.

property report The mandatory federal and/or state documents compiled by developers to provide potential purchasers with material facts about a property prior to its purchase.

proprietary lease A lease given by the corporation that owns a cooperative apartment building to the shareholder for the shareholder's right as a tenant to an individual apartment.

prorations Shared expenses, either prepaid or paid in arrears, that are divided equitably between buyer and seller at settlement.

protected class Any group of people designated as such by statute in consideration of federal and state civil rights and lending legislation; currently includes familial status, marital status, age, race, gender, handicapping condition, color, religion, source of income, and national origin.

protection agreement An agreement between an unlisted property owner and a broker to secure payment for the broker if the property is sold to the particular buyer named in the agreement; it does not create a general listing, and may not create agency at all—only compensation for a buyer's agent. Sometimes called a "one-shot" listing.

provisional broker A real estate licensee who performs real estate activities under the supervision of a licensed real estate broker-in-charge. Must complete post-licensing courses to remove the provisional license status.

public offering statement The document all prospective time-share purchasers must receive before signing a sales contract. The statement must disclose all material facts about the property, as required by the state.

puffing Exaggerated or superlative comments or opinions: e.g. "This house has the best view in town!".

pur autre vie For the life of another. A life estate pur autre vie is a life estate that is measured by the life of a person other than the grantee.

purchase-money mortgage A note secured by a mortgage or deed of trust given by a buyer, as borrower, to a seller, as lender, as part of the purchase price of the real estate.

quantity-survey method The appraisal method of estimating building costs by calculating the cost of all of the physical components in the improvements, adding the cost to assemble them, and then including the indirect costs associated with such construction.

quiet title A court action to remove a cloud on the title.

quitclaim deed A conveyance by which the grantor transfers interest in the real estate, if any, without warranties or obligations; frequently used to remove clouds on the title.

radon A colorless, odorless radioactive gas that naturally occurs in all areas of the state from the decay of radioactive minerals in the ground; EPA suggests that a reading of 4.0 picocuries or higher is cause for a mitigation system. Considered to be one of the leading causes of lung cancer.

rafter One of a series of sloping beams that extends from the center ridge board to an exterior wall and provides the main support for the roof.

rate cap The limit on the amount the interest rate can be increased at each adjustment period in an adjustable rate loan. The cap may also set the maximum interest rate that can be charged during the life of the loan.

ratification A method of creating an agency relationship in which the principal accepts/confirms the conduct of someone who acted without prior authorization as the principal's agent.

ready, willing, and able buyer One who is prepared to buy property on the seller's terms and is ready to take positive steps to consummate the transaction; one of the agent's requirements for entitlement to commission.

real estate Land; a portion of the earth's surface extending downward to the center of the earth and upward infinitely into space, including all things permanently attached to it, whether naturally or artificially.

real estate investment syndicate *See* syndicate.

real estate investment trust (REIT) Trust ownership of real estate by a group of individuals who purchase certificates of ownership in the trust, which in turn invests the money in real property and distributes the profits back to the investors free of corporate income tax.

real estate license law The state law enacted to protect the public from fraud, dishonesty, and incompetence when dealing with real estate licensees in the purchase and sale of real estate.

real estate mortgage investment conduit (REMIC) A tax entity that issues multiple classes of investor interests (securities) backed by a pool of mortgages.

real estate recovery fund A fund established in some states from real estate license revenues to cover claims of aggrieved parties who have suffered monetary damage through the actions of a real estate licensee.

Real Estate Settlement Procedures Act (RESPA) Federal law that ensures that residential buyers and sellers receive full disclosure of all settlement charges when a 1–4 family unit residence is financed by federally-related first mortgage loans. The Act mandates a HUD booklet about closing costs, a good-faith estimate of closing costs, and a standardized HUD-1 closing statement. The Act also prohibits kickbacks from lenders.

reality of consent If misrepresentation, fraud, mistake of fact, undue influence or duress are absent in contract formation, good contract is formed.

real property The land plus permanent improvements and the interests, benefits, and rights inherent in real estate ownership.

REALTOR® A registered trademark term reserved for the sole use of active members of local REALTORS® boards affiliated with the National Association of REALTORS®.

reconciliation The final step in the appraisal process, in which the appraiser combines the estimates of value received from the sales comparison, cost, and income capitalization approaches to arrive at a final estimate of market value for the subject property.

recording The act of entering or recording documents into the public record at the recorder's office established in each county. Until recorded, a deed or mortgage ordinarily is not effective against third parties, such as subsequent purchasers or mortgagees.

rectangular (government) survey system A system established in 1785 by the federal government, providing for surveying and describing land by reference to principal meridians and base lines; used mainly west of the Mississippi River.

redemption period A 10-day period of time after a foreclosure auction during which a property owner in default has the right to redeem the pledged real estate by paying the loan balance plus interest, and costs; also called the upset bid period.

redlining The illegal practice of a lending institution denying loans or restricting their number for certain areas of a community.

reduction certificate (payoff statement) The document signed by a lender indicating the amount required to pay a loan balance in full and satisfy the debt; used in the settlement process to protect both the seller's and the buyer's interests.

reference to recorded plat *See* lot-and-block (recorded plat) system.

registration certificate The document that developers of time-shares in North Carolina must obtain from the North Carolina Real Estate Commission before they can offer a project's time-shares for sale to the public.

regression An appraisal principle that states that between dissimilar properties, the value of the better quality property is affected adversely by the presence of the lesser quality property.

Regulation Z Implements the Truth-in-Lending Act requiring credit institutions to inform borrowers of the true cost of obtaining credit.

reliction Gradual recession of water which uncovers land that usually belongs to the riparian owner.

remainder interest A future interest in real estate created by the grantor for some third party that will be enjoyed after the termination of a prior estate, such as when an owner conveys a life estate to one party and the remainder to another.

remainderman One entitled to receive a remainder interest in some estate sometime in the future.

rent A fixed, periodic payment made by a tenant of a property to the owner for possession and use, usually by prior agreement of the parties.

rent schedule A statement of proposed rental rates, determined by the owner, or the property manager, or both, based on a building's estimated expenses, market supply and demand, and the owner's long-range goals for the property.

replacement cost The construction cost at current prices of a property that is not necessarily an exact duplicate of the subject property but serves the same purpose or function as the original.

reproduction cost The construction cost at current prices of an exact duplicate of the subject property.

rescission The legal remedy of canceling, terminating, or annulling a contract and restoring the parties to their original positions. Contracts may be rescinded due to mistake, fraud, or misrepresentation. There is no need to show any money damage.

Residential Rental Agreement Act The state law that mandates delivery of habitable residential rental units; obligations of the landlord and the tenant are mutually dependent. Provides tenant with rights and remedies such as the Retaliatory Eviction Doctrine.

Resolution Trust Corporation The organization created by the Financial Institutions Reform, Recovery, and Enforcement Act (FIRREA) to liquidate the assets of failed savings and loan associations.

restrictive covenant Private agreements usually imposed by the owner when property is sold that limits the way the real estate ownership may be used; frequently used by owner/developer to maintain specific standards in a subdivision. The covenants are appurtenant. Also called protective covenants.

retainer fee A small fee paid by the client upon creation of a buyer agency relationship as an advance partial compensation for services; it may be non-refundable or applied to final compensation due depending on the agency agreement.

retaliatory eviction Illegal eviction of a tenant that has exercised protected rights under the law.

revenue stamps *See* excise tax.

reverse-annuity mortgage (RAM) A loan under which the homeowner receives monthly payments based on the homeowner's accumulated equity rather than a lump sum. The loan must be repaid at a prearranged date, upon the death of the owner, or the sale of the property.

reversionary interest A future estate that the grantor holds while granting a life estate to another person.

ridge board A heavy horizontal board, set on edge at the apex of the roof, to which the rafters are attached.

right of first refusal The right of a person to have the first opportunity to either purchase or lease real property, if the owner ever decides to sell or lease; no terms are negotiated.

right of survivorship *See* tenancy by the entirety.

right-of-way The right given by a landowner to another to use the land as a pathway, without actually transferring ownership.

riparian rights An owner's rights in land that borders on or includes a stream, river, or lake. These rights include access to and use of the water.

roofing felt Sheets of flat or other close-woven, heavy material placed on top of the roof boards to insulate and waterproof the roof.

roofing shingle Thin, small sheet of wood, asbestos, fiberglass, slate, metal, clay, or other material used as the outer covering for a roof. Shingles are laid in overlapping rows to completely cover the roof surface. Shingles are sometimes used as an outer covering for exterior walls.

rules and regulations Real estate licensing authority orders that govern licensees' activities. They usually have the same force and effect as statutory law.

R-value The insulation value of materials. The higher the R-value, the more resistant the material is to the transfer of heat.

sale and leaseback A transaction in which an owner sells improved property and, as part of the same transaction, signs a long-term lease to remain in possession of the premises.

sales comparison approach The process of estimating the value of a property by examining and comparing actual sales of comparable properties.

satisfaction of mortgage A document acknowledging the full repayment of a mortgage debt.

secondary mortgage market A market for the purchase and sale of existing mortgages, designed to provide greater liquidity for mortgages; also called the secondary money market. Mortgages are first originated in the primary mortgage market.

security agreement *See* Uniform Commercial Code.

security deposit A payment by a tenant, held by the landlord during the lease term and kept (wholly or partially) on default or destruction of the premises by the tenant.

self-help eviction Illegal eviction practices used by landlords instead of lawful use of summary ejectment.

servient tenement Land on which an easement exists in favor of an adjacent property (called the dominant tenement); also called a servient estate or tract. Easement runs with the land.

setback The amount of space local zoning regulations require between a lot line and a building line.

settlement The process of adjusting and prorating credits, debits, and closing expenses to conclude a real estate transaction; referred to as closing.

severalty The ownership of real property by only one person or entity; also called sole ownership.

severance Changing an item of real estate to personal property by detaching it from the land; for example, cutting down a tree.

sharecropping In an agricultural lease, the agreement between the landowner and the tenant farmer to split the crop or the profit from its sale, actually sharing the crop.

shared-appreciation mortgage (SAM) A mortgage loan in which the lender, in exchange for a loan with a lower interest rate, participates in the profits (if any) the borrower receives when the property is eventually sold.

sheathing Insulating material that is applied to the wall framing; siding is applied on top of the sheathing.

shingles Exterior roofing material frequently made of fiberglass, asphalt, or wood.

short sale When a lender allows a borrower in default on mortgage loan payments to sell the mortgaged property for less money than necessary to satisfy the loan to avoid the delay and expense of a foreclosure sale; lender usually "forgives" the balance owed after the sale, although the IRS will frequently consider the forgiven amount to be taxable income for the borrower.

siding Boards nailed horizontally to the vertical studs, with or without intervening sheathing, to form the exposed surface of the outside walls of the building. Siding may be made of wood, metal, or masonry sheets.

sill The lowest horizontal member of the house frame, which rests atop the foundation wall and forms a base for the studs. The term can also refer to the lowest horizontal member in the frame for a window or door.

situs The personal preference of people for one location over another, not necessarily based on objective facts and knowledge.

slab A flat, horizontal reinforced concrete area, usually the interior floor of a building but also an exterior or a roof area.

soffit The external underside of the eave; usually contains ventilation for the attic and/or roof.

soil suitability test An engineer's test to determine the ability of the ground to absorb and drain water; used to determine suitability and location of septic system; also called a percolation or perk test.

sole plate The bottom of the wall frame that connects the studs to the flooring.

special agent One who is authorized by a principal to perform a single act or transaction. A real estate broker is usually a special agent of the seller authorized to find a ready, willing, and able buyer for a particular property, or a special agent of the buyer to find a specific type of property to purchase. Special agent has limited authority and cannot bind his principal.

special assessment A tax or levy customarily imposed against only those specific parcels of real estate that will benefit from a proposed public improvement like a street or sewer.

special warranty deed A deed in which the grantor only warrants, or guarantees, the title against defects arising during the period of the grantor's tenure and ownership of the property and not against defects existing before that time, generally using the language *by, through or under the grantor but not otherwise.*

specific lien A lien affecting or attaching only to a specific parcel of land or piece of real property; i.e. mortgage lien.

specific performance A legal action to compel a party to carry out the terms of a contract.

split-level Usually a house in which two or more floors are located directly above one another, and one or more additional floors, adjacent to them, are placed at a different level; a tri-level.

spot zoning Zoning that illegally singles out property for either special or more restrictive treatment than is usual under the area zoning ordinance.

square-foot method The appraisal method of estimating building costs by multiplying the number of square feet in the improvements being appraised by the cost per square foot for recently constructed similar improvements.

statute of frauds A state law that requires that certain instruments that convey interest in real estate be in writing to be legally enforceable, such as deeds, real estate sales contracts, and certain leases.

statute of limitations That law pertaining to the period of time within which certain actions must be brought to court or be lost.

statutory right of redemption The right of a defaulted property owner to recover the property after its sale by paying the appropriate fees and charges.

steering The illegal practice of channeling home seekers to particular areas, either to maintain the homogeneity of an area or to change the character of an area, which limits their choices of where they can live.

stigmatized property Property regarded as undesirable because of events that occurred there; also called psychologically impacted property. Some conditions that typically stigmatize a property are murder, gang-related activity, proximity to a nuclear plant, and even the alleged presence of ghosts.

straight-line method   A method of calculating depreciation for tax purposes, computed by dividing the adjusted basis of a property by the estimated number of years of remaining useful life.

stud   The vertical members in the wall framing; usually placed 16–24 inches apart and serve as main support for the roof and/or the story above.

subagent   One who is employed by a person already acting as an agent; typically a reference to a provisional broker licensed under a broker (agent) who is employed under the terms of a listing agreement. A subagent has the same duties to the client as the agent.

subdivision   A tract of land divided into two or more parcels by the owner, known as the subdivider, for the purpose of sale or development (either now or in the future); all land division involving the dedication of a new street or a change in an existing street.

subdivision and development ordinances   Municipal ordinances that establish requirements for subdivisions and development.

subdivision plat   *See* plat map.

subflooring   Boards or plywood sheets nailed directly to the floor joists, serving as a base for the finish flooring. Subflooring is usually made of rough boards, although some houses have concrete subflooring.

subjacent support   The support of the surface of land by the land's subsurface; duty of the owner of subsurface rights to support the surface of the land.

sublease/sublet   The leasing of premises by a tenant to a third party for part of the lessee's remaining term. *See* assignment.

subordination   Relegation to a lesser position, usually in respect to a right or security.

subordination agreement   A written agreement between holders of liens on a property that changes the priority of mortgage, judgment, and other liens under certain circumstances.

subprime loan   A loan made to a borrower with a credit rating below what is required for regular loans creating greater risk liability for the lender that is countered by higher interest rates and fees; called B, C, or D paper.

subrogation clause   Any rights the insured had to sue the person who caused the damage are assigned to the insurance company that has already paid the insured for the damages.

substitution   An appraisal principle that states that the maximum value of a property tends to be set by the cost of purchasing an equally desirable and valuable substitute

property, assuming that no costly delay is encountered in making the substitution.

subsurface rights   Ownership rights in a parcel of real estate to the water, minerals, gas, oil, and so forth that lie beneath the surface of the property.

suit to quiet title   A court action intended to establish or settle the title to a particular property, especially when a cloud on the title exists.

summary ejectment   Legal eviction procedure heard before a magistrate for removal of a tenant that has breached the lease terms.

supply   The amount of goods available in the market to be sold at a given price. The term is often coupled with demand.

supply and demand   The appraisal principle that follows the interrelationship of the supply of and demand for real estate. As appraising is based on economic concepts, this principle recognizes that real property is subject to the influences of the marketplace, as is any other commodity.

surety bond   An agreement by an insurance or a bonding company to be responsible for certain possible defaults, debts, or obligations contracted for by an insured party; in essence, a policy insuring one's personal or financial integrity. In the real estate business, a surety bond is generally used to ensure that a particular project will be completed at a certain date or that a contract will be performed as stated.

surface rights   Ownership rights in a parcel of real estate that are limited to the surface of the property and do not include the air above it (air rights) or the minerals below the surface (subsurface rights).

survey   The process by which boundaries are measured and land areas are determined; the on-site measurement of lot lines, dimensions, and position of a house on a lot, including the determination of any existing encroachments or easements.

success fee   Compensation that is due and payable upon the creation of a valid sales contract for property located by the buyer's agent.

tacking   Adding or combining successive periods of continuous occupation of real property by adverse possessors. This concept enables someone who has not been in possession for the entire statutory period to establish a claim of adverse possession.

taxation   The process by which a government or municipal quasi-public body raises monies to fund its operation.

tax credit   An amount by which tax owed is reduced directly.

tax deed An instrument, similar to a certificate of sale, given to a purchaser at a tax sale. *See* also certificate of sale.

tax lien A statutory lien against real property for non-payment of taxes. Real and personal property tax liens and assessments take priority over all other liens. Real property tax and assessment liens are specific liens; personal property tax liens are general liens.

tax sale A court-ordered sale of real property to raise money to cover delinquent taxes.

tenancy by the entirety A concurrent form of ownership reserved for property owned by husband and wife. Right of survivorship is mandatory; making the surviving spouse owner in severalty immediately upon the death of a spouse.

tenancy in common A concurrent form of ownership in which each owner holds an undivided interest in the real property. Ownership interests can be unequal and the right of survivorship is not allowed.

Tenant Security Deposit Act The state act that regulates the amount and use of money that can be required as a security deposit and how the landlord holds that deposit. The maximum amount of the deposit depends on the term of the tenancy.

term loan A loan in which only interest is paid during the term of the loan, with the entire principal due with the final interest payment; also called a straight loan.

testate Having made and left a valid will.

"time is of the essence" A phrase in a contract that requires the performance of a certain act no later than a stated time or the noncompliant party is in breach and the contract may be voidable by the opposite party.

time-share Any right to occupy a unit of real property during five or more separated time periods over a period of at least five years.

title (1) The right to or ownership of land. (2) The evidence of ownership of land.

title insurance A policy insuring the owner and/or mortgagee against loss by reason of defects in the title to a parcel of real estate, other than encumbrances, defects, and matters specifically excluded by the policy.

title search The search of public records to determine the current state of ownership of real estate; examining chain of title.

title theory Describing those states like North Carolina that interpret a mortgage to mean that the lender is the owner of mortgaged land who vests the legal title with the trustee while borrower holds equitable title. Borrower regains legal title upon full payment of the mortgage debt.

top plate The top part of the wall framing that connects the stud to the ceiling framing.

topographic survey A survey that measures the features of the earth's surfaces such as hills and valleys plus the location of roads.

Torrens system A method of evidencing title by registration with the proper public authority, generally called the registrar, named for its founder, Sir Robert Torrens.

tort A wrongful act, injury or violation of legal right to the person or property of another.

townhouse A hybrid form of ownership where the owner holds fee title to their unit and the ground beneath; horizontal ownership. Frequent use of party walls; row houses. Common areas are usually owned and maintained with other unit owners through a homeowners' association.

trade fixture An article installed by a tenant under the terms of a lease and removable by the tenant before the lease expires.

transfer tax Tax stamps required to be affixed to a deed by state or local law; excise tax, formerly know as revenue stamps.

trust A fiduciary arrangement whereby property is conveyed to a person or an institution, called a trustee, to be held and administered on behalf of another person, called a beneficiary. The one who conveys the trust is called the trustor.

trustee The holder of bare, legal title in a deed of trust loan transaction on behalf of a beneficiary.

trustee's deed A deed executed by a trustee conveying land held in a trust.

trust funds Those monies received on behalf of others by a real estate licensee while acting as an agent in a real estate transaction. Generally, trust funds include earnest money deposits, down payments, tenant security deposits, rents, and monies received from final settlements and must be deposited into a trust account in accordance with NC Real Estate Commission Rules.

Truth-in-Lending Act *See* Regulation Z.

underground storage tank (UST) A tank and any underground piping connected to the tank that has at least 10 percent of its combined volume underground; federal UST regulations apply to only those storing either petroleum or certain hazardous substances.

undivided interest *See* tenancy in common.

unenforceable contract A contract that has all the elements of a valid contract, yet neither party can sue the other to force performance of it. For example, a verbal contract is generally unenforceable.

Uniform Commercial Code   A codification of commercial law, adopted in most states, that attempts to make uniform all laws relating to commercial transactions, including chattel mortgages and bulk transfers. When chattels are purchased on credit, security interests are created by an instrument known as a security agreement. To give notice of the security interest, a financing statement must be recorded. Article 6 of the code regulates bulk transfers—the sale of a business as a whole, including all fixtures, chattels, and merchandise.

Uniform Electronic Transactions Act (UETA)   North Carolina version of the federal E-sign legislation that validates electronic contracts, documents and signatures.

Uniform Settlement Statement   The standard HUD-1 closing statement form required to be given to the borrower, lender, and seller at or before settlement by the closing agent in a transaction covered under the Real Estate Settlement Procedures Act.

unilateral contract   A one-sided contract wherein one party makes a promise to induce a second party to do something. The second party is not legally bound to perform; however, if the second party does comply, the first party is obligated to keep the promise.

unit-in-place method   The appraisal method of estimating building costs by calculating the costs of all of the physical components in the structure, with the cost of each item including its proper installation, connection, etc.; also called the segregated cost method.

universal agent   Person empowered to do anything the principal could do personally; unlimited authority; unusual in real estate.

urea-formaldehyde foam insulation (UFFI)   A 1970s foam insulation that released gases that can cause respiratory problems such as skin irritations or asthma attacks.

usury   Charging interest at a higher rate than the maximum rate established by state law.

valid contract   A contract that complies with all the essentials of a contract and is binding and enforceable on all parties to it.

VA-guaranteed loan   A mortgage loan on approved property made to a qualified veteran by an authorized lender and guaranteed by the Department of Veterans Affairs to limit the lender's possible loss.

value   The power of a good or service to command other goods in exchange for the present worth of future rights to its income or amenities.

variance   Permission obtained from zoning authorities to build a structure or conduct a use that is expressly prohibited by the current zoning laws; an exemption from ordinances due to unique hardship not created by the property owner.

vendee/vendor   Vendee is a buyer, usually under the terms of a land contract; vendor is a seller, usually in a land contract.

voidable contract   A contract that seems to be valid on the surface but may be rejected or disaffirmed by one or both of the parties.

void contract   A contract that has no legal force or effect because it does not meet the essential elements of a contract.

voluntary lien   A lien placed on property with the knowledge and consent of the property owner; such as a mortgage lien.

walk-through   The final inspection of the property by the buyer prior to closing to assure that the seller has vacated, made required repairs satisfactorily, and delivered the property in the condition it was in at contract.

waste   An improper use or abuse of a property by a possessor who holds less than fee ownership, such as a tenant, life tenant, mortgagor, or vendee. Such waste ordinarily impairs the value of the land or the interest of the person holding the title or the reversionary rights.

water table   Natural water level whether it is above or below ground level.

wetlands   Areas periodically inundated or saturated to the extent that they can or do support vegetation adapted to aquatic conditions.

will   A written document, properly witnessed, providing for the transfer of title to property owned by the deceased.

willful misrepresentation   Intentionally misinforming any party involved in a transaction about a material fact.

willful omission   Intentionally failing to disclose a material fact to any party involved in a transaction.

Working with Real Estate Agents   A mandatory agency information brochure that a licensee must give to and review with consumers in all real estate sales transactions no later than first substantial contact; it does not create agency.

wraparound loan   A method of refinancing in which the new mortgage is placed in a secondary, or subordinate, position. The new mortgage includes both the unpaid principal balance of the first mortgage and whatever additional sums are advanced by the lender. In essence, it is an additional mortgage in which another lender refinances a borrower by lending an amount exceeding the existing first mortgage amount without disturbing the existence of the first mortgage.

yield   The return on investment; amount of profit.

zoning ordinance   An exercise of police power by a municipality to regulate and control the character and use of property. Zoning is local in nature.

Answer Key for End-of-Chapter Questions

Detailed rationales for the end-of-chapter questions are available online at *www.dearbornRE.com* under the Instructor Resources material for this title.

CHAPTER 1
Basic Real Estate Concepts

1. c (2)
2. b (3–4)
3. b (4)
4. c (4)
5. a (4–5)
6. d (5)
7. b (9)
8. c (12)
9. b (9)
10. a (12–13)
11. d (11)
12. c (6)
13. b (10)
14. d (10)
15. d (12–13)
16. d (11)
17. a (5)

CHAPTER 2
Property Ownership and Interests

1. b (18)
2. c (19)
3. c (19)
4. b (20)
5. d (20)
6. c (22)
7. b (22)
8. b (23)
9. b (21)
10. c (23)
11. d (23)
12. a (23)
13. a (24)
14. a (26)
15. d (26)
16. b (26)
17. c (27–28)

18. a (27–28)
19. b (26–27)
20. c (26–27)
21. d (25–26)
22. c (29)
23. a (29)
24. c (30–31)
25. a (31)
26. b (31)
27. a (33)
28. d (30–33)
29. d (31–33)
30. b (31–33)
31. b (34)
32. b (36)
33. c (35)
34. a (35)
35. c (34–35)

CHAPTER 3
Encumbrances on Real Property

1. b (43–44)
2. d (43–44)
3. d (44)
4. c (45)
5. b (45)
6. d (43–44)
7. b (45)
8. a (46)
9. a (46)
10. b (46–48)
11. c (49)
12. a (50)
13. a (50) $0.80 + 0.50 = $1.30 city + county tax rate ÷ 100 = 0.013; $1,600 annual taxes ÷ 0.013 = $123,076.92 assessed value
14. b (50) $133,000 assessed value × 0.01678 tax rate = $2,231.74 annual taxes ÷ 12 months = $185.97833 = $185.98 monthly tax liability
15. b (50) $2,000 annual taxes ÷ $183,500 assessed value = 0.010899 × $100 = $1.0899 = $1.09 per $100 of assessed value

16. b (50) $129,000 appraised value × 75% = $96,750 assessed value

17. c (50) $389,000 appraised value × 85% = $330,650 assessed value x $0.011 tax rate = $3,376.15 annual tax liability

18. a (50) $295,000 market value × 80% = $236,000 assessed value × $0.0063 county tax rate = $1,486.80 annual tax bill ÷ 12 months = $123.90 monthly tax bill

19. a (50) $7,248,000 total taxes ÷ $11,325,000 ÷ 100 = $ 0.64 per $100 assessed value

CHAPTER 4
Property Description

1. c (56)
2. b (56)
3. b (56–57)
4. c (57)
5. a (59)
6. c (63)
7. c (63)
8. c (63)
9. d (63)
10. a (60) 21,780 square feet ÷ 43,560 number of sq. ft. in acre = 0.5 acre × $25,000 per acre = $12,500

CHAPTER 5
Transfer of Title to Real Property

1. c (77)
2. d (76) $75,000 sales price ÷ 500 = 150 × $1 = $150
3. d (76) $185,900 sales price ÷ 500 = 371.80 × $1 = $371.80; round up to $372.00
4. c (65, 77–78)
5. b (67, 70)
6. c (65–66, 77–78)
7. d (75)
8. d (76–77)
9. a (65)
10. d (67)
11. c (79)
12. a (81)
13. a (81–82)
14. d (78)
15. c (81)
16. c (77)
17. b (77)
18. b (82)

19. d (82)
20. a (77)

CHAPTER 6
Land-Use Controls

1. a (97)
2. d (89)
3. b (88, 97)
4. a (89)
5. b (90)
6. b (90)
7. c (88–89)
8. b (96)
9. a (91)
10. b (97)
11. a (90)
12. d (90)
13. b (94, 97–98)
14. a (98)
15. b (90–91)
16. a (89)
17. a (91)
18. c (94)
19. c (95)
20. d (98)
21. b (90–91)
22. d (90)
23. d (92)
24. b (96)

CHAPTER 7
Real Estate Brokerage and the Law of Agency

1. a (122)
2. b (115)
3. b (122)
4. b (107)
5. a (108)
6. b (108)
7. b (122–123)
8. a (110)
9. d (131)
10. a (110)
11. c (129–130)
12. c (130)
13. b (130)
14. d (122–124)
15. b (110)
16. d (120)
17. c (120)

18. b (122–124)
19. c (124)
20. d (123–124)
21. c (130)
22. c (107–109)
23. b (109–110)
24. d (128, 130)
25. c (112–116)
26. d (126, 129)
27. c (131)
28. c (117–122)

CHAPTER 8
Basic Contract Law

1. b (145–146)
2. b (151)
3. b (150)
4. b (145)
5. d (143)
6. b (144)
7. a (149)
8. c (144–145)
9. b (143)
10. d (150)
11. d (146)
12. c (146)
13. c (148)
14. b (144)

CHAPTER 9
Agency Contracts

1. d (156)
2. c (159)
3. c (161–162)
4. b (156)
5. a (156)
6. d (164)
7. a (159)
8. c (157)
9. a (143–144) (Rule A.0104)
10. a (164)
11. d (164)
12. d (159)
13. a (168–169)
14. b (169)
15. b (159) $125,000 sales price × 6% commission rate = $7,500 commission × 60% (100% – 40% other firm's split) = $4500 ABC's share

16. a (159) $4287.50 commission portion ÷ 70% = $6125 Listing firm split ÷ 50% = $12,250 total commission ÷ 5% commission rate =$245,000
17. d (167) $120,000 + $1000 +$50,000 = $171,000 net amount seller needs ÷ 95% (100% – 5% comm. rate) = $180,000
18. d (167) $85,000 seller desired net + $1,000 closing costs + $65,000 loan payoff = $151,000 net amount seller needs ÷ 0.93 (100% – 7% comm. rate) = $162,365.59 sales price (rounded up to $162,366.00)

CHAPTER 10
Sales Contracts and Practices

1. b (183)
2. b (186–187)
3. d (183–184)
4. b (181)
5. d (181)
6. a (177, 179)
7. d (180)
8. b (181)
9. a (187–188)
10. c (185)
11. d (185)
12. b (180)
13. b (186)
14. a (180)
15. c (184)

CHAPTER 11
Landlord and Tenant

1. b (207)
2. b (206)
3. a (200)
4. c (201–202)
5. d (203)
6. b (201)
7. c (201–202)
8. b (205)
9. d (196)
10. a (198–199)
11. d (195)
12. c (194–195)
13. c (203)
14. b (203)
15. b (207)
16. c (197)
17. c (196)

18. b (195)
19. b (199–200)
20. c (201)
21. d (200–201)
22. b (195)
23. a (197–198)
24. b (200)
25. a (205)
26. a (206–207)
27. b (203)
28. c (202) $900 monthly rent × 12 months = $10,800 base rent; $275,000 gross sales – $150,000 = $125,000 sales subject to percentage rent × 4% = $5,000 percentage rent + $10,800 base rent = $15,800 total annual rent

Property Management

1. a (217)
2. c (216)
3. c (217)
4. c (217–218)
5. b (220)
6. d (216, 218)
7. c (218) $750 monthly rent × 12 months × 20 units= $180,000 total rent × 8% = $14,400 commission
8. b (214–215)
9. c (218)
10. c (214–215)
11. c (216) 2-4BR × $1,000/mo. = $2,000 × 12 mos. = $24,000 rent received; 25–3BR × $850/mo. = $21,250 × 12 mos. = $255,000 × 0.95 (5% vacancy) = $242,250 rent received; 10–2BR × $750/mo. = $7,500 × 12 mos. = $90,000 × 0.95 (5% vacancy) = $85,500 rent received; 11–1BR × $650/mo. = $7,150 × 12 mos. = $85,800 × 0.90 (10% vacancy) = $77,220; Total rent received = $428,970 × 0.12 mgmt. fee = $51,476
12. c (217)
13. a (213)
14. b (214)

CHAPTER 13
Real Estate Financing: Principles

1. b (227)
2. a (230)
3. b (227)

4. b (234) $120,000 loan × 0.03 (3 discount points) = $3,600
5. b (227)
6. c (235–236)
7. b (233)
8. b (234) $2,700 points ÷ $90,000 loan = 0.03 = 3 points
9. a (245)
10. d (230)
11. c (227–229)
12. a (228)
13. b (233–234)
14. c (230)
15. d (244)
16. b (244)
17. c (245)
18. b (245–246)
19. a (235)
20. c (237)
21. b (230, 235)
22. b (245)
23. b (238)
24. a (229)
25. b (227)
26. b (246)

CHAPTER 14
Real Estate Financing: Practices

1. a (255)
2. a (265)
3. c (259)
4. b (266)
5. b (272)
6. d (263)
7. c (267)
8. b (265)
9. a (263–264)
10. b (265)
11. c (259)
12. b (273)
13. c (262)
14. d (255, 274)
15. c (268–269)
16. b (267)
17. c (269–270) Housing Expense = $750 ÷ 0.28 = $2,678.57, rounded up to $2,679 for income ratio; Recurring Obligations $750 + $500 = $1,250 ÷ 0.36 = $3,472.222 rounded to $3,472 for debt ratio = higher income need

18. a (273)
19. c (259)
20. d (255)
21. d (254)
22. c (266)
23. a (272)
24. c (262)
25. c (184–185, 265)
26. d (267)
27. d (273)
28. b (257) $114,500 appraised value × 0.80 = $91,600 loan amount
29. c (257)
30. c (269–270) $847 PITI + $745 recurring obligations = $1,592 ÷ 0.36 = $4,422.22 × 12 months = $53,066.66 annual income; rounds to $53,067
31. a (269–270) $60,000 annual income ÷ 12 months = $5,000 monthly income × 0.36 = $1,800 maximum PITI and Recurring obligations; $1,800 − ($160 taxes + $700 recurring debts) = $940 maximum PI ÷ 6.67 loan factor = $140.92953 × $1,000 = $140,929.53
32. a (269–270) $42,000 annual gross income ÷ 12 months = $3,500 × 0.36 = $1,260 − $500 = $760

CHAPTER 15
Closing the Real Estate Transaction

1. b (292–293)
2. d (291)
3. c (285)
4. d (294–295) $1,800 annual taxes ÷ 360 days = $5.00 per day; Jan 1–Sep 15 = 255 days × $5 = $1,275 seller's liability; Seller prepaid $1,800 − $1,275 = $525 credit seller/debit buyer
5. b (296) $450 rent ÷ 30 days = $15 × 23 days = $345 seller's portion; $450 − $345 =$105 debit seller/credit buyer
6. c (234, 257, 291) $150,000 sales price × 0.90 = $135,000 (loan amount) × 0.03 = $4,050 (loan fees) + $15,000 (down payment) = $19,050
7. b (293)
8. d (297)
9. a (298)
10. d (297)
11. b (298)
12. c (297)
13. d (285)
14. b (286)

15. b (298)
16. d (297–298)
17. d (297–298)
18. a (287)
19. b (297)
20. c (297)
21. b (642)
22. c (642)
23. c (641)
24. a (641)

CHAPTER 16
Basic Residential Construction

1. a (316)
2. b (310)
3. d (312)
4. c (308)
5. c (315)
6. a (311)
7. c (319)
8. a (312)
9. c (312)
10. c (312)

CHAPTER 17
Real Property Valuation

1. b (324)
2. c (340–341)
3. b (336)
4. a (338–339) Net operating income (NOI) of $24,000 ÷ $300,000 value = 0.08 = 8%
5. c (338–339)
6. b (325)
7. c (338)
8. b (338)
9. c (336)
10. b (329, 333)
11. b (337)
12. d (337)
13. c (338)
14. a (324)
15. b (326)
16. b (338–339)
17. a (335)
18. c (333)
19. b (338)
20. b (339)
21. b (337)
22. a (340)

23. a (335)
24. b (338)
25. d (337)
26. a (326)
27. c (338) Gross income of $6,000 – $1,000 mgt. ex. – $300 taxes – $1,100 repairs = $3,600 (Debt service is not an operating expense.)
28. d (329, 333)
29. c (333–334)

Subject	Comparable		Sold for **$140,000**
2,100 SF	1,900 SF (200 × $72)	=	+ 14,400
4BR	3 BR (1 × $2,000)	=	+ 2,000
2 CG	1 CG (1 × $1,500)	=	+ 1,500
No patio	Patio (1 × $2,000)	=	– 2,000
No pool	Pool (1 × $14,000)	=	– 14,000
2.5 baths	2 baths (½ = $800)	=	+ 800
1 acre	1.5 acres (½ = $15,000)	=	– 15,000
Subject Property		=	$127,700

30. c (333–334)

Comp A	Comp B	Comp C	Comp D
$73,000	$74,000	$62,000	$71,000
–$3,000	–$2,000	+$3,500	–$5,000
$70,000	$72,000	$65,500	$66,000
Range = $65,500 low to $72,000 high			

31. b (333–334)

CHAPTER **18**
Property Insurance

1. d (349, 353)
2. b (352)
3. a (353)
4. a (352–353)
5. d (354)
6. c (350–352)
7. b (352) ($175,00 × 50% bought coverage) ÷ ($175,000 × 80% required coverage) × $82,000 claim = $51,250
8. b (354–355)
9. c (354–355)
10. b (352)

CHAPTER **19**
Federal Income Taxation of Real Property Ownership

1. c (361)

2. a (361)
3. c (361)
4. b (362)
5. d (360–361)
6. b (360–362)
7. a (362)
8. a (360–362)
9. a (361–362) $127,500 sales price less selling expenses of $750 = $126,750 amount realized – $75,000 original cost = $51,750
10. c (362–364)
11. b (361–362) $72,000 basis + $15,000 addition + $3,000 deck = $90,000. Repairs and painting would be considered ordinary repairs or maintenance and would not increase the adjusted basis.
12. d (364–365)
13. c (364)

CHAPTER **20**
Fair Housing and Ethical Practices

1. c (370–371)
2. d (377)
3. d (370)
4. b (381)
5. c (381)
6. a (382)
7. b (374–375)
8. c (375)
9. d (381–382)
10. b (370)
11. a (370–373)
12. b (370)
13. c (372–373)
14. b (378–379)
15. b (377)
16. b (378–379)
17. b (374–375)
18. b (381)
19. b (376)

CHAPTER **21**
Environmental Issues and the Real Estate Transaction

1. b (390–392)
2. c (392)
3. c (392–394, 402)
4. a (392)
5. b (397–398)
6. c (395)

7. b (398)
8. d (400)
9. c (395)
10. d (393–394)
11. b (393)
12. c (393–394)

CHAPTER 22
Real Estate Mathematics

1. b $123,000 sales price × 0.05 down payment = $6,150 down payment amt.

2. a $73,000 sales price × 0.06 = $4,380 gross commission ÷ 2 = $2,190 listing firm's share × 0.30 Janice's share = $657

3. b $356,000 loan amt. ÷ $1,200,000 value = 0.2966666 = 29.67% LTV

4. d $135,000 SP × 0.065 = $8,775 gross commission × 0.55 selling broker's share = $4,826.25 × 0.60 your share = $2,895.75

5. b 2% + 5%+ 3% = 10% total commission rate; $2,000 total comm. ÷ 0.10 comm. rate = $20,000 sales price
   Al: $20,000 × 0.02 = $400
   Broker: $20,000 × 0.05 = $1,000
   Betty: $20,000 × 0.03 = $600

6. a $75,000 lot + $250,000 house = $325,000 new assessed value × 0.01678 rate = $5,453.50 ÷ 12 months = $454.46 monthly tax

7. b 350 acres × 43,560 (sq. ft./acre) = 15,246,000 sq. ft. ÷ 1,300' = 11,727.692' depth; 11,727.692 × 6,000' frontage = 70,366,152 sq. ft. ÷ divided by 43,560 = 1,615.4 acres rounded

8. c 660' × 660' = 435,600 sq. ft. ÷ 43,560 = 10 acres ÷ 2 = 5 acres in each lot

9. b $5,000 profit ÷ $20,000 original price = 25% profit

10. c $20,000 × 5 lots = $100,000 original value; $17,000 × 9 lots = $153,000 present value − $100,000 = $53,000 profit ÷ $100,000 original value = 0.53 = 53% profit

11. d $135,000 net + $950 closing costs + $53,500 loan payoff = $189,450 ÷ 0.935 (100% − 6.5%) = $202,620.32 minimum sales price

12. c $180,000 SP × 0.85 = $153,000 loan amount ÷ 1,000 = 153 × 6.65 factor = $1,017.45 PI; Taxes: $996 ÷ 12 months = $83. Insurance: $480 ÷ 12 months = $40; $1,017.45 PI + $83 T + $40 I = $1,140.45 monthly PITI

13. b $1,017.45 monthly PI × 360 payments = $366,282 PI − $153,000 original P = $213,282 total interest

14. b $153,000 LV × 0.07 = $10,710 I ÷ 12 months = $892.50 I; $1,017.45 PI − $892.50 I = $124.95 P; $153,000 P − $124.95 P = $152,875.05 new LV

15. d $185,500 SP × 0.80 = $148,400 loan × 0.01 = $1,484 origination fee; $148,400 × 0.02 = $2,968 discount points; $1,484 + $2,968 = $4,452 loan fees

16. d $37,100 down payment + $400 attorney fees + $4,452 loan fees = $41,952

17. c $105,000 × 0.90 = $94,500 original debt; $105,000 − $94,500 = $10,500 original equity; $105,000 × 1.20 = $126,000 new value; $94,500 × 0.92 (100% − 8%) = $86,940 new debt; $126,000 − $86,940 = $39,060 new equity; $39,060 − $10,500 = $28,560 increase in equity; $28,560 ÷ $10,500 = 2.72 = 272%

18. a $40,800 ÷ 12 months = $3,400 monthly gross income; Housing: $895 ÷ $3,400 = 0.26 = 26%: Yes; Recurring Obligations: $895 housing + $425 debt = $1,320 ÷ $3,400 = 0.39 = 39%: No

19. c $719.32 PI + $135 TI + $500 debt = $1,354.32 total debt ÷ 0.36 = $3,762 monthly income × 12 months = $45,144

20. b $53,000 ÷ 12 = $4,416.67 monthly income; $4,416.67 × 0.36 = $1,590 maximum recurring obligations; $1,590 − $150 TI − $650 recurring obligations = $790 maximum PI; $790 ÷ 8.0462 = $98.182993 × 1,000 = $98,182.99

21. a $38,500 ÷ 12 months = $3,208.33 monthly income; $3,208.33 × 0.36 = $1,155 maximum recurring obligations; $1,155 − $700 PITI = $455 other debt

22. d $575 × 3 = $1,725 ÷ 30 = $57.50/day Nov 1 to Nov 14 = 14 days × $57.50 = $805 seller retains $1,725 − $805 = $920 credit buyer/debit seller

23. a $82,000 × 0.07 = $5,740 annual interest ÷ 360 days = $15.944/daily interest; Aug 1 to Aug 11 = 11 days × $15.944 = $175.38 seller's interest portion

24. b $1,260 ÷ 360 days = $3.50/day; Jan 1 to Nov 15 = 315 days × $3.50 = $1,102.50 seller's share of taxes; $1,260 total tax – $1,102.50 seller's share = $157.50 credit seller/debit buyer for buyer's share

Math for 25 through 28:
Commission: $150,000 SP × 0.075 = $11,250
Interim interest: $90,000 LV × 0.07 = $6,300 annual interest ÷ 360 days = $17.50/day; Feb 15 to end of month = 16 days × $17.50 = $280
Origination fee: $90,000 LV × 0.01 = $900
Discount points: $90,000 LV × 0.01 = $900
Tax proration: $1,260 annual tax ÷ 360 days = $3.50/day × 45 days (Jan 1 to Feb 15) = $157.50 seller's share
Excise tax: $150,000 SP ÷ 500 = $300

25. d Buyer's settlement charges: $900 origination fee + $900 discount points + $280 interim interest + $185 title insurance + $380 insurance policy + $550 attorney fees = $3,195

26. c Seller's settlement charges: $11,250 commission + $150 deed preparation + $300 excise tax = $11,700

27. c Cash from buyer: $150,000 sales price + $3,195 settlement charges – $90,000 loan – $3,000 earnest money deposit – $157.50 taxes = $60,037.50

28. b Cash to seller: $150,000 sales price – $11,700 settlement charges – $50,000 loan payoff – $157.50 taxes = $88,142.50

29. b Comps #1 and #2 are the same except for square footage: $110,000 – $100,000 = $10,000 ÷ 200 sq. ft. (3,000 – 2,800) = $50 per sq. ft.

Comp #2 and Comp #3:

$110,000 – $86,000 =	$24,000
3,000 sq. ft. – 2,600 sq. ft. = 400 sq. ft. × $50 =	–$20,000
Value of garage:	$4,000

	Comp #1	Comp #2	Comp #3
	$100,000	$110,000	$86,000
Sq. ft.	+$10,000	-0-	+$20,000
Garage	–$4,000	–$4,000	-0-
	$106,000	$106,000	$106,000

30. b $120,000 SP + $2,600 CC = $122,600 basis
31. c $120,000 + $2,600 + $16,000 = $138,600
32. d $165,000 SP × 0.93 – $1,300 = $152,150
33. a $152,150 amount realized – $138,600 adjusted basis = $13,550 gain

34. b 120 × $2,000 = $240,000 SP
35. a 120,000 feet ÷ 1,200 feet = 100 feet × $200 = $20,000 SP
36. d (120,000 ÷ 43,560) × $10,000 = $27,548.21
37. c 4 acres × 43,560 sq. ft. = 174,240 sq. ft. ÷ 22,500 sq. ft. (150' × 150') = 7.744 lots = 7 lots
38. b 22,500 sq. ft. ÷ 43,560 = 0.516528925 (approximately 0.517 acres)
39. b 174,240 sq. ft. – 157,500 sq. ft. (7 lots × 22,500 sq. ft.) = 16,740 sq. ft. ÷ 43,560 sq. ft. = 0.38429752 (approx. 0.384 acres)
40. d $205,000 – $115,000 = $90,000 profit
41. d $90,000 profit ÷ $115,000 original cost = 78.26%
42. c $115,000 × 0.20 = $23,000 original equity
$205,000 – $51,000 = $154,000 present equity
$154,000 – $23,000 = $131,000 equity change
$131,000 ÷ $23,000 = 570% equity change
43. a $205,000 SP × 0.046 = $9,430 commission + $51,000 loan payoff + $410 excise tax ($205,000 ÷ 500) + $15 release + $40 courier = $60,895
$205,000 SP – $60,895 = $144,105 net
44. a $285,000 SP – $249,000 original value = $36,000 profit
$36,000 ÷ $249,000 = 14% profit
45. a $149,000 SP – $185,000 original value = $36,000 loss
$36,000 ÷ $185,000 = 19% loss
46. b 321.74% profit + 100% original price = 421.74% ratio of current value to original value
$97,000 current value ÷ 421.74% = $23,000 original value
47. b $64,090 ÷ 12 = $5,340.83 monthly income × 0.29 = $1,548.84 maximum housing expense per income ratio; $5,340.83 × 0.41 = $2,189.74 maximum long-term recurring debt – $575 non-housing debt = $1,614.74 maximum housing expense per debt ratio; $1,548.84 < $1,614.74; lesser rules.
48. a 0.29 × $1,900 = $551 income ratio;
0.41 × $1,900 = $779 – $150 debt = $629 debt ratio; $551 < $629; lesser rules
49. d $120,000 LV × 0.095 ÷ 12 = $950 first month's interest payment; $1,009.20 PI – $950 I = $59.20 principal payment for the month
$120,000 beginning loan balance – $59.20 P payment = $119,940.80 new loan balance
50. d $273,750 sales price ÷ 500 = $547.50; must round up to next dollar → $548.00 excise tax

Practice Exam

1. b (56)
2. c (50)
3. c (56–57)
4. d (65)
5. d (26–28)
6. b (70)
7. d (22)
8. b (82)
9. a (67)
10. a (27–28)
11. b (199–200)
12. a (90)
13. d (207)
14. b (88)
15. a (70)
16. b (43–44)
17. c (90–91)
18. d (19–20)
19. b (200)
20. a (291)
21. d (181)
22. b (149)
23. c (145–146)
24. c (164)
25. d (187–188)
26. d (180)
27. a (144–145)
28. a (297)
29. d (158)
30. a (181)
31. c (159)
32. c (147)
33. d (298)
34. c (120)
35. d (213–214)
36. b (146, 180)
37. a (22–24)
38. b (46)
39. d (92)
40. d (117–122)
41. b (163–164)
42. a (111–112)
43. a (360-361, 365)
44. b (362)
45. a (381)
46. c (378-379, 381)
47. a (381)
48. d (312)
49. a (392–393)
50. d (168–169)
51. b (352–353)
52. a (93A.6)
53. d (93A.2)
54. a (A.0105)
55. a (A.0107)
56. a (A.0105)
57. b (A.0110)
58. a (A.0101, A.0503)
59. a (A.0110)
60. c (A.0503)
61. d (A.1902)
62. b (A.1902)
63. a (A.1902)
64. a (93A Article 4)
65. c (237)
66. a (227)
67. b (227)
68. c (230)
69. c (235–236)
70. c (233–234)
71. d (185)
72. a (239)
73. d (233–234)
74. b (230)
75. b (230)
76. c (245)
77. d (235)
78. b (265)
79. a (273)
80. b (273)
81. b (336)
82. a (324)
83. b (329, 333)
84. d (339)
85. d (338)
86. c (326)
87. c (335)
88. d (324)
89. c (325)
90. a (329)
91. b (337)
92. d (340–341)
93. a (338)
94. c (420) $98,763 loan balance × 5.75% annual interest rate ÷ 360 days × 30 days = $473.24 monthly interest; $584 monthly PI − $473.24 monthly I = $110.76 monthly P; $98,763 loan

balance – \$110.76 P = \$98,652.24 new loan balance

95. d (76) \$143,900 sales price ÷ 500 = \$287.80 rounds up to \$288.00

96. b (414) 150' × 375' = 56,250 square feet ÷ 43,560 = 1.2913 acres × \$50,000 price per acre = \$64,565 sales price ÷ 150 front feet = \$430.43 per front foot

97. c (410–411) \$412.50 monthly interest × 12 months = \$4,950 annual interest ÷ \$60,000 loan amount = 0.0825 = 8.25%

98. c (415–416) \$2,593.50 × 2 = \$5,187 gross commission ÷ 0.065 (6.5%) = \$79,800 SP

99. d (418, 423) \$65,000 seller net ÷ 0.94 (100% – 6%) = \$69,148.936 rounded to \$69,149

100. b (415–416) Sales price of \$50,000 × 0.0775 (7¾%) = \$3,875 commission

101. b (420) \$107,000 sales price × 0.80 (80%) = \$85,600 loan × 0.025 = \$2,140 points

102. a (294, 420) \$64,000 assessed value × 0.0072 tax rate ÷ 360 days × 118 days that seller is responsible for tax = \$151.04 seller debit/buyer credit

103. a (415–416) \$84,500 sales price × 0.07 (7%) = \$5,915 gross commission × 0.40 (40% to listing broker) = \$2,366 × 0.50 (50% of the 40%)= \$1,183 to listing licensee

104. c (296–297) \$138,000 loan amount × 6.5% interest rate = \$8970 annual interest ÷ 360 days × 4 days = \$99.67 interim interest

105. c (333–334) \$166,200 comp's sales price – \$2750 (50 extra square feet × \$55) – \$1000 (extra ½ bath) + \$2500 (short 1-car garage) + \$1662 (\$166,200 × 6% annual appreciation ÷ 12 months × 2 months) = \$166,612 indication of value

106. c (418, 423) Seller net of \$72,000 ÷ 0.94 (100% – 6%) = \$76,595.744 rounded to \$76,596

107. a (292–293, 297–298) \$84,500 purchase price less \$67,600 loan, less \$2,000 deposit, less \$183.53 prorated taxes, plus \$1,250 closing costs = \$15,966.47 rounded to \$15,966; proration of taxes: \$880.96 ÷ 360 days = \$2.447 per day × 75 days (Jan 1–Mar 15) = \$183.25 credit buyer/debit seller

108. c (416–418) \$105,000 sales price (present value) ÷ 1.25 (100% + 25%) = \$84,000

109. b (269) \$1386 housing expense ÷ 28% income ratio = \$4,950 minimum income; \$1,386 + \$725 debt = \$2,111 long term recurring debt ÷ 36% debt ratio = \$5,864 minimum income; chose larger income amount because must qualify on both ratios

110. b (219) \$2364 payment × 360 total # of payments = \$851,040 total P&I – \$394,000 original principal amount = \$457,040 total interest paid

APPENDIX C
Real Estate License Law*

1. c (93A-6)(A.0113)
2. d (93A-2)
3. a (A.0503)
4. d (93A-6)(A.0105)
5. a (93A-2)
6. c (93A-6)
7. a (A.1900)
8. c (A.0105)
9. d (A.0105)(93A.6)
10. c (93A-40)(58B.0103)
11. b (93A-40 & 45)
12. b (93A-8)
13. a (A.0112)
14. c (93A-3)
15. a (93A-3)
16. b (A.0107)
17. b (A.0503)
18. d (A.0601)
19. a (A.0107)
20. b (A.0104)
21. c (A.0107)
22. d (A.0104)
23. d (A.0107)
24. b (A.0107)
25. a (93A-4.2)
26. d (A.0110)

* Answers to these and all license law questions can be found in Appendix C: Real Estate License Law and Commission Rules.

Answer key to closing statement worksheet from Chapter 15

A. Settlement Statement

U.S. Department of Housing
and Urban Development

B. Type of Loan

1. ☐ FHA 2. ☐ FmHA 3. ☐ Conv. Unins.	6. File Number:	7. Loan Number:	8. Mortgage Insurance Case Number:
4. ☐ VA 5. ☐ Conv. Ins.			

C. Note: This form is furnished to give you a statement of actual settlement costs. Amounts paid to and by the settlement agent are shown. Items marked "(p.o.c.)" were paid outside the closing; they are shown here for informational purposes and are not included in the totals.

D. Name & Address of Borrower:	E. Name & Address of Seller:	F. Name & Address of Lender:

G. Property Location:	H. Settlement Agent:	
	Place of Settlement:	I. Settlement Date:

J. Summary of Borrower's Transaction		K. Summary of Seller's Transaction	
100. Gross Amount Due From Borrower		**400. Gross Amount Due To Seller**	
101. Contract sales price	110,000	401. Contract sales price	110,000
102. Personal property		402. Personal property	
103. Settlement charges to borrower (line 1400)	4,904.14	403.	
104.		404.	
105.		405.	
Adjustments for items paid by seller in advance		**Adjustments for items paid by seller in advance**	
106. City/town taxes to		406. City/town taxes to	
107. County taxes to		407. County taxes to	
108. Assessments to		408. Assessments to	
109.		409.	
110.		410.	
111.		411.	
112.		412.	
			110,000
120. Gross Amount Due From Borrower	114,904.14	**420. Gross Amount Due To Seller**	110,000
200. Amounts Paid By Or In Behalf Of Borrower		**500. Reductions In Amount Due To Seller**	
201. Deposit or earnest money	5,000	501. Excess deposit (see instructions)	
202. Principal amount of new loan(s)	88,000	502. Settlement charges to seller (line 1400)	7,747.96
203. Existing loan(s) taken subject to		503. Existing loan(s) taken subject to	
204.		504. Payoff of first mortgage loan	82,750.00
205.		505. Payoff of second mortgage loan	
206.		506. Accrued Interest- mortgage	344.79
207.		507.	
208.		508.	
209.		509.	
Adjustments for items unpaid by seller		**Adjustments for items unpaid by seller**	
210. City/town taxes to		510. City/town taxes to	
211. County taxes to		511. County taxes to	
212. Assessments to		512. Assessments to	
213.		513.	
214.		514.	
215.		515.	
216.		516.	
217.		517.	
218.		518.	
219.		519.	
			90,842.75
220. Total Paid By/For Borrower	93,000	**520. Total Reduction Amount Due Seller**	
300. Cash At Settlement From/To Borrower		**600. Cash At Settlement To/From Seller**	
301. Gross Amount due from borrower (line 120)	114,904.14	601. Gross amount due to seller (line 420)	110,000
302. Less amounts paid by/for borrower (line 220)	(93,000)	602. Less reductions in amt. due seller (line 520)	(90,842.75)
303. Cash ☐ From ☐ To Borrower	21,904.14	**603. Cash** ☐ To ☐ From Seller	19,157.25

Section 5 of the Real Estate Settlement Procedures Act (RESPA) requires the following: • HUD must develop a Special Information Booklet to help persons borrowing money to finance the purchase of residential real estate to better understand the nature and costs of real estate settlement services; • Each lender must provide the booklet to all applicants from whom it receives or for whom it prepares a written application to borrow money to finance the purchase of residential real estate; • Lenders must prepare and distribute with the Booklet a Good Faith Estimate of the settlement costs that the borrower is likely to incur in connection with the settlement. These disclosures are manadatory.

Section 4(a) of RESPA mandates that HUD develop and prescribe this standard form to be used at the time of loan settlement to provide full disclosure of all charges imposed upon the borrower and seller. These are third party disclosures that are designed to provide the borrower with pertinent information during the settlement process in order to be a better shopper.

The Public Reporting Burden for this collection of information is estimated to average one hour per response, including the time for reviewing instructions, searching existing data sources, gathering and maintaining the data needed, and completing and reviewing the collection of information.

This agency may not collect this information, and you are not required to complete this form, unless it displays a currently valid OMB control number.

The information requested does not lend itself to confidentiality.

L. Settlement Charges

700. Total Sales/Broker's Commission based on price $ 110,000 @ 6.00 % = $6,600	Paid From Borrowers Funds at Settlement	Paid From Seller's Funds at Settlement
Division of Commission (line 700) as follows:		
701. $ to		
702. $ to		
703. Commission paid at Settlement		6,600
704.		
800. Items Payable In Connection With Loan		
801. Loan Origination Fee 1.00 %	880.00	
802. Loan Discount 1.5 %	1,320.00	
803. Appraisal Fee to	150.00	
804. Credit Report to	50.00	
805. Lender's Inspection Fee		
806. Mortgage Insurance Application Fee to		
807. Assumption Fee		
808.		
809.		
810.		
811.		
900. Items Required By Lender To Be Paid In Advance		
901. Interest from 10/15 to 10/30 @$ 24.444 /day	391.10	
902. Mortgage Insurance Premium for months to		
903. Hazard Insurance Premium for 1.0 years to	345.00	
904. years to		
905.		
1000. Reserves Deposited With Lender		
1001. Hazard insurance months @$ per month		
1002. Mortgage insurance months @$ per month		
1003. City property taxes months @$ per month		
1004. County property taxes months @$ per month		
1005. Annual assessments months @$ per month		
1006. Escrow account deposit months @$ per month	500.00	
1007. months @$ per month		
1008. months @$ per month		
1100. Title Charges		
1101. Settlement or closing fee to		
1102. Abstract or title search to		
1103. Title examination to	250.00	
1104. Title insurance binder to		
1105. Document preparation to		50.00
1106. Notary fees to		
1107. Attorney's fees to	500.00	
(includes above items numbers:)		
1108. Title insurance to		
(includes above items numbers:)		
1109. Lender's coverage $		
1110. Owner's coverage $		
1111.		
1112.		
1113.		
1200. Government Recording and Transfer Charges		
1201. Recording fees: Deed $ 7.00 ; Mortgage $ 7.00 ; Releases $ 7.00	14.00	7.00
1202. City/county tax/stamps: Deed $; Mortgage $		
1203. State tax/stamps: Deed $ 220.00 ; Mortgage $		220.00
1204.		
1205.		
1300. Additional Settlement Charges		
1301. Survey to	200.00	
1302. Pest inspection to	75.00	
1303. buyer's property tax 10/16 to 12/30	229.04	
1304. seller's property tax 1/1 to 10/15		870.96
1305.		
1400. Total Settlement Charges (enter on lines 103, Section J and 502, Section K)	4904.14	7,747.96

636

Computation of figures on settlement statement:

Principal amount of new loan: $110,000 sales price × 80% loan = $88,000 loan

Buyer's interim interest:
$88,000 loan amount × 10% = $8,800 annual interest
$8,800 annual interest ÷ 360 days = $24.444 daily interest
$24.444 daily interest × 16 days (Oct 15 to Oct 30) = $391.10 interest

Seller's accrued interest:
$82,750 loan balance × 10% = $8,275 annual interest
$8,275 annual interest ÷ 360 days = $22.986 daily interest
$22.986 daily interest × 15 days (Oct 1 to Oct 15) = $344.79 interest

Property taxes:
$1,100 ÷ 360 days = $3.056 daily taxes
January 1 to October 15 = 285 days
285 × $3.056 = $870.96 (seller's taxes)
$1,100.00 − $870.96 = $229.04 (buyer's taxes)

Revenue stamps: $110,000 ÷ $500 = 220 × $1 = $220

Broker's commission: $110,000 × 6% = $6,600

Loan origination fee: $88,000 × 1% = $880

Discount points: $88,000 × 1.5% = $1,320

Buyer's statement:

Buyer's debits	$114,904.14
− Buyer's credits	$93,000.00
	$21,904.14 balance (cash) due from buyer

Seller's statement:

Seller's credits	$110,000.00
− Seller's debits	$90,842.75
	$19,157.25 balance (cash) due to seller

Index